Palgrave Studies in Economic History

Series editor
Kent Deng
London School of Economics
London, United Kingdom

Palgrave Studies in Economic History is designed to illuminate and enrich our understanding of economies and economic phenomena of the past. The series covers a vast range of topics including financial history, labour history, development economics, commercialisation, urbanisation, industrialisation, modernisation, globalisation, and changes in world economic orders.

More information about this series at
http://www.palgrave.com/gp/series/14632

Vicente Pinilla • Henry Willebald
Editors

Agricultural Development in the World Periphery

A Global Economic History Approach

palgrave
macmillan

Editors
Vicente Pinilla
Department of Applied Economics
and Economic History
Universidad de Zaragoza
Zaragoza, Spain

Henry Willebald
Department of Economics
Universidad de la República
Montevideo, Uruguay

Palgrave Studies in Economic History
ISBN 978-3-319-66019-6 ISBN 978-3-319-66020-2 (eBook)
https://doi.org/10.1007/978-3-319-66020-2

Library of Congress Control Number: 2017956115

Cover illustration: Y H Lim / Alamy Stock Photo

Printed on acid-free paper

This Palgrave Macmillan imprint is published by Springer Nature
The registered company is Springer International Publishing AG
The registered company address is: Gewerbestrasse 11, 6330 Cham, Switzerland

Preface

After the Second World War (WWII), economic development emerged as a prominent field of study within economics. The culmination of the industrialisation processes in Western European countries and in North America enabled their populations to earn high per-capita incomes and enjoy standards of living that were substantially better than in the past. For Asian and African countries, which were then undergoing their processes of decolonisation, or for the Latin American republics with more than a century of independence behind them, industrialisation became the primary economic objective. Furthermore, the fact that the Soviet Union had transformed from being an essentially agricultural economy to an industrial and military power in just a few decades reinforced the idea that, irrespective of the prevailing economic system of each country, implementing a similar structural change was the only path towards economic progress.

For the economists who, at that time, specialised in formulating an economic development theory, analysing the role that agriculture should have in this development was an important issue. To do this they found inspiration in the vision that the British economic historians had provided regarding the role that this sector had played in the English industrialisation process. In turn, the theoretical developments of the economists in this field would influence the perspective that the economic historians had over the following decades with respect to how the agriculture of each country had influenced the development of modern economic growth.

As from the 1980s, the view that economic historians had of the interactions between agriculture and economic growth changed drastically. Initially, an in-depth review of the British case was made and subsequently in many other countries the paradigms of the past were questioned. As part of this revival of the study of agricultural economic history, certain studies particularly stood out that sought to offer a broad view of the agricultural transformation over the preceding two centuries, analysing the developed countries as a whole (*The Dynamics of Agricultural Change* by David Grigg in 1982 and *L'agriculture des pays développés, 1800 à nos jours* by Paul Bairoch in 1992). Without a doubt, the book by Giovanni Federico, *Feeding the World, An Economic History of Agriculture, 1800–2000,* published in 2005, constituted a vital contribution to economic history. This book offered an ambitious and highly systematic view of the agricultural transformations throughout the whole world over the long term. It has been the most influential work published in this field, decisively stimulating the economic analysis of the history of agriculture in many countries around the world.

In the wake of these previous studies and also seeking the revival of this field, the book *Agriculture and Economic Development in Europe since 1870* (edited by Pedro Lains and Vicente Pinilla) was published in 2009. This book offered a review of publications from a broad range of European countries on the traditional roles assigned to agriculture during growth processes. Its objective was to provide economic historians, and also growth development economists, with an updated view of a subject in which considerable progress had been made and which is still vital for the comprehension of the situation of developing countries. Along the same lines, in the year 2013, another book was published (*Agricultural Transformation in a Global History Perspective* edited by Ellen Hillbom and Patrick Svensson) which, through the study of the agricultural transformation processes in different countries around the world, sought to illustrate the diversity of agricultural growth and its influence on economic development on a global scale in the long term with a strong emphasis on the microeconomic aspects of the process.

We believe that the publication of this book should be understood within this context. It initially arose as a session organised by Sandra Kuntz and Vicente Pinilla in the World Economic History Congress held in Kyoto in August 2015. The interest of Palgrave Macmillan in this subject and the enthusiasm of Laura Pacey for the organisers of the session to consider the more ambitious project of writing a book on the subject were key in the development of the project.

This book, then, has a very clear objective: to present analytical historical narratives that help us to understand the diversity of the roles that agriculture has played in the economic development processes of the periphery countries and to study these agricultural transformations. To do this, the book has formulated chapters that analyse transversal themes for all of the periphery countries (Chaps. 2, 3, and 4), others that analyse large regional groups of countries (Chaps. 8, 9, 13, and 17) and finally, national cases studies (Chaps. 5, 6, 7, 10,11, 12, 14, 15, 16, and 18). We believe that the geographical coverage is very broad: the four periphery countries included in the group now known as the BRICS (Brazil, India, China and South Africa) are considered. Furthermore, the largest Asian countries are studied along with the two remaining countries of the Indian subcontinent, and Indonesia and Vietnam, as well as the whole of Southeast Asia. With respect to Latin America, in addition to studying the region as a whole, Argentina, Brazil, Peru and Uruguay are studied individually. The cases of Ghana and Zambia are analysed for Africa together with South Africa. Finally, countries which began by forming part of the world periphery, but now clearly form part of the core countries (Australia, Canada and New Zealand), are also studied.

The editors owe a great debt of gratitude to the many people who have enabled this project to finally culminate in the book that follows this preface. First and foremost, our gratitude is for the authors. They have not only worked with enthusiasm preparing their respective chapters, but have also collaborated with the editors, cross-reviewing the chapters written by the other authors, and finally they have been enormously receptive to modifying and improving their chapters following the recommendations of the editors and colleagues who have acted as referees of their work.[1] We had the opportunity to hold a conference in Zaragoza to discuss the first versions of the chapters in March 2017, thanks to the finance received from GLOCRED (a Research Network of Eight R&D Projects Sponsored by Spanish Ministry of Economy and Competitiveness) and the research project led by Iñaki Iriarte and Vicente Pinilla 'The integration of the international economy and its effects: agri-food production, natural resources, society and environment (nineteenth–twenty-first centuries)' (sponsored by the Spanish Ministry of Economy and Competitiveness). We also extend our thanks, of course, to the team at Palgrave Macmillan. Their support, encouragement and help during the whole process of writing the book have been paramount. Last, but not least, the editors owe an enormous personal debt to their families from whom they have robbed a lot of time in order to complete this book.

Department of Applied Economics and Economic History, Universidad de Zaragoza, Zaragoza, Spain — Vicente Pinilla

Department of Economics, Universidad de la Repúlbica, Montevideo, Uruguay — Henry Willebald

Notes

1. The list of the reviewers is the following: Ch. 2: D. Byerlee; Ch. 3: K. Anderson; Ch. 4: A. Booth; Ch. 5: J. Velazco; Ch. 6: N. Vink and J. Greyling; Ch. 7: E. Hillbom; Ch. 8: P.K. Viswanathan; Ch. 9: T. Axelsson; Ch. 10: T. Kurosaki; Ch. 11: A. Booth; Ch. 12: M. Anderson; Ch. 13: B. Mueller; Ch. 14: J. Alvarez; Ch. 15: E.R. Till; Ch. 16: M. Lopez Jerez; Ch. 17: A. Palacios; Ch. 18: M. Martin-Retortillo.

Contents

Abbreviations

ABARES	Australian Bureau of Agricultural and Resource Economics and Sciences
ABS	Australian Bureau of Statistics
ADLI	Agricultural demand-led industrialisation
APEC	Asia-Pacific Economic Cooperation
APRA	American Popular Revolutionary Alliance
ASEAN	Association of Southeast Asian Nations
AUD	Australian Dollar
BAP	Banco Agrario del Perú
BSAC	British South Africa Company
CA	Central Agency
CAP	Common Agricultural Policy
CAP	Cooperativas Agrarias de Producción
CBS	Central Bureau of Statistics
CCP	Chinese Communist Party
CCP	Conventions People's Party
CDC	Colonial (now Commonwealth) Development Corporation
COCOBOD	Ghana Cocoa Board
CPCS	Central Purchase and Centre Supply
DAC	Development Assistance Committee
DEA	Data Envelopment Analysis

DFI	Direct Foreign Investment
DUA	Domestic-use Agriculture
EAP	Economically Active Population
EC	European Community
ECLA	Economic Commission for Latin America
EMBRAPA	Empresa Brasileira de Pesquisa Agropecuária
ENAHO	Encuesta Nacional de Hogares
FAO	Food and Agricultural Organization
FAOSTAT	Food and Agricultural Organization Statistics
FELDA	Federal Land Development Authority (Malaysia)
FDI	Foreign Direct Investment
FRA	Food Reserve Agency
GATT	General Agreement on Tariffs and Trade
GDP	Gross Domestic Product
GGDC	Groningen Growth and Development Centre
GIS	Geographic Information Systems
GMD	Guomindang
GSTP	Global System of Trade Preferences for developing countries
HLET	High-Level Equilibrium
IFC	International Finance Corporation
ILO	International Labour Organization
INEI	Instituto Nacional de Estadística e Informática
ISA	Import Substitution Agriculture
ISI	Import Substitution Industrialisation
JEL	Journal of Economic Literature
KTDA	Kenyan Tea Development Authority
LTT	Land to the Tiller
M	Million
MRD	Mekong River Delta (Vietnam)
MT	Million Tonnes
NES	Nucleus plantation estate with outgrowers
NIC	newly industrialised country
NP	National Party
NRA	Nominal Rate of Assistance
NSRC	National System of Rural Credit

OLS	Ordinary Less Squares
OPEC	Organization of the Petroleum Exporting Countries
PORIM	Palm Oil Research Institute of Malaysia
PPF	Production Possibility Frontier
PRC	People's Republic of China
RRA	Relative Rate of Assistance
R&D	Research and Development
RRD	Northern Red River Delta (Vietnam)
RRIM	Rubber Research Institute of Malaya
RST	Residence Superior in Tonkin
SAAU	South African Agricultural Union
SAIS	Sociedades Agrarias de Interés Social
SAP	South African Party
SASC	South American Southern Cone
SRI	Stanford Research Institute
SSCI	Social Science Citation Index
STCP	Sustainable Tree Crop Programme
UN	United Nations
UK	United Kingdom
US	United States (of America) (adjective)
USA	United States of America (noun)
US$	United States of America Dollar
USD	United States of America Dollar
USSR	Union of Soviet Socialist Republics
WTO	World Trade Organization
WWI	First War World
WWII	Second War World

List of Figures

List of Tables

Part I

Introduction, Theory and World Approaches

1

Agricultural Development in the World Periphery: A General Overview

Vicente Pinilla and Henry Willebald

1 Development, Agriculture and Periphery

The aim of this book is to provide a long-term perspective that allows a better understanding of the process of agricultural transformations and their interaction with the rest of the economy. During the 1950s and 1960s, most growth economists considered that agriculture played a negligible role in promoting economic development (Lains & Pinilla, 2009). This view, influenced by the impulse toward industrialisation in the global periphery, has only seldom been revisited, even though many recent studies have indicated the existence of positive relationships between agriculture and economic growth. These relationships derive from inter-sectoral

V. Pinilla
Department of Applied Economics and Economic History, Universidad de Zaragoza, Zaragoza, Spain

H. Willebald (✉)
Department of Economics, Universidad de la República, Montevideo, Uruguay

V. Pinilla, H. Willebald (eds.), *Agricultural Development in the World Periphery*, Palgrave Studies in Economic History, https://doi.org/10.1007/978-3-319-66020-2_1

links (Delgado, Hopkins, & Kelly, 1994; Hazell & Haggblade, 1993; Timmer, 2009), the strengthening of domestic markets (Adelman, 1984), technological (Hayami & Ruttan, 1985; Ruttan, 2002) and organisational improvements, or simply the exploitation of comparative advantage in the rural setting. Of particular interest is the analysis of changes in agricultural production and productivity and their relationship to per capita income levels, in order to assess the possible contribution of agriculture to economic growth. Also of interest is the analysis of the relationships between agriculture and other economic sectors during this process, the use of resources (land, labour, capital) and the influence of institutional and technological factors in the long-run performance of agricultural activity.

The structural transformation process, both as an analytical concept and as a historical event, implies a sustained improvement in agricultural productivity (Hillbom & Svensson, 2013). As productivity grows, the economy creates conditions to process a real structural change in which the transference of resources to other sectors with higher productivity is possible, and the final consequence is an increase in the total factor productivity (TFP). This structural transformation requires a highly productive agricultural sector that employs a small proportion of the whole workforce (Timmer, 2009). Despite the fact that relative prices may, at certain times, deteriorate for the agricultural sector as a whole—an issue raised initially by Raul Presbich and Oscar Singer eight decades ago—productivity growth also offers an opportunity to increase farm household incomes and, in consequence, improve living conditions and poverty alleviation in rural areas.[1]

Obtaining higher productivity in agriculture—in individual crops or animal husbandry, as well as in the whole sector—allows for increasing incomes within agriculture and, at the same time, more resources allocated to other activities. There is a long tradition of studying agricultural transformation as a universal process, and numerous attempts have been made to model the various stages, with, so far, no great success (Federico, 2008). Specifically, the starting point for this book is that structural transformation is a process of great diversity (Hillbom & Svensson, 2013). An overall comprehension of the variety of trajectories leaves much still to be learned, especially concerning the drivers of change in regions with low levels of development, institutional restrictions, a variety of distance to the technological frontiers, and different modalities of participation in the international markets.

Geographical descriptions of the world make use of various metaphors: expressions such as centre–periphery, North–South, or First/Second/Third World have the capacity to characterise, rapidly and intuitively, the spatial organisation of the global economic system (Vanolo, 2010). Given the wide circulation of these concepts, they play a fundamental role in the building of our personal geographical images (Baudrillard, 1983), and these representations are often determinant in the comprehension of the evolution and performance of countries and regions.

The core–periphery metaphor—applied on a global scale—has referred to the unequal distribution of power in the economy, in society, and in the polity, stressing the domination/dependency relationships between different regions of the world (Rodríguez, 2006). Because that metaphor was developed in a structuralist scientific framework,[2] the core–periphery approach emphasises the relational dimension of the spatial organisation of the economic scenario, which is the uneven power structure (sometimes expressed as polarisation) that reproduces differentiations in the economic role of territories (Vanolo, 2010). The understanding of modern economic growth, also from a core–periphery perspective, resurfaced in the 1990s from Paul Krugman in his seminal work of 1991 (Krugman, 1991), which was based on two initially identical regional economies, specialising respectively in modern (the core) or traditional (the periphery) activities in a scenario of sufficiently low trade costs, whenever manufacturing operates under increasing returns to scale, and the market for these goods is monopolistically competitive. The agglomeration of forces generates a mechanism of circular causation that produces an intense polarisation between both regions. The generalisation of the core–periphery pattern resulted "in the emergence of persistent differences in the economic structure of the industrial core as compared to the agricultural periphery" (Ascani, Crescenzi, & Iammarino, 2012).

Economic historians subsequently extended these ideas to the economic development of the world since the early nineteenth century, distinguishing between an industrialised centre and a periphery specialising in the production and export of primary products. For most of the periphery countries (the so-called poor periphery) this specialisation, together with their participation in the economy of the First Globalisation, would have produced long-term negative results due to de-industrialisation, increased inequality, and the volatility of commodity prices (Jacks, O'Rourke, & Williamson, 2011).

In the core–periphery metaphor, the emphasis is on the role and position of such areas in the world economy, emphasising dimensions other than the simple "rich–poor" dichotomy (historically, it is possible to identify "poor periphery" and "rich periphery", Lindert & Williamson, 2003). The use of this terminology implies the building of analogies with the economic marginality of certain territories and the need to research the spatial interactions between geographical regions (and not just the mere historical evolution of "stages" of development) in order to explain the "underdevelopment" phenomenon. This approach considers the dynamics between cores and peripheries, and allows for influences moving in both directions, and thus for truly comparative narratives based on mutual exchange and interaction (Hanns Reill & Szelényi, 2011).

2 Agriculture in the Periphery: Big Trends and Stylised Facts

Agricultural output has increased in the long run, enough to provide more food per capita to a population more than six times greater than at the beginning of the nineteenth century (Federico, 2004). Factor endowments—land, labour, capital—and institutions have mutually interacted to obtain this result (Hillbom & Svensson, 2013).

Agricultural production grew, thanks mainly to the increase in inputs ("extensive" growth) in the nineteenth century and to TFP growth ("intensive" growth) in the twentieth century. Unlike other productive activities, agriculture is vulnerable to and restricted by natural pre-conditions. Land quality matters through its determination of settlement patterns and possibilities of agricultural expansion and growth. The relationship between land and labour affects the options of technical and institutional arrangements, creates the organisation of production systems, and promotes the functioning of factorial markets.

"Traditional" property rights over land, which still prevailed throughout the world in 1800, have gradually been replaced by "modern" ownership, but the process is not yet over (Federico, 2004) and, many times, determines the very notion of periphery. Most states implemented land and tenancy reforms in the twentieth century, with mixed results. Family farms were already fairly diffused in the nineteenth century and their share substantially increased in the twentieth century. Agriculture has always been a very competitive sector because the economies of scale have been modest and large farms have shown a multiplicity of serious incentive problems (the *latifundio–minifundio* problem). In spite of this, the size of farms in the core countries increased in the second half of the twentieth century, in large part due to the prevailing technological change and an increasing "industrialisation" of primary production.

The organisation of labour constitutes the other pillar of the system of production (Hillbom & Svensson, 2013). Power relations, the access to other production activities and alternative occupations, as well as the institutions that regulate the relationship between workers, capitalists, and landowners, are of vital importance in the evolution of agriculture in the long run.

The government can make a difference in terms of the transformation process. The 1930s marked a watershed in agriculture policies, from a period of almost perfect "benign neglect" to an era of massive intervention (Pinilla, 2009a). After 1950, agricultural policies in the core countries favoured agriculture, at the expense of consumers, while, in the periphery, they sacrificed agriculture in the service of rapid structural change (Federico, 2004).

Market opportunities provide powerful incentives. Farmers respond positively to price incentives and demand patterns when they have access to the appropriate infrastructure and well-functioning local, regional, national, and international market institutions (Pinilla, 2009b). The extent and structure of the market is therefore of vital importance for change and growth in agriculture. Farmers set up numerous strategies to access and exploit endowments; diverse strategies are formed, restricted by existing pre-conditions in the form both of institutions, primarily property rights, and of factor endowments.

Following Federico (2004, 2008) and our own calculations, we have divided the last 145 years into two periods: previous to (1870–1938)[3] and subsequent (1950–2010) to WWII, and we propose estimates of indices of agricultural output in real terms for the world core and periphery.

The performances of both regions were similar prior to WWII, with annual growth rates of 1.1 and 1.2 per cent in the core and periphery, respectively (Fig. 1.1, Panel a). The variability of production in the periphery was notoriously greater, with large growth rates in the First Globalisation (1880s, 1890s and 1900s until WWI), low rates in the extremes of the period—prior to the Belle Époque (the 1870s)—and during the Great Depression (the 1930s) and a profound contraction during WWI (comparing the levels of 1913 and 1920) (Fig. 1.1, Panel b).

The performance of agriculture prior to WWI was undoubtedly good compared with the stagnation of the preceding centuries, but it loses historical relevance somewhat when compared to the growth of the post-1950 era (Bairoch, 1999; Federico, 2008).

According to estimates by the FAO, from 1950 to 2010,[4] world agricultural production grew 2.3 per cent annually—in other words, production tripled—and in this process the performance of the world periphery was absolutely determinant of the expansion (Fig. 1.2, Panel a). As the core

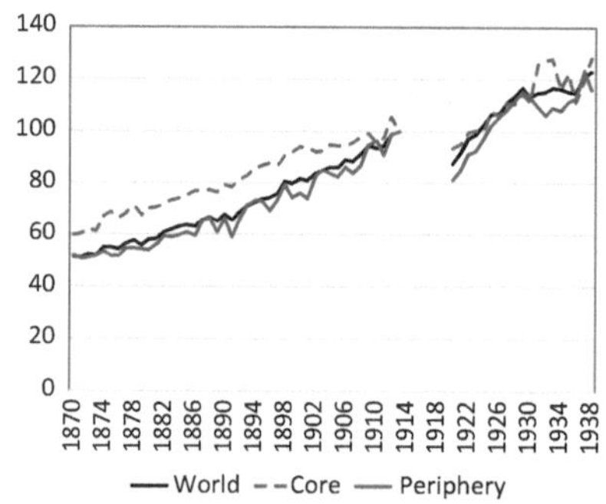

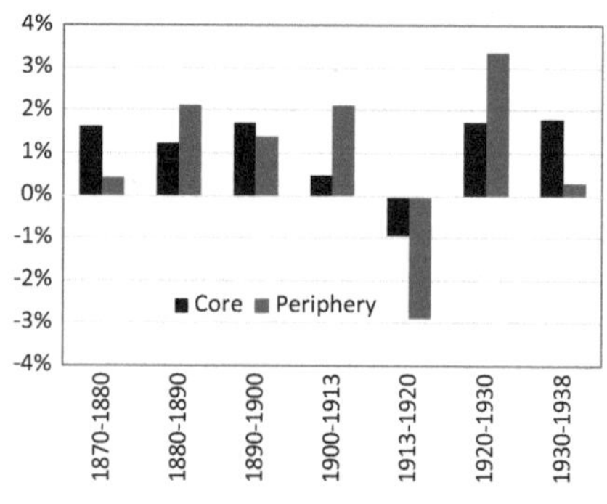

Fig. 1.1 Agricultural production in the world core and periphery 1870–1938. **(a)** Output real index 1913 = 100. **(b)** Growth rates in agricultural production. Source: Federico (2004, 2008) and own calculations

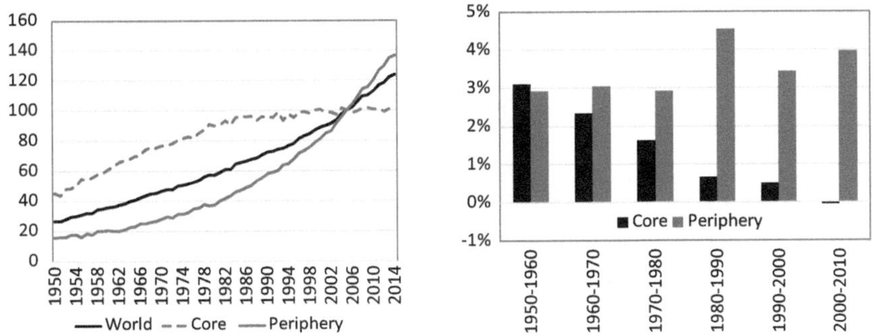

Fig. 1.2 Agricultural production in the world core and periphery 1950–2010. **(a)** Output real index 1991–1993 = 100. **(b)** Growth rates in agricultural production. Source: FAO and own calculations

grew 1.3 per cent annually, the periphery experienced an annual growth rate of 3.4 per cent, outperforming the industrially advanced countries with a notable upswing of Asian production (Federico, 2008). The result was a progressive acceleration of the periphery production—interrupted by the collapse of agriculture in the "transition economies" (the former Soviet Union and other Eastern European countries)—that contrasts distinctly with the slowing-down of production in the core (Fig. 1.2, Panel b).

3 What Can We Learn from History?

According to the previous concepts and considerations, we have selected economies and regions historically identified with the "world periphery" and considered the agricultural evolution of these countries or regions in the long run. On this basis, we have included three countries from Africa (Ghana, South Africa, and Zambia), thirteen from Asia (Bangladesh, Cambodia, China, India, Indonesia, Laos, Malaya, Myanmar, Pakistan, Philippines, Taiwan, Thailand, and Vietnam), two from Oceania (Australia and New Zealand), Canada and the whole of Latin America (see Fig. 1.3).

As a whole, this group of countries represents over 40 per cent of the total world area, with decreasing trends in the population and GDP shares until the mid-twentieth century, and a significant recovery after WWII (Fig. 1.4). Our sample involves, historically, over one half of the world

Fig. 1.3 World periphery: our sample. Source: own elaboration based on CC BY-SA 3.0, https://commons.wikimedia.org/w/index.php?curid=407551

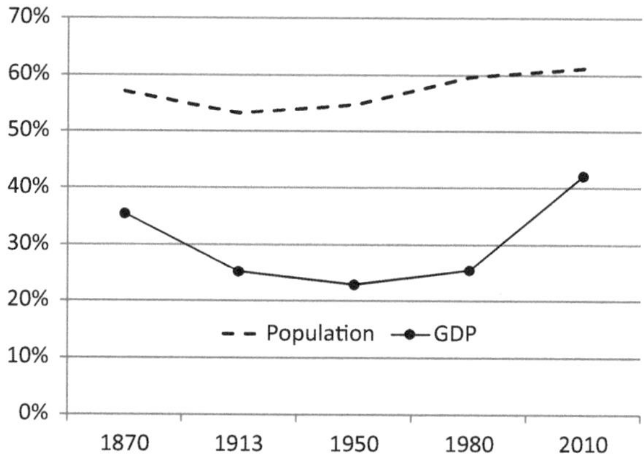

Fig. 1.4 World periphery: main indicators of our sample. Shares of world population and GDP. Source: The Maddison-Project

population, reaching 60 per cent by the beginning of the twenty-first century. In terms of world GDP shares, the trajectory of our sample draws a clearer U-shape evolution. In the 1870s, the sum of the GDPs of our sample represented one third of the world product but, by the mid-twentieth century, that ratio had declined to one quarter of the world GDP. The recovery of the second half of the twentieth century—noted previously for agriculture in Fig. 1.2—was impressive, and the GDP share achieved almost 45 per cent in the first decade of the twenty-first century.

What can we learn from history? A conceptual discussion is a suitable starting point to begin finding answers to this question.

In Chapter 2, Andersson and Till discuss the most influential views of the role of agriculture in development theory, as well as explaining the fluctuating scholarly attention to agriculture over time. This chapter identifies four main influential views on agriculture: agriculture as the fifth wheel; as a distorted sector with rational economic agents; as inherently important via trade (as injection or break); and as an engine of economic development. Today's agro-sceptics appear to be rooted in the fifth wheel school of thought, while the agro-proponents are more inclined to the "agriculture as engine, via structural transformation" school. It appears as if this view has been reinforced by the overall shift of objective within the development debate, from aggregate growth to pro-poor growth.

A possible positive contribution of agriculture to economic development is related to the role played by the export of agricultural products in the last two hundred years. Chapter 3, by Aparicio, González-Esteban, Pinilla and Serrano, is devoted to this topic. In the last two centuries, agricultural trade has grown at a remarkably rapid rate. In the first globalising wave, international trade was based on the exchange of primary products for manufactured goods. This provided important opportunities for complementarity in certain countries on the periphery that took advantage of the opportunity to base their economic development on the growth of their exports, and the linkages between them and the rest of the economy. However, most of the agricultural exporting countries obtained few benefits from this model of development (this pattern of trade was increasingly replaced by an intra-industrial one after WWII). In addition, the more developed countries tended to protect their own agricultural production, which was a major obstacle to agricultural trade at least until the end of the twentieth century. The beginning of the twenty-first century entailed significant changes, combining a higher incidence of market forces, "industrialisation" of agricultural production, and real structural changes within agriculture, offering non-traditional export goods that have opened new opportunities for growth and development.

In most of the tropical regions of the world, this agricultural reorientation toward foreign markets was generally directed in the colonies by an elite of large metropolitan landowners of large plantations. As we can see in Chapter 4, by Byerlee and Viswanathan, the evolution of plantations in the twentieth century has been remarkable. Plantations re-invented themselves and evolved from the earlier system of forced labour and colonial extraction into modern near-industrial firms operating in global markets. Additionally, while during the colonial period the record of plantations was often poor in terms of economic development and poverty reduction, it steadily improved over the century. Finally, and most importantly, these authors conclude that, in the early twenty-first century the plantation era is ending. By far the most important factor has been the rise of smallholders in the traditional plantation areas, due to a combination of their inherent efficiency, a more level playing field in policy support, institutional innovations to coordinate smallholder production with large mills and raise yields, and the reduced costs of entry after the pioneering stage of development. At the same time, transaction costs to plantations of accessing large amounts of cheap labour and land steadily rose over time. African countries are good examples of the long-run evolution of these traditional export crops of the periphery, although plantations were not always the technological option.

As Gunnarsson states in Chapter 5, cocoa in Ghana was predominantly a smallholder activity from the beginning, and it largely remained so over the course of the twentieth century. Ninety per cent of total production is today grown on smallholdings owned by individual farmers and operated, largely, by household labour. Cocoa in Ghana is indeed an export commodity, but it is not a plantation crop and the cocoa industry does not constitute an enclave economy. A fairly equitable distribution of assets among cocoa-producing households should have been an advantage in a drive towards industrialisation, as was the case in the East Asian "miracle" countries. Explanations as to why the Ghana case is different combine specific institutional and technological factors and conditions. Considering institutional issues, the distribution of assets is more unequal than we have been led to believe and, additionally, protection of property and regulation of profit accumulation (taxation and market arrangements) have been insufficient or have worked against the interest of the farmers. Considering technological issues, obstacles to productivity upgrades are related to physical factor endowments (type of commodity, soil conditions, man–land ratio etc.) that may have complicated or inhibited productivity improvements to be dispersed among a broad cross-section of farming households.

In contrast with the previous focus on institutional and technological issues, the starting point of Hillbom and Jenkin in Chapter 6 is the abundance of natural endowments—mineral deposits and land suitable for profitable agriculture—that characterised the historical evolution of Zambia (named Northern Rhodesia before independence in 1964). The authors present evidence of the extent to which, and through what mechanisms, natural resource endowments have influenced state policies and how these policies have determined the state of the contemporary Zambian agricultural sector. The discovery of mineral riches in the early colonial era, and the geographical location of those deposits, as well as that of fertile agricultural soils, have encouraged the extension of the railways, the settlement of large-scale farms, and government agricultural policies focused on securing food for a growing urban population. Maize has been given the role of a social contract crop, but agricultural policies have distorted opportunities for widespread agricultural diversification, creating instead a dual agricultural sector. The fundamental role of the agricultural sector has been to service the mining areas and the growing urban populations. With the government's consistent dependency on copper export revenues, Zambia remains caught in a reliance on two inter-dependent primary sectors, neither of which is dynamic enough to drive a structural transformation process. This kind of inter-dependence, and consequent interaction between diverse agents, with particular interests and different political power, opens interesting analyses of the political economy that dominates peripheral agriculture. South Africa is a good illustration of this notion.

Greyling, Vink and Var der Merwe trace, in Chapter 7, the progression from "suppression to support" of South African agriculture during the early twentieth century (1886 to 1948), revisiting the early part of the development of the South African agricultural sector, examining the nature of the alliance between "gold" and "maize", its subsequent disintegration, and the ability of either party to capture the state. The focus is on the evolution of political tensions stemming from the converging and diverging interests of groupings within the mining and agricultural sectors, and specifically how this facilitated the transition from "squeezing" a large but marginalised group of smaller white farmers, as well as black famers in general, to the reluctant "squeezing" of the mining industry by the state and the eventual complete marginalisation of black farmers. The South African case illustrates the complexity of the political tensions created during the transformation process and their long-term impact, since these played a significant role in putting the country on the path to apartheid.

In the Asian continent, agriculture has undergone profound transformations from the colonial period to the present day. In Chapter 8, Kurosaki examines the agriculture–macroeconomic growth link in India, Pakistan, and Bangladesh, using unusually long-term data that correspond to the current borders for the period c.1900–2000. The empirical results show two structural changes. The first occurred between pre- and post-1947 periods in India and Bangladesh. The portion of non-agricultural growth that can be attributable to agricultural growth increased substantially after independence/partition in 1947. The second occurred around the 1970s–1980s in all three countries, where non-agricultural growth that appeared to have occurred autonomously became the main engine of macroeconomic growth, with a secondary role for agriculture, at least until the end of the twentieth century.

Moving from the Indian subcontinent to Southeast Asia, Booth, in Chapter 9, argues that the key drivers of agricultural growth in Southeast Asia have been population growth, and increased involvement in international trade, which in this region led to the rapid growth in production of a number of crops for global, as well as domestic, markets. A third driver has been technological change, which increased output per unit of factor input. Institutional changes have also been important, but those changes have occurred mainly in response to the aforementioned (confirming the extended idea that the institutional framework is an endogenous process). Several of the following chapters delve into this region and present a more detailed description and analysis.

In Chapter 10, López Jerez focuses on the often-neglected role of agriculture in creating the basis for changing Vietnam's economy from one based on agriculture to one based on manufacturing industries. To do so, she compares two rice economies: the Northern Red River Delta and the Mekong River Delta in the South. The modern transformation of the South, with significant improvements in technology, specialisation, and increased income per capita suggests that agriculture became a driving force of the further industrialisation of the South, especially in terms of rural industrialisation. This chapter offers evidence in favour of the agro-proponent approach mentioned previously, which identifies the legacy of the "agriculture as engine, via structural transformation" school.

One of the most successful economies of the second half of the twentieth century was Indonesia, which is analysed by Axelsson and Palacio in Chapter 11. The authors measure structural change by looking at the gap between the share of agricultural GDP and employment for the whole country and its regions. Indonesia has been transformed from a predominantly agricultural economy to one based on industry and services. However, in a global comparison, particularly in relation to other Asian countries, the structural transformation has been sluggish, and poverty lingers, a consequence of the weak linkages across sectors and regions, and an indication that the process was fundamentally dependent on the state and its needs. In the 1970s, the state pushed for the transformation process with food security as the principal goal. This was coupled with an industrial policy that prioritised output rather than the creation of labour opportunities and the rise of the new entrepreneurial class. In the 1980s, when structural transformation slowed, in particular labour re-allocation, it coincided with diminishing state support for agriculture. It was not until a shift in industrial policy, forced by a decline in oil prices, when more labour-intensive manufacturing was promoted, that an acceleration in the process recurred. With the financial crisis and its political aftermath, a brief stagnation set in, but this was replaced by strong indications of a resurgence of agriculture that may be a sign that the structural transformation has been triggered again.

In Chapter 12, Ash, Du and King analyse the historical forces which shaped China's agricultural development during the Qing Dynasty and into the post-1911 Republican period. They then turn to post-1949 developments, where their focus is the government's attempt to resolve tensions between maintaining basic rural welfare and fulfilling its imperative of rapid industrial growth. The reforms which were instituted at the end of 1978 constitute a watershed in China's agricultural development as market forces and price signals began to make themselves felt, and farmers' decisions were no longer led by planning imperatives, but were increasingly shaped by changing prices. Simultaneously, rapid urbanisation, accelerated industrial development and large-scale infrastructural construction encroached on an already limited arable land base, whilst also encouraging massive inter-regional labour flows. Overall, grain output growth since 1978 has been impressive.

In the countries of Latin America, agriculture has also undergone profound transformations in the last two centuries, for reasons that have to do with the development models followed, as studied by Martín-Retortillo, Pinilla, Velazco and Willebald in Chapter 13. Initially, Latin American countries followed a commodity export-led growth model, based on agriculture and mining, that extended from the last third of the nineteenth century to the 1920s, with very varied results. After WWII, these countries moved to the progressive creation of the so-called inward-looking development model, in which agriculture definitively lost its once-leading role. However, since the beginning of the 1990s, a new strategy has been adopted that includes structural reforms and a return to the international market in agricultural products, with successful trajectories that tend to identify this stage with another prosperous era of globalisation (the authors recognise the period as a "real resurrection of the goose that laid the golden eggs"). The cases of Peru and Brazil illustrate these concepts.

In Chapter 14, Anderson seeks to shed light on the extent to which Australia's agricultural, mining, and manufacturing sectors have changed their contributions to GDP, employment, and exports in the course of Australia's economic growth over the past two centuries, with a particular focus on periods of mining booms and slumps. A key fact highlighted in this chapter is the persistence of agriculture in the overall economy for 100 years, and even during the latest mining boom, a process that responds to several factors: a large land frontier that took more than a century for settlers to exploit, declines in initially crippling domestic and ocean trade costs for farm products, innovations by farmers via a strong public agricultural R&D system, and reasonably sound macroeconomic policies that avoided the "resource curse" that afflicted so many other natural resource-rich economies. It is true that manufacturing protection policies reduced the prosperity of primary production, but for farmers and graziers that was, at least to some extent, offset by the ban on iron ore exports between the late 1930s and early 1960s and a boom in wool prices in the early 1950s.

Latin American evolution is expressed, in the case of Brazil, in a transition from a clear agricultural backwardness to its current global leadership. According to Mueller and Mueller, in Chapter 15, until the early 1960s, frontier expansion was the main determinant of agricultural growth, but beginning in the early 1970s, modernisation accelerated substantially, and the expansion of the frontier assumed a subsidiary role. The authors argue that the initial process of modernisation up to the 1990s can be represented as a top-down technocratic policy imposing a series of reforms that sought to modernise the sector and remove the bottlenecks and inefficiencies that hindered agriculture and created obstacles for industry and the macroeconomy, which were the central objectives of the policymakers. This chapter shows how these interventions succeeded in creating a productive agribusiness sector, for example by investing heavily in technology adapted to Brazilian reality. But at the same time, the interventions also led to further distortions and inefficiencies in agriculture, as they were used as an instrument for generating foreign exchange, controlling inflation, and other subsidiary objectives. The final transformation into a major world agricultural producer only took place after the mid-1990s, once the country had inflation under control and had reformed political institutions, allowing a less interventionist policy, in which induced innovation could finally thrive.

As Velazco and Pinilla explain in Chapter 16, throughout its history, Peru, as a small open economy, has undergone cycles of crisis and recovery, usually linked to fluctuations in the international market. The Peruvian economy has always been an exporter of primary products and an importer of manufactured goods. Development strategy models have ranged from the diversification of primary exports, to import-substitution industrialisation, and the promotion of non-traditional exports, which is the current model. These strategies have determined the outcome for agriculture. The sector was an axis of accumulation for the economy in the context of the model of primary exports of agricultural products (cotton and sugar) and minerals. This situation changed radically in the late 1950s, when an import-substitution industrialisation process was encouraged. This marked a turning point, when the growth of agriculture became dependent on the expansion of industry. The evidence discussed, particularly the growth in agricultural labour productivity and the performance of TFP, seems to suggest another change in the 1990s, in how agriculture related to and connected with other economic sectors. The structural reforms of the 1990s, particularly the policies promoting the development of agro-industry, created favourable conditions for non-traditional export agriculture to expand and consolidate. This growth was led by the coastal region, thanks to its climate, the expansion of agricultural frontiers based on irrigation, proximity to the markets, and improvements in infrastructure.

The importance of frontier expansion in agricultural evolution is analysed by Willebald and Juambeltz in Chapter 17. The expansion of the Atlantic economy from the mid-nineteenth century up to WWI, the incorporation of new regions into the global economy, and the formation of markets for goods and factors on a world scale are three of the main features of the First Globalisation. The new settlement economies followed parallel paths based on similar dynamic relationships between waves of immigration, the marginalisation of native populations, European capital inflows, an abundance of land, free labour, socially-useful political institutions, and neo-European cultures. These "temperate economies" include a group of non-European countries which, at the beginning of the twentieth century, could be classified as developed: Argentina, Uruguay, and Chile in South America, Canada in North America, South Africa in Africa, and Australia and New Zealand in Oceania. However, in this characterisation, the South American Southern Cone countries were the "failures" in the settler club, with slower development paths and lower living standards. The authors focus on the incorporation of "new" land into production, from 1850 to 1950, which had consequences for structural change, income distribution, and the intensity of the use of production factors. Settler economies conformed to different modalities of land incorporation into production, and they faced different conditions that involved adopting extensive or intensive processes of expansion. Those settler economies that evolved intensively through the process of land frontier extension, applying labour as intensification factor, fell behind in the long-run performance and constituted the "impoverished cousins" of the club: Argentina, Chile, and Uruguay. Those countries where the land frontier expansion adopted a different pattern—probably based on capital intensification—consolidated as the rich countries of the club: Australia, Canada and New Zealand. South Africa shared features of both groups.

Alvarez Scanniello, in Chapter 18, illustrates those differences, with an in-depth analysis of the cases of New Zealand and Uruguay. He argues that the different economic performances reflect dissimilar growth patterns of physical productivity in livestock production and, especially, in the productivity of agrarian land. A particular issue was the different rates at which the two countries implemented technologies that improved the land factor. While in New Zealand the livestock system was based on transforming the soil and creating pasture land, in Uruguay livestock rearing was based on natural grassland with only a small proportion of artificially produced or improved pasture land. Uruguay had better natural conditions for livestock production, which became apparent in the nineteenth century, and, therefore, it had less incentive than New Zealand to develop technologies to improve the productivity of land devoted to livestock production. The interaction among institutions (land market regulation), public policy (subsidy and credit schemes to stimulate the intensification of livestock production), agrarian innovation systems, and the geographical context, all played a key role in the development of technological change.

4 Concluding Remarks

Agriculture has played a relevant role in the economic development processes of peripheral countries. But this has not been its only role and it has not had the same importance in all countries. The wide variety of possibilities in its contribution to economic development has depended on numerous factors, including the initial conditions of each country (factor endowments, both in quantity and quality; institutional quality; the degree of technological development; the weight of non-agricultural traditional activities; agro-climatic factors; market accessibility; etc.), the mode of entry into international markets, with its positive and negative impacts, the economic policies and development models implemented by each country and the type of industrialisation or modernisation process experienced.

For many countries, external markets have been highly significant for the expansion of their agricultural activities. A rapid expansion of exports has constituted, for some peripheral economies, an important growth engine, as in the case of Argentina, Australia, New Zealand or Uruguay. However, in other countries, despite the growth of exports, the resulting inducement for development has been very weak, as in the cases of Ghana or Peru until quite recently. This shows the importance of the linkages of the export sector with the rest of the economy. Inter-sectoral and inter-regional (as in the case of Indonesia) links are absolutely vital for the potentiality of an export-driven model to work and produce significant results in terms of increasing per capita incomes and economic development.

These linkages are also fundamental so that the growth of industry and services and the expansion of the domestic market can generate, in turn, relevant agricultural growth and modernisation.

Furthermore, income distribution and the existing degree of inequality can influence whether agricultural growth to generates a greater or lesser effect on the growth of the economy as a whole, due to their incidence on the creation of markets and their relevance in the contention and management of conflicts. The institutional matrix is undoubtedly paramount in this type of process.

In fact, institutions can help us to understand the development of agriculture and its capacity to generate growth in the economy as a whole, while taking into account its often predominant endogenous nature. That is, although the establishment of appropriate property rights regarding natural resources, their enforcement and the respect of the rule of law are fundamental for implementing the structural change, the institutions have often arisen as a result of the different dimensions of the economic system and particularly in response to technological progress (as in the case of Southeast Asia). Technology has been a fundamental factor, particularly during the second half of the twentieth century, for the modernisation of the agricultural sectors of peripheral countries. The different paces at which the innovations have been adopted have depended on a whole range of factors: resource endowments, investment in R&D by public institutions, economic policies and the successful entry into international markets. These factors have acted as facilitators of the process or challenges to overcome, giving rise to trial and error and learning processes. In this sense, the role of the State has had transcendental importance.

As well as providing financial and technical resources to enable agricultural growth, the State has often been targeted by the different power groups acting in the economy (see the case of South Africa) and, particularly, those most closely related to natural resources (farmland, water, minerals). As before, the resolution of these conflicts illustrates and explains an adequate or deficient agricultural performance.

This book highlights the diversity of the results arising from the different paths followed by the periphery countries in the different world regions:

- In the export era (first wave of globalisation), the economies of the settler countries (Argentina, Australia, Canada, New Zealand, Uruguay) experienced spectacular growth, largely based on the development of the agricultural export sector, with good knock-on effects on other activities. In the lead-up to WWI, they were among the economies with the highest per capita income, despite having lower levels of industrialisation and being exposed to relatively volatile international markets. The agricultural sector has continued to be important in the majority of these countries, although restricted in some of them, and its development has been based on the persistence of primary production in the economic and exporting structure. There are many examples of truncated structural changes in periphery economies, which are particularly prominent in Latin American and African cases.
- In general terms, in the first wave of globalisation, the boost derived from exports was significant, but in some countries the results were fairly poor (as was the case of exporting economies in Latin America, except in the Southern Cone or Southeast Asia, which did not change drastically). With respect to the plantation economies, a few of them captured the

majority of the benefits to be gained from exporting, with the predominance of logic of the enclave and low-transformation structures.

- Since the end of WWII, the role of the agricultural sector and its contribution to development dwindled. This can be explained by the inward-looking development policies, but also by the high level of protectionism of the developed countries. In the latter, the high productivity of agriculture, which enabled them to have a higher level of self-sufficiency, and their policies for supporting domestic production, affected the development of periphery.
- However, in the final decades of the twentieth century, the agricultural sector recovered its leading role. Some countries opened up to external markets and since then a second export era has been taking place (the majority of Latin American countries, Ghana and South Africa in Africa, Vietnam in Asia). There has been a change in their policies, a greater exposure to international markets, new options for specialising in non-traditional products and closer links between the exporting sectors and the rest of the economy.
- Technology plays a relevant role in the second half of the twentieth century. The green revolution and other innovations have increased agricultural output and productivity substantially, with cases such as Brazil, where the sector has experienced a process which some identify with an "industrialisation" of agriculture.
- The institutional factors and, especially, the ownership structure and a better management of natural resources have played a significant role. This is the case with Vietnam with the Mekong Delta or the end of the plantation era with the definitive predominance of the smallholders.
- The State is a key agent in the agricultural development. The State implements economic policies that can promote or restrict agriculture (or the sectors linked with it), creates specific programmes (of production, technical assistance, financial support, price support), and it is the field where interests conflicts are solved.

Finally, the book also contemplates the conceptual category used as an argumentative and analytical guide. The notion of world periphery is dynamic. The starting point of this book is identifying economies which, given the conditions prevailing in the international economic system of the second half of the nineteenth century, could be considered as being marginal to the world economic core, due to their position with respect to the technological frontier and their incidence in the relationships of global power. However, the very process of structural transformation—to which the agricultural and mining industry decisively contributed—has led to several economies of our sample losing (or starting to lose) their status as periphery economies and now being classified as core economies (while being fully aware that the core concept is also a dynamic notion). Economies of the "rich" periphery, such as Canada, Australia or New Zealand, can hardly be called peripheral economies nowadays, but there are also several peripheral regions that were definitively poor at the end of the nineteenth century which are on the path not only to losing this status, but to becoming leaders of a model that seems to accept several centres in its constitution; this is the case with China, India, Brazil and some Southeast Asian economies. Nowadays, the international economy is subject to transcendental changes and, as it happened in the second half of the nineteenth century, the world periphery is the protagonist of this global transformation.

Notes

1. The debate on the deterioration of the terms of trade of primary products has generated a large number of studies, most of which have concluded that this deterioration did not exist in the period indicated by Prebisch and Singer (at least until 1914), but has been very important since the First World War (WWI). The deterioration has been more marked in certain periods in the form of shocks (the inter-war years and the 1980s), without a return to the initial situation in any persistent and continuous way as predicted by those authors. See Prebisch (1950), Singer (1950), Grilli and Yang (1988), Hadass and Williamson (2003), Ocampo and Parra-Lancourt (2010) and Serrano and Pinilla (2011).
2. Latin American structuralism, characterised especially by the economic thought developed by the ECLAC, is one of the most important representatives of this theoretical conceptualisation.

3. 1870–1938. We consider the data presented in Federico (2004) referred to agricultural output, real index (1913 = 100) (Statistical Appendix, Table I) and "world" shares in (Table 6) regarding North Western Europe, Southern Europe, the USA and Japan as the "core" and the rest of countries as the "periphery". For this we deducted Japan from Asia and the USA from Western Settlement. For Japan, we used three series: Gross Domestic Product by Industry at Market Prices (1985–1940), Deflator Agriculture, Forestry and Fishery (1985–1940) and Value Added in Agriculture: 1934–1936 Prices (1874–1936) from the Long-Term Economic Statistics (LTES) Database. For the USA, we used three series: Farm Gross Product (Million Dollars, 1913 prices); Gross Farm Income (Million Dollars, 1913 prices), and Gross Farm Income (Million Dollars 1913 prices, chained) from the Historical Statistics of the United States, Millennial Edition Online.
4. 1950–2010. As Federico (2008), we consider information of Gross production in agriculture (2004–2006 = 100) from FAO statistical database from 1961 to 2010, and complement the previous—partial—data with Federico (2008)'s estimates for the 1950s. We select the same "Core" countries that for the period 1870–1938 y consider the rest of the countries as "Periphery". We elaborate weighted indices according to the shares that represented the Gross Production Values (current million US$) in 1991–1992.

References

Adelman, I. (1984). Beyond Export-Led Growth. *World Development, 12*(9), 937–949.

Ascani, A., Crescenzi, R., & Iammarino, S. (2012). *New Economic Geography and Economic Integration: A Review.* WP 1/02 Search Working Paper.

Bairoch, P. (1999). *L'agriculture des pays développés. 1800 à nos jours.* Paris: Economica.

Baudrillard, J. (1983). *Simulations.* New York: Semiotext(e).

Delgado, C. Hopkins, J., & Kelly, V. (1994). *Agricultural Growth Linkages in Sub-Saharan Africa: A Synthesis.* IFPRI Report to USAID, Africa Bureau. Washington, DC: International Food Policy Research Institute.

Federico, G. (2004). The Growth of World Agricultural Production, 1800–1938. *Research in Economic History, 22*, 125–181.

Federico, G. (2008). *Feeding the World. An Economic History of Agriculture, 1800–2000*. Princeton, NJ: Princeton University Press.
Grilli, E. R., & Yang, M. C. (1988). Primary Commodity Prices, Manufactured Good Prices, and the Terms of Trades of Developing Countries: What the Long Run Shows. *The World Bank Economic Review, 2*(1), 1–47.
Hadass, Y. S., & Williamson, J. G. (2003). Terms-of-Trade Shocks and Economic Performance, 1870–1940: Prebisch and Singer Revisited. *Economic Development and Cultural Change, 51*(3), 629–656.
Hanns Reill, P., & Szelényi, B. A. (Eds.). (2011). *Cores, Peripheries and Globalization. Essays in Honor of Ivan T. Berend*. Budapest and New York: Central European University Press.
Hayami, Y., & Ruttan, V. (1985). *Agricultural Development: An International Perspective* (Revised and expanded ed.). Baltimore: Johns Hopkins University Press.
Hazell, P., & Haggblade, S. (1993). Farm-Nonfarm Growth Linkages and the Welfare of the Poor. In M. Lipton & J. van der Gaag (Eds.), *Including the Poor: Proceedings of a Symposium Organized by the World Bank and the International Food Policy Research Institute*. Washington, DC: The World Bank.
Hillbom, E., & Svensson, P. (Eds.). (2013). *Agricultural Transformation in a Global History Perspective, Routledge Explorations in Economic History*. London and New York: Taylor & Francis Group.
Jacks, D., O'Rourke, K., & Williamson, J. G. (2011). Commodity Price Volatility and World Market Integration Since 1700. *The Review of Economics and Statistics, 93*(3), 800–813.
Krugman, P. (1991). Increasing Returns and Economic Geography. *Journal of Political Economy, 99*(3), 483–499.
Lains, P., & Pinilla, V. (Eds.). (2009). *Agriculture and Economic Development in Europe Since 1870*. London and New York: Routledge Taylor and Francis Group.
Lindert, P., & Williamson, J. (2003). Does Globalization Make the World More Unequal? In M. Bordo, A. Taylor, & J. Williamson (Eds.), *Globalization in Historical Perspective* (pp. 227–275). Cambridge, MA: National Bureau of Economic Research.
Ocampo, J. A., & Parra-Lancourt, M. A. (2010). The Terms of Trade for Commodities Since the Mid-19th Century. Revista de Historia Económica. *Journal of Iberian and Latin American Economic History, 28*(1), 11–44.

Pinilla, V. (2009a). The Impact of Markets in the Management of Rural Land. In V. Pinilla (Ed.), *Markets and Agricultural Change in Europe from the 13th to the 20th Century* (pp. 11–36). Turnhout: Brepols Publishers.
Pinilla, V. (Ed.). (2009b). *Markets and Agricultural Change in Europe from the 13th to the 20th century*. Turnhout: Brepols Publishers.
Rodríguez, O. (2006). *El estructuralismo latinoamericano*. Mexico: SigloXXI-CEPAL/Naciones Unidas.
Ruttan, V. W. (2002). Productivity Growth in World Agriculture: Sources and Constraints. *The Journal of Economic Perspectives, 16*(4), 161–184.
Serrano, R., & Pinilla, V. (2011). Terms of Trade for Agricultural and Food Products, 1951–2000. *Revista de Historia Económica-Journal of Iberian and Latin American Economic History, 29*(2), 213–243.
Singer, H. W. (1950). *The Distribution of Gains between Investing and Borrowing Countries*. The American Economic Review, 40, 2, Papers and Proceedings of the Sixty-second Annual Meeting of the American Economic Asociation, pp. 473–485.
Timmer, C. P. (2009). *A World Without Agriculture: The Structural Transformation in Historical Perspective*. Washington, DC: AEI Press.
Vanolo, A. (2010). The Border Between Core and Periphery: Geographical Representations of the World System. *Tijdschrift voor Economische en Sociale Geografie, 101*(1), 26–36.

Sources

CC BY-SA 3.0., https://commons.wikimedia.org/w/index.php?curid=407551
Historical Statistics of the United States, Millennial Edition Online, Agriculture (http://hsus.cambridge.org/HSUSWeb/toc/showChapter.do?id=Da).
Food and Agriculture Organization of the United Nations (FAO).: http://www.fao.org/faostat/en/#home
Long-Term Economic Statistics (LTES) Database: Institute of Economic Research (http://www.ier.hit-u.ac.jp/English/databases/ltes.html) Series: J0125__001, J0130__007 and J0913__005.
The Maddison-Project, http://www.ggdc.net/maddison/maddison-project/home.htm, 2013 version.

Vicente Pinilla is Professor of Economic History at the University of Zaragoza and a Fellow of the Instituto Agroalimentario de Aragón (IA2). His research interests lies in international trade in agricultural products, long-term agricultural changes, environmental history, and migration. He is the author of *Peaceful Surrender: The Depopulation of Rural Spain in the Twentieth Century*, and editor of the books *Agriculture and Economic Development in Europe since 1870*, *Markets and Agricultural Change in Europe from the Thirteenth to the Twentieth Century*, *Natural Resources and Economic Growth: Learning from History*, and *Wine Globalization: A New Comparative History*.

Henry Willebald is Professor of Economic History and Economic Development at the Universidad de la República, Uruguay. His research interests lie in natural resources, international trade, regional development and inequalities in the long run (nineteenth and twentieth centuries). He is an editor of the book *Natural Resources and Economic Growth: Learning from History*, has written chapters in books edited by international publishers and has published articles in the main economic history journals.

2

Between the Engine and the Fifth Wheel: An Analytical Survey of the Shifting Roles of Agriculture in Development Theory

Martin Andersson and Emelie Rohne Till

1 Introduction

Over the last decade, agricultural development in less developed countries has increasingly become the talk of the town. International donors and national governments have increased their attention to the rural economy, agriculture has attracted raising commercial investments and the interest among scholars, media and the public seems to have risen, leading some to predict an "agricultural renaissance" in the twenty-first century (Pingali, 2010). However, two diametrically opposing views on the role of agriculture in economic development exist within the

The authors benefitted from comments on an earlier version of this chapter at seminars at University of Queensland and University of Zaragoza, as well as from the editors and Derek Byerlee. The authors also gratefully acknowledge research funding from Marianne and Marcus Wallenberg Foundation, The Wenner-Gren Foundations and The Crafoord Foundation.

M. Andersson • E. Rohne Till (✉)
Department of Economic History, Lund University, Lund, Sweden

V. Pinilla, H. Willebald (eds.), *Agricultural Development in the World Periphery*, Palgrave Studies in Economic History, https://doi.org/10.1007/978-3-319-66020-2_2

scholarly debate. According to the agro-proponents, agriculture plays a crucial role for both aggregate and pro-poor growth (Adelman, 1984; Christiaensen, Demery, & Kuhl, 2011; de Janvry & Sadoulet, 2010; Lipton, 2012; Ravallion & Chen, 2007; Timmer, 2009). They hold that agricultural development has been essential for long-term growth and industrialisation in the past (Diao, Hazell, Resnick, & Thurlow, 2007; Gollin, Parente, & Rogerson, 2002; Mellor, 1999; Timmer, 1988). Concurrently, the agro-sceptics argue that agriculture is unlikely to lift poor countries out of poverty and to stimulate sustained increase in income growth (Ashley & Maxwell, 2001; Collier & Dercon, 2009). They question the idea that agricultural growth is generally efficient in reducing poverty (Hasan & Quibria, 2004), that agriculture typically has been a precursor of development (Ellis, 2004), and that agriculture was as an engine of growth historically in now-developed countries (Dercon & Gollin, 2014). As such, in today's scholarly debate, agriculture is seen as both the engine and the fifth wheel in economic development.

The purpose of this chapter is to trace how the role of agriculture in theories of economic development has shifted over time, and to explore possible reasons as to why scholarly attention vis-à-vis agriculture fluctuates. Methodologically, our approach is based on reviewing key literature in Development Economics, and in Agricultural Economics with regard to developing countries. The key source and principle guide to the literature on agriculture in economic development up to the early 1990s is the Survey of Economics Literature volume IV (Martin 1992), devoted entirely to agriculture in developing countries. For the general tendencies we based our approach on the Handbook of Development Economics volumes I–V (from 1988 to 2010), the Handbook of Agricultural Economics volumes I–IV (2001–2010), and World Bank Reports (World Bank 1982; 1986; 2007)—as well as previous survey efforts (Barrett, Carter, & Timmer, 2010; Dethier & Effenberger, 2012; Federico, 2005; Johnston, 1970; Lains & Pinilla, 2009; Rao, 1985; Reynolds, 1975; Staatz & Eicher, 1998). Further, we have used a bibliometric methodology to estimate the shifting scholarly attention, which considers all economic literature published on EconLit, 1969–2015.

2 Perspectives on Agriculture in Development

Among the range of perspectives on the role of agriculture in development since the birth of Development Economics, four major views in the literature are identified as having been particularly influential.

2.1 Fifth Wheel: Duality and Agricultural Labour Surplus

At the centre of early development theory is the idea of duality, typically between the modern industrial sector and the traditional agricultural. Two of the most influential perspectives on dualism are Boeke's (1953) study of colonial Indonesia and Lewis's classic Economic Development with Unlimited Supplies of Labour (1954). For Boeke, dualism meant the different workings of the modern vz the agricultural sectors, and of the developed vz developing world, respectively. According to him, the social structures of developing countries were so different from Western countries, that Western development strategies were simply not applicable. This type of "cultural" dualism should not be confused with the dualism connected with Arthur Lewis. The fundamental difference between these two conceptualisations is that in Boeke's duality, labour supply is either backwards bending or totally inelastic, whereas in Lewis's model it is perfectly elastic. Lewis's model is most relevant here, as it had a profound legacy on development theory. The model's duality meant that neoclassical assumptions had to be abandoned and therefore the approach to the study of the economy of developing countries needed a particular kind of economics: Development Economics.

In Lewis's two-sector model (as in the models of Fei and Ranis (1964) and Jorgenson (1961)), the subsistence sector holds an unlimited supply of labour, readily transferrable at a relatively low cost to the modern industrial sector. While farmers in Boeke's world are content with a target income, for Lewis, subsistence farmers are ready to accept moving to other sectors for an income slightly higher than in agriculture but well below marginal productivity in the modern sector. According to this view, agriculture's contribution to development is to reallocate labour and indirectly contribute to much needed savings and investments in the modern sector. As such, agriculture is important but more implicitly, than explicitly, analysed.

While Lewis did not equate the agricultural sector with subsistence, his theory maintains that it is the agricultural sector that typically holds the largest amount of subsistence labour. The surplus labour was conceptually close to, for instance, Rosenstein-Rodan (1943) and Nurkse's *disguised unemployment* in agriculture, which meant that *agrarian excess population* could be removed from agriculture without reducing output. Since labour was a valuable yet underutilised resource it could be reallocated to the modern sector for the capital formation necessary for industrialisation to evolve. This view, which is at the core of early development thinking, was classical economics applied to underdeveloped economies to which orthodox neoclassical economics made little sense. Although Lewis (1954, p. 433) himself did not neglect the importance of the agricultural sector, holding that industrial and agrarian revolutions always go together, the legacy of this school is that agriculture does not drive industrialisation and the development process. If neglected, agriculture might stifle the entire process, but by itself it does not stimulate economic development—rather it acts as a fifth wheel.

2.2 Chicago School Rationality and Anti-distortion

A major influence on the perception of how agriculture functions in developing countries came with Theodore Schultz. He recognised neither cultural dualism nor surplus agricultural labour. Instead, Schultz went to great trouble to restore the neoclassical position that the marginal productivity of agricultural labour was not zero, using a microeconomic approach focusing on the behaviour of individual farmers. He convincingly argued that peasants were as rational as any other economic agent (a point already made by Bauer and Yamey in their (1959) study on Nigerian farmers), and that while farmers in developing countries might be poor they use the available resources efficiently. By implication the supply curve of labour is neither flat nor backwards bending (Schultz, 1964).

Farmers were poor because traditional agriculture tends "to approximate the economic equilibrium of the stationary state" (1964, p. 6) and it would require new knowledge or technology to break away from this equilibrium. As such, investment in farmers' knowledge and technology would support productivity increases in the agricultural sector. In Schultz's view, agriculture, if not upgraded, will slow down overall growth. But if its productivity increases, which it will if proper incentives are given to it, agriculture can be as efficient as any other sector.

That rational behaviour and market incentives are applicable also to smallholder farmers might not be particularly controversial today. As Falcon (1988, p. 199) points out, however, this was viewed as radical at a time when agriculture was largely seen as a passive sector populated by small farmers held back by traditionalism and inertia. For example, Myrdal's (1968) influential "Asian Drama" argued that smallholder agriculture lacked spread effects and that agriculture was not likely to develop without large-scale land reforms.

A second policy legacy of Schultz, in addition to the investment in public goods to improve farmers' access to knowledge and technology, is a strong hands-off attitude to agricultural regulatory policies, for example on price stabilisation and international trade. This inference logically follows the rationality perspective, and has been forcefully argued by Schultz and his followers. Proponents of this reasoning have shown the lack of economic reason for agriculture to be overly taxed in poor countries and excessively subsidised in rich countries, as this effectively closes the door for producers in the developing world (Anderson, 2009; Bauer, 1954; Johnson, 1973; Krueger, Schiff, & Valdés, 1988, 1991; Schultz, 1978). However, it is less clear what this view suggests in terms of agricultural development after distortions are wiped away. The implication of this perspective is that Agricultural Economics is very much like regular economics, which functions the same in developing countries as developed ones.

2.3 Agriculture and Trade: Break or Injection

A third main view concerns itself with the role of agriculture in trade, where agriculture is seen as either a break or an injection. Regarding the first, the works of Raúl Prebisch and followers have been particularly influential for the developing world. As most development economists of the 1950s–1960s, they were concerned with rapid industrialisation in the developing world, which required substantial state planning to encourage necessary capital formation and reallocation towards the modern sector. The core concept was the Prebisch–Singer thesis, suggesting deteriorating terms of trade for primary products in relation to industrial goods. By implication, concentration on agriculture has long-term adverse effects on developing countries' ability to catch-up. The import-substitutive policies that followed had a clear anti-agriculture bias and were widely adopted in the developing world. This perspective did not regard agriculture to be able to generate employment or to develop linkages to the rest of the economy, nor to play any major role in stimulating domestic industrial production. Instead, all agricultural labour needed to be transferred to industry due to its low marginal productivity (Baran, 1952; De Janvry, 1975).

In contrast to the strand seeing agricultural trade as a block to development, the opposite view was formulated by Myint's (1958) vent-for-surplus thesis. This states that increased effective demand from trade enables use of surplus resources (land and/or family labour) existing in developing countries. This particularly applies to countries where the land frontier is not closed. Rather than trade as a function of comparative advantage, this "surplus productive capacity" is a relatively inexpensive way to increase growth in poor countries.[1]

2.4 Agriculture as Engine

The fourth main view sees agriculture as a potential driver—engine—of growth. According to this view, agriculture can play such a crucial role via the structural transformation; the strengthening of the domestic market; or productivity enhancing technological change.

The first strand among the perspectives that sees agriculture as a major force in the growth process has its roots in the structural change analysis understanding the relative decline of agriculture in the process of modern economic growth, and agriculture's contribution of food, labour and capital in this process (Chenery & Syrquin, 1975; Clark, 1940; Kuznets,

1961). Within this, two angles exist, emphasising either the specific contributions of agriculture, or the wider linkages of agricultural growth in the rest of the economy. In the first, based on Kuznets (1961), agriculture makes specific and significant contributions to the growth process through the direct contribution of factors (labour, capital), commodities (food), and market expansion (via increased domestic demand). In the second, agricultural growth underpins aggregate and pro-poor growth through providing strong and varied linkages to the rest of the economy. This interaction creates linkages from the agricultural to the industrial and service sectors, via factor, commodity and financial flows, as first developed by Johnston and Mellor (1961); further strengthened by Peter Timmer (1988, 2002, 2005, 2009); and Nicholls (1964), King & Byerlee (1978), Mellor & Johnston (1984), Hazell & Haggblade (1993), Ranis & Stewart (1993), and Delgado, Hopkins, & Kelly (1994).

A second, closely related, strand, emphasises agricultural growth's potential to strengthen the domestic market, thereby stimulating aggregate growth—first advanced by Singer (1979), and further developed by Adelman (1984) and her concept of "agricultural demand-led industrialisation" (ADLI). Under ADLI, agriculture contributes through effective demand for non-tradable industrial goods created by rising agricultural incomes, induced by the ADLI strategy. According to this strategy, development should be agriculture driven rather than export driven, as increased agricultural growth leads to more domestic demand for domestically produced intermediate goods and commodities, than growth in other sectors does (Adelman, 1984).

A third strand, seeing agriculture as an engine for growth, partly stems from Schultz's emphasis on technological change to get agriculture moving, as advanced by Yujiro Hayami and Vernon Ruttan. While they acknowledge the impact of Schultz's rational farmer thesis and subsequent enthusiasm for investing in farmers' education, agricultural knowledge and technology, they found it to be an incomplete theory of agricultural change (Ruttan, 2002). In response they developed the "induced innovation model," which has since become the dominant theory on how more productive technologies for low-income agriculture emerge (Ruttan & Hayami, 1984). In this model, technical innovations are driven by changes in relative factor prices, which induce profit-seeking innovations either by private firms or the public sector. This is different from the view of Boserup (1965), who was more concerned with how changing factor prices in light of population pressure spurs technological progress. As such, Ruttan and Hayami remain analytically quite close to Schultz, emphasising the role that rationality and changing incentives play in the development of the agricultural sector, which in turn plays a role in economic development.

To conclude, it seems that today's agro-sceptics are rooted in the fifth-wheel view, where agriculture is perceived as insufficient to generate transformative economic growth. Gollin (2010, p. 3860), recognises this legacy himself, stating that: "This general story—told convincingly in the early agricultural development literature—seems in large measure to be right." The agro-proponents on the other hand, have a closer tie to the "agriculture as engine, via structural transformation" school. Like the early scholars, who saw agriculture as an engine for growth, the current agro-proponents seek to show the tremendous growth potential that agricultural growth can have to aggregate economic growth, and especially pro-poor growth, via the sector's multiple linkages to the overall economy.

3 Patterns in Academic Attention to Agriculture

3.1 Bibliometric Methodology

To explore the shifting levels of attention to agriculture in the scholarly debate, a three-pronged bibliometric approach is used, organising and analysing the collective scholarly work in the field.

The first approach maps all articles in the field of interest as a share of all articles published in economics, using the Journal of Economic Literature (JEL) classification. The database is compiled from EconLit (American Economic Association's database of economic literature), and through drawing on Kelly & Bruestle's (2011) classification of the database per each JEL-code, 1969–2007 (extending this to 2015). The mapping calculates the share of articles published in each of the relevant JEL-codes, including the categories O (Economic Development) and Q (Agriculture and Natural Resource Economics).[2] The database has two main caveats: adjustments made so that the extended database (for 2007–2015) is comparable with that of 1969–2007, and the change of JEL classifications in 1991. Firstly, every article may have up to 7 JEL-codes, meaning that a simple tabulation of JEL-codes may inflate the share of relevant articles. To avoid this, Kelly & Bruestle (2011) treats an article with *n* different codes as *n* different articles with each assigned a weight of 1/*n* of an article (for an article with 3 JEL-codes, each JEL-code is treated as 1/3 (=0.33) article with that JEL-code). Through this, the total number of JEL-codes correspond to the total number of articles published. To make the extension (2007–2015) comparable, the same method is used. However, the extension does not have access to the exact number of JEL-codes for each article. Instead, the articles are weighted by the average number of JEL-codes. As the average number of JEL-codes are 2.73 (Kosnik, 2016), each JEL-code is weighted by 0.366 (1/2.73). For 2005, 2006 and 2007, both techniques are used in order to test if the average JEL-codes give comparable results. Overall, they do[3] and the method is accepted as strong enough to reveal the research trends that this chapter is interested in, despite its drawbacks. The second caveat is the change in the classification system in 1991. Here, the paper relies on Kelly & Bruestle's (2011) effort to merge the two systems, which benefits from the fact that in 1991–1999 authors assigned both old and new codes. Using the shares from this double-entry, they develop a weighting scheme to track the development pre-1991. While this paper relies on this method, it should be noted that the stark trend-breaks around 1991 may have been inflated due to the recoding, and the pre- and post-1991 comparisons should be interpreted with care.

The second bibliometric approach tracks the shifting attention in a more tailored manner, by identifying specifically relevant journals. As Alafiatayo (1989) discusses, for any field there are a number of journals considered "core journals" and therefore referred to much more frequently than other journals. Due to the multi-disciplinary nature of the topic of interest, "core journals" are identified across three disciplines: Agricultural Economics, Development Economics and Economics. The journals in each discipline are selected based on a qualitative assessment of the journals' relevance, coupled with a consideration of their impact factor (in the Journal Citation Report). This was done by: identifying the top 10 highest impact factor journals in each discipline; qualitatively assessing the relevance of these journals for this chapter (highly relevant/semi-relevant/not relevant); and selecting, from those that were assessed as "highly relevant", the journals with highest impact factor. As such, these journals were selected:

- Agricultural Economics
  - *Journal Of Agricultural Economics* (Impact Factor: 1.545)
  - *American Journal Of Agricultural Economics* (1.436)
- Development Economics
  - *World Development* (2.438)
  - *Journal Of Development Economics* (1.837)
- Economics
  - *Quarterly Journal Of Economics* (5.538)
  - *American Economic Review* (3.833)

To trace the scholarly attention to the role of agriculture in these journals, the frequency of articles with certain keywords in the topic were mapped for each journal. For the journals in Development Economics and Economics, the keyword "agricultur*" was mapped. For the Agricultural Economics journals, the keyword "developing" was mapped instead, in an effort to trace the most relevant articles. However, as Silva and Teixeira (2009) highlight, bibliometric exercises always are limited with regard to the chosen keyword's inability to embrace the entire reality under analysis, which affects the analysis.

The third bibliometric approach is to select seminal articles and map the influence of these over time, via citation analysis. The seminal articles were selected through a qualitative assessment, based on the literature review covered in Sect. 2. One article for each main view identified in Sect. 2 was selected:

- Fifth wheel: Ranis and Fei (1961)
- Rational but distorted: Krueger, Schiff, and Valdés (1988)

- Trade, as injection: Myint (1958)
- Trade, as break: Prebisch (1959)
- Engine, via structural transformation: Johnston and Mellor (1961)
- Engine, via technology: Ruttan and Hayami (1984)
- Engine, via demand: Adelman (1984).

Next, the citations of the selected articles were mapped over time, using the Web of Science's (WoS) Social Science Citation Index (SSCI). This index was used instead of EconLit as it spans a longer time (from 1956), and because it offers more comprehensive citation data of the published literature.

3.2 Bibliometric Results

Graph 2.1 traces the relative attention to agriculture's role in economic development (O13) and in international trade (Q17), as a share of all articles published in EconLit, 1969–2015. The share is the number of articles in the sub-discipline in a specific year, divided by all articles published that year available on EconLit. For reference, in 1969 the total number of articles is 4474; 13,091 in 1992; and 42,298 in 2015.

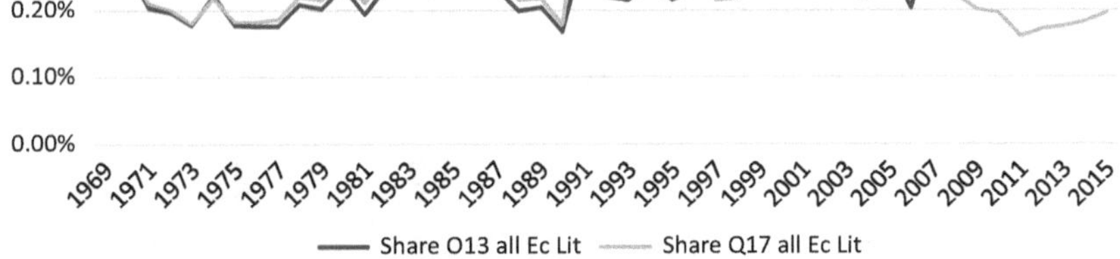

Graph 2.1 Relative importance of sub-disciplines O13 (Development Economics: Agriculture) and Q17 (Agricultural Economics: Agriculture in International Trade) in total articles in Economic Literature (published in EconLit), 1969–2015

As depicted, the scholarly attention to agriculture's role in development was high in the initial part of the period (1969–1970), lower during 1970s–1990s, and it increased for a short period after 1991 before stagnating around 1995–2005. Regarding the last decade (2005–2015), the graph confirms that the attention to the role of agriculture in economic development has increased sharply, while the attention to the role of agriculture in international trade has decreased to some of the lowest levels in the period.

Graph 2.2 displays the attention in the core journals to the agricultural sector (development and economics journals), or to developing economies (agricultural journals). As is shown, agriculture enjoyed a relatively high share of attention in high-impact Economics journals in the 1960s, but has since received less attention. For Development Economics journals, agriculture received more attention from the 1990s onwards, at the same time as development was receiving even more attention in high-impact agricultural journals.

Graph 2.3 displays the number of citations for each selected article, over time. The pattern indicates relatively frequent citations in the 1960s; decline after the mid-1970s; relatively low level of citation during the 1980s; a sharp increase 1991–1995; a further increase after 2005. More specifically, the graph indicates that Ranis and Fei (1961)—as an article

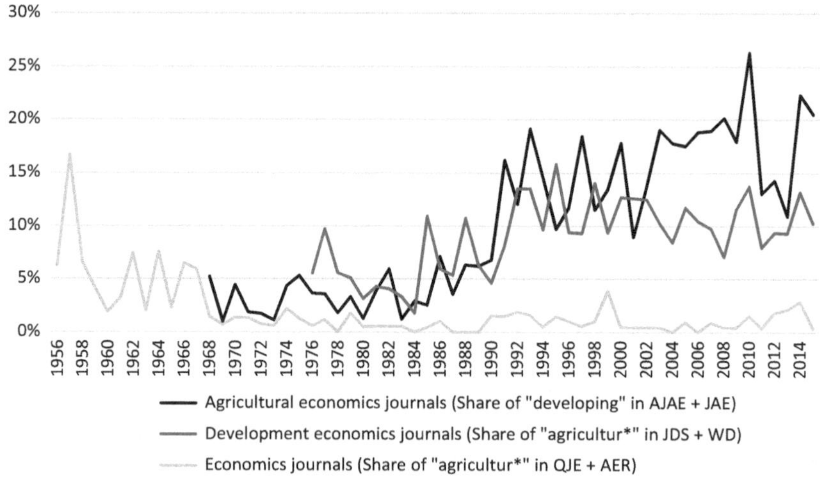

Graph 2.2 Share of relevant articles in core journals

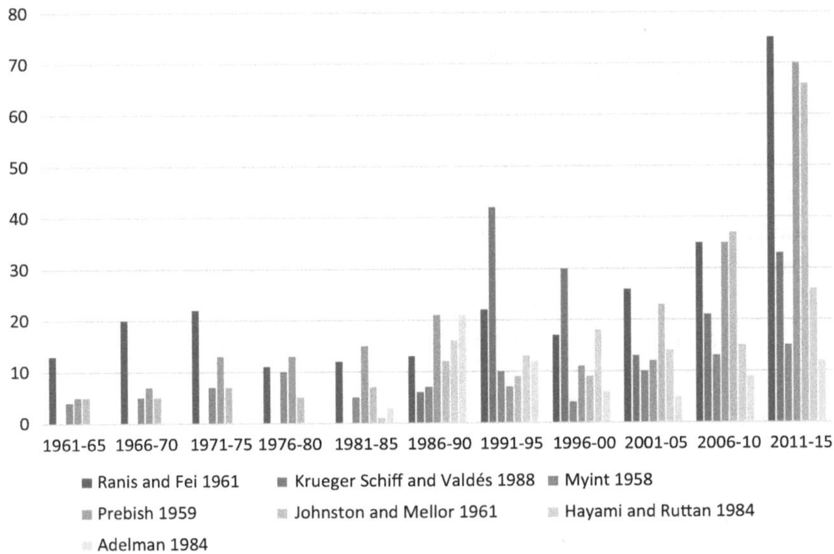

Graph 2.3 Number of citations on WoS SSCI, per key article, in 5-year intervals

within the "agriculture as fifth wheel"—was frequently cited around 1965–1975 and again post-2005. We see that Krueger et al. (1988) within the "agriculture as rational but distorted" enjoyed only a short time of attention 1991–1995. Citations of Adelman (1984) and "agriculture as engine, via demand" have increased since 2000. Further, Johnston and Mellor (1961) and the "agriculture as engine, via structural transformation" was most cited during the 1960s and post-2005; while Myint's (1958) view of agriculture as an injection to trade has been moderately cited throughout the period. Prebisch's view on agriculture as a break via trade was the most cited key article in the late 1970s and the 1980s, and has again been cited in the last decade. Lastly, concerning Ruttan and Hayami (1984), representing the "agriculture as engine, via technology," this was well cited during the 1990s but has since lost ground to both Johnston and Mellor (1961) and Ranis and Fei (1961).

In addition a regional analysis is conducted, estimating the articles published concerning the three major regions Africa, Asia and Latin America.[4] This shows that before 1980 there was no pronounced difference in interest in agricultural research between the regions, and that the interest in agriculture in Africa has outpaced that of the other regions since the mid-1980s, and with a slight acceleration of the gap in the post-2005 period. Since the 1990s there has been some increased interest also in agriculture in Asia (possibly driven be an interest in South Asia), whereas the interest in agriculture in Latin America has been stagnant.

Analysing the results, we find that there have been five main phases of interest: higher interest in the late 1960s, early 1990s and post-2005, and lower in the 1970–1980s and around 1995–2005. In the late 1960s and early 1970s, the scholarly attention to the subject was relatively high, indicated by high attention to articles on the role of agriculture in economic development (JEL-code O13) and the role of agriculture in international trade (JEL-code Q17) as a share in all economic literature published on EconLit. Further, this was also a time of a relatively high attention to Agricultural Economics within high-impact Economics journals, and relatively frequent citations of seminal articles. From the mid-1970s until late 1980s, the scholarly attention to the role of agriculture was low, both in the overall economic literature, and within relevant high-impact journals. Further, among the selected key articles, only Ranis and Fei's (1961) article on 'agriculture as fifth wheel' remained relatively well cited, whereas the other seminal articles were much less cited. There was a break around 1989–1990, as the scholarly attention to agriculture saw an upswing during 1989–1995. Graph 2.3 indicates that this was driven by attention to Krueger, Schiff and Valdés (1988)-type literature, on the need to treat agriculture as a rational sector and to eliminate distortions. This is also reflected in that this period saw an upswing of attention to the JEL-code Q17 (agriculture in international trade). However, this upswing was relatively short, and 1995–2005 saw lower scholarly attention to agriculture, as seen in the decreasing share of agricultural-related articles within Development Economics literature, the stagnant share of relevant articles in high-impact journals, and the decreasing number of citations of all selected key articles. In the last period there is a marked shift towards more scholarly attention, with a high share of articles with JEL-code O13, a high share of articles on developing contexts in Agricultural Economics journals, and frequent citations to Fei and Ranis, Johnston and Mellor, and Hayami and Ruttan.

4 Explaining the Shifting Academic Attention to Agriculture

To explore why the shifts in scholarly attention have taken place, we put forth five explanations that are featured as possible drivers in the literature on the role of agriculture reviewed for this chapter. Each potential driver is explored below, in an effort to identify the extent to which they represent reasonable explanations behind shifts in attention to agriculture. Our assessment is based on how these five explanations align with other notable trends in the development discussion.

4.1 Fluctuations of Agricultural Commodity Prices

In much of the recent literature on agriculture in development, there is a perception that the resurgence of interest of agriculture since around 2005, is driven by increased world food prices since the early 2000s. Due to a combination of structural changes in world demand (increased demand from emerging economies, continuing urbanisation) and supply (increased competition for water and land, slowing down of growth of agricultural R&D investments), and exacerbated by weather shocks and rising energy prices, global grain consumption exceeded global production for most of the early 2000s, depleting stocks worldwide. Subsequently, the global food prices spiked around 2008 and have since remained at a higher level than pre-crisis (Diaz-Bonilla & Robinson, 2010).

Turning to the data however, the correspondence between high food prices and high attention does not hold for any of the other periods identified in Sect. 3. As can be seen in Graph 2.4, food prices were high at the end of the 1950s to mid-1960s, in the 1970s, and relatively high (after a long period of decline) after the mid-2000s.[5] Recalling that agricultural interest was found to be high in the late 1960s, the first half of the 1990s and after 2005, it does not appear that high food prices themselves were driving the shifts between high and low attention to agriculture, even with the expectation that there would be a certain lag in the attention to agriculture that food price changes would cause. The high food prices in the 1970s cannot be connected to an increased interest in the 1970s or

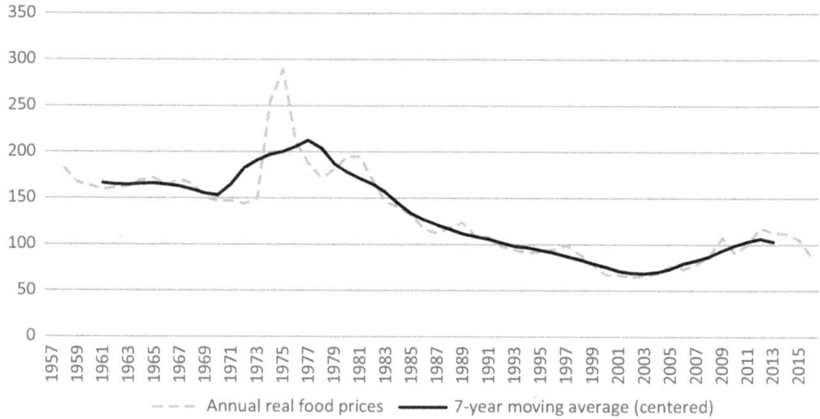

Graph 2.4 Annual Real Food Price Index (2010 = 100), 1957–2015. Note: Following the approach of OECD (2015, p. 12), nominal food prices are deflated by seasonally adjusted GDP deflator for the USA, to convert to real prices. Source: Author's calculation based on IMF IFS database 2016

1980s, and neither of the periods of high interest on the late 1960s or early 1990s was marked by increasing prices.

However, prices' role should not be understated: the extended period of declining food prices in the 1980s and 1990s (associated with slumping world growth, increased agricultural support in developed countries lowering demand, and the continued expansion of the Green Revolution increasing supply) led to many developing countries starting to discourage domestic production of staples and investments to agriculture (Diaz-Bonilla & Robinson, 2010). This indicates that extended periods of low or high prices affect the general trend in attention to the role of agriculture in development, but it is not sufficient to confirm that world food prices is a main driver, historically and universally, for the shifts in attention to the role of agriculture.

4.2 Concern for Food Security

The second potential driver discussed relates to the most elementary role of agriculture: the ability to deliver food and nutrition to an expanding global population.

In the 1960s and 1970s, the view on food security gradually shifted from rather widespread Malthusian concern, to optimism that food security could actually be achieved, in light of the Green Revolution across Asia. Its success in both helping to avoid famines and contributing to aggregate growth (Lipton, 1989) possibly led to less concern with food security. However, from the 1980s onwards, food security was no longer seen as a primary concern, but instead seen as something that could be achieved via trade, targeted development programmes, or urban migration—not via strengthening the agricultural sector (De Janvry, 2010). During this time, agriculture was neglected in policy, and public investments to agriculture diminished. That said, the period did see some increased attention to access (rather than production) of food with Sen's (1981) influential writings emphasising the need to understand the demand and distributional side of food security, and in light of the 1968–1974 Sahelian drought and the Great African Famine 1984–1985.

After twenty years of playing second fiddle, food security again became a central policy concern from 2005 onwards. Its re-emergence as a central policy concern is mainly rooted in the new global challenges, and in the resurgence of optimism that food security can be achieved via technological improvements. In terms of the challenges, the changing patterns of global food production and consumption, changing diets, new technologies, and liberalisation of trade and FDI vis-à-vis agriculture is putting enormous pressure on the largely small-scale and relatively low-productive agriculture that predominates in most developing countries. Among the 3.38 billion people living in rural areas in the world, 3.16 billion live in low- and middle-income countries, and a vast majority of them are small-scale farmers relying on agriculture for food and income (WDI, 2017). Unless these small-scale farmers are enabled to cope with the pressures that the new global food system is putting on them, it might be premature to write off the Malthusian concern, common among pre-Green Revolution scholars, as invalid. However, at the same time as the increased challenges to food security are placing it on the agenda, technological improvements and renewed optimism towards achieving food security have also supported the recent increased attention to agriculture. The technology for it is already in place, and for some a Green (or Gene) Revolution in Africa is no longer unrealistic wishful thinking but a process that has already started (The Economist, 2016a, 2016b). In addition to the challenges and opportunities for agriculture in the developing world, the global concern for food security has also increased in connection with the drive to examine agriculture's role in energy and environment concerns—for example, its ability to provide biofuel and to economically sequester carbon (Pingali, 2010).

Overall, it appears as the fluctuating interest in food security is reflected in the scholarly attention to agriculture in economic development.

4.3 Influence of Historical Development Experiences

A third potential driver is the perception of the role of agriculture in historical development experiences, particularly those in England in the eighteenth and nineteenth centuries, in the Soviet Union in the first half of the twentieth century and in various part of the developing world in the second half of the twentieth century.

As summarised in Lains and Pinilla (2009), there was a general consensus among European economic historians in the 1950s until 1980s, that the agricultural revolution was a crucial factor for industrialisation and economic growth in England and Europe. The industrial revolution in England had been preceded by an agricultural revolution—increasing agricultural productivity and enabling modern manufacturing to emerge—by several decades. Although this understanding was later questioned by, for example, Allen (1994) and Clark (2007), it was influential in shaping the understanding of the scholars such as Lewis and Nurkse that industrial and agrarian revolutions always go together. According to Timmer (1988), this understanding of the English development experience contributed to the view of agriculture as a fifth wheel, as it does not see the agricultural sector itself as actively driving economic development.

The interpretation of the role that agriculture played in the Soviet experience from the 1930s to the 1950s, further came to strengthen the views of agriculture as a fifth wheel (Timmer, 1992). The apparent success of the forced industrialisation campaign, relying on the State's capacity to extract surpluses from agriculture, offered support to the views that neglected the role of agriculture, such as most interpretations of Lewis's (1954) model, the structuralist views of Prebisch, as well as Gerschenkron's understanding of the role of agriculture in the Soviet development. However, after the collapse of the centrally planned economies in Eastern Europe and the Soviet Union, the understanding of the role of agriculture in the Soviet Union has instead contributed to an extractive view of agriculture losing support.

In second half of the twentieth century, development experiences within the developing countries may have contributed to the shifting attention to agriculture. The rapid development experience of East Asia likely contributed to a positive view of agriculture, as agricultural growth is seen to have provided a foundation for the rapid growth from the 1960s onwards. Drawing especially on Taiwan, the agricultural sector is seen to have played an important role in the early development phase through the land reforms of the 1950s, the strengthening of rural cooperatives in finance, credit, and marketing in the 1960s, and the market-oriented reforms that were introduced for agriculture in the late 1970s and 1980s. Coupled with the adoption of high-yielding varieties and use of chemical fertilisers, pesticides, and irrigation, agricultural growth was rapid in the region (Fan and Brzeska, 2010). As for Latin America, the early approach to agriculture was heavily influenced by Prebisch and the theory on deteriorating terms of trade, leading to an environment of protectionism and neglect of agriculture, implemented through: overvalued currencies; limitation of exports via export taxes, export quotas and embargos; limited investment in agricultural R&D and rural education; and food price manipulation (Schuh & Brandão, 1992, pp. 567, 571, 586). The failure of these development policies to yield the desired economic development may have contributed to the increased attention to agriculture in the last decade. As for Africa in this period, agriculture was largely overshadowed by concerns for industrialisation, as well as for education, aid and nation-building (Eicher & Baker, 1992, p. 22). The underperformance of both agricultural and aggregate economic growth in this period (Binswanger-Mkhize & McCalla, 2010), and agriculture's substantially larger share of GDP in Africa compared to other regions (WDI, 2017), may have contributed to the increased interest in agriculture in development in Africa, as shown in the regional analysis in Sect. 3.2. Overall, the understanding of the role of agriculture in previous development experiences, may have contributed to the broad shifts in scholarly attention to agriculture, leading towards a more prioritised role in the twenty-first century.

4.4 Shifting Paradigms in Development Assistance

The fourth potential driver is that changes in development assistance may have affected scholarly attention to agriculture. Overall, this assistance has reflected the movements of the field of Development Economics (usefully synthesised by Thorbecke 2006). The early development assistance of the 1950s, with the exception of US aid to East Asia, was guided by the general development objective of the time: to achieve growth via industrialisation, largely subordinating agriculture to the needs of industrialisation. The 1960s and 1970s kept with the framework of industrialisation and import-substitution, by which support to agriculture was mostly viewed as a way to reach poverty-stricken groups. This concern for poverty was mostly crowded out in the 1980s and 1990s (De Janvry, 2010), although the 1980s was also when the international organisations, led by the World Bank, started to increase their attention to the role of agriculture in economic development (WDR, 1982, 1986). Around 2000, poverty returned as a major policy concern for the international community, as exemplified by the Millennium Development Goals. As most of the world's poor are in agriculture, the sector received increased attention, for example illustrated by the 2008 World Development Report—fully dedicated to the role of agriculture for economic development. In this last period, new actors promoting the role of agriculture in development have also emerged, such as the Bill and Melinda Gates Foundation, which has committed more than US$2 billion to increase agricultural productivity (Gates Foundation, 2016).

To illustrate how these paradigm shifts in development assistance have influenced the attention to the agricultural sector, Graph 2.5 tracks development assistance directed at agriculture, 1967–2015, exploring if "donors' interest" has mirrored "scholarly interest" to agriculture. As displayed, agricultural aid increased throughout the 1970s until it peaked in

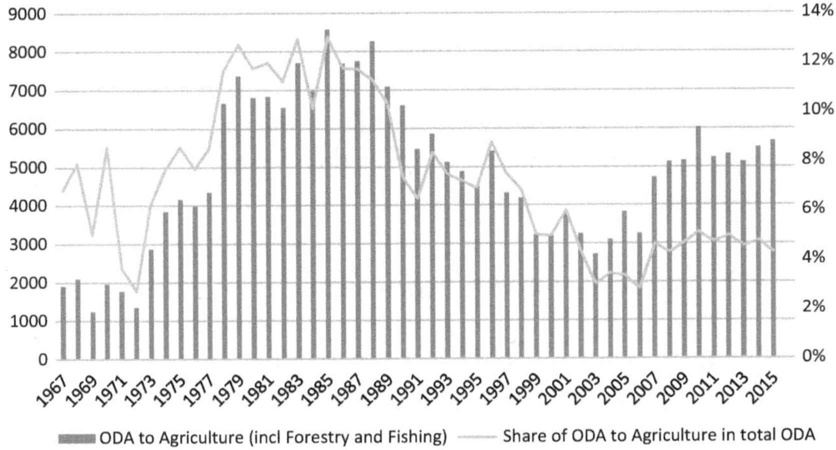

Graph 2.5 DAC Official Development Assistance to Agriculture, 1967–2015 (Constant Prices, 2014 US Dollar, in millions). Source: OECD.stat

the mid-1980s. It then decreased for almost two decades, until it started to increase after 2007, albeit with a period of plateaued or even slight recovery of aid level around 1993–1997.

In addition to the development of DAC-aid, the landscape of development agencies has also shifted in the last decade with the entrance of former aid recipients as aid donors—China being the largest of these new players. As China has opted out of global aid reporting systems, information on this is scarce (Parks, 2015). Beyond concluding that Chinese agricultural aid has become more influential in the last 6–10 years, and that it focuses on Africa—based on the data available from AidData (china.aiddata.org), it is beyond the scope of this chapter to assess its influence.

Overall, the attention to agriculture by development agencies has moved in tandem with scholarly attention, rather than preceding it. One exception may be the upswing of scholarly attention to agriculture around 1990–1995, which was preceded by a period of higher attention to agriculture among development agencies, starting from about 1985. This decade saw high agricultural aid flows, and an increased interest among development donors to agriculture, indicated by the World Bank Reports on agriculture in 1982 and 1986. Both scholarly attention and agricultural aid then waned after the mid-1990s, and increased again after a 10 year slump in the mid-2000s—perhaps partly driven by China's emergence as a donor. However, the development assistance did not precede the shift in scholarly attention at these times, and the high interest of development agencies in agriculture in the 1970s does not correspond to the level of scholarly attention at that time.

4.5 Changing Policy Environment

The fifth potential driver is that the shifts in scholarly attention to agriculture have been driven by the policy environment for agriculture, in terms of subsidies and taxes.

Graph 2.6 depicts the average agricultural support or taxation of agriculture, over time, based on Anderson and Nelgen's (2013) database on distortions to agricultural incentives, 1955 to 2011. The graph demonstrates the Nominal Rate of Assistance for all primary agricultural products, where a positive rate of assistance indicates that agriculture is subsidised and a negative number indicates that it is taxed.

As shown, there has been a general shift from discrimination towards support for agriculture, albeit with regional differences, where the developing regions tax substantially more than the developed regions. In Africa, taxation of agriculture has been persistent, while Latin America and Asia have eased the burden on agriculture since the 1990s. However, the most successful Asian countries—Korea, Taiwan and Japan—have been net supporters of the agricultural sector throughout the post-war era (mostly driven by Japan's high support). Graph 2.6 indicates: that tax policies towards agriculture were discriminatory in the developing world from 1950s until the mid-1980s, and even still today in Africa; that the developed and the successful developing countries have supported agriculture instead of taxing it; and that the discrimination towards agriculture has gradually decreased. As such, there seems to be some correlation between the heavy taxation of agriculture in the developing world during the period of low attention in the 1970s and 1980s, and less taxation in the last decade during the increased attention. One could argue, however, that the changing policy environment should not be seen as a driver of

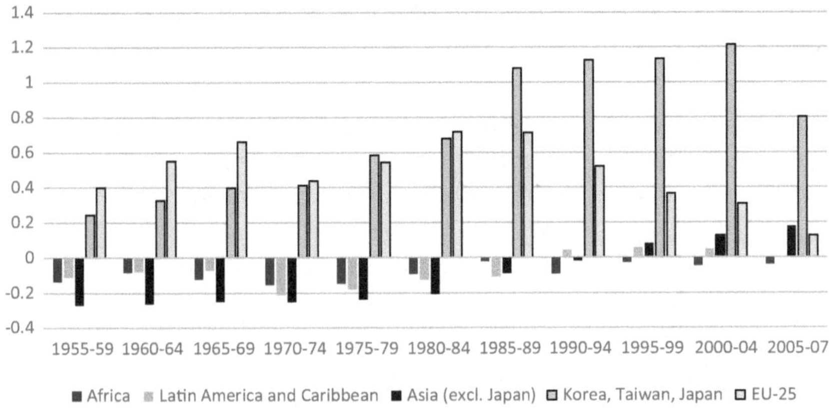

Graph 2.6 Nominal rates of assistance to agriculture, by regions, over time 1955–2007. Note: Weighted average for each country, including non-product specific assistance and estimates for non-covered farm products, with weights based on gross value of agricultural production at undistorted prices. Source: Anderson and Nelgen (2013)

scholarly attention, but rather as the result of the scholarly debate. The correlations that can be identified between the long period of low scholarly attention and high taxation of agriculture, and recent scholarly attention and less taxation are more likely to be the result of the scholarly debate affecting policies, rather than the other way around.

4.6 Discipline-Specific Developments in Agricultural and Development Economics

In addition to the above five identified and explored potential drivers of the shifting attention, the analysis of the source material revealed that the view on agriculture has developed differently within the subdisciplines Agricultural Economics and Development Economics. Within Agricultural Economics, efforts to understand agriculture's role in developing countries has increased over time. Comparing the volumes in the Handbook of Agricultural Economics, shows that volume 1 (2001) has an explicit focus on the development of the agricultural sector itself, rather than how the agricultural sector can play a role in economic development, while in volume 2 (2002), 2 of the total of 21 chapters are devoted to agriculture in economic development; and by the publication of Volume 4 in 2010, almost all chapters are devoted to the role of agriculture in economic development, rather than to agricultural development per se. Turning to the changing attention to agriculture within Development Economics, no such strengthening can be discerned. In both the latest Handbooks of Development Economics (Volume 4 in 2007, and Volume 5 in 2010), no chapter is specifically devoted to the role of agriculture in economic development. Volume 5 explicitly aims to design research agendas that are informed by policy questions—but yet, agriculture did not qualify. This might be a sign of the current state of Development Economics, in which there has been a significant re-orientation towards microeconomic issues, as seen particularly in Volume 4. As Meier (2002, p. 14) has stated, this perspective struggles to deal with development as a dynamic and historically contextualised process, and as such it could be one reason why the discipline has not been able to address the complex issue of the role of agriculture in development.

5 Conclusions

Taking as a point of departure the contrary opinions of the role of agriculture for future development, this chapter set out to trace influential viewpoints of the role of agriculture in development theory, as well as assessing and explaining the pattern of fluctuating scholarly attention to agriculture over time.

Four main influential views on agriculture have been identified: agriculture as fifth wheel; as a distorted sector with rational economic agents; as important via trade (as injection or break); and as an engine of economic development. Today's agro-sceptics appear rooted in the fifth wheel school of thought, while the agro-proponents have a legacy more derived from the "agriculture as engine, via structural transformation" school. It seems as if this view has been reinforced by the overall shift of objective within the development debate, from aggregate growth to pro-poor growth.

In terms of the shifting attention to agriculture, there have been five main phases: two short periods of higher attention in the late 1960s, and the first half of the 1990s; two longer periods of lower attention around 1970–1990, and 1995–2005; and one long period of higher attention from 2005 onwards. Among the five explored potential drivers to explain the ups and downs, our analysis supports the perception that the most elementary role of agriculture—the ability to deliver food and nutrition to an expanding global population—has played an important role. As such, the shifts in food security concern, in combination with food price fluctuations, appear as a possible driver of the shifting attention. The first period of higher scholarly attention in agriculture was concurrent to food security optimism in the wake of the Green Revolution; the long downturn of attention in 1970–2005 coexisted with a weaker concern for food security and an almost three-decade long decrease in food prices; and the latest increase in scholarly attention was again connected to increased concern for food security coupled with the trend break towards increasing food prices in the early 2000s. However, the short upswing of interest around 1990–1995 does not seem connected to these food aspects, but may instead be related to the shift in development assistance objectives among international organisations.

This chapter has also noted that it appears that the discussion of agriculture in economic development has shifted from being rooted in Development Economics earlier in the period, to that the recent attention to agriculture in developing countries is increasingly driven by Agricultural Economics.

At the end of the 1960s, although agriculture received attention it did not last, as the food security concerns were less acute in light of the successful start of the Green Revolution. When agriculture regained attention in the 1989–1995 period development theory was dominated by the neoclassical reasoning of the "agriculture as a sector with rational economic agents" view, prescribing that no special attention needed to be given to agriculture, and that the low productive sector of agriculture should not be prioritised. During this most recent period of increased attention, since around 2005, there seems to have been a strong association between pro-agriculture theoretical views, particularly the structural transformation perspective, and increased concern for food security.

Further, the other forces discussed may be reinforcing the interest in this period, through learning from historical experiences, the emphasis on agriculture within development assistance as part of poverty reduction objectives, and fewer policies discriminating against agriculture in developing countries. This apparent consolidation of forces viewing agriculture as an important sector in economic development, may lend weight to Pingali's (2010) prediction that we are indeed moving towards an "agricultural renaissance" in the twenty-first century.

Notes

1. A similar theoretical strand, emphasising the potential ability of agriculture to contribute to growth via exports, is staple theory, as developed by W. A. Mackintosh and Harold Innis. In this, demand for staple products (products that can be produced in surplus of domestic demand) is crucial for growth, together with a country's ability to reduce its cost to supply these products. If achieved, staple exports are seen to spur investments and consumption throughout the domestic economy. A main difference to "vent-for-surplus" is that staple theory emphasise different productivity-generating capacities of products, where staple products yield more output than focusing on less export-oriented products. As such, it places more emphasis on agricultural productivity increase than "vent-for-surplus."
2. The JEL-codes of relevance are:
   O: Economic Development, Innovation, Technological Change, and Growth/O1 Economic Development/O13 Agriculture, Natural Resources, Energy, Environment, Other Primary Products.
   Q: Agricultural and Natural Resource Economics, Environmental and Ecological Economics/Q1 Agriculture/Q17 Agriculture in International Trade.
3. The method generates a slightly higher number of articles for JEL-code O (1972 vs 1869, in 2005), and lower for JEL-code Q (514 vs 684, in 2005), but the difference is not enough to alter any trends in the three years when both versions are used.
4. The analysis traces the share of articles published with the keyword "agricultur*" and a specific geographic region (Africa, Asia, Latin America),

out of all the articles with the keyword "agriculture*" in WoS SSCI, 1957–2015.

5. The graph displays food prices based on IMF IFS annual data to provide an indication of the long-term trend. This trend is similar to that of agriculture's terms of trade, which strengthened in the 1970s, followed by a long decline, until it turned upwards in the early 2000s (Ocampo and Parra-Lancourt, 2009). For a more thorough assessment of the price development of agricultural commodities since the 1950s, see Serrano and Pinilla (2011).

References

Adelman, I. (1984). Beyond Export-Led Growth. *World Development, 12*(9), 937–949.

Alafiatayo, B. (1989). The Research Literature of Agricultural Economics. *International Library Review, 21*, 463–479.

Allen, R. (1994). Agriculture During the Industrial Revolution. In R. Floud & D. McCloskey (Eds.), *The Economic History of Britain Since 1700* (Vol. I: 1700–1800, 2nd ed., pp. 96–122). Cambridge: Cambridge University Press.

Anderson, K. (2009). Distorted Agricultural Incentives and Economic Development: Asia's Experience. *The World Economy, 32*(3), 351–384.

Anderson, K., & Nelgen, S. (2013). Updated National and Global Estimates of Distortions to Agricultural Incentives, 1955 to 2011, Regional Aggregates. Spreadsheet at www.worldbank.org/agdistortions. Washington, DC: World Bank.

Ashley, C., & Maxwell, S. (2001). Rethinking Rural Development. *Development Policy Review, 19*, 395–425.

Baran, P. A. (1952). On the Political Economy of Backwardness. *Manchester School Economic and Social Studies, 20*, 66–84.

Barrett, C., Carter, M. R., & Timmer, C. P. (2010). A Century-Long Perspective on Agricultural Development. *American Journal of Agricultural Economics, 92*, 447–468.

Bauer, P. T. (1954). *West African Trade: A Study of Competition, Oligopoly and Monopoly in a Changing Economy*. London: Cambridge University Press.

Bauer, P. T., & Yamey, B. S. (1959). A Case Study of Response to Price in an Underdeveloped Country. *Economic Journal, 69*, 800–805.

Binswanger-Mkhize, H., & McCalla, A.F. (2010). Chapter 70: The Changing Context and Prospects for Agricultural and Rural Development in Africa (pp. 3571–3712). In *Handbook of Agricultural Economics*. Amsterdam: Elsevier.

Boeke, J. H. (1953). *Economics and Public Policy as Exemplified by Indonesia.* New York: Institute of Pacific Relations.

Boserup, E. (1965). *The Conditions of Agricultural Growth.* Chicago: Aldine.

Chenery, H., & Syrquin, M. (1975). *Patterns of Development, 1950–1970.* Oxford: Oxford University Press.

Christiaensen, L., Demery, L., & Kuhl, J. (2011). The (Evolving) Role of Agriculture in Poverty Reduction—An Empirical Perspective. *Journal of Development Economics, 96*(2), 239–254.

Clark, C. (1940). *The Conditions of Economic Progress.* London: Macmillan.

Clark, G. (2007). *A Farewell to Alms: A Brief Economic History of the World.* Princeton, NJ: Princeton University Press.

Collier, P., & Dercon, S. (2009). *African Agriculture In 50 Years: Smallholders In A Rapidly Changing World?* Background paper for the Expert Meeting on How to Feed the World in 2050, FAO.

De Janvry, A. (1975). The Political Economy of Rural Development of Rural Development in Latin America: An Interpretation. *American Journal of Agricultural Economics, 57*, 490–499.

De Janvry, A. (2010). Agriculture for Development: New Paradigm and Options for Success. *Agricultural Economics, 41*(1), 17–36.

De Janvry, A., & Sadoulet, E. (2010). Agricultural Growth and Poverty Reduction: Additional Evidence. *World Bank Research Observer, 25*(1), 1–20.

Delgado, C., Hopkins, J. and Kelly, V. (1994). *Agricultural Growth Linkages in Sub-Saharan Africa: A Synthesis.* IFPRI Report to USAID, Africa Bureau. Washington DC: International Food Policy Research Institute.

Dethier, J. J., & Effenberger, A. (2012). Agriculture and Development: A Brief Review of the Literature. *Economic Systems, 36*, 175–205.

Dercon, S., & Gollin, D. (2014). Agriculture in African Development: Theories and Strategies. *Annual Review of Resource Economics, 6*(1), 471–492.

Diao, X., Hazell, P., Resnick, D., & Thurlow, J. (2007). *The Role of Agriculture in Development. Implications for Sub-Saharan Africa.* IFPRI Research Report No. 153. Washington, DC: International Food Policy Research Institute.

Diaz-Bonilla, E., & Robinson, S. (2010). Chapter 61: Macroeconomics, Macrosectoral Policies, and Agriculture in Developing Countries (pp. 3035–3213). In *Handbook of Agricultural Economics*. Amsterdam: Elsevier.

The Economist. (2016a, March 12). *Farming in Africa: Miracle Grow*.

The Economist. (2016b, June 11). *Technology Quarterly: The Future of Agriculture*.

Eicher, C. K., & Baker, D. C. (1992). Agricultural Development in Sub-Saharan Africa: A Critical Survey. In L. Martin (Ed.), *A Survey of Agricultural Economics Literature, Volume 4: Agriculture in Economic Development 1940s to 1990s* (pp. 3–328). Minneapolis: University of Minnesota Press.

Ellis, F. (2004). *Occupational Diversification in Developing Countries and the Implications for Agricultural Policy*. Programme of Advisory and Support Services to DFID (PASS). Project No. WB0207.

Falcon, W. P. (1988). Book Review. *American Journal of Agricultural Economics, 70*(1), 198–200.

Fan, S., & Brzeska, J. (2010). Chapter 66: Production, Productivity, and Public Investment in East Asian Agriculture (pp. 3401–3434). In *Handbook of Agricultural Economics*. Amsterdam: Elsevier.

Fei, J. C., & Ranis, G. (1964). *Development of the Labor Surplus Economy; Theory and Policy*. Homewood, IL: Richard D. Irwin for the Economic Growth Center, Yale University.

Federico, G. (2005). *Feeding the World: An Economic History of Agriculture, 1800–2000*. Princeton: Princeton University Press.

Gates Foundation. (2016). Agricultural Development Strategy Overview. Retrieved February 21, 2017, from http://www.gatesfoundation.org/What-We-Do/Global-Development/Agricultural-Development

Gollin, D., Parente, S., & Rogerson, R. (2002). The Role of Agriculture in Development. *American Economic Review, 92*(2), 160–164.

Gollin, D. (2010). Chapter 73: Agricultural Productivity and Economic Growth (pp. 3825–3866). In *Handbook of Agricultural Economics*. Amsterdam: Elsevier.

Handbook of Agricultural Economics. (2001, 2002, 2007, 2010). Elsevier. Volume I–IV, 1–3894.

Handbook of Development Economics (1988, 1989, 1995, 2007, 2010). Elsevier. Volume I–V, 3–5061.

Hasan, R., & Quibria, M. G. (2004). Industry Matters for Poverty: A Critique of Agricultural Fundamentalism. *Kyklos, 57*(2), 253–264.

Hazell, P., & Haggblade, S. (1993). Farm-Nonfarm Growth Linkages and the Welfare of the Poor. In M. Lipton & J. van der Gaag (Eds.), *Including the Poor: Proceedings of a Symposium Organized by the World Bank and the International Food Policy Research Institute*. Washington, DC: The World Bank.

Johnson, D. G. (1973). *World Agriculture in Disarray. World Economic Issues.* Macmillan: London.

Johnston, B. (1970). Agriculture and Structural Transformation in Developing Countries: A Survey of Research. *Journal of Economic Literature, 8*(2), 369–404.

Johnston, B. F., & Mellor, J. W. (1961). The Role of Agriculture in Economic Development. *The American Economic Review, 51*(4), 566–593.

Jorgenson, D. (1961). The Development of a Dual Economy. *Economic Journal, 71*, 309–334.

Kelly, M. A., & Bruestle, S. (2011). Trend of Subjects Published in Economics Journals 1969–2007. *Economic Inquiry, 49*(3), 658–673.

King, R. P., & Byerlee, D. (1978). Factor Intensities and Locational Linkages of Rural Consumption Patterns in Sierra Leone. *American Journal of Agricultural Economics, 60*(2), 197–206.

Kosnik, L.R. (2016). *A Survey of JEL Codes: What do They Mean and are They Used Consistently?* Working Paper, Department of Economics, University of Missouri-St. Louis

Krueger, A. O., Schiff, M., & Valdés, A. (1988). Agricultural Incentives in Developing Countries: Measuring the Effect of Sectoral and Economywide Policies. *The World Bank Economic Review, 2*(3), 255–271.

Krueger, A. O., Schiff, M., & Valdés, A. (Eds.). (1991). *The Political Economy of Agricultural Pricing Policy*. Baltimore: John Hopkins University Press.

Kuznets, S. (1961). Economic Growth and the Contribution of Agriculture: Notes on Measurement. *International Journal of Agrarian Affairs, 3*, 59–75.

Lains, P., & Pinilla, V. (2009). Introduction. In P. Lains & V. Pinilla (Eds.), *Agriculture and Economic Development in Europe Since 1870* (pp. 1–24). Abindon, Oxon: Routledge.

Lewis, W. A. (1954). Economic Development with Unlimited Supplies of Labour. *The Manchester School, 22*(2), 139–191.

Lipton, M. (1989). *New Seeds and Poor People (with Richard Longhurst)*. London: Unwin Hyman.

Lipton, M. (2012). *Income from Work: The Food-Population-Resource Crisis in the 'Short Africa'*. Medford, MA: Leontief Prize Lecture, Tufts University.

Martin, L. (Ed.). (1992). *A Survey of Agricultural Economics Literature, Volume 4: Agriculture in Economic Development 1940s to 1990s. American Agricultural Economic Association*. Minneapolis: University of Minnesota Press.

Meier, G. (2002). *Sir Arthur Lewis and Development Economics—Fifty Years On. The VII Sir Arthur Lewis Memorial Lecture*. Kingstown: St Vincent and the Grenadines.

Mellor, J. W. (1999). *Faster, More Equitable Growth—The Relation Between Growth in Agriculture and Poverty Reduction. CAER*. Cambridge, MA: Harvard University Press.

Mellor, J. W., & Johnston, B. F. (1984). The World Food Equation: Interrelations Among Development, Employment, and Food Consumption. *Journal of Economic Literature, 22*(2), 531–574.

Myint, H. (1958). The "Classical Theory" of International Trade and the Underdeveloped Countries. *The Economic Journal, 68*(270), 317–337.

Myrdal, G. (1968). *Asian Drama, An Inquiry Into the Poverty of Nations*. London: The Penguin Press.

Nicholls, W. H. (1964). The Place of Agriculture in Economic Development. In C. K. Eicher & L. W. Witt (Eds.), *Agriculture in Economic Development* (pp. 11–44). New York: McGraw-Hill.

Ocampo, J., & Parra-Lancourt, M. (2009). The Terms of Trade for Commodities since the mid-19th Century. *Revista de Historia Económica, Journal of lberian and Latin American Economic History, 28*(1), 11–43.

OECD. (2015). *Issues in Agricultural Trade Policy Proceedings of the 2014 OECD Global Forum on Agriculture*. Paris: OECD Publishing.

Parks, B. (2015, November 30). 10 Essential Facts about Chinese Aid in Africa. *The National Interest*. Retrieved February 21, 2017, from http://nationalinterest.org/feature/10-essential-facts-about-chinese-aid-africa-14456

Pingali, P. (2010). Agriculture Renaissance: Making "Agriculture for Development" Work in the 21st Century. In P. E. Pingali & R. E. Evenson (Eds.), *Handbook of Agricultural Economics* (pp. 3867–3894). Amsterdam: Elsevier.

Prebisch, R. (1959). International Trade and Payments in an Era of Coexistence. *The American Economic Review, 49*(2), 251–273.

Ravallion, M., & Chen, S. (2007). China's (Uneven) Progress Against Poverty. *Journal of Development Economics, 82*(1), 1–42.

Ranis, G., & Fei, J. C. (1961). A Theory of Economic Development. *The American Economic Review*, 533–565.

Ranis, G., & Stewart, F. (1993). Rural Nonagricultural Activities in Development: Theory and Application. *Journal of Development Economics, 40*(1), 75–101.

Rao, J. M. (1985). Agriculture in Recent Development Theory. *Journal of Development Economics, 22*, 41–86.

Reynolds, L. G. (1975). *Agriculture in Development Theory: An Overview, 1–26, in: Agriculture in Development Theory*. New Haven: Yale University Press.

Rosenstein-Rodan, P. N. (1943). Problems of Industrialisation of Eastern and South-eastern Europe. *The Economic Journal, 53*(210/211), 202–211.

Ruttan, V. W. (2002). Productivity Growth in World Agriculture: Sources and Constraints. *The Journal of Economic Perspectives, 16*(4), 161–184.

Ruttan, V. W., & Hayami, Y. (1984). Toward a Theory of Induced Institutional Innovation. *The Journal of Development Studies, 20*(4), 203–223.

Schuh, E., & Brandão, A. S. (1992). The Theory, Empirical Evidence, and Debates on Agricultural Development Issues in Latin America: A Selective Survey. In L. Martin (Ed.), *A Survey of Agricultural Economics Literature, Volume 4: Agriculture in Economic Development 1940s to 1990s* (pp. 545–967). Minneapolis: University of Minnesota Press.

Schultz, T. W. (1964). *Transforming Traditional Agriculture*. New Haven: Yale University Press.

Schultz, T. W. (Ed.). (1978). *Distortions of Agricultural Incentives*. Bloomington, IN: University of Indiana Press.

Sen, A. (1981). *Poverty and Famines*. Oxford: Clarendon Press.

Serrano, R., & Pinilla, V. (2011). The Terms of Trade for Agricultural and Food Products, 1951–2000. *Revista de Historia Económica, Journal of lberian and Latin American Economic History, 29*(2), 213–243.

Silva, S. T., & Teixeira, A. A. (2009). On the Divergence of Evolutionary Research Paths in the Past 50 Years: A Comprehensive Bibliometric Account. *Journal of Evolutionary Economics, 19*(5), 605–642.

Singer, H. (1979). Policy Implications of the Lima Target. *Industry and Development, 3*, 17–32.

Staatz, J. M., & Eicher, C. K. (1998). Agricultural Development Ideas in Historical Perspective. In C. K. Eicher & J. M. Staatz (Eds.), *International Agricultural Development* (pp. 8–38). Baltimore: Johns Hopkins University Press.

Thorbecke, E. (2006). *The Evolution of the Development Doctrine, 1950–2005*. Research Paper 2006/155, UNU-WIDER, 1–37.

Timmer, P. (1988). Chapter 08: The Agricultural Transformation (pp. 275–331). In *Handbook of Development Economics*. Amsterden: Elsevier.

Timmer, P. (1992). Agriculture and Economic Development Revisited. *Agricultural Systems, 40*(1), 21–58.

Timmer, P. (2002). Chapter 29: Agriculture and Economic Development (pp. 1487–1546). In *Handbook of Agricultural Economics*. Amsterden: Elsevier.

Timmer, P. (2005). *Agriculture and Pro-Poor Growth: an Asian Perspective*. Retrieved February 23, 2017, from http://papers.ssrn.com/sol3/papers.cfm?abstract_id=1114155

Timmer, P. (2009). *A World Without Agriculture: The Structural Transformation in Historical Perspective*. Washington, DC: Aei Press.

World Bank. (1982). *World Development Report 1982*. New York: Oxford University Press.

World Bank. (1986). *World Development Report 1986*. New York: Oxford University Press.

World Bank. (2007). *World Development Report 2008: Agriculture for Development*. Washington, DC: World Bank.

WDI. (2017). *World Development Indicators*. The World Bank. Retrieved February 24, 2017, from http://data.worldbank.org/indicator/SP.RUR.TOTL?locations=XO

Martin Andersson's research interests include the role of agriculture for economic development and the relation between economic growth, poverty reduction, and distribution of income in the developing world. He has worked as a consultant for the World Bank and the African Center for Economic Transformation and has been a Marie Curie post-doc at EUI in Florence and a visiting scholar at UC Berkeley and the University of Queensland. He is currently an Associate Professor in Economic History at Lund University.

Emelie Rohne Till is a PhD candidate at the Department of Economic History, at Lund University. Her main research area is development economics approached from an economic history perspective, focusing on the role of structural transformation and of the agricultural sector in economic development, in Sub-Saharan Africa. Her PhD project concerns the role of agriculture in Ethiopia's economic development, during the implementation of an Agricultural Development Led Industrialisation (ADLI) strategy since 1993.

3

The World Periphery in Global Agricultural and Food Trade, 1900–2000

Gema Aparicio, Ángel Luis González-Esteban, Vicente Pinilla, and Raúl Serrano

This study has received financial support from Spain's Ministry of Science and Innovation, project ECO2015-65582-P, and from the Government of Aragon, through the Research Group "Agri-food Economic History (nineteenth and twentieth centuries)". The authors wish to thank Kym Anderson, Henry Willebald, and participants at the meeting "Agricultural development in the world periphery. A global economic history approach" (University of Zaragoza, April 2017) for their help and advice. The usual disclaimers apply.

G. Aparicio
Independent Scholar, New York, USA

Á. L. González-Esteban
Department of Economics, Universitat Pompeu i Fabra, Barcelona, Spain

V. Pinilla (✉)
Department of Applied Economics and Economic History, Universidad de Zaragoza, Zaragoza, Spain

R. Serrano
Faculty of Economy and Business, Department of Business Administration, Universidad de Zaragoza, Zaragoza, Spain

V. Pinilla, H. Willebald (eds.), *Agricultural Development in the World Periphery*, Palgrave Studies in Economic History, https://doi.org/10.1007/978-3-319-66020-2_3

1 Introduction

Between 1870 and 2000, international trade in food and agricultural raw materials underwent unprecedented growth. This long period may be divided into two distinct stages. In the first of these, lasting until WWII, agricultural and food trade grew at a very similar rate to that of total trade. In the second period, however, its relative growth, both in terms of volume and value, was considerably lower, to the extent that, by the end of the period, it represented a very minor part of trade as a whole.

International trade expanded continuously from the end of the Napoleonic wars until WWI, and the reasons for this growth are clear: incomes rose as the cost of maritime and overland transport fell, resulting in market integration and a general trend towards free trade, encouraged most particularly by the UK. Moreover, a highly stable international monetary system, based on the gold standard, gradually included more and more countries (Estevadeordal, Frantz, & Taylor, 2003; O'Rourke & Williamson, 1999). Farm products were a key component of the increase in international trade, approximately half of which consisted of food products and agricultural commodities. Moreover, inter-industrial trade (i.e. between manufactured goods and primary goods) is fundamental to the explanation of international exchanges of goods. In the first wave of globalisation, many economies of the non-industrialised periphery based their development on export-led growth models (Anderson, 2018; Martín-Retortillo et al., 2018; Pinilla & Rayes, 2017). Therefore, as their economies specialised in that direction, their weight in world trade, and especially in agricultural and food products, increased.

WWI and, above all, the disruption of the international economy caused by the crisis of 1929 and the collapse of the free trade system, radically affected trade patterns (Findlay & O'Rourke, 2007). First, the war caused a temporary contraction of trade, which gradually recovered during the 1920s and resumed a clear growth path by the end of the decade. The 1929 crash, however, had far-reaching effects; international trade shrank in terms of both volume and value. Agricultural products were not immune to these problems, suffering heavily from falling prices and the protectionist barriers erected in this period.

Following WWII, and especially during the years of the "golden age of capitalism", the world economy accelerated at an unprecedented pace. Generalised growth, the liberalisation of international trade, improvements in transport and communications, and exchange-rate stability provided a tremendous boost to international trade. Furthermore, trade grew at a faster rate than production, causing markets to become intensively integrated.

Thus, agricultural trade experienced unprecedented growth between 1951 and 2000, expanding much faster than in earlier periods (Aparicio, Pinilla, & Serrano, 2009). This period also witnessed changes in the direction, constitution and structure of international trade, in favour of the exchange of manufactured goods between industrialised nations. Thus, trade between the developed countries increasingly took the form of exchanges of differentiated products and the circulation of semi-finished goods and parts between the subsidiaries of vertically integrated multinational companies. Consequently, the percentage of total international trade represented by agricultural goods declined sharply in this period. Thus, the North–South trade pattern forged in the period of the first globalisation was gradually replaced by a pattern based principally on exchanges of manufactured goods. In the case of agricultural trade, flows of processed goods between high-income countries grew significantly.

2 International Agricultural and Food Trade in the First Wave of Globalisation

2.1 Globalisation and Agricultural Trade

In the second half of the nineteenth century, international trade expanded rapidly. The estimations performed by Lewis (1952, 1981) for primary products as a whole indicate an annual growth rate of 3.7 per cent between 1850 and 1900. This rate of expansion was considerably higher in the third quarter of the century than in the fourth, which is logical when we take into account the first globalisation, which began around 1850, the low initial level of exchanges, and the return to protectionism that took place in the last two decades of the century, as a result of the "invasion" of Europe by agricultural products from overseas and the Russian Empire (O'Rourke, 1997).

Rising incomes, technological change, and falling transport costs were key factors in this pronounced growth in international trade (Meissner, Jacks, & Novy, 2011; O'Rourke & Williamson, 1999; Pinilla & Ayuda, 2010). The trend towards liberalism, in the form of a multilateral trade network in which bilateral treaties played a central role, and the existence of the gold standard, which other countries (following the example of Great Britain) progressively adopted, smoothed the way for this expansion of world trade (Jacks, 2005, 2006).

Between 1900 and 1913, trade in agricultural and food products prolonged the growth trend witnessed in the preceding century, which then fell sharply during WWI, to then recover and expand rapidly until the crash of 1929, when it initially dipped and then stagnated (Table 3.1 and Fig. 3.1). Over this period as a whole, agricultural trade grew at an annual

Table 3.1 World agricultural and food trade (by volume) (annual growth rate)

1850–1902	**3.7**
1850–1875	4.6
1875–1902	3.0
1903–1938	**1.4**
1903–1913	3.3
1913–1918	−10.9
1918–1929	7.8
1929–1938	−1.1
1951–2000	**4.0**
1951–1973	4.6
1974–2000	3.5
2000–2010	3.4

Source: 1850–1902, Lewis (1981); 1903–2000, Aparicio et al. (2009); 2000–2010, own calculation based on United Nations COMTRADE database. The Lewis data for 1850–1902 are all for primary products and include non-agricultural commodities as minerals. Neither the Lewis data nor its main source, which is the publication of the League of Nations, Industrialisation and Foreign Trade, distinguish between agricultural commodities and the rest. Therefore, in this table and in Figs. 3.1 and 3.2, we have assumed that the growth rate of the agricultural trade was similar to that of the primary commodity trade. From this assumption we have used the index numbers of the Lewis series to push back our agricultural trade data from the early twentieth century.

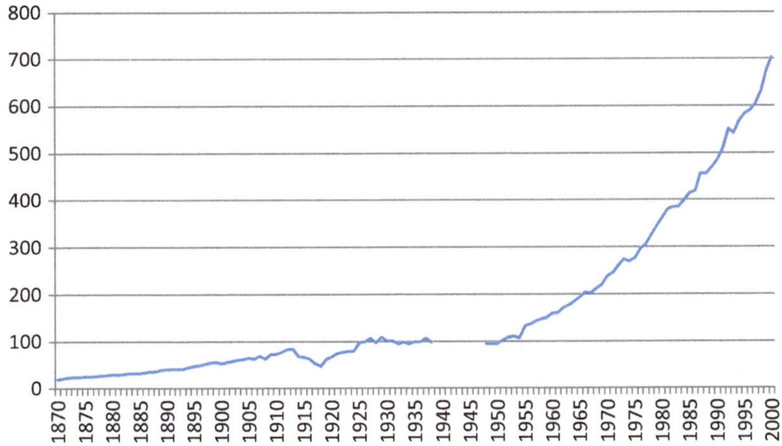

Fig. 3.1 International agricultural and food trade (by volume) (1952–1954 = 100). Source: 1870–1902, Lewis (1952, 1981); 1903–1938 and 1951–2000, Aparicio et al. (2009); 1949–1954, González, Pinilla, and Serrano (2016)

rate of 1.4 per cent, considerably less than the rate of 3.7 per cent achieved in the second half of the nineteenth century. Thus, the pattern of international trade until 1914 was very similar to that of the late nineteenth century, and was only interrupted by the outbreak of war.

Initially, trade plunged during these years, since Europe (the principal importer of agricultural products in this period) was the region most affected by the war, and its countries were obliged to divert huge sums of money in order to finance the conflict. Consequently, there was little cash available to fund food imports, although these were needed more than ever to compensate for the distortion of production caused by the war; money, if available, was spent on war materials. And then, one of the Allied strategies was to blockade Germany, in the hope of achieving a swift victory by undermining the morale of soldiers at the front through war-weariness and food shortages at home and the effects of hunger on the civilian population (Offer, 1989). Finally, the shortage of merchant shipping to carry cargoes not directly related to the conflict, and the potential risk to maritime traffic, considerably increased transport costs, further depressing agricultural trade.

The period between the end of WWI and the beginning of the Depression was marked by a rapid recovery in international trade in physical terms. This process commenced in 1919 and by 1925 trade was once again at 1913 levels, and between 1921 and 1929 the world volume of exports grew at an annual rate of 7 per cent.

The recovery in the volume of trade was mainly due, in the short term, to strong European demand. After the war the blockade was lifted, while other obstacles to trade that were directly related to the war disappeared. Furthermore, European agricultural production had suffered severely from the war, and countries had no alternative but to purchase food or agricultural raw materials in international markets until output recovered. Despite strong growth in the world demand for food, problems soon became apparent in the countries producing and exporting primary goods. European agriculture began to recover during the 1920s, although international prices for some foodstuffs and agricultural commodities fell. At the same time, many European countries erected tariff barriers against food imports, thereby intensifying protectionism.

The USA also played its part in the consolidation of protectionism, raising import tariffs, after the 1929 crash, to their highest ever level. By 1931, almost all European countries had significantly increased their own import tariffs in response; the average level of tariffs in continental Europe rose to 39.5 per cent in 1931, compared to 24.6 per cent in 1913 and 24.9 per cent in 1927 (Bairoch, 1989, pp. 91–92). The agrarian tariffs were even higher, with levels over 50 per cent. In the three greatest agrarian import markets of continental Europe (Germany, France and Italy) the increase in tariff levels was enormous, reaching in Germany a general agrarian tariff level of 82.5 per cent (Liepmann, 1938, p. 106). The tendency to seek protection from economic depression by insulating domestic markets gained strength in the following years, as further restrictions on foreign trade, such as quotas, import licenses, exchange controls, etc. were adopted.

Economic crisis, and the general spread of protectionism worldwide, caused average international prices to fall by approximately 50 per cent, which particularly affected countries producing agricultural goods (Ocampo & Parra-Lancount, 2010); between 1929 and 1932, the value of international trade declined even more sharply than its volume, a phenomenon known as the contractive spiral of international trade.

From 1929 to 1934 the volume of international trade in agricultural products diminished by 13 per cent in absolute terms, although a slight recovery in the latter years of the decade resulted in an annual negative growth rate of 1.2 per cent for the 1930s as a whole.

2.2 The Role of the Periphery in International Trade in Agricultural and Food Products

Since the mid-nineteenth century, non-European countries, such as the Latin American republics, British Dominions, and the territories colonised by the European powers, tended to place themselves as exporters of primary products in the international division of labour that took place in the first globalisation. European demand for these products, in the context of the reduction of international transport prices and of trade liberalisation, generated interesting opportunities to increase exports from those countries specialising in such products.

To achieve the increase in exports, it was first necessary to reorientate land towards crops for which there was demand in the international market, or to cultivate new lands. In certain countries, such as the settler economies (Argentina, Australia, Canada, New Zealand, Uruguay) the vast plains, used until then by the indigenous populations, had first to be conquered. Subsequently, there commenced a formidable process of agricultural frontier expansion usually carried out by European immigrants (Willebald & Juambeltz, 2018).[1] In the tropical regions of the world, this agricultural reorientation was generally directed in the colonies by an elite of large metropolitan landowners, and in the Central American republics by multinational companies, with large plantations being the most common way of organising production for export (Byerlee & Viswanathan, 2018). However, in some countries, small local farmers were also actively involved in the development of export-oriented production, stimulated by expectations of greater profit.

The most successful cases for the economic development of this type of specialisation were the countries recently colonised by European powers (New Europes), including Argentina, Australia, Canada, New Zealand, and Uruguay, which undertook in this period an intense process of territorial colonisation and expansion of their exports.[2] An abundant provision of land capable of being designated for agricultural production, characteristic of temperate zones, a significant supply of workers proceeding from Europe, and a considerable entry of foreign capital, facilitated and stimulated this process of export-led growth.

In the case of settler countries, the rapid development of their exports of primary products and the linkages between the export base and the rest of the economy produced spectacular economic growth and substantial diversification of their economies. In 1913, these countries had the highest per capita income in the world, along with the first-comers of European industrialisation, and the USA. Their industrialisation had already clearly taken off, very often with the support of protectionist measures, as for example in the case of Australia after 1900.

Most of the remaining non-European world oriented their economies in this same direction, although the results were much more modest. The growth of exports was much slower and the linkages with the rest of the economy were very weak. As a consequence, income levels remained low and the economy did not experience deep transformations. A comparison of the levels of per capita exports and per capita income for the Latin American republics shows a clear correlation between both variables (Bulmer-Thomas, 1994; Martín-Retortillo et al., 2018).

Up to the beginning of the twentieth century, we have no data on agricultural trade that would allow us to analyse its evolution on a global scale. However, the new data for total trade provided by Federico and Tena-Junguito (2016) show that, until 1890, there were improvements in the shares of trade for Oceania, Africa, and Latin America. Between 1850 and 1914, exports from the Latin American countries increased at an impressive annual rate of 3.5 per cent (Bértola & Williamson, 2006, p. 28). Since 1890, the growth of exports from the periphery was substantial and all non-European regions, except Oceania, gained substantial weight in world trade (Federico & Tena-Junguito, 2016).

Figure 3.2 shows that after WWI the world trade in agricultural products underwent crucial changes. The dynamism of the countries of the periphery contrasts with the stagnation and subsequent fall of the core countries.[3] The countries of the periphery increased their agricultural export specialisation, while the more developed countries turned to

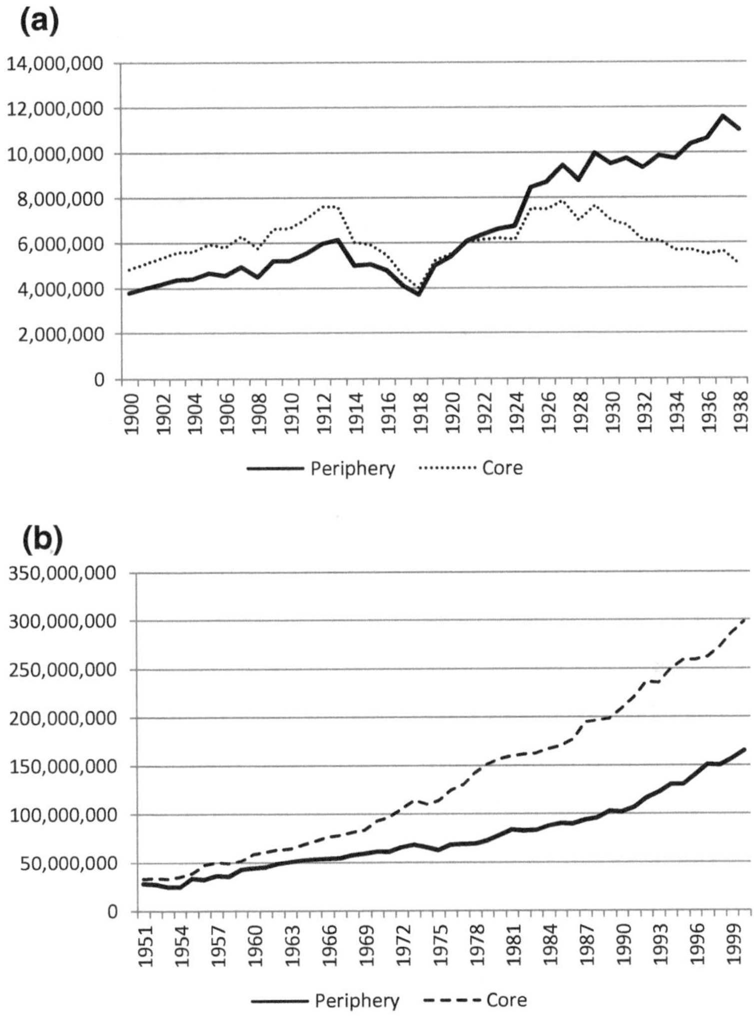

Fig. 3.2 World agricultural exports: The Periphery vs. the Core countries. (**a**) 1900–1938 constant prices USA $ 1925. (**b**) 1951–2000 constant prices USA $ 1980. Source: Own calculation based on I.I.A. (1910–1939) and FAO (1947–2000) and FAOSTAT (2009)

industry. In addition, the problems of some large European agricultural exporters, such as Russia after 1917, seriously affected the results of the central countries.

Figure 3.3 allows for a greater degree of regional disaggregation. Until 1929, all regions of the world, except Europe, substantially increased their exports of agricultural products. Especially important was the case of Asia, which surpassed all others in its expansion. The impact of the crisis and the 1930s depression was very uneven. Paradoxically, the most dynamic behaviour during the 1930s took place in the European colonies (and the British dominions), while the independent republics of Latin America saw their exports stagnate. The developed countries experienced a much greater impact on their exports of agricultural products and food. This diversity of results could be explained mainly by the impact of the growing protectionism of the European countries and the USA. The colonies usually had privileged access to the metropolitan markets, which greatly alleviated the effect of protectionism on their exports, while the territories located in tropical areas had the advantage that their products did not compete with European or North American production, which also facilitated the maintenance or increase of their exports.

Finally, it should be noted that the expansion of export agriculture in Africa and Asia was later than in Latin America. This explains why their productive capacity grew very quickly after WWI.

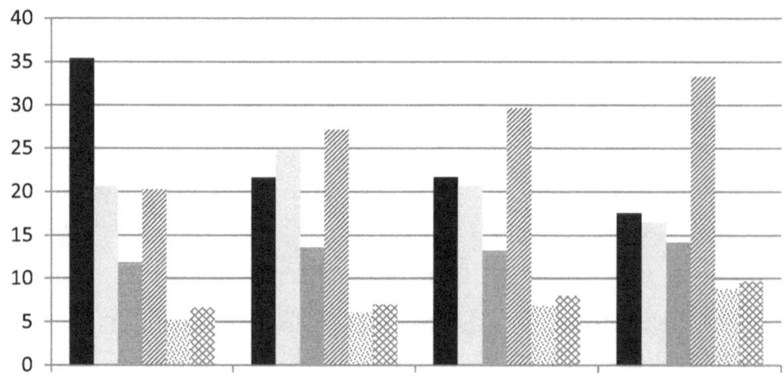

Fig. 3.3 Breakdown by regions of world trade of agricultural and food products, 1900–1938 (exports at 1925 prices) (%). Source: Own calculation based on I.I.A. (1910–1939)

2.3 The Structure of Agro-Food Exports in the Periphery

The structure of agro-food exports in the different regions of the periphery shows clearly differentiated profiles. South America, for example, was specialised in food, which accounted for more than two-thirds of its agro-food exports (Table 3.2). Within this group of products, the two most important were cereals and tropical products, particularly coffee, and meat also had significant weight. In fact, this specialisation reflected the profiles of two very different sub-regions. On the one hand, the Southern Cone, and particularly Argentina and Uruguay, were large exporters of wheat, maize, linseed oil, and meat. On the other hand, countries in the tropical latitudes, such as Brazil or Colombia, exported mainly plantation products and had a significant weight in world coffee exports.

Africa and Asia were, however, specialised in the export of agricultural raw materials. The trajectory of both regions in the first third of the twentieth century diverged. While in Africa, the weight of agricultural raw materials declined, because of the rapid increase in exports of plantation products such as coffee, cocoa, and tea, the opposite happened in Asia, especially from the boom in rubber exports.

3 World Agricultural Trade in the Second Wave of Globalisation, 1950–2000

3.1 The Evolution of Agricultural and Food Trade

WWII profoundly affected world trade in general, and both agricultural production and its commerce. The effects of the war varied greatly: on the one hand, the war zones, mainly Europe, were the most affected; imports were reduced and these regions suffered massive devastation of their agriculture (Brassley, 2012). Elsewhere, other regions were only indirectly affected by the war, since their traditional export markets were radically reduced. Thus, the volume of exports of agricultural and food products from South America fell overall by 42 per cent from the late 1930s to the mid-1940s (Pinilla & Aparicio, 2015).

Table 3.2 Breakdown of exports in agricultural and food products, 1900–1938 (at 1925 prices) (%)

	Africa		Asia		Oceania		South America	
	1909–13	1934–38	1909–13	1934–38	1909–13	1934–38	1909–13	1934–38
Food and live animals chiefly for food	21.4	35.5	46.6	32.1	42.6	58.1	69.5	71.2
Meat and meat preparations	0.1	0.8	0.2	0.1	12.2	11.7	10.7	10.9
Dairy products and eggs	1.9	1.5	2.1	1.1	7.5	18.2	0.3	0.6
Cereals and cereal preparations	5.9	6.1	16.6	10.5	11.9	13.0	24.1	26.4
Vegetables and fruit	2.5	4.9	2.8	2.7	0.9	2.0	3.1	3.0
Sugar, sugar preparations and honey	6.3	7.3	10.5	8.6	9.9	13.0	3.0	4.2
Coffee, tea, cocoa, spices and manufactures thereof	3.6	11.9	13.8	8.0	0.2	0.2	27.7	25.0
Beverages and tobacco	9.3	8.6	2.1	1.4	0.0	0.1	0.9	0.9
Crude materials, inedible, except fuels	64.9	50.8	50.5	63.9	57.3	41.8	29.6	27.7
Oil seeds and oleaginous fruit	15.4	15.7	11.4	8.5	1.2	1.9	5.0	7.8
Crude rubber	4.1	0.7	4.7	31.2	0.0	0.1	4.4	1.0
Textile fibres	45.4	34.4	34.4	24.2	56.0	39.9	20.2	18.9
Animal and vegetable oils, fats and waxes	4.4	5.1	0.8	2.6	0.1	0.0	0.0	0.2
Total	100.0	100.0	100.0	100.0	100.0	100.0	100.0	100.0

Source: Own calculation based on I.I.A. (1910–1939)

The return to pre-war trade levels occurred in a relatively short time. According to our estimates (Fig. 3.1), between 1934–1938 and 1948–1950, international agricultural trade had contracted by 4.4 per cent, which means that the recovery after 1945 was quite fast, considering that its fall during the war was so dramatic (Brassley, 2012). Since 1951, the pre-war volume of trade was exceeded. Thus, in 1952–1954 it was already 9.2 per cent higher than in 1934–1938.

The second half of the twentieth century saw unprecedented economic growth, particularly in the decades of capitalism's golden age. *Per capita* incomes rose, generally, the world over until the crisis of the 1970s, and that expansion continued overall in the ensuing decades, although the pattern of development varied widely. This phenomenon is reflected in the spectacular growth of international trade. In this context, agricultural trade experienced unparalleled growth between 1951 and 2000, expanding much faster than in earlier periods.

Two clearly distinct phases can be observed in this evolution. The first of these took place between 1951 and 1973 (the years of the "golden age"), when international agricultural trade grew continuously, at an annual growth rate of 4.6 per cent. Farm trade grew faster in this period than it had at any other time since the early nineteenth century. The second, between 1973 and 2000, saw trade grow at an annual rate of 3.5 per cent, a pace somewhat lower and less stable than in the preceding years.

The strong economic growth that had begun after WWII came to an end in the early 1970s. The world economy was wracked by the energy crisis, inflation, exchange-rate instability, slower growth in the industrialised nations and a general atmosphere of uncertainty. Despite recession, instability, and increased trade barriers, agricultural exports responded strongly to the first energy crisis, and average annual growth of 5.1 per cent was achieved between 1974 and 1980, the highest figure in the second half of the twentieth century. This vitality of trade was encouraged by a very rapid improvement in the real prices of agricultural products after their gentle but persistent decline from 1951 until 1972.[4]

The second oil crisis forced governments to toughen their monetary and fiscal policy, resulting in a painful economic slowdown that particularly affected developing countries. Demand for imports fell and problems of overcapacity emerged, reflected in the steep fall in international commodity prices (Serrano & Pinilla, 2011). Structural adjustment programmes were launched to mitigate the effects of the crisis, and agricultural trade increased only very slowly in the early 1980s. The poor performance of trade compared to the economy in general suggests the existence of significant constraints. Trade growth slowed, in part, due to the stagnation of demand. The two main reasons for the stagnation of demand for foodstuffs were the decline in the rate of growth in the world population and the saturation of what had become a mature market. At the same time, growth in agricultural trade was blocked by increasing protectionism. In an effort to shield farmers from the crisis, Europe, Japan, and the USA, among others, raised non-tariff barriers sharply and sought to isolate their agriculture from falling prices and volatility. In addition, real prices of agricultural products experienced a downward trend that persisted until the mid-1980s, when prices tended to stabilise (Serrano & Pinilla, 2011).

Finally, the years between the 1980s and 2000 could be described as the most significant political transformation since the end of WWII. A sequence of extraordinary events resulted in the collapse of communism in the Soviet Union and Eastern Europe, and the emergence of a new political, economic, and trade order (Findlay & O'Rourke, 2007). The 1990s were characterised by wide divergence in the economies of the leading industrialised nations, the drive toward European integration, rapid economic growth in the USA, a severe recession in Japan, and growth in many developing countries, especially China. Two consequences of events in the preceding period were to have a positive influence on agricultural trade. These were the massive debt loads of many developing countries, and the deterioration in the terms of trade. Those countries that had formerly operated policies penalising the agro-export sector now sought to expand production for export as a way of increasing revenues, despite slack international demand for agricultural goods in this period. This rise in agro-food trade was enhanced by lower trade barriers resulting from the liberalisation of international markets in agricultural products and commodities, the impact of Regional Trade Agreements covering agricultural trade, and accelerating income growth after the crisis, especially in Asia, which would gradually become a major importer of agricultural products.

The primary cause of agricultural trade growth during the second half of the twentieth century was the growth in world income, although Regional Trade Agreements and, especially, the creation of the European Union, also played a major role. Finally, falling agricultural prices and the exchange rate stability that lasted until the early 1970s also contributed to growth in agricultural trade, although to a much lesser extent (Serrano & Pinilla, 2010).

It was also in this period that the direction, make-up, and structure of international trade shifted in favour of exchanges of manufactured goods between industrialised nations. In fact, the percentage of total international trade represented by agricultural goods declined sharply over this period. While agricultural and food products accounted for 43.0 per cent in 1951, this share had shrunk to just 6.7 per cent at current values by 2000. Among the reasons for this significant loss of importance, and doubtless one of the most important, is the relative fall in prices. This is evident when we consider the difference between the drastic loss of share of agricultural trade in terms of value, compared to the more moderate (albeit important) decline in terms of volume, which demonstrates an extremely serious fall in relative prices. This occurred most sharply between 1973 and 1982, and especially conditioned the incomes of countries specialised in the export of the most basic products (Serrano & Pinilla, 2011b).

With regard to the causes of the loss of share in terms of volume, one reason was the generalised protectionism in the international markets for agricultural products (Anderson, 2009, 2016). While other types of trade, such as manufacturing, enjoyed greater multilateral liberalisation of their markets, strong market intervention caused agricultural trade growth to be based on the proliferation and success of regional trade agreements, in addition to important changes in consumption patterns related to rising income levels. Thus, the slower growth in farm trade had much to do with the significant fall in agriculture's share of world GDP. The smaller share of intra-industrial trade for the majority of agricultural products was also crucial. The home market effect for agricultural exchanges had an extremely limited importance, which explains why these markets grew less dynamically than those of manufactured goods and total trade (Serrano & Pinilla, 2012).

The period also witnessed changes in the direction, composition, and structure of international agricultural trade. On the one hand, agricultural trade became increasingly concentrated among the developed countries. On the other, trade in high-value-added products and processed foods grew ever more important, tending to displace basic products (Serrano & Pinilla, 2014).

3.2 Changes in the Geographical Distribution of Trade: The Reversal of Traditional Roles in Agricultural and Food Trade

International economic integration made a comeback in the second half of the twentieth century, but the North–South pattern forged in the period of the first globalisation was gradually replaced by a trade pattern based principally on exchanges of manufactured goods between developed nations. In the case of agricultural trade, flows of processed goods between high-income countries grew significantly. In general, the industrialised nations supported their agriculture in pursuit of food self-sufficiency, a goal that most had adopted after the scarcity of the war and post-war years. Importantly, widespread state support of the agricultural sector in these countries was also driven by the aim of tackling the so-called "farm-income problem", thus trying to guarantee farmers a "fair" income (Tracy, 1964).

This strategy, which Díaz-Bonilla and Tin (2002) call Import Substitution Agriculture (ISA), was deployed by all of the world's leading countries, with Europe and Japan at the forefront (González et al., 2016). Access to new technologies made self-sufficiency possible, reduced the volume of imports, and even allowed these countries to become net exporters of agricultural products from very early on in the period. To take into account how much these protectionist policies distorted agricultural trade, we can use the nominal rate of assistance (NRA), defined as "the percentage by which government policies have raised gross returns to producers above what they would be without government intervention (or lowered them, if the NRA is below zero)". Reasonably reliable estimates exist of the impact of these polices on agriculture, in a significant group of European and developed countries since 1955. The figures are telling: the NRA was positive in weighted average terms in the developed world, at least since 1955, the first year for which data are available. Thus, developed countries' public policies increased farm incomes by 44 per cent in Western Europe, 39 per cent in Japan, and 13 per cent in the USA, in the years 1955–1959. In later years, support to farmers grew considerably, especially in Western Europe and Japan. On the contrary, developing countries heavily discriminated against their farmers, specifically by setting strong anti-trade biases in the structure of assistance (Anderson, 2009, 2016).

The above-described set of national and international policies led to a major "disarray" in world agriculture (Johnson, 1987; Tyres & Anderson, 1992). The farm subsidies operating in rich countries tended to distort production and trade. On the one hand, agricultural trade was severely restricted by import control measures, but on the other hand it was actually expanded by the use of export subsidies and restitutions. When it comes to developing countries, some implemented import subsidies—which could foster farm trade to a certain extent—but they also, and commonly, taxed food exports. The net effect of government intervention on farm trade was probably negative, mainly because the assistance to import-competing commodities was, on average, significantly more important than that conceded to exportables (Anderson, 2016; GATT, 1958). The disarray in world agriculture was visibly significant because of the distortions in prices and trade, the large cost imposed upon taxpayers and consumers, the uneconomic expansion of farm output in the industrial countries, and the associated effects on the developing countries.

The fall in European imports, especially bulk products, in relative terms is a clear example of this process, as may be observed in Table 3.3, which reflects the main changes in the regional distribution of trade in agro-food products. The counterpoint was the rise in food imports to Asia, which was undergoing a far-reaching process of industrialisation, demographic growth, and urbanisation. Thus, Asian imports of farm products and foodstuffs grew across the board, and the continent's share increased in the four product categories considered.

Table 3.3 Percentage regional distribution of trade of agricultural and food products (US dollars, 1980)

Region	1952–1959	1966–1973	1980–1987	1994–2000
A. Exports				
Europe	32	36	41	44
North and Central America	24	24	25	21
Oceania	8	6	6	5
Asia	14	14	14	17
South America	13	9	9	9
Africa	8	10	5	4
Total	100	100	100	100
B. Imports				
Europe	59	58	54	48
North and Central America	19	16	13	14
Oceania	1	1	1	1
Asia	14	18	24	29
South America	4	2	2	3
Africa	3	4	6	5
Total	100	100	100	100

Source: Own work based on FAO (1947–2000) and FAOSTAT (2009).
Europe includes the Soviet Union and, after 1991, Russia and the ex-Soviet economies

In the case of exports, changes in the geographical make-up of trade flows are even more marked. Governments in the developed nations provided agriculture with more support than any other sector, while many developing nations discriminated against farmers. This was especially the case in South America, where many countries opted early on for policies based on industrialisation and import substitution, which severely penalised their agro-export sectors (Serrano & Pinilla, 2016).

As a result, the regions that were most dependent on the export of bulk products (Africa, Oceania, and South America) saw their share in world agricultural trade fall. Thus, both Africa and South America experienced a progressive decline in relative share in the regional distribution of exports. Moreover, some of these countries not only saw their exports fall in relative terms, but also experienced a sharp deterioration in the ratio of agricultural exports to imports. Thus, Africa and Asia became net importers of agricultural products, where they had once been net exporters.

The flip-side of this decline was the increasing share of high-income nations, and in particular the rise of European exports, which grew from 32 per cent of the world total in the 1950s to 44 per cent by the end of the century.

The lion's share of this increase is explained by the combination of two factors. First, the rise in self-sufficiency was made possible by technological progress, high levels of protectionism, and support for farming through the Common Agricultural Policy (CAP). Second, domestic markets were progressively deregulated, which greatly favoured the increase in intra-regional trade. The creation of the European Union as a common market is a case in point, as it brought about a spectacular increase in farm trade between the member states (Pinilla & Serrano, 2009; Serrano & Pinilla, 2011a).

The antithesis of the European case is Latin America. The significant decline in this region's share is explained by four factors, namely the retention of exports due to the demographic boom, specialisation in low income-elasticity products, the failure of agreements aimed at achieving regional economic integration, and the anti-export bias of economic policies (Serrano & Pinilla, 2016).

Figure 3.2 clearly shows the differences in export behaviour between the countries of the centre and the periphery. Both groups of countries began in 1950 with a similar volume of exports of agricultural and food products. However, by the end of the twentieth century, the exports of the centre's countries were almost double those of the periphery.

4 Final Remarks

In the last two hundred years, agricultural trade has grown at a remarkably rapid rate. Trade has also grown faster than production, which has led to greater international integration of the agricultural and food markets. However, there are notable differences between the two waves of globalisation. In the first globalising wave, international trade was based on the exchange of primary products for manufactured goods, with an international division of labour based on the comparative advantages of the respective countries. This provided important opportunities for complementarity in certain countries on the periphery that took advantage of the opportunity to base their economic development on the growth of their exports and the linkages between them and the rest of the economy to boost their industrialisation. However, most of the agricultural exporting countries, mainly located in the tropics, obtained few benefits from this model of development.

In the second wave of globalisation, this pattern of trade was increasingly replaced by an intra-industrial trade, in which the exchange of manufactured goods was its most dynamic engine. In addition, the more developed countries tended to protect their agricultural production with high protectionist barriers, which have been a major obstacle to agricultural trade. Finally, the developing countries themselves turned to the inward-looking models of economic growth, mainly based on the substitution of industrial imports, penalising their agrarian export sectors and also damaging the agricultural trade. As a result, the second half of the twentieth century saw an important increase in the participation of the developed world in the export of agricultural products and foodstuffs, at the same time as its share in agricultural imports declined. Logically, traditional exporters of agricultural products saw their participation in world agricultural trade fall significantly.

The final years of the twentieth century and the first decade of the twenty-first century seem to mark an appreciable change of trend. Trade in agricultural and food products has continued to grow at a rate similar to that of the last quarter of the twentieth century (Table 3.1), but a change in development models in the 1990s, a certain smoothing of agricultural protectionism in more developed countries, and a strong boost in the demand for agricultural products from emerging countries, mainly China, has favoured developing countries regaining prominence in such trade. Between 2000 and 2010, the share of the periphery in world exports of agricultural products and food has increased by about eight percentage points. The regions of the developing world that have been the stronger protagonists of this new export dynamism have been South America and Asia, while the rest of Latin America and Africa have not experienced a similar expansion of their trade in agricultural products and foodstuffs.[5]

Notes

1. In settler economies, the agricultural sector's share of GDP remained fairly constant, and until trade costs fell substantially, exports were concentrated in a small number of high-volume goods (Anderson, 2018).
2. We include in this group only the settler economies whose development was based on the exploitation of under-utilised natural resources and the export of the products obtained to the core countries, and where the European immigrant population ended up being a large majority of the population. See Sutch (2013). The Europeans had hardly colonised these countries until the nineteenth century and, given the high transport costs, it was not profitable to export agricultural products that were similar to the European ones. All of these countries were ranked among the world's top fifteen economies in terms of per capita income in 1913.
3. We consider countries on the periphery to be those located outside the European continent that did not experience a significant process of industrialisation in the nineteenth century, including those in Africa, Latin America and the Caribbean, Asia (excluding Japan), and Oceania.
4. On the evolution of the terms of trade of agricultural products, see Serrano and Pinilla (2011b) and Pfaffenzeller, Newbold, and Rayner (2007).
5. Based on United Nations COMTRADE database.

References

Anderson, K. (2009). *Distortions to Agricultural Incentives. A Global Perspective, 1955–2007*. Washington and New York: Palgrave Macmillan and the World Bank.

Anderson, K. (2016). *Agricultural Trade, Policy Reforms, and Global Food Security*. London and New York: Palgrave Macmillan.

Anderson, K. (2018). Agricultural Development in Australia in the Face of Occasional Mining Booms: 1845 to 2015. In V. Pinilla & H. Willebald (Eds.), *Agricultural Development in the World Periphery: A Global Economic History Approach*. London and New York: Palgrave Macmillan.

Aparicio, G., Pinilla, V., & Serrano, R. (2009). Europe and the International Agricultural and Food Trade, 1870–2000. In P. Lains & V. Pinilla (Eds.), *Agriculture and Economic Development in Europe Since 1870* (pp. 52–75). London: Routledge.

Bairoch, P. (1989). European Trade Policy, 1815–1914. In P. Mathias & S. Pollard (Eds.), *The Cambridge Economic History of Europe* (Vol. VIII, pp. 1–160). Cambridge: Cambridge University Press.

Bértola, L., & Williamson, J. (2006). Globalization in Latin America Before 1940. In V. Bulmer-Thomas, J. H. Coatsworth, & R. Cortés-Conde (Eds.), *The Cambridge Economic History of Latin America, vol. II. The Long Twentieth Century* (pp. 11–56). Cambridge: Cambridge University Press.

Brassley, P. (2012). International Trade in Agricultural Products, 1935–1955. In P. Brassley, Y. Segers, & L. Van Molle (Eds.), *War, Agriculture, and Food. Rural Europe from the 1930s to the 1950s* (pp. 33–54). London: Routledge.

Bulmer-Thomas, V. (1994). *The Economic History of Latin America Since Independence*. Cambridge: Cambridge University Press.

Byerlee, D., & Viswanathan, P. K. (2018). Plantations and Economic Development in the Twentieth Century: End of an Era? In V. Pinilla & H. Willebald (Eds.), *Agricultural Development in the World Periphery: A Global Economic History Approach*. London and New York: Palgrave Macmillan.

Diaz-Bonilla, E. & Tin, J. (2002). *That was Then but this is Now: Multifunctionality in Industry and Agriculture*. TMD Discussion Paper 94.

Estevadeordal, A., Frantz, B., & Taylor, A. M. (2003). The Rise and Fall of World Trade, 1870–1939. *Quarterly Journal of Economics, CXVIII, 2*, 359–407.

FAOSTAT. (2009) FAO. Retrieved April, 2010, from http://www.fao.org/faostat/en/#home

Federico, G., & Tena-Junguito, A. (2016). World trade, 1800–1938: A New Data-Set, European Historical Economics Society Working Paper 93.

Findlay, R., & O'Rourke, K. (2007). *Power and Plenty: Trade, War, and the World Economy in the Second Millennium*. Princeton: Princeton University Press.

Food and Agriculture Organization of the United Nations. (1947–2000). *FAO Trade Yearbook*. Rome: FAO.

Food and Agriculture Organization of the United Nations. (1956). *Yearbook of Food and Agricultural Statistics 1955, vol. IX(Part 2)*. Rome: FAO.

GATT. (1958). *Trends in International Trade. Report by a Panel of Experts*. Geneva: The Contracting Parties of the General Agreement on Tariffs and Trade.
González, A. L., Pinilla, V., & Serrano, R. (2016). International agricultural markets after the War, 1945–1960. In C. Martiin, J. Pan-Montojo, & P. Brassley (Eds.), *Agriculture in Capitalist Europe, 1945–1960. From food shortages to food surpluses* (pp. 64–84). London: Routledge.
Institut International d'Agriculture. (1910–1939). *International Yearbook of Agricultural Statistics*. Rome: International Institute of Agriculture.
Institut International d'Agriculture & Bureau de la FAO à Rome. (1947). *Annuaire International de Statistique Agricola 1941–42 à 1945–46*. Rome: IIA and FAO.
Jacks, D. (2005). Intra- and International Commodity Market Integration in the Atlantic Economy, 1800–1913. *Explorations in Economic History, 42*(3), 381–413.
Jacks, D. (2006). What Drove Nineteenth Century Commodity Market Integration? *Explorations in Economic History, 43*(3), 386–412.
Johnson, D. G. (1987). *World Agriculture in Disarray*. London: Macmillan.
Lewis, A. W. (1952). World Production, Prices and Trade, 1870–1960. *The Manchester School of Economic and Social Studies, XX*(2), 105–138.
Lewis, A. W. (1981). The Rate of Growth of World Trade, 1830–1973. In L. S. Grassman & E. Lundberg (Eds.), *The World Economic Order*. London: Palgrave Macmillan.
Liepmann, H. (1938). *Tariff Levels and the Economic Unity of Europe*. London: George Allen & Unwin.
Maddison, A. (2001). *The World Economy: A Millennial Perspective*. Paris: OECD.
Martín-Retortillo, M., Pinilla, V., Velazco, J., & Willebald, H. (2018). The Goose That Laid the Golden Eggs? Agricultural Development in Latin America in the Twentieth Century? In V. Pinilla & H. Willebald (Eds.), *Agricultural Development in the World Periphery: A Global Economic History Approach*. London and New York: Palgrave Macmillan.
Meissner, C. M., Jacks, D. S., & Novy, D. (2011). Trade Booms, Trade Busts, and Trade Costs. *Journal of International Economics, 83*(2), 185–201.
O'Rourke, K. H. (1997). The European Grain Invasion, 1870–1913. *Journal of Economic History, 57*(4), 775–801.

O'Rourke, K. H., & Williamson, J. G. (1999). *Globalization and History. The Evolution of a Nineteenth-Century Atlantic Economy*. Cambridge, MA: The MIT Press.

Ocampo, J. A., & Parra-Lancourt, M. A. (2010). The Terms of Trade for Commodities Since the Mid-Nineteenth Century. *Revista de Historia Económica. Journal of Iberian and Latin American Economic History, 28*(1), 11–44.

Offer, A. (1989). *The First World War: An Agricultural Interpretation*. New York: Oxford University Press.

Pfaffenzeller, S., Newbold, P., & Rayner, A. (2007). A Short Note on Updating the Grilli and Yang Commodity Price Index. *The World Bank Review, 21*(1), 151–163.

Pinilla, V., & Aparicio, G. (2015). Navigating in Troubled Waters: South American Exports of Food and Agricultural Products, 1900–1950. *Revista de Historia Económica-Journal of Iberian and Latin American Economic History, 33*, 2.

Pinilla, V., & Ayuda, M. I. (2010). Taking Advantage of Globalization? Spain and the Building of the International Market in Mediterranean Horticultural Products, 1850–1935. *European Review of Economic History, 14*(2), 239–274.

Pinilla, V., & Rayes, A. (2017). *Why Did Argentina Become a Super-Exporter of Agricultural and Food Products During the Belle Époque (1880–1929)?* EHES Working Papers in Economic History, 107.

Pinilla, V., & Serrano, R. (2009). Agricultural and Food Trade in the European Union since 1963. In K. Patel (Ed.), *Fertile Ground por Europe? The History of European Integration and the Common Agricultural Policy Since 1945* (pp. 273–300). Baden-Baden: Nomos.

Serrano, R., & Pinilla, V. (2010). Causes of World Trade Growth in Agricultural and Food Products, 1951–2000: A Demand Function Approach. *Applied Economics, 42*(27), 3503–3518.

Serrano, R., & Pinilla, V. (2011a). Agricultural and Food Trade in European Union Countries, 1963–2000: A Gravity Equation Approach. *Économies et SociÉtÉs, SÉrie AF Histoire Économique Quantitative, 43*(1), 191–219.

Serrano, R., & Pinilla, V. (2011b). Terms of Trade for Agricultural and Food Products, 1951–2000. *Revista de Historia Económica-Journal of Iberian and Latin American Economic History, 29*(2), 213–243.

Serrano, R., & Pinilla, V. (2012). The Long-Run Decline in the Share of Agricultural and Food Products in International Trade: A Gravity Equation Approach of its Causes. *Applied Economics, 44*(32), 2199–2210.

Serrano, R., & Pinilla, V. (2014). Changes in the Structure of World Trade in the Agrifood Industry: The Impact of the Home Market Effect and Regional Liberalization from a Long Term Perspective, 1963–2010. *Agribusiness: An International Journal, 30*(2), 165–183.

Serrano, R., & Pinilla, V. (2016). The Declining Role of Latin America in Global Agricultural Trade, 1963–2000. *Journal of Latin American Studies, 48*(1), 115–146.

Sutch, R. (2013). Introduction. In C. Lloyd, J. Metzer, & R. Sutch (Eds.), *Settler Economies in World History* (pp. 1–36). Leiden: Brill.

Tracy, M. (1964). *Agriculture in Western Europe*. New York: Praeger.

Tyres, R., & Anderson, K. (1992). *Disarray in World Food Markets: A Quantitative Assessment*. Hong Kong: Cambridge University Press.

Willebald, H., & Juambelz, J. (2018). Land Frontier Expansion in Settler Economies (1830–1950): Was It a Ricardian process? In V. Pinilla & H. Willebald (Eds.), *Agricultural Development in the World Periphery: A Global Economic History Approach*. London and New York: Palgrave Macmillan.

Gema Aparicio is an independent researcher. She holds an MA in Economic History from the London School of Economics and a PhD in Economics from the University of Zaragoza. Her research interests lies in international trade in agricultural products between 1900 and 1938. She has published some articles and book chapters on this topic.

Ángel Luis González-Esteban is a lecturer in Economic History at the University Pompeu Fabra. He graduated in Economics at the University of Salamanca and then took a Master's degree in Latin American Studies (Usal) and a Master's degree in Economic History (UB). His PhD (University of Barcelona) was on the world wheat economy (1939–2010) and he was awarded the Ramón Carande (AEHE) prize for young researchers.

Vicente Pinilla is Professor of Economic History at the University of Zaragoza and Fellow at Instituto Agroalimentario de Aragón (IA2). His research interests lies in international trade in agricultural products, long-term agricultural changes, environmental history, and migration. His is the author of *Peaceful*

Surrender: The Depopulation of Rural Spain in the Twentieth Century, and is an editor of the books *Agriculture and Economic Development in Europe since 1870*, *Markets and Agricultural Change in Europe from the Thirteenth to the Twentieth Century*, *Natural Resources and Economic Growth: Learning from History*, and *Wine Globalization: A New Comparative History.*

Raúl Serrano is Assistant Professor at the University of Zaragoza (Spain). He has a PhD in Economics from the University of Zaragoza (2007). His research is focused on international trade and firm internationalisation, especially in the agro-food industry. He has written some articles and book chapters about these topics.

4

Plantations and Economic Development in the Twentieth Century: The End of an Era?

Derek Byerlee and P.K. Viswanathan

1 Introduction

Plantations are generally understood to be a way of mobilising land, labour and capital to produce tropical commodities in large operational units under central management (Graham & Foering 1984; Tiffen & Mortimore, 1990). In 1900, the plantation was the accepted approach to producing tropical commodities such as tea, coffee, cocoa, sugar cane and sisal, often using imported indentured labour in frontier regions (Wickizer, 1958). In the early twentieth century, other tropical commodities—rubber, oil palm and bananas—began to be cultivated

Valuable comments from Vicente Pinilla and Anne Booth are appreciated.

D. Byerlee (✉)
School of Foreign Service, Georgetown University, Washington, DC, USA

P.K. Viswanathan
Department of Management, Amrita University, Kochi, Kerala, India

V. Pinilla, H. Willebald (eds.), *Agricultural Development in the World Periphery*,
Palgrave Studies in Economic History, https://doi.org/10.1007/978-3-319-66020-2_4

using the plantation mode of production. Associated with these new crops and the phasing out of indentured labour, the "modern plantation system" emerged as a near-industrial form of year-round commodity production employing significant foreign capital, hired labour, and scientific knowledge and logistics (Courtenay, 1969). This modern plantation system contrasted with the overwhelming dominance in tropical agriculture of smallholder farmers using mostly family labour.

Today, the plantation system in the tropics carries a strong negative imagery in the history of agriculture in economic development, given its association with the shameful era of slave labour in the Americas and the period of exploitation of land and labour by European imperial powers in their colonies to provision their home markets. With the independence of colonies after WWII, the negative perception of plantations was reinforced by influential writings on plantations, most notably by the West Indian economist, George Beckford (1972), and the American anthropologist, Sidney Mintz (1985).

Nonetheless, after independence, a few authors saw virtues in modern plantations as providing much needed capital and modern technology into "backward societies" especially when combined with rising standards for hired labour (Graham & Foering 1984; Wickizer, 1958). However, these writings have largely been forgotten and over the past three decades, scholarship on plantations has waned.

The purpose of this chapter is to fill the gap in recent literature by providing an overview of the evolution of plantations in the twentieth century as a way of supplying tropical commodities, whilst paying particular attention to agrarian structure and land and labour relations. The chapter covers a broad canvas drawing on our knowledge of three tropical commodities—namely tea, rubber, and oil palm—that are mainly grown in Asia and to some extent in Africa. We also include the experience of the Americas by drawing on the extensive literature on bananas in that region. Further, given the dominance of sugar cane as the most important tropical commodity prior to the twentieth century and in the historical literature, we also refer to the twentieth-century sugar cane experience. These five crops were among the most important plantation crops in the early part of the twentieth century and make up most of the area covered by plantations today.

2 Defining the Modern Plantation

After the demise of slavery and indentured labour, the organisational structure of plantations evolved considerably in the early twentieth century into the "modern plantation" defined by ten characteristic features (Courtenay, 1969; Goldthorpe, 1988; Graham & Foering, 1984):

1. A corporate structure often with financing from outside the sector. Such capital may be important to produce tree crops, with extensive upfront establishment costs, capital costs for milling, and a long gestation period for payback.
2. Professional management separated from ownership. Professional managers were mostly expatriates (i.e., European) in the colonial period, but most are nationals today.
3. A hierarchical management structure to supervise operations, especially labour. Oil palm plantations in Malaysia, for example, may have up to seven levels of management (Goldthorpe, 1988).
4. Specialisation in one commodity that allows hiring of the requisite technical expertise (e.g., agronomy, pest control) and standardisation of labour operations in the field.
5. Investment in data, logistics and science allowing continuous improvements in productivity, through careful monitoring of plantation sub-units and investment in R&D either within the company, or collectively through industry research organisations.
6. Vertical integration with first-stage processing of raw materials on the plantation. Many plantation companies are also horizontally integrated through ownership of plantations by parent companies that are spatially dispersed, sometimes across countries.
7. Relatively low seasonality of production due to the humid tropical climate that allows field operations to be built around an almost continual harvest season to make full use of mill capacity.
8. Labour intensive, as many operations, especially harvesting, are manual, requiring a large labour force that is often recruited externally, sometimes from abroad, and that is usually housed on the plantation.

9. A large and contiguous land area although this varies enormously from a minimum of about forty hectares (the definition of a plantation in Malaysia) to tens of thousands of hectares. The size of a vertically integrated operation is determined largely by mill capacity.
10. Orientation of output toward export markets, after initial processing and sometimes second-stage processing.

These organisational features that are akin to industrial processes in manufacturing are atypical of the vast majority of agriculture that is still characterised by family farming,[1] with family ownership of a significant share of, albeit limited, assets, and most labour provided by family members. There are, of course, many variations of both plantation and smallholder systems that will be noted later in the chapter.

3 The Major Plantation Crops of the Twentieth Century

Plantation crops grown in the twentieth century can be divided into five groups (three of which are dealt with in Table 4.1). The first group includes the traditional beverage crops of tea, coffee and cocoa that were already well established in tropical agriculture and world trade by 1900 and have steadily expanded their markets during the twentieth century. However, there were large geographical and even inter-continental shifts in production. Around 1900, cocoa moved decisively from the Americas and the Portuguese- and Spanish-ruled islands of São Tomé and Fernando Po, respectively, before moving to smallholders in West Africa, notably Ghana and Côte d'Ivoire, and then Indonesia—the three leading producers today. In the early 1900s, Brazil dominated world coffee markets but since WWII has steadily lost share to Colombia and Vietnam, where smallholders dominate production. India remains the major producer of tea, but Sri Lanka and Kenya are now the major exporters. Importantly, all three of the beverages and especially coffee have evolved from bulk (that is, undifferentiated and relatively low value) commodities to more specialised niche markets based on quality and geographical origin that pay premium prices.

Table 4.1 Evolution of exports (million tons) of major tropical commodities in the twentieth century

	≈1900		1961		2010	
	Exports (Mt)	Top exporters	Exports (Mt)	Top exporters	Exports (Mt)	Top exporters
Beverages						
Black tea	0.38	India, Sri Lanka	0.47	India, Sri Lanka	1.27	Kenya, Sri Lanka
Coffee	1.25	Brazil, Venezuela Colombia	2.69	Brazil, Colombia	5.91	Brazil, Vietnam
Cocoa	0.26	Ecuador, São Tomé, Brazil	1.05	Ghana, Nigeria	3.20	Côte d'Ivoire, Indonesia
Sugarcane	5.2	Indonesia, Cuba, USA	14.51	Brazil, Thailand	47.60	Brazil, Thailand
New commodities						
Rubber	0.22	Brazil, Peru	2.08	Malaysia, Indonesia	7.42	Indonesia, Thailand
Palm oil	0.21	Nigeria, French W. Africa	0.66	Congo DR, Nigeria	36.16	Indonesia, Malaysia
Bananas	0.82	NA	3.57	Ecuador, Honduras	14.0	Ecuador, Costa Rica

Source: FAOSTAT for 1961 and 2010. Estimates for 1900 are from V. Pinilla (pers comm)

Notes: Palm oil includes palm kernels and palm kernel oil. All tea exports from South Asia and Africa assumed to be black tea

Sugar cane is in a group of its own. From the 1700s, sugar was the most important tropical commodity in world trade and like beverages, its production has expanded steadily in the twentieth century. However, unlike beverages, it remains a bulk commodity in international trade. Sugar exports have shifted decisively from Cuba and Java together with several British island colonies in the early 1900s to be dominated today by Brazil.

The third group of commodities have entered plantation production in the first part of the twentieth century. Rubber and palm oil were extensively traded in world markets in the nineteenth century based on the harvesting of wild or semi-wild trees. Starting at around 1900, rubber cultivated on plantations in Malaysia quickly displaced wild rubber, mostly from the Americas; and from the 1920s, Indonesia and Malaysia also entered the palm oil market by establishing plantations that eventually captured markets from West African producers. Bananas had long been grown for local food needs, but, starting at around 1900, vertically integrated companies established a major export market initially in the USA based on cultivation of bananas in large plantations in Central America. All three of these new commodities are still largely marketed as bulk commodities.

The fourth group of plantation commodities (not considered in this chapter) were produced at the beginning of the century but suffered as the industry declined or disappeared. The best example is sisal and its variant henequen grown on plantations in Yucatan State of Mexico, which took off in the late nineteenth century to produce twine for the emerging mechanical harvesting and binding of wheat. After an extraordinary boom, the industry declined from the 1920s as wheat harvesting became fully mechanised. Indigo is another plantation industry in India and elsewhere in Asia that died with the invention of synthetic dyes in the early 1900s. Coconuts were also a significant plantation industry in Southeast Asia and the Pacific as a supplier of vegetable oil for margarine in the early 1900s, but their share of world markets has declined precipitously as more efficient oil crops—oil palm and soybean—captured the edible oil market.

Finally, new export industries in recent decades such as horticultural products and flowers have some of the characteristics of plantations but usually involve relatively small land areas and employ local labour. Given these differences and their recent origin, they are not considered in this chapter.

4 Factors Determining Agrarian Structure: Plantations vs Smallholders[2]

In 1900 about 90 per cent of agricultural exports from the tropics were produced on plantations (Pim, 1946). Over the course of twentieth century there was a notable shift in most tropical commodities from plantations to smallholder production (Table 4.2). In the early 1900s, the prevailing wisdom was that plantations linked to global capital and product markets were the most efficient production system (Wickizer, 1958). However, the rapid and spontaneous expansion of smallholder cocoa in West Africa, followed by the growth and eventual domination of smallholder rubber in Asia refuted the myths of smallholder backwardness and antipathy to market forces. Trends for other major commodities indicate a similar shift, although less so for oil palm and tea (Table 4.2).

Many authors have discussed the unique attributes of agriculture favouring the inherent efficiency of family farms (Allen & Lueck, 1998). Diversified family farms using family labour have advantages in managing production risks, the seasonality of labour demand, labour supervision and low overhead costs. Given these advantages of family farming, why then did plantations emerge at all for export commodities?

Table 4.2 Cultivated area of export crops by percent under large plantations in the major producing region at three time periods: circa 1900, 1930 and 2010 (numbers in bold indicate the dominant exporting region at the time)

Crop	Year	Africa	Americas	Asia
	1900	NR		**100**
Tea (black)	1930	100		**100**
	2010	**30 (Kenya)**		**72 (India)**
				28 (Sri Lanka)
	1905			**100**
Rubber (cultivated)	1930			**55**
	2010			**17**
	1905	>95	**>95**	
Cocoa	1930	**78**	>95	
	2010	**15**		<10
	1900	**NR**		NR
Oil palm (cultivated)	1930	**10–15**[a]		100
	2010	8		**≈60**
	1900		**100**	
Bananas (for export)[a]	1930		**100**	
	2010		**≈35**[b]	

Source: 1905 data for rubber from Drabble (1973). Data for 1930 from Greaves (1935). Data for 2010 estimated by the authors from various sources

NR indicates not relevant since not cultivated

[a]Based on quantity exported. There were 50,000 ha of plantations in the Congo

[b]Data for Ecuador and Costa Rica only

4.1 Economic Fundamentals

The most widely accepted economic argument for large plantations derives from a combination of significant economies of size in processing, the need to process perishable products immediately after harvest, and the bulky nature of the harvested product relative to the processed product. These characteristics put a premium on large contiguous areas around a mill to reduce transport costs of raw materials and on central management to coordinate harvesting with mill capacity utilisation (Binswanger & Rosenzweig, 1986). Sugar cane, oil palm, tea, and sisal require processing within about 24 hours after harvest, and bananas require quick shipping after harvest; and all except tea are based on bulky raw materials.[3] Further, large economies of scale in milling or shipping these products and high transactions costs of organising smallholders to a tight delivery schedule to fit mill (or ship) capacity favours vertical integration of production with processing of these commodities. Except for tea, the scale of milling has increased enormously over the century. For oil palm, a modern mill in 1934 required about 2,000 ha to fill capacity (Tate, 1996) and this had reached about 10,000 ha by 2000. The area to supply a sugar mill increased in Cuba from around 500 ha in 1900 to 3,250 ha in 1916, and 6,000 ha in 1929 (Dye, 1994); today it is as high as 70,000 ha in Brazil. Notably with the development of simple processing techniques by smallholders, rubber could be processed in small-scale artisan factories and smallholder production took off spontaneously and rapidly.

Sugar cane is the only perennial crop in the tropics where production can be fully mechanised. The breakthrough came with the development of mechanical harvesting in the 1920s for the high-wage economies of the USA and Australia. However, by the early twenty first century it had spread to the large sugar producers of Latin America, notably Brazil, cutting labour for harvesting by over 95 per cent. For oil palm, rubber and especially tea, labour for manual harvesting remains the major cost on plantations today.

Another economic fundamental relates to the pioneering cost and risks of introducing new commodities in new areas (Collier & Venables, 2012). This favours large companies with relevant experience, their own R&D capacity, and ready access to capital. Pioneering costs and risks are highest when a crop is being domesticated for cultivation for the first time and in frontier areas, where infrastructure and services are poorly developed and new crops are being tried. Techniques of cultivation had to be developed in the early1900s for rubber and oil palm that were previously harvested from wild and semi-wild plants. Cultivation and processing of bananas for export was also a new venture with high start-up costs and risks. However, after an industry was established and the basic processing and export logistics and infrastructure were in place, pioneering costs and risks fell, opening space for smallholders, as in rubber.

4.2 Biased Economic Policies

Beyond economic fundamentals, the rise of plantations often reflected policies that distorted the underlying costs in their favour (Binswanger, Deininger, & Feder, 1995). Policies that reduced prices for key production factors (land, labour and capital) to large operations relative to the prices faced by smallholders obviously favoured plantations. For example, investors in plantations were abetted by an almost universal policy under the colonial empires of providing cheap land through concessions carved out of "wastelands", generally in forested areas with low population density. Land policies were complemented by labour policies that facilitated cheap immigrant labour from poor and densely populated regions, often across colonial borders. Head taxes were also employed to encourage migration to obtain cash combined with prohibitions on smallholders growing cash crops (e.g., Kenya until the 1950s; Indonesia until the 1920s) (Bosma, 2013; Deininger & Binswanger, 1995). Finally, colonial governments often provided considerable support in the form of cheap loans, as well as outright grants in times of depressed prices (e.g., as in Malaya) (Jackson, 1968).

Prevailing ideologies and beliefs shaped these policies. Colonial officials widely believed that plantations linked to global capital and product markets and under European management were the most efficient system (Wickizer, 1958). Accordingly, colonial governments often openly discouraged smallholder participation in the production of tropical exports, such as rubber (Bauer, 1948). In India until quite recently, registration requirements for tea producers had inhibited smallholder participation in the industry (Borah, 2013). These beliefs persisted despite the fact that colonial texts on tropical agriculture had recognised by the 1930s the inherent competitiveness of smallholders (e.g., Greaves, 1935; Pim, 1946).

Notably Thailand, which was never colonised, resisted requests to grant large land concessions, and instead consistently supported smallholder development, emerging after 1950 as the world's leading rubber producer, the second exporter of sugar, and the third largest oil palm producer. The Thai success with "plantation crops" amply demonstrated the global competitiveness of smallholders.

Independence in Asia and Africa and a new nationalistic spirit in Latin America after WWII brought in new policy regimes, and plantations became the "whipping boy" for many political leaders (Wickizer, 1958). The high visibility of foreign-owned and foreign-managed plantations together with a strong dose of nationalism and socialism in the post-independence era resulted in the nationalisation of plantations in many countries. Where plantations were taken over by the state, inefficient management and corruption only hastened their demise, as in the case of oil palm in Democratic Republic of Congo, tea and rubber in Sri Lanka, and sugar cane in Cuba. Malaysia was one of the very few countries that was able to orchestrate an orderly transition from foreign ownership of plantations to national ownership through its sovereign wealth fund and smallholder equity buy-ins.

4.3 Institutional Innovations to Support Smallholders

Meanwhile, independent governments gave more support to smallholders, through research, extension, marketing support, land reform, and formula pricing, depending on the country and commodity. Combined, these trends raised the transaction costs of plantations in accessing land and labour, and pushed private companies to look for other institutional arrangements, including contracting by mills or procurement of raw materials in the open market. In the Americas, United Fruit, the dominant banana company, facing a major backlash against the practice of holding giant land tracts of about 1.4 Mha combined with trade union activism after WWII, sharply reduced its plantations and moved to contracting small and medium producers. Ecuador, which prevented land alienation to foreign investors and encouraged local entrepreneurship, emerged as the world's leading banana exporter in the 1950s based on small- and medium-sized producers (Southgate & Roberts, 2016).[4] In Kenya, which was facing an insurrection before independence, the Swynnerton Plan in 1954 reversed anti-smallholder policies and actively promoted their participation in cash crop production. In the UK, the Colonial (now Commonwealth) Development Corporation (CDC) was established in 1958 to promote investment in tropical commodities involving smallholders.

Despite the success of smallholders in several plantation commodities, they often obtained lower yields than large plantations due to lack of capital, little experience with the new crops, and the use of poor quality seedlings (International Finance Corporation (IFC), 2013; Tiffen & Mortimore, 1990; Zen, Barlow, & Gondowarisito, 2005). They also often obtained lower prices since they generally sold through an intermediary that coordinated delivery to the mill (IFC, 2013; Ramsay, 1987). These results in turn reflected weak financial markets, insecure land rights, poor advisory services, and lack of strong farmer organisations to negotiate fair deals with mills.

Starting even in colonial states, there was much experimentation with models linking smallholders to state agencies and/or private agribusiness companies to overcome their asset deficits. These can be analysed within a framework that recognises the contribution of various resources employed in the value chain—capital, labour, land, and management—and the distribution of ownership of those resources among various stakeholder groups—namely, smallholders and their communities, migrants, private investors, and the state (Fig. 4.1). The assets owned by different stakeholder groups are often complementary, giving rise to mutually beneficial opportunities for partnerships.

One approach used a plantation management model for smallholders. In 1956 Malaysia established the Federal Land Development Authority (FELDA), a parastatal to resettle poor and landless households by

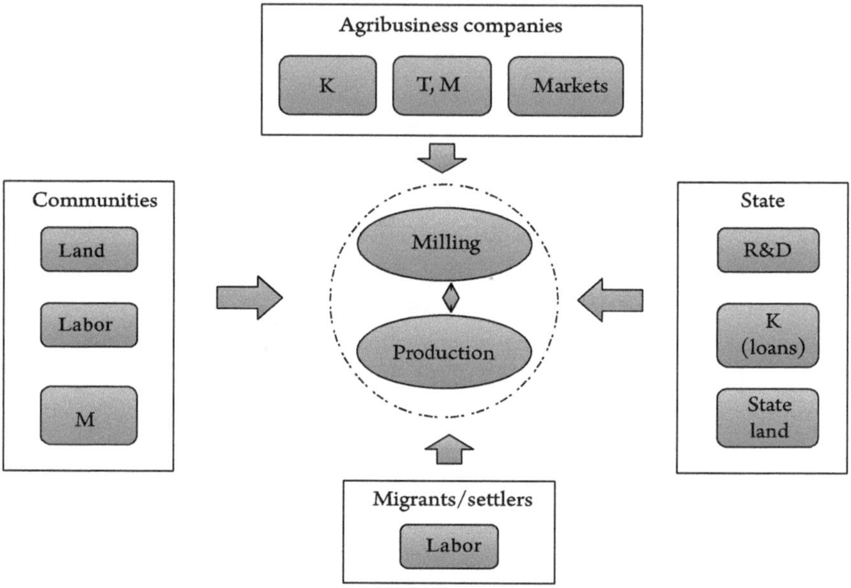

Fig. 4.1 Simplified framework showing the relative asset position of various stakeholder groups in commodity production. *M* management, *K* capital, *T* technology. Source: Authors' elaboration

converting large contiguous blocks in state forest land into oil palm and rubber plantations. The blocks were centrally managed by FELDA, with the settlers contributing labour in the early years. After repaying the land development debt, they received full title to their individual plots and took on limited management tasks. FELDA has generally been rated a success as an anti-poverty programme (Pletcher, 1991). FELDA subsequently transformed these plantations into one of the world's largest palm oil producers, FELDA Global Ventures, in which settler households hold the largest equity.

Another approach using a plantation organisation model is the association of a nucleus plantation estate with outgrowers (NES) that was pioneered in the British colonies of West Africa, under the CDC, and has been used extensively in Indonesia. The state or donors financed the establishment costs of a contiguous area of smallholder plots around a nucleus plantation that was state owned in the early years.

Most evaluations have graded the NES as reasonably successful (Zen et al., 2005). However, in many cases smallholders were little more than labourers on a centrally managed plantation, even though they received a share of profits besides wages.

In other cases, plantation companies have entered joint ventures with local communities to access land and labour. In the early 1900s, Java the second largest sugar exporter used a system where sugar companies negotiated with villagers to rent land on an annual basis and to hire labour, albeit with highly unequal distribution of the benefits (Bosma, 2013). Recently, oil palm companies in Sarawak, Malaysia and Indonesia have entered into long-term ventures with communities to access land again with few tangible benefits to communities (Cramb, 2013; McCarthy, 2010).

In other models, smallholders retain considerable management autonomy except for the timing of mill delivery. Contract farming is common for short-cycle crops such as sugar cane and bananas, so that mills or packers depend entirely on purchased fruit under contract with surrounding growers. Mills often provided working capital and a guaranteed price for delivery. The state, as in India, may also regulate zones for each mill to provide them quasi-monopoly powers to ensure that they utilise mill capacity. The delivery price is often negotiated by the state as a percentage of the export price, as in Thailand for sugar cane.

Export levies (or cess) on tropical commodities controlled by a parastatal has also been used to provide technical services and replanting grants to smallholders. One of the earliest examples is the Federation of Coffee Growers of Colombia, established in 1927 through a levy on coffee exports, providing a wide variety of services to its half a million members, overwhelmingly smallholders. Similarly, the Smallholder Tea Development Authority of Sri Lanka raised levies to transform their tea industry from a production base of large plantations to one of smallholders (Byerlee, 2014). In Thailand, the Office of Rubber Replanting Aid Fund, established in 1960 and funded by a cess on rubber exports, led to smallholders' wide adoption of high-yielding clonal material and enabled Thailand to become the world's largest rubber producer (Viswanathan, 2008).

Where the industry is sufficiently well organised, these parastatals have been privatised under majority smallholder ownership. The Kenyan Tea

Development Authority (KTDA), established as a parastatal in 1964, provided a range of services to growers, including processing. Fully privatised in 2000, KTDA is owned by more than half a million smallholders, who produce and process 70 per cent of Kenya's tea and is now the world's largest tea company (Mitchell, 2012).

Finally, smallholders can vertically integrate downstream to large mills through cooperative ownership of mills with the cooperative coordinating supply by members. This approach was pioneered in Bombay Presidency (now Maharashtra) in colonial India for sugar cane and continues today (Bosma, 2013). In oil palm, the cooperative model is widely used in Thailand and in Latin America. One of the most successful cooperatives is Hondupalma in Honduras, which, along with its own mills, owns several downstream industries, including a biodiesel plant.

These institutional innovations have played a critical role in increasing the competitiveness of smallholders. Yield gaps for tea in Kenya between smallholders and plantations have been reduced from 70 per cent in the 1970s to about 15 per cent today through the KTDA. By using high-yielding clones, Thailand increased rubber yields fourfold and has the highest yields of any major rubber producer today. Yields of Oil palm produced by smallholders in Nucleus Estate schemes sometimes exceeds that on the estate in Indonesia. Strong political support for a smallholder approach has generally been a prerequisite for the success of these models.

5 Land Rights

The reliance of plantations on large land concessions both historically and today risks conflicts over land with local communities. In frontier areas where tropical commodities were largely produced and shifting cultivation was traditionally practised by local communities, customary land rights were and still are poorly recognised. However, in British West Africa, colonial authorities gave precedence to local land rights over land concession for oil palm and rubber plantations, as did the colonial government of Sarawak, which was nominally under the British (Cleary, 1992; Martin, 1988). There were tensions in Peninsular Malaysia but, overall, land laws that secured tenure for local communities and prohibited alienation of land to plantation companies prevented serious conflicts (Kratoska, 1985)

By contrast, for bananas in Central America and oil palm in the Belgian Congo before WWII and in independent Indonesia in recent years, land conflicts were inevitable, given the very large areas allocated to plantation companies. In general, conflicts were less frequent when investments generally took place in sparsely populated forested areas, although there were exceptions such as rubber in Vietnam (Booth, 2007; Cleary, 2003).[5]

Land concession policies frequently encouraged speculation by plantation companies in land resources. For example, from 1840 to 1940, some 4.7 Mha was allocated for tea plantations in India although only 0.45 Mha of tea was planted (Siddique, 1990). Similarly, only one third of concessions in French Indo-China were cultivated in 1931 (Murray, 1980) and an even smaller share of the 1.4 Mha of land concessions mostly awarded to United Fruit in Central America in return for railway construction, was ever planted with bananas (Southgate & Roberts, 2016). With the commodity boom in the early twenty-first century there has been a resurgence of speculative investments in large land holdings in those countries with the weakest land and forest governance, abetted by policies providing cheap land through concessions (Byerlee, 2014).

Overall, the issue of land rights was in part muted by the rise of smallholder production systems for export commodities over the past century. Thailand, the world's leading producer of a number of tropical commodities (rubber, oil palm, sugar cane), had long given priority to land tenure security even in areas demarcated as state forests, and managed to increase world market share through smallholder systems with fewer conflicts. However, in situations of tenure insecurity and unequal power relations, smallholders too may become "land grabbers", sometimes with serious land conflicts as seen in the recent civil war resulting from struggles over cocoa lands in Côte d'Ivoire and conflicts related to cocoa expansion in Indonesia (Li, 2014; Woods, 2003).

6 Labour Rights and Conditions

Besides vast tracts of land, development of plantations required access to cheap and plentiful labour. While large-scale employment of labour can make significant positive impacts on economic development, the recruitment and housing of large numbers of unskilled labour on isolated plantations also invited abuses of labour rights

While no reliable statistics are collected on global employment in plantations, the International Labour Organization (ILO), using a broad definition of plantation crops (including annual cash crops), estimated that some 20 million were employed around 1990 (Table 4.3). At that time, the largest plantation labour forces were in India and Sri Lanka, mainly in tea, and in Brazil, mainly in coffee and sugar cane. Since then there have been major shifts in employment, with a sharp decline in Brazil through mechanisation of both sugar cane and coffee, and a major surge in Indonesia and Malaysia, where over 2 million workers are employed as labourers on oil palm plantations (Byerlee, Falcon, & Naylor, 2017).

As plantations were often developed on the sparsely populated frontier, labour needed to be brought in from distant places, including migrant workers from other countries or colonies. In Malaysia and other immigrant plantation economies, the commodification of labour resulted in an ethnic division, with immigrant labour concentrated in plantations and Malays in peasant production. Still, wage rates of immigrants were 75 per cent above wages in the origin region in India (Bauer, 1948). However, with the depression of the 1930s wages fell and immigration reversed as many migrants were repatriated. In recent years with the growth of oil palm industry and growing labour scarcity in Malaysia, there has been a resurgence of international migration and Malaysia continues to have one of the highest percentages of migrant workers in the region. Over 80 per cent of the labour force is recruited contractually from surrounding countries, mostly from Java in Indonesia, where rural wages are only about one quarter of those in Malaysia (Wiggins & Keats, 2014). Although Malaysia has formal rules and processes for contracting labour from abroad, these are loosely enforced, and many workers are illegal immigrants.

In India over a million people were working in the colonial plantations with "indentured" features of labour control in the early 1900s. Since workers' accounts (wages less costs of food and other minimal living expenses provided in plantation stores) were settled only at the end of the contract, the system led to abuses in terms of debt accumulation and

Table 4.3 Number ('000s) of plantation workers by crop for selected countries, 1987–1992

	Bananas	Coffee & cocoa	Rubber	Sugar	Tea	Tobacco	Other	Total
Africa								
Kenya		52		13	100		21	186
Malawi					47	90		137
Mauritius				40	3			43
Sub-total	0	52	0	53	150	90	21	366
Asia								
Bangladesh					114			114
India		376	247		987			1,610
Indonesia			143		93		77	313
Malaysia		55	98		2		115	270
Philippines	30			200		80		310
Sri Lanka			190		426		244	860
Sub-total	30	431	678	200	1,622	80	436	3,477
Latin America								
Brazil		675		557		49	78	1,359
Costa Rica	45	136						181
Cuba	18	64		237		40	48	407
Guatemala		53		13			11	77
Honduras	27	25		5				57
Panama	15	1		4				20
Sub-total	105	954	0	816	0	89	137	2,101
Grand Total	135	1,437	678	1,069	1,772	259	594	5,944

Source: ILO (1994)

incidence of debt-bondage preventing workers from leaving. The system was finally abolished by the Tea Districts Emigration Act of 1933 that required employers to pay repatriation costs.

In Africa, with few landless labourers, colonial authorities used a variety of practices to "recruit" labour, including forced labour and head taxes to "encourage" villagers to enter the cash economy. A League of Nations enquiry in 1928 censored Liberia for forced labour practices to supply both the Firestone Rubber plantation (the largest in the world) and cocoa plantations in São Tomé and Principe. In 1956, one review of the Firestone operation in Liberia by a former US high government official, Wayne Chatfield-Taylor, noted that "In a country like Liberia where the bulk of the population still lives largely in self sufficient tribal society, the recruitment of labour cannot be left to the automatic operation of the market forces" (Chatfield-Taylor, 1956, p. 66). Firestone, the major employer, paid village chiefs for decades to "send" labour to work on its plantations.

Participation of women workers depended on the type of crop, as well as prevailing cultural patterns, education and literacy among women, and the wages paid to men (ILO, 1994). Available evidence (though dated) suggests that today women workers comprise between 20 and 50 per cent of plantation wage employment across countries and crops. They are particularly high in the tea industry, where women are widely considered as superior tea pluckers (ILO, 1994). The male–female wage gap has declined across countries thanks to the implementation of the Equal Remuneration Convention, 1951 (ILO, 1994).

Most colonial governments took action to gradually improve labour welfare or at least stem the most abusive practices. Often these actions were initiated by the metropolitan power based on reports from civil society, the press and others in the colonies, and despite the protests of the plantation industry. These include the Rhemev enquiry in 1904 in the Dutch East Indies, the Ainsworth Report in Australian-ruled Papua New Guinea in 1924, the Doan report in 1928 in French Indochina, and the Royal Commission on Labour in India in 1929, all of which were focused on labour rights in plantations.

Colonial governments responded through a number of measures. Malaysia, for example, implemented a minimum wage law in 1924 and full labour legislation by 1929 (Bauer, 1948). United Plantations, then a leading plantation company, made a strong commitment to labour standards from the 1920s, including provision of health and schooling (Martin, 2004). Elsewhere progress was slower, with continuing controversy over labour rights and conditions in the Netherlands Indies that led to negative media exposure in the metropolitan powers, and official enquiries by the metropolitan government. After independence, countries introduced new laws to protect rights of plantation workers such as India's Plantation Act of 1951.

The gradual spread of trade unions was also a factor in improved labour rights and conditions. Trade unions were established in the 1920s in many plantation economies (Malaysia, India, Colombia) often in an atmosphere of hostility from both companies and governments. Strikes by tea workers in Northeast India in 1921 and by United Fruit Company workers in Colombia in 1928 were brutally suppressed with the loss of many lives in each case. Trade unionism lost ground in the depression years but resurged after WWII and was especially militant in Sri Lanka on tea and Central America for bananas. Trade union activism and strikes resulted in many companies divesting their plantations and moving to contract smallholders.

After independence, and with the rise of the former colonies as members of the UN, the ILO revamped its efforts on plantation labour. In 1958 it formulated its ambitious Convention 110 on Conditions of Employment of Plantation Workers that laid out multiple rights of plantation workers covering the recruitment and engagement of migrant workers and afforded protection to plantation workers in respect of employment contracts, wages, working time, medical care, maternity protection, employment accident compensation, freedom of association, labour inspection, and housing. ILO followed this report by annual monitoring reports on plantation conditions, summarised by Sajhau and Muralt (1987). However, only 12 countries ratified the convention and these did not include large plantation economies such as India, Indonesia and Malaysia; and Brazil and Sri Lanka subsequently renounced it after ratification.

By the end of the twentieth century, a variety of voluntary certification systems emerged to respond to social and environmental concerns of global consumers and civil society. Most of these standards have been developed by non-governmental organisations, such as Fairtrade, Rainforest Alliance, Utz, and the Ethical Tea partnership. Others are the result of industry collective efforts, such as the Roundtable on Sustainable Palm Oil, or are government initiatives such as Trustea in India.

All of these certification standards stipulate minimum labour standards. For instance, under the Fairtrade Hired Labour Standard, employers commit to pay workers decent wages, guarantee their right to join trade unions, and adhere to health, safety and environmental principles. However, in India the 34 Fairtrade certified tea plantations with 78,000 workers—compared to the more than 1,000 large tea estates, and more than one million workers they employ—is too small to make a visible impact (Neilson & Pritchard, 2011).

By contrast in bananas, 100 per cent of Chiquita's (formerly United Fruit) bananas are certified, and an increasing share of shipments by other companies are also certified. Ventura (2007) showed how the certification has been able to reduce worker rights' violations on the Chiquita plantations, including the protection of minors, in accordance with local laws and international norms such as the conventions of the ILO (Milder & Newsom, 2015).

Today child labour is one of the most intransigent problems in tropical commodity production. Child labour has historically been a major part of the plantation labour force—nearly half of tea labourers in Assam in 1940 were children (Siddique, 1990). Since the wage payment system for plantation workers was often linked to output, workers looked for an increase in daily output by taking help from children to finish their daily task.

ILO estimates around 1990 showed that children accounted for 7 to 12 per cent of the total plantation wage labour force (Ashagrie, 1993). A Tea Board of India review in 1987 estimated that children and adolescents formed about 12 per cent of the workforce in Assam and 7.5 per cent in West Bengal. However, there was a subsequent reduction in the proportions of child labour in India to 6.5 per cent (Sivananthiran & Venkataratnam, 2002).

The 1999 ILO convention on child labour was quickly ratified by most countries with large plantations and has met with significant progress in some countries. In Malaysia, under the 1966 Children and Young Persons (Employment) Act, children under the age of 14 have been effectively prohibited on plantations. However, Liberia, with a generally poor history of labour rights has been the subject of UN and US government reports centred on the use of child labour on plantations. Also child labour is more common today on small- and medium-sized family holdings, as in the cocoa smallholdings of West Africa and bananas in Ecuador (Anti-Slavery International, 2004; Southgate & Roberts, 2016).

Finally, plantations as repositories of large numbers of unskilled labour have long been associated in much of the development literature with high incidence of poverty. Evidence suggests that this has been the case in the past and in some cases continues until today. In the world's major tea producing area of Northeast India, especially Assam, real wages appear to have risen little for a century (Fig. 4.2) and plantation workers there today receive only about half of the wage rate of tea plantation workers in South India (Sarkar, 2015). Poverty rates among tea workers in Northeast India continue to be among the highest in the world.

However, the relationship between plantation agriculture and poverty varies enormously across time, regions and crops. Malaysia, more than most other countries, has achieved impressive rates of growth based on plantation agriculture and its downstream industries, and one of the best records anywhere of rapid reduction in rural poverty. Rural wages have risen sharply and would have risen much more without large-scale migrant labour from the region. Similarly, rural wages are much higher and poverty rates lower in rural Sumatra where plantation agriculture and smallholder tree crop production dominate than they are in rural Java. There is considerable evidence that poverty reduction in Sumatra has been greatest in districts where the oil palm sector is most dynamic (Edwards, 2015).

Although labour rights have continued to be an issue in plantation agriculture, the focus by civil society, international bodies and some governments has undoubtedly led to steady progress in improving labour standards and livelihoods on plantations. Progress has been most visible on plantations owned by large national and multinational companies selling to markets that put pay a premium for social justice. Permanent labourers hired under minimum wage laws that are enforced have also benefited relative to temporary and seasonal workers. At the bottom of the ladder are illegal immigrants under informal contracts, many of whom continue in a situation of debt bondage reminiscent of earlier colonial experiences.

7 Conclusion

In several ways, the evolution of plantations in the twentieth century has been remarkable. First, plantations re-invented themselves and evolved from the earlier system of forced labour and colonial extraction into modern near-industrial firms operating in global markets. The rubber and oil palm plantations in Southeast Asia and banana plantations in

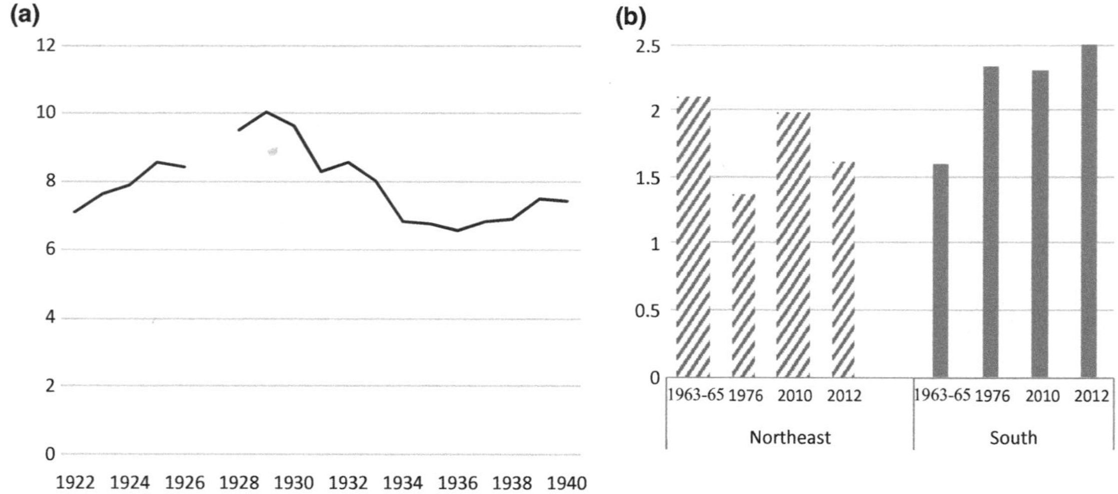

Fig. 4.2 Wages of tea plantation workers in India. (**a**) Nominal wages in Assam (Rupess per month), 1920–1940. (**b**) Real wages in Northeast and South India (Rupees 1960/day), 1963–2013, Source: Siddique (1990) and Indian Labour Journal, February, 2013. Wages may not include subsidised rations

Central America established in the early twentieth century paved the way. Other crops that had been cultivated under the old plantation system, such as tea and sugar, also evolved, albeit more slowly, into market-based operations during the first half of the twentieth century.

Second, while during the colonial period the record of plantations was often poor in terms of economic development and poverty reduction, it steadily improved over the century. In particular, after independence some countries (notably Malaysia) successfully transformed their plantation-based economy into a vehicle for economic development through improved labour standards, involvement of smallholders, and development of downstream industries. However, there are also counter-examples of limited progress, such as the world's largest tea-growing area in Northeast India, where extreme poverty remains high until today.

Third, and most important, we conclude that by the early twenty-first century the plantation era is ending. By far the most important factor has been the rise of smallholders in the traditional plantation areas due to a combination of their inherent efficiency, a more level playing field in policy support, institutional innovations to coordinate smallholder production with large mills and raise yields, and the reduced costs of entry after the pioneering stage of development. At the same time, transactions costs to plantations of accessing large amounts of cheap labour and land have risen steadily over time.

Today, smallholders dominate exports of rubber, cocoa, coffee and bananas that a century ago were largely produced on plantations. Remaining plantations are state-owned holdovers from a period of nationalisation (as in the case of rubber in Indonesia) or have re-emerged in the commodity boom of the early twenty-first century in countries and areas with poor land governance and cheap land concessions, notably Myanmar, Laos and Cambodia. In sugar cane in Latin America, notably Brazil, operations have been almost completely mechanised, mitigating the need to hire and house large numbers of workers, and sugar cane operations no longer fit our definition of a plantation system.

Today by far the largest areas of plantations are for tea in South Asia and for oil palm in Malaysia and Indonesia. The two largest tea exporters, Sri Lanka and Kenya, have used innovative institutional mechanism to convert the bulk of their exports to smallholder systems. Only in India, the largest tea producer, are plantations still dominant. However, with rising costs and continuing labour unrest, policy support is now shifting to smallholders.

In oil palm, the fact that smallholders now account for over 40 per cent of the oil palm area in Indonesia, the largest producer, and 80 per cent in Thailand, the third largest producer, indicates that the structure of the industry has already shifted. In well-established areas with a high density of mills, such as in Sumatra, independent small- and medium-sized producers are now the most dynamic sector. With appropriate support, we see no reason why oil palm will not follow the same trajectory to smallholder production as other plantation crops. Indeed, with the passing of the commodity boom, oil palm plantations with their high cost structure will face increasing competitive pressures from smallholders.

The passing of the plantation era, however, does not solve all of the problems of tropical commodity production. Land scarcity and poor land governance are features of tropical commodity systems, and in times of high prices, smallholder expansion carries high risks of conflicts. Likewise, small and medium growers also depend on hired labour, and labour rights and conditions are often poorer than on plantations and harder to monitor. Further, the rise in global standards, both public and private, raises transactions costs for smallholders to participate in global markets for certified produce. Finally, for sustained poverty reduction, smallholders need to diversify and "decommodify" by adding value through speciality markets.

Notes

1. Another exception is intensive indoor livestock production (poultry and pigs) although this requires little land.
2. Parts of this section are based on Byerlee (2014).
3. The processed product constitutes about 10% of the raw materials for sugar cane and 20% for oil palm.
4. Given the high volume of exports, the frequency of shipping has mitigated the need for contractual delivery of the harvest.
5. At the time, transforming forest "wastelands" into productive plantations was part of the development ethos and only in the later part of the

twentieth century was the global value of tropical forests recognised. See Byerlee and Rueda (2015) for a review.

References

Allen, D., & Lueck, D. (1998). The Nature of the Farm. *The Journal of Law & Economics, 41*, 343–386.

Anti-Slavery International. (2004). *The Cocoa Industry in West Africa: A History of Exploitation*. Retrieved May 1, 2017, from http://www.antislavery.org/includes/documents/cm_docs/2008/c/cocoa_report_2004.pdf

Ashagrie, K. (1993). Statistics on Child Labour. *Bulletin of Labour Statistics, 3*, 663–679.

Bauer, P. T. (1948). *The Rubber Industry: A Study in Competition and Monopoly*. Cambridge: Harvard University Press.

Beckford, G. L. (1972). *Persistent Poverty: Underdevelopment in Plantation Economies of the Third World*. New York: Oxford University Press.

Binswanger, H. P., Deininger, K., & Feder, G. (1995). Power, Distortions, Revolt and Reform in Agricultural Land Relations. In J. Behrman & T. Srinivasan (Eds.), *Handbook of Development Economics* (Vol. 3B, pp. 2659–772). Amsterdam: North-Holland.

Binswanger, H. P., & Rosenzweig, M. R. (1986). Behavioural and Material Determinants of Production Relations in Agriculture. *Journal of Development Studies, 22*(3), 503–539.

Booth, A. (2007). *Colonial Legacies Economic and Social Development in East and Southeast Asia*. Honolulu: University of Hawaii Press.

Borah, K. (2013). Entrepreneurship in Small Tea Plantation: A Case of Assam. *The Echo, 1*, 79–90.

Bosma, U. (2013). *Sugar Plantation in India and Indonesia: Industrial Production, 1770–2010*. Cambridge: Cambridge University Press.

Byerlee, D. (2014). The Fall and Rise Again of Plantations in Tropical Asia: History Repeated? *Land, 3*(3), 574–597.

Byerlee, D., Falcon, W. P., & Naylor, R. L. (2017). *The Tropical Oil Crop Revolution: Food, Fuel, Farms and Forests*. New York: Oxford University Press.

Byerlee, D., & Rueda, X. (2015). A Century of Global Discourse on Tropical Commodities on the Forest Frontier: From Public to Private Standards. *Forests, 6*(4), 1301–1324.

Chatfield-Taylor, W. (1956). *Firestone Operations in Liberia*. Washington, DC: National Planning Association.

Cleary, M. (2003). Land Codes and the State in French Cochin-China c. 1900–1940. *Journal of Historical Geography, 29*, 356–375.
Cleary, M. C. (1992). Plantation Agriculture and the Formulation of Native Land Rights in British North Borneo c. 1880–1930. *Geographical Journal, 158*(2), 170–181.
Collier, P., & Venables, A. J. (2012). Land Deals in Africa: Pioneers and Speculators. *Journal of Globalization and Development, 3*(1), 1–22.
Courtenay, P. P. (1969). *Plantation Agriculture*. London: G. Bell and Sons.
Cramb, R. A. (2013). Palmed Off: Incentive Problems with Joint-Venture Schemes for Oil Palm Development on Customary Land. *World Development, 43*, 84–99.
Deininger, K., & Binswanger, H. P. (1995). Rent Seeking and the Development of Large-Scale Agriculture in Kenya, South Africa, and Zimbabwe. *Economic Development and Cultural Change, 43*, 493–522.
Drabble, J. H. (1973). *Rubber in Malaya, 1876–1922; The Genesis of the Industry*. Kuala Lumpur: Oxford University Press.
Dye, A. (1994). Avoiding Holdup: Asset Specificity and Technical Change in the Cuban Sugar Industry, 1899–1929. *The Journal of Economic History, 54*(03), 628–653.
Edwards, R. (2015). *Is Plantation Agriculture Good for the Poor? Evidence from Indonesia's Palm Oil Expansion?* Paper No. 2015-12, Arndt-Corden Department of Economics, Australian National University.
Goldthorpe, C. C. (1988). A Definition and Typology of Plantation Agriculture. *Singapore Journal of Tropical Geography, 8*, 26–43.
Graham, E., & Foering, I. (1984). *The Modern Plantation in the Third World*. New York: St Matins Press.
Greaves, I. C. (1935). *Modern Production Among Backward Peoples*. London: G. Allen & Unwin.
International Finance Corporation. (2013). *Diagnostic Study on Indonesian Oil Palm Smallholders*. Washington, DC: International Finance Corporation.
International Labour Organization. (1994). *Recent Developments in the Plantations Sector*. Committee on Work on Plantations, International Labour Organization, Sectoral Activities Programme—Tenth Session Geneva—1994, Report I.
Jackson, J. C. (1968). *Planters and Speculators: Chinese and European Agricultural Enterprise in Malaya, 1786–1921*. Kuala Lumpur: University of Malaya Press.

Kratoska, P. H. (1985). The Peripatetic Peasant and Land Tenure in British Malaya. *Journal of Southeast Asian Studies, 16*, 16–45.

Li, T. M. (2014). *Land's End: Capitalist Relations on an Indigenous Frontier*. Durham: Duke University Press.

Martin, S. M. (1988). *Palm Oil and Protest: An Economic History of the Ngwa Region, South-Eastern Nigeria, 1800–1980*. Cambridge: Cambridge University Press.

Martin, S. M. (2004). *The UP Saga*. Copenhagen: NIAS Press.

McCarthy, J. F. (2010). Processes of Inclusion and Adverse Incorporation: Oil Palm and Agrarian Change in Sumatra, Indonesia. *The Journal of Peasant Studies, 37*(4), 821–850.

Milder, Jeffrey C., & Newsom Deanna (2015). *Evaluating the Effects of the SAN/Rainforest Alliance Certification System on Farms, People, and the Environment*. SAN/Rainforest Alliance Impacts Report, Sustainable Agriculture Network, Mexico & Rainforest Alliance, New York.

Mintz, S. W. (1985). *Sweetness and Power: The Place of Sugar in Modern History*. New York: Viking.

Mitchell, D. (2012). Kenya Smallholder Coffee and Tea: Divergent Trends Following Liberalization. In M. A. Aksoy (Ed.), *African Agricultural Reforms: The Role of Consensus and Institutions* (pp. 247–270). Washington, DC: World Bank.

Murray, M. J. (1980). *The Development of Capitalism in Colonial Indochina (1870–1940)*. Berkeley: University of California Press.

Neilson, J., & Pritchard, B. (2011). *Value Chain Struggles: Institutions and Governance in the Plantation Districts of South India*. New York, NY: Wiley.

Pim, A. (1946). *Colonial Agricultural Production*. London: Oxford University Press.

Pletcher, J. (1991). Regulation with Growth: The Political Economy of Palm Oil in Malaysia. *World Development, 19*, 623–636.

Ramsay, A. (1987). The Political Economy of Sugar in Thailand. *Pacific Affairs, 60*, 248–270.

Sajhau, J. P., & Muralt, J. V. (1987). *Plantations and Plantation Workers*. Geneva: International Labour Organization.

Sarkar, K. (2015). *Wages, Mobility, and Labour Market Institutions in Tea Plantations: The Case of West Bengal and Assam*. Discussion Paper No. 46, Centre for Development Studies, Trivandrum, India.

Siddique, M. A. B. (1990). *Evolution of Land Grants and Labour Policy of Government: The Growth of the Tea Industry in Assam, 1834–1940*. New Delhi: South Asian Publishers.

Sivananthiran, A., & Venkataratnam, C. S. (Eds.). (2002). *Labour and Social Issues in Plantations in South Asia: Role of Social Dialogue*. New Delhi: International Labour Organisation & Indian Industrial Relations Association.

Southgate, D. W., & Roberts, L. J. (2016). *Globalized Fruit, Local Entrepreneurs: How One Banana-Exporting Country Achieved Worldwide Reach*. Philadelphia: University of Pennsylvania Press.

Tate, D. J. M. (1996). *The RGA History of the Plantation Industry in the Malay Peninsula*. New York: Oxford University Press.

Tiffen, M., & Mortimore, M. (1990). *Theory and Practice in Plantation Agriculture*. Boulder: Westview Press.

Ventura, F. (2007). *Examining the Rainforest Alliance's Agricultural Certification Robustness*. IR/PS CSR Case 07-07 https://gps.ucsd.edu/_files/faculty/gourevitch/gourevitch_cs_ventura.pdf

Viswanathan, P. K. (2008). Emerging Smallholder Rubber Farming Systems in India and Thailand: A Comparative Economic Analysis. *Asian Journal of Agriculture and Development, 5*, 1–19.

Wickizer, V. D. (1958). The Plantation System in the Development of Tropical Economies. *Journal of Farm Economics, 40*, 63–77.

Wiggins, S., & Keats, S. (2014). *Rural Wages in Asia*. London: Overseas Development Institute.

Woods, D. (2003). The Tragedy of the Cocoa Pod: Rent-Seeking, Land and Ethnic Conflict in Ivory Coast. *The Journal of Modern African Studies, 41*, 641–655.

Zen, Z., Barlow, C., & Gondowarsito, R. (2005). Oil Palm in Indonesian Socio-Economic Improvement: A Review of Options. *Oil Palm Industry Economic Journal, 6*, 18–29.

Derek Byerlee is Adjunct Professor in the School of Foreign Service, Georgetown University and Editor-in-Chief of the journal, Global Food Security. Over the past decade, he has published widely on large-scale farming and land rights and is the co-author of *Rising Global Interest in Farmland: Can It Yield Sustainable and Equitable Benefits*, published by the World Bank in 2011, and *The Tropical Oil Crop Revolution,* published by Oxford University Press in 2017. He is a Fellow of the Agricultural and Applied Economics Association, and was awarded a D. Econ (Hon), University of Adelaide in 2016.

P.K. Viswanathan is Professor (Economics and Sustainability) at the Department of Management, Amrita University, Kochi, India. His research and teaching interests relate to: the economics of natural resources management and sustainability; agrarian transformation and rural livelihoods; aspects of technology, institutions, policies and governance; climate change impacts; welfare impacts of trade certifications in India's plantation sector, among others. He has authored/co-authored about thirty articles in journals and 40 chapters in edited volumes. He has recently co-edited two books: *Globalisation, Development and Plantation Labour in India*, published in 2016 by Routledge India (New Delhi) and *Micro Irrigation Systems in India: Emergence, Status and Impacts*, published in 2016 by Springer Science + Business Media (Singapore).

Part II

Africa

5

Ghana's Recurrent Miracle: Cocoa Cycles and Deficient Structural Change

Christer Gunnarsson

1 Introduction

The first decade of the twentieth-first century witnessed what for a long time gave the impression of an emerging African economic "miracle". Over a period of some fifteen years the economic growth record of the major part of Sub-Saharan Africa outpaced all other regions. This African growth "miracle" appeared to defy a conventional image of Africa as a persistent no-growth region. There were high expectations that Africa had eventually embarked on a process of economic transformation that promised to greatly raise the region's competitiveness and forever lift its masses out of extreme poverty. Great progress had indeed been made in terms of poverty reduction and the continent had certainly become more attractive to foreign investors. However, since around 2015, economic growth rates have slowed down markedly, which raises questions about the sustainability of the African growth process. Have the high growth figures been driven largely by a global commodity boom and have African

C. Gunnarsson (✉)
Department of Economic History, Lund University, Lund, Sweden

V. Pinilla, H. Willebald (eds.), *Agricultural Development in the World Periphery*, Palgrave Studies in Economic History, https://doi.org/10.1007/978-3-319-66020-2_5

economies thereby remained trapped in their habitual dependence on primary commodity exports? Or has the process involved observable and manifest elements of macroeconomic structural change?

African economies are in large degree agricultural. In most African countries, agriculture contributes a large share of GDP and an even higher share of employment. That the world's lowest per capita income levels are found in Africa is largely due to low levels of productivity in agriculture and deficient structural change within and between sectors. Productivity growth, specifically labour productivity, forms a key component of structural change. Labour productivity growth can be intra-sectoral through capital accumulation or technological change within agriculture; it can also take the shape of labour moving from low-productivity to high-productivity activities within and outside agriculture, by which overall labour productivity in the economy will be raised.

This chapter examines the potential of, and obstacles to, productivity growth and structural change in one of the African "miracle" economies, viz. Ghana. The focus is on long-term growth mechanisms and obstacles to structural change within the leading sector of Ghana's agricultural economy, the cocoa industry. The cocoa industry constitutes the backbone of Ghana's economy and it has been so since early colonial times. Cocoa is the country's most important export crop, accounting for some 8 per cent of GDP and 30 per cent of export earnings in the peak year of 2010 (Ghana Statistical Service, 2010). The number of cocoa farmers is estimated to be about 700,000 while as many as six million people (25 per cent of the population) may in varying degrees be dependent on the cocoa sector (Anthonio & Aikins, 2009). Cocoa in Ghana was predominantly a smallholder activity from the beginning, and it largely remained so during the course of the twentieth century. Ninety per cent of total production is today grown on smallholdings owned by individual farmers and operated predominantly by household labour. The average size of holdings is about 2.25 ha and a majority of farms are smaller than the average.

The growth of the cocoa sector can unquestionably be said to have been decisive when Ghana reached status as a middle-income country in 2010. Continued growth of the sector is of vital importance since, even with growth in other sectors, cocoa will continue to dominate agricultural exports, at least over the medium term (Breisinger et al., 2008).

Ghana is today reckoned as one of the most successful and comparatively prosperous economies of Sub-Saharan Africa. This is not news; the same has been said several times over the past century. But Ghana's economic history also exhibits an extraordinary pattern of recurrent booms and busts in the cocoa industry with episodes of great economic success followed by long periods of stagnation and decline. The cocoa industry displays a manifest historical cyclical pattern, with two marked production cycles over the past century. The first cycle is associated with the establishment and consolidation phase, culminating in the mid-1930s and followed by a downturn throughout the 1940s. The second cycle began in the 1950s, reaching a production peak in 1965, followed by a long decline during the course of the 1970s and early 1980s. Since then, the industry has recovered, albeit slowly to begin with, and after the turn of the century growth acceleration has followed, which culminated in a production peak of over 1 million tons in 2010 (Fig. 5.1). However, thereafter output has again stalled, which raises questions about the future sustainabil-

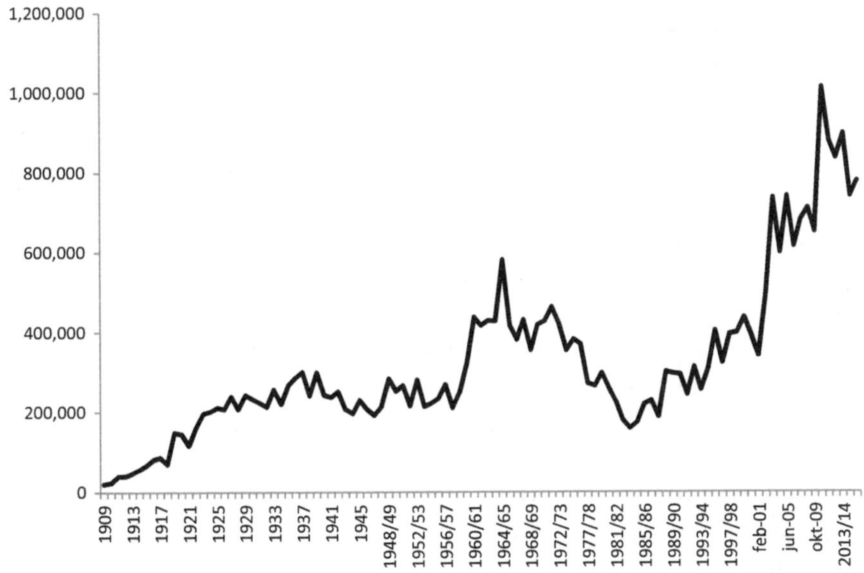

Fig. 5.1 Ghanaian cocoa production (tons) 1909–2016. Source: FAO commodity Series, no 27, Cacao, 1955 (for 1909 to 1946); COCOBOD (for 1947/48 to 2015/16)

ity of the industry. A crucial question is whether we are now witnessing a third cycle. The record growth from the trough in the early 1980s to the peak in 2010 is truly remarkable, but a deceleration of growth might be equally worrisome if it marks the beginning of a new long recession.

The questions is whether the cocoa industry has the potential to avoid repeating the historical cyclical pattern. The two long cycles are associated with an effective absence of structural change in the cocoa industry and in the economy at large. Explanations for this deficient structural change can be sought for among specific institutional and technological factors and conditions. An institutional element might be that the distribution of assets is more unequal than we have been led to believe, which may have left the many small farmers in a vulnerable position. It can also be that institutional arrangements with regard to protection of property and regulation of profit accumulation (taxation and market arrangements) have been insufficient or working against the interest of the farmers in general. The technological element entails obstacles to upgrading productivity that concern physical factor endowments (type of commodity, soil conditions, man-land ratio, etc.) that may have complicated productivity improvements or prevented them from being dispersed among a broad cross-section of farming households.

In the following we shall attempt to demonstrate how some of these institutional and technological elements have been at work in the past and we shall attempt an assessment of whether observed obstacles to structural change are in the process of being overcome. We begin by focusing on whether past dynamics of growth have been extensive or intensive—in this case whether the expansion has been due to specialisation or to a utilisation of a vent-for-surplus and exploitation of forest rent. Connected to this is the question of migration of cocoa farmers, and whether they represent the typical cocoa farmer or if they are a special category. The institutional factors dealt with are land tenure arrangements, labour deployment, and the marketing system, including price policy. A profoundly important question that needs to be answered is why yields on many large farms have not been significantly higher than those on smaller units.

There is necessarily a special emphasis on the drivers of growth during the first cycle, the period of establishment and consolidation. It was then that the basic structure of the smallholder-based economy was formed, a structure that remained largely intact over the second cycle. As shall be demonstrated in the following, the two historical cycles can be characterised by extensive growth dynamics with the production expansion made possible by enlargement of both the area under cultivation and the workforce, while labour productivity remained essentially unchanged. Migration played an important role for leading this extensive growth but the migrant cocoa farmer was not a typical or average farmer. What needs to be investigated is whether the basic structure of the industry may be undergoing a process of change in the current boom. If the recent boom is driven by land expansion and increased use of labour rather than by productivity growth, doubts can indeed be raised about the sustainability of Ghanaian cocoa production (Teal, Zeitlin & Maamah, 2006). Productivity growth and structural change will also involve social change, which raises the question of whether we are witnessing the beginning of the end of the typical small cocoa farm.

2 The Boom-Bust Pattern of Ghana's Cocoa Industry

Ghana became the world's leading cocoa exporter before WWI, which is particularly remarkable since the crop was only introduced into the country as late as in the 1880s. After more than four decades of continuous growth, a production peak of over 300,000 tons was reached in the mid-1930s. Ghana (at that time the Gold Coast and Ashanti) with its outstanding export growth was rightly considered the growth "success story" of British colonial Africa. The expansion essentially occurred under free market conditions. The links with the consumer markets were created by the presence of European merchant capital, but the tie between them and the farmers was made up by indigenous traders. The crop was purchased from the producers by a class of indigenous merchants or middlemen who brought the incentives of the market to the farmers and also functioned as creditors. Many of these brokers were large-scale merchants, although in terms of numbers the vast majority consisted of petty traders dealing in small quantities. These petty traders or sub-brokers purchased the cocoa from the producers and sold it to the large brokers who in turn sold it to the European firms. The producer was supplied with capital during the off-season for which he was to deliver a certain amount of cocoa at the current market price.

This system functioned relatively well up until the 1930s when market prices were falling as a result of the global economic crisis, profit margins were shrinking, and competition was hardening. Producer prices (prices paid to the cocoa producing community, not necessarily the prices received by the farmer) were declining in the 1930s; the gap between export price and producer price appears to have been widening, which indicates that hardship was felt among farmers and brokers. The terms of trade (cocoa prices in relation to prices on a basket of imported consumer goods bought by the rural community) went against cocoa producers in the 1930s and gradually discontent was growing and insurgence lurking (Gunnarsson, 1978). In 1937, as a reaction to a buying agreement between the larger European trading companies and a simultaneous decline in cocoa prices, the indigenous cocoa community revolted by refusing to market the cocoa crop. This hold-up lasted for six months and was accompanied by a total boycott of imported goods handled by European firms. To resolve the situation the Secretary of State for the Colonies appointed a commission of inquiry, the Nowell Commission, to visit West Africa to assess the situation. The commission delivered a report that can be seen as a first step towards statutory marketing. The report proposed a marketing scheme, which was to "clear up all abuses" in the cocoa trade and strengthen the position of the producers vis-à-vis the buyers. All cocoa farmers would become members of a Cocoa Farmers Association and the Association would assemble and sell the entire crop of cocoa on behalf of the producers. The Association was also to be used for agricultural and economic education of the producers, and would assist in the preparation of crop estimates and promote schemes for agricultural credit facilities (Nowell, 1938).

The proposals of the Nowell Commission did not result in the actual establishment of a statutory monopoly and, as it turned out, it is doubtful whether it would have functioned. However, the advent of WWII turned out to be decisive in the drive towards government intervention. During the war the government agreed to buy the entire produce at a fixed price.

The long growth period was interrupted by falling demand during WWII, and by increasing incidences of cocoa tree disease. Under such conditions government intervention may have been required in order to avoid a total demise of the cocoa industry. After the war, the statutory Cocoa Marketing Board, later renamed the Ghana Cocoa Board (COCOBOD), was established to organise purchases and regulate producer prices. Soon it had developed into a complete statutory buying monopoly.

After a long stagnation during WWII and its aftermath, cocoa output picked up again in the mid-1950s and a new production peak of close to 600,000 tons was attained in 1965: that is, double the pre-war peak level. Ghana was by the time of independence in 1957 among the most economically advanced countries in Sub-Saharan Africa and expectations were set high as the country started her drive towards industrialisation and modernisation under the reign of Nkrumah's Conventions People's Party (CCP). But then again the cocoa industry stalled and was not to pick up decisively until some 25 years later. In the 1970s, the cocoa industry underwent a period of disastrous deterioration. Ghana's position as the world's leading producer was lost to the Cote d'Ivoire and in 1984 Ghana's cocoa output volume just about exceeded one fourth of the 1965 level, reaching an all-time low of 159,000 tons. Much of the decline of Ghana's cocoa industry has been explained by harmful consequences of the marketing board system. The control system during the war had been motivated largely by access concerns (Bauer & Yamey, 1968) while the marketing board was thought necessary for price stabilisation in a highly volatile market. In practice, it developed into an instrument of excessive taxation to siphon resources away from the agricultural sector (Killick, 1990; Williams, 2009). Surpluses accumulated were mainly used to finance industrialisation and development projects while incentives to farmers were effectively reduced (Bates, 2005; Bauer & Yamey, 1968). By setting farmgate prices well below world prices, the marketing board effectively levied a tax on farmers, which discouraged production and reduced farmers' income. Although very little of the funds accumulated were brought back to the average farmer in the 1950s, producer prices were actually increased, evidently as part of a strategy to round up support for the CCP in upcoming elections (Akoto, 1987). After independence, producer prices were lowered and the little state support there was to the cocoa industry was transferred to newly launched state farms (Akoto, 1987).

Excessive taxation and low real producer prices were clearly important for the long decay of the industry from the mid-1960s. Although the socialist industrialisation project was abandoned after the overthrow of Nkrumah in 1966, the control system remained intact for another two decades. The combination of the control system and a constantly overvalued exchange rate made it virtually impossible to offer effectively high prices. Even if nominal prices increased, the real producer price would remain low. The gradual and partial return after 1983 to a freer market system—as part of the Structural Adjustment Program—with some resemblance to the system prevailing during the first cycle, appears to have been an important incentive mechanism in the recent boom period. Clearly, the statutory marketing system had an important role in reducing farmers' incentives over the course of the second cocoa cycle between the 1950s and the 1980s. But the fact remains, even during the recent boom, under a more liberalised marketing system, little appears to have happened in terms of productivity growth and structural change. In order to understand this, we must turn to more fundamental institutional factors and to those relating to choices of technology.

3 The Small-Scale Structure Established

Ghana by the time of colonisation was a land-abundant economy. The expansion involved access to cheap land in the forest belt and cocoa cultivation practices were spread by migrants from the south. Migration was a characteristic feature of the cocoa industry from the beginning and has remained so ever since. Cocoa was first planted for commercial purposes around 1890 in Akwapim in the south of what is now the Central Province. Planting spread rapidly and had reached the Ashanti region before WWI. From then onwards Ashanti was gradually to become the leading cocoa-producing region. It later spread to neighbouring Brong Ahafo and to the Western region. In the latest expansion from the 1990s, production has been moving further westward so that today the Western region has become the leading cocoa district (Fig. 5.2).

Migration is closely connected with land abundance in that cocoa cycles have been moving in concurrence with and caused by movement of people and exploitation of new land rather than by replanting on existing land. Ruf (1995) has coined this process 'exploitation of forest rent' meaning that it has usually been more profitable to plant cocoa trees on virgin land rather than on existing cocoa land after felling of old trees. In connection with this, the expansion has also been explained as a case of vent-for-surplus utilisation of previously underutilised resources (Hopkins, 1973; Myint, 1958; Szereszewski, 1965). In such a process, productivity improvements are negligible or play a subordinate role vis-à-vis land expansion. Against this, others (Austin, 2014; Hill, 1963) have argued that cocoa production was based on at least some degree of specialisation and reallocation of resources from the onset of the expansion, which would indicate productivity growth but also a risk of being trapped in monoculture (Amin, 1972; Ward, 1960). It shall be argued here that for the two observed historical cycles, the first approach—a combination of vent-for-surplus and exploitation of forest rent through migration—offers a better explanation of the booms and busts in the Ghanaian cocoa industry than a specialisation approach. The absence of productivity

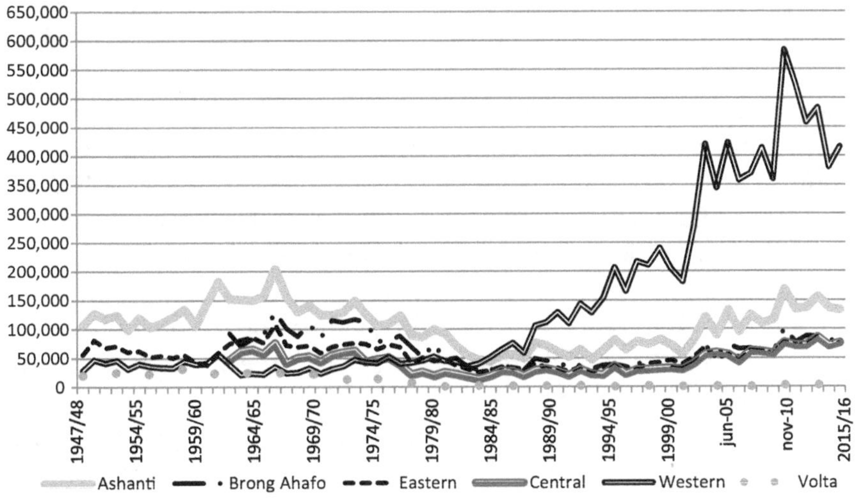

Fig. 5.2 Regional distribution of COCOBOD purchases 1947/48–2015/16 (tons). Source: COCOBOD 2017

improvement inherent in such a process would also be a core factor explaining the non-existence of major structural changes within the industry and in the economy at large.

What was it that, from the late nineteenth century, induced smallholding farmers to take up production for export of a previously unknown non-staple commodity? Was it coercion as argued by dependency theory (Amin, 1972)? Coercion would include: monetary taxation of peasants, forcing them to produce more; political support for the social strata and classes that were allowed to appropriate part of the surplus and which were in charge of organising pools of labour; and a political alliance of colonial interests with social groups which saw a chance to commercialise the tribute they were already levying on the peasants. On a more general level, Ward (1960) argued that a number of commodities exchanged in the world market as cash crops were not initially intended for sale by the peasant producers, but were produced to pay pre-existing debts. The merchants who set out to link local production systems to the world market found that the producers had no surplus to offer and no cash available. So, the merchants advanced cash and commodities on credit to the farmers and when the producers had become indebted, they were drawn into a process of production for debt payment (Ward, 1960, pp. 148–163).

In the real world, the introduction of cocoa among smallholders was fundamentally voluntary. The rural economy responded positively to economic incentives and it did so relying largely on indigenous institutional arrangements. A suggestion that "the traditional society was distorted to the point of being unrecognizable" is clearly a misrepresentation (Amin, 1972). Nor can it be credibly argued, as done by aficionados of the colonial interventions (McPhee, 1926), that the expansion of cocoa was due to "safe pilotage" of the peasant by colonial authorities and that the cocoa industry was the "foster child of the Government" (McPhee, 1926, p. 41). The colonial government did nothing to convert land tenure systems and its contribution to the spread of technology and know-how appears to have been next to negligible. English capital built railways and harbours and channels, roads and towns, and it advanced cash on credit to the middlemen, but it surely did not bring new cultures or carefully nurse the industry "by distribution of plants, by its instructors, by its experiments as to the best species and the means of fighting fungoid and insect pests" (McPhee, 1926, p. 48).

Nor is there any evidence that a commercial specialisation was necessary for the expansion of production among a majority of the smallholdings. It can be argued that non-specialisation was in effect *the necessary* prerequisite for the adoption of cocoa production among farming households. In order to understand how the smallholder economy could become market oriented without a radical reallocation of resources or without coercion we turn to Adam Smith's vent-for-surplus theory, as outlined by Myint (1958). This theory postulates that an economy may have a dormant capacity for surplus production, but that this capacity could only be realised by an extension of the market, preferably by external trade. According to the Ricardian comparative cost principle, relative costs will function as instruments of allocation, directing resources to activities or sectors with lower costs and higher productivity. In vent-for-surplus theory the function of trade is to create an effective demand for a *potential* surplus capacity. The expansion does not entail a reallocation problem, the basic necessary precondition being that there are no obstacles to the transformation from potential surplus to real surplus realisation. Thus, the economy is initially producing inside the production possibility frontier (PPF). If the economy had been on the PPF, cocoa could only have been introduced by a movement on the curve, that is, by sacrificing some commodity or activity for production of cocoa. Alternatively, there should be some technological change so that the PPF shifts outward indicating higher productivity in all activities (Fig. 5.3).

In principle, orthodox economic theory does not accept the idea that an outlet could exist for surplus production in any economy (Findlay, 1970, pp. 70–73). An economy could not produce at a point inside the production possibility curve. Although unoccupied land may exist, there is never a surplus productive capacity available at the point of equilibrium since the relatively scarce resource, labour, will be fully employed. The fact that land is lying idle is due to labour being fully employed. Idle land resources have, then, no surplus capacity. Conversely, there can be plenty of underemployed labour without surplus capacity when land is fully utilised, as in the Lewis model (Lewis, 1954). Contrary to this, vent-for-surplus theory holds that surplus capacity consists of *both land and labour resources.* That Ghana was a land-abundant economy is evident from the fact that the introduction of cocoa production resulted in a dramatic extension of cultivated acreage, but the question of surplus labour requires a more careful examination. The implications of surplus labour were that abundant labour could be put to work at the same time as abundant land became available. As Teal (2002) explains, this means in concrete terms that the profitability of cocoa farming stems from the crop being both more valuable than others to cultivate and that the costs of cultivating it are low. Under such conditions there is an incentive to expand output by a combination of additional labour and newly cultivated land.

It is also conceivable that output will continue increasing even if there is a fall in real prices as long as costs remain lower and profits higher than alternative crops. This does not mean that prices are unimportant. That cocoa farmers respond to price incentives is well established empirically (Ady, 1949; Bateman, 1965). For tree crops such as cocoa, prices are not reflected directly in outputs but initially in the rate of planting and later in output. Planting occurs as a response to favourable producer prices while, given that the cocoa tree has a gestation period before reaching full

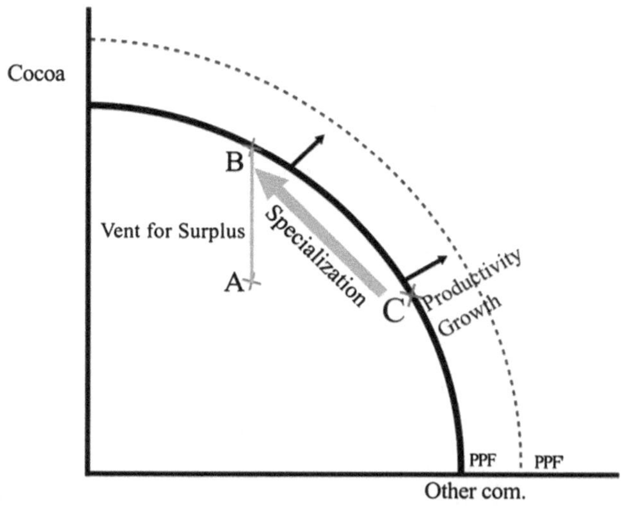

Fig. 5.3 Production Possibility Frontier at the introduction of cocoa in Ghana. Source: own elaboration

maturity, prices will tend to be considerably lower once the tree reaches fruit-bearing age (Fig. 5.4). Output will remain high for a period even if prices are falling, but if they are depressed for long, planting will slow down or even come to a halt and will not expand again until producer prices recover. In the early period, prices were initially high, which encouraged new planting until around 1930. The production peak in 1936 was the outcome of a long period of expansion of planting. After the establishment of the statutory Cocoa Marketing Board, prices to the farmers remained stable but low until the early 1950s, which kept the planting rate low, but after producer prices had become more favourable, planting increased dramatically, which formed the foundation for the coming production boom with its peak in 1965. By then farmgate prices had already been reduced significantly. Real producer prices in the 1970s collapsed when an overvalued exchange rate made it impossible for the government to pursue a realistic cocoa pricing policy. Any major increase in producer prices would have meant that the government was faced with a decline in cocoa revenue. Farmers responded to the decline in real producer prices by not replanting. Change began with the policy change in

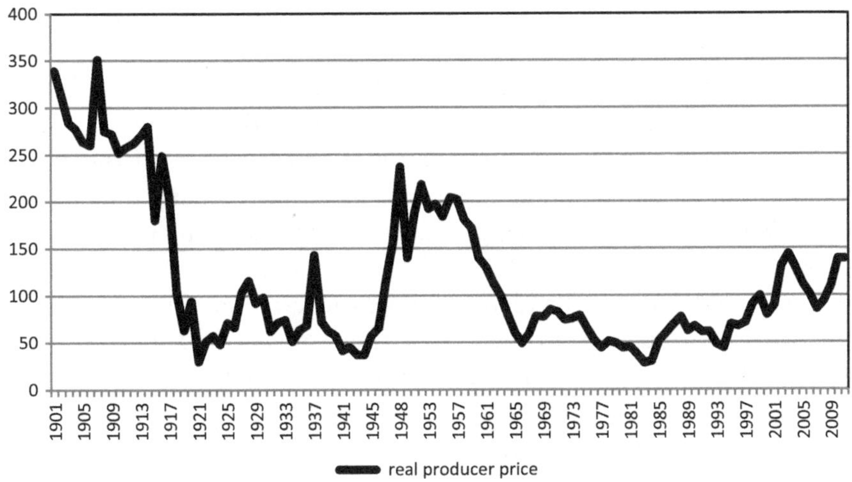

Fig. 5.4 Real Producer Prices 1901–2011 (Index 1963=100). Source: Prices for 1901–1971 from Bateman (1974); Prices for 1972–2011 from FAOSTAT

1983, which included higher farmgate prices and a currency devaluation reducing both direct and indirect taxation of cocoa producers (Kolavalli et al., 2012).

Low incentives due to excessive taxation and depressed prices were factors behind the long downturn of the cocoa industry from the mid-1960s. It can be argued that Ghana's long crisis was a crisis of political economy, and as such principally a result of inhibited growth and predatory economic institutions (Bauer & Yamey, 1954; Bates, 2005; Frimpong-Ansah, 1991). When the buying system was liberated in 1983 it did not mean a full return to the type of completely free market competition prevailing before WWII. However, the system seems to have allowed farmers a higher share of the export price. Real prices trebled between 1980 and 2001 and farmers' share of export price increased to around 50 per cent (Leturque & Wiggins, 2011). The COCOBOD sets the floor price that needs to be paid to growers, and even in the absence of price competition, farmers have benefitted. Payments to farmers have become more reliable, corruption and cheating has come down and there is no apparent sign of a return to the old problem of indebtedness among farmers that plagued the industry in the first cocoa cycle. Since cocoa is now bought with cash throughout the year, farmers are supplied with working capital to buy labour and other inputs all year around. In the old free-market times cash was advanced by buying firms via local brokers and had to be met by delivery of cocoa. Farmers had to supply an amount of cocoa which corresponded to the ruling market price. If the market quotation of cocoa was 6d per load at the time of receiving the loan, the moneylender would advance 3d, that is half the market value (Shepard, 1936, p. 38). If the market price during the season fell to 3d per load, the farmer would have to hand over his entire crop to the moneylender (Shepard, 1936, p. 40). In such cases, the farmer would need increased advances for the next season with the result that short-term credit would tend to develop into long-term credit, that is, indebtedness. Obviously, the present marketing and credit system is more favourable to the farmers. Incentives have been brought back but since liberalisation has been partial, the volatility and insecurity of the older free-market system has been avoided, mainly due to the guaranteed floor price.

4 The Advantage of Being Small

The simple technology of cocoa farming made it well suited as a complementary activity in the village economy. The fact that large capital outlays were unnecessary and labour requirements small meant that the farmers could cultivate their cocoa farms with traditional tools. Cocoa production was well suited to small-scale cultivation since it did not interfere with the subsistence economy but served as an addition to it. The farmers did not have to give up food farming to become specialised cash-crop farmers, so the initial risks involved in engaging in cocoa production were minimal. Establishment of a cocoa farm was a relatively simple process. After land area had been acquired, it was cleared by felling and burning, and food crops and cocoa plants were inter-planted. The food crops were cultivated for some years until the cocoa trees reached such a height as to render food cultivation impossible. At that stage, the food farm was abandoned and the cocoa trees left unattended until they came into full bearing, which for the amelonado variety that was planted in the early period took some seven to eight years (Shepard, 1936).[1]

In the 1930s, Shepard estimated that the number of trees per acre (one acre is 0.40 hectares) amounted to about 700 (Shepard, 1936, p. 2). The nursing of the younger trees seems to have been more thorough on plantations where weed growth was checked by the planting of banana and cassava plants (as in Trinidad). In Ghana, such plantings were made only in the first years after the planting of cocoa and never on an entirely planned scale. Drainage systems were rare on smaller farms; the natural drainage in the West African forest belt appears to have been sufficient (Shepard, 1936, pp. 3–4). The absence of technological innovations did not, however, mean lower yields in comparison with the West Indian plantations. The yield was probably twice that of the Trinidad plantations and quite in parity with the yields obtained by highly intensive methods in Grenada. It should also be noted that the cocoa farmers normally had their own food farms. In Beckett's study of the village of Akokoaso (a survey carried out between 1932 and 1935) the bulk of the staple food (mainly plantain and cocoyam) was produced in the village. Only 8 out of 267 independent farmers had no food farms. Most cocoa farmers produced a sufficient amount of food for own consumption while only very small amounts were sold in the local market (Beckett, 1944, p. 18).

Myint's version of the vent-for-surplus theory appears to offer a reasonable understanding of the rapid spread of cocoa production among smallholders, at least up until the 1930s. The best-known application of the vent-for-surplus theory is Szereszewski (1965) who argues that "the expansion into the forest was an expression of the natural resource-intensity of cocoa farming; the capitalisation of current labour into cocoa farms was another labour-saving procedure" (Szereszewski, 1965, pp. 104–105). This was "an underemployment situation in the sense that the resources of the economy—land and labour—were at the low level of physical utilisation determined by the preference of the population for income and leisure, and the available conversion rates between these two" (Szereszewski, 1965, pp. 84–85). The fundamental importance of this is that the cocoa boom took place without structural change. Although the employment of previously underemployed labour resources led to increased productivity per man, productivity per man-hour or per acre remained unchanged (Hopkins, 1973, p. 233).

The vent-for-surplus theory is sometimes treated as a micro-concept while others see it as a concept for understanding a macro-level process. Although a changing conversion rate between income and leisure depicts the choice mechanisms of farmers at a point of equilibrium it gives no hint with regard to long-term macro-processes. No account is taken of population growth or of spatial and social mobility. In the long run, given the fundamentals outlined, continued expansion of production would have to rely on an enlargement of both land area and workforce. The diffusion of cocoa also involved migration of people for exploiting new land. Since the 1890s, the extension of the area of cocoa production has continued, with recurrent periods of reduction, and this is also characteristic of the very latest cocoa boom in the Western Province. Area extension involves important elements of migration and indigenous entrepreneurship. Although cocoa production became a smallholder activity, the first initiatives came from enterprising people with a long tradition of non-agrarian activity (Hill, 1963, pp. 118 and 178–192). It seems that migrants have continued to play a similar role in later developments as well. Migrants and their behaviour have such an important role to play in the diffusion of cocoa production that it is sometimes misleadingly argued that it is the migrant, not the sedentary farmer, who is the typical cocoa farmer.

Social stratification over time is another issue. In Myint's version of the vent-for-surplus theory, the initial stage of complementarity between subsistence agriculture and export production is later gradually replaced by an increasing degree of specialisation. This occurs as certain farmers, encouraged by their early success, decide to devote more of their time and efforts to cocoa production and abandon food crop production. One could assume that only the more successful and prosperous farmers, encouraged by their previous success, would decide to devote more of their time and efforts to specialised cash-crop export production. They acquire more land, by purchase or lease, they hire labour from outside the family, and they start buying food at the market. Their farms are likely to be bigger while at the other end of the spectrum the number of dependent small farmers would be increasing. Inequality would thereby surge.

Big farms were known already in the 1930s. The Nowell Commission observed that: "the original conception of the Gold Coast farmer…one of a peasant cultivator who, with his own labour and the help of his family grows his food and tends to an acre or two of cocoa trees…is no longer true of more than a minority of farms and these of the smallest size" (Nowell, 1938). In his study of the village of Koransang, Beckett noted that large farms were becoming common in certain parts of the country, mainly in the Eastern Province (Beckett, 1945b). In a report from 1945 he wrote: "The general term peasant production has been used above to describe the structure but the organization is not so simple. There are true peasant proprietors in villages in the Western and Central Provinces and parts of Ashanti, there are also the 'caretakers' or crop-share tenants in established farms, there are the laborers working on a daily rate of pay. There is also the townsman absentee landlord" (Beckett, 1945a).

During the 1960s and 1970s much policy emphasis was laid upon larger farms. A sample census undertaken by the Ministry of Agriculture in 1970 gave an estimate of 290,000 cocoa "holders" controlling 3.5 million acres of land, which would give an average of 12 acres per holder (Okali, Owusu Ansah & Rourke, 1974). This is probably a gross overestimation since it would mean an average size about 2.5 times the average (2.2 hectares) recorded in 2008 (Leturque &

Wiggins, 2011). Possibly, it is also an underestimation of the number of farmers, since the Nowell Commission estimated a number of 300,000 farmers in 1938. The 1960s and 1970s were, however, the period when large farms were often supported while smaller farms were largely neglected, almost as a remnant of the past. In The Seven-Year Plan of 1964 a quarter of total planned investment expenditure on agriculture was allocated to public agricultural institutions for large-scale mechanised state-farms. Even after the overthrow of the Nkrumah regime, the beneficiaries of public resources allocated to agriculture were the specialist mechanised large-scale holdings (Akoto, 1987).

5 Migrants as Key Actors

There had been specialised farmers all along. Hill (1963) has demonstrated that cocoa production was initiated and diffused by commercially oriented migrating farmers in the Akwapin area, and that by the time Ghana had become the world's largest cocoa producer in 1911, these southern migrants produced the bulk of the output. During the last years of the nineteenth century, some Akwapim farmers started buying land in various parts of Akim Abuakwa, west of the Densu River. Some of the areas acquired were large, amounting to several square miles. The land was often purchased jointly in "companies" or "families" (Hill, 1963, pp. 15–18). Hill found that the chiefs were quite willing to sell land to strangers. In Hill's words, "the cash received for the land seemed like a windfall for the vendor chiefs and if payment instalments, following an initial down-payment, was the best the purchasers could offer, such terms were accepted with alacrity" (Hill, 1963, p. 15). Selling of land is evidenced by later studies (Beckett, 1945a; Austin, 2005). Sometimes land was combined with land rents paid to the local chief (normally 1d per tree planted), sometimes land was rented without any sale involved. Cocoa production consequently spurred the rise of a land market and individualisation of ownership to land.

Hill (1970) believes that a central part of the Ghanaian cocoa industry came to be dominated by this group of rural capitalists who accounted for a major share of the total output. On the other hand, she maintains that "the migrant cocoa farmers and their families who were mainly responsible for the development of cocoa farming during 1891–1911 were able to continue growing nearly all their own foodstuffs as they had done at home, cocoa farming being fitted in as a complementary activity" (Hill, 1963, p. 132). This is as close as one could get to a vent-for-surplus approach. Regardless of how susceptible to market incentives the traditional economy may have been, cocoa would not have been adopted unless it had been introduced to the rural community by outsiders, or strangers as they were called. The enterprising migrants did this. However, although these migrants were the initiators of cocoa production, the fact remains that the majority of the cocoa farmers were, and have remained, smallholders with only small plots of land at their disposal.

Migration is a recurrent phenomenon in Ghana's cocoa industry. From the very beginning the geographical relocation of cocoa production has involved and in large degree been led by migrants. The migrant cocoa farmer is usually younger than the average farmer, he is likely to be more specialised in cocoa farming, and the frequency of migrant "capitalists" is probably somewhat higher than among farmers in general (Arhin, 1988). But the migrant farmers do not constitute a homogeneous category. As for all farmers, land ownership largely determines the status of the migrant. Some migrants can access land by direct purchase, others by leasehold under customary land tenure as tenants (Benneh, 1988). There are, and have been, capitalist-like business-oriented farmers with larger farms and many dependents. Most likely they make up a small minority. There is also the average landowning farmer with dependents of various kinds, labourers, caretakers, et cetera, and there is the dependent farmer who doesn't own his own land. As land has gradually become scarcer, sharecropping arrangements have become common practice. It is, and has always been, difficult to assess the size of these groups. Some migrants come to the new area with accumulated funds from previous farms which they can invest in land purchases. Other migrants have no accumulated funds and cannot afford to buy new land. They have left their home area in search of better livelihood and will have to settle down as some form of tenant (Arhin, 1988).

6 Land Constraint and Forest Rent

Hill (1963) assumes that there was a land constraint in the Akwapim district, where the first migrants came from, and that in order to find an outlet for their economic aspirations the Akwapims had to migrate westward. Thus, migration was induced by a land constraint in the area of origin. It is very likely that the migratory processes that have been a typical feature of the cocoa industry ever since have been driven by a land constraint and moving of the land frontier (for an empirical application of this concept, see Willebald & Juambeltz, 2018, Chap. 17 of this volume). The vent-for-surplus would be approaching exhaustion when one or both factors of production become relatively scarce. The surplus capacity is exhausted when planting and harvesting of cocoa cannot be done without sacrificing labour time needed for food production. Alternatively, it can be exhausted if land becomes relatively scarce and thereby more expensive to acquire for the planting of new cocoa trees.

The cocoa industry developed largely through a combination of migration and deforestation. The best supply of available land is found in sparsely populated forests. The economic advantage that comes from growing a crop after forest clearing Ruf interprets as a "differential forest rent". The differential forest rent applied to cocoa is defined as the difference in production cost and investment costs between a ton of cocoa produced on a farm established just after a forest was cleared and a ton of cocoa produced by replanting on fallow land or after the felling of the first plantation (Ruf, 1995). When trees grow older and when the forest has been largely cleared, cultivation becomes more difficult. Farmers have to face more weeds, more pests and diseases, lower soil moisture content and fertility, physical erosion, more wind, possibly disturbed rainfall patterns, at the least less effective rainfall, fewer timber resources, which may increase housing costs and less game resources, thus increasing the cost of living and the labour costs. At that point the forest rent has vanished. Weeds, pests, loss of fertility, lower yields and shortened economic life mean more labour and inputs, thus a higher average production cost. The older the tree, the higher the costs. If the farmer waits too long before taking the decision, he cannot face replanting costs.

Ruf's forest rent is perfectly compatible with both the specialisation approach and with the vent-for-surplus theory. The differential rent will start shrinking at a point when aggregate costs of replanting exceed the benefits of new planting. This is most likely to happen when the economy is approaching the land frontier, when land resources are becoming more expensive. This is also a point when the vent-for-surplus begins to shrink. If the expansion takes place within a vent-for-surplus condition, this surplus capacity will be exhausted precisely at the point when the differential rent has vanished. Evidence seems to suggest that farmers may still find it more economical to expand on new land than replace old and diseased trees. A major reason is that labour requirements are higher in replanting than for clearing new forest land (Ruf, 1995). In addition, for securing ownership to land it may be rational to migrate and claim new land than to stay on the old farm and face high investments costs that perhaps cannot be met. When the land is not used the farmer can no longer claim ownership to it according to customary rules. Therefore, it may be rational to abandon an old farm and access new land and claim ownership of it (Amanor, 2010). Migration and sharecropping arrangements seem to have become more common, which may not be a good sign. Continued migration means extending the area under cultivation, which entails risks of continued deforestation. In addition, sharecropping, which means paying rent in kind, is disadvantageous for the tenant who would prefer paying pecuniary rents.

In case specialisation was the fundamental driver of the cocoa expansion it is likely that shrinking differential rents would have been felt earlier than if there was a vent for surplus. Specifically, specialised farmers would have faced high investment costs while at the same having to struggle with a food shortage. In a long-term perspective, it is very likely that the vent-for-surplus/forest rent has gradually been moving towards exhaustion in one region after the other, as illustrated by the geographical movement of cocoa production over the past century. At some point, land acquisition in the old areas would have become more expensive and excessive planting may have led to deforestation with serious implications for complementary livelihoods, including food shortage. Continued expansion in the old area would then have had to rely upon an increasing degree of specialisation, accompanied by technological change and noticeable economies of scale. Instead, what has followed is deterioration and long-term stagnation.

7 Productivity Growth with Structural Change?

Substantial progress has been made in the latest boom period. Cocoa farming households are generally relatively better off than the average rural household, and the large decrease in poverty levels among cocoa producers since the 1990s coincides with the period of positive development of cocoa prices. In the early 1990s (after the trough of the second cocoa cycle) poverty rates among cocoa-producing households were higher than the national average, 60 per cent vs 51 per cent. By 2006, the poverty rate among cocoa households had come down well below the national average, 23.9 per cent vs 28.5 per cent (Ghana Statistical Service, 2010). However, if the fall in poverty is more associated with favourable prices and volume growth than with growth in labour productivity there will be reason to fear that the industry is going to exhibit a downward phase of a third long-term cycle, with potentially serious consequences regarding prospects for both structural change and rural livelihoods.

While the COCOBOD is often given credit for its role in the upswing in cocoa production, it is quite possible that the boom after 2000 has been a result of high prices rather than the removal of constraints in the production sphere. When recovery has arrived, as in the late 1950s, and specifically, from the 1990s onwards, it has come with moving of the land frontier. The question is to what extent this has been combined with rejuvenation and productivity rise on a large scale in all cocoa producing regions. There appear to have been manifest changes in the industry with regard to adoption of hybrid cocoa varieties, and new technology of production such as increased use of fertilisers, and greater control of pests and diseased trees (Teal et al., 2006; Vigneri & Santos, 2008). Hybrid cocoa varieties were introduced in 1984 as part of the government supported

Cocoa Rehabilitation Project to replace the traditional amelonado variety and the amazons variety that had been introduced during the 1950s. Hybrids produce more pods per tree and come to maturity in three years compared to between five and eight years for the older varieties. Traditional amelonado cocoa trees may have disappeared entirely from all fields planted after 1995. Edwin and Masters (2005), using data from a 2002 survey of 192 fields, found that planting the more recently released varieties is associated with at least 42 per cent higher yields than fields planted with traditional trees. Fertiliser use is also very important, being associated with 19 per cent higher cocoa yield per 50 kg bag of fertiliser. In addition, they found no evidence of a decline in the yield advantage of the new varieties over the 17-year age span observed in their sample (Edwin & Masters, 2005).

Hybrids give higher yields but potentially also involve higher costs. They require the application of chemical inputs and since the crop can be harvested all year around it is important to hire labour on a regular rather than seasonal basis. Despite this, farmers have increasingly adopted hybrids. Vigneri (2005) estimates that already by 2002, 57 per cent of farmers from the three main areas of production were growing hybrid trees (Vigneri, 2005). Unlike traditional trees that still need shade, hybrids can be grown in full-sun conditions. This is more common in the newer areas planted, such as in the Western region. Farmers prefer full-sun systems because of the higher short-term profitability, which is linked to their much shorter growing cycle (Ruf, 2011). Farmers also prefer complete clearing of the forest before planting, a strategy used as an attempt to enhance security of land ownership. The downside of a full-sun system is that the yield period of the cocoa tree becomes shorter and that the effects on soil depletion are more pronounced.

In spite of continued movement of the land frontier, the effect of these improved practices has been an increase in productivity of about 30 per cent, which has brought productivity back to the levels achieved in the 1980s. The first big jump in productivity occurred in 1980s (corresponding to the year of the CPR) and the second more recently with improved practices. Teal and Vigneri (2004) identifies higher input of family labour into production and favourable weather conditions as major causes of yield increases. Teale (2002) has shown that per capita output of Ghanaian cocoa has been declining since around 1930. This is calculated on total national population. However, estimates show that there are today some 700,000 farmers as compared to about 300,000 in the 1930s. The number of farmers has indeed doubled, but when the peak of 1 million tons was reached it meant that output had more than trebled. Thus, output per farmer has increased by some 30 per cent. Yields per hectare have increased as well, but extension of planted area seems to have been an equally important factor. Possibly then, what we see is a process in which productivity per man has increased, while productivity per man-hour or per acre may have remained unchanged. If this is so, the drivers of growth are likely to be identical to those prevailing in early expansion more than a hundred years ago (Hopkins, 1973, p. 233).

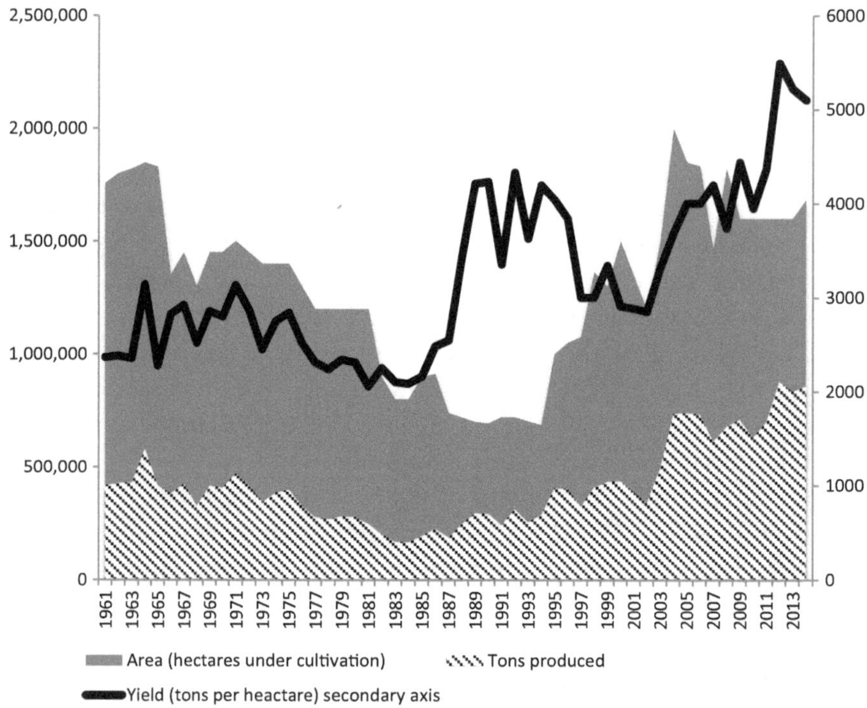

Fig. 5.5 Cocoa Area and Yields 1961–2014. Source: FAOSTAT

8 The Future of Small Farms

In comparison with its main competitors, Côte d'Ivoire and Indonesia, Ghana's yields are very low (Gockowski, 2007). Moreover, Vigneri holds that calculations suggest that in 2006 net cocoa profits on bearing farms were actually 6 per cent lower than those obtained in 1996, indicating that on average cocoa production has not become more profitable to the farmer over time (Vigneri, 2008). Unsurprisingly, this has prompted the question of the future viability of cocoa on small farms. Farm-level productivity growth is assumed to come from farmers' adoption of new production technology (e.g. improved planting material, pest management, soil fertility management, etc.). Evidence shows clearly that the use of chemical inputs increases efficiency more if combined with mechanisation. They also show that farms with large areas become efficient when they use mechanisation or when they specialise in the production of cocoa instead of combining with food production on small units.

A 2001 survey conducted by the Sustainable Tree Crop Programme (STCP) showed that in all four cocoa-producing countries in West Africa, the top 25 per cent of households (ranked by the amount of cocoa produced) had on average costs of production four times lower and yields nearly four times greater than the bottom 25 per cent, and that a significant share of smaller cocoa farms incurred losses (Gockowski, 2007). The study recommends the adoption of policies to differentiate between larger and more efficient farms. The recommendation is to target production innovations to the larger producers through a strategic distribution of improved planting material (hybrid pods) in the most densely populated regions of the cocoa belt. This could result in the replanting of up to 24,000 ha of land, and integrating this intervention with the expansion of fertiliser use would achieve a productivity gain of above 50 per cent.

A relevant question is of course why farmers often hesitate to apply techniques that are known to give higher yields. One problem might be that older cocoa farmers are generally unwilling to risks investing in yield upgrading strategies. Low land prices might be the potential answer since it would be cheaper in the short run to increase output extensively rather than intensively. In the long run, farmers who do not apply modern techniques will eventually face higher input prices or be constrained by limited credit so that they will be prevented from accessing inputs the day it would be rational for them to apply them. On the other hand, there is no reason why small farms should benefit from modern techniques. Using the same techniques, small farms usually have high higher labour input per hectare than large farms, which leads to higher yields per hectare.

Neglect or failure to adopt modern technology might mean the end of the smallest farms. Perhaps this is also inevitable given the imperative of structural change. One option for less efficient farmers would be the conversion from a no-shade cocoa system to a partial-shade cocoa system with cocoa and non-cocoa trees intercropped so that producers could supplement their incomes with the sale of forest products. This would mean a fine-tuning of the old complementary production system that could prove viable to some extent. For many others, the alternative would have to be to leave cocoa production altogether. In all likelihood, this is already happening with the ongoing generational shift. The average cocoa farmer is ageing and the younger and more educated generation prefers living in urban and globalised environments to tilling the land of their ancestors. However, the other extreme, to go for large-scale mechanisation of mega-sized farms is a risky enterprise and it is not evident that it would be the best strategy for achieving macro-economic structural change. A strategy supporting the medium-sized specialised farms remains to be seen. This is regrettable since, as suggested by historical evidence, it is often the safest way to incentivise macro-economic structural change by means of agricultural growth.

9 Conclusion: A Unimodal Economy with Delayed Structural Change

High and sustained rates of agricultural growth, largely driven by productivity growth, will be necessary if African countries are to accelerate poverty reduction, and increase export earnings, which would have a lasting positive spill-over effect on sustained economic development. It took

Ghana more than fifty years after independence to join the ranks of middle-income countries and when it finally did, its level of industrialisation was low and the country as dependent as ever on primary commodity exports. This is at least in some measure remarkable. Given the level of prosperity attained in the boom periods, one would not expect Ghana to have had worse preconditions for structural change than a comparable economy like Malaysia. The economy was initially clearly unimodal in character, that is, land was fairly evenly distributed and possession of land appears not to have been a major source of political authority. Nor was acquisition of land problematic—expansion came with greater and more widespread economic opportunities, including diffusion of de facto property rights to individual farming households. The institutions that made expansion possible were for the most part indigenous in origin but the traditional tribute appropriating elite was not involved in the expansion, at least not as leading actors.

Relative smallness is not necessarily a disadvantage. Historical evidence from Europe, the USA, and East Asia suggests that an agricultural economy dominated by family smallholdings may be comparatively better equipped for structural change than one in which access to land is unequally distributed and production dominated by large estates or plantations. As argued by Adelman (1984), the dynamics of economic growth and structural change will be dependent on the pre-existing distribution of income and wealth in agriculture. In a process of structural change driven by agriculture, small and medium-sized farmers should be emphasised since they are more likely to use domestically produced intermediate goods, while large-scale producers might import machinery and other inputs, which might weaken the linkages between agriculture and other sectors (Adelman, 1984).

In a similar vein, North (1961) argues that if the initial distribution of assets in agriculture (land and capital) is uneven, income inequality within agriculture will increase since the income gap between those who gain and those who lose will grow. In contrast, with a more equitable distribution of incomes, there is a demand for a broad range of goods and services, which will induce investment in other types of economic activity. "Trading centers will tend to develop to provide these goods and services, in contrast to the plantation economy, which will merely develop a few urban areas devoted to export of the staple commodity" (North, 1961). Normally, this requires that productivity improvement in agriculture is widespread and involving a broad cross-section of the farming households. Characteristically, in this process technological and institutional change allows income and productivity improvements to be dispersed among a stratum of medium-income households.

Cocoa in Ghana is indeed an export commodity, but it is not a plantation crop and the cocoa industry does not constitute an enclave economy. It might be that very smallest farms will disappear with the advent of high-yielding technologies but there is no reason to believe that large mechanised farms are the only and most viable way forward. A fairly equitable distribution of assets among cocoa producing households would be an advantage in a drive towards macroeconomic structural change and industrialisation, as was the case in the East Asian "miracle" countries. The only way that this can be achieved is through a substantial and lasting productivity increase on medium-sized farms.

Notes

1. Gestation periods have become shorter over time. In the first cocoa cycle, the dominant variety was amelonado with a maturation period of seven to eight years. During the second cycle, the Amazon variety with a gestation period of about five years become dominant and in since the 1990s Amazon hybrid varieties with a gestation period of about three years have become more frequent and totally dominant in the newer cocoa areas in the Western region.

References

Adelman, I. (1984). Beyond Export-Led Growth. *World Development, 12*(9), 937–949.

Ady, P. (1949). Trends in Cocoa Production in British West Africa. *Oxford Bulletin of Statistics, 11*(4), 399–404.

Akoto, O. A. (1987). Agricultural Development Policy in Ghana. *Food Policy, 12*(3), 243–254.

Amanor, K. (2010). Family Values, Land Sales and Agricultural Commodification in Rural Ghana. *Africa, 80*(1), 104–125.

Amin, S. (1972). Underdevelopment and Dependence in Black Africa-Origins and Contemporary Forms. *The Journal of Modern African Studies, 10*(4), 503–524.

Anthonio, D. C., & Aikins, E. D. (2009). *Reforming Ghana's Cocoa Sector: An Evaluation of Private Participation in Marketing*. Master Thesis, Luleå University of Technology.

Arhin, K. (1988). *Economic Differentiation Among Ghanaian Migrant Cocoa Farmers*. Economic Research Review NS 4(1). Accessed through Michigan State University Library.

Austin, G. (2014). Vent for Surplus or Productivity Breakthrough? The Ghanaian Cocoa Take-Off, c.1890–1936. *Economic History Review, 67*(4), 1035–1064.

Bateman, M. (1965). Aggregate and Regional Supply Functions for Ghanaian Cocoa: 1946–1962. *Journal of Farm Economics, 47*(2), 384–401.

Bateman, M. (1974). An Econometric Analysis of Ghanaian Cocoa Supply. In R. A. Kotey, C. Okali, & B. E. Rourke (Eds.), *Economics of Cocoa Production and Marketing*. Legon: University of Ghana.

Bates, R. H. (2005). *Markets and States in Tropical Africa: The Political Basis of Agricultural Policies*. Berkeley, CA: University of California Press.

Bauer, P. T., & Yamey, B. S. (1954). *West African Trade: A Study of Competition, Oligopoly and Monopoly in a Changing Economy*. Cambridge: Cambridge University Press.

Bauer, P. T., & Yamey, B. S. (1968). *Markets, Market Control and Marketing Reform: Selected Papers*. London: Weidenfeld and Nicolson.

Beckett, W. H. (1944). *Akokoaso: A Survey of a Gold Coast Village*. London: P. Lund, Humphries.

Beckett, W. H. (1945a). *Research and the Peasant Producer: Reports and Proceedings of the Cocoa Research Conference*.

Beckett, W. H. (1945b). *Koransang: A Gold Coast Cocoa Farm*. Accra: Government Printer.

Breisinger, C., Diao, X., Kolavalli, S., & Thurlow, J. (2008). *The Role of Cocoa in Ghana's Future Development*. Ghana Strategy Support Program (GSSP) Background Paper No. GSSP 0011.

Edwin, J., & Masters, W. (2005). Genetic Improvement and Cocoa Yields in Ghana. *Experimental Agriculture, 41*(4), 491–503.

Findlay, R. (1970). *Trade and Specialization*. Harmondsworth: Penguin.

Frimpong-Ansah, J. H. (1991). *The Vampire State in Africa: The Political Economy of Decline in Ghana*. London and Trenton, NY: James Curry Publishers and Africa World Press.

Ghana Statistical Service. (2010). Accra: Ghana—Population and Housing Census 2010.

Gockowski, J. (2007). *The Analysis of Policies, Productivity and Agricultural Transformation in the Cocoa-Producing Rural Economies of West Africa*. STCP Technical Report Executive Summary.

Gunnarsson, C. (1978). *The Gold Coast Cocoa Industry 1900–1939: Production, Prices and Structural Change*. Ph D Dissertation, Lund University.

Hill, P. (1963). *The Migrant Cocoa-Farmers of Southern Ghana*. Cambridge: Cambridge Univesity Press.

Hill, P. (1970). *Studies in Rural Capitalism in West Africa*. Cambridge: Cambridge University Press.

Hopkins, A. G. (1973). *An Economic History of West Africa*. London: Longman.

Killick, T. (1990). *Markets and Governments in Agricultural and Industrial Adjustment*. ODI Working Paper 34. London: Overseas Development Institute.

Kolavalli, S., Vigneri, M., Maamah, H., & Poku, J. (2012). *The Partially Liberalized Cocoa Sector in Ghana: Producer Price Determination, Quality Control and Service Provision*. Accra: International Food Policy Research Institute.

Leturque, H. & Wiggins, S. (2011). *Ghana's Sustained Agricultural Growth: Putting Underused Resources to Work*. ODI Research Reports and Studies. London: Overseas Development Institute.

Lewis, W. A. (1954). Economic Development with Unlimited Supplies of Labour. *Manchester School of Economic and Social Studies, 22*(2), 139–191.

Manshard, W., & Morgan, W. B. (Eds.). (1988). *Agricultural Expansion and Pioneer Settlements in the Humid Tropics*. Tokyo: United Nations University (UNU).

McPhee, A. (1926). *The Economic Revolution in West Africa*. London: G. Routledge & Sons, Ltd.

Myint, H. (1958). The "Classical Theory" of International Trade and the Underdeveloped Countries. *The Economic Journal, 68*(2), 317–337.

North, D. (1961). *The Economic Growth of the United States, 1790–1860*. Englewood Cliffs, NJ: Prentice-Hall, Inc.

Nowell, W. (1938). *Report of the Commission on the Marketing of West African Cocoa*. London: His Majesty's Stationery Office.

Okali, C., Owusu Ansah, M., & Rourke, B. E. (1974). The development pattern of some large cocoa holdings in Ghana. In R. A. Kotey, C. Okali, & B. E. Rourke (Eds.), *Economics of Cocoa Production and Marketing*. Legon: University of Ghana.

Ruf, F. (1995). From the Forest Rent to the Tree Capital: Basic laws of Cocoa Cycles. In F. Ruf & P. S. Siswoputranto (Eds.), *Cocoa Cycles. The Economics of Cocoa Supply*. Cambridge: Woodhead Publishing Ltd.

Shepard, C. Y. (1936). *Report on the Economics of Peasant Agriculture*. Accra: Gold Coast Government.

Szereszewski, R. (1965). *Structural Changes in the Economy of Ghana, 1891–1911*. London: Weidenfeld and Nicolson.

Teal, F. (2002). Export Growth and Trade Policy in Ghana in the Twentieth Century. *The World Economy, 25*(9), 1319–1337.

Teal, F., Zeitlin, A., & Maamah, H. (2006). *Ghana Cocoa Farmers Survey 2004: Report to Ghana Cocoa Board*. Accra: ECAM Consultancy Ltd.

Vigneri, M. (2008). *Drivers of Change in Ghana's Cocoa Sector*. IFPRI-GSSP Background Paper number 13. Washington, DC: International Food Policy Research Institute.

Vigneri, M., & Santos, P. (2008). *What Does Liberalization without Price Competition Achieve? The Case of Cocoa Marketing in Rural Ghana*. IFPRI-GSSP Background Paper 14. Washington, DC: International Food Policy Research Institute.

Vigneri M., Teal, F., & Maamah, H. (2004). *Coping with Market Reforms: Winners and Losers Among Ghanaian Cocoa Farmers*. Report to the Ghana Cocoa Board.

Ward, B. E. (1960). Cash or Credit Crops? An Examination of Some Implications of Peasant Commercial Production with Special Reference to the Multiplicity of Traders and Middlemen. *Economic Development and Cultural Change, 8*(2), 148–163.

Willebald, H., & Juambeltz, J. (2018). Land Frontier Expansion in Settler Economies (1830–1950): Was it a Ricardian Process? In V. Pinilla & H. Willebald (Eds.), *Agricultural Development in the World Periphery: A Global Economic History Approach*. London and New York: Palgrave Macmillan.

Williams, T. (2009). *An African Success Story: Ghana's Cocoa Marketing System*. IDS Working Paper No. 318. Brighton, UK: Institute of Development Studies.

Christer Gunnarsson is an economic historian in the Department of Economic History at Lund University, Sweden. Within African and Asian Economic History, he has dedicated a long trajectory specialised in colonial history, inequality and structural change in agriculture. His specific interests lie in social stratification, the elaboration of social tables, and the typology of agricultural transformation.

6

Initial Conditions and Agricultural Development in Zambia, 1915–2015

Ellen Hillbom and Samuel Jenkin

1 Introduction

Austin (2010) noted that many African colonies were short of both mineral deposits and land suitable for profitable agriculture. Northern Rhodesia, Zambia after independence in 1964, is an exception to this observation in having had an abundance of both. In the early twentieth century, mining, and especially the copper industry, became the leading earner of export revenues as well as the main source of wage employment. Meanwhile, there was an excess of good farmland and the development of the mining sector resulted in, at least in an African context, an early and exceptional urbanisation providing a consistent internal market for agricultural products.

Hillbom conducted this research within the Marcus and Marianne Wallenberg funded project "Growing more unequal: Long-term trends in inequality in Africa". Both authors would like to thank participants in the session New Approaches in African Agricultural and Rural History at the African Economic History Meeting in Brighton in 2016 as well as colleagues Martin Andersson and Emelie Till for their comments on draft versions of this text.

E. Hillbom (✉) • S. Jenkin
Department of Economic History, Lund University, Lund, Sweden

V. Pinilla, H. Willebald (eds.), *Agricultural Development in the World Periphery*, Palgrave Studies in Economic History, https://doi.org/10.1007/978-3-319-66020-2_6

Until the 1970s, natural resource abundance was generally understood by economists as favourable, providing pre-conditions for economic progress including sectorial change (Habakkuk, 1962; Nurkse, 1953). The actual outcome, however, proved generally to be a negative correlation between richness in natural resources and economic growth (Sachs & Warner, 1995). The poor economic performance of natural-resource-rich countries has since been repeatedly investigated and debated (Gylafson, Herbertsson, & Zoega, 1999; van der Ploeg, 2011; Willebald, Badia-Miró, & Pinilla, 2015). Zambia provides a pertinent example where generous initial conditions appeared to offer opportunities for economic growth and agricultural development, but the outcome has been poor.

During the colonial era, Northern Rhodesia became a mono-mineral economy and, after independence, the failure to manage copper incomes and lack of sectorial change caused certain scholars to understand Zambia as an example of a natural resource curse (see du Pleiss & du Pleiss, 2006 for a review of the literature, and Robinson, Govereh, & Ndlela, 2009 for the distortionary impact of copper-driven exchange rates). Meanwhile, state authorities, during both the colonial and independence eras, have had as their primary ambition for the agricultural sector to secure food, maize and to some extent beef, for domestic urban workers. For the past century, agricultural policies have exhibited a remarkable consistency towards this end. The result has been the creation of a dual agricultural sector comprising of, on the one hand, a commercial sector initially based on settler estates, but with time including a growing number of indigenous large-scale and emergent farmers and, on the other hand, a larger subsistence sector harbouring the majority of indigenous smallholders.

The aim of our study is to present evidence on to what extent and through what mechanisms: (1) initial natural resource endowments have influenced state policies; and (2) how those policies have determined the state of the contemporary Zambian agricultural sector. We assess a 100-year period from 1915 to the present day, linking the colonial and independence eras. To examine path-dependency in agricultural policies and identify possible critical junctures we apply a political–economy framework incorporating initial conditions, economic and political institutions, and agency represented by government, and commercial and subsistence farmers.

2 A Political Economy Framework

Our analytical framework (see Fig. 6.1) rests on three pillars: (1) initial conditions in the form of quantity and quality of natural resource endowments,[1] and location in relation to the challenges of remoteness; (2) political and economic institutions providing a framework for policy development; and (3) agency by representatives of the government as well as commercial and subsistence farmers in the agricultural sector.

Theoretically, we expect a multi-causal relationship between, on the one hand, geography in the form of natural resource endowments and location as the initial conditions for playing the game and, on the other hand, institutions as the rules of the game (Austin, 2008; North, 1990; van der Ploeg, 2011). Empirically, the intricate puzzle is to disentangle in what way these factors interact and to identify under what conditions and time periods one factor can dominate and be the prime mover of change in a specific historical setting (Austin, 2008; Willebald, Badia-Miró, & Pinilla, 2015). In this study, we show how, in the case of Zambia, initial conditions with an abundance of valuable minerals and agricultural land guided economic and political strategies during both the colonial and independence eras; in addition, how these policies developed into a path-dependent behaviour with two overarching characteristics. First, a consistent reliance on the primary sector and a crowding out of efforts that could have led to sectorial change. Second, that instead of encouraging

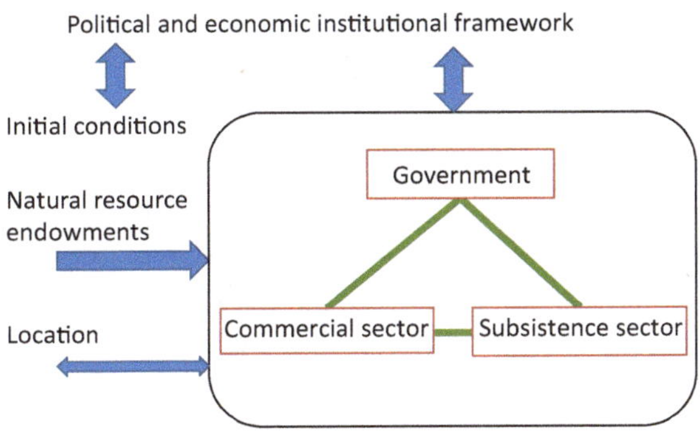

Fig. 6.1 Analytical model. Source: own elaboration

broad-based agricultural development the State has had as its primary ambition the creation of a limited commercial agricultural sector with the main objective of supporting the export generating mining sector.

Related to the debate on the governance of natural resource abundance is the issue of location and remoteness. A land-locked country such as Zambia is understood to be at a particular disadvantage as transport costs for international trade are high (Gallup, Sachs, & Mellinger, 1999), a condition that puts pressure on the development of key infrastructure. A similar argument about the disadvantage of remoteness goes for agricultural producers' opportunities to access domestic markets. That being said, where there is domestic demand for farm products from an urban population, as was the case in Zambia, remoteness and being land locked can also work as an advantage as it provides protection from foreign competition.

New Economic Geography analysis developed by Krugman (1991) emphasises the cumulative forces of endogenous agglomeration of manufacturing industries exhibiting increasing returns to scale. Initially constructed in contrast to an agriculture sector exhibiting constant returns to scale, the theory might at a first glance seem to offer little to a discussion of agricultural development. However, the underlying essence of the model, the reduction of transport costs and the mobility of factors of production, are convertible. Just as manufacturers will seek to locate close to main markets where transport costs are reduced, agriculture producers will react to transaction costs such as transportation costs, closeness to population clusters, and access to inputs and information when commercialising. Throughout our analysis we will consistently return to how the location of natural resources, infrastructure development and commercialisation relate to sectorial interaction and agricultural policies.

Moving on, the establishment of the commercial agriculture sector in Northern Rhodesia was based on the invitation to settlers of European descent by the colonial administration. The last decades have seen a growing literature quantifying the impact of such policies arguing that, on a global plane, it had a significant and substantially positive effect on long-term economic performance, including agricultural growth and sectorial change (Acemoglu, Johnson, & Robinson, 2001; Easterly & Levine, 2012; Putterman & Weil, 2010) and that this happened through three interrelated transmission channels. First, the diffusion and access to European agricultural technology is argued to have enhanced productivity and facilitated commercial exploitation of natural resource abundance (Easterly & Levine, 2012). Second, the accumulation of human capital through the education, skills and knowledge of European migrants improved agricultural production and productivity (Fourie, 2012; Woodberry, 2012). Third, and most contested, the implementation of "developmental" or "inclusive" institutions from the mother country in settler colonies meant that broad access to economic and political markets, secure property rights and use of tax revenues for provision of development enhancing public goods was guaranteed (Acemoglu, Johnson, & Robinson, 2001, 2002).

Notwithstanding that numerous in-depth empirical studies have shown Africa to be an outlier in global cross-country regression frameworks (Bowden, Chiripanhura, & Mosley, 2008; Frankema & van Waijenburg, 2012; de Zwart, 2011) these transmission channels have routinely been assumed relevant for the region. For Northern Rhodesia they may be especially questioned since the focus of commercial production was maize, a crop that was introduced to the region some 500 years ago. From the late nineteenth century, that is the period of the arrival of settlers in Northern Rhodesia, and onwards, maize has been successively supplanting the continent's own historical grain crops such as sorghum and millet, and supporting population increase (McCann, 2005). Rather than viewing the transfer of technology, the accumulation of human capital and the design of development-enhancing institutions as a one-way traffic, the agency of indigenous societies needs to be factored into the analyses (Austin, 2008; Bayly, 2008; Frankema, Green, & Hillbom, 2016).

The arguments for or against exogenous factors' influence on agricultural development in Africa has not, however, been restricted to the colonial legacies debate. The literature on contemporary Foreign Direct Investment (FDI) identifies the same transmission channels as it focuses on knowledge spill-overs and diffusion taking practical shape in the form of technological transmission. The potential knowledge diffusion from FDI spill-overs is, however, contingent upon absorptive capacity, that being the ability of local producers to actually internalise the potential benefits arising from proximity to foreign producers. In addition, the

FDI theory's emphasis on regional effects, that is spatial proximity, ties it back to arguments presented by the New Economic Geography (Crespo & Fontoura, 2007; Smeets, 2008) and we shall provide evidence for how the development of key infrastructure is correlated to a spatial path-dependency in the establishment of colonial settlement and contemporary agricultural FDI in Zambia.

Finally, after independence, African states developed agricultural policies to ensure the spread of technology and knowledge to both the commercial and smallholder sectors. Since the turn of the millennium those efforts that initially were tied to broad ambitions for poverty reduction and development of agricultural-based economies have rested on two pillars. First, the theoretical arguments claiming that smallholders relying on family labour have the economic incentives to be efficient agricultural producers and have the potential for commercialisation if they can access functioning markets (Haggblade & Hazell, 2010; Byerlee, 2018, Chap. 4 of this volume). Second, the empirical experience of the Asian Green Revolution in the 1960s–1970s, showing that political strategies aiming to promote pro-poor agricultural growth among smallholders can result in broad-based development processes leading to agricultural transformation and structural change (Hazell et al., 2010; Timmer, 2009). In Sect. 5.2 we will discuss to what extent such ambitions have actually managed to create change in Zambia's dual agricultural sector.

3 Background: The Establishment of Northern Rhodesia

In the early 1870s diamond mines were opening in Kimberly and gold was discovered in Witwatersrand in the 1880s. These riches created expectations that there would also be valuable mineral deposits in other parts of Southern Africa, and Cecil Rhodes, having made a fortune at Kimberley, strove to continue the European expansion northward. Meanwhile, the European powers were involved in their "Scramble for Africa" and the British wished to put a stop to further German expansion after the country's annexation of German West Africa (Namibia). In

1889 Rhodes received a British royal charter for his newly funded British South Africa Company (BSAC). It ran for 25 years and gave him the right to colonise the area that became known as "the three Rhodesias", containing Southern Rhodesia (Zimbabwe) as well as North-Western Rhodesia and North-Eastern Rhodesia, which became protectorates in 1891 and 1900 respectively and in 1911 were merged into Northern Rhodesia. The charter was renewed for a 10-year term in 1914, but in 1924 Northern Rhodesia was put directly under British administration, which lasted until the establishment of Zambia as an independent nation in 1964 (Parsons, 1993: Chaps. 10, 11).

Amongst the indigenous populations that inhabited the area at the time two diverse agricultural systems of production dominated: (1) in the south, a tradition of cattle-keeping and permanent cultivation; (2) in the north, *chitemene,* a form of slash-and-burn agriculture. The latter production system, with its inherent impact on soil conditions and necessitating large areas for shifting agriculture, was seen as inherently inefficient by most Europeans and was significantly restricted by colonial administrators from 1910 onwards. Later studies have, however, shown that it was surprisingly productive, yielding up to three times more than hoe cultivation (Baldwin, 1966; Chinene et al., 1998; Scott, 1995).

The initial focus of the BSAC was to develop mining and commercial agriculture in Southern Rhodesia. However, in the 1890s and first years of the twentieth century the potential for copper mining in Northern Rhodesia was discovered and within the next two decades the area developed its own mining sector. In this land-abundant area, mustering and retaining sufficient labour proved challenging. When the BSAC gradually introduced the hut tax from 1901, the local economy of the indigenous population was progressively monetised and finding wage employment became increasingly important (Vickery, 1986). Meanwhile, mineral extraction became the main source of government revenues and the rural areas were primarily considered as labour reserves for the mining sector.

The protectorates were land locked and the issue of transportation had to be solved before copper exports could become feasible. According to the original charter, the BSAC was obliged to invest in rail to the extremity of the Zambezi River. The railway's primary purpose, configuration and ultimate destination were determined almost exclusively by the desire to facilitate the extraction of mineral resources. In 1904, the railway, extending from Southern Rhodesia, reached Victoria Falls and the following year the small administrative centre of Livingstone. By 1906 it had been gradually extended to Broken Hill, the locality of zinc deposits that could now be exploited, then made a westward shift towards the copper rich areas of what would become the Copperbelt by 1909, and finally crossing the Congo border to cater for the Katanga District (Gann, 1958, 1969) (Map 6.1).

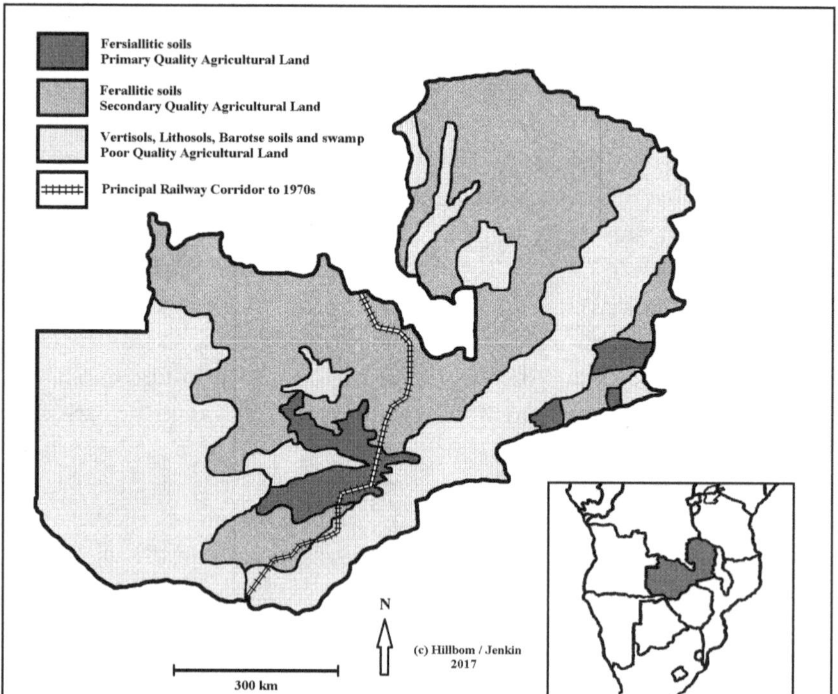

Map 6.1 Northern Rhodesia in c. 1915. Source: Authors' own

4 Minerals, Maize and Men, c. 1915–1964

4.1 Settler Farming

In the early colonial period, indigenous production in close proximity to the mining areas catered for food provisions (Gann, 1969), but soon it became insufficient to meet growing demand. Consequently, around 1915 the BSAC started inviting settlers from different parts of Southern Africa and Europe to ensure sufficient commercial production for the domestic market. From then onwards settler estates were seen as the core of the commercial sector. While the stretch of the railway was determined by ambitions to reach mineral deposits, chance would have it that it also traversed some of Northern Rhodesia's most fertile soils, and the administration established Crown Lands along the railway line reserved for settler agriculture (see Map 6.1). Thereby the railway corridor provided settlers with primary agricultural land, proximity to road and railway networks and access to urban areas with high food demand (Chinene et al., 1998). In essence, the railway became the geographic focal point for the development of cumulative agglomerations (Krugman, 1991) for both primary sectors, mining and settler farming.

In the spirit of the colonial era and as later argued in the colonial legacies literature, it was expected that settlers, through their superior technologies and knowledge would be significantly more productive and successful compared to indigenous farmers (Easterly & Levine, 2012; Fourie, 2012). The BSAC administration saw settlers as an opportunity to diversify incomes and make better use of existing investments in mining. The British Colonial Office that took over after 1924 was, however, less optimistic as it knew from experiences in Kenya, South Rhodesia and elsewhere that the success of settler communities generally depended on political and financial support from the administration (Frankema, Green, & Hillbom, 2016; Gann, 1958). Notwithstanding, quick results were considered vital and when local indigenous producers could not meet demand, strategies of land alienation and promotion of the settler sector continued. Subsequently, Northern Rhodesia has been marked as a "settler economy" by Mosley (1983).[2] However, unlike in other such

African colonies, settler farming was not expected to secure export revenues by producing high-value export-oriented cash crops. Instead it was to focus on internal demand for low-value, high-volume food staples, primarily maize and to a lesser degree beef, to provide for labour employed in mining, the export earning primary sector (Baldwin, 1966; Gann, 1969).

While estimates from the time are limited, it is understood that by 1910 there were some 60–75 farm units occupied by Europeans in North-Western Rhodesia, with a combined land size of between 240,000 and 280,000 acres (one acre is 0.40 hectares) (Vickery, 1986). By the time of the 1921 census of the territory, some 504 European males listed "farmer" as their occupation, most of them based along the railway north and south of Lusaka. At the time, there were 29,000 acres of land under maize cultivation, with a yield of 145,000 bags (of 200 pounds each—a pound being 0.45 of a kilo). The only additional substantial settler population was found in the east of the country around modern Chipata, where by 1921 there were 30 tobacco producers (Northern Rhodesia Annual Reports, 1925).

Early settler agriculture was extensive in nature, and the lack of markets beyond the Congo mines, combined with the difficulty of getting goods to markets beyond the immediate vicinity of the railway line, made conditions difficult. With the opening up of the Copperbelt mines from the 1920s, however, new ready markets for maize production were provided. Soon the mining areas' appetite for agricultural products exceeded settler production, which created market opportunities for surplus-generating indigenous farmers (Vickery, 1985). Differently from other colonies where the marketable crop was a newly introduced cash crop, maize was already widely produced and consumed by the indigenous population. Therefore, it is logical that settlers' technological advantage and superiority in knowledge, as well as the importance of transmission channels from the settlers to the indigenous smallholders, were of limited significance. During the early colonial era, prior to large-scale mechanisation and with modest access to improved seeds and chemical fertilizer, the settler advantage lay rather in access to fertile land, infrastructure and markets.

The competition from indigenous farmers was not appreciated by the settler community, and, as in other colonies in the region, it began pressuring the administration to restrict Africans' opportunities for commercialisation. Frankema, Green, & Hillbom (2016) have shown that throughout the colonial era, administrations were generally pragmatic in their support of settlers and where the settler sector did not deliver it could lose its preferential treatment. However, despite initial scepticism the administration in Northern Rhodesia decided on protecting the settlers and was channelling what limited resources it had for agricultural improvement towards them at the expense of African producers (Vickery, 1985). The reason was the administration's dependency on settlers to secure food for the urban mining centres.

4.2 Indigenous Labour Supply and Agricultural Production

Meanwhile, the colonial administration was primarily interested in the African population as a source of mining labour, and any effort to encourage agricultural specialisation and commercialisation of indigenous farmers was thought of as putting at risk the mining sector's heavy capital investments. In terms of direct labour control the administration established Barotseland as a Native Reserve and strictly regulated the urban areas such as the townships surrounding the mines. Still, the large majority of Africans lived on customary land controlled by traditional authorities, in which they accessed abundant agricultural land (although not always of the highest quality) and enjoyed a fair amount of freedom. Consequently, the administration needed indirect ways of ensuring labour movements towards the wage-earning sectors. This was accomplished through the introduction of a tax regime which drew Africans into the cash economy, necessitating labour migration to the mines and, later, waged labour on settler farms (Vickery, 1986). For the indigenous population wage labour provided cash for the payment of taxes and helped in supporting remaining family members who stayed in subsistence farming. Due to absence of labour-saving technological change, labour migration also resulted in labour scarcity in many areas, which prevented agricultural growth.

The establishment of Crown Land along the railway line had created a geographic exclusion of the large majority of indigenous farmers located further away from markets and transport opportunities. A few, however, did live in proximity to markets, often adjacent to settler farmers, and could compete in the production of maize, which was a low-capital product. There is clear evidence that given the right conditions, indigenous farmers through their own agency could thrive in the market economy, responding to price incentives and available opportunities for improvements (Baldwin, 1966; Vickery, 1985). The capacity of African farmers to compete at the aggregate level from an early stage is evidenced when comparing marketed maize levels between 1930 and 1935. In this period, settler production increased by 25 per cent, from 168,000 bags to 210,000 bags while African sales increased more than threefold from 30,000 bags to 100,000 bags (Baldwin, 1966). In addition, by 1930, the Annual Report notes the increase in the use of plough technology by indigenous producers, and with it an increasing competition in the maize market (Northern Rhodesia Annual Reports, 1932).

Instead of embracing this success and creating inclusive economic institutions to encourage further broad-based agricultural growth, colonial authorities, under pressure from settlers, distorted the market against local producers. From 1936, the newly established Maize Control Board set quotas for the internal market, whereby indigenous farmers would produce 25 per cent and settlers the remainder. While prevailing international and local market forces prevented the policy from significantly restricting African production in the immediate term, indigenous producers continued to be directly disadvantaged by productions prices, being paid up to a third less per bag than settlers (Vickery, 1986). When the often higher market prices obtained by the Board were received, appropriate supplementary distributions were made to settler producers, but this process was deemed impractical for African producers.

The late colonial period saw a change in policy approaches towards indigenous agriculture and in 1949 a significant surplus built up over time by the Board was transferred to an African Farming Improvement Fund. The supporting operations of the Fund provided a foundation for an emerging African commercial class. The differentiation of the African agriculture sector into commercial and subsistence already in place based on location and access to marketing opportunities, was now further enhanced by the introduction of the African Improved Farmer Scheme (financed by the Fund). It has been argued that the focus of fund allocations was not on increasing production, but rather on soil and water conservation primarily on land adjoining settler farms. Nevertheless, for indigenous farmers included in the scheme it meant access to a higher maize price (Makings, 1966; Vickery, 1986). The number of improved indigenous farmers rose from less than one hundred in the first year to 1,000 in 1955 and to over 3,000 in 1960, with the participation in an accompanying peasant scheme rising from 651 to 2,443 between 1955 and 1960 (Makings, 1966). Despite impressive growth, these figures must be compared against a general population by this time of over three million, of which only around 80,000 were non-Africans, leaving a significant number of indigenous farmers outside the government support system.

Technological advances in the post-war years that could only be taken advantage of by those already of a sufficient scale further reinforced the increasing differentiation. This is well articulated in the case of the SR-52 maize variety introduced after WWII. Imported from Southern Rhodesia, the productivity of the new grain far exceeded existing varieties, but required specific sowing patterns that only mechanised farmers using tractors could accomplish. Its success also relied on regular and heavy use of fertilisers, not readily available at the time to smaller producers. The new grain however, enabled commercial producers and more advanced African farmers to increase yields fivefold (Scott, 1995; Vickery, 1986) (see Fig. 6.2). Despite a number of indigenous farmers moving into the commercial sector, the increasing maize production and productivity did not foster broad-based agricultural development. Rather it further strengthened the duality of the agricultural sector separating the commercial and progressive classes from the overwhelming majority of subsistence farmers.

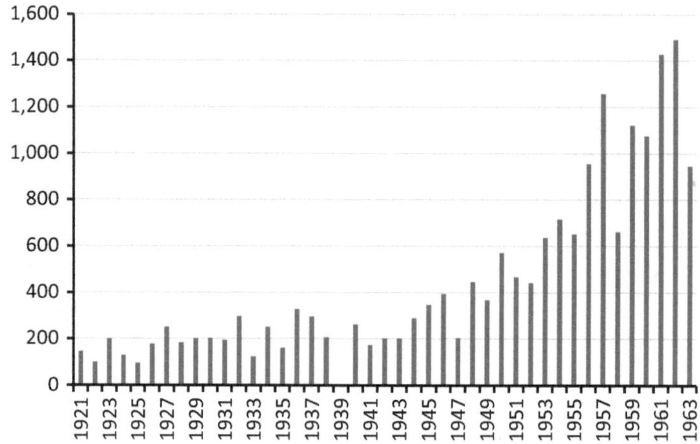

Fig. 6.2 Annual maize production (in 200 pound equivalent) by commercial farmers in Northern Rhodesia, 1921–1963 (in thousands). Source: Litschauer and Rowe (1995)

5 Independence Era: 1964 to Present

5.1 Sectorial Developments and Economic Crisis

The post-independence Zambian government continued to rely on the two well-established primary sectors—mining for export revenues and commercial farming for food security. Agricultural policies continued to include subsidising agricultural inputs to stimulate maize production, as well as distorting markets and stabilising prices. Differently from the colonial era though, the government now also wanted to stimulate the smallholder sector and the National Agricultural Marketing Board was directed to reverse colonial policies favouring settlers. For the sector as a whole there was significant progress based on mechanisation, new hybrid varieties, fertilisers and farming on marginal lands. As in many other parts of Africa at the time, the combination of technological change and government policies resulted in significant agricultural growth (McCann, 2005, pp. 162–165).

From the early 1960s to the late 1980s Zambian farmers increased their maize production by 300 per cent (see Fig. 6.3), although the last years of the 1980s appear extreme and should be treated with caution.[3]

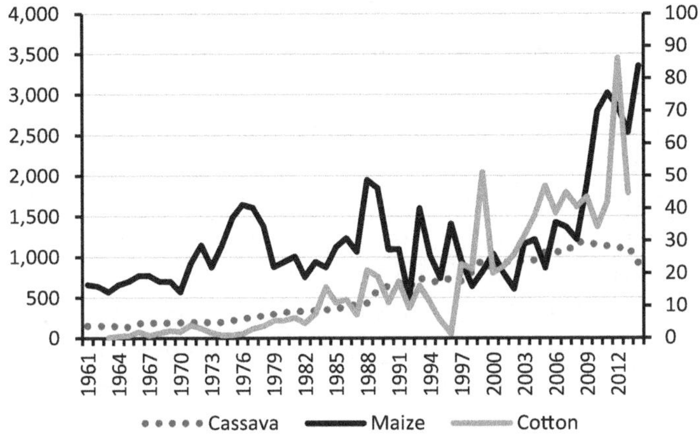

Fig. 6.3 Agricultural production in tons 1961–2014 (cassava and maize on the left hand axis and cotton on the right hand axis) (in thousands). Source: FAOSTAT (2016)

The social and economic patterns established in the 60 years of colonial rule, however, persisted into the independence era. In 1968, despite there being only 700 registered settler farmers, this group accounted for 62 per cent of total marketed output (Saasa, 1987). Nevertheless, the new agricultural policies encouraged smallholder production to a higher degree than before and in 1990 small- and medium-sized farmers were providing as much as 80 per cent of total maize production (McCann, 2005). Behind these numbers we find a growing and increasingly successful group of indigenous emergent medium-scale farmers, while the majority of indigenous smallholders continued to produce maize primarily for subsistence.

While government maize-biased agricultural policies influenced total production, it also contributed to a shift to maize as a staple crop in traditional cassava-growing regions. Maize strengthened its position as the "social contract crop" and the government prioritised spending on supporting maize production and marketing, to the detriment of other crop varieties, the main goal being to maintain stability in maize-meal pricing in urban centres (Scott, 1995). This position of maize as the social contract crop persists today, despite the fact that the relative value of maize production to total agricultural production continues to decrease. Figure 6.3 shows that during the first decades after independence agricultural production growth primarily took place in the maize sector, though cassava (alternative staple crop) and cotton (primary non-food cash crop) experienced a modest take-off.

Meanwhile, the government continued to expect incomes from mining generally and copper specifically to provide the main source of government revenue. In 1966, agriculture accounted for 15 per cent and manufacturing and construction combined for roughly 11 per cent of Zambia's GDP, while the mining sector alone accounted for 49.6 per cent (Saasa, 1987; WDI, 2016). Mining also accounted for a significant proportion of government revenue, copper alone accounting for in excess of 50 per cent of tax incomes in the years before 1970 (Saasa, 1987). The dependency on copper and lack of diversification proved detrimental. Although copper prices were increasing in absolute terms on the world market, in relative terms in relation to other industrial products and key natural resources that Zambia imported, such as oil, copper prices experienced a long-term decline from the 1970s onwards (WDI, 2016). Declining terms of trade and disastrous management of the economy due to the poor quality of economic and political institutions lead to a severe economic crisis in the mid-1980s through to the early 1990s (du Pleiss & du Pleiss, 2006). More recently, rising Chinese demand during the commodity boom in the early twenty-first century led to increasing copper prices and a recovery by the Zambian copper sector.

The economic crisis compelled the Zambian government in 1991 to accept structural adjustment reforms which included requirements for a significant reduction of agricultural subsidies, although they were never fully abandoned (Govereh, Jayne, & Chapato, 2008; Jayne & Jones, 1997). Rather, agriculture was accorded a higher priority in government planning and accounted for a significant proportion of government expenditure, rising from 11 per cent in 1974–1975 to 30 per cent in the late 1980s (Moyo, O'Keefe, & Sill, 1993). Nevertheless, there was a temporary loss of focus on maize in government policies causing many smallholders to abandon their attempts at commercial maize farming. Despite cut-backs during structural adjustment, the reliance on government support in the form of input subsidies persisted into the 1990s. In the late 1990s, preceding the renewed emphasis on small-scale agriculture as the key to broad-based agricultural development in developing regions

(World Bank, 2007), the Zambian government returned to agricultural policies focused on market distortion and subsidies.

5.2 Revival of the Agricultural Sector

In 1995 a new government maize agency was established—the Food Reserve Agency (FRA). This parastatal strategic food reserve/marketing board was given a mission to buy maize at a pan-territorial price exceeding wholesale prices in major maize producing areas. FRA's market-distorting price policies include offering farmers above market prices, subsidising prices to select large-scale millers, exporting to neighbouring countries at prices below the FRA purchasing price, and so on. Between 2004–2005 and 2010–2011 FRA purchased up to 86 per cent of maize marketed by smallholders costing the government roughly 25 per cent of annual total agricultural sector expenditures. FRA activities made maize prices more stable and raised them above average maize market prices by as much as 17–19 per cent between 2003 and 2008. These strategies have primarily favoured maize net-sellers, that is, the commercial sector (Mason & Myers, 2013).

In addition, the Fertilizer Credit Programme was created in 1997–1998 and in the 2002–2003 season large-scale fertiliser subsidies were reintroduced. Participating farmers could obtain 200 to 800 kg on credit and during the three years of the program an average 29,000 MT of fertiliser were distributed annually, particularly to the major maize producing regions in the Central, Eastern and Southern Provinces. Repayment rates were poor however and the next program, the Fertilizer Support Programme, was designed as a cash-only input subsidy program targeting selected beneficiary farmers. A standard package including 400 kg of fertilisers and 20 kg of hybrid maize seeds to plant one hectare of maize was designed. Annual volumes were slightly more than double those of the previous program, and beneficiaries were more evenly distributed over the country. In 2009–2010, the program was renamed the Farmers Input Support Programme, which continues in the present. While package sizes were halved, the total volume and number of recipients increased substantially (Ricker-Gilbert, Jayne, & Shively, 2013, pp. 8, 11) from 48,000

MT of fertilisers and 120,000 farmers in 2002–2003 to 180,000 MT and 900,000 farmers ten years later (MAL 2012 quoted in Ricker-Gilbert, Jayne, & Shively 2013, p. 2).

Numerous factors such as the above-market prices offered by the parastatal FRA, the increase in fertilisers distributed through various schemes and consecutive years of favourable weather, seem to have contributed to the sharp increase in Zambian maize production the last 10 years (see Fig. 6.3) (Ricker-Gilbert, Jayne, & Shively, 2013). It is primarily subsidised fertilisers that have been deemed to have had a statistically significant positive impact on long-term trends in output and yields (Mason, Jayne, & Myers, 2012; Prowse & Hillbom, 2018). This significant increase in production has also resulted in a sustained period of strong maize exports, which has seen Zambia become a net exporter of maize in all but one year since 2007 at the time of writing, a situation not seen since the 1970s (FAOSTAT, 2016). Despite the persistent maize focus, the rearticulation of agricultural policies seems to have also encouraged diversification of staple crops with an increase in both hectares dedicated to cassava (see Fig. 6.4) and total cassava and cotton production (see Fig. 6.3). In addition, while production of alternative high value crops such as vegetables has proven to involve higher risks, they also bring considerably higher profits (Chapoto et al., 2013). Sitko and Jayne (2014), however, warn against interpreting agricultural growth as evidence of an initial agricultural transformation process. They point out that while there has been a rapid increase in the number of medium-scale, so called "emergent", farmers cultivating 5–20 hectares of land since the turn of the millennium, this is not due to successful accumulation by subsistence farmers starting below 5 hectares, the smallholder group in which more than 95 per cent of farmers are found. Rather, it is primarily attributed to land acquisitions and commercialisation by salaried urbanites and privileged rural dwellers.

The last quarter of a century has also seen a renewed surge in agricultural FDI in Zambia. As discussed previously, foreign investments have played a long-standing role in the shaping of Zambia's agricultural sector, both arising as a consequence of natural resource endowments and being further encouraged by policy decisions. The building of the railway and subsequent allocation of fertile land to settlers along the railway created a

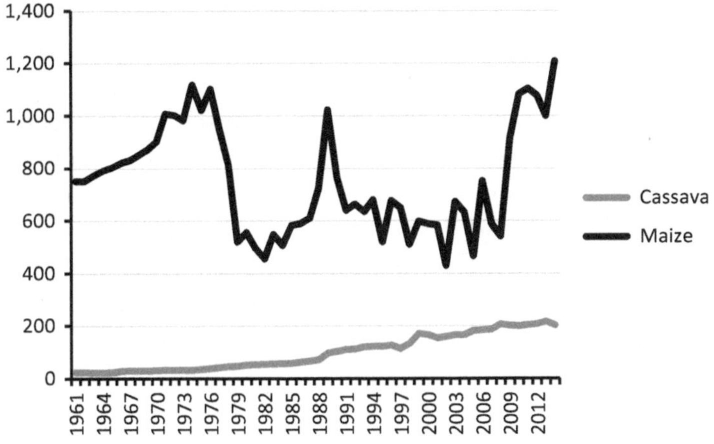

Fig. 6.4 Hectares under production 1961–2014. Source: FAOSTAT 2016

corridor for cumulative agglomeration. Map 6.2 shows that the regional effects of, on the one hand, urbanisation, infrastructure development and market access and, on the other hand, agricultural FDI is reproduced in a spatial path-dependent pattern. Ninety-four per cent of total proposed agricultural FDI in 1992–2009 was directed to the four Zambian provinces along the central rail and road corridor between Livingstone and the Copperbelt. As theorised by Krugman (1991) there is a spatial path-dependency and agglomeration directing the growth of urban settings in the Copperbelt, Lusaka, Central and Southern provinces, and the location of foreign investment in agriculture.

Despite more than a century of development of the mining sector and urbanisation, the most recent data available shows that more than 55 per cent of Zambia's population remains engaged in the agriculture sector, while almost 60 per cent of the population live in rural areas (WDI, 2016). From the point of view of the sectorial location of the labour force, the country's economy is still agriculture-based. At the same time, 54 per cent of the population resides in the four provinces which border the main rail line running north from the Southern province border town of Livingstone through Lusaka and Central provinces to the Copperbelt. These are also the areas where the commercial farmers of the dual agricultural sector are found. Covering only 30.9 per cent of the country's land area, these four provinces accounted for 53.2 per cent of total maize production in 2016 (Zambia Data Portal, 2017). Zambia, however, still has a significant amount of unexploited arable land, and fertile land is not restricted to this corridor (see Map 6.1). Due to limited infrastructure development, however, other areas are remote, severed from the markets that could initiate commercial activities. The remote areas are populated by subsistence farmers and despite half a century of agricultural policies to encourage smallholder food production, it is estimated that the agriculture sector is producing at well below its potential based on its natural resource endowments. The ratio of cultivated land to total suitable area is below 30 per cent and the yield gap (potential yield minus actual yield)

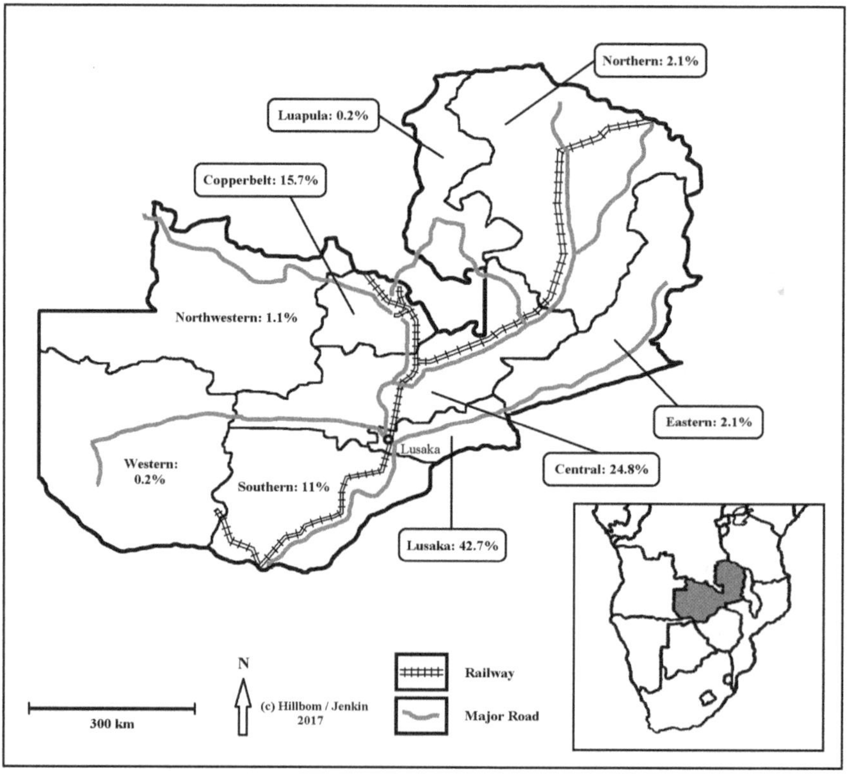

Map 6.2 Percentage of Proposed Foreign Investment in Agriculture 1992–2009, by Province. Source: own elaboration

is in excess of 80 per cent (World Bank, 2011). These numbers clearly indicate the limitations of agricultural growth and absence of broad-based agricultural transformation.

6 Concluding Remarks

Our aim was to present evidence on the extent to which, and through what mechanisms, initial natural resource endowments have influenced state policies and how those policies have determined the state of the contemporary Zambian agricultural sector. We have argued that the discovery of mineral richness in the early colonial era, and the geographic location of those deposits as well as that of fertile agricultural soils have informed: first, the extension of the railway; second, the settlement of large-scale farmers; and third, government agricultural policies focusing on securing food for a growing urban population. We have further analysed path-dependency in policies, investments and spatial patterns in the agricultural sector, showing how maize has been given the role of social contract crop and how agricultural policies have distorted opportunities for widespread agricultural diversification, creating instead a dual agricultural sector. While we have seen a century of political and financial efforts being invested in encouraging agricultural growth, the fundamental role of the agricultural sector has throughout our period of investigation been to service the mining areas and growing urban population. With the government's consistent dependency on copper export revenues, Zambia remains caught in a reliance on two interdependent primary sectors, neither of which is dynamic enough to drive a structural transform process.

Notes

1. In our study, we present natural resource endowments as an exogenous initial condition, but this is not the only assertion. Instead, the endogeneity of natural resources is a rising issue in the literature Willebald, Badia-Miró, Pinilla (2015).
2. The definition of settler colonies is contested. One dividing line is between the modern settler economies of the Neo-European type, e.g. USA and Australia, and the colonial territories that were under European political and

military control but attracted limited numbers of settlers, e.g. Africa (Loyd & Metzer 2013). For further diversity within the African context, one approach is the recognition of major shifts in the ratio of settlers to natives (in both directions), but then bearing in mind that settler–native ratios change over time. Another approach is estimating the settler communities' influence on colonial politics (Frankema, Green, & Hillbom, 2016).

3. The same caution goes for Fig. 6.4 and the statistics on hectares under maize production.

References

Acemoglu, D., Johnson, S., & Robinson, J. A. (2001). The Colonial Origins of Comparative Development: An Empirical Investigation. *American Economic Review, 91*(5), 1369–1401.

Acemoglu, D., Johnson, S., & Robinson, J. A. (2002). Reversal of Fortune: Geography and Institutions in the Making of the Modern World Income Distribution. *Quarterly Journal of Economics, 117*(4), 1231–1294.

Austin, G. (2008). The 'Reversal of Fortune' Thesis and the Compression of History: Perspectives from African and Comparative Economic History. *Journal of International Development, 20*, 996–1027.

Austin, G. (2010). African Economic Development and Colonial Legacies. *International Development Policy, 1*, 11–32.

Baldwin, R. (1966). *Economic Development and Export Growth: A study of Northern Rhodesia, 1920–1960*. Berkley: University of California Press.

Bayly, C. (2008). *Indigenous and Colonial Origins of Comparative Economic Development: The Case of Colonial India and Africa*. Policy Research Working Papers No 4474, World Bank, Washington, DC.

Bowden, S., Chiripanhura, B., & Mosley, P. (2008). Measuring and Explaining Poverty in Six African Countries: A Long-Period Approach. *Journal of International Development, 20*(8), 1049–1079.

Byerlee, D. (2018, forthcoming). Plantations, Tropical Commodities and Economic Development over the 20th Century: End of an Era. In V. Pinilla & H. Willebald (Eds.), *Agricultural Development in the World Periphery: A Global Economic History Approach*. Basingstoke: Palgrave Macmillan.

Chapoto, A., Haggblade, S., Hichaambwa, M., Kabwe, S., Longabaugh, S., Sitko, N. J., & Tschirley, D. (2013). Institutional Models for Accelerating Agricultural Commercialization: Evidence from Post-Independence Zambia,

1965–2012. In E. Hillbom & P. Svensson (Eds.), *Agricultural Transformation in a Global History Perspective*. Abingdon: Routledge.

Chinene, V., Maimbo, F., Banda, D., & Msune, S. (1998). *A Comparison of Customary and Leasehold Tenure: Agriculture and Development in Zambia. Land Reform, Land Settlement and Cooperatives* (Vol. 2, pp. 88–99). Rome: Food and Agriculture Organization.

Crespo, N., & Fontoura, M. P. (2007). Determinant Factors of FDI Spillovers—What do we Really Know? *World Development, 35*(3), 410–425.

Easterly, W., & Levine, R. (2012). *The European Origins of Economic Development*. NBER Working Paper 18162, National Bureau of Economic Research, Cambridge.

FAOSTAT. (2016). Retrieved April 13, 2017, from http://www.fao.org/faostat/en/#home

Fourie, J. (2012). The Remarkable Wealth of the Dutch Cape Colony: Measurements from Eighteenth-Century Probate Inventories. *The Economic History Review, 66*(2), 419–448.

Frankema, E., Green, E., & Hillbom, E. (2016). Success and Failure of European Settler Farming in Africa. *Revista de Historia Económica, 34*(2), 237–265.

Frankema, E., & van Waijenburg, M. (2012). Structural Impediments to African Growth? New Evidence from Real Wages in British Africa, 1880–1965. *Journal of Economic History, 72*(4), 895–926.

Gallup, J. L., Sachs, J. D., & Mellinger, A. D. (1999). Geography and Economic Development. *International Regional Science Review, 22*(2), 179–232.

Gann, L. (1958). *The Birth of a Plural Society: The development of Northern Rhodesia under the British South Africa Company 1894-1914*. Manchester: Manchester University Press.

Gann, L. (1969). *A History of Northern Rhodesia: Early days to 1953*. New York: Humanities Press.

Govereh, J., Jayne, T. S., & Chapato, A. (2008). *Assessment of Alternative Maize Trade and Market Policy Interventions in Zambia*. Working Paper 33, Food Security Research Project.

Gylafson, T., Herbertsson, T. T., & Zoega, G. (1999). A Mixed Blessing: Natural Resources and Economic Growth. *Macroeconomic Dynamics, 3*, 204–225.

Habakkuk, H. J. (1962). *American and British Technology in the Nineteenth Century*. Cambridge: Cambridge University Press.

Haggblade, S., & Hazell, P. (2010). *Success in African Agriculture*. Baltimore: Johns Hopkins.

Hazell, P., Poulton, C., Wiggins, S., & Dorward, A. (2010). The Future of Small Farms: Trajectories and policy priorities. *World Development, 38*(10), 1349–1361.

Jayne, T. S., & Jones, S. (1997). Food Marketing and Price Policy in Eastern and Southern Africa: A survey. *World Development, 25*, 1005–1027.
Krugman, P. (1991). *Geography and Trade*. Cambridge: MIT Press.
Litschauer, J., & Rowe, J. (1995). Zambia's Agricultural Data System: A Review of the Agricultural Time Series Data. In M. Roth & S. Smith (Eds.), *Land Tenure, Land Markets, and Institutional Transformation in Zambia*. LTC Research Paper 124.
Loyd, C., & Metzer, J. (2013). Settler Colonization and Societies in World History: Patterns and concepts. In C. Loyd, J. Metzer, & R. Sutch (Eds.), *Settler Economies in World History* (pp. 1–34). Leiden: Brill.
Makings, S. (1966). *Agricultural Change in Northern Rhodesia/Zambia: 1945–1965*. Food Research Institute Studies, 6(2), Stamford University.
Mason, N. M., Jayne, T. S., & Myers, R. J. (2012, August 18–24). *Smallholders Behavioral Response to Marketing Board Activities and a Dual Channel Marketing System: The case of maize in Zambia*. Paper presented at the 28th International Association of Agricultural Economics Triennial Conference, Foz do Iguacu, Brazil.
Mason, N. M., & Myers, R. J. (2013). The Effects of the Food Reserve Agency on Maize Prices in Zambia. *Agricultural Economics, 44*, 203–216.
McCann, J. C. (2005). *Maize and Grace: Africa's Encounter with a New World crop 1500–2000*. Cambridge, MA and London: Harvard University Press.
Mosley, P. (1983). *The Settler Economies: Studies in the Economic History of Kenya and Southern Rhodesia 1900–1963*. Cambridge: Cambridge University Press.
Moyo, S., O'Keefe, P., & Sill, M. (1993). *The Southern African Environment: Profiles of the SADC Countries*. London: Earthscan Publications.
North, D. (1990). *Institutions, Institutional Change and Economic Performance*. Cambridge: Cambridge University Press.
Northern Rhodesia Annual Report 1923. (1925). His Majesty's Stationary Office.
Northern Rhodesia Annual Report 1930. (1932). His Majesty's Stationary Office.
Nurkse, R. (1953). *Problems of Capital Formation in Underdeveloped Countries*. Cambridge: Cambridge University Press.
Parsons, N. (1993). *A New History of Southern Africa*. London: Macmillan.
Du Pleiss, S., & Du Pleiss, S. (2006). Explanations for Zambia's Economic Decline. *Development Southern Africa, 23*(3), 351–369.
Prowse, M., & Hillbom, E. (2018, forthcoming). Prices or Policies? A gendered analysis of drivers of maize production in Malawi and Zambia, 2002–2013. In A. Andersson Djurfeldt, F. Dzanku, & A. Isinika (Eds.), *Agriculture, Diversification, and Gender in Rural Africa: Longitudinal Perspectives from Six Countries*.

Putterman, L., & Weil, D. N. (2010). Post-1500 Population Flows and the Long-Run Determinants of Economic Growth and Inequality. *The Quarterly Journal of Economics, 125*(4), 1627–1682.

Ricker-Gilbert, J., Jayne, T. S., & Shively, G. (2013). Addressing the "Wicked Problem" of Input Subsidy Programs in Africa. *Applied Economics Perspectives and Policy, 35*(2), 322–340.

Robinson, P., Govereh, J., & Ndlela, D. (2009). Zambia. In K. Anderson & W. Masters (Eds.), *Distortions to Agricultural Incentives in Africa*. Washington: World Bank.

Saasa, O. (1987). *Zambia's Policies Towards Foreign Investment: The Case of the Mining and Non-mining Sectors*. Research Report 79, Nordafrika Institutet, Uppsala

Sachs, J. D., & Warner, A. M. (1995). *Natural Resource Abundance and Economic Growth*. Development Discussion Paper No. 517a, Harvard Institute for International Development, Harvard University.

Scott, G. (1995). *Agricultural Transformation in Zambia: Past Experience and Future Prospects*. Workshop on Agricultural Transformation in Africa, Abidjan,

Sikto, N. J., & Jayne, T. S. (2014). Structural Transformation or Elite Land Capture? The Growth of "Emergent" Farmers in Zambia. *Food Policy, 48*, 194–202.

Smeets, R. (2008). Collecting the Pieces of the FDI Knowledge Spillovers Puzzle. *World Bank Research Observer, 23*(2), 107–138.

Timmer, C. P. (2009). *A World Without Agriculture: The Structural Transformation in Historical Perspective*. Washington, DC: AEI Press.

van der Ploeg, F. (2011). Natural Resources: Curse or Blessing? *Journal of Economic Literature, 49*(2), 366–420.

Vickery, K. (1985). Saving Settlers: Maize Control in Northern Rhodesia. *Journal of Southern African Studies, 11*(2), 212–234.

Vickery, K. (1986). *Black and White in Southern Africa: The Tonga Plateau Economy and British Imperialism, 1890–1939*. Westport: Greenwood Press.

Willebald, H., Badia-Miró, M., & Pinilla, V. (2015). Introduction. In M. Badia-Miró, V. Pinilla, & H. Willebald (Eds.), *Natural Resources and Economic Growth: Learning from History* (pp. 1–25). London: Routledge.

Woodberry, R. (2012). The Missionary Roots of Liberal Democracy. *American Political Science Review, 106*(2), 244–274.

World Bank. (2007). *World Bank Development Report 2008: Agriculture for development*. Washington, DC: World Bank.

World Bank. (2011). *Rising Global Interest in Farmland: Can it yield sustainable and equitable benefits?* Washington, DC: World Bank.
World Development Indicators, WDI. (2016). Retrieved April 13, 2017, from http://databank.worldbank.org/data/reports.aspx?source=world-development-indicators
Zambia Data Portal. (2017). Retrieved March 23, 2017, from http://zambia.africadata.org/
de Zwart, P. (2011). South African Living Standards in Global Perspective, 1835–1910. *Economic History of Developing Regions, 26*(1), 49–74.

Ellen Hillbom is an economic historian at Lund University in Sweden. Within the broader field of African Economic History, she has over the years specialised in colonial history, rural and agricultural development as well as in long-term changes in inequality and structural transformation. She also conducts research on current development challenges, both macroeconomic structures and local agricultural systems of production, primarily in Botswana, Tanzania, Zambia and Malawi.

Samuel Jenkin is a PhD candidate with the Department of Economic History at Lund University. His research interests include the role of agricultural transformation in supporting long-term economic development, and the capacity of foreign direct investment and infrastructure development to support structural change in agriculture.

7

Maize and Gold: South African Agriculture's Transition from Suppression to Support, 1886–1948

Jan C. Greyling, Nick Vink, and Emily van der Merwe

1 Introduction

This chapter traces the progression from "suppression to support" of South African agriculture during the early twentieth century (1886 to 1948), revisiting the early part of the development of the South African agricultural sector from the perspective of the structural transformation framework. To this end the nature of the alliance between "gold" and "maize" (as coined by Trapido, 1971), and its subsequent disintegration (as documented by Morrel, 1988) is re-examined. The focus is on the evolution of political tensions stemming from the converging and diverging interests of groupings within the mining and agricultural sectors, and

J.C. Greyling (✉) • N. Vink
Department of Agricultural Economics, Stellenbosch University, Stellenbosch, Western Cape, South Africa

E. van der Merwe
Department of Economics, Stellenbosch University, Stellenbosch, Western Cape, South Africa

V. Pinilla, H. Willebald (eds.), *Agricultural Development in the World Periphery*, Palgrave Studies in Economic History, https://doi.org/10.1007/978-3-319-66020-2_7

specifically how this facilitated the transition from "squeezing" a large but marginalised group of smaller white farmers, as well as black famers in general, to the reluctant "squeezing" of the mining industry by the state and the eventual complete marginalisation of black farmers.

The chapter contributes to the recent expansion of the structural transformation literature that stresses the importance of taking underlying country fundamentals into account with development policy formation. The South African case illustrates the complexity of the political tensions created during the transformation process and their long-term impact, since these played a significant role in putting the country on the path to grand apartheid. In addition, a newly compiled long-term dataset on agricultural prices, output and public spending is provided, to add a quantitative perspective to the ability of either party to capture the state and a more precise estimate of the timing of the disintegration of the alliance. Two previously underemphasised aspects of stakeholder interactions at the time are also explored: the nature and policy impact of the interaction between white and black farmers and the mines within the context of shared and conflicting interests; and the changes in the nature and extent of support to white farmers during this period.

In what follows, Sect. 2 provides an overview of the structural transformation literature employed as theoretical framework for this study, while Sect. 3 expands on the historical background and state capture. The fourth Section describes the measures put in place by white farmers to stem the competition from black farmers. This is followed in Sect. 5 by a closely related discussion on the land and labour market interventions by the State. In Sects. 6 and 7 the transition to the controlled marketing of maize and other agricultural produce, and increased direct subsidies to the commercial farming sector are discussed, followed by a brief discussion of the post-1948 consolidation of support and its eventual decline towards the 1990s. The ninth and last Section provides a summary and conclusion.

2 Theoretical Framework

The structural transformation of economies during development has shown itself to be a "remarkably uniform" process through the work of Clark (1940), Lewis (1954), Kuznets (1966) and Chenery & Syrquin

(1975). This transformation is paramount since it is regarded as a defining characteristic of economic growth, both as cause and as effect (Syrquin, 2006).

The trajectory of the transformation that industrialised economies transition through can be summarised as follows (Timmer, 1988): prior to the structural transformation, the economy is dominated by farming, largely subsistence farming, since it constitutes the bulk of economic output and the labour force. During the initial stages of development, the productivity of the agricultural sector is required to increase sufficiently for the sector to be able to generate surpluses. These surpluses enable the sector to meet the domestic demand for food, produce exportable surpluses, release labour to the rest of the economy, and serve as a source for capital and a market for manufactured inputs and consumables (Johnston & Mellor, 1961). At this point some countries could opt to "squeeze" the agricultural sector through depressing commodity prices or increased taxation to raise greater surpluses from the sector, since these could earn a greater return if employed by non-farm industries with a greater productivity (Timmer, 1988). Examples include the suppression of peasants in the Soviet Union (see e.g. Allen, 1996).

Collectively these enable faster productivity growth in the non-farm economy relative to the farm economy, thereby resulting in farm incomes that increasingly fall behind incomes earned in the rest of the economy. "This lag in real earnings from agriculture is the fundamental cause of the *deep political tensions generated* by the structural transformation" (Timmer, 2009, p. 6, emphasis in original). Given sufficient political influence the sector can lobby for policy interventions directed at narrowing the earnings gap, mostly through import protection, price support measures and direct transfers to farmers (Lindert, 1991). Finally, the agricultural sector transitions to the last phase in the transformation process following the removal of price interventions and other support measures, and continued agricultural productivity growth. At this point the agricultural sector is fully integrated into the rest of the economy given indistinguishable productivity levels (Timmer, 1988). The income disparity between farm and non-farm labour also starts to converge and is eventually equalised (Barrett, Carter, & Timmer, 2010).

Whilst this constitutes the general trajectory of the transformation, the heterogeneity in the underlying fundamentals of individual countries results in different productivity expansion paths and development outcomes (Timmer, 2007). This sentiment is also shared by the authors of a five-year World Bank study on the structural transformation of late developing African countries. They stress the importance of taking national characteristics such as "…country assets, market functionality, business climate, institutional arrangements, overall governance, and political stability…" into account when formulating policy since these determine the constraints faced by households who are struggling to escape poverty (Losch, Freguin-Gresh, & White, 2011, p. xxii). Ultimately these determine the timing and extent of the eventual convergence of the urban–rural productivity and income gaps, where successful countries such as China and South Korea achieve a classic transformation, whilst progress is stunted in others such as India or fails as with South Africa (Binswanger-Mkhize, 2014).

3 Historical Background and Capturing the State

Subsistence farming dominated South Africa's agricultural landscape for most of the nineteenth century, with the exception of the wool- and wine-exporting settler farmers of the Cape (Ross, 1986). After starting their migration to the interior with the "Great Trek" of 1838, the newly established settlers of the northern interior could not readily join their exporting Cape compatriots given a coastline straddled by mountains and the lack of navigable rivers.

The discovery of diamonds at Hopetown near Kimberley in 1866 and gold at the Witwatersrand in 1886 put this initial steady state in flux. Whilst this development posed an economic and political threat to the predominantly farming community of the newly established Boer republics of the Free State and South African Republic (later Transvaal), the fortunes of some farmers were greatly improved through the substantial and growing market for agricultural produce in the interior.

By the 1890s a "marriage of convenience" had developed between wealthy mine owners of the Witwatersrand and some of the larger farmers of the interior, especially those of the eastern Transvaal. Likened to the union of "iron and rye" of Imperial Germany (Trapido, 1971), the marriage between maize and gold rested on two main pillars. One, because the gold mines also had responsibility for housing and feeding mineworkers, there was a mutual interest in a regular supply of, and dependable market for, maize. Two, the two sectors had a shared interest in the creation and maintenance of a constant supply of cheap black labour (Morrel, 1988; Trapido, 1971; Wolpe, 1972).

The development and prosperity that came with the mines was followed closely by the struggle for the control of the Boer Republics. Conflict manifested itself in the Jameson Raid (1896) that the Republics managed to subdue, ultimately culminating in the Second Anglo-Boer War (1899–1902) from which Great Britain emerged as victor (Davenport & Saunders, 2000).

The "scorched earth" strategy employed by Britain towards the end of the war wiped out the livestock that was the main source of traction and transport for farmers, and brought agriculture in the two Boer republics to its knees. After the war, Lord Alfred Milner as Governor of the Orange River and Transvaal colonies was tasked with the reconstruction efforts of the agricultural sector. This took the form of the provision of credit for buying land and equipment, as well as loans to import expensive cattle, but these efforts were directed at the larger farmers who were deemed to have a greater ability to repay loans and the potential to provide the gold mines with produce (Morrel, 1988).

With smaller farmers left unsupported, this gave rise to a class of so-called "*Boer notables*" who employed modern production techniques and made use of hired labour. At the time, a second group of prosperous Transvaal farmers established themselves as major actors in the industry. This emergent group of mostly English-speaking "progressive" famers consisted of immigrants or former Rand businessmen whose social capital offered them greater access to financing, the mining market and land from landholding companies (Morrell, 1986).

Whilst the larger farmers played a dominant role in supplying the mines, the balance was supplied by rival smaller white and black farmers. At the time land and labour served as the major production inputs, with a sufficient supply of labour the greatest hurdle faced by white famers. Conversely, black farmers faced major challenges in accessing land.[1]

In dealing with the convergent and conflicting interests, both the mining and broader agricultural interest groups lobbied the state to turn its machinery in their favour. During the early part of the twentieth century, most of the larger farmers in Transvaal supported Botha and Smuts' *Het Volk* party, which favoured the mining interests. *Het Volk* amalgamated with the Cape Colony South African Party (SAP) and other smaller parties to form the South African Party (SAP) after the formation of the Union in 1910 and became the party of the progressive Afrikaner farmers who supported the policy to restore relations between the historically estranged Boers and British. By 1911 the structural transformation of the economy had progressed beyond its agrarian roots to one where the agricultural sector represented 22 per cent of GDP and mining 27 per cent (Nattrass & Seekings, 2010, p. 4).

In reaction to SAP's pro-British and pro-mines stance, Hertzog established the National Party (NP) in 1914 to promote republicanism and Afrikaner nationalism, and secession from Britain for the two former Boer republics. The party was particularly popular amongst smaller white farmers who felt left behind by Smuts. The NP's victory in 1924 through a coalition with the (white) Labour Party served as a turning point in the popular imagination as the era of a "…white workers government antagonistic to the interest of mining capital…" (Davenport & Saunders, 2000, p. 300). Morell (1988) argues that this victory added momentum to the disintegration of the maize and gold alliance already in motion.

Figure 7.1 provides a visual summary of the main stakeholders as well as the resource and influence flows. The main stakeholders, namely the white and black farmers, the mines and the state, are shown at the extremities. Maize is at the centre of this system, with both black and white farmers competing to supply the commodity. All three parties competed for both black labour and land, whilst only white farmers and the mines could lobby the state, as represented by the dotted lines. The nature of this lobbying warrants further exposition since at least four distinct groupings can be found in this process. This includes the larger farmers and the mine owners, amongst whom the informal alliance emerged, the initially disenfranchised small farmers, and the often-overlooked blue-collar white mineworkers.

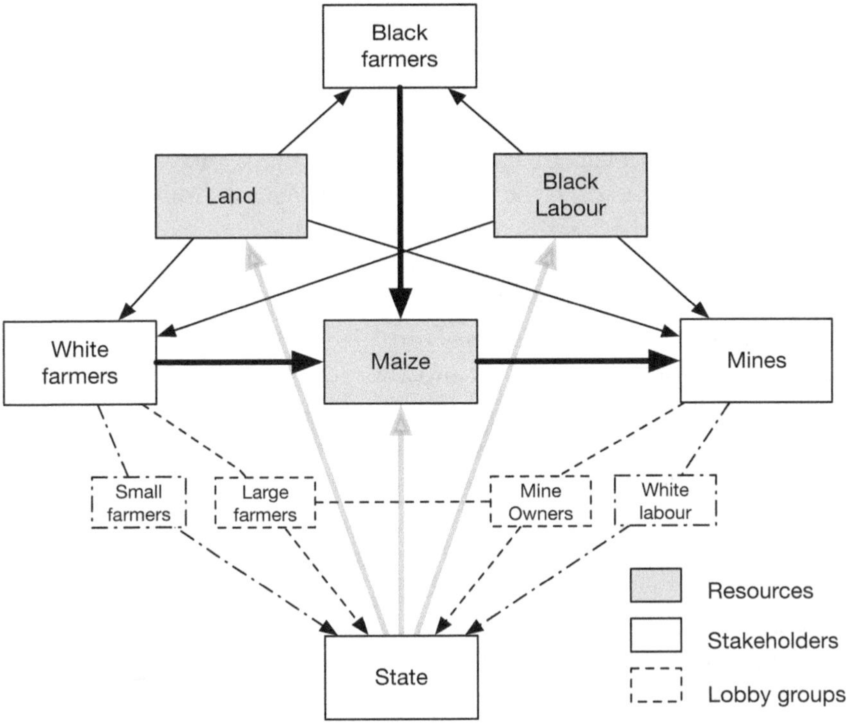

Fig. 7.1 The stakeholders with their resource and influence flows. Source: our elaboration

4 Stemming the Competition from Black Farmers

The impact of the discovery of diamonds and gold was not limited to white farmers. In the rush to supply these new markets, African farmers proved themselves more than capable of producing substantial surpluses. For example, their output in Natal expanded two-and-a-half fold between 1867 and 1894, resulting in a nearly doubling of average per capita output (Lenta, 1983). Numerous examples of similar patterns can be found in other parts of South Africa (Beinart, 1982; Bundy, 1972; Keegan, 1986; Lacey, 1982; Morris, 1976; Trapido, 1978; Wilson, 1971).

The success of these farmers created a problem for the white farmers. With simple technology and relatively abundant arable land, labour was the critical factor. Capital-constrained settler farmers found it difficult to offer wages that were high enough to attract indigenous labour, resulting in labour shortages in many regions of the country. They tried to resolve this by persuading the colonial government to limit African competition through the creation of reserves, to bring about an artificial land shortage using measures such as: livestock, hut and poll taxes; road rents; location, vagrancy and pass laws; and confinement to the reserves. In the process they invoked a Nieboer–Domar system of serfdom, given the context of an abundance of land and a shortage of labour (Domar, 1970; Nieboer, 1900).

In response to the pressure to reduce such competition, the state intervened in the land rental market and sought to reduce the number of rent-paying African tenant farmers, with the Glen Grey Act of 1894 the precursor of things to come (see e.g. Thompson & Nicholls, 1993). It attempted to levy a labour tax on all men living in the reserves, and banned the sale, rental or subdivision of land by introducing a perverted form of communal tenure. Whilst Africans could not access land through official channels during this period, many bought land as individuals and in groups as land syndicates. No exact information is available regarding the amount of land bought, but there was some speculation that Africans would succeed in buying back all that they had lost during the colonial wars (Plaatje, 1987).

From the perspective of the maize and gold alliance the parties faced the usual mix of shared and competing objectives: both parties had an incentive to suppress black farmers since black self-subsistence posed a threat to the maintenance of the cheap labour system (Marcus, 1989). Conversely, the mines had an incentive to act in favour of black farmers for two reasons. One, the mines and other land speculation companies owned vast tracts of land and favoured leasing to black tenants who were deemed more dependable with rent payments. The amount of land accessed in this way is substantial given that land holding companies alone owned more than 1300 farms in the Transvaal at the turn of the century with a single tribe renting more than twenty-two of these (Bundy, 1972).

Two, the mines had a possible (probable?) incentive to support some black farmers since their competition weakened the bargaining position of white farmers, thereby lowering commodity prices.

White farmers were opposed to black famers in principle given the competition they posed for accessing land, cheap labour and the disposal of produce. Conversely, capital-constrained farmers at the turn of the twentieth century opted for various tenure arrangements that enabled black families to access land and produce crops since access to labour was the most constraining production factor.

5 Land and Labour Market Interventions

The existing racial discrimination in access to land was consolidated by the Land Act of 1913, which made it explicit that "natives" were only allowed to buy, rent or acquire by other means land from other "natives", and white farmers from other whites, thereby creating a parallel land market and outlawing other forms of contract such as labour tenancy and sharecropping. This caused much disruption to the farm production of the black peasantry (Keegan, 1981; Matsetela, 1981; Plaatje, 1987; Willan, 1984). The main intention of the law, which was "almost exclusively the basis of the country's future policy of apartheid" (Wilson, 1971), was to transform tenants into wageworkers for the mines, thereby earning it the title of the "…law made for the mining houses…" (Davenport, 1987). The law was also intended to "curb black farming practices at a time when white farming was beginning to pick up…to check black sharecropping…and to prevent the purchase of land by syndicates of blacks who…were beginning to move ahead fast" (Davenport, 1987).

The immediate effect of the law was to force those African families who were formerly independent farmers on sharecropped land to accept wage labour and give up their equipment. The longer-term effect was to end African farming above the subsistence level and to degrade the reserves to "dormitories" (Hendricks, 1990) for a cheap African labour force. The results were catastrophic: by 1918 agricultural production in the reserves covered at most 45 per cent of subsistence requirements, declining to 20 per cent in the 1950s (Simkins, 1984), while by the 1920s increasing population pressure caused African households in the reserves to spend 60 per cent of their income on food.

Appointed under provisions of the Land Act, the Beaumont Commission reported that land scheduled for African occupation in terms of the Act was only sufficient for about half of the native population, and recommended that further land be released, specifying the areas which should be added. As indicated in Table 7.1, the reserves were limited to 7.8 per cent of the total land area before 1936. Outside the reserves, Africans owned only 0.7 per cent of the land and lived on state and European-owned lands (another 0.6 and 2.9 per cent); thus the total land technically available for their use was 12 per cent, excluding the mission reserves. This remained unchanged until the establishment of the Native Land Trust by the Native Trust and Land Act No. 18 of 1936. The Trust was meant to release a further 6.2 million hectares (later to be known as "released land") and add it to the original scheduled land to increase the size of the reserves to 13.7 per cent of the country.

Table 7.1 Land areas by land tenure systems, 1916

Tenure system	Area (hectares)	Percentage
Native reserves	9,538,300	7.8
Mission reserves	460,000	0.4
Native-owned lands	856,100	0.7
Crown lands occupied	805,100	0.6
EOL[a]: Occupied by Europeans	90,314,000	73.7
EOL[a]: Occupied by Africans	3,550,900	2.9
Vacant Crown land[b], reserve[c] and other	17,002,400	13.9
Total:	122,526,800	100.0

Source: Beaumont Commission (1916) pp. 3–4; DBSA (1990), p. 34. It excludes Walvis Bay

[a]EOL: European-Owned Land

[b]Now called State Land: mountains, beaches, etc. where ownership is not allowed

[c]Nature reserves

6 Towards Controlled Marketing

Having traced the initial "squeeze" and eventual marginalisation of black farmers, we now turn to the remaining stakeholders, namely the State, white farmers and mine owners, and show the multiple complexities of structural transformation in South African agriculture's progression "from suppression to support".

South African maize farmers, both black and white, made rapid strides towards achieving domestic maize self-sufficiency after the Second Anglo-Boer War. Production more than doubled from 360,000 to 860,000 tons between 1904 and 1911, and continued to trend upwards to reach a high of 2.9 million tons by 1948. The area planted to maize showed a steady increase from the 1.5 million hectares planted in 1911 to peak at 5.6 million hectares in 1932 (second panel of Fig. 7.2). The average area planted levelled off during the 1930s as shown by the fitted trend, but continued upwards during the 1940s.

With neither the mines nor the greater Southern-African market able to absorb the expanding harvest, farmers were forced to seek alternatives for their crop. For this they turned to the State, under whose supervision just over 42,000 tons where exported to the UK in 1907 and 1908 (see third panel of Fig. 7.2). These exports where in part facilitated by the proclamation of "Government grades" for maize that ensured the exportability of the 463,000 bags of 200 pounds each (Bosman & Osborn, 1924, p. 42). Maize exports took off in earnest during WWI, given the substantial premium that South African farmers could earn on the world market, as reflected in the second panel of Fig. 7.2.

The first cooperatives were established in 1908 and jointly formed the Central Agency (CA) for the marketing of their maize. The mines supported the establishment of the CA since they hoped that it would facilitate effective marketing and promote efficiency in general, and the evidence suggests that they were indeed well served by the CA (Morrel, 1988). It was also hoped that such an agency would strengthen the bargaining position of cash-strapped small farmers who had to accept the price offered by their local merchant or travelling buyers (Brits, 1969). Cooperatives did not buy or sell the maize on their own account but merely acted as agents on behalf of their members. Farmers were paid an

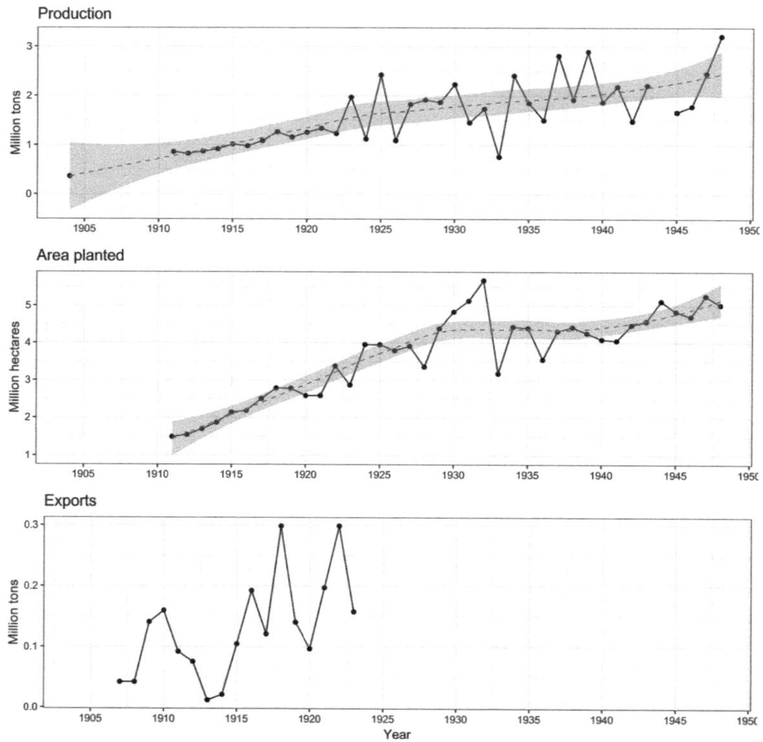

Fig. 7.2 South African maize production, area planted and exports. Source: Compiled from Bosman and Osborn (1924); Union of South Africa (1960) and Agricultural Census Reports (1918 to 1950). Notes: The greyed area around the fitted plots shown in the first and second panels portrays the 95 per cent confidence interval of the respective plots

advance by the cooperatives upon delivery, and received the balance at the end of the marketing season once the relevant costs were deducted. This practice proved problematic since cooperatives often found themselves in a difficult financial position because of either paying out overgenerous advances and/or inefficient management and administration. As a result, the cooperative movement struggled to gain traction among bigger farmers: by 1922 membership totalled some 6,300 farmers who sold but 10 per cent of the total crop (Brits, 1969).

The export expansion failed to support the South African maize price during the war however, since it trailed the US price by more than 42 per cent ($250) at its 1916 peak. South African farmers struggled to gain traction on the world market given their low yields and limited infrastructure: South African farmers averaged a yield of 0.7 ton per ha nationally in 1925 with their counterparts in Argentina and the USA achieving more than double that at 1.6 and 1.5 respectively (Saunders, 1930). Whilst the main rail lines from the ports to the interior had been completed by 1902, most of the branch lines critical for agricultural exports on a substantial scale were only added between 1905 and 1930. The expansion was substantial with 12,460 km of track added during this period, representing 64 per cent of all the lines built in South Africa up to that point (De Swardt, 1983). The construction of grain silos (elevators) by South African Railways along the branch lines of the main maize-producing regions followed during the 1920s. Four elevators had been completed by 1925 in the eastern Transvaal towns of Bethal, Balfour, Kinross, and Middelburg (De Swardt, 1983; Morrel, 1988). Attempts were also made to stimulate exports through preferential rail rates from interior sellers to the ports and subsidised ocean freight rates. The state went so far as to task a Union Government representative in London with marketing all unsold maize handled through the railway authorities (Brits, 1969).

South African maize prices trended continually downwards during the 1920s to reach a low of $160 per ton by 1932, following the onset of the Great Depression (see first panel of Fig. 7.3). In fact, the South African price declined by 28 per cent and 50 per cent relative to 1931 and 1929 respectively, 68 per cent below the high of 1921. This hardship was amplified by the 1933 drought that reduced total production by 56 per cent or a million tons (1.73 versus 0.76) relative to the previous year.

Figure 7.3 clearly shows that South African farmers on average got the short end of the stick during the WWI, given their limited political power, but this was also the case during most of the WWII. Whist South African farmers where somewhat sheltered against the decline pursuant on the Great Depression, they also missed out on the post-Depression boom.

Having failed to benefit from WWI price increases and a growing impatience with the inability of the CA to counter the continued price decline, farmers lobbied the State through the South African Agricultural Union (SAAU) for support and domestic price controls, while mine owners opposed the move in the interest of profitability (Morrel, 1988). The National Party government, as the torchbearer of the small farmer, was in favour of protecting domestic production and promoting self-sufficiency, as evidenced by a 1926 report which described agricultural protection as a "necessary evil" required to stimulate production in a stagnating economy (Department of Agriculture, 1926, p. 12)

The CA was rendered obsolete by the Marketing Act of 1931, which expanded state involvement in the maize market, and the CA was dissolved in 1934. This was followed by the promulgation of the Marketing Act of 1937, which established the (pro-farmer) State as the sole buyer and seller of numerous agricultural commodities, including maize. So influential and far-reaching were the effects of the 1937 Act that it was at one point described as the "Magna Carta of agriculture in South Africa" (Stanwix 2012, p. 8). Morrel (1988) regards the promulgation of the 1937 Act as marking the breakdown of the maize and gold alliance since (progressive) farmers no longer required the mines to ensure their success. This Act followed on the back of a growing divide between the mines and the progressive farmer group who increasingly cast their lot with that of the smaller farmers (Morrel, 1988). This manifested itself in the growing prominence of the farmer cooperative movement (cooperative societies that facilitated the collective marketing of maize, of which membership grew to 86,700 by the mid-1930s, Department of Agriculture, 1934, p. 478).

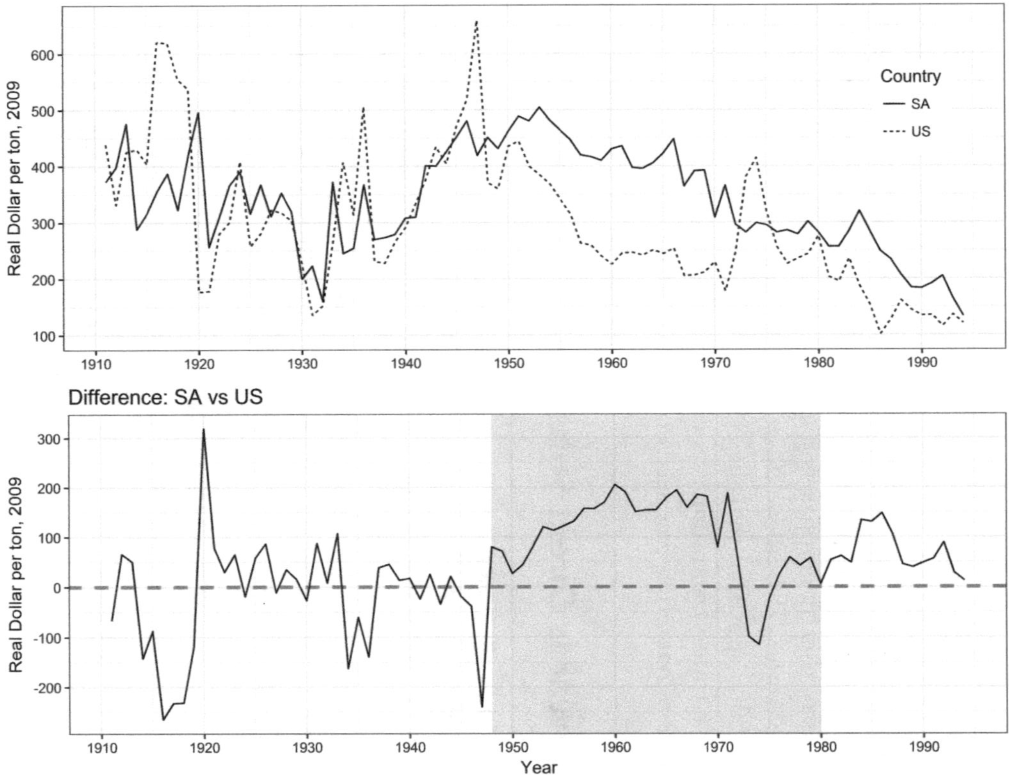

Fig. 7.3 Real maize prices: South Africa vs USA. Source: South African Data: price data compiled by Liebenberg (2012); deflated by the South African Reserve Bank 2009 GDP deflator and exchange adjusted with average 2009 South African exchange rate as published by The World Bank Databank (2016). US Data: USDA (2016) and deflated with the US deflator as published by Barro (2010)

Morris (1976) argues that the 1924 NP victory tipped the scales in the farmers' favour, but that the 1937 Marketing Act decoupled their success from that of the mines. Morrel (1988) does not provide a specific date for the solemnisation of the divorce of the maize and gold alliance. Such a definite separation was not possible given the State's unwillingness to "...sacrifice mining profitability for agricultural viability" (Morrel, 1988, p. 634). Davenport and Saunders (2000) also stress the importance of maintaining mining profits, specifically for the sake of white blue-collar workers who made a crucial contribution to the NP at the polls. Trapido (1978) adds to this by emphasising the importance of mining tax revenue to the state. The above therefore strengthens Davenport and Saunders' (2000) position that the NP's 1924 victory was not as important to the farming community as has often been argued, especially if viewed from a marketing perspective.

7 Towards Direct Subsidies

Stanwix (2012, p. 1) describes South Africa's agricultural history as a "marathon of government intervention". Built around the cornerstone provided by the 1937 Marketing Act, South African agricultural policy transitioned into its second phase after WWII. Various policy instruments set the scene for the almost total segregation of agriculture and for a comprehensive system of support measures to white farmers. Between 1910 and 1935, 87 Acts were passed in the Union Parliament rendering permanent assistance to farmers (Minnaar, 1990). State support to white farmers also came in the form of disaster relief, the construction of irrigation infrastructure, water subsidies, soil conservation, research, consumer price subsidies and soft interest rates.

Table 7.2 provides an overview of the various leases and purchases granted to white farmers in 1916 (Union of South Africa, 1916). Between 1910 and 1936, an average of about 700 farmers were settled per year and supported by substantial state subsidies. Loans were also made to help white farmers obtain working capital and farming requisites. One result of this period of strong government support was the growth of the number of white farms from 81,432 in 1921 to a peak of 119,556 in 1952.

Figure 7.4 shows changes in the different forms of state support to farmers over the period 1910 to 1994.[2] It is clear from both the first and second panel that the agricultural sector enjoyed limited support prior to 1924, with expenditure on the sector averaging close to 2.5 per cent of total public outlay.

The early growth in non-subsidy and research spending (the dotted line of the first panel of Fig. 7.4) can be explained by the establishment of the Land and Agricultural Development Bank (or "Land Bank") in 1912.[3] The Bank was not created with a commercial aim, but rather to use public funds to promote agriculture, *inter alia* by making capital available to white farmers at below-market rates (Bertelsmann et al., 2008, p. 645). As the NP came to power in 1924, subsidy and assistance spending increased for the first time in 10 years, from zero to R24 million (in 2005 values).

Table 7.2 Allotment of agricultural holdings during 1916

	No. of holdings	No. of settlers	Area (hectares)	Amount (£)	Rent (£)
Land Settlement Act, 1912	141	210	168,636	110,053	–
Crown Land Disposal Ordinance (Transvaal)	123	134	90,557	58,215	–
Crown Land Disposal Ordinance 1903 (Transvaal)	26	26	21,414	10,654	–
Act 15 of 1887 (Cape): Sales	12	13	4,356	993	–
Act 26 of 1891 (Cape): Leases	24	25	19,291	–	523
Act 26 of 1891 (Cape): Sales	2	1	7,621	395	–
Natal Proclamation	36	35	28,711	13,026	53
Irrigation Settlement Act 31 of 1909	22	22	120	3,353	–
Act 13 of 1908 (OFS): Leases	3	7	2,085	–	145
Total Land Alienated	389	473	322,791	196,689	721

Source: Union of South Africa (1916).

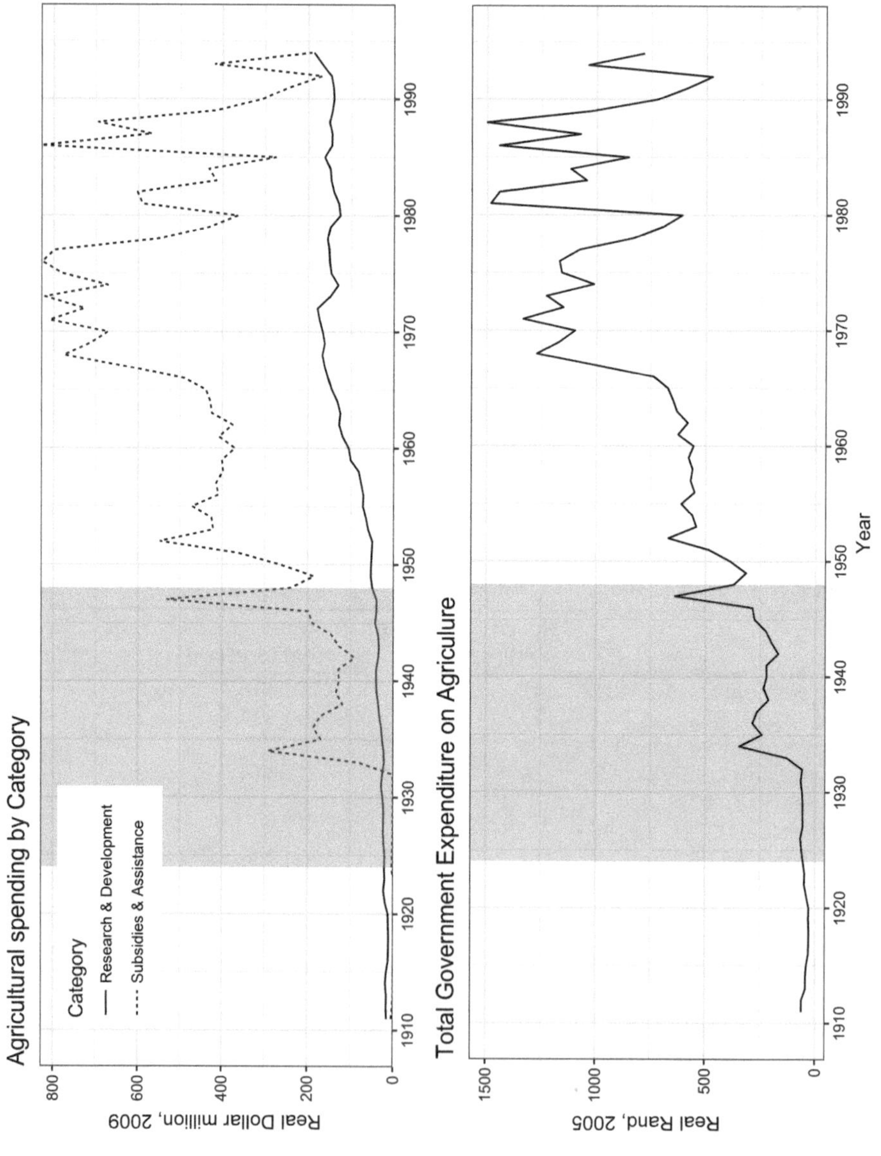

Fig. 7.4 Government expenditure on agriculture. Source: Liebenberg (2012)

The public expenditure share of the agricultural sector shows a clear albeit short-term uptick in 1924 following the election victory of the NP in that year. This provides credence to Morrel's (1988) hypothesis that it marked the start of the disintegration of the maize and gold alliance with the scales tipping in favour of farmers in general, following the growing disenchantment of the select group of large-scale progressive farmers with the mines.

Public support of the agricultural sector only took off in earnest with the Great Depression and the accompanying drought when its public expenditure share reached an all-time high of close to 20 per cent. Droughts played a significant role in the level of State support at different times. Unsurprisingly, in response to the Great Depression and a severe drought that lasted three years, Hertzog's government increased State support to agriculture immensely from 1929 onwards, as shown in Fig. 7.4., assistance and subsidy spending increasing 72-fold between 1932 and 1933. In the following year, subsidies more than trebled from R504 million to R1836 million (2005 values). Subsidy and assistance spending on the sector declined immediately thereafter but remained at historically high levels throughout the 1930s and 40s.

8 Post-1948 Support Consolidation and Eventual Reversal

Built around the cornerstone provided by the 1937 Marketing Act, South African agricultural policy transitioned into its third phase after WWII. The sector, or at least the white farmers, enjoyed far higher levels of direct and indirect support until around 1983 (see Fig. 7.4). Examples of direct support measures include disaster relief, the construction of irrigation infrastructure, water subsidies, soil conservation, research, consumer price subsidies and soft interest rates. Indirect measures took the form of greater control over the marketing of agricultural commodities through the Marketing Act of 1968 (Van Zyl, Fényes, & Vink 1992; Vink & Kirsten, 2003). On the other hand, black maize famers were doubly affected by these marketing measures since they were excluded from access to urban markets, to the extent that they were forced to sell via a white farmer when they had a surplus, while most (95 per cent) small-scale producers had to buy maize at a premium since they were not self-sufficient in production (Van Zyl & Coetzee, 1990). The introduction of the interest rate subsidy in conjunction with the ability to write off capital purchases in the year of acquisition also contributed to the rapid adoption of combine harvesters during the 1960s and 1970s, which resulted in significant productivity increases but at the expense of employment (see e.g. De Klerk 1984; Van Zyl, Vink, & Fenyes 1987).

These measures stayed in place until the 1980s, after which agricultural policy was gradually restructured towards lower subsidies, market-related interest rates and the deregulation of controlled marketing schemes (Kirsten, Edwards, & Vink, 2009; Van Zyl, Fényes & Vink, 1992). This process was hastened by the split in the NP in 1983 that saw the farmers siding with the breakaway Conservative Party, rendering them vulnerable to increased subordination by corporate agribusiness and their "own" farmer cooperatives (Bernstein, 2004). This process was only completed by the late 1990s and resulted in substantial efficiency gains through the removal of marginal land from production and greater access to international markets (Vink & Kirsten, 2000). Having stalled at high levels of support for an extended period these measures could not generate sufficient momentum for the completion of the structural transformation of the economy, which serves as a possible explanation for Binswanger-Mkhize's (2014) conclusion that South Africa offers an example of a failed transformation.

9 Discussion and Conclusion

At first glance the structural transformation of the South African economy during the late nineteenth to mid-twentieth century seems to fit the textbook example: farming in the South African interior initially faced numerous challenges in the absence of sizable markets, transport networks and sufficient labour supply. This status quo was disrupted by the discovery of diamonds and gold, which kick-started commercial farming through increased productivity and eventually an expansion to food exports. This resulted in substantial gains for some farmers, but the mining industry was initially effective in "squeezing" the broader sector through suppressing maize prices, given weak international integration and competitiveness. This, together with growing competition for labour and land between white and black farmers on the one hand and white farmers and the mines on the other, gave rise to growing tension between maize and gold. White farmers could now use their increased political power to secure the transition to the "second phase" of the structural transformation as increased product market intervention and direct subsidies improved their profitability.

However, the South African case also illustrates several important divergences from the standard framework, particularly in the complexity of stakeholder interactions and resource flows. Shortly after the discovery of gold on the Witwatersrand a strategic alliance developed between the gold mines and a group of larger "progressive" maize farmers. This followed from their mutual interest in the maize market and the securing of black labour. However, this relationship showed a gradual deterioration over time because of the depression of maize prices by the mines, thereby forcing the "progressive" farmers to increasingly cast their lot with that of their smaller compatriots. Eventually this broader white farmer grouping managed to gain control of the State with the support of blue-collar mineworkers, thereby gaining direct support for themselves and product price support through the centrally controlled marketing of most agricultural products. These farmers also applied the State machinery to help stem competition from black famers by increasing control over their access to land and to produce markets. South African agriculture enjoyed high levels of direct and indirect support until the 1980s, but these lasted only until the early 1980s.

Notes

1. The market competition between black and white farmers and the land challenges faced by black farmers have received relatively little attention within the context of the maize and gold debate, so this will be expanded upon in Sect. 4.

2. Prior to 1910, agricultural policy was managed by each of the four provinces separately.
3. Still in existence today, the institution is now governed by the Land and Agricultural Development Bank Act 15 of 2002, with land redistribution, food security and agricultural growth as its primary objectives.

References

Allen, R. C. (1996). *Farm to Factory: A Reinterpretation of the Soviet Industrial Revolution*. Princeton: Princeton University Press.

Barrett, C. B., Carter, M. R., & Timmer, C. P. (2010). A Century-Long Perspective on Agricultural Development. *American Journal of Agricultural Economics, 92*(2), 447–468.

Beinart, W. (1982). *The Political Economy of Pondoland, 1860–1930*. Cambridge: Cambridge University Press.

Bernstein, H. (2004). The Boys from Bothaville, or the Rise and Fall of King Maize: A South African Story. *Journal of Agrarian Change, 4*(4), 492–508.

Bertelsmann, E., Evans, R. G., Harris, A., Kelly-Louw, M., Loubser, A., Roetstoff, M., Smith, A. D., & Stander, L. (2008). *Mars: The Law of Insolvency in South Africa*. Claremont, CA: Juta.

Binswanger-Mkhize, H. P. (2014). *Three forms of Structural Transformation: Classic, Stunted and Failed*. Institute of Rural Management Anand (IRMA): Gujarat.

Bosman, G. J., & Osborn, I. B. (1924). *The Maize Industry of South Africa*. March: The SUN and Agriculutural Journal of South Africa.

Brits, R. N. (1969). The Marketing of South African Maize. *South African Journal of Economics, 37*(3), 198–218.

Bundy, C. (1972). The Emergence and Decline of a South African Peasantry. *African Affairs, 71*(285), 369–388.

Chenery, H., & Syrquin, M. (1975). *Patterns of Development, 1950–1970*. Oxford: Oxford University Press.

Clark, C. (1940). *The Conditions of Economic Progress*. New York: Macmillan.

Davenport, T. R. H. (1987). Can Sacred Cows be Culled? A Historical Review of Land Policy in South Africa with Some Questions About the Future. *Development Southern Africa, 4*(3), 388–400.

Davenport, T., & Saunders, C. (2000). *South Africa: A Modern History* (5th ed.). London: Palgrave Macmillan.

Department of Agriculture. (1926). *Annual Report*. Pretoria: Union of South Africa.

Department of Agriculture. (1934). *Annual Report*. Pretoria: Union of South Africa.

Domar, E. (1970). The Causes of Slavery or Serfdom: A Hypothesis. *The Journal of Economic History, 30*(1), 18–32.

Hendricks, F. (1990). *The Pillars of Apartheid: Land Tenure, Rural Planning and the Chieftaincy*. Uppsala: Acta Universitatis Upsaliensis, Studia Sociologica Upsaliensia.

Johnston, B. F., & Mellor, J. W. (1961). The Role of Agriculture in Economic Development. *The American Economic Review, 51*(4), 566–593.

Keegan, T. (1981). *The Transformation of Agrarian Society and Economy in Industrializing South Africa: The Orange Free State Grain Belt in the Early Twentieth Century*. London: University of London.

Keegan, T. (1986). *Rural Transformations in Industrialising South Africa: The Southern Highveld to 1914*. Johannesburg: Ravan Press.

Kirsten, J., Edwards, L., & Vink, N. (2009). South Africa. In K. Anderson & W. A. Masters (Eds.), *Distortions to Agricultural Incentives in Africa* (pp. 147–174). Washington, DC: World Bank Publications.

De Klerk, M. (1984). Seasons That Will Never Return: The Impact of Farm Mechanization on Employment, Incomes and Population Distribution in the Western Transvaal. *Journal of Southern African Studies, 11*(1), 84–105.

Kuznets, S. S. (1966). *Modern Economic Growth: Rate, Structure, and Spread*. New York: Yale University Press.

Lacey, M. (1982). *Working for Boroko: The Origins of a Coercive Labour System in Southern Africa*. Johannesburg: Ravan Press.

Lenta, G. (1983). Reserved Land in South Africa: A Century of Declining Productivity. *Perspectives in Economic History, 2*, 13–24.

Lewis, W. (1954). Economic Development with Unlimited Supplies of Labour. *The Manchester School, 22*(2), 139–191.

Lindert, P. H. (1991). Historical Patterns of Agricultural Policy. In P. C. Timmer (Ed.), *Agriculture and the State: Growth, Employment and Poverty in Developing Countries* (pp. 29–83). Ithaca: Cornell University Press.

Losch, B., Freguin-Gresh, S., & White, E. (2011). *Rural Transformation and Late Developing Countries in a Globalizing World*. The World Bank: Washington, DC.

Marcus, T. (1989). *Modernising Super-Exploitation*. London: Zed Books.

Matsetela, T. (1981). *Rural Change Among Africans in the Ventersdorp District of 1910–1935: A Case Study of Bakwena-ba-ga-Mogopa*. London: University of London.

Minnaar, A. (1990). The Effects of the Great Depression (1929–1934) on South African White Agriculture. *South African Journal of Economic History, 5*(2), 83–108.

Morrell, R. (1986). Competition and Cooperation in Middelburg, 1900–1930. In *Putting a Plough to the Ground* (pp. 373–419). Braamfontein: Ravan Press.

Morrel, R. (1988). The Disintegration of the Gold and Maize Alliance in South Africa in the 1920s. *The International Journal of African Historical Studies, 21*(4), 619–635.

Morris, M. (1976). Apartheid, Agriculture and the State: The Farm Labour Question. In *SALDRU Farm Labour Conference*. Cape Town: Southern Africa Labour and Development Research Unit (SALDRU).

Nattrass, N., & Seekings, J. (2010). *The Economy and Poverty in the Twentieth Century in South Africa* (Vol. 276). Cape Town: Centre for Social Science Research.

Nieboer, H. J. (1900). *Slavery as an Industrial System: Ethnological Researches*. The Hague: Martinus Nijhoff.

Plaatje, S. (1987). *Native Life in South Africa*. London: Longman.

Ross, R. (1986). The Origins of Capitalist Agriculture in the Cape Colony. In W. Beinart, P. Delius, & S. Trapido (Eds.), *Putting a plough to the ground*. Braamfontein: Ravan Press.

Saunders, A. R. (1930). *Maize in South Africa*. Pretoria: Central News Agency South Africa.

Simkins, C. (1984). What has been Happening to Income Distribution and Poverty in the Homelands. *Development Southern Africa, 1*(2), 42–152.

De Swardt, S. J. J. (1983). Agricultural Marketing Problems in the Nineteen Thirties. *South African Journal of Economics, 51*(1), 1–18.

Syrquin, M. (2006). Structural Transformation. In D. Clark (Ed.), *The Elgar Companion to Development Studies* (pp. 601–606). Massachusetts: Edward Elgar Publishing Limited.

Thompson, R. J., & Nicholls, B. M. (1993). The Glen Grey Act: Forgotten Dimensions in an Old Theme. *South African Journal of Economic History, 8*(2), 58–70.

Timmer, C. P. (1988). The Agricultural Transformation. In V. I. H. Chenery & T. N. Srinivasan (Eds.), *Handbook of Development Economics*. Amsterdam: Elsevier Science Publishers.

Timmer, C. P. (2007). *The Structural Transformation and the Changing Role of Agriculture in Economic Development: Empirics and Implications*. Washington DC: American Enterprise Institute.

Trapido, S. (1971). South Africa in a Comparative Study of Industrialization. *The Journal of Development Studies, 7*(3), 309–320.

Trapido, S. (1978). Landlord and Tenant in a Colonial Economy: The Transvaal 1880–1910. *Journal of Southern African Studies, 5*(1), 26–58.

Van Zyl, J., & Coetzee, G. (1990). Food Security and Structural Adjustment: Empirical Evidence on the Food Price Dilemma in Southern Africa. *Development Southern Africa, 7*(1), 105–116.

Van Zyl, J., Fényes, T. I., & Vink, N. (1992). Effects of the Farmer Support Programme and Changes in Marketing. *Journal of Agricultural Economics, 43*(3), 466–476.

Van Zyl, J., Vink, N., & Fenyes, T. I. (1987). Labour-Related Structural Trends in South African Maize Production. *Agricultural Economics, 1*, 241–258.

Vink, N., & Kirsten, J. (2000). *Deregulation of Agricultural Marketing in South Africa*. Sandton: Development Bank of Southern Africa.

Vink, N., & Kirsten, J. (2003). Policy Successes and Policy Failures in Agriculture and Land Reform in South Africa The 1990s. *South African Journal of Economic History, 18*(1), 96–117.

Willan, B. (1984). *Sol Plaatje: A biography*. Johannesburg: Ravan Press.

Wilson, F. (1971). Farming, 1866–1966. In M. Wilson & L. Thompson (Eds.), *Oxford History of South Africa* (pp. 104–171). Oxford: Oxford University Press.

Wolpe, H. (1972). Capitalism and Cheap Labour-Power in South Africa: From Segregation to Apartheid. *Economy and Society, 4*(1), 425–456.

Jan C. Greyling is a lecturer in the Department of Agricultural Economics at Stellenbosch University. His research interests include: long-term agricultural development; agricultural employment and labour; technological and structural change; and land reform.

Nick Vink is Chair of the Department of Agricultural Economics at Stellenbosch University. He has served as President of the South African and the African Agricultural Economics Associations and is currently the President-elect of the International Association of Agricultural Economists. His main research interests include: agricultural development on the African continent; land reform and structural change in South African agriculture; agricultural policy and wine economics.

Emily van der Merwe is a graduate student in the Department of Economics at Stellenbosch University. Her research interests include: climate change and resource adaptation; African economic history; poverty, inequality and sustainable development in rural areas; policy and the political economy of natural resource management.

Part III

Asia

8

The Agriculture–Macroeconomy Growth Link in India, Pakistan, and Bangladesh: 1900–2000

Takashi Kurosaki

1 Introduction

To achieve sustainable agricultural development with due considerations for the interaction between population, resources, and environment, a long-term historical viewpoint focusing on economic institutions is necessary. Development economists as well as comparative historians have analysed the long-term effect of economic institutions on economic performance (e.g. Acemoglu & Robinson, 2012). When the economy

The author is grateful to Ann Booth, Sandra Kuntz-Ficker, Masaki Nakabayashi, Tetsuji Okazaki, Vicente Pinilla, Tomoko Shiroyama, Kaoru Sugihara, Masayuki Tanimoto, P.K. Viswanatan, Henry Wilelbald, and participants at the 17th World Economic History Congress, the 2016 TNAU Conference "Toward Sustainable Development of India and South Asia: Population, Resources, and Environment," and the Economic History Seminar at the University of Tokyo, for their useful comments on the earlier version of this chapter. Funding from a JSPS Grant-in-Aid for Scientific Research-S (22223003) is gratefully acknowledged.

T. Kurosaki (✉)
Hitotsubashi University, Tokyo, Japan

V. Pinilla, H. Willebald (eds.), *Agricultural Development in the World Periphery*, Palgrave Studies in Economic History, https://doi.org/10.1007/978-3-319-66020-2_8

under study has experienced colonisation by global powers, such effect is often examined in the context of colonial legacies. As shown by Banerjee and Iyer (2005), for an example of a negative colonial legacy, the regions inside India where proprietary rights in land were given to large landlords had significantly lower productivity in the post-independence period.

The Indian subcontinent is an interesting place for such an analysis, as united Pakistan (today's Pakistan and Bangladesh) was partitioned out from India in August 1947, suddenly and without any considerations for economic networks (Sadullah, Mujahid, & Ahmad, 1993). The complete absence of economic considerations such as market or irrigation or electricity networks at the time of Partition provides us with a unique opportunity to investigate the impact of political regime changes on economic performance using a framework of natural experiments (Kurosaki, 2015).

With this big picture in mind, this study attempts to deepen our understanding on long-term growth performance of India (such as the work by Sivasubramonian, 2000) with its focus on agriculture and its growth linkage with non-agriculture. The case of India is of great interest from a different aspect as well, as India has recently been emerging as a fast-growing tiger economy. This makes it more interesting to understand the long-term performance of Indian economy in comparative perspectives. In the recent literature, such a comparison is to be found, for example, between India and China in Bosworth and Collins (2008), and between India and the UK in Broadberry and Gupta (2010).

However, there are only a few studies with due attention paid to the regional diversity within the Indian subcontinent, if we restrict the survey to those studies analysing long-term development at the semi-macro level. As an exceptional work, Caruana-Galizia (2013) estimated regional GDP for the period 1875–1911, showing convergence across Indian regions. The convergence found by Caruana-Galizia (2013) is consistent with the economic integration caused by railroads, as demonstrated by Donaldson (2010). At the same time, it seems that there is no quantitative study on sectoral linkages at the regional level within the Indian subcontinent. Especially, peripheral regions within the Indian subcontinent have not been analysed in detail. Such information would give us insights into the long-term development of markets and the impacts of institutions in the subcontinent.

Research on the sectoral growth linkages between agriculture and non-agriculture has seen a recent rise in development economics, because non-farm rural economy is growing in developing countries (Christiaensen, Demery, & Kuhl, 2011; Haggblade, Hazell, & Dorosh, 2007). Agricultural growth contributes to poverty reduction not only through its direct impact on the economy but also through its indirect route of enhancing non-agricultural growth. Based on this idea, Christiaensen et al. (2011) analysed cross-country panel data and showed that the indirect route was particularly strong among poorest countries. Such analysis, however, has rarely been applied to historical data.

To fill in these research gaps in the literature, this study investigates the agriculture–macroeconomy growth link in India, Pakistan, and Bangladesh in the twentieth century. Areas currently in Pakistan and Bangladesh were a typical periphery in the second half of the nineteenth century when the whole subcontinent came under British rule. For this reason, quantitative historical work on these regions during the colonial era is worth attempting. The use of unusually long-term data that correspond to the current borders for the period c.1900–2000 distinguishes this study from those already existing. A completely new dataset is presented for the pre-1947 period, which divides the estimates for the undivided India provided by Sivasubramonian (2000) into components corresponding to the three regions, viz. India, Pakistan, and Bangladesh, with the help of information compiled by Kurosaki (2011) and Kurosaki (2015). In the quantitative analysis of this chapter, three measures of the agriculture–macroeconomy linkage are examined: (1) agricultural share in GDP; (2) correlation of agricultural and non-agricultural growth; and (3) decomposition of GDP growth into direct contribution of agriculture, its indirect contribution, and autonomous contribution of non-agriculture.[1] Although it is true that the nation-state of Pakistan did not exist before 1947 and the nation-state of Bangladesh did not exist before 1971, investigating agricultural roles for "fictitious" Pakistan before 1947 and "fictitious" Bangladesh before 1971 would give us valuable insights, since farming is carried out on land, which is immovable by definition, and many economic activities in non-agriculture are linked with agriculture.

The rest of the chapter is organised as follows. The next section (2) describes the data used in this study. Section 3 explains the analytical framework. Section 4 presents empirical results, followed by discussion on the colonial period. Section 5 concludes the chapter.

2 Data

2.1 Data Coverage

Agriculture in this chapter refers to the sum of crops and livestock subsectors within the primary sector. The fishing and forestry subsectors are not included, but treated as non-agriculture.[2] Seven time-series variables are compiled for each of the areas currently in India, Pakistan, and Bangladesh (country subscript k and year subscript t): Population (pop_{kt}), GDP and its components in nominal terms (gdp_n_{kt}, $agri\_n_{kt}$ and $nonag\_n_{kt}$), and GDP and its components in real terms (index) (gdp_r_{kt}, $agri\_r_{kt}$, and $nonag\_r_{kt}$). The pre-1947 deflators are borrowed from Sivasubramonian (2000) with regional adjustments and the post-1947 deflators are taken from the government statistics. The year is in fiscal year (July 1 to June 30 [Pakistan and Bangladesh] or April 1 to March 31 [India]).[3] The idea is to compile a balanced panel dataset of 7 variables × 3 countries × 101 years (from 1900/1901 to 2000/2001).

We restrict our attention to this period as data availability is highly limited during the nineteenth century. Furthermore, territorial redefinitions occurred frequently during the nineteenth century, which makes it almost impossible to estimate statistics corresponding to areas currently in India, Pakistan, and Bangladesh out of the available statistics, which are, moreover, reported in different formats. The formats were dependent on whether the region was a British Province of India or a Princely State. Our starting year of 1900/1901 implies, however, that we cannot examine the agriculture–macroeconomy linkage during the period when the first wave of textile-based industrialisation occurred in India. The first railroad arrived in 1853, followed by the first cotton textile mill in Bombay in 1854 and the first jute mill in Calcutta in 1855. Our analysis begins when India had already achieved some extent of textile-based industrialisation. This point needs to be taken care of when we interpret the empirical results.

The estimates for population, pop_{kt}, are based on decade-wise estimates taken from government sources and interpolated exponentially (Kurosaki, 2011). The original source of information of these government estimates is population censuses conducted every 10 years.

2.2 Estimating the Post-1947 Series

Six GDP figures for independent India are basically taken from estimates by the Government of India. Regarding the period 1950/1951–2000/2001, the latest series, which is re-estimated based on the 2004/2005 base-year methodology (Government of India, 2011), is adopted without any revision. GDP estimates for 1947/1948, 1948/1949, and 1949/1950 are taken from Sivasubramonian (2000) and connected with the government estimates beginning in 1950/1951 using fixed adjustment factors.

For Pakistan and Bangladesh since independence, the governments' statistical bureaus have not prepared the back series after they changed the base year and improved the GDP estimation procedure. Therefore, we cannot obtain official long-term statistics even for its post-independence period (post 1949/1950 for Pakistan and post 1972/1973 for Bangladesh). Therefore, we compiled the long-term nominal series by using the latest figures appended by earlier series directly. We compiled the long-term real series by using the latest figures appended by earlier series indirectly through using the adjustment factors for two different base years calculated from observations overlapping the two different base-year series. The data sources are the Government of Pakistan (various issues), Government of Pakistan (2000), Government of Bangladesh (various issues), and Government of Bangladesh (1993).

For Bangladesh areas during the united Pakistan period (the East Pakistan era), there is no official GDP estimate. As the Government of Pakistan estimated the real GDP series for the period 1949/1950–1970/1971 corresponding to West Pakistan, we compiled the long-term real series for Bangladesh (East Pakistan) by subtraction. The long-term nominal series for Bangladesh (East Pakistan) was estimated from the nominal series for united Pakistan using the East's share in real terms and benchmark adjustment factors. This portion of the dataset is thus highly preliminary but the regional disparity shown in our estimates is consistent with the one shown by Papanek (1967).

From these sources, we compiled the post-Partition dataset based on official data with several gaps. For Pakistan, there are no data for 1947/1948 and 1948/1949. For Bangladesh, there are no data for 1947/1948, 1948/1949, and 1971/1972. We filled in the missing values by combining our estimates for the crop sub-sector value-added and interpolated estimates for the rest of the economy. These estimates are thus highly preliminary.

2.3 Estimating the Pre-1947 Series

Before August 1947, the sum of areas currently in India, Pakistan, and Bangladesh formed the undivided India, for which Sivasubramonian (2000) presented his GDP estimates. Sivasubramonian's estimates are regarded as the best among the existing ones (Broadberry & Gupta, 2010; Caruana-Galizia, 2013). The task of this study is to divide the six GDP series for undivided India, estimated by Sivasubramonian (2000), into components attributable to areas currently in India, Pakistan, and Bangladesh.

Let Y_t be either GDP or agricultural value-added or non-agricultural value-added in year t for undivided India and Y_{kt} be its regional components (k = India, Pakistan, and Bangladesh). As identity, the total can be decomposed as

$$Y_t = \Sigma_k Y_{kt} = \Sigma_k \alpha_{kt} s_{kt} Y_t, \tag{8.1}$$

where $\alpha_{kt} = (Y_{kt}/L_{kt})/(Y_t/L_t)$, which shows region k's relative productivity in comparison to the overall average, and $s_{kt} = L_{kt}/L_t$, which is region k's share in the production factor L. In the estimation, we adopt labour force (number of workers engaged in agriculture/non-agriculture) as the production factor, as was done by Geary and Stark (2002) and Caruana-Galizia (2013). For the Indian subcontinent during the colonial period, we have rich information on s_{kt}, regional distribution of labour force distinguished by sectors. We used figures based on population census data interpolated for non-census years (Kurosaki, 2011).

To estimate the key parameter α_{kt}, Geary and Stark (2002) proposed a short-cut method using the information contained in relative wages. This approximation is valid only when relative wages across regions accurately reflect relative productivity differentials across regions. This assumption may not hold true in colonial India.

We, therefore, directly estimated α_{kt} for each of k in all t for the crops subsector using the database in Kurosaki (2011). From the database, three share series can be calculated, differentiated by the base year for real price aggregation. In this chapter, the 1938/1939 base year is employed, although the results were highly similar when alternative base years were used. By applying $\alpha_{kt}s_{kt}$ to Sivasubramonian's (2000) estimates for "Agriculture" (his term for the crops subsector), we obtained the three series of Y_{kt} (k = India, Pakistan, and Bangladesh) regarding the crops subsector.

Regarding the livestock subsector, as most farmers in the Indian subcontinent produce crops and livestock products in the same farm (in other words, specialised livestock producers are exceptional), we assume that α_{kt} for the livestock subsector is a fixed multiple of α_{kt} for the crops subsector. The multiplication adjustment parameter was calculated using the data in the earliest five years after Partition. By combining the value-added from the crops subsector and the livestock subsector thus compiled, we obtained the complete time series for agricultural value-added for the three regions.

Regarding the rest (i.e., non-agricultural sector), we separately estimated value-added from non-agricultural primary sector, the secondary sector ("construction", "manufacturing" [manufacturing conducted in registered factories], and "small-scale and cottage industries" [manufacturing in non-registered factories and households]), and the tertiary sector (services). As information is highly limited, we adopted a version of the short-cut method proposed by Geary and Stark (2002). More concretely, for each of these three series, we estimated α_{kt} in three benchmark years of 1900, 1911 (adapted from Caruana-Galizia, 2013), and 1946, and then interpolated the parameter. The benchmark parameters were multiplied by fixed numbers so that the terminal year of 1946 smoothly connected with the earliest five years after Partition. As shown in this construction, the estimates for the pre-1947 non-agricultural value-added series are highly preliminary.

2.4 Long-Term Series Compiled

Seven time-series variables (population, real and nominal GDP, real and nominal value-added from agriculture, and real and nominal value-added from non-agriculture) were thus compiled for each of the areas currently in India, Pakistan, and Bangladesh, for the period from 1900/1901 to 2000/2001.[4] The dataset is available from the author on request.

The nominal series until 1946/1947 can be linked directly with the post-1947 nominal series. On the other hand, the real series cannot be linked directly as they are based on different base years. To examine the movement of the real series, the whole time series of real GDP was tentatively linked using fixed factors to express them in 1948/1949 prices.[5] The fixed prices of 1948/1949 were used by Sivasubramonian (2000) to link his estimates for undivided India and post-1947 statistics for India.

The results are shown in Fig. 8.1. The per-capita GDP in the first decade of the twentieth century was highest in Bangladesh and lowest in Pakistan. Just before Partition, the order was reversed as Pakistan areas experienced a sustained growth led by irrigated agriculture during the first half of the twentieth century, while Bangladesh areas experienced a continuous decline in per-capita GDP. After Partition, Pakistan grew more rapidly than India and Bangladesh, especially during the 1960s and 1970s, enjoying the highest per-capita GDP in the 1980s. After stagnation during the East Pakistan era and the period immediately after independence, the Bangladeshi economy began to grow rapidly in the 1990s. At the end of the twentieth century, per-capita GDP of India and Pakistan were similar, ahead of Bangladesh's by a big margin.[6]

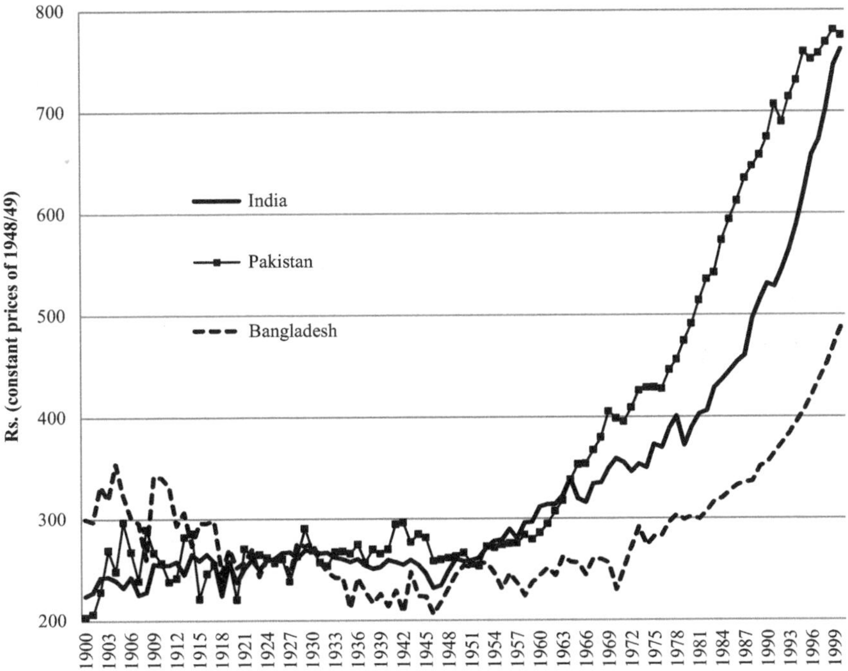

Fig. 8.1 Per-capita GDP (constant prices) in the long-run

3 Measures to Analyse the Agriculture–Macroeconomy Linkage

Three descriptive measures for the agriculture–macroeconomy linkage are calculated from the data thus compiled. As the focus of this chapter is on the linkage in the real economy, we mainly use time series in real terms for the empirical analysis and the nominal series for robustness check. First, s_{kt}, the share of agricultural output in GDP in real terms, is calculated as a time series. It is defined as

$$s_{kt} = agri\_r_{kt} / gdp\_r_{kt}, \tag{8.2}$$

for $k = I$ (India), P (Pakistan), and B (Bangladesh). As s_{kt} becomes bigger, agriculture's presence in the macroeconomy becomes larger.[7]

The second measure attempts to capture the inter-sectoral linkage. By definition, gdp_r_{kt} is the sum of $agri\_r_{kt}$ and $nonag\_r_{kt}$, which is value-added from non-agriculture (including fishery and forestry in the primary sector, the whole secondary sector, and the whole tertiary sector). In an agricultural economy, a growth in the agricultural sector is likely to accelerate the growth in the non-agricultural sector through the forward linkage in an input-output table. Based on this idea, time series regression is run

$$g\_nonag_{kt} = b_{k0} + b_{k1} g\_agrig_{kt} + u_{kt}, \tag{8.3}$$

where $g\_agri_{kt} = (agri\_r_{kt} - agri\_r_{k,\,t-1})/agri\_r_{k,\,t-1}$, and $g\_nonag_{kt} = (nonag\_r_{kt} - nonag\_r_{k,\,t-1})/nonag\_r_{k,\,t-1}$. The empirical model can be understood as a simplified version used by Christiaensen et al. (2011). Unlike their specification, we cannot include other covariate factors due to the lack of detailed information before 1947, and we do not use lags due to the low degrees of freedom.

The Ordinary Least Squares (OLS) estimate of parameter b_{k1} is meant to capture the strength of spillover effects from agriculture to non-agriculture. Let us call b_{k1} the linkage parameter. Econometrically, however, it only shows the strength of correlation between agricultural and non-agricultural growth. It increases when the forward linkage in an input-output table from agriculture to non-agriculture becomes stronger but it also increases when the backward linkage in the opposite direction becomes stronger. Furthermore, an increase in agricultural income shifts up the demand curve for non-agricultural products, contributing to the non-agricultural growth (income effect). Rigorously controlling for the backward linkage and the income effect for the clean identification of the forward linkage effect is left for further study. Considering the fact that very little manufacturing input was used in agricultural production during the colonial period, the backward linkage factor is likely to be negligible. We thus estimate the parameter for each decade and examine its magnitude and statistical significance, as showing the strength of the forward linkage effect and the income effect mixed.

Third, if b_{k1} is significant, we can decompose the observed growth rate in GDP into three components as

$$g\_gdp\_r_{kt} = \underset{(\text{i})}{s_{kt} g\_agri_{kt}} + \underset{(\text{ii})}{(1-s_{kt}) b_{k1} g\_agri_{kt}} + \underset{(\text{iii})}{(1-s_{kt})(b_{k0}+u_{kt})}, \quad (8.4)$$

where b_{k0}, b_{k1}, and u_{kt} are replaced by its predicted values from OLS regression of Eq. (8.3). We call each of the three components as contributions to macroeconomic growth from (i) agriculture, direct, (ii) agriculture, indirect, and (iii) non-agriculture, autonomous. We calculate this decomposition for each decade, when b_{k1} is statistically significant at the 10 per cent level or lower. When b_{k1} is statistically insignificant, we set the component (ii) at zero. The sum of (i) and (ii) is one measure of how large the total contribution of agriculture to the macroeconomic growth.

4 Empirical Results

4.1 Agriculture's Share in the Macroeconomy

The agricultural share in real GDP is shown in Fig. 8.2., which shows an overall decline in all three regions throughout the twentieth century.

During the colonial period, the decline was slower in areas currently in Pakistan than in the other two. The decline occurred in areas currently in Bangladesh and India, even though per-capita GDP stagnated in areas currently in India and declined in areas currently in Bangladesh (compare Figs. 8.1 and 8.2). This pattern is unexpected because in the standard development economics textbook, a declining share of agriculture is usually associated with increasing per-capita GDP. The textbook pattern occurs when per-worker productivity is much higher in non-agriculture than in agriculture so that the economic growth is led by growing non-agriculture. During the colonial period, too, per-worker productivity in non-agriculture was indeed higher than in agriculture. However, the relative position of non-agriculture against agriculture deteriorated during the colonial period, which was completely different from the textbook

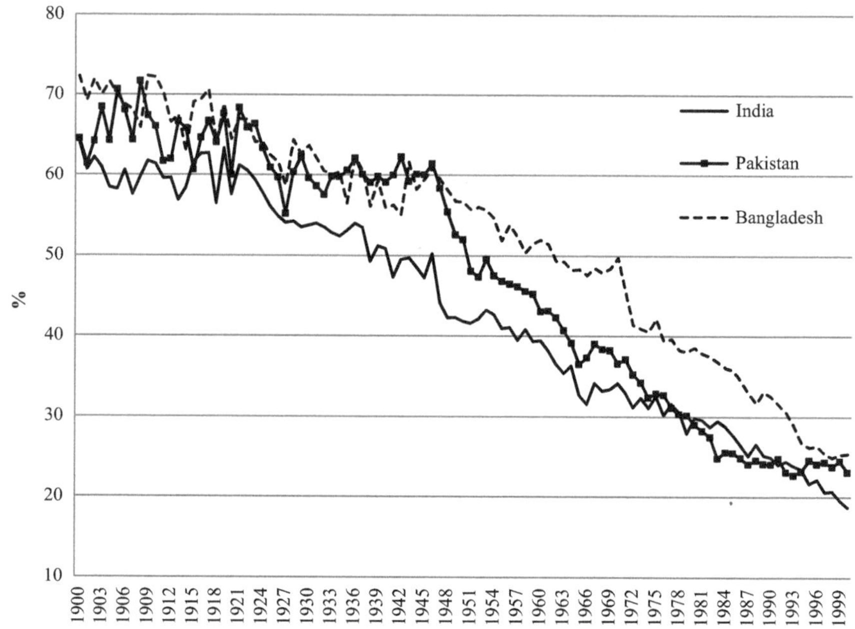

Fig. 8.2 Agricultural share in real GDP in the long-run

pattern of economic development through industrialisation. Especially in areas currently in Pakistan, per-worker productivity in agriculture increased steadily, not only in absolute terms but also in relative terms against non-agriculture. As a result, Pakistan areas during the colonial period experienced the highest growth in per-capita GDP and the slowest decline in the agricultural share in GDP. In areas currently in Bangladesh, deindustrialisation continued from the late nineteenth century, resulting in the absolute as well as relative decline of per-worker productivity during the colonial era.

After Partition, the agricultural share declined faster when the per-capita GDP grew faster, the pattern consistent with the development economics textbook. This association is the clearest for Pakistan, where a high growth together with a rapidly declining agricultural share in GDP occurred in the 1950–1960s. In all the three countries, non-agriculture grew faster than agriculture and some of the earlier spurt in non-agricultural growth was facilitated by import substitution industrialisation in India and Pakistan. The Bangladesh case was somewhat different as its manufacturing industries (first jute textile, then replaced by ready-made garments) were export-oriented from the beginning.

These results were robust when the agriculture share was re-calculated using nominal GDP (available on request from the author). As expected, more short-run fluctuations were observed due to transient price shocks if we use nominal GDP.

4.2 Agricultural Growth's Spillover to Non-agricultural Growth

Parameter estimates for b_{k1} are reported in Table 8.1. In most decades, the absolute value of parameter b_{k1} is small and statistically insignificant during the colonial period. The parameter became positive in India and Bangladesh after Partition and statistically significant in the 1970s–1980s in India and the 1950s–1960s in Bangladesh. The significant parameter b_{k1} for Bangladesh in the 1950s–1960s reflect the establishment of jute industries in East Pakistan.[8]

The parameter is negative and significant in Bangladesh in the 1990s. This is consistent with the latest development in the country, when the export-oriented, non-agriculture-based garment industry grew rapidly. As the main engine of non-agricultural growth is not based on agriculture, non-agricultural growth may be accelerated when agricultural production declines, through abundant supply of cheaper labour for the industry.

4.3 Agricultural Contribution to Macroeconomic Growth

Table 8.1 also reports decomposition results of macroeconomic growth into direct contribution of agriculture, its indirect contribution, and autonomous contribution of non-agriculture. The decomposition equation is (8.4) when the linkage parameter was statistically significant,

Table 8.1 Decomposition of real GDP growth into direct and indirect contributions of agriculture

	Annual growth rate in *Y* (%)			Linkage parameter[a]		Relative contribution[b] (%)		
	GDP	Agriculture	Non-agriculture	Parameter estimate	(standard error)	Agri-culture, direct	Agri-culture, indirect	Non-agriculture, autonomous
Areas currently in India (–1946/1947), India (1950/51–)								
1900/1901–1910/1911	1.93	1.49	2.68	0.013	(0.197)	50.0	0.0	50.0
1910/1911–1920/1921	−0.62	−1.26	0.33	−0.135	(0.111)	119.5	0.0	−19.5
1920/1921–1930/1931	2.29	1.60	3.15	−0.143	(0.278)	40.8	0.0	59.2
1930/1931–1940/1941	1.02	0.47	1.63	−0.046	(0.236)	25.2	0.0	74.8
1940/1941–1946/1947	−0.67	−0.88	−0.47	−0.734	(0.555)	66.0	0.0	34.0
1950/1951–1960/1961	3.83	3.24	4.24	0.145	(0.110)	35.5	0.0	64.5
1960/1961–1970/1971	3.63	2.20	4.46	0.088	(0.059)	24.3	0.0	75.7
1970/1971–1980/1981	3.03	1.67	3.67	0.169**	(0.068)	19.1	6.2	74.6
1980/1981–1990/1991	5.24	3.45	5.91	0.112*	(0.063)	19.9	5.2	74.9
1990/1991–2000/2001	5.55	2.68	6.35	0.058	(0.162)	12.3	0.0	87.7
Areas currently in Pakistan (–1946/1947), Pakistan (1950/1951–)								
1900/1901–1910/1911	3.90	4.14	3.46	−0.072	(0.070)	68.5	0.0	31.5
1910/1911–1920/1921	−0.67	−1.63	0.96	0.030	(0.098)	143.5	0.0	−43.5
1920/1921–1930/1931	3.08	3.01	3.17	−0.108	(0.066)	58.8	0.0	41.2
1930/1931–1940/1941	1.88	1.79	2.01	0.149	(0.205)	56.8	0.0	43.2
1940/1941–1946/1947	1.73	2.38	0.73	0.350	(0.346)	82.5	0.0	17.5
1950/1951–1960/1961	3.15	1.26	4.85	−0.017	(0.128)	22.0	0.0	78.0
1960/1961–1970/1971	6.18	4.55	7.25	−0.086	(0.303)	32.2	0.0	67.8
1970/1971–1980/1981	5.24	2.92	6.37	−0.217	(0.496)	20.9	0.0	79.1
1980/1981–1990/1991	5.83	3.97	6.51	−0.059	(0.113)	19.9	0.0	80.1
1990/1991–2000/2001	4.04	3.62	4.16	0.134	(0.076)	21.6	0.0	78.4

(*continued*)

Table 8.1 (continued)

	Annual growth rate in Y (%)			Linkage parameter[a]		Relative contribution[b] (%)		
	GDP	Agriculture	Non-agriculture	Parameter estimate	(standard error)	Agri-culture, direct	Agri-culture, indirect	Non-agriculture, autonomous
Areas currently in Bangladesh (–1946/1947), East Pakistan (1950/1951–), Bangladesh (1972/1973–)								
1900/1901–1910/1911	2.37	2.36	2.41	0.166*	(0.080)	71.8	4.6	23.6
1910/1911–1920/1921	−2.12	−3.24	0.31	−0.075	(0.104)	103.9	0.0	−3.9
1920/1921–1930/1931	1.89	1.76	2.12	−0.041	(0.125)	60.1	0.0	39.9
1930/1931–1940/1941	−1.41	−2.70	0.51	−0.037	(0.083)	112.1	0.0	−12.1
1940/1941–1946/1947	−0.53	0.87	−2.51	0.192	(0.150)	−79.4	0.0	179.4
1950/1951–1960/1961	2.11	1.24	3.26	0.180***	(0.039)	33.2	4.6	62.2
1960/1961–1970/1971	2.07	1.64	2.56	0.745**	(0.236)	40.9	28.1	31.0
1972/1973–1980/1981	3.60	2.72	4.19	0.335	(0.291)	31.4	0.0	68.6
1980/1981–1990/1991	3.76	2.07	4.70	0.040	(0.108)	21.6	0.0	78.4
1990/1991–2000/2001	4.79	2.30	5.80	−0.201***	(0.052)	16.1	−6.7	90.7

Notes: The component "Agriculture, indirect" is set at zero if the parameter is statistically insignificant. "Non-agriculture, autonomous" is calculated as the residual.

[a]Estimated by OLS using Eq. (8.3). Statistically significant at 10% (*), 5% (**), and 1% (***)

[b]Decomposition is conducted using Eq. (8.4) when the linkage parameter is statistically significant

whereas the indirect agricultural contribution is set at zero if the parameter was insignificant.

Throughout the periods in all three regions, except for the latest decades, "Agriculture, direct" was the main driver of macroeconomic growth. "Agriculture, indirect" significantly contributed to macroeconomic growth only in India in the 1970s–1980s and in Bangladesh in the 1950s–1960s.

"Non-agriculture, autonomous" became the main driver of macroeconomic growth in all three countries after the 1970s–1980s. Although agricultural share in GDP remained large during the 1970s–1980s, agricultural growth rate was much lower than non-agricultural growth rate. As a result, the contribution from "Non-agriculture, autonomous" to the GDP growth became much more substantial than that from "Agriculture, direct" in the last decades of the century. This shows that these countries reached the stage of normal economic development with the non-agricultural growth leading the macroeconomic growth.

"Non-agriculture, autonomous" contributed to the macroeconomic growth in the 1900s and the 1920s as well. These decades are known as the period of colonial industrialisation in India (Sivasubramonian, 2000; Roy, 1996). Therefore, our methodology is able to confirm the contribution of industrialisation even when it occurred under the colonial institutions. If the second half of the nineteenth century had been analysed, more contribution from "agriculture, indirect" and "non-agriculture, autonomous" could have been shown from our methodology. The nineteenth-century industrialisation in India could be compared with the Japanese experience during the same period. The current data available do not allow us to conduct these exercises. These are left for further research.

4.4 Discussion on the Results Regarding the Colonial Period

The results reported in Table 8.1 were found robust to changes in decadal classification, addition of a time trend in Eq. (8.3), and changes of base years in the calculation of relative productivity differential parameters for agriculture.

Table 8.2 Contributions of agriculture to growth in undivided India

	Annual growth rate in Y (%)			Linkage parameter		Relative contribution (%)		
	GDP	Agri-culture	Non-agri-culture	Para-meter estimate	(standard error)	Agriculture, direct	Agriculture, indirect	Non-agriculture, autonomous
Undivided India								
1900/1901–1910/1911	2.11	1.78	2.70	0.057	(0.208)	55.3	0.0	44.7
1910/1911–1920/1921	−0.81	−1.57	0.36	−0.171	(0.118)	115.7	0.0	−15.7
1920/1921–1930/1931	2.29	1.72	3.05	−0.218	(0.246)	44.3	0.0	55.7
1930/1931–1940/1941	0.84	0.22	1.55	−0.046	(0.236)	14.9	0.0	85.1
1940/1941–1946/1947	−0.46	−0.39	−0.54	−0.434	(0.790)	43.6	0.0	56.4

Notes: See Table 8.1

Table 8.3 Decomposition of real GDP growth, colonial period readjusted with a one-year lag

	Annual growth rate in Y (%)			Linkage parameter		Relative contribution (%)		
	GDP	Agri-culture	Non-agri-culture	Parameter estimate	(standard error)	Agriculture, direct	Agriculture, indirect	Non-agriculture, autonomous
Areas currently in India (–1946/1947)								
1900/1901–1910/1911	1.93	1.49	2.68	0.172	(0.138)	50.0	0.0	50.0
1910/1911–1920/1921	−0.62	−1.26	0.33	0.056	(0.130)	119.5	0.0	−19.5
1920/1921–1930/1931	2.29	1.60	3.15	0.173	(0.174)	40.8	0.0	59.2
1930/1931–1940/1941	1.02	0.47	1.63	0.173	(0.305)	25.2	0.0	74.8
1940/1941–1946/1947	−0.67	−0.88	−0.47	0.976*	(0.390)	66.0	62.2	−28.2
Areas currently in Pakistan (–1946/1947)								
1900/1901–1910/1911	3.90	4.14	3.46	0.095*	(0.047)	68.5	3.6	27.9
1910/1911–1920/1921	−0.67	−1.63	0.96	0.060	(0.107)	143.5	0.0	−43.5
1920/1921–1930/1931	3.08	3.01	3.17	0.102	(0.060)	58.8	0.0	41.2
1930/1931–1940/1941	1.88	1.79	2.01	−0.180	(0.161)	56.8	0.0	43.2
1940/1941–1946/1947	1.73	2.38	0.73	−0.132	(0.413)	82.5	0.0	17.5
Areas currently in Bangladesh (–1946/1947)								
1900/1901–1910/1911	2.37	2.36	2.41	−0.046	(0.083)	71.8	0.0	28.2
1910/1911–1920/1921	−2.12	−3.24	0.31	0.183	(0.091)	103.9	0.0	−3.9
1920/1921–1930/1931	1.89	1.76	2.12	0.093	(0.112)	60.1	0.0	39.9
1930/1931–1940/1941	−1.41	−2.70	0.51	−0.024	(0.085)	112.1	0.0	−12.1
1940/1941–1946/1947	−0.53	0.87	−2.51	−0.087	(0.168)	−79.4	0.0	179.4

Notes: See Table 8.1

Table 8.4 Contributions of cotton/jute growth to textile growth in undivided India

	Annual growth rate in *Y* (%)		Linkage parameter, from crop output to textile value-added			
			No time lag for crop output		1-year lag for crop output	
	Agri output quantity	Textile, real value-added	Parameter estimate	(standard error)	Parameter estimate	(standard error)
Cotton						
1900/1901–1910/1911	3.62	1.79	−0.082	(0.134)	0.044	(0.158)
1910/1911–1920/1921	0.75	0.00	−0.024	(0.114)	0.005	(0.123)
1920/1921–1930/1931	1.19	3.38	0.286	(0.609)	−0.537	(0.428)
1930/1931–1940/1941	2.95	3.40	−0.171	(0.203)	−0.308	(0.219)
1940/1941–1946/1947	−12.75	−0.69	0.323	(0.425)	−0.074	(0.353)
1900/1901–1946/1947	0.99	2.60	0.005	(0.106)	−0.117	(0.106)
Jute						
1900/1901–1910/1911	0.91	5.48	0.177	(0.233)	−0.410*	(0.206)
1910/1911–1920/1921	−3.41	3.20	−0.043	(0.152)	0.074	(0.173)
1920/1921–1930/1931	9.50	2.06	0.209	(0.170)	0.169	(0.156)
1930/1931–1940/1941	5.81	4.46	0.103	(0.133)	−0.047	(0.146)
1940/1941–1946/1947	−1.66	−2.91	−0.081	(0.056)	0.031	(0.066)
1900/1901–1946/1947	−0.01	1.24	0.046	(0.061)	0.016	(0.063)

Notes: See Table 8.1

This may appear a puzzle. The colonial industrialisation in India was led by cotton textile, jute, and sugar industries, all agriculture-based. The service sector, especially the trade subsector, was also dependent on agricultural marketing. Then we would expect a strong inter-sectoral linkage (highly positive b_{k1}). But parameter estimate for b_{k1} was insignificant. Using the current data, we can examine two potential reasons behind the absence of the linkage.

First, the artificial division into three regions without considering marketing networks could be the reason for the puzzle. During the colonial period, a portion of raw cotton produced in West Punjab and Sind (now in Pakistan) was exported from Karachi (now in Pakistan) but the rest was sent to textile mills in Bombay or Ahmedabad (now in India); raw jute produced in East Bengal (now in Bangladesh) was either exported from Calcutta Port (now in India) or sent to jute mills in Calcutta areas (now in India). Before Partition, there was no jute mill in areas currently in Bangladesh and there were only three small cotton textile mills in areas currently in Pakistan (Kochanek, 1983, p. 88). Dividing the undivided India into three areas according to the current borders could have cut such linkages, resulting in insignificant linkage parameter.

If the artificial division was the culprit, a positive b_{k1} is expected if we use the data for undivided India during the colonial period. With this motivation in mind, Eq. (8.3) was re-estimated for undivided India. The results are reported in Table 8.2. Against our expectation, b_{k1} remains insignificant. Therefore, the artificial division was not the culprit.

Second, due to the time taken in agricultural marketing and processing, agricultural growth in a year cannot accelerate non-agricultural growth in the same year but does so a year after. This type of a lag should be more substantial during the colonial period, when transport facilities were less developed. In Punjab, cotton is harvested in October–November, ginned in November–January, and then sent to spinning mills. Therefore, the impact of a bumper cotton harvest on textile spinning industries could realise in the next fiscal year. Wheat is harvested in March–May so that the impact of a bumper wheat harvest on wheat mills could be delayed, too. Regarding sugar cane, as it should be processed immediately after harvest, direct mill production of sugar should not be associated with a time lag. On the other hand, indirect mill production through refining farmer-made *gur* (jaggery made from sugar canes) into white sugar may take some time. As jute is harvested and sent to retting in September, it is least likely to have a one-year lag.

For these reasons, we re-estimated Eq. (8.3) with g_agrig_{kt} in the right-hand-side replaced by $g\_agrig_{k,t-1}$. The results for the colonial period are reported in Table 8.3.[9] With a one year lag, b_{k1} becomes more positive and sometimes significant. Therefore, the time lag taken for agricultural marketing has some explanatory power. Nevertheless, the absolute value of parameter b_{k1} in Table 8.3 is still small so that the indirect contribution from agricultural growth to non-agricultural growth was still not very substantial.

Among value-added series estimated by Sivasubramonian (2000), those for factory-sector cotton and jute textile industries are based on actual production data collected annually. Therefore, we expect the series to be more reliable than those for other subsectors within secondary and tertiary sectors. If the lack of the agriculture non-agriculture growth linkage was due to the data problem only, we would expect the linkage parameter b_{k1} to become significantly positive when we restrict our attention to cotton and jute only.

For this reason, we re-estimate Eq. (8.3) by replacing g_nonag_{kt} on the left-hand side by the growth rate in real value-added in cotton (jute) textile industry and g_agrig_{kt} on the right-hand side by the growth rate in real gross output of cotton (jute). We also estimate the version with a one-year time lag for the explanatory variable.

The regression results are reported in Table 8.4. As before, the parameter takes both positive and negative values depending on the decade and statistically insignificant. This suggests that cotton and jute industries in the colonial India did not grow faster when cotton or jute production in the agricultural sector grew faster in the same year or in the year before. This does not mean, however, that cotton/jute textile industries' growth was isolated from that of cotton/jute raw production. In the longer run, they were positively correlated. For instance, decadal growth rates of raw cotton (jute) production and cotton (jute) textile industries were slightly positively correlated, as shown in the first two columns of Table 8.4.

In this chapter, we provide three more possibilities for the absence of strong agriculture–macroeconomy linkage during the colonial period, all of which cannot be tested rigorously using the current dataset. Therefore, three possibilities are presented as a pure conjecture at this stage of the research.

First, growth in non-agriculture during the colonial period may not have been driven by agriculture much. There are several reasons for this. The first is international trade. It is possible that when the majority of a bumper harvest of cotton or jute was exported, the agricultural growth due to the bumper harvest did not lead to an increase in industrial output of cotton and jute textile factories. Furthermore, if trade policies were such that domestic production of cotton and jute could be encouraged at the cost of domestic manufacturers, even a negative impact of agricultural growth on manufacturing growth could happen. The trade factor needs to be investigated further using primary data and reports during the colonial period, which is left for further study.[10] The second is the nature of important non-agricultural activities in the peripheral regions. In areas currently in Pakistan, army and railroad activities were important (Kochanek, 1983, p. 19). The growth in income earned by persons engaged in the army and the railroad could be negatively correlated with agricultural growth, cancelling the positive correlation between agriculture and agri-based trades and industries. The third is the nature of manufacturing industries in colonial India. In areas currently in India, the major source of industrial growth in the first half of the twentieth century came from new industries such as steel/metal, chemical, and engineering, which are not very agriculture-based. In other words, cotton/jute textile and sugar industries, which are highly based on agriculture, already became so mature at the beginning of the twentieth century that their growth did not contribute much to the manufacturing growth during the period analysed in this chapter.

Second, estimates for value-added from secondary and tertiary sectors by Sivasubramonian (2000) could be inappropriate for the purpose of this chapter. Although GDP estimates by Sivasubramonian (2000) are regarded as the best available and used by several authors to extend his analysis (e.g., Broadberry & Gupta, 2010; Caruana-Galizia, 2013), their reliability could be applicable only to the long-term trends. Short-run fluctuations regarding production in secondary and tertiary sectors could not be reliable. This is because of the estimation methodology adopted by

Sivasubramonian (2000). Within nine subsectors in secondary and tertiary sectors, only four (mining, manufacturing in the organised sector, railways/communication, and government services) were based on actual data that had valid annual fluctuations, either based on commodity-wise production or government expenditure details. All other subsectors were estimated using benchmark estimates, interpolation, and extrapolation. The most worrying is that such imputation was applied to manufacturing in the unorganised sector and trades. The former includes rice mills in both West Punjab and East Bengal and cotton ginning factories in West Punjab and Sind. The latter includes agricultural traders whose business should fluctuate in a procyclic way with agricultural output.

Third, our regional estimates for the pre-1947 period could be biased due to the simplified assumption of homogeneous prices of agricultural produce over undivided India and integrated labour markets within each region (i.e., each of the areas currently in India, Pakistan, and Bangladesh). Using more heterogeneous prices and wages according to the colonial economic geography, which reflects connectivity and transport costs differently from the post-1947 ones, could change the results reported in this chapter.

5 Conclusion

In this chapter, the agriculture–macroeconomy growth link in India, Pakistan, and Bangladesh was examined using unusually long-term data that correspond to the current borders for the period c.1900–2000. From the new dataset, a long-term decline in the share of agriculture in GDP was demonstrated in all three countries, including the period when per-capita GDP declined during the colonial period in areas currently in Bangladesh. The empirical results also showed two structural changes. The first one occurred between pre- and post-1947 periods in India and Bangladesh. The portion of non-agricultural growth that can be attributable to agricultural growth increased substantially after the independence/partition in 1947. The second one occurred around the 1970s–1980s in all the three countries, where non-agricultural growth that appeared to have occurred autonomously became the main engine of macroeconomic growth.

Overall, the analyses in this chapter showed that all the three countries are already in the modern stage of agricultural transformation, in which agricultural share in GDP and labour force is decreasing at a sustained pace. This process is expected to continue in the twenty-first century, as predicted by Briones and Felipe (2013). Non-agricultural growth in the twenty-first century is expected to be more isolated from agricultural growth, as well. Looking at the heterogeneity among the three countries, the contrast shown in the twentieth century suggests that the areas currently in Bangladesh suffered most from wrong policies and institutions during the colonial period and the united Pakistan period. With this double burden emancipated, how long Bangladesh can maintain the current growth momentum remains an interesting question to explore.

The analysis in this chapter robustly showed the absence of the growth linkage between agriculture and non-agriculture during the colonial period. The absence could be attributable to a time lag taken for agricultural marketing/processing, the nature of industrialisation, and the lack of quality data on annual fluctuations in non-agriculture and on the regional structure of economic geography. Regarding the nature of industrialisation, more micro-investigations of non-agricultural growth in areas currently in Pakistan and Bangladesh are called for. Regarding the data, non-agricultural value-added in three regions, 1901/1902–1946/1947, could be based on more frequent benchmark years and more disaggregated regional prices. GDP estimates for Bangladesh (East Pakistan for the period from 1949/1950 to 1970/1971) need to be revised as well. Furthermore, alternative estimates are called for regarding tertiary and secondary sectors in the pre-1947 period, to replace estimates by Sivasubramonian (2000). With these further works, our understanding of long-term impact of economic institutions on economic performance in the Indian subcontinent will be deepened.

Notes

1. It should be noted that these three linkage measures only partially characterise the long-term process of agricultural transformation. For the three South Asian countries, other aspects of agricultural transformation

can be analysed. See Kurosaki (2015) for changes in crop composition at the macro level, Kurosaki (2017) for regional dynamics in agriculture, and Thapa, Viswanathan, Routray, and Ahmad (2010) and Briones and Felipe (2013) for the effects of agricultural transformation on poverty reduction or employment generation and the comparison of the South Asian experiences with other Asian economies.

2. The main reason for this treatment is that we have more reliable data for crops and livestock subsectors than for fishing and forestry subsectors (Sivasubramonian, 2000). Because the GDP share of fishing and forestry subsectors is very small, whether we classify them into agriculture or non-agriculture does not make any difference as far as the analysis of this chapter is concerned.
3. Agricultural output in pre-1947 corresponds to the agricultural year for all the three regions, beginning on July 1 and ending on June 30 next year. In figures with limited space, the fiscal (agricultural) year 1900/1901 is shown as "1900."
4. The dataset is available from the author on request.
5. The long linked series in real terms are not used in Sects. 3 and 4. As shown below, the three measures of agriculture–macroeconomy linkage are calculated using static compositions or growth rates within a decade. Therefore, the tentative nature of the long-term linkage in Fig. 8.1 does not affect the main analysis of this chapter.
6. In Fig. 8.1, which is based on 1948/1949 prices, Pakistan's per-capita GDP in 2000/2001 was slightly higher than India's. When real GDP is evaluated using more recent base years (e.g., 2000/2001), per-capita GDP in India in 2000/2001 is higher than in Pakistan. For this reason, per-capita GDP of India and Pakistan were "similar", as written in the text.
7. Alternative measures of agriculture's presence in the macroeconomy could be the share in labour force or in export earnings. We do not use the labour shares because the available data for the colonial period are based on population censuses conducted every ten years, lacking in annual fluctuations. In all three regions before Partition, the agricultural share in labour force was stable throughout the period (however, as the crude activity rate was going down, the agricultural labour share in the population was declining). We do not use the export shares because of their dependence on trade and foreign exchange policies.
8. Jute mills established in East Pakistan during this period were mostly owned by West Pakistan capitalists (Kochanek, 1983). Therefore,

although industrial production of these factories contributed to GDP in East Pakistan, it did not contribute much to GNP in East Pakistan, as most of the industrial profits were remitted from East to West Pakistan. There is no credible estimate for GNP in East Pakistan, however.

9. For the comparison purpose, we re-estimated the same model with a time lag using the post-1947 data. We were not able to obtain statistically significant results at all for all the three countries.
10. As a preliminary step towards this investigation, a similar version of Eq. (8.3) between cotton/jute production in the agricultural sector and raw cotton/jute export quantity was estimated. This is because data do not exist for value-added in trade separately for raw cotton and jute. Similar insignificant relations were found (details are available on request).

References

Acemoglu, D., & Robinson, J. A. (2012). *Why Nations Fail: The Origins of Power, Prosperity, and Poverty*. London: Profile Books.

Banerjee, A., & Iyer, L. (2005). History, Institutions and Economic Performance: The Legacy of Colonial Land Tenure Systems in India. *American Economic Review, 95*(4), 1190–1213.

Bosworth, B., & Collins, S. M. (2008). Accounting for Growth: Comparing China and India. *Journal of Economic Perspectives, 22*, 45–66.

Briones, R., & Felipe, J. (2013). *Agriculture and Structural Transformation in Developing Asia: Review and Outlook*. ADB Economics Working Paper, No. 363. Manila: Asian Development Bank.

Broadberry, S., & Gupta, B. (2010). The Historical Roots of India's Service-Led Development: A Sectoral Analysis of Anglo-Indian Productivity Differences, 1870–2000. *Explorations in Economic History, 47*, 259–368.

Caruana-Galizia, P. (2013). Indian Regional Income Inequality: Estimates of Provincial GDP, 1875–1911. *Economic History of Developing Regions, 28*(1), 1–27.

Christiaensen, L., Demery, L., & Kuhl, J. (2011). The (Evolving) Role of Agriculture in Poverty Reduction: An Empirical Perspective. *Journal of Development Economics, 96*(2), 239–254.

Donaldson, D. (2010). *Railroads of the Raj: Estimating the Impact of Transportation Infrastructure*. NBER Working Paper No. w16487 (forthcoming in American Economic Review).

Geary, F., & Stark, T. (2002). Examining Ireland's Post-Famine Economic Growth Performance. *Economic Journal, 112*, 919–935.

Government of Bangladesh. (various issues). *National Accounts Statistics*. Dhaka: Bangladesh Bureau of Statistics, Government of Bangladesh.

Government of Bangladesh. (1993). *Twenty Years of National Accounting of Bangladesh (1972–73 to 1991–92)*. Dhaka: Bangladesh Bureau of Statistics, Government of Bangladesh.

Government of India. (2011). *National Accounts Statistics Back Series 2011 (1950–51 to 2004–05)*. New Delhi: The Central Statistical Organisation, Government of India.

Government of Pakistan. (various issues). *National Accounts Statistics*. Islamabad: Pakistan Bureau of Statistics/Federal Bureau of Statistics, Government of Pakistan.

Government of Pakistan. (2000). *50 Years of Pakistan in Statistics*. Islamabad: Federal Bureau of Statistics, Government of Pakistan.

Haggblade, S., Hazell, P. B. R., &. Dorosh, P.A. (2007). Sectoral Growth Linkages Between Agriculture and the Rural Nonfarm Economy. In S. Haggblade, P.B.R. Hazell, & T. Reardon (eds.), *Transforming the Rural Nonfarm Economy: Opportunities and Threats in the Developing World* (pp. 141–182). Baltimore: Johns Hopkins University Press.

Kochanek, S. A. (1983). *Interest Groups and Development: Business and Politics in Pakistan*. Karachi: Oxford University Press.

Kurosaki, T. (2011). *Compilation of Agricultural Production Data in Areas Currently in India, Pakistan, and Bangladesh from 1901/02 to 2001/02*. PRIMCED Discussion Paper, No. 6, Hitotsubashi University. http://www.ier.hit-u.ac.jp/primced/

Kurosaki, T. (2015). Long-Term Agricultural Growth in India, Pakistan, and Bangladesh from 1901/2 to 2001/2. *International Journal of South Asian Studies, 7*, 61–86.

Kurosaki, T. (2017). *Comparative Economic Development in India, Pakistan, and Bangladesh: Agriculture in the 20th Century*. Tokyo: Maruzen Publishers.

Papanek, G. F. (1967). *Pakistan's Development: Social Goals and Private Incentives*. Cambridge, MA: Harvard University Press.

Roy, B. (1996). *An Analysis of Long Term Growth of National Income and Capital Formation in India (1850–51 to 1950–51)*. Calcutta: Firma KLM Private Ltd..

Sadullah, M. M., Mujahid, S., & Ahmad, A. (Eds.). (1993). *The Partition of the Punjab 1947: A Compilation of Official Documents*. Lahore: Sang-e-Meel Publications.

Sivasubramonian, S. (2000). *National Income of India in the Twentieth Century*. Delhi: Oxford University Press.
Thapa, G. B., Viswanathan, P. K., Routray, J. K., & Ahmad, M. M. (Eds.). (2010). *Agricultural Transition in Asia: Trajectories and Challenges*. Bangkok: Asian Institute of Technology.

Takashi Kurosaki is Professor at the Institute of Economic Research, Hitotsubashi University, Tokyo, Japan. He holds a PhD from Stanford University (1995) in food research. He has been conducting theoretical and empirical work from a microeconomic perspective on questions of economic development and poverty reduction in South Asia.

9

Southeast Asian Agricultural Growth: 1930–2010

Anne Booth

1 The Role of Agriculture in Economic Development in Southeast Asia

The purpose of this chapter is to examine the changing role of agricultural production in Southeast Asia from the early decades of the twentieth century to the first decade of the twenty-first century. The chapter argues that the key drivers of agricultural growth in Southeast Asia have been population growth, leading to increased domestic demand for food, and increased involvement in international trade which in Southeast Asia led to the rapid growth in production of a number of crops for global as well as domestic markets. Many of these crops were not indigenous to the region, but were introduced from other parts of Asia, Central and South America and Africa. A third driver has been technological change, which increased output per unit of factor input (both land and labour).

A. Booth (✉)
Department of Economics, University of London, London, UK

V. Pinilla, H. Willebald (eds.), *Agricultural Development in the World Periphery*,
Palgrave Studies in Economic History, https://doi.org/10.1007/978-3-319-66020-2_9

Institutional changes, including changes in land tenure systems, changes in labour contracts and changes in government policies towards agriculture have also been important, but these changes have occurred mainly in response to the changes brought about by population growth, international trade and technological change.

2 Growth of Population and Foodcrop Production in Southeast Asia

Although there is still some doubt about the figures, it is probable that in 1820 the population of the ten countries which now comprise Southeast Asia was around 40 million, or about 10–12 per cent that of China. By 1930, a figure of 130 million is plausible for the whole region; in mid-2016, the population of the Association of Southeast Asian Nations (ASEAN-10) is estimated to be around 633 million, about 46 per cent of China's and almost half that of India.[1] Although immigration from India and China did contribute to population growth in parts of Southeast Asia, especially in British Malaya, much of the population growth over the past two centuries must have been due to higher fertility and falling mortality. An important factor in falling mortality was the increased availability of new foodcrops, which found their way to Southeast Asia, as well as to Africa, from parts of the Americas as a result of the "Columbian exchange" (Boomgaard, 2014, pp. 138–139; Nunn and Qian, 2010). The most important were maize, sweet potatoes and cassava, which had become important sources of calories in many parts of Southeast Asia by the early twentieth century, especially for the low-income groups. Growing populations were accommodated by extending the land frontier, often into forests or upland regions where these crops were easier to grow and yielded more calories per hectare than upland rice. There is little evidence of serious famine anywhere in Southeast Asia after 1850, in contrast to both China and India. But as more evidence on food consumption became available in the early twentieth century, colonial officials were worried that population was growing faster than food supply in densely settled regions in Java, the Philippines and Vietnam.

By the early twentieth century, colonial governments in most parts of Southeast Asia were collecting data on food production and consumption, and for the main foodcrops, especially rice, it is possible to compare yields per hectare, output growth and per-capita availability (Booth, 2012a: Table 1). The considerable variation in the per-capita consumption of the main food staples across Southeast Asia by the 1930s was the result of differences in both preferences and purchasing power of the populations. In the case of both Java and the Philippines, where per-capita rice consumption was relatively low, other food staples including corn, vegetables, beans and rootcrops were consumed. This was also true in other parts of Southeast Asia to varying extents. Mears, Agabin, Anden, & Marquez (1974: Appendix 4.1) estimated per-capita availability of rice and corn in the Philippines from 1910 to 1940; they found that it reached a maximum in the mid-1920s and fell thereafter. Rice and corn consumption per-capita tended to move together which suggests that corn was not just a substitute for rice. Consumption of both staples was determined by changes in purchasing power, which fell for many people in the Philippines over the 1930s.

3 The Impact of International Trade

The second crucial driver of agricultural change in Southeast Asia has been growing involvement in international trade. Sugar, coffee, pepper and spices had been exported from Southeast Asia for centuries; by the end of the nineteenth century these crops were supplemented by others, including tobacco, abaca, tea and rice.[2] Until the latter part of the nineteenth century, these crops were usually grown by smallholders, sometimes under coercion, and sometimes by free cultivators responding to global market opportunities. As trade between Europe, America and Asia accelerated after 1870, new crops and new production methods were introduced. Plantations operated by companies based in Europe and North America began to cultivate large tracts of land, usually on long leases in Northeast Sumatra, peninsular Malaya, South Vietnam and the Philippines. By the early twentieth century, these plantations were cultivating crops such as rubber, palm oil, and pineapples, which had been introduced from South America and Africa.

The British, Dutch and French colonial governments expected that non-food export crop production would be dominated by large estates. Smallholders were expected to grow foodcrops for their own use and for local markets. But in fact smallholder production of rice for export grew rapidly in the three deltas in Central Thailand, Southern Vietnam and Southern Burma in the latter part of the nineteenth and early twentieth centuries (Owen, 1971). Much of the rice grown in the three deltas went into markets in other parts of Asia including India, China and the rice-deficit regions of Southeast Asia, especially British Malaya, the Philippines and Indonesia. Until the early twentieth century, crops such as sugar, tea and coffee were mainly grown on estates, as were the new crops introduced after 1900, especially rubber and palm oil. In Java, the largest sugar-producing region in Southeast Asia until the depression of the 1930s, the estates rented land from indigenous cultivators, while in the Philippines most of the land under sugar was owned by the companies. In contrast to Indonesia, British Malaya and French Indochina, many of the large estates in the Philippines were owned by local rather than foreign interests (Booth, 2007, p. 55). In addition the Philippines benefited from protected market in the USA, into which its sugar could be sold, up to a quota limit. Java producers had to sell into world markets, and as protection increased in the 1930s, they were forced to cut output (Van Gelderen, 1939, pp. 58–62).

Restrictions on output over the 1930s also affected producers of rubber, tea and tin, in Southeast Asia and elsewhere. In the case of rubber, production by smallholders began to take off in Sumatra and Kalimantan (Dutch-controlled Borneo) in the 1920s. The collapse in world prices in the early 1930s led the Dutch and British governments to agree on a restriction scheme, which involved a high export tax on smallholder producers. This was so unpopular that it was removed after two years, and by the end of the 1930s output from smallholder producers, whose fixed costs were very low, had almost caught up with that of large estates (Creutzberg, 1975, p. 4). Although much of the growth in smallholder cash-crop production was a response to market conditions, some government officials outside Java were supportive of attempts by indigenous producers to diversify sources of income (Touwen, 2001, pp. 279–281).

The supportive approach of at least some Dutch officials in the 1930s can be contrasted with the attitudes of British officials in Malaya, who reserved large tracts of land for the exclusive use of Malay farmers, but were reluctant to allow smallholders to grow "speculative" cash crops. Malays had to concentrate on paddy production, which was in the words of one economic historian the "least profitable" of all major occupations (Lim, 1977, p. 176). Malays were also prevented from migrating to non-agricultural occupations. According to the 1931 census, indigenous Malays comprised less than ten per cent of the non-agricultural labour force in both the Straits Settlements and the Federated Malay States. This was a much lower proportion than in other colonies in the region (Booth, 2007: Table 6.2). The policy of trapping the majority of the Malay population in foodcrop agriculture was to cause serious problems for post-independence governments.

In spite of the attempts to regulate export production, exports from the region continued to grow over the 1930s relative to the rest of Asia and to what Lewis (1969) defined as the tropical world (Booth, 2004: Tables 2 and 3). In 1860, Southeast Asia accounted for around 17 per cent of exports from Asia (excluding Japan). By 1937, the proportion had grown to 37 per cent. One important legacy of the growth of Southeast Asia's export economy relative to that of both China and India was the large influx of labourers from both countries. Although Dutch and American officials in the Netherlands Indies and the Philippines imposed some controls on in-migration after 1900, numbers continued to increase until the 1930s. Chinese and Indian migrants accounted for a majority of the population only in British Malaya by 1930, but they comprised significant minorities elsewhere, especially in urban areas. They often dominated wholesale and retail trade and took a disproportionate share of administrative, professional and clerical jobs not occupied by nationals of the colonial power. The resulting "plural economy" was another legacy which successive governments had to deal with across Southeast Asia after 1945.

Between 1946 and 1957, almost all the colonies in Southeast Asia either became fully independent or were granted self-government. As Myint (1972, p. 28) pointed out, the new states were determined to break with the colonial model of economic development, in which a narrow range of primary products were exported and manufactured goods imported. Building up a modern industrial sector was viewed as essential; in addition, most governments wanted to transfer a greater share of national income to their indigenous populations. But how were these aims to be achieved in new nations where popular expectations for a better life were often running ahead of economic growth? With the exception of Thailand, per-capita GDP in other parts of Southeast Asia in 1950 was well below the levels achieved in the late 1930s, and by 1960 several countries had still not caught up. Myint concluded that the more successful countries over the 1950s, at least in terms of economic growth, were the Philippines, Thailand and what was soon to become the Federation of Malaysia. In Indonesia and Burma, where in his words, the reaction against the colonial economic pattern had been most violent, growth was slower and economic nationalism more extreme. In Indonesia, most Dutch enterprises were nationalised in the late 1950s, including plantations, banks, trading houses and manufacturing enterprises. Foreign investment was reduced to a trickle, and the rupiah became increasingly overvalued, so that smuggling of export products from Sumatra and Sulawesi became widespread. After the military took power in Burma, even more extreme policies were pursued, which effectively isolated the country from the international economy for several decades.

Even in those economies which Myint characterised as outward-looking, governments often pursued policies which penalised the agricultural sector. Export taxes were widely used across the region. Some officials appeared to think that elasticities of supply and demand were such that the incidence would fall on foreign buyers of crops such as rice and rubber, but the evidence showed that in fact the burden of export taxes fell mainly on domestic producers (Booth, 1980). This was politically acceptable in the case of large plantations, but increasingly after 1950, export crops were produced by smallholders. Even where governments earmarked funds from export taxes for research and agricultural extension, economists were critical of the heavy taxation of export producers, especially given the assistance afforded the industrial sector in the form of high tariffs and quantitative restrictions on imports. Studies of effective rates of protection in Southeast Asia carried out over the 1970s and 1980s all found that manufacturing industry was protected while agriculture was often taxed (Findlay & Garnaut, 1986).

In spite of the urban/industrial bias of trade policy in most parts of Southeast Asia from the 1950s to the 1980s, smallholder growers continued to increase production of crops such as rubber, coffee, cocoa, pepper and other spices.[3] By the 1980s, rubber had become largely a smallholder crop in Thailand, Malaysia and Indonesia; these three countries, together with Vietnam, accounted for over 70 per cent of the world's production of natural rubber in 2010.[4] Large agricultural estates only survived for crops which required rapid processing after harvest, including sugar, tea and palm oil. World demand for vegetable oils has grown rapidly over the last three decades, driven especially by India and China, and in response to this demand production in both Malaysia and Indonesia expanded rapidly. By the end of the twentieth century, the large estate sector in both countries was dominated by palm oil production. In Indonesia, area under palm oil has continued to grow rapidly and the country is now the largest producer in the world. The growth of land under palm oil in Indonesia has been viewed as an important cause of the rapid loss of pristine forest, although some studies have argued that palm oil alone cannot explain all the reported loss of primary forest (Wicke, Sikkema, Domburg, & Faaij, 2008, p. 1).

Patterns of export and import of rice in Southeast Asia established in the early decades of the twentieth century have broadly persisted, but with some important changes. After 1950, the exportable surplus of rice declined in both Vietnam and Burma/Myanmar, although by the early twenty-first century, Vietnam once again became a major exporter together with Thailand (Booth, 2016: Table 6.7). Both Myanmar and Cambodia have also re-emerged as rice exporters, while Indonesia, the Philippines and Malaysia remain dependent on imports.[5] Indonesia, Malaysia and Vietnam are also significant importers of corn, while Indonesia, the Philippines, Thailand and Vietnam are all importing considerable quantities of wheat, a grain that cannot be grown in the humid tropics. In recent years diets have diversified across the region and in most countries rice accounted for a lower proportion of total calorie consumption in the early twenty-first century than in the 1960s (Table 9.1). Especially in urban areas both bread and noodles are now widely consumed. In recent years, Indonesia has become the largest wheat importer in Asia and one of the largest in the world. Southeast Asia as a

Table 9.1 Percentage of calories derived from rice and rice yields, 1960s to 2000s

	Rice calories as % of total		Yields (tons per hectare)[a]	
Country	1961	2000	1965	2010
Laos	83	66	0.8	3.7
Cambodia	78	75	1.1	2.9
Philippines	47	42	1.3	3.6
Myanmar	74	71	1.6	4.1
Thailand	71	44	1.8	2.9
Vietnam	72	66	1.9	5.4
Indonesia	47	50	2.0	5.0
Malaysia	49	30	2.2	3.8
China	30	30	3.0	6.6
South Korea	50	31	4.3	7.3
Japan	47	23	4.8	5.3

Source: IRRI, World Rice Statistics (www.irri.org)
[a]Three year averages for 2009 to 2011

whole now accounts for over ten per cent of global wheat imports, a figure which is likely to increase in coming years.

The trends in imports and exports of agricultural commodities across Southeast Asia in recent decades should be viewed in the context of rapid changes in the composition of total trade. All Southeast Asian countries have diversified their exports and imports away from agricultural commodities. Thailand, Malaysia, the Philippines, Vietnam and Cambodia are now all important exporters of a range of manufactures including automobile, electronic and other components, footwear and garments. Indonesia is now a net importer of petroleum products, but still an important exporter of gas and coal and other minerals as well as manufactures. Recent reforms in Myanmar are likely to lead to diversification of the country's export base into labour-intensive manufactures. Several countries in Southeast Asia export labour, and remittances play a significant role in the balance of payments in the Philippines and Indonesia. Tourism is an important source of foreign exchange in Thailand, Malaysia, Vietnam, Cambodia and Indonesia. This diversification means that most economies in the region are less vulnerable to prices of a narrow range of commodities. But has it discouraged governments from investing in new technologies in agriculture, whether export oriented or import substituting? The next section looks at trends in the adoption of new technologies in Southeast Asia over the last century.

4 Changes in Production Technologies

A frequent criticism of agricultural policies pursued by the various colonial regimes in Southeast Asia has been that their priorities in agricultural research were directed largely, if not exclusively, towards the export crops grown on large estates. While most colonial agricultural officials were aware of the yields gap in rice which existed between Northeast Asia and Southeast Asia, there was little attempt to develop new higher yielding varieties of rice which were suitable for the humid tropics. The Dutch did disseminate some new varieties based on crossing local with Chinese strains, and they did increase yields in well-irrigated areas of Java (Barker & Herdt, 1985, pp. 57–58). But average rice yields in Java showed little increase until 1940, partly because cultivation was being extended onto marginal lands, and partly because farmers could not afford to apply fertiliser. The lack of progress in rice agriculture can be contrasted with the impressive growth in sugar yields on Java between 1880 and 1930, as a result of the development of higher yielding varieties at research stations funded in large part by the sugar companies. Unfortunately, the benefits from increased yields were largely lost through declining prices so that by the end of the 1930s, the real value of output per hectare was much the same as at the end of the nineteenth century (Booth, 1988, p. 223).

In British Malaya, the Rubber Research Institute of Malaya (RRIM) was established in the 1920s, but as Barlow (1978, p. 74) has pointed out, funding was limited, and there was always tension between research and extension activities. After independence, extension work was transferred to other agencies, and the RRIM became an important centre for research into the breeding of higher yielding clones, which were planted not just by the large estates, but also by smallholders. Even before the adoption of the New Economic Policy, the government adopted several policies designed to improve output and yields among smallholder growers; by the early 1970s, smallholder yields per mature hectare were well above the levels of the 1930s, although still below those achieved by the large estates (Barlow, 1978: Appendix Table 3.2). In 1979, the Palm Oil Research Institute of Malaysia (PORIM) was established, financed by a levy on producers (Martin, 2003, pp. 245–246). It made important contributions not just to the development of new varieties and cultivation techniques but also to new processing technologies.

By the 1970s, the Malaysian government had achieved considerable success in improving yields of smallholder producers of rubber, through replanting schemes, and the spread of improved cultivation techniques. Smallholders were also encouraged to grow other export crops such as palm oil. But other governments across Southeast Asia had less success. In Indonesia, where by the late 1960s the area under rubber cultivation was considerably larger than in Malaysia, total production was only 60 per cent of the Malaysian figure (Barlow, 1978, p. 106). The disparity was due to the much lower yields, especially of smallholders who had gone on replicating the same production technologies over more land since the 1920s. Smallholder yields were less than half those in Malaysia in the 1970s. Most other cash crops grown by smallholders, including cloves, kapok, copra and nutmeg, had much the same history after 1950 as rubber; production expanded because more land was cultivated but yields were either constant or fell (Booth, 1988, pp. 212–213).

Since the 1980s, there has been some success in increasing smallholder yields of rubber and other treecrops through government extension support; by the early twenty-first century smallholder rubber yields had reached 710 tons per planted hectare, which is comparable to Malaysian yields in the 1970s. Rubber has become largely a smallholder crop in Indonesia, with smallholders accounting for around 80 per cent of production (Table 9.2). Indonesia is now the second largest producer of natural rubber after Thailand, where production has always been dominated by smallholders. Indonesia has also emerged as the world's largest producer of palm oil; until the 1980s it was mainly grown on estates and yields were as high as in Malaysia. Improved cultivation technologies developed at PORIM spread rapidly to Indonesian estates. Since the 1980s, land under smallholder palm oil in Indonesia has grown rapidly. This is partly the result of the Nucleus Estate Program initiated in the Suharto era; yields on the "plasma" smallholdings developed close to the large estates are only slightly lower than for estates. But other smallholdings have much lower yields, only about half those on the estates (Zen, Barlow, & Gondowarsito, 2005, p. 24).[6]

It has already been argued that by the 1960s, several countries in Southeast Asia were dependent on rice imports, while in others (Burma and Vietnam) the exportable surplus of rice had declined compared with the 1930s. There was growing anxiety about food, and especially rice, availability; in both Indonesia and the Philippines food imports were using up a considerable part of scarce foreign exchange. In the 1960s new higher yielding varieties of rice were developed at the International Rice Research Institute by crossing the dwarf variety grown in Japan with local Southeast Asian cultivars. Trials on test plots showed that in irrigated areas, with high application of fertiliser, much higher yields could be achieved. The challenge for governments across the region was to persuade millions of farmers to grow the new seeds, and also to use appropriate amounts of fertiliser. At first, many observers argued that farmers were too risk averse to use the new varieties, and that only the better off farmers would be able to afford fertiliser. The new technologies would thus lead to higher incomes for the richest farmers who cultivated irrigated land, while smaller farmers and farm labourers were unlikely to benefit. Overall it was argued that the "Green Revolution" in rice agriculture would aggravate income disparities in rural areas, and would not greatly increase output.

In fact these arguments were too pessimistic. The new varieties were adopted by many millions of farmers across the region, including those cultivating small parcels of land. Fertiliser use did increase, especially in those countries (such as Indonesia) where governments subsidised its farmgate price. If we compare rice yields in the main rice-growing countries of Asia in the 1960s with those achieved in the early twenty-first century, it is clear that many countries have seen at least a doubling of

Table 9.2 Area, output and yields of estates and smallholders: Indonesia (four year annual average 2010–2013)

	Area ('000 hectares)	Output ('000 tons)	Yields (tons/hectare)
Palm oil			
Estates	5,654	19,343	3.42
Smallholders	3,908	10,990	2.81
Rubber			
Estates	518	584	1.13
Smallholders	2,973	2,410	0.81

Source: Central Statistics Board, Statistical Yearbook of Indonesia, 2015, 234–237

yields (Table 9.1). These figures refer to averages on all types of land; while it is broadly true that farmers cultivating well-irrigated land have achieved greater increases in yields, the evidence suggests that there have also been increases on rain-fed land. Yields growth has also occurred in corn, although less progress has occurred in rootcrops, which are still consumed quite widely among poorer groups.

The impact of the new rice technologies was probably most dramatic in Indonesia where production growth was rapid in the 1970s and 1980s, and the country moved from being the world's largest rice importer in the 1970s to a rice exporter in the latter part of the 1980s. This achievement was hailed by the Suharto government, and also by many international experts.[7] But by the end of the 1980s, critics were raising concerns about the resource costs of the Indonesian "rice miracle". Domestic prices of rice were above world levels, and when Indonesia exported its surplus, world prices fell. Thus the Indonesian government was subsidising its farmers to grow rice, through the provision of cheap fertiliser and free irrigation water, and then subsidising the sale on world markets of the surplus above domestic requirements of about 500,000 tons (Timmer, 1989, pp. 54–55). Economists questioned the government's rice policy, pointing out that heavy subsidies to one part of the agricultural economy, the rice sector, distorted producer incentives and also led to problems of equity. To the extent that domestic rice prices were higher in Indonesia than what they would have been had there been no interventions in the rice market, this penalised rice consumers in both rural and urban areas, who were often poorer than the rice farmers with a marketed surplus. The policy of protecting other food producers, including the sugar sector, also pushed up domestic costs for the food-processing industries where sugar was an important input. Similar arguments were made in the Philippines where protection for major import-competing crops, including rice and corn, increased from the mid-1980s (David, Intal, & Balisacan, 2009, pp. 250–251). In both Indonesia and the Philippines, high food prices have pushed up wages which made labour-intensive industries less competitive than in Thailand, where domestic rice prices were closer to international levels.[8]

Thus the rapid growth in rice yields shown in Table 9.1, while impressive, has been achieved at some cost in terms of market distortions.[9] Economists continue to debate the extent and impact of interventions in markets for food and other agricultural commodities across Southeast Asia including Vietnam, Laos and Cambodia, where market reforms were introduced more recently and have had a considerable impact on output and yields of a range of agricultural commodities, including rice, coffee, rubber, sugar and pig meat (Athukorala, Huong, & Thanh, 2009). That government policies affecting the prices of both agricultural output and inputs have been important in encouraging the adoption of new production technologies is not disputed. But the longer term impact of these policies on both economic growth and equity within and between sectors is often controversial. In the Indonesian context the achievement of rice self-sufficiency was short-lived; by the 1990s the country was once again importing rice, and imports have continued in more recent years (Booth, 2016, pp. 114–115). Attempts to increase domestic output through import controls have led to domestic price increases which have had an adverse affect on both urban and rural poverty. While Indonesia is still a net exporter of agricultural products, thanks mainly to the rapid growth of palm oil exports, it remains very dependent on international markets for food, as does the Philippines. This situation is unlikely to change in future, unless further breakthroughs can be made in the development of new varieties of rice and corn.

Such breakthroughs will depend on more research, at both the international and national level. Recent studies indicate that expenditure on research and development in most Southeast Asian countries is low relative to GDP, with the exception of Singapore. As the agricultural sector declines relative to GDP, the proportion devoted to agricultural research is very low indeed. A study of agricultural research expenditure in Indonesia has found that there was a considerable increase between 1971–1975 and 1991–1995, from 111 to 230 million dollars (1990 international dollars). In spite of the budgetary problems brought about by the crisis, the real value of agricultural research expenditures stayed constant until 2001–2003. But relative to the numbers of scientists working in agriculturally related activities, expenditure in Indonesia has been declining. Budgetary expenditures on agricultural development as a proportion of total budgetary development expenditures reached a peak in the years from 1975 to 1985, when they were around 13 per cent of GDP from the agricultural sector. This fell to around three per cent in 2001–2003 (Fuglie & Piggott, 2006). While private research expenditures might be growing, these are largely oriented to the perennial crop sector. Rada, Buccola, and Fuglie (2010) found that most of the technological progress in this sector was due to private incentives and trade liberalisation measures; there was little evidence of government-sponsored research playing a significant role.

5 Responses to Growing Populations: Changing Systems of Land Tenure and Labour Use

This chapter has argued that population growth, international trade and new technologies have together driven agricultural growth across Southeast Asia since the nineteenth century. The three forces have been inter-related; rapid population growth has led to the adoption of new crops and more labour-intensive cultivation practices. Where demand for food has outstripped supply, international trade has increased. From colonial times to the present, Thai, Vietnamese and Burmese farmers have supplied rice to farmers growing rubber, coffee and other cash crops for export in other parts of Southeast Asia. Farmers in many parts of Asia have been ready and willing to adopt new crops and new cultivation technologies when they have been profitable; adoption has also been facilitated by well-organised extension services. Inevitably, given the magnitude of the changes which have occurred in both population and agricultural production since the nineteenth century, systems of land tenure and labour use in agriculture have had to adapt.

In the colonial era, officials tried to establish agrarian systems based on small owner-cultivators with secure tenure, while at the same time accommodating the demands of large estates, which often had powerful connections in the metropolitan countries. They were at best partially successful. Various attempts at land titling were attempted although often the new titling arrangements allowed opportunistic individuals to cheat their less sophisticated neighbours, and then exit the traditional system and use the new system to obtain legal safeguards for their land acquisitions (Booth, 2007, pp. 35–50). After independence, governments across Southeast Asia tried to unify the different systems of land rights which had evolved during the late nineteenth and early twentieth centuries. Continuing rapid growth in rural populations led not just to more tenancy but also to a larger share of the rural population controlling very small plots of land, or no land at all. Most of their income was derived from agricultural labour, or from a mixture of wage labour and self-employment in activities such as small-scale manufacturing, construction and trade. Although there were some attempts at land reform in Indonesia, Thailand and the Philippines after 1950, the impact on the distribution of land by holding size was far less than in Taiwan.

In many parts of Southeast Asia, the problem of rural landlessness appears to have become worse in recent decades. Although censuses and labour force surveys showed that a declining proportion of the labour force was employed in agriculture, the absolute size of the labour force has often been either stable or, in some regions, growing.[10] In some areas, the growing populations have been accommodated by bringing more land under cultivation. Several governments encouraged migration from densely settled agricultural regions to those areas considered to have reserves of "empty" land suitable for cultivation. The most ambitious of the various land settlement policies was the Indonesian transmigration programme, which was greatly expanded in the 1980s with donor funding from the World Bank and other bilateral aid agencies. But its implementation proved controversial and funding was cut back in the 1990s. While it is true that cultivation ratios are still low in many parts of Southeast Asia, and more land could be brought into agricultural production, the challenge for governments will be to increase arable area while at the same time protecting the rights and livelihoods of both local people, and migrant workers.

6 What of the Future?

Behind the various controversies which have been attracting attention in Southeast Asia in recent years lie a number of difficult policy problems. Many governments in the region argue that agriculture now accounts for less than one-fifth of GDP and is not seen as a priority for investment expenditure. Productivity per worker in agriculture is estimated to be lower than in other sectors of the economy, so it is argued that government policies should be directed towards creating more employment in other sectors of the economy where productivity is higher. The problem with this reasoning is that labour force data, as reported in censuses and surveys, classify people according to their "principal" source of income, but in many cases this is not their only source of income. For many decades, rural households across Southeast Asia have been deriving their incomes from a range of activities. As far as we can tell from the available evidence, many households categorised as "agricultural" now derive half or more of their income from off the holding, especially if they are cultivating small holdings. Much of this income may be derived from agricultural labour, or from trade and transport of agricultural products. To that extent the incomes of many rural households are still dependent on the agricultural sector, although agricultural output itself is falling as a share of total output.[11] But estimates of "labour productivity" in agriculture are usually derived by taking data on agricultural output from the national accounts data and dividing this figure by numbers employed in agriculture from a census, with no attempt to correct for occupational multiplicity. The result is that "labour productivity" in agriculture is often understated compared with other sectors of the economy.

But even if allowance is made for these problems, is it not true that in coming decades, the agricultural sector will account for a falling proportion of output, employment and exports across Southeast Asia? Can governments justify increasing protection for the sector, which will lead to higher prices for food, thus penalising the poor? On the other hand, can they neglect investments which might increase agricultural output in the medium term? Given increasing population growth, such neglect would inevitably lead to lower exportable surpluses or higher imports. If world prices for agricultural products are likely to increase in the medium term, is this not a reason for increasing agricultural output either through expanding the land frontier or through increasing output per hectare on land already under cultivation? But if more land is to be brought under agricultural cultivation, what are the environmental consequences of forest lost and loss of both animal and vegetable species? These questions are likely to become more important across Southeast Asia in coming decades.

Notes

1. Population data for Southeast Asia in the early nineteenth century are taken from Boomgaard (2014). The population of China in 1820 and 1930 is taken from Maddison (2003). Figures for August 2016 are taken from Population Reference Bureau, 2016.
2. Bulbeck, Reid, Tan, & Wu (1998) document the growth of production and export of cloves, pepper, coffee and sugar from Southeast Asia from the fourteenth to the twentieth centuries. De Zwart (2016) examines the impact of spices and pepper on indigenous populations in Indonesia in the VOC era.
3. In many parts of Southeast Asia, it was difficult to establish how much land was under smallholder non-food agriculture, at least until new technologies including satellite mapping became available. Growth rates of both area and output could be overstated because of underestimates in earlier decades.
4. Thai rubber production was, and continues to be, entirely smallholder, and largely based in the south of the country. Production began in the 1930s, and increased rapidly after 1950. Smallholders received little government assistance until the 1970s, but since then the Rubber Research Institute of Thailand has been successful in encouraging replanting with higher yielding plants. Over the past four decades average yield of trees has increased by a factor of five (Delarue, 2011).
5. Indonesia managed to achieve "self-sufficiency" in rice in the 1980s, but began to import again in the 1990s. In recent years, imports have been controlled, which has caused a rapid increase in local prices relative to

international prices. Average wholesale prices in Indonesia in 2016 were around double the price of ex-Bangkok five per cent broken.

6. Cramb & McCarthy (2016, pp. 42–43) report that over four million workers are involved in the palm oil industry in Indonesia and Malaysia; most are Indonesians. Smallholders typically divide their time between palm oil cultivation and other activities.
7. Fuglie (2010: Table 6) estimated that between 1961 and 2006 growth in total agricultural output was 3.6 per cent per annum, of which half came from total factor productivity growth, and half from growth in inputs.
8. Ingram (1971, p. 256) suggested that the rice premium in Thailand, by depressing domestic rice prices, could have held down wages and facilitated the growth of the industrial and service sector. But it also aggravated income differentials between Bangkok and the north of the country. In Indonesia, rice prices have moved well above world prices in recent years (see footnote 5). This in turn has encouraged the government to increase the minimum wage. If rice prices were to follow global trends, it is probable that domestic production of rice would fall in periods of low world prices. On the other hand, poverty would fall, and employment in non-agricultural activities would increase, especially if the government was able to moderate increases in the minimum wage
9. Detailed analyses of distortions in agricultural markets across Asia can be found in Anderson and Martin (2009).
10. Where the proportion of the labour force in agriculture is falling in Southeast Asia in recent years, it appears that most of the increase in non-agricultural employment has been in services rather than manufacturing industry. The proportion of the non-agricultural labour force in services is higher in most parts of Southeast Asia than in Japan, Taiwan or South Korea when those countries had roughly similar levels of per-capita GDP (Booth, 2002: Table 6).
11. According to the 2003 Agricultural Census, on average farm households derived 44 per cent of their income directly from the farm holding, although there was considerable variation across provinces (Booth, 2012b, p. 65). Income from the holding accounted for under 40 per cent of household incomes in Java and Bali and over 60 per cent in Central Kalimantan, Riau, South Sumatra, and Papua. Estimates from Thailand in 1998/1999 suggest that only 32 per cent of farm household cash income came from farm activities.

References

Anderson, K., & Martin, W. (Eds.). (2009). *Distortions to Agricultural Incentives in Asia*. Washington, DC: World Bank.

Athukorala, P.-C., Lan Huong, P., & Tri Thanh, V. (2009). Vietnam. In K. Anderson & W. Martin (Eds.), *Distortions to Agricultural Incentives in Asia* (pp. 281–302). Washington: World Bank.

Barker, R., & Herdt, R. with Rose, B. (1985). *The Rice Economy of Asia*. Washington, DC: Resources for the Future.

Barlow, C. (1978). *The Natural Industry: Its Development, Technology and Economy in Malaysia*. Kuala Lumpur: Oxford University Press.

Boomgaard, P. (2014). Population Growth and Environmental Change: A Two-Track Model. In N. Owen (Ed.), *Routledge Handbook of Southeast Asian History* (pp. 113–143). Abingdon: Routledge.

Booth, A. (1980). The economic Impact of Export Taxes in ASEAN. *Malayan Economic Review, 25*(1), 36–61.

Booth, A. E. (1988). *Agricultural Development in Indonesia*. Sydney: Allen and Unwin.

Booth, A. (2002). Rethinking the Role of Agriculture in the "East Asian" Model. *ASEAN Economic Bulletin, 19*(1), 40–51.

Booth, A. E. (2004). Linking, De-linking and Re-linking: Southeast Asia in the Global Economy in the 20th Century. *Australian Economic History Review, 44*(1), 35–51.

Booth, A. E. (2007). *Colonial Legacies: Economic and Social Development in East and Southeast Asia*. Honolulu: University of Hawaii Press.

Booth, A. E. (2012a). Measuring Living Standards in Different Colonial Systems: Some Evidence from South East Asia, 1900–1942. *Modern Asian Studies, 46*(5), 1145–1181.

Booth, A. (2012b). The Performance of the Indonesian Agricultural Sector: Twelve Questions and Some Tentative Answers. In A. Booth, C. Mannig, & T. Kian Wie (Eds.), *Land, Livelihood, The Economy and the Environment in Indonesia: Essays in Honour of Joan Hardjono* (pp. 51–84). Jakarta: Yayasan Pustaka Obor Indonesia.

Booth, A. (2016). *Economic Change in Modern Indonesia: Colonial and Post-Colonial Comparisons*. Cambridge: Cambridge University Press.

Bulbeck, D., Reid, A., Cheng Tan, L., & Wu, Y. (1998). *Southeast Asian Exports Since the 14th Century: Cloves, Pepper, Coffee and Sugar*. Leiden: KITLV Press.

Cramb, R., & McCarthy, J. F. (2016). Characterising Oil Palm Production in Indonesia. In R. Cramb & J. F. McCarthy (Eds.), *The Oil Palm Complex: Smallholders, Agribusiness and the State in Indonesia and Malaysia* (pp. 27–77). Singapore: NUS Press.

Creutzberg, P. (Ed.). (1975). *Changing Economy in Indonesia: Volume 1: Indonesia's Export Crops, 1816–1940*. The Hague: M. Nijhoff.

David, C., Intal, P., & Balisacan, A. M. (2009). Philippines. In K. Anderson & W. Martin (Eds.), *Distortions to Agricultural Incentives in Asia* (pp. 223–254). Washington: World Bank.

Delarue, J. (2011). *Thailand: The World's Leading Exporter of Natural Rubber owing to its Smallholders*. Working Paper. Agence francaise de développement, January, Paris.

Findlay, C., & Garnaut, R. (Eds.). (1986). *The Political Economy of Manufacturing Protection: Experiences of ASEAN and Australia*. Sydney: Allen and Unwin.

Fuglie, K. O. (2010). Sources of Growth in Indonesian Agriculture. *Journal of Productivity Analysis, 33*, 225–240.

Fuglie, K. O., & Piggott, R. (2006). Indonesia: Coping with Economic and Political Instability. In P. Pardey, J. Alston, & R. Piggott (Eds.), *Agricultural R&D In the Developing World: Too Little, Too Late?* (pp. 65–104). Washington: International Food Policy Research Institute.

van Gelderen, J. (1939). *The Recent Development of Economic Foreign Policy in the Netherlands East Indies*. London: Longmans, Green and Co.

Ingram, J. C. (1971). *Economic Change in Thailand, 1850–1970*. Kuala Lumpur: Oxford University Press.

Lewis, W. A. (1969). *Aspects of Tropical Trade, 1883–1965*. Stockholm: Almqvist and Wiksell.

Lim, T.-G. (1977). *Peasants and their Agricultural Economy in Colonial Malaya: 1874–1941*. Kuala Lumpur: Oxford University Press.

Maddison, A. (2003). *The World Economy: Historical Statistics*. Paris: OECD Development Centre Studies.

Mears, L., Agabin, M., Anden, T. L., & Marquez, R. C. (1974). *The Rice Economy of the Philippines*. Manila: University of the Philippines Press.

Myint, H. (1972). *Southeast Asia's Economy: Development Policies in the 1970s*. Harmondsworth: Penguin Books.

Nunn, N., & Qian, N. (2010). The Columbian Exchange: A History of Disease, Food and Ideas. *Journal of Economic Perspectives, 24*(2), 163–188.

Owen, N. G. (1971). The Rice Industry in Mainland Southeast Asia 1850–1914. *Journal of the Siam Society, 59*(2), 75–143.

Rada, N., Buccola, S. T. & Fuglie, S. T. (2010). *Uncovering Productivity Growth in the Disaggregate: Indonesia's Duelling Agricultural Sub-sectors*. Selected Paper Presented to the Agricultural and Applied Economics Association Joint Meetings, Denver

Timmer, P. (1989). Indonesia: Transition from Food Importer to Exporter. In T. Sicular (Ed.), *Food Price Policy in Asia: A Comparative Study*. Ithaca: Cornell University Press.

Touwen, J. (2001). *Extremes in the Archipelago: Trade and Economic Development in the Outer Islands of Indonesia, 1900–1942*. Leiden: KITLV Press.

Wicke, B., Sikkema, R., Domburg, V., & Faaij, A. (2008). Exploring Land Use Changes and the Role of Palm Oil Production in Indonesia and Malaysia. *Land Use Policy, 28*(1), 193–206.

Zen, Z., Barlow, C., & Gondowarsito, R. (2005). *Oil Palm in Indonesia Socio-Economic Improvement A Review of Options*. Working Paper No 2005/11, Working Papers in Trade and Development. Division of Economics Australian National University, Canberra.

de Zwart, P. (2016). *Globalization and the Colonial Origins of the Great Divergence*. Leiden: Brill.

Anne Booth was born in New Zealand and was educated in New Zealand and at the Australian National University in Canberra. She has been studying processes of economic development in Southeast Asia since the 1970s. She has held academic positions at the University of Singapore, the Australian National University and the School of Oriental and African Studies in the University of London, and is currently Professor Emerita, University of London. She is currently working on a study of living standards in Southeast Asia from the end of the nineteenth to the beginning of the twenty-first century.

10

The Two Rice Deltas of Vietnam: A Century of Failure and Success

Montserrat López Jerez

1 Introduction

Vietnam's remarkable economic transformation, from one of the poorest countries in the world in the 1980s to a low middle-income country in 2011, has been achieved by a substantial reduction of the relative weight of agriculture to manufacturing industry. This might be understood as the first steps on Vietnam's path to industrialisation and structural change. This chapter, however, focuses on the often-neglected role of agriculture in creating the premises for such a change, but argues that examining only the recent transformation might be insufficient to understand the

I acknowledge funding by Handelsbanken and the project "Tracing the Institutional Roots of Economic Development? The Impact of Colonial Extraction" led by Christer Gunnarsson (*Vetenskapsrådet* 2011–2137). This chapter is based on my dissertation: "Deltas Apart. Factor Endowments, Colonial Extraction and Pathways of Agricultural Development in Vietnam" defended on 19 December 2014 (opponent: Prof Peter Timmer). I am grateful to Takashi Kurosaki, Anne Booth, and the editors for comments. Any mistakes are mine.

M.L. Jerez (✉)
Department of Economic History, Lund University, Lund, Sweden

V. Pinilla, H. Willebald (eds.), *Agricultural Development in the World Periphery*, Palgrave Studies in Economic History, https://doi.org/10.1007/978-3-319-66020-2_10

initial mechanisms at play. We take a historical institutional perspective, based on Adelman (1986), to provide a potential explanation of this ongoing success story while identifying constraints. We do so by comparing the two rice economies: the Northern Red River Delta (RRD) and the Mekong River Delta (MRD) in the South. Both regions constitute the rice bowls of Vietnam and have experienced, especially the South, export booms during the twentieth century.

Vietnam has experienced an average 7 per cent GDP per capita growth for more than a decade, while managing to reduce income inequalities and poverty. Headcount poverty decreased from 58 per cent in the early 1990s to around 10 per cent in 2010 (World Bank Indicators). Income inequality, measured with a Gini coefficient, went from 0.45 in 1993 to 0.38 in 2006. This reduction was a result of improvements in the distribution across regions and sectors (McCaig, Benjamin, & Brandt, 2009, p. 32). This is outstanding indeed.

The main reason for the fall of poverty rates was increased earnings of agricultural workers (Benjamin & Brandt, 2004; Ravallion & van de Walle, 2008). Given that 70 per cent of the population was employed in agriculture in 1990, the growth in the sector is reflected in the decreased rural poverty headcount ratio: from 70.9 in 1993 to 8.4 in 2006 (McCaig et al., 2009). This means that absolute poverty in rural areas has almost been eliminated, and the living standards of its population improved. In 2015, 44 per cent of the population was employed in agriculture, indicating that labour had been released but the sector remained economically significant.

Rice played a fundamental role in this transformation. First, the recovery and sustained increases in rice production allowed the target of food security for the country to be reached, a major concern after the war devastation. Second, its exports became an engine of growth. Based on Young, Wailes, Cramer, and Khiem (2002), during the period 1976–1980, right after Reunification in 1975, the area under rice cultivation increased by one per cent, but production stagnated at 11 million tonnes. For the period 1988 to 1995, rice production increased by five per cent yearly. By 1997, Vietnam had become the second largest exporter of rice in the world.

Rice remains the most important crop and occupies the majority of arable land in the two Deltas, which, in turn, jointly account for 70 per cent of all rice produced (International Rice Research Institute (IRRI)

Vietnam). Improvements in production and land productivity, along with increases in real incomes for farmers, have been experienced in both Deltas. The difference is, however, that the South has greatly outperformed the North. That is, not only have the paths of the Deltas diverged; the differences are probably not about to disappear soon.

2 A Tale of Two Deltas

The explanation for this transformation, and what the majority of the current literature focuses on, is the reform known as Doi Moi. From 1986 a series of reforms started to dismantle a centrally planned economy, having at their core rural-oriented development strategies (Timmer, 2009, p. 42). Amongst the most important changes that took place were: the liberalisation of domestic input and output markets; increased rice prices; expansion of export quotas; and, in 1998, the devaluation of the currency by 10 per cent, favouring exporters. All these policy changes were preceded by significant investments in irrigation and other infrastructures that had previously been destroyed by the war.

The de-collectivisation of farming has thus been highlighted as the main driver (Pingali & Xuan, 1992). This is only applicable to the North however, where collectivisation started in 1955 (e.g. White, 1970). In the South, there is a commonly shared understanding that collectivisation was weak, and that most farmers went back to farming the land they had historical rights to, or that they had handed over to the cooperative or collective (Beresford, 1985; Kerkvliet & Selden, 1998). Consequently, the initial land distribution would be a fundamental factor influencing the dynamics of the transformation at household level, an aspect nonetheless controversial since the extent of latifundia in Cochinchina (South Vietnam during colonial times) was considered one of the most extensive in Asia.

In the North, the response to de-collectivisation was positive (Fig. 10.1). Crop income increased by 7.16 per cent from 1993 to 1998. The difference is that the South experienced a 95 per cent increase in real income per capita (14.3 per year), versus 55 per cent in the North (9.2 per year) during the 1990s (Benjamin & Brandt, 2004). Considering that Northern rural households' initial average income was 87 per cent of the Southerners', the difference grew.

During the 1990s, the households that benefited most followed two characteristics: they were in the South and had more irrigated land (Glewwe, Gragnolatti, & Zaman, 2000). This development relates to the extent of the agricultural transformation. Crop production grew annually by 8.9 per cent in the South compared to 2.7 per cent in the North (Benjamin & Brandt, 2004, pp. 17, 20). Further, the increases in rice production did not hinder the growth of other crops (such as coffee) in the South, while in the North non-rice production grew at a slower rate than rice. Consequently, the surplus capacity of an average Southern household was significantly larger than in the North; by 1998, more than two-thirds of all farm output was marketed in relation to one-third respectively.

This output growth in the South was due to land intensification. The land frontier was practically closed. It is estimated that only 10 per cent of the increases in cultivated land came from marginal lands. The rest was a result of greater cropping intensity and higher yields (Benjamin & Brandt, 2004; Young et al., 2002).

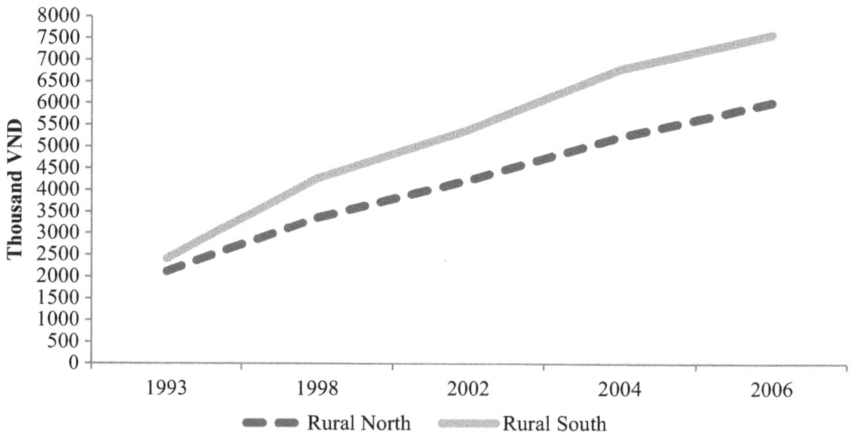

Fig. 10.1 Mean Real per Capita Income. Source: McCaig et al. (2009)

Whereas the transformation of the country as a whole has been attributed to the liberalisation effect of Doi Moi, this chapter claims that it is insufficient to explain the differences in outcomes in North and South, more specifically in the Deltas. The literature normally attributes these differences to the variance in initial conditions between the two regions. Ravallion & van de Walle point at "a legacy of the lower penetration of market institutions in the North during French rule, the longer period of collective organization in the North, and village economies that have been traditionally less open to outsiders" (2008, p. 33). This is a valid account of observed phenomena. Their approach puts emphasis on political institutions as exogenous forces, but it leaves unanswered the question of why the North followed that path or why the South, in contrast, had greater penetration of market institutions. A similar question could be asked for the 1920s. Why was the Southern (Cochinchinese) rice farmer more able to take advantage of the commercialisation opportunities brought during French colonialism than the Northern (Tonkinese) farmer? During that period, Cochinchina became the third largest exporter of rice in the world, but substantially worsened after the Great Depression.

This chapter proposes an explanation for how history may matter for these economies. After all, these initial conditions are the outcome of previous processes.

3 An Interpretation of the Initial Conditions: Colonialism, Division, and Inclusiveness

According to Adelman (1986, p. 54): "[H]ow the poor fare during the course of economic development depends on how the distribution of assets, the institutions for asset accumulation, and the institutions for access to markets by the poor all interact with the development strategies chosen". She claims that the effects on the poor are critically dependent on land tenure conditions and the size distribution of landholdings; land is a fundamental asset for the rural majority (besides their labour). When new commercial and/or technological opportunities arise for populations with unequal possibilities of responding to them, inequalities widen (Adelman, 1986, p. 55). This is representative of the long-term evolution of the Deltas (the growing differences), and it is equally significant for the understanding of the transformation for each region. Due to the differences in factor endowments (land scarcity in the North versus a frontier economy in the South until mid-twentieth century), we argue that the barriers for transformation varied between the two. This chapter claims that, despite the major institutional reforms that had taken place in North Vietnam, the size of the landholdings remains a constant and fundamental obstacle for the complete modernisation of its agriculture. A theoretical model to explain the mechanisms of such factor constraints is presented below. The South, on the contrary, seems to experience a more transformative growth than during its previous export booms. This requires further exploration.

4 Red River Delta: The Involutionary Delta?

One commonly observed economic phenomenon in the past, and today, is that in areas with high population densities and at subsistence, a seemingly excess labour force did/does not leave agriculture. The RRD, with population densities above 1000 habitants/km^2 in some of the provinces during colonial times, is a case in point.

In López Jerez (2014, forthcoming) a model based on Elvin's (1973) High-Level Equilibrium (HLET) for medieval China is developed (see a representation of the two models in Figs. 10.2, 10.3). Briefly, the model qualifies and operationalises the HLET via an interpretation of involutionary processes as Boserupian. Starting with a premise of constant land (a closed arable frontier), the potential agricultural surplus shrinks, first relatively and then absolutely, as population grows given the existing technology and practice. As population grows, and returns to labour, technology, and practice diminish, the output potential surplus shrinks. This leads to an equilibrium where population is at subsistence level. This is a high-level equilibrium trap as land productivity is at its highest given the existing technology and input-output relationship, but *at low levels of welfare*.

Elvin's HLET was taken further by Huang (1990), arguing that China suffered from involutionary processes. He defines involution as a process of growth without development. That is, output increases but at the cost of diminished marginal returns per workday, which negatively affects labour productivity and income per capita (Huang, 1990, p. 11). Huang's view of involution is as a process which makes the concept less taxonomical than previous works (i.e. Geertz), and that it is one of three patterns of development, along with intensification and development. He considers that intensification is Boserupian, driven by population pressure, while development requires "efficient division of labor, increased capital inputs per unit labor, or technological advance" (Huang, 1990, p. 12). Whilst this statement does not affect his definition of involution, it differs from our interpretation of involutionary processes as Boserupian. Boserup claims that population pressure leads to processes of land use intensification (otherwise, as the population grows, people would either

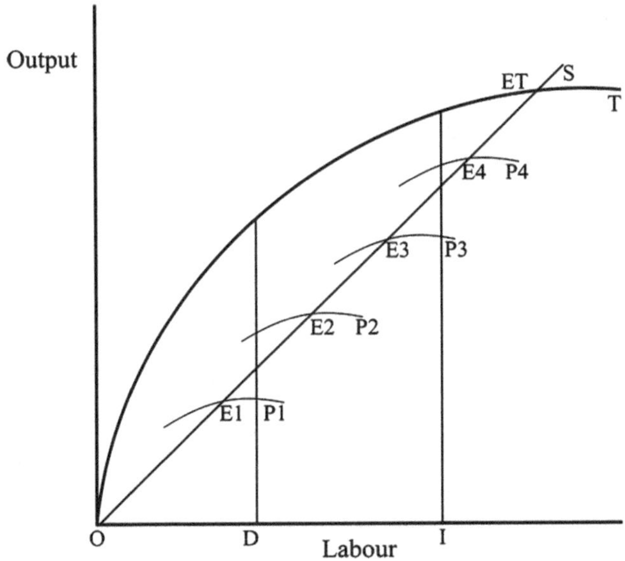

Fig. 10.2 The high level equilibrium trap. Source: Elvin (1973, p. 313)

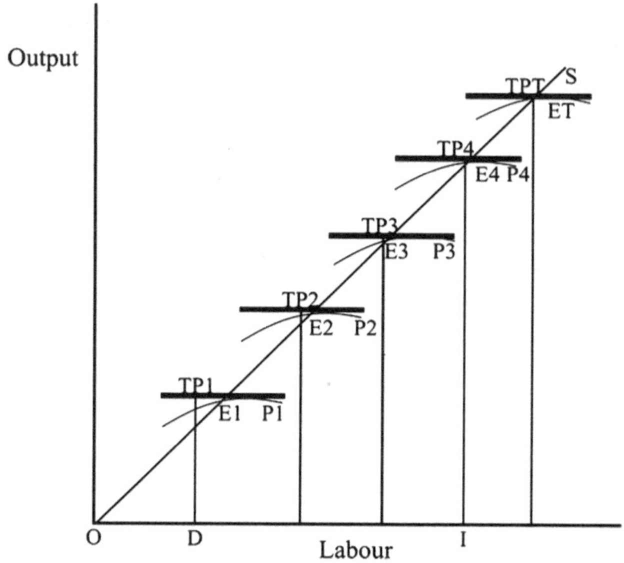

Fig. 10.3 Alternative representation (TP: total production given a level of technology *i* = 1 to T). Source: Author

starve or migrate). However, she points out that output per person-hour is more likely to decline initially (Boserup, 1965, p. 41).

Our position is that diminishing marginal returns to labour (closing on zero) are necessary but not sufficient for involution to take place. Huang (1990) himself presents a potential mechanism via the *familisation of rural production*. Women and children become more active and indispensible in the economic activities of the household. Household production leads to a common trait of subsistence households: diversification of economic activities within but with minimal commercialisation (Eicher, 1969).

HLET does not exclude opportunities of economic growth. Nonetheless, being in the trap means that technological innovations are not sufficient to outrun population pressure, leading to involution and pushing the population towards subsistence. Elvin's HLET is concerned with macroprocesses, but there is a microlevel implication. If land, as a closed factor at a given technological level, is exposed to population growth for a prolonged period of time, an expected outcome is intense land fragmentation. This tends to become more acute if, due to inheritance practices, land is distributed amongst heirs. The consequence is excessive parcelling (within-household land fragmentation), which, in turn, may make investments in modern inputs unprofitable, independently of the existence of technology. This, consequently, shifts the focus of the problem towards the profitability of such investments. There are two aspects to consider. These famers are at subsistence with limited disposable incomes to purchase modern inputs, but, equally important, there may be economies of scale in utilising modern inputs that the farmers, due to the land fragmentation, cannot achieve.

The problem of excessive parcelling tends to be overlooked by much of the literature on agricultural transformation, since land per household or farm is normally used. Here, we contend that excessive parcelling may create suboptimal conditions that are likely to be path dependent and intrinsically linked to high population pressure.

In order to ascertain that a region was reaching HLET, the following indicators should be identified in analytical terms. At the **macro** level: (1) a high land use system, given traditional technology; (2) a labour-intensive agrarian system, but affected by decreasing returns to labour; (3) as population grows, a reduction in the surplus available above subsistence per household. These hinder investments and the creation of effective markets for goods and services. The outcome is that there is little surplus of marketable products, and in any case the homogeneity of the production pushes prices down. Indicators at **micro** level would be: (1) the familisation of rural production, even with below subsistence returns to labour (Chayanov, 1966; Huang, 1990); (2) excessive fragmentation of household land; (3) diversified production to meet subsistence requirements.

This has clear implications for industrialisation. First, labour is not released, while other linkage effects, such as savings or excess production for a non-rural population are compromised due to the limited surplus capacity. Under these conditions, it is hypothesised that the majority of the population will be consequently driven towards subsistence.

5 The Red River Delta: Then and Now

Arguing that the RRD has been in a form of HLET is arduous, as it requires a thorough discussion and analysis of fragmented and incomplete data. This can be found in López Jerez (2014, pp. 79–104). The key findings are that the degree of specialisation (nurseries, use of manure and azolla, variety of seeds, high cropping index), knowledge of cultivation techniques, and the adaptability to changing climate conditions that was practiced there conform more to a HLET than a backward rice economy in a low-level equilibrium trap. In this chapter, we focus on one aspect less dealt with in the literature but that has remained constant over the century: land parcelling.

Due to inheritance, cultivation practices, and increasing population pressure on barely increasing arable land, land became increasingly fragmented during the century. Tonkin's Residence Superior (RST) reported that there were 16 million parcels in 1937, with less than 0.089 ha on average, increasing to 17.7 million in 1941. To put this into perspective, the number of parcels in the province of Bac Ninh was greater than in the whole of Cochinchina, which was 60 times larger (Gourou, 1945, p. 276).

The problems of excessive land fragmentation are well-known (e.g. Binswanger & Elgin, 1984). They can be summarised as the difficulty of rationalising production costs, which leads to inefficiencies of labour, and hinders the use of animal power and mechanisation.

One could argue that a solution by the French and successive governments would have been to consolidate farming land per household by a redistribution of parcels, while trying to maintain the number of hectares per household. Without being able to test exactly how the settlement in this region took place, we cannot be certain, but it is plausible that the most fertile land was cultivated first (given the form of irrigation); as population put pressure on existing land, new land was cultivated, leading to more fragmentation. Thus, families may have had plots with different fertilities, making consolidation impossible. Some families would have lost out on yields, and, considering how vulnerable they were, there would have been a natural resistance to such reform. There was no proper insurance market, which led to farmers hedging their risks via parcelling and relative diversification.

Currently, the World Bank (1998, p. 10) reports farms in the RRD comprised, on average, eight or nine non-contiguous plots often no larger than 200 to 500 square metres each (see also Duong & Izumida, 2002). This excessive fragmentation, and its negative effect on production, arguably resulted from "equitable" allocation of land after the 1988 reform (Markussen, 2017). The fundamental cause might not be the allocation per se, but the excessive population pressure that the region still suffers. Indeed, the reform did not alter the fragmentation, but it was not the fundamental cause. This fragmentation was likely not altered by the decades of collectivisation, since land remained cultivated by the traditional farming households (Larsen, 1965; White, 1970).

The initial surplus generated in the 1990s, thanks to de-collectivisation, allowed the incorporation of new technologies into cultivation, especially new seeds that shortened the fallow, and chemical fertilisers and pesticides. The investments in irrigation and better dikes improved the cultivation and reduced the cultivation hazards that had characterised this region. This led to greater intensification of land use.

In the RRD, the area under cultivation of rice has remained mostly unaltered since 1960 (626,000 ha arable and approximately 1 million cultivated). Land productivity (tonnes/ha) increased from 2.42 in the period 1975–1979 to 3.81 in 1990–1994, reaching 4.91 in 1995–1999 (Tran et al., 2004, p. 218). This is an average for the whole Delta.

Rambo, Cuc, and Gillogly (1993) reported from Nguyen Xa. This village in Thai Binh province had, in 1990, greater productivity than the provincial average, with cropping intensity index of 2.31. Paddy productivity was 6.45 tonnes/ha for the spring crop and 4.68 for the fall crop. The village has a density of 2030 persons/km^2 of *cultivated* land (Le and Rambo, 1993, p. 12). This makes it amongst the most populated villages in the world, and means that each hectare must support 20 people. This pressure also means that a failure in one of the crops could put the population under threat. This happened in 1991, when farmers had to resort (as they had done many times in the past) to the produce of their vegetable gardens and the sale of household husbandry to survive.

Land intensification in rice has traditionally been achieved via labour intensification (Booth & Sundrum, 1984). Rice is transplanted from nurseries and, farmers spend 220 to 280 8-hour person-days/ha/crop and almost all of it manual family labour (Tran, Chien, Thoa, Dobermann, & Witt, 2004). This makes the RRD one of the most labour-intensive irrigated rice areas in Asia.

The implication, as in the past, is that the seasonality of rice cultivation determines when labour is released. The effect is a lower opportunity cost of labour (Rambo et al., 1993), which in turns hinders their labour opportunities and incomes.

Consequently, the probable result of increased population pressure and land partition is a limited surplus capacity of the farming households. Rice remains the dominant crop to guarantee subsistence, along with the small vegetable gardens and ponds (to supplement the diet). This chapter suggests that, under other conditions (in relation to provision of public goods, allocation of labour), large parts of the Delta remain at HLET, probably experience involutionary processes, and likely hindering the release of labour for industrialisation, which was a concern already raised during colonial times.

6 Mekong River Delta: The Transformative Delta?

The transformation of the colonial South has been explained by the vent for surplus theory (Myint, 1958; Hayami, 2001). Briefly, the opening up of the economy to more extensive foreign trade, along with investments in infrastructures, led to an allocation of surplus labour (seasonal migration trading off subsistence activities) to frontier lands. It seems that the land frontier closed sometime during the 1930s (Sansom, 1970). This process of land intensification has been achieved using traditional technology. Yields remained low, ca 1.2 tonnes/ha and double-cropping was not frequent (with the exception of areas around Saigon). This means that the incentives for intensifying land use were almost inexistent as long as new land was made available. The shortcoming of this theory, however, is that the distribution effects of the surplus generated are not included. There were likely processes of stratification (a more dynamic socioeconomic peasant structure associated to rice, including Chinese milling houses and traders) but polarisation happened after the Great Depression (López Jerez, 2014, pp. 140–143). This could also mean that the farming majority did not have the incentives and/or opportunities to invest. After all, Cochinchina was considered one of the most unequal rice economies of Asia. The fundamental aspect is that these colonial outcomes do not seem to fit with the transformation of the South during the past decades. More on the colonial period can be found in López Jerez (2014), but here we return to Adelman (1986) to identify which institutions were altered so as to facilitate the transformation. Since size of landholdings (with barely any fragmentation) was not an obstacle in the 1980s, we focus on distribution and tenure.

7 Breaking Down the Landed Elites

The importance of the distribution of land, more than income, as an initial condition for long-term economic growth has been investigated by numerous authors (e.g. Birdsall & Londono, 1997; Carter, 2000). These authors have stressed different mechanisms, but generally focused on the negative correlation between unequal access to land and difficulties of accumulating assets, such as acquisition of technologies, credit, and education. These affect the security of investments and increase transaction costs.

At the onset of Doi Moi, land inequality in the Mekong and Southeast (measured by a Gini coefficient) was 0.51. This was high in relation to the 0.37 in the RRD (Deininger & Jin, 2003, p. 12). In a mono-causal approach to the recent transformation of Vietnam, it is possible to reject the hypothesis that land inequality is negative to economic growth. After all, the RRD had a more egalitarian distribution. This finding, however, should be contextualised.

First, the process of titling had been slightly more cumbersome in some provinces in the South. Second, the comparison should not be made to the RRD (due to the factor proportions), but to other economies that had similar unequal structures in the form of land distribution. According to FAO statistics (2008), based on a median of eight Latin American countries, the land Gini coefficients were approximately 0.8 in 1990. Consequently, land inequality in South Vietnam was only slightly higher than other East Asian economies, but better than those Latin American countries.

7.1 Steps Towards Unimodalism?

Johnston and Kilby (1975) discuss the distribution of land in terms of the extent of unimodalism, as opposed to bimodalism. In the South, two major land reforms aimed at altering the extremely unequal distribution of land ownership were undertaken. However, it is likely the land abundance relative to labour kept bimodalism lower than in the North, where tenancy was widespread (Gourou, 1945). That is, even though they were tenants, they had access to a sufficient landholding to pay rent and their subsistence. There is evidence indicating that some might have been capable of accumulation, especially during the boom years of the 1920s, resulting in a middle-class of farmers. There is also the scarcely recorded period when the Viet Minh took over rural areas in Cochinchina and redistributed land to the tillers. No deeds were ever issued and, as areas became secured, some of these tenancy contracts were re-established (Fall, 1967).

The first land reform came as a response to a worsening situation in the countryside. Infrastructures had been destroyed as a result of conflict during the period 1945–1954, and 600,000 to 800,000 ha were abandoned. Insecurity made many migrate to urban centres (Salter, 1970, p. 726). Exports ceased and at some point rice had to be imported.

From 1956, the Diem administration attempted to first distribute (French) land and second formalise landlord and tenant relationships so as to bring land under cultivation immediately. In this respect, a small recovery took place: the rice area cultivated in the Delta reached 1,810,000 ha in 1959, and rice exports resumed (Callison, 1974).

Nonetheless, the reform was extensively criticised for failing to curb the power of the wealthy landed elites in Saigon, to reduce rents (de facto), and to redistribute land to the cultivators (Callison, 1974, p. 46). By 1968, under both Ordinance 57 and the French land purchase programme together, about 12 per cent of the French lands (approximately 245,000 ha) had been distributed and only 132,208 farmers (10 per cent of all tenants in the country) had received title to their land or could expect it someday (Bredo, 1970, p. 742).

This said, the data available shows an improvement in the land distribution to tenants and owners (Fig. 10.4).

The Lorenz curves do not start at zero because landless tenants were given zero land. This is of course accurate as they did not own it, but it would have been useful to know this group's land size distribution. Independently of that, the numbers of tenants was reduced by half (from 222,110 to 134,155). Based only on ownership, the Gini coefficient decreases from 0.69 to 0.65. This is a small reduction. However, when tenants are included, the Gini coefficient is 0.84 reducing to 0.80; a greater reduction, but pointing at large inequalities. The SRI survey of 1968 (limited to 440 operating farms) reported a Gini coefficient of 0.59 for land in ownership (Callison, 1974, p. 361).

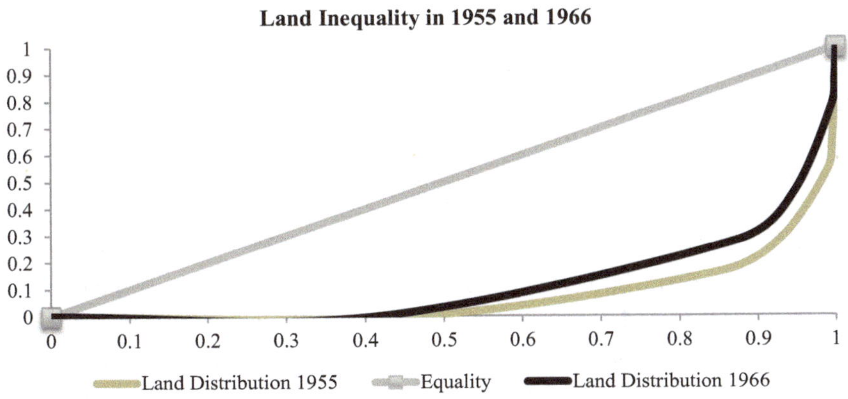

Fig. 10.4 Lorenz Curves, 1955 and 1966, in Republic of Vietnam. Source: Data for landowners taken from SRI (1968), estimates of landless from Callison (1974, pp. 359–360)

8 Missed Opportunities After Independence

The intensification of the conflict during the 1960s must have made the possibilities of collecting rents more limited. This could have led to some improvement of the disposable income of the farmers, *ceteris paribus*. The 1968 SRI survey indicates that absentee landlords who sold their land started to invest in commerce, industry and real estate development (Callison, 1974). During this period, the urbanisation rate is estimated at 14 per cent (compared to less than half for the North). This could explain why there was a degree of rural–urban inequality already prior to Doi Moi. It is also indicative of the limited private investments in agriculture of the time. Those that had the incentives were the tenants who remained under the burdens of insecurity and high rents.

It is conceivable that the period up the early 1960s could have been decisive in turning the situation around. But the fear of losing legitimacy by alienating the political and economic forces in Saigon, which were rooted in land, was seen as strong reason to postpone a land reform (Prosterman, 1970). The US advisors and administration were divided on the degree of intervention in other non-military aspects. But some steps were taken after 1965 to provide, through technical assistance, fertilisers and pesticides, and introduce the IR-8 rice (the so called "miracle rice") after a devastating flood in 1967. This led a dramatic change via increased rice prices in cities and favourable exchanges rates to facilitate the purchase of fertilisers (Logan, 1971). In 1969, the rice production increased by 17 per cent and, in the winter of 1971, the total production was 5.6 million tonnes. This transformation came together with increasing land intensification to 5.1 per cent all land (SRI, 1968, p. 30, vol. 5), and by 1975 300,000 ha of the cultivated land was being double cropped (USAID, 1975, p. 15, vol. 1).

Logan (1971) argues this improvement was the outcome of the Green Revolution and increased prices, while Prosterman (1970), amongst others, suggest that it is the effect of the 1971 Land to the Tiller (LTT) Reform. This cannot be an either–or question, however. It is plausible that those large landholders who were in the villages could put land aside to try the new varieties, and had incentives to increase production in all their lands. Nonetheless the situation with absentee landlords was a different scenario. The tenant was reluctant to invest if land were to be reclaimed by the owner, and the landowner could not be certain whether the Viet Cong would confiscate the land. The war played its role in influencing the behaviour of farmers and landlords.

While the policies of the late 1960s would have spread new technologies and restored production, Sansom's (1970) fieldwork in the Delta suggests that changes in cultivation had already been taking place. The peaks of the cultivation seasonality were reduced, which helped to absorb labour. Labour became more expensive partly as a result of political changes (the Viet Cong pushed for a minimum wage) and shortage due to military draft, migration, and human casualties. Sansom (1970) maintains that because of the production and monitoring costs, there was an optimal size for landholding (5 ha) for the first time in the modern history of the South. His analysis shows that the previous abundance of relatively cheap labour and land availability, which could be cultivated at low capitalisation, did not constrain the preferred land size. It is probable that during this period there were islands of land use intensification.

The fact is that there is not much evidence to assess how successful the LTT Reform was. Since there were barely any land records, the distribution of land had to be done using area maps. One has to bear in mind that the US troops were withdrawing from Vietnam at the same as the Viet Cong were going ahead with their own land reform. Nonetheless Callison's (1974, pp. 387–374) work, which takes us to the same villages as Sansom (1970) and Hickey (1964/1967), allows us to see a "before and after" the reform. The outcome seemed to be positive. Hayami (1994) provides anecdotal evidence that relatively larger landowners had to redistribute land before Reunification, whereas Wiegersma (1988) reveals that, in areas where landlords had a strong presence, there was a greater bias. It is hard to be certain. After all, records were not kept, and many farmers were displaced during the war (villages had been moved for security reasons to isolate the Viet Cong). The process of reallocation of land by approval of the village members should have restrained the possibilities of absentee landlords to claim land. And it likely did. Allocating land to old veterans or families who migrated could have been problematic and might have led to conflict (Kolko, 1997).

In sum, 1954–1975 was a period of great uncertainty, but we can identify two overall processes: a tendency to a reduction of inequalities in land distribution and processes of land intensification as the factor proportion and relative prices changed (both land and labour were becoming scarce). The impossibilities for previous larger owners to claim their land after Reunification allowed former tenants to keep their access, and further reduced the inequalities in distribution. Needless to say, the displacement of people as a result of the war left many landless, but land seems to have remained abundant in relation to man for rice cultivation. This could have allowed a reallocation of labour and better pre-conditions in which to respond to the liberalisation of the economy.

9 A Reinterpretation of the Initial Conditions and Processes

One may think that, in the RRD, the one of Adelman's pre-conditions (asset distribution, institutions for accumulation and access to markets) that had been granted, vis-à-vis Doi Moi, was secured individual rights over land. But land was too fragmented in highly densely populated villages. The outcome of the reform, in terms of being equitable, was merely a reflection of the factor proportions. Considering the small size of farmland, 0.23 ha on average (Kerkvliet & Selden, 1998), the possibilities of surplus generation and accumulation were short-lived. Indeed, in the first years after the 1986 reform, incomes per capita increased, but crop production per capita stagnated. An indicator of such constraints can be found in the fact that inequalities in the RRD were not driven by land size (McCaig, Benjamin, & Brandt, 2009). That is, there was no variation of land size amongst rural households in different quintiles of the income distribution. This was probably due to the extensive fragmentation of the land, which put a ceiling on the surplus capacity of each household. The differences in income, according to this source, resulted from off-farm opportunities. This phenomenon is unusual in such a large rice economy and likely continues, as the median operated farm area remains unaltered (Markussen, 2017).

The reforms aimed at generating a land market, and the expectation was to have processes of land accumulation via market-mechanisms. Nonetheless, land transactions in the North were barely taking place (Deininger & Jin, 2003). Ravallion and van de Walle (2008) referred to studies that point at the resistance from local officials to selling-off land, while others indicate that banks did not accept the titles because of the impossibility of selling them. These authors take this more as anecdotal evidence, since no systematic study had been done to quantify these instances. The reality is, however, that land was not being traded as much as in the South. Although land was a scarce factor (and hence more expensive vis-à-vis labour), the excessive land fragmentation likely made a plot of land almost untradeable. This had already been a problem during colonial times.

The outcome was that those farming households that could release labour would have kept land as collateral for survival. If households were forced to consolidate land, considering how scattered plots were, the transaction and political costs would have been high.

The South was certainly more complex. The initial conditions in the 1980s, with greater landlessness and land inequalities than the North, could have led to the interpretation that these aspects were not per se detrimental for growth. We, however, have claimed that these values have to be contextualised with the onset of the war. By 1940 the land frontier had probably closed, and factor proportions changed. Land use was intensified (double-cropping) and new technologies were introduced during the 1960s. The surplus capacity of the South had increased since colonial times, as shown by the record high production of 1971. The average farm size was estimated 1.2 ha (World Bank, 1998), which was four times the average of the RRD; this was enough for the households to take advantage of the reforms. However, as this chapter has argued, that would not have been sufficient. Land ownership was the most important issue for farmers during the period (besides survival), and was mentioned in all surveys conducted since the 1950s. Land was a political weapon for the Viet Cong. The land reforms of the time, along with the war, led to a redistribution of land. This is the important pre-condition discussed by Adelman, which she calls "redistribution before growth" (Adelman, 1986, p. 57). If productivity can be increased, as it did during the 1980s onwards, the adverse effects of unequal asset distribution are reduced and assets become more valuable, which might partly explain the greater exchange of land titles in the South.

This chapter shows that, in the South, land inequalities decreased from the 1950s to the early 1990s while the economy grew via increases in factor productivity. Indeed, more detailed study is required to understand how land was distributed after Reunification, but there is the added complexity of displaced populations. A significant indicator that the process was initially relatively more inclusive was that incomes of the poor increased as income inequalities were reduced. Landlessness, though higher than in the North, did not have to be negative (Ravallion & van de Walle, 2006; Doung & Izumida, 2002). While some smallholders sold their land to shift towards services and crafts, other landless acquired land to become self-cultivators. The positive effects of inter-provincial migration in the South are supportive (Phan & Coxhead, 2010). The picture was thus more nuanced in the South than in the North.

The modern transformation of the South, with significant improvements in technology, specialisation, and increased income per capita suggests that agriculture became a driving force of the further industrialisation of the South, especially rural industrialisation. Paraphrasing Timmer (2009, p. 41), agriculture since the early 1980s not only has got moving, it has been a contributor to growth. This implies that the rural transformation had some resemblance to that of the other East Asian economies, the so-called miracle economies (Japan, Taiwan, and South Korea). They are the empirical base of the model "growth with equity" (Adelman, 1984; Andersson & Gunnarsson, 2003; Booth, 1999). Indeed, the international conditions of Vietnam since the 1990s have differed substantially from those of the other economies, but the dynamics of transformation are illustrative. We have argued that the bottlenecks in the North and the more dynamic and transformative South cannot be *exclusively* understood by the liberalisation reform but by understanding the historical processes that set the conditions for it.

References

Adelman, I. (1984). Beyond Export-Led Growth. *World Development, 12*(9), 937–949.

Adelman, I. (1986). A Poverty-Focused Approach to Development Policy. In J. J. P. Lewis & V. Kallab (Eds.), *Development Strategies Reconsidered* (pp. 11–34). Washington, DC: Overseas Development Council.

Andersson, M., & Gunnarsson, C. (2003). *Development and Structural Change in Asia-Pacific: Globalising Miracles or the End of a Model?* London: RoutledgeCurzon.

Benjamin, D., & Brandt, L. (2004). Agriculture and Income Distribution in Rural Vietnam under Economic Reforms: A Tale Of Two Regions. In P. Glewwe, N. Agrawal, & D. Dollar (Eds.), *Economic Growth, Poverty and Household Welfare in Vietnam* (pp. 133–186). Washington, DC: World Bank.

Beresford, M. (1985). Agriculture in the Transition to Socialism: The Case of South Vietnam. In M. Lundahl (Ed.), *The Primary Sector in Economic Development* (pp. 370–395). Sydney: Croom Helm Ltd.

Binswanger, H. P., & Elgin, M. (1984). Reflections on Land Reform and Farm Size. In C. K. Eicher & J. M. Staatz (Eds.), *International Agricultural Development* (3rd ed., pp. 316–328). London: The John Hopkins Press.

Birdsall, N., & Londono, J. L. (1997). Asset Inequality Matters: An Assessment of the World Bank's Approach to Poverty Reduction. *The American Review, 87*(2), 32–37.

Booth, A. (1999). Initial Conditions and Miraculous Growth: Why is South East Asia Different from Taiwan and South Korea? *World Development, 27*(2), 301–321.

Booth, A., & Sundrum, R. M. (1984). *Labor Absorption in Agriculture: Theoretical Analysis and Empirical Investigation.* Oxford: Oxford University Press.

Boserup, E. (1965). *The Conditions of Agricultural Growth: The Economics of Agrarian Change Under Population Pressure.* London: George Allen & Unwin Ltd.

Bredo, W. (1970). Agrarian Reform in Vietnam: Vietcong and Government of Vietnam Strategies in Conflict. *Asian Survey, 10*(8), 738–750.

Callison, C. S. (1974). *The Land-to-the-tiller Program.* Athens, OH: Ohio University, Centre for International Studies.

Carter, M. R. (2000). *Land Ownership Inequality and the Income Distribution Consequences of Economic Growth.* Helsinki: UNU-WIDER.

Chayanov, A. V. (1966). *The Theory of Peasant Economy*. In D. Thorner, B. Kerblay, & R.E.F Smith. Homewood: Richard D. Irwin, INC (First published in 1923).

Deininger, K., & Jin, S. (2003). *Land Sales and Rental Markets in Transition—Evidence from Rural Viet Nam*. World Bank Policy Research Working Paper 3013.

Duong, P. B., & Izumida, Y. (2002). Landholdings and Household Income in the Vietnamese Villages. *Japanese Journal of Farm Management, 40*(2), 23–37.

Eicher, C. K. (1969). The Subsistence Farmer in Traditional Economies. In C. R. Wharton (Ed.), *Subsistence Agriculture and Economic Development* (pp. 227–228). Chicago: Aldine Publishing Company.

Elvin, M. (1973). *The Pattern of the Chinese Past: A Social and Economic Interpretation*. Stanford: Stanford University Press.

Fall, B. B. (1967). *The Two Viet-Nams: A Political and Military Analysis* (3rd ed.). London: Praeger.

FAO. (2008). Trends in Land 2008. Retrieved from http://www.un.org/esa/sustdev/publications/trends2008/land.pdf

Glewwe, P., Gragnolatti, M., & Zaman, H. (2000). *Who Gained from Vietnam's Boom in the 1990s? An Analysis of Poverty and Inequality Trends*. World Bank Policy Research Working Paper 2275

Gourou, P. (1945). *The Standard of Living in the Delta of the Tonkin: (French Indo-China)*. New York: Institute of Pacific Relations.

Hayami, Y. (1994). Strategies for the Reform of Land Policy Relations. In R. Baker (Ed.), *Agricultural Policy Analysis for Transition to a Market-Oriented Economy in Viet Nam*. FAO Economic and Social Development Paper, no. 123

Hayami, Y. (2001). Ecology, History, and Development: A Perspective from Rural Southeast Asia. *The World Bank Research Observer, 16*(2), 169–198.

Hickey, G. C. (1964/1967). *Village in Vietnam*. Massachusetts: Yale University Press. 6th Print.

Huang, P. C. (1990). *The Peasant Family and Rural Development in the Yangzi Delta, 1350–1988*. Stanford: Stanford University Press.

Johnston, B. F., & Kilby, P. (1975). *Agriculture and Structural Transformation: Economic Strategies in Late Developing Countries*. New York: Oxford University Press.

Kerkvliet, B. J. T., & Selden, M. (1998). Agrarian Transformation in China and Vietnam. *The China Journal, 40*, 37–58.

Kolko, G. (1997). *Vietnam: Anatomy of a Peace*. London: Routledge.

Larsen, M. R. (1965). *Agricultural Economy of North Vietnam*. US Department of Agriculture, Economic Research Service.

Le, T.C. & Rambo, A.T. (1993). Too Many People, Too Little Land: The Human Ecology of a Wet Rice-Growing Village in the Red River Delta of Vietnam. *Occasional Paper No. 15*, East-West Center Honolulu.

Logan, W. J. C. (1971). How Deep is the Green Revolution in South Vietnam?: The Story of the Agricultural Turn-Around in South Vietnam. *Asian Survey, 11*(4), 321–330.

López Jerez, M. (2014). *Deltas Apart—Factor Endowments, Colonial Extraction and Pathways of Agricultural Development in Vietnam*. Lund Studies in Economic History (69) (PhD).

López Jerez, M. (forthcoming). Factor Endowments and Two Stylised Dynamics of Growth Without Development. Under Revision.

Markussen, T. (2017). Land Issues 2006–14: Property Rights and Investment. In F. Tarp (Ed.), *Growth, Structural Transformation, and Rural Change in Viet Nam: A Rising Dragon on the Move* (pp. 117–138). Oxford: Oxford University Press.

McCaig, B., Benjamin, D., & Brandt, L. (2009). *The Evolution of Income Inequality in Vietnam, 1993–2006*. Mimeo: Australian National University and University.

Myint, H. (1958). The "Classical Theory" of International Trade and the Underdeveloped Countries. *The Economic Journal, 68*(270), 317–337.

Phan, D., & Coxhead, I. (2010). Inter-Provincial Migration and Inequality During Vietnam's Transition. *Journal of Development Economics, 91*, 100–112.

Pingali, P. L., & Xuan, V. T. (1992). Vietnam: Decollectivization and Rice Productivity Growth. *Economic Development and Cultural Change, 40*(4), 697–718.

Prosterman, R. L. (1970). Land-to-the-Tiller in South Vietnam: The Tables Turn. *Asian Survey, 10*(8), 751–764.

Rambo, A. T., Cuc, L. T., & Gillogly, K. (1993). Nguyen Xa Village and its Agroecosystem. In T. C. Le & A. T. Rambo (Eds.), *Too Many People, Too Little Land: The Human Ecology of a Wet Rice-Growing Village in the Red River Delta of Vietnam* (pp. 11–31). Honolulu: East-West Center.

Ravallion, M., & van de Walle, D. (2006). *Does Rising Landlessness Signal Success or Failure for Vietnam's Agrarian Transformation?* World Bank Policy Research Working Paper.

Ravallion, M., & van de Walle, D. (2008). *Land in Transition: Reform and Poverty in Rural Vietnam*. Washington: World Bank.

Salter, M. (1970). The Broadening Base of Land Reform in South Vietnam. *Asian Survey, 10*(8), 724–737.

Sansom, R. L. (1970). *The Economics of Insurgency in the Mekong Delta of Vietnam*. Cambridge, MA: MIT Press.

SRI. (1968). *Land reform in Vietnam*. Menlo Park, CA: Stanford Research Institute.

Timmer, C. P. (2009). *A World Without Agriculture: The Structural Transformation in Historical Perspective*. Washington, DC: AEI Press.

Tran, T. S., Chien, N. V., Thoa, V. T. K., Dobermann, A., & Witt, C. (2004). Site-Specific Nutrient Management in Irrigited Rice Systems of the Red River Delta of Vietnam. In A. Dobermann, C. Witt, & D. Dawe (Eds.), *Increasing Productivity of Intensive Rice Systems Through Site-Specific Nutrient Management* (pp. 217–242). Manila: IRRI.

USAID. (1975). *US Economic Assitance to South Vietnam* (Vol. 1 and 2). Washington, DC: USAID.

White, C. P. (1970). *Land Reform in North Vietnam*. Washington, DC: Agency for International Development.

Wiegersma, N. (1988). *Vietnam: Peasant Land, Peasant Revolution: Patriarchy and Collectivity in the Rural Economy*. London: Palgrave Macmillan.

World Bank, Vietnam. (1998). *Vietnam—Advancing Rural Development for Vision to Action*. Working Paper 18628.

Young, K. B., Wailes, E., Cramer, G., & Khiem, N. T. (2002). *Vietnam's Rice Economy: Developments and Prospects*. Research Report 968, Arkansas Agricultural Experiment Station.

Montserrat López Jerez is a Wallander Postdoctoral Research Fellow at the Department of Economic History, Lund University, where she obtained her PhD in 2015. Her research focuses on the role of institutions in shaping economic behaviour in the long-term, especially in relation to colonialism, agricultural transformation, and inclusiveness in Asia. She has extensive teaching experience on institutional and development economics.

11

Transforming Indonesia: Structural Change from a Regional Perspective, 1968–2010

Tobias Axelsson and Andrés Palacio

1 Introduction

Indonesia was a shambles in the late 1960s. It was among the poorest countries in the developing world, with 68 per cent of its labour in agriculture (GGDC, 2015). Almost three decades later, the World Bank included the country as one of the Asian tigers in its East Asia Miracle report (World Bank, 1993). Under the authoritarian regime of president Suharto, income per capita in 2011 US dollars grew by a factor of three, from 959 USD in 1968 to 3,119 USD in 1993 (TED, 2014). Even though it was low compared to its neighbours, and 50 per cent of its labour force was still in agriculture, the country was on its way into the group of middle-income economies and not even the 1997s crisis could

Andrés Palacio acknowledges financial support from: The Marianne and Marcus Wallenberg Foundation.

T. Axelsson (✉) • A. Palacio
Department of Economic History, Lund University, Lund, Sweden

V. Pinilla, H. Willebald (eds.), *Agricultural Development in the World Periphery*,
Palgrave Studies in Economic History, https://doi.org/10.1007/978-3-319-66020-2_11

stop it. Indonesia forged ahead joining the G20 in 2008. At the same time the political voice of the Indonesians was enhanced with democratisation and decentralisation (Hall & Vidyattama, 2016).

However, over a decade into the twenty-first century, absolute poverty is still a major issue. Using the $3.10 a day benchmark, 112 million people were living in poverty in 2010 (WDI, 2017). Using the $1.90 a day benchmark, Indonesia, together with China and India, is also a main contributor to the new Bottom Billion, a term coined by Paul Collier more than a decade ago (Sumner, 2010).[1] In addition, surplus labour is still a main feature of the Indonesian economy, with 38 per cent of the labour force working in agriculture[2] in 2010 (GGDC, 2015). In a global comparison, the pattern of reallocation of agricultural labour for the period 1995–2010, which coincides with the most recent commodity boom, places Indonesia behind most Asian and Latin-American countries (Andersson & Palacio, 2016).

In this context, we ask to what extent the dual nature of growth has stimulated structural change, or just rewarded a particular sector or region of the Indonesian economy. To answer these questions, we apply a structural change perspective and examine the role of agriculture in the Indonesian economy over the period 1968–2010. By structural change we mean the reallocation of output and labour to other sectors of the economy (Lewis, 1954; Kuznets, 1955). The failure to allocate resources across economic sectors is a clear sign of weak structural change and therefore low productivity.

The measure of structural change used in this chapter, the Inter-Sectoral Gini, is the gap between the share of agricultural employment and GDP (Timmer, 2004). This gap indicates that there is room for growth if labour reallocation continues. We acknowledge the problem of occupational multiplicity or diversification of farm income into non-agricultural activities, which can lead to underestimating the size of the gap. Evidence suggests that around 70 per cent of agricultural households in 2003 still consider agriculture the main source of income (Booth, 2012). We also set out to complement the sectoral perspective of structural change with the geographical, or better said regional, one.

The regional distribution of growth in Indonesia, the world's largest archipelagic state, is linked to historically poor areas, at least in relative terms (Hill & Vidyattama, 2016). Similar patterns can be observed in parts of northeastern India, northern Nigeria and the northeast of Brazil, but Indonesia is more interesting given the weight of agriculture in the development policy in the 1970s and 1980s (GOI, Repelita I–V). Furthermore, Indonesia is one of the few developing countries with a steady growth at 5 per cent for almost three decades (Booth, 2016).

A caveat is the difficulties in presenting geographical boundaries that speak to the many political and administrative changes at the provincial level in Indonesia. To avoid these changes in provincial boundaries, we divide Indonesia into five regions[3]: Sumatra, Java, Kalimantan, Sulawesi and Eastern Indonesia. The aim is to identify the similarities and dissimilarities among regions in their process of structural change over the period 1968–2010. Java sticks out with 60 per cent of the national GDP, followed by Sumatra at 20 per cent and Kalimantan at 10 per cent (Hill, Resosudarmo, & Vidyattama 2008; Hill & Vidyattama, 2014).

We find that, with the exception of Jakarta, labour productivity growth in agriculture is indeed the main driver of the structural change during 1995–2010, but surplus labour remains a main feature of the economy. We see that the state provided support to agriculture in the 1970s and 1980s, without tapping the potential growth coming from greater labour reallocation. Labour-intensive manufacturing in the late 1980s did grow, especially in Java, but not enough to absorb the excess labour of the whole country. Since the 1970s, the GDP share of agriculture has declined at the expense of that of the service sector, with traditional services as the largest absorber of agricultural labour. Yet, Sumatra and Kalimantan, without their reource-rich provinces (Riau and East Kalimantan), have experienced weak structural change, or little labour reallocation. Although there is also evidence of diversification both within and outside agriculture (Booth, 2002, 2012), the linkages between sectors and regions have been weak. Not surprisingly, poverty is still high in Indonesia, at least by international standards.

2 Structural Transformation 1968–2010

One of the main propositions in economic history is that development implies structural change. Broadly speaking, structural change can be understood as "long term changes in the composition of output and employment across economic sectors" (Krüger, 2008). In other words, economic sectors do not grow at the same pace, and therefore these changes have effects on the labour market, with clear implications on the income distribution, that is, poverty and inequality. The analysis of the relationship between structural change and income distribution goes back to the work of Lewis (1954) and Kuznets (1955). The main argument is that the reallocation of agricultural labour and other resources into more productive sectors is the major structural change in a developing economy, leading to overall convergence in productivity between agriculture and non-agriculture and therefore to long-term changes in the income distribution.

To set the discussion, Fig. 11.1 presents the evolution of the sectoral value added, meassured in constant 2011 US Dollars, as a proportion of GDP since 1960. Studies show that the share of agricultural GDP in Indonesia fell quicker than in other fast-growing economies in East Asia (Manning, 1998, p. 6). It declined from 43 per cent to 14 per cent of total GDP during this period. At the same time the share of people employed in agriculture declined from almost 66 per cent in 1971 to 38 per cent in 2010 (see Fig. 11.2). Closing the gap between the share of agricultural employment and GDP reflects the improvement in the financial and labour markets in the economy (Timmer, 2004). Yet, this dimension of structural change appears to be developing slowly: 38 per cent of the Indonesian labour force with 14 per cent of the income, a gap of 24 units. Even if the agricultural labour force is adjusted down by 30 per cent to compensate for the multiplicity of occupation, the gap is still 12 units.

A brief comparison of the speed of reallocation of agricultural labour for the period 1960–2010 puts Indonesia on a par with Thailand and the Philippines, and behind almost every country in Latin America (Andersson & Palacio, 2016). In line with other Asian countries, the

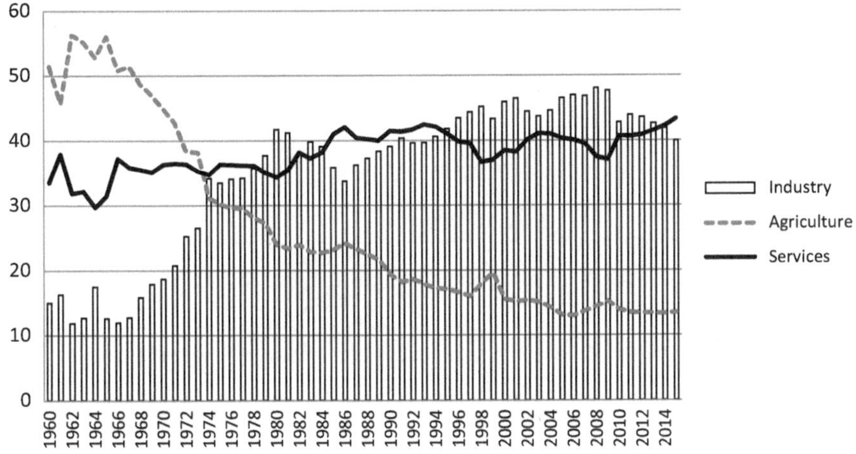

Fig. 11.1 Evolution of sectoral value added as proportion of GDP, 1960–2011 (%). Source: World Bank Development Indicators (2017)

evolution of labour productivity in Indonesia, which can be broken down into its within-sectoral productivity and a reallocation component, provides evidence that reallocation has been important for growth. For the period 1975–1990, the contribution of reallocation to labour productivity growth is 75 per cent (De Vries, Timmer, & de Vries, 2015). It falls to 20 per cent for the period 1990–2010, but remains healthy in contrast to most Latin-American countries.

To capture the nature of the structural transformation over time, we divide our period into three sub periods. The starting point is 1968, when Suharto came into power and Indonesia took shape as a centralised and unitary state. This first period ends in 1984 when the agricultural development strategy had arguably reached its pinnacle with the achievement, albeit only temporary, of rice self-sufficiency. The second period, 1984–1996, encapsulates the rise of Indonesia as a manufacturing powerhouse, which ends in economic calamity and political turmoil. The final period starts off out of the ashes of the Suharto regime in 1998, and ends in 2010.

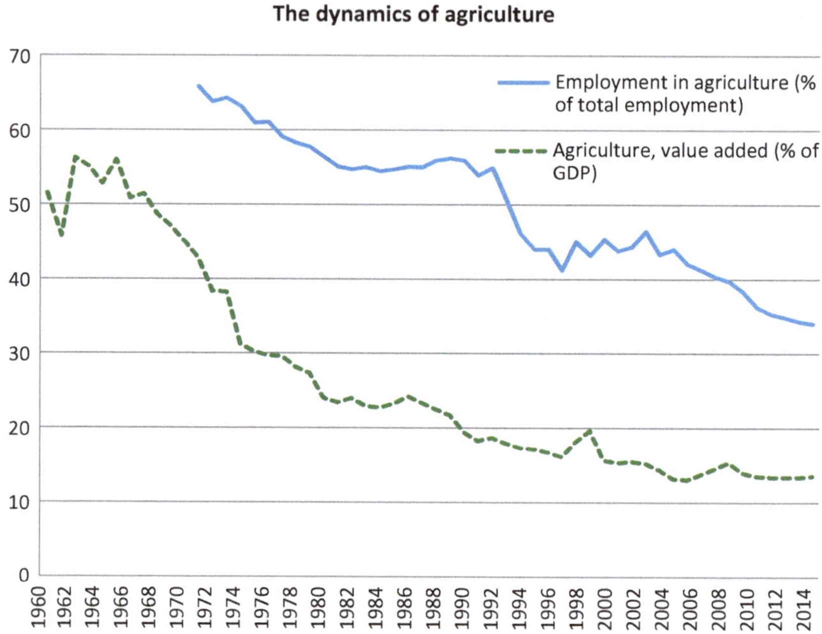

Fig. 11.2 Structural change: the gap between agricultural employment and GDP (%). Source: World Bank Development Indicators (2017)

2.1 A New Order 1968–1984

In an international comparison the Indonesian GDP per capita was the equivalent of many African countries of the time and ranked very low in an Asian context (Booth, 2016). The industrial sector was small. Agriculture accounted for over 50 per cent of total GDP and employed more than 60 per cent of the labour force (Fig. 11.2). To further aggravate the situation, food production could not keep up with demand (Bresnan, 1993).

By 1984 the picture had changed significantly. The value added from agriculture had halved to 20 per cent of GDP. Industry and services accounted for just below 40 per cent of GDP each. The decline in the agricultural labour force fell too, but the gap between shares remained as wide as before. In 1984 agriculture still accounted for 55 per cent of total farm household income (Booth, 2002). Given that centralisation under

Suharto was strong, the main reason behind the productivity increase in Indonesia is to be found in state policy (Booth, 1988; Axelsson, 2008). Some even argue that failing to put food, particularly rice, on the table would have risked Suharto losing power (Bresnan, 1993). The production of food crops was not driven by the expansion of land under cultivation but rather a result of state-led land intensification programmes (Simatupang & Timmer, 2008).

These programmes, known as Bimas, and later Insus, gained momentum in 1973 when funding through the windfall oil revenue meant that the agricultural extension system could be expanded. The programmes gave access to new modern agricultural inputs, cheap credit and instructions in modern cultivation practices. While the programmes had coercive elements (Axelsson, 2008), the adoption rate of new technology was impressive and by 1984 the high yielding varieties dominated. Initially, the programmes focused on Java but expanded further afield as they gained momentum (Booth, 1988). By 1985, 77 per cent of rice cultivation was under these intensification programmes (Sawit & Manwan, 1991). The dramatic increase in yields came with a rise in labour productivity.

Regarding cash crops, the Suharto regime inherited a crippled sector (Bresnan, 1993; Hill, 2000). Over the period there was a fast growth in the production of cash crops such as sugar in Java, and rubber and palm oil in Sumatra (Hill, 2000). A success story during this time is the palm oil sector; production had seen a more than fivefold increase by 1984. Yet, extension programmes were to a large degree absent until the end of the 1970s and even after that most smallholders did not participate. Instead, prices were the driving force with farmers increasing their production through working longer hours (Booth, 1988).

The period 1968–1984 saw the expansion of industry.[4] Given that the industrial base was only about 10 per cent of GDP at the time of Suharto's takeover, a top priority was to kick start the industrialisation process. As with agriculture, the opportunity for change came with the oil boom in 1973. The nature of the industrial policy and thereby the outcome was to have great impact on prospects for the structural transformation. Like in many other developing countries of the time, industrialisation was led through state initiatives and import substitution. The focus was on capital rather than labour-intensive industries (Hill, 1990, 2000). This being said, the import substitution policies also benefitted the expanding manufacturing industries, making the Indonesian industrial sector much more diversified in the middle of the 1980s. Yet industries, such as textiles, which did expand in output, did so through technological upgrading (Hill, 1990).

2.2 Manufacturing Indonesia 1985–1996

After the slowdown in the structural transformation in the early 1980s, the pace of growth picked up once again in the second half of the decade; yet at a much slower rate than in the previous period. By the end of the Suharto era 18 per cent of GDP came from agriculture and it remained a major source of employment. The share of households declaring agriculture as the principal source of income only declined from 81 to 78 per cent between 1983 and 1993 (Booth, 2002).

True, the effects from the intensification programmes in agriculture had slowed down, partly because the political role of agriculture had changed with the achievement of self-sufficiency in 1984 (Bresnan, 1993), and public investments decreased as oil revenues declined, making it difficult to support agriculture (Simatupang & Timmer, 2008). It was also a consequence of the fact that the vast majority of farmers at this point were using modern technologies (Sawit & Manwan, 1991). At the same time cultivated land was being increasingly used for non-agricultural purposes. The response, the Supra Insus programme built on previous ones but had greater suport for technological adaptation. By 1992, the area under intensification programmes had increased to over 80 per cent (Hill, 2000). Again, these programmes focused on yields and production while mechanisation took secondary priority (Axelsson, 2013). In fact, with the new cultivation practices there is evidence of increased labour intensity, thus even hindering the shedding of labour (Sawit & Manwan, 1991). Yet in the early 1990s there is a dramatic decline in the agriculture labour force. This indicates that labour-saving technologies were used and therefore driving the transformation forward. In the cash crop sector there was little state support until the early 1990s, but we see a steady increase in production (Booth, 2012; Hill, 2000). This is accompanied by the increasing importance of smallholders in the cash crop sector.

The industrial sector grew in importance and hovered around 40 per cent of GDP. The collapse in the oil price also had implications for industry. Indonesia could no longer sustain an oil-fed and inefficient industrial policy. For Indonesia to maintain the industrial share of GDP, a shift away from the industrial policy of the 1970s was needed (Bresnan, 1993; Hill, 2000). This shift was not done overnight and was often met with resistance from the industrial elites that had benefited from their close ties with Suharto (Vatikiotis, 1993). While there was an internal pressure for change, the regional dynamics in Asia had also changed with the Plaza Accord in 1985, which opened the gates for increased capital flows to feed manufacturing. The result was a shift in the drivers of the industrialisation process away from the oil-driven state-led industrialisation project towards an export-oriented manufacturing sector fuelled by foreign direct investment. It is this process that took off in the early 1990s with labour-intensive industries (Hill, 2000). Given the geographical concentration of non-natural resource, or labour-intensive, industries in Java, the spatial distribution of growth was set.

2.3 Out of the Ashes 1997–2010

The financial crisis in 1997 stopped the Indonesian economy dead in its tracks. Arguably the following decade was little more than a recovery, with GDP per capita not returning to pre-crisis levels until 2005 (WDI, 2017). Perhaps surprisingly, with the exception of the crisis years, the agricultural GDP continued to decrease at the same pace until 2005. After that, the process seems to have reversed and by 2010 it was back at levels seen a decade earlier. At the same time, agricultural labour share remained stagnant between 1995 and 2005. From then onwards, the steep decrease indicates labour productivity increases in agriculture and a strengthening off linkages to other sectors (shown in the next section). Here we also see the increase of diversification with the share of households deriving their income primarily from agriculture decreasing from 78 per cent to 69 per cent between 1993 and 2003 (Booth, 2002).

The 1997 crisis had far-reaching consequences beyond the economic scope. After three decades Suharto was forced to step down. Indonesia had under Suharto become increasingly centralised (Booth, 2014). Revenues from the regions, bar a few minor ones, were transferred to the national budget. The funds were then returned to the regions through subsidies or presidential decrees. Although the regime directed an increasing amount of funds towards the provinces, there was a growing dissent in the provinces in the last years of the Suharto regime, not least from the resource-rich provinces that felt cheated on their wealth (World Bank, 2003).

When Suharto stepped down in 1998, Indonesia embarked on a road towards democratisation. With democratisation came demands from regional governments for more power and the discussion on regional autonomy was reignited as the regions pressed for greater autonomy (Usman 2001; World Bank, 2003). In 1999, Law 22 and Law 25 were passed. Two years later decentralisation and regional autonomy was effectuated (World Bank, 2003). The "big bang" of decentralisation meant that the old top-down approach to development no longer applied. In concrete terms, for the agricultural sector this has meant an end to the broad and encompassing agricultural modernisation schemes of the past. Instead it was a decentralised system whereby each region was responsible for its own funding, which of course also meant that poor agricultural regions would be struggling to maintain its services especially in expensive project like irrigation (Firman 2009; Simatupang & Timmer, 2008). Consequently the organised efforts of the past were no longer in place. Instead we saw the old extension system struggling while NGOs and private interests gained ground promoting new cultivation practices, mechanisation of agriculture and, more importantly, focus had shifted towards agri-business and the marketing of agricultural products (World Bank, 2007).

In addition, the decentralisation process had, at least partially coincided with the commodity boom. The resource-rich regions saw their income from natural resources soar. This resurgence of agriculture was partly fuelled by the growing demand for "flexible crops", such as palm oil, soybeans, sugar cane, palm oil and corn. Flexible crops have multiple uses like food, feed, fuel and industrial material, which makes the agricultural sector less vulnerable to price fluctuations (Da Silva, Gómez, & Castañeda, 2010) and allows it to diversify risks within a single crop sector (Borras et al., 2012). Among flexible crops, Indonesia is the world's largest producer of palm oil and among the top 20 producers of sugar cane, soybeans and maize (FAO, 2016). Indonesia is also among the top 20 producers of rice, rubber and coffee. In this context, most of these agricultural crops are labour intensive and therefore likely to have increased labour demand, especially in areas with palm oil and rubber.[5]

In this context, a debate on deindustrialisation has risen in recent years. Industrial GDP has grown slower than actual GDP (Basri, 2009). However, for this time period we do not see deindustrialisation as a concern because value added from industry was above 40 per cent on average. At the same time, there are indications that foreign investments are increasing and that the quality of industrial production is improving (Narjoko, 2014).

The new era emerging from the crisis has led to a changing role of the central state. The process is now in the hands of the provinces, and decentralisation has brought increasing conflicts between local stakeholders. For instance, local governments today exploit their resources to a much larger extent than they did before. The greater freedom has led to greater local possibilities but there are also signs that the development policies of the past have been replaced with more fragmented and short-sighted ones (Firman, 2009). Perhaps now, more than ever, it becomes important to look at the regional diversity within Indonesia.

3 Identifying Regional Structural Change in Indonesia

Here we explore the possible causes of regional diversity in growth experiences within Indonesia by using a structural change perspective to identify and highlight relationships among key economic variables. For comparability over time, the data is organised into five regional groups, which are composed of 26 provinces (see the list of provinces by region in footnote 3). Labour data is taken from the official website of the Central Bureau of Statistics (CBS), sectoral value-added data from the Indonesian regional data at the World Bank, and national account data from the Groningen Growth and Development Centre (GGDC).[6]

While we are examining the whole period, we focus particularly on the years after 1995. Following De Vries, Timmer, and de Vries, (2015), we can run a decomposition exercise of labour productivity to examine which sectors are driving the performance of the Indonesian economy. However, we view structural change as the interplay between the two terms: without increases in sectoral productivity, reallocation does not contribute to growth as labour goes into low-productivity non-agricultural sectors.

Agriculture has been the largest contributor to overall labour productivity over manufacturing and traditional services.[7] We also confirmed the finding that labour reallocation explained around 20 per cent of the productivity growth while within sector productivity accounts for the remaining 80 per cent (De Vries, Timmer, and de Vries, 2015). In other words, Indonesia like most developing economies experienced a resurgence of agriculture during the recent commodity boom.[8] Yet, as noted earlier, the rate of reallocation of agricultural labour during the period 1995–2010 was among the lowest in the developing world: −1.4 per cent. Thus higher prices are the starting point of the explanation for people staying in agriculture. Indeed, even though the share of households engaged with agricultural commodities declined by more than 25 per cent between 2003 and 2013, the share of households engaged in the production of crops such as palm oil, sugar cane, rubber and cocoa grew by more than 27 per cent on average, and the income per capita of this group more than doubled during the period and outcompeted any other agricultural subsector.[9]

The income per capita allows the identification of three cohorts of regions that had similar patterns of growth. Table 11.1 shows the income per capita by region normalised to the national average. Part A in the table shows that there is *sustained growth* in the regions of Java and Kalimantan, *stagnation* in Sumatra and Sulawesi and *shrinking* in Eastern Indonesia.

Table 11.1 Income per capita as the share of the national income average

	1975	1990	2000	2010
A. Regional gross product per capita with rich provinces				
Sumatra	198	127	111	103
Java, incl. Jakarta	74	94	100	102
Kalimantan	139	169	178	158
Sulawesi	66	56	58	62
Eastern Indonesia	74	57	60	58
B. Regional gross product per capita without rich provinces				
Sumatra, w/out Riau	86	89	87	83
Java, w/out Jakarta	63	75	76	78
Kalimantan, w/out East	78	85	83	71
Sulawesi	66	56	58	62
Eastern Indonesia, w/out Papua	42	41	38	36

Source: Author's calculation based on data from the Indonesian Central Bureau Statistics and estimates from Hill and Vidyattama (2016)

3.1 Sustained Growth

Java accounts for over 60 per cent of the national GDP. The gap between agricultural GDP and labour fell by 20 per cent to 16 units for the period 1980–2010 (Table 11.2). Below 10 units characterises an advanced economy. The state support to agriculture slowed down the reallocation of labour into non-agriculture (see Figs. 11.3 and 11.4). With the exception of Jakarta, the provinces within Java had 29 per cent of the labour force in agriculture in 2010. Even though off farm income overestimates the number of people employed in agriculture, by the early 1990s around 40 per cent of agricultural households in Java considered agriculture their main source of income (Booth, 2002). Adjusting agricultural labour by 60 per cent, the gap is close to 4 units. Java, which dominates the rice and sugar cane markets in Indonesia, has indeed transformed its economy. However, the proximity to Jakarta has not been enough to converge in terms of income per capita. Without Jakarta, the mean income is 80 per cent of the national mean.

Kalimantan, the richest region by income per capita, has diverged upwards continuously from the rest of Indonesia. 47 per cent of the labour force in 2010 worked in agriculture, and the mean income was 58 per cent higher than the average. Twenty-seven per cent of the national

Table 11.2 Regional structural change, the gap between agricultural employment and GDP

	1980	1990	2000	2010	where, 1980–2010
A. Share of agricultural labour (%)					
Sumatra	68	67	56	47	−31%
Java	50	46	36	29	−42%
Kalimantan	68	61	50	47	−31%
Sulawesi	61	65	56	48	−21%
Eastern Indonesia	65	69	59	56	−14%
B. Share of agricultural regional gross product (%)					
Sumatra	28	25	24	24	−14%
Java	30	21	16	13	−57%
Kalimantan	40	26	24	21	−48%
Sulawesi	43	34	39	33	−23%
Eastern Indonesia	48	38	31	27	−44%
C. Difference between both shares = the gap					
Sumatra	40	42	32	23	−43%
Java	20	25	20	16	−20%
Kalimantan	28	35	26	26	−7%
Sulawesi	18	31	17	15	−17%
Eastern Indonesia	17	31	28	29	71%

Source: Author's calculation based on data from the Indonesian Central Bureau Statistics and sectoral GDP data from the Indonesian database at the World Bank (2017).

production of palm oil was concentrated in the region in 2014 (Indonesian Palm Oil Statistics, 2015), as was 18 per cent of the national production of rubber (Indonesian Rubber Statistics, 2015). Smallholdings dominated 82 per cent of the rubber production, and private estates, 84 per cent of palm oil. The gap indicates however that structural change is slow: it fell by 7 per cent for the period 1980–2010. The level is 26 units. Without East Kalimantan, its most diversified province, the income per capita of the region was 30 per cent below the national average income.

3.2 Stagnation

Sumatra lost ground to Java and Kalimantan. The income per capita had been halved between 1970 and 2010. The end of the oil boom is part of the explanation, yet the region still accounts for over 20 per cent of the national GDP. The agricultural sector, which used to employ almost 70 per cent of the workforce in the 1980s, provided for almost 50 per cent

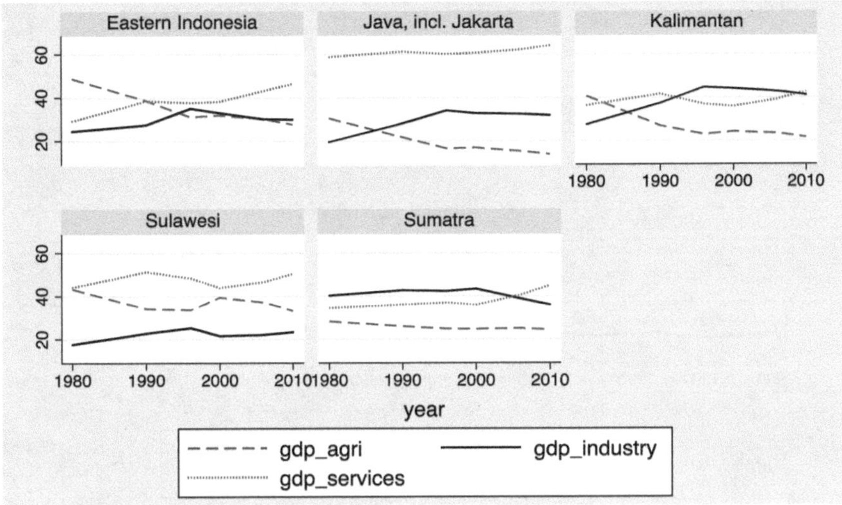

Fig. 11.3 The diversification of the economic structure. Shares of regional GDP (%). Source: Indonesia Database for Policy and Economic Research, World Bank (2017)

in 2010. The fact that smallholdings account for around 43 per cent of the production of palm oil and over 60 per cent of the production of rubber is a clear sign that agricultural households are participating in the commodity market. The agricultural GDP had barely fallen during the last three decades and accounts for 25 per cent of the regional GDP (70 per cent of the palm oil production and 74 per cent of the rubber production). The gap between agricultural GDP and labour, which fell by 43 per cent in the period 1980–2010, indicates that structural change had indeed occurred but income per capita had not increased. Without its wealthiest province of Riau, the mean income had remained over 80 per cent of the national one throughout the period.

In the same way, Sulawesi also showed little variation in the mean income. Its mean income was around 60 per cent of the national one. As in Sumatra, almost 50 per cent of the labour was in agriculture in 2010, but they were not engaged in the production of cash crops or flexible

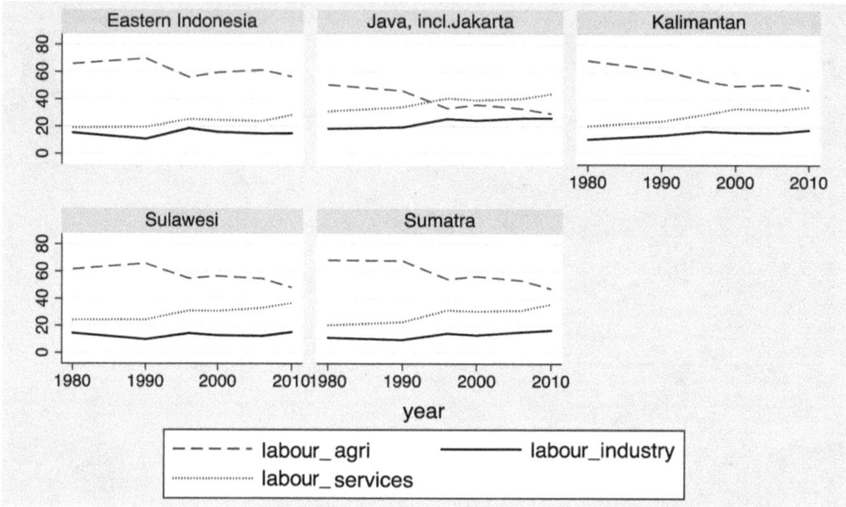

Fig. 11.4 Labour reallocation across regions and time. Shares of regional Labour (%). Source: Indonesia Database for Policy and Economic Research World Bank (2017)

crops. The gap between shares of agricultural labour and GDP had barely fallen and was at 15 units in 2010. There were no rich provinces that could serve as regional growth poles.

3.3 Shrinking

Agriculture is the main sector in Eastern Indonesia, with 56 per cent of the labour force in 2010 working in it. The decline in agricultural GDP in Eastern Indonesia was faster than in other regions, and that of labour slower. The gap between both remained at 30 units over the period, and income per capita was in decline. The region did not produce the most important commodities such as rice, palm oil, rubber, sugar cane and cocoa. Some of its provinces, for instance, West Nusa Tenggara and Papua, had grown at a fair rate, but others like Maluku had experienced continuous shrinking.

In conclusion, relative to total population, agriculture was a net source of labour supply in all regions, with positive contributions to labour that outpaced other sectors in the economy. In general, regional income per capita indicates that transformation has been slow. We believe that some sort of trap within agriculture has been strengthened by the recent decade of high commodity prices. The flexible crops, especially palm oil and rubber, for instance, increase the labour demand, and their multiple uses provides opportunities to diversify the risks. The concern lies in the long-term downward trend in the prices of agricultural commodities. After all, the expansion of palm oil is not exclusive to Indonesia, and those with the lowest labour costs set the world prices. Take the example of coffee, in which Indonesia is also among the top 20 producers in the world, but the households engaged in the production of coffee have declined by almost 20 per cent in the last decade. If people do stay in agriculture, the gap between the share of employment and GDP persists, and therefore the mobility of labour and capital may not ensure the full connection of agriculture to the rest of the economy. A result in the short run may be higher unemployment and poverty unless the non-agricultural sector provides new employment opportunities and a strong focus on the needs of the poorest population groups and regions. On the other hand, decentralisation seems to make little difference in the regional dynamics of structural transformation.

4 Indonesian and the Asian Development Model

In the discussion on the rise of post-war Asia Pacific, the role of an East Asian model of development is often referred (Kuznets, 1988; World Bank, 1993; Birdsall, 2005). This model thinking is useful when studying the transformation of Southeast Asia. Not least because although there may have been no explicit model for the first-tier countries to follow, the second-tier developers looked at countries like Japan and Taiwan for inspiration. Suharto, and the technocrats surrounding him, looked for inspiration and have often been put together with the first-tier newly industrialised country (NIC) economies when explaining the East Asian miracle (Bresnan, 1993; World Bank, 1993).

At the core of the East Asian model and thereby the transformation process we find a dynamic agricultural sector. In the first-tier countries we saw significant increases in agricultural productivity and strong linkages to other sectors of the economy. These linkages meant that labour could shift into other sectors of the economy, resulting in an overall productivity increase and surplus capital available for other sectors of the economy. This was done through, among other things, pricing policies in favour of the growing industrial sector but with farmers keeping a sizable share of the increased income, resulting in a sharp decline in rural poverty (World Bank, 1993). In this way, agriculture could serve as a source of labour, capital, and food, and also become an important domestic market for domestically produced manufactured goods.

Indonesia has shown signs of dynamism in agriculture since the 1970s. The state did support the sector through subsidies and technical expertise, but it was not able to create the linkages that were strong enough to ensure a sustained transformation of agriculture. This was apparent already in the 1980s when the sector, despite becoming a less important contributor to GDP, continued to employ over half of the population. The oil boom allowed Indonesia to finance both the rise of industry and the modernisation of agriculture, but without the emergence of a new class of rural entrepreneurs linked to other sectors of the economy.

The East Asian model also stresses the equal distribution of income and land. This manifested itself in land reforms that set the preconditions for a more inclusive growth model. The land reform laws of 1960 aimed at limiting land ownership and tenancy, but they never bore fruit and therefore the more equal initial conditions that we had seen in the first-tier miracle economies were not present (Booth, 2012). The reasons for the failure relate to inadequate legislative framework, bureaucratic deficiencies, vested interests and corruption (Neilson, 2016). In addition, there were ideological differences, which after the coup that failed in 1965 became stronger and pushed land reforms down the public agenda (Bresnan, 1993). Finally, the land scarcity was also a constraint for implementing the 1960 land reforms. Instead Indonesia attempted to equalise the access to agricultural inputs regardless of the income level across social groups (Axelsson, 2008). True, it did compensate the smallholders to a certain extent for the lack of land reform, but that does not qualify as equality. Furthermore, the industrial policy until the mid-1980s was not inclusive as it did not pull the broad base out of agriculture. The more equal countries were able to reallocate their productive assets more efficiently (Bourguignon, 2004). So, Indonesia has not succeeded in creating these egalitarian preconditions for sustained growth. In addition, the state support for agriculture was geographically unbalanced, favouring Java.

In spite of uneven regional growth and little transformation outside Java, political conflicts were kept in check by returning more funds to the regions as well as maintaining a strong military presence. These features make up for political stability during the Suharto regime. In this respect, Indonesia differs little from other Asian countries. Suharto and his technocrats built a development strategy based on the three aspects: growth, stability and equal distribution (Sajogyo & Wiradi, 1985), but the latter fell by the wayside and led to very different outcomes in terms of structural transformation compared to the country's Asian peers.

Given our estimates of labour decomposition, trends of diversification and regional trends of growth, and the history of the country, Indonesia still has much work to do. First, the integration of the outer regions into the economy goes through the agricultural sector. Our estimates of labour productivity indicate that the sector has indeed outpaced other sectors of the economy. Thus flexible crops with a high share of value in labour provide an opportunity to diversify income risks and generate higher farm income in rural areas. The experience so far shows that smallholding farmers have been able to deal with the task, at least in Java, Sumatra and Kalimantan. Similar experiences should be promoted and supported in Sulawesi and the Outer Eastern islands, given the relative abundance of land. Support services inspired by the spirit of the Suharto era, particularly in the food crop sector, should be encouraged in order to provide agricultural inputs, including high yielding seeds and land, within competitive markets. This is particularly important given the new institutional challenges that the transformation of agriculture entails in terms of size and productivity and the local capability issues tied to the decentralisation process.

Second, successful regional economies have enabled the labour force to move out of agriculture. The labour-displacing effect of the agricultural sector has at least partially been offset by an increase in the demand for labour coming from off-farm activities. In regions where stagnation dominates, the State must facilitate the transition out of agriculture into other sectors by investing in human capital and infrastructure. Furthermore, the State must focus on the delicate balance between the substitution of technology and labour as the national agricultural sector becomes more productive. Thus, where surplus labour is related to stagnation, strategies inspired by the old transmigration programmes must identify the differences across provinces in terms of factor endowments (land quality, labour and technology) and indicate the most suitable strategies for growth. Sometimes they might relate to the type of activities needed to trigger growth, or the quantity and quality of labour that needs to be retrained in other activities or the kind of institutional capabilities that need to be developed at the local level to ensure a better distribution of income across regions.

In sum, Indonesia only partially followed the Asian model. It did favour agriculture in its early stages, but failed to create the dynamics for a sustained transformation process independent of the State as a driving force for modernisation of both agriculture and industry. Furthermore, the process has been uneven given that the so-called pre-conditions for growth have been hampered by the unequal distribution of resources and the lack of linkages across sectors and regions. Java has indeed been able to diversify its economy and experience a sustained process of growth and transformation while the other regions seem to lag at least twenty years behind.

5 Conclusion

Since 1968, Indonesia has displayed an impressive growth record. We measure structural change by looking at the gap between the share of agricultural GDP and employment for Indonesia and its regions. Indonesia has transformed from a predominantly agricultural economy to one based on industry and services. Yet in a global comparison, particularly in relation to other Asian countries, the structural transformation has been sluggish and poverty lingers. We argue that this is a consequence of the weak linkages across sectors and regions. The process was dependent on the State, and its needs. In the 1970s the State was pushing for the transformation process with food security as the principal goal. This was coupled with an industrial policy that prioritised output rather than creating labour opportunities or aiding the rise of the new entrepreneurial class. In the 1980s when structural transformation slowed down, in particular regarding labour reallocation, it coincided with waning state support for agriculture. It was not until a shift in industrial policy, forced by a decline in oil prices, that there was more labour-intensive manufacturing and an acceleration in the process once again.

With the financial crisis and its political aftermath a brief stagnation set in but as this was replaced by strong indications of the resurgence of agriculture, it was possible to believe that the structural transformation had been triggered again. However, at the regional level the process was clearly uneven. With decentralisation the role of the central government became less dominant, but the process of structural transformation was more reliant on local governments. True, local government may be closer to the people, but it is less organised and communities are eager to fend for themselves rather than coordinating policies across regions. More advanced regions like Java have greater opportunities to forge ahead. This means that at least 25 per cent of the Indonesian labour force is not fully taking part in the transformation process. If Indonesia is serious about turning from half to full miracle, the transformation process has to be more inclusive. In other words, the State must create policy to achieve a balancing act between the technology needed to catch up and the amount and type that will be good for labour, whilst also creating the social policies to safeguard the rights and satisfy the needs of those left behind across the regions.

Notes

1. The poverty estimates must be treated with caution because of the data limitations of the World Bank dataset.

2. By agriculture we mean farming, livestock, forestry, fishery and agro-business that processes and transports the output.
3. Sumatra (Aceh, Sumatera Utara, Sumatera Barat, Riau, Jambi, Sumatera Selatan, Bengkulu, and Lampung); Java (DKI Jakarta, Jawa Barat, Jawa Tengah, DI Yogyakarta, Jawa Timur and Bali) Kalimantan (Barat, Tengah, Selatan and Timur); Sulawesi (Utara, Tengah, Selatan and Tenggara); Eastern outer islands (Nusa Tenggara Barat, Nusa Tenggara Timur, Maluku and Papua).
4. By industry we mean mining, manufacturing, construction and public utilities.
5. Palm oil is to provide on average 350 jobs per 1000 ha and rubber 420 (Rising Global Interest in Farmland: can it yield sustainable and equitable benefits?).
6. We recognise the limitations of the data sources listed here. First, there are no reliable time series data on working hours in the labour data. Second, the data cannot be disaggregated by sources of income. We used household declaration of principal source of income and shares of income from agricultural censuses. Third, the sectoral data from GGDC does not capture the informal sector.
7. Agriculture 0.53%, mining 0%, manufacturing 0.23%, public utilities 0.02%, construction 0.08%, wholesale, retail and trade 0.35%, transport and communications, 0.15%, financial services 0% and personal and community services 0.13%.
8. Fuglie (2012) estimated agricultural TFP for Indonesia to have grown by a factor of 3.6 between 1991–2000 and 2001–2009.
9. Perennial crops, period 2003-2013: palm oil grew by 115%, rubber 71.7%, sugar cane 26.3% and cocoa 15.1%. Coffee fell by 18.6% (CBS, 2015).

References

Andersson, M., & Palacio, A. (2016). *Structural Change and Income Inequality–Agricultural Development and Inter-sectoral Dualism in the Developing World, 1960–2010*. Revista OASIS, 23, pp. 99–122

Axelsson, T. (2008). *Peasants and Policymakers, Agricultural Transformation in Java Under Suharto*. Holmbergs: Lund.

Axelsson, T. (2013). State Led Agricultural Development and Change in Yogyakarta 1973–1996. In E. Hillbom & P. Svensson (Eds.), *Agricultural*

Transformation in a Global History Perspective (pp. 86–107). Abingdon: Routledge.

Basri, F. (2009, Nov, 29). 'Deindustrialisasi betul-betul serius!' [Deindustrialisation is Really Serious!]. Kompasiana.

Birdsall, N. (2005) *The World is Not Flat: Inequality and Injustice in Our Global Economy*. Annual Lecture, UNU-WIDER.

Booth, A. (2002). The Changing Role of Non-farm Activities in Agricultural Households in Indonesia: Some Insights from the Agricultural Censuses. *Bulletin of Indonesian Economic Studies, 38*(2), 179–200.

Booth, A. (2012). Land, Livelihood, the Economy and the Environment in Indonesia: Essays. In A. Booth, C. Manning, & T. Kian Wie (Eds.), *Honour of Joan Hardjono, Chapter 4* (pp. 51–84). Jakarta: Yayasan Pustaka Obor Indonesia.

Booth, A. (2014). Before the 'Big Bang' Decentralisation Debates and Practise in Indonesia 1949–1999. In H. Hill (Ed.), *Regional Dynamics in Decentralized Indonesia* (pp. 25–44). Singapore: Institute of Southeast Asian Studies.

Booth, A. (2016). *Economic Change in Modern Indonesia, Colonial and Post-Colonial Comparisons*. Cambridge: Cambridge University Press.

Borras, S. M., Jr., Franco, J. C., Gómez, S., Kay, C., & Spoor, M. (2012). Land Grabbing in Latin America and the Caribbean. *Journal of Peasant Studies, 39*(3–4), 845–872.

Bourguignon, F. (2004). The Poverty-Growth-Inequality Triangle. *Poverty, Inequality and Growth,* 69–64.

Bresnan, J. (1993). *Managing Indonesia, The Modern Political Economy*. New York: Columbia University.

CBS (Central Bureau of Statistics), BPS (Badan Pusat Statistik). (1986–2013). *Published volumes*. Jakarta: BPS.

Da Silva, J. G., Gómez, S., & Castañeda, R. (2010). Boom agrícola y persistencia de la pobreza rural en América Latina. Algunas reflexiones. *Revista Austral de Ciencias Sociales, 18*, 5–20.

De Vries, G., Timmer, M., & de Vries, K. (2015). Structural Transformation in Africa: Static Gains, Dynamic Losses. *The Journal of Development Studies, 51*(6), 674–688.

FAO. (2016). *The State of Food and Agriculture*. Rome: United Nations.

Firman, T. (2009). Decentralization Reform and Local-Government Proliferation in Indonesia: Towards A Fragmentation of Regional Development. *Review of Urban and Regional Studies, 21*(2/3), 143–157.

Fuglie, K. O. (2012). Productivity Growth and Technology Capital in the Global Agricultural Economy. In K. O. Fuglie, S. L. Wang, & V. E. Ball

(Eds.), *Productivity Growth in Agriculture: An International Perspective* (pp. 335–368). Washington: CABI.

GOI, Government of Indonesia. (various years). *Repelita I–V*. Jakarta: Bappenas.

Groningen Growth Development Centre. (2015). National Accounts Data for Indonesia.

Hill, H. (1990). Indonesia's Industrial Transformation Part I. *Bulletin of Indonesian Economic Studies, 26*(2), 79–120.

Hill, H. (2000). *The Indonesian Economy* (2 nd ed.). Cambridge: Cambridge University Press.

Hill, H., Resosudarmo, B., & Vidyattama, Y. (2008). Indonesia's Changing Economic Geography. *Bulletin of Indonesian Economic Studies, 44*(3), 407–435.

Hill, H., & Vidyattama, Y. (2014). Hares and Tortoises: Regional Development Dynamics in Indonesia. In H. Hill (Ed.), *Regional Dynamics in Decentralized Indonesia* (pp. 68–97). Singapore: Institute of Southeast Asian Studies.

Hill, H., & Vidyattama, Y. (2016). Regional Development Dynamics in Indonesia Before and After the 'Big Bang' Decentralization. *The Singapore Economic Review, 61*(2), 26.

Indonesia Database for Policy and Economic Research, World Bank. (2017).

Indonesian Palm Oil Statistics. (2015). Central Bureau of Statistics of Indonesia.

Indonesian Rubber Statistics. (2015). Central Bureau of Statistics of Indonesia.

Krüger, J. J. (2008). Productivity and Structural Change: A Review of the Literature. *Journal of Economic Surveys, 22*(2), 330–363.

Kuznets, P. W. (1988). An East Asian Model of Economic Development: Japan, Taiwan, and South Korea. *Economic Development and Cultural Change, 36*(S3), S11–S43.

Kuznets, S. (1955). Economic Growth and Income Inequality. *The American Economic Review*, 1–28.

Lewis, W. A. (1954). Economic Development with Unlimited Supplies of Labour. *The Manchester School, 22*, 3–42.

Manning, C. (1998). *Indonesian Labour in Transition: An East Asian Success Story?* Cambridge: Cambridge University Press.

Narjoko, D. (2014). Did Better firm Enter the Indonesian Manufacturing Sector After the 1997–998 Crisis? *Bulletin of Indoensian Economic Studies, 50*(3), 371–391.

Neilson, J. (2016). Agrarian Transformations and Land Reform in Indonesia. In J. F. McCarthy & K. Robinson (Eds.), *Land and Development in Indonensia: Searching for the People's Sovereignity* (pp. 245–264). Singapore: ISEAS—Yusof Ishak Institute.

Sajogyo, P., & Wiradi, G. (1985). *Rural Poverty and Efforts for Its Alleviation in Indonesia, WCARRD Follow-Up Programme*. Rome: FAO.

Sawit, M. H., & Manwan, I. (1991). The Beginnings of the New Supra Insus Rice Intensification Program: The Case of the North Coast of West Java and South Sulawesi 1. *Bulletin of Indonesian Economic Studies, 27*(1), 81–103.

Simatupang, P., & Timmer, C. P. (2008). Indonesian Rice Production: Policies and Realities. *Bulletin of Indonesian Economic Studies, 44*(1), 65–80.

Sumner, A. (2010). *Global Poverty and the New Bottom Billion: What if Three-quarters of the World's Poor Live in Middle-income Countries?* IDS Working Paper, vol. 2010 (349).

The Conference Board Total Economy Database™, (TED). (2014, January).

Timmer, C. P. (2004). The Road to Pro-Poor Growth: The Indonesian Experience in Regional Perspective. *Bulletin of Indonesian Economic Studies, 40*(2), 177–207.

Usman, S. (2001). *Indonesia's Decentralization Policy: Initial Experiences and Emerging Problems*. SMERU Working Paper, the SMERU Research Institute, Jakarta.

Vatikiotis, M. R. J. (1993). *Indonesian Politics Under Suharto, Order Development and Pressure of Change*. London: Routledge.

World Bank. (2007). *Agricultural Extension Services In Indonesia: New Approaches and Emerging Issues*. Decentralizing Indonesiae: A Regional Public Expenditure Review Overview Report.

World Bank. (1993). *The East Asian Miracle*. Oxford: Oxford University Press.

World Development Indicators. (2017). Washington, US: World Bank.

Tobias Axelsson is Assistant Professor at the Department of Economic History, Lund University. He has his BA in Indonesian studies and an MA in Economic History from Lund University, where he also did his doctoral degree. He is researching and publishing on agricultural transformation processes and colonial origins of inequality. He has been a guest researcher at ISEAS in Singapore and a guest research fellow at the International Institute for Asian Studies, Leiden.

Andrés Palacio is Lecturer in the Department of Economic History at Lund University, Sweden, and Research Fellow in the Department of Finance, Government and International Affairs at Externado de Colombia University in Bogotá. He holds a PhD from Lund University and an MSc from the London School of Economics and Political Science. He has been Deputy Minister of Labour Affairs in Colombia, and has published on development economics and social demography.

12

Perspectives on Agricultural and Grain Output Growth in China from the 19th Century to the Present Day

Robert Ash, Jun Du, and Cheng King

Until well after the establishment of the People's Republic in 1949, agriculture was the dominant sector of the Chinese economy. For more than two thousand years of recorded history, China's core economic challenge was how to generate sufficient grain supplies to feed an expanding population. In the first two sections we touch on some of the historical forces which shaped China's agricultural development during the Qing Dynasty and into the post-1911 Republican period. We then turn to post-1949 developments, where our focus is the government's attempt to resolve tensions between maintaining basic rural welfare and fulfilling its imperative of rapid industrial growth.

R. Ash (✉)
SOAS China Institute, SOAS, University of London, London, UK

J. Du • C. King
National University of Singapore, Singapore, Singapore

V. Pinilla, H. Willebald (eds.), *Agricultural Development in the World Periphery*, Palgrave Studies in Economic History, https://doi.org/10.1007/978-3-319-66020-2_12

1 Historical Perspectives: Agricultural Development in the Qing Dynasty

1.1 Qing Agriculture: Land and Population

Until the process of encroachment on Chinese territory at the hands of western powers and Japan during the nineteenth century, the territory controlled by the Qing Dynasty embraced "China Proper" (*Zhongguo benbu* [中国本部], also known as the "Eighteen Provinces"), "Outer China" (Manchuria, Mongolia, Chinese Turkestan [today's Xinjiang]) and Tibet. China Proper contained the bulk of the population, and it was the bedrock of agriculture throughout the Qing Dynasty (1644–1911). By contrast, Outer China's contribution to agricultural growth remained fairly limited, and the full exploitation of the rich farming potential of Manchuria and Xinjiang only began to be realised in the twentieth century.

Population loss in Manchuria resulting from military conflict during the transition from the Ming to the Qing Dynasty initially encouraged large-scale migration into the region. By 1668, Manchuria had absorbed some 14 million migrants (Deng, 2011, p. 20, 2015, pp. 7–9), although thereafter until 1860 permanent immigration was banned. This was detrimental to agricultural production, since migrants brought with them knowledge of more advanced farming techniques than those available to the indigenous population.[1] Thanks to the ban on migrants, the region's man–land ratio remained low, limiting improvements in land productivity and preventing its agricultural export potential from being realised.

By the mid-eighteenth century the Qing government had established direct control over Xinjiang (literally "new borders"), where it introduced a distinctive government structure and currency regime. As in Manchuria, permanent settlement by Chinese migrants was banned and severe restrictions imposed on outside contacts with the local population. As a result, despite a significant expansion in Xinjiang's arable area (Wang, 1911, pp. 1–5), agriculture remained underdeveloped. Output instability also limited the farm sector's capacity to generate tax revenue, and constrained the expansion of trade (Na, n.d.).

By contrast, by the early eighteenth century agriculture in China Proper had reached the apotheosis of its pre-modern development, achieving a degree of prosperity unprecedented in previous Imperial Chinese history. This was reflected in stable and sustained farm output growth, and—at least in the core agricultural regions—in yields approaching their putative ceiling, subject to the constraints of pre-modern farming technology and organisation.

Several factors contributed to the growing prosperity. One was the absence during most of the Qing of any major external threat from beyond the northern and northwestern borders of China Proper. This facilitated renewed output growth on the North China Plain—arguably the most important agricultural zone. Another was the reduction in migration and land reclamation costs, encouraged partly by access to new imported crops (Ho, 1955, pp. 191–201) and partly by the impact of climate change (Zhu, 1972). Warmer weather and the introduction of new plants suitable for dry climates and/or rough and hilly terrain assisted post-Ming recovery in the Yangtze Delta region and on the North China Plain. The same factors facilitated agricultural development by expanding the area of high-yielding farmland in the Pearl River Delta (Guangdong) and around Dongting Lake (Hunan).

There is a strong consensus that China's arable land base expanded by a large margin during the Qing period.[2] However, quantifying the increase is extremely hazardous, not only because of difficulties in interpreting available land estimates, but also because of a lack of standardisation of the basic Chinese land measure (the *mou*).[3] Suffice to say here that an authoritative Chinese source suggests that in 1840 the arable land base of China Proper was about 76.5 million ha (Shi, 1989), but that a significant margin of error (perhaps as high as 15–20 per cent) needs to be allowed for in interpreting this figure.

Estimates of China's population offer a firmer basis for interpreting and assessing changes in agriculture during much of the Qing Dynasty. There is widespread agreement that between the 1730s and the mid-eighteenth century there was a major acceleration of population growth in China, although not all sources are agreed on the magnitude of this spurt.[4] It seems clear too that in the second half of the eighteenth century, population growth in China slowed and may in some years even have declined. Military conflicts and upheavals, as well as the impact of natural disasters, were the primary causes of such population losses.[5]

Accelerated population growth during the eighteenth and first half of the nineteenth centuries had major demand and supply implications for China's agriculture. On the one hand, there was rapid growth in the number of mouths to feed, ensuring that food (i.e., grain) production came overwhelmingly to dominate the farm economy. On the other hand, with farmers constituting the overwhelming majority—well over 90 per cent—of the population, increased numbers also made available a larger agricultural labour force. Accordingly, the main response to demographic change, at least in China Proper, was a shift towards labour intensification in farming and a steady decline in the man–land ratio.

Wet field techniques had been used to grow rice in the Yangtze Delta region since the Tang dynasty (618–907), and, in particular, between the eighth and thirteenth centuries major breakthroughs were achieved in agriculture (Elvin, 1973: Chaps. 9–13). Part of the narrative of agricultural development during this period was the displacement of millet by wheat as the main crop in the dry cropping regions of northern China—a process facilitated by the introduction of more efficient milling machinery (Myers, 1970, p. 179). But at the heart of farming revolution was the mastery of wet-field, or paddy, rice cultivation. This single development—"the dynamic driving force behind an era of economic revolution" (Elvin, 1973, p. 133)—made possible the opening-up of the hitherto underdeveloped, but extremely fertile, southern half of the country, and encouraged large-scale migrations from the north.[6]

Important though this breakthrough was, diffusion of the new technology beyond the Yangtze Delta region to other parts of southern China proceeded quite slowly. The main reason for this seems to have been the absence of sufficient farm labour, demand for which only began to be met in many southern regions of China when population growth began to accelerate during the eighteenth century.[7] This was especially the case in the rich Pearl River Delta and Dongting Lake agricultural regions, where rapid population growth facilitated a strong shift towards high-productivity wet rice cultivation during the eighteenth and nineteenth centuries (Cao, 2009, pp. 828–829 and 832; also Liang, 2008).

Not all Chinese farmers were engaged in crop farming.[8] Fishing, husbandry (especially pig rearing) and poultry farming were integral parts of the agricultural economy. Nutrients from paddy fields were used to fatten pigs, chicken, ducks and geese, as well as to feed fish. In return, organic fertilisers from animal and human waste, as well as silt accumulated in fish ponds were used to enrich the soil. In addition to grain and other forms of crop cultivation, other agricultural activities, such as silk farming and forestry, thrived. In particular, the wet-field rice cultivation practised in conjunction with animal and fish husbandry maintained soil fertility and was the basis of agricultural prosperity in the rich Yangtze Delta region throughout and beyond the Qing Dynasty. The transferability of this system to Southern China, with its plentiful supply of water supplies and favourable climatic conditions, facilitated accelerating output growth and generated sufficient food supplies to support a high density and rising population comparable with those of European countries in the early stages of their Industrial Revolutions.

1.2 Quantifying Agricultural Growth

It seems likely that once recovery from the military dislocation surrounding the establishment of the Qing Dynasty in 1644 had been completed, yield and area growth combined to generate a steady increase in total grain output. This process came to an end only when, in the mid-nineteenth century, the political authority of the Qing administration began to weaken under the impact of China's defeat in the first Opium War and severe dislocation occasioned by the Taiping Rebellion.

A recent study suggests that between the reign of Shun Zhi (1644–1661) and the eve of the Rebellion grain production rose more than two-and-a-half fold (see Table 12.1)

If these figures are to be believed, they suggest that from the beginning of the Qing Dynasty until 1850 total grain output grew, on average, by around 0.5 per cent p.a. Expansion of the cultivated area[9] under grain contributed more than half of this increase. But *can* the figures be believed? Without a great deal more evidence it is impossible to know. We merely observe here that a comparison of these figures with estimates

Table 12.1 Grain production trends in China, 1573–1850

	Area under grain (m ha)	Average yield (kg/ha)	Total output (m tonnes)
Ming Emperor Wan Li (1573–1620)	47.9	1,825.7	87.5
Qing Emperor Shun Zhi (1644–61)	38.4	1,828.1	70.2
End of reign of Qing Emperor Kang Xi (1720)	60.7	2,093.1	127.1
End of reign of Qing Emperor Daoguang (1850)	75.3	2,439.6	183.7

Source: Zhihong Shi (1989)
Notes: Original estimates given in *shi mou* (area) (1 *shi mou* = c. 1/15 ha), and *shi jin* (yield and output) (1 *shi jin* = c. 0.5 kg)

of grain production after 1949 leaves room for some doubt. If they *are* accepted, they raise interesting questions about the trajectory of grain output growth after 1949, bearing in mind that official estimates show that China's total production of grain in 1957 (the final year of the First Five-Year Plan) was 195.1 million tonnes, or a mere 6.2 per cent higher than Shi's putative figure for 1850.[10]

In the face of such uncertain figures, it is safest to take refuge in a *qualitative* conclusion: namely, that circumstantial evidence suggests that increased yields reinforced an expanding acreage under grain to generate a significant rise in total grain output from the beginning of the Qing Dynasty until the mid-nineteenth century. Until more detailed and/or reliable information becomes available, it is impossible to quantify any of these increases with any confidence.

If anything, the difficulties of quantifying output change after 1850 are even greater, thanks to the impact on farm production of dislocation caused by major political upheavals (above all, the Taiping Rebellion). The depredations of the Taiping regime were felt most acutely in the rich agricultural regions of the Yangtze Delta—Jiangsu and Zhejiang—but also in neighbouring provinces in the middle and lower Yangtze River valley, such as Anhui and Jiangxi. Such turmoil made it difficult to maintain vital farm infrastructure and took a serious toll on agricultural labour supply. The outcome was a sharp narrowing of the balance between population and food supplies.[11]

Meanwhile, under the impact of increasing exposure of China (above all, coastal regions) to international political forces, an important development in the latter part of the nineteenth century was the formation of new linkages between Chinese farmers and the outside world. In particular, demand for cash crops encouraged agricultural specialisation, which—aided also by improvements in transport and communications—facilitated growing integration of China nationally and internationally. Not least, international forces for the first time in China's history exerted a significant influence on domestic farm prices. Given the continental scope of the Chinese economy, this impact was not a uniform one throughout the country, although it could be felt many hundreds of miles inland from the coast (Brandt, 1989, p. 50).

2 Agriculture During the Republican Period (1912–1949)

It is a truism that the years of the Republican period on mainland China were a period of enormous political upheaval and social dislocation, which inevitably impacted on the economy—and especially its dominant sector, agriculture. Between 1911 and 1928 warlordism and conflict between the Chinese Communist Party (CCP) and Guomindang (GMD) made unified rule impossible; from 1937 war against Japan (1937–1945) and Civil War between the forces of the CCP and GMD had a hugely dislocating effect on the farm economy, especially in the eastern half of the country. Only during the 'Nanking Decade' (1928–1937) did China approximate to being a unified country.

For many years the prevailing view of pre-1949 rural society in China was shaped by the belief that institutional barriers were responsible for holding back agricultural growth. The unequal distribution of land and a rise in the number of landless peasants, increasing indebtedness, harsh exploitation of tenant farmers by landlords and local authorities, infrastructural neglect and deficient investment—all these factors, it was argued, impeded farm output growth and led to a steady deterioration in rural living standards.

Such views were captured in what used to be called the "distributionist" school of thought. Subsequently, this orthodoxy was challenged by scholars who proposed a more positive interpretation of pre-1949 agricultural growth—sometimes referred to as the "eclectic" approach—that suggested that, at least in some regions, the farm economy "performed remarkably well in supporting a population expansion without a reduction of living standards (except during wartime), providing labour for the expanding urban economy, and exporting food and industrial crops to the cities" (Myers, 1970, p. 293).[12] The emergence of a more commercialised agriculture, with its payoff in terms of specialisation, is one factor that promoted the buoyant performance to which Myers refers, although he is at pains also to stress the technological constraints on output growth.

Suggesting that there exists a clear demarcation between "distributionist" and "eclectic" approaches is, however, ultimately misleading. Given the huge physical scale of China, its resource, climatic, institutional and economic conditions are sufficiently varied to be fully capable of embracing both optimistic and pessimistic interpretations of what was happening in China between 1912 and 1949.[13]

Quite detailed estimates of the sown area, yield and total output of major grain crops are available from a variety of Chinese sources for every province during 1914–1918, 1924–1929 (average), 1931–1937 and 1946–1947 (Xu, 1983, pp. 12–87). However, they pose formidable interpretative difficulties, which limit their usefulness for a study of limited scope such as the present one. Instead, we draw on the findings of some recent research conducted by Chinese colleagues in an attempt to identify factors shaping agricultural development during the Republican period, some of which have been largely ignored in previous analysis.

There is evidence that during the Republican period, measured in value terms, the rural economy achieved quite buoyant growth (Sheng, 2002), with the sale of agricultural products recording average annual growth of around 5 per cent between the mid-1890s and 1930s (Ding, 1985). There is, however, also evidence that a number of forces intervened to undermine this growth momentum.

The first of these was a change in the tax regime facing farmers. During the Qing Dynasty tax payments—both the central government's formal agricultural tax and local authorities' additional exactions—seem not to have been a major burden on farmers (Zhang, 2006).[14] Following its establishment of a strong, nominally unified government in 1928, the GMD ceded most tax-raising responsibilities to local—essentially provincial—government authorities. Since the remit of local governments was exercised most strongly in the rural sector, agricultural taxes became the main formal source of financing provincial expenditure. As a result, agricultural taxes rose sharply (Buck, 1968, pp. 324–332),[15] with some part of North China experiencing a threefold rise between 1928 and 1933 (ibid.). According to one source, the increased tax burden was the main factor contributing to worsening rural poverty in Gansu (Huang, 2009), while elsewhere higher taxes had a similar though less severe impact through their knock-on effect on rents (Liu, 2016). One study (Zhang, 1957, pp. 9–11) reveals that by 1934 the average tax burden per unit area of paddy and dry-crop land in China had risen by 83 and 79 per cent, respectively. It is true that the GMD later acknowledged the negative impact of its fiscal policies, and there is evidence of a declining burden in 1935–1936, although on the eve of the outbreak of war against Japan farm taxes were still two-thirds or more higher than at the beginning of the Republican period (ibid.).

For those of a "distributionist" persuasion the rate and burden of tenancy were critically important factors shaping developments in the farm sector in the 1920s and 1930s. In general, land distribution was more equal in northern than in southern China (Shi, 2002). But even in the south, where landlordism was more common, for hundreds of years the right to *use* the land had traditionally taken precedence over ownership rights.[16] By contrast, with the establishment of GMD rule, the government began to adopt a Western-style code of law, which favoured those in possession of the ownership rights to land and made it easier to dispossess farmers of their use rights. In short, under the GMD regime changes in the legal code increased tenants' vulnerability.

While there appears to be little evidence of a significant increase in the incidence of tenancy during the 1920s and 1930s, there *is* evidence of a deterioration in conditions for farm tenants. Security of tenure weakened, as tenants were forced to renegotiate contracts more frequently—a development which imposed an increasing financial burden, since a new contract required the payment of a new deposit and was frequently accompanied by a rise in rent. Nor were rent receipts used for farm investment; more often than not, they were channelled into consumption or speculation, especially among growing numbers of absentee landlords.[17]

As for type and level of rent, the heterogeneity of conditions in China make it impossible to generalise. Rents might be paid in cash or in kind (or sometimes converted from kind to cash), as a fixed amount or as a share of the harvest of the main crop. Typically, rents seem to have absorbed between 40 and 50 per cent of tenants' annual output, although there were significant variations depending on geography, land quality and the type of rental system. There is some evidence that during the 1920s and 1930s the burden of rent was rising.[18]

Rural indebtedness was also rising, especially under the impact of the Great Depression of the early 1930s, when the incidence of farm bankruptcy increased sharply. Almost 40 per cent of farmers surveyed during 1929–1933 by J.L. Buck in his famous study, which is generally thought to have contained a bias towards richer farmers, were in debt—most of the credit having been used for consumption rather than for productive purposes (Buck, 1968, p. 461 *et seq*). In the absence of a national credit market, most loans were from local and personal sources, and incurred annual interest rates typically of 30 per cent or more. By contrast, only about 20 per cent of farmers reported having any savings, most of which were in the form of money loans (ibid., p. 466).

The government of the Republic of China under Chiang Kai-shek did not precipitate disaster on the scale, whether in economic or human terms, that was comparable with that which was to follow the collapse of Mao Zedong's Great Leap Forward in 1959–1961. Nevertheless, during the Republican period the farm sector *was* largely neglected. This was not by intent, but by default—the consequence of political rather than economic factors. The evidence suggests that despite the formulation of rational and comprehensive rural reform initiatives—embracing land reform, land reclamation, irrigation extension, reforestation, pest control, seed improvements, etc.—little progress was made towards raising productivity and farm efficiency, let alone improving farmers' welfare.

The reason why the potential benefits of productivity enhancing initiatives were left unfulfilled lies largely in the nature of the GMD's social and political allegiances. The leadership unequivocally identified with the rural landowning class, and its political authority in the countryside was dependent on support of the rural gentry. Thus:

> A true agrarian reform [in pre-1949 China] would have...challenged the social and political relationships that were at the basis of the rural order. The landlord élite was...a sort of rural aristocracy that dominated and exploited village society...[I]t held economic power...and, by virtue of this fact, political influence. Rather than attack all these privileges and risk antagonising a class that controlled almost all of village society, the Kuomintang preferred to jettison this part of Sun Yat-sen's programme [i.e., the policy of 'land to the tiller' [*gengzhe you tian*, 耕者有其田]]. (Bianco, 2001, p. 39)[19]

A reasonable summing up would be that in the Nanking Decade the GMD deserves quite high marks for farm policy formulation and content; but low marks for implementation. Perhaps the most damning indictment of all is in the finding that the share of the national budget directed to rural reconstruction during 1931–1936 averaged less than 3 per cent. By contrast, in Taiwan under the Japanese colonial government, by 1930–1934 just over a quarter of all fixed investment was allocated to agriculture (Ho, 1978, pp. 35–36).

3 Agricultural Development in the People's Republic (1949–2016)

3.1 China's Agriculture Under Mao Zedong

The destruction caused by the war against Japan (1937–1945) and the subsequent Chinese Civil War (1946–1949) caused agricultural production to fall to a crisis level at the end of the 1940s. Following the establishment of the People's Republic of China (PRC) in 1949, agriculture was a priority concern of government planners. A lagging agricultural performance not only limited rural development, it also affected the country's ability to fulfil the long-term macroeconomic goal of rapid industrialisation. Within the farm sector itself, the core challenge was how to generate sufficiently rapid grain output growth to meet the nutritional needs of a growing population (especially the urban proletariat).

The evolution of agricultural policy after 1949 was dominated by institutional change. Once land reform had been completed, the rural economy and society were transformed by rapid agricultural collectivisation, which eventually culminated in the emergence of the three-tier system of communes, brigades and production teams. These changes fundamentally changed the way in which agricultural production was organised in China.

The shift towards a collectivised agriculture began in the early 1950s. It reached its apogee during the "high tide" of 1955–1956, and the Great Leap Forward of 1958. Mismanagement of the Leap led directly to the catastrophic famine of 1959–1961. In general, however, the shift towards a collective agriculture—in particular, the labour mobilisational capacity that resulted from the reorganisation of farm production—was accompanied by rising farm output. Once recovery from the post-Leap famine had been completed, from the late 1960s until the mid-1970s total output steadily increased. In general, China's agricultural growth throughout the Mao Era (1949–1978) compares quite favourably with that of many other developing countries during the same period.

The defining feature of this performance is that it was ultimately based on the use of massive inputs of labour. These were mobilised within the new institutional framework of farming. Crucially, however, farmers' decision-making power was abrogated to higher-levels of authority within this framework.[20] Contributions from capital investment and technological innovation were less significant, although improvements in water control and irrigation (Vermeer, 1977), and the more extensive use of chemical fertilisers and machinery (Dawson, 1970; Kuo, 1970; Liu, 1970; Stavis, 1978) helped promote farm output growth, especially from the mid-1960s.

Nevertheless, official production estimates suggest that the mobilisation and intensive use of China's abundant farm labour force were insufficient to generate sustained growth in per capita grain output. Even if its output impact was positive, institutional change, assisted from the mid-1960s by increased availability of some modern inputs, appears eventually to have been accompanied by diminishing returns (Perkins, 1975).

In interpreting these estimates, note that during the Mao Era an average per capita grain allocation of 270–310 kg of raw grain would have been sufficient to meet rural subsistence requirements (including allowances for feed and seed) (Walker, 1984, pp. 3–4). As Fig. 12.1 shows, between the 1950s and 1970s per capita output failed to meet this criterion until the mid-1970s, with domestic food output barely keeping pace with population growth. In this regard, the collapse of agriculture caused by mismanagement in the Great Leap Forward marked a watershed, forcing the government for the first time since 1949 to resort to grain imports in 1960. Thereafter, for most of the rest of the Mao Era, China's status as a net importer of food grains necessitated large-scale outflows of foreign exchange (see Table 12.2).

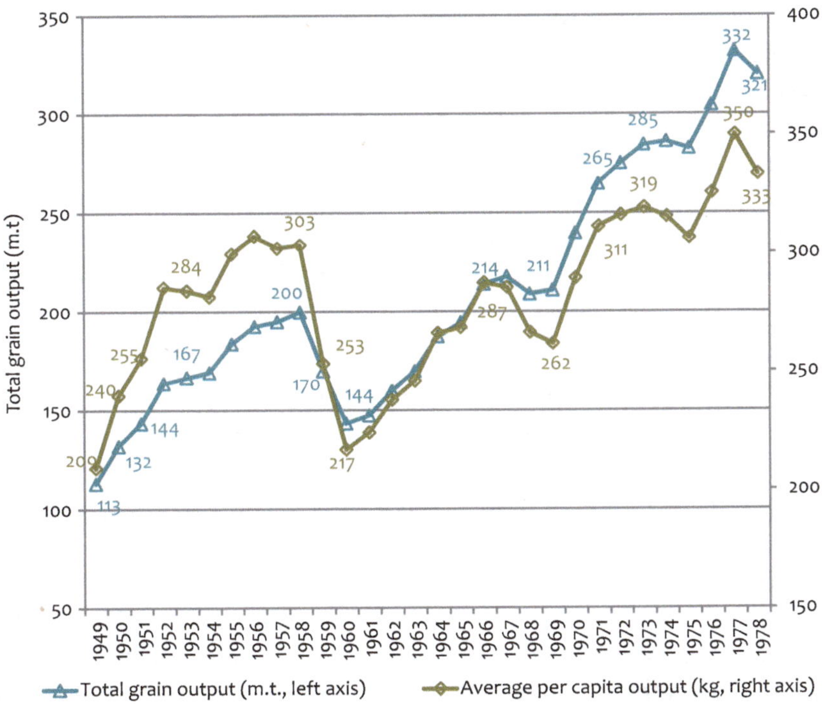

Fig. 12.1 Changes in total and per capita grain output, 1949–1978. Note: These estimates refer to raw grain. Source: Derived from estimates of population and total production in NBS, various years

Table 12.2 China's food import-export balance, 1953–1978

	South China	North China	Total
Pre-collectivisation			
1953–1955	6.89	2.04	8.93
Post-collectivisation			
1956–1960	19.51	−4.72	14.79
1961–1965	6.70	−20.14	−13.44
1966–1970	9.42	−7.97	1.45
1971–1975	9.53	−11.59	−2.06
1976–1978	−0.23	−11.06	−11.29

Source: Data derived from Du, Jun and Deng, Keng (2017)
Note: All figures in million tones. Negative figures indicate the need for food imports to bridge domestic food deficits

Neither the re-organisation of farming and rural society, nor somewhat belated efforts to modernise agriculture through increased provision of modern inputs succeeded in promoting sufficiently rapid output growth. On the contrary, emergence of food deficits and enforced recourse to grain imports highlight low levels of productivity and efficiency that persisted in agriculture. Meanwhile, the central government's introduction in 1953 of monopoly grain procurement ensured that welfare gains accrued exclusively to industrial workers in the urban sector. A further corollary of the heavy industrialisation imperative was a distorted output structure within agriculture (Fan and Nolan, 1994; Lin, 1989; Perkins, 1988).

3.2 The Performance of the Grain Sector Under the Impact of Post-1978 Reforms

Overall, grain output growth since 1978 has been impressive, even allowing for some significant, largely policy-induced, fluctuations in production (see Fig. 12.2). The sharpest downturn in total output occurred between 1998 and 2003, but with recovery completed in 2008 there followed a series of record bumper harvests which was interrupted only in 2016. However, the previous peak level of *per capita* production—that of 1996—was re-attained as recently as 2011, although it subsequently rose to a historic peak of more than 450 kg in 2016.[21] The fact that during the most recent downturn China was not, except in 2004, forced to resort to large-scale imports highlights the critical role played by its enormous domestic grain stocks.

Output growth reflects changes in sown area and/or yields. Examination of both in respect to cereals and soya beans reveals that yields of all four crops have risen (Fig. 12.3a), but that the sown area under rice and wheat has contracted, while that of corn and soya has expanded (Fig. 12.3b). The net result is that rising yields have more than offset sown area declines for rice and wheat, while for corn and soya higher yields have reinforced the output effect of expanding sown areas.

Deng Xiaoping's reforms began in agriculture, where they were most dramatically embodied in the reintroduction of household-based production activities. This reversal of the previous collectivist thrust of agricultural policy was no doubt the most eye-catching aspect of government efforts to revive China's farm economy after 1978. But institutional change was only one aspect of a *package* of policy measures which characterised the first agricultural reforms. Indeed, it was the combined impact of several simultaneous initiatives—enhanced incentives among farmers, higher grain procurement prices, the delegation of decision making powers to producers, and stronger direct links between effort and rewards—that facilitated increases in agricultural total factor productivity (Fan, 1991).

Farmers are famously rational and sophisticated in their decision making (Cheung, 1969). Having been dormant since the early 1950s, the reintroduction of market forces in the 1980s encouraged farmers' price sensitivity to re-emerge, enabling input adjustments to increased procurement prices to facilitate rapid grain output growth (1979–1984). In addition, rural market reforms had a significant technological pay-off. They were instrumental in freeing the market for farm inputs and making industrial and technology-based inputs—chemical fertilisers, new seed varieties and better farm machinery—available to the agricultural sector. The use of such inputs and application of other benefits of advances in agricultural technology contributed significantly to rising grain output during and after the 1980s (ibid., also Lin, 1991; Huang & Rozelle, 1996).

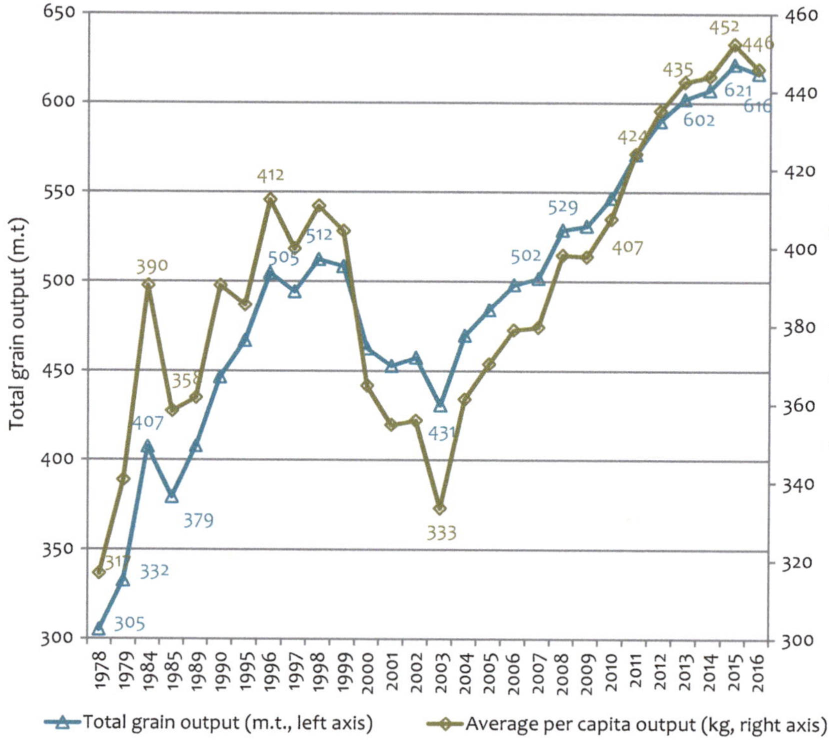

Fig. 12.2 Trends in total and per capita grain production (1978–2016). Sources: China, National Bureau of Statistics, *Zhongguo tongji nianjian* (China Statistical Yearbook), 2016 and various previous issues; NBS (2009), NBS (2017)

3.3 Opening Up the Market and Controlling the Surplus

Compared with the Mao Era, one of the most distinctive changes that took place after 1978 was the re-activation of the price mechanism, enabling the government to use price adjustments to encourage output growth. However, the government's strategic priority—maximisation of industrial growth—remained basically unchanged.

In pursuit of this goal, the government sought, as it had done in the past, to hold down wage costs in the industrial sector through maintaining a net resource transfer from the rural to the urban sector. Since the

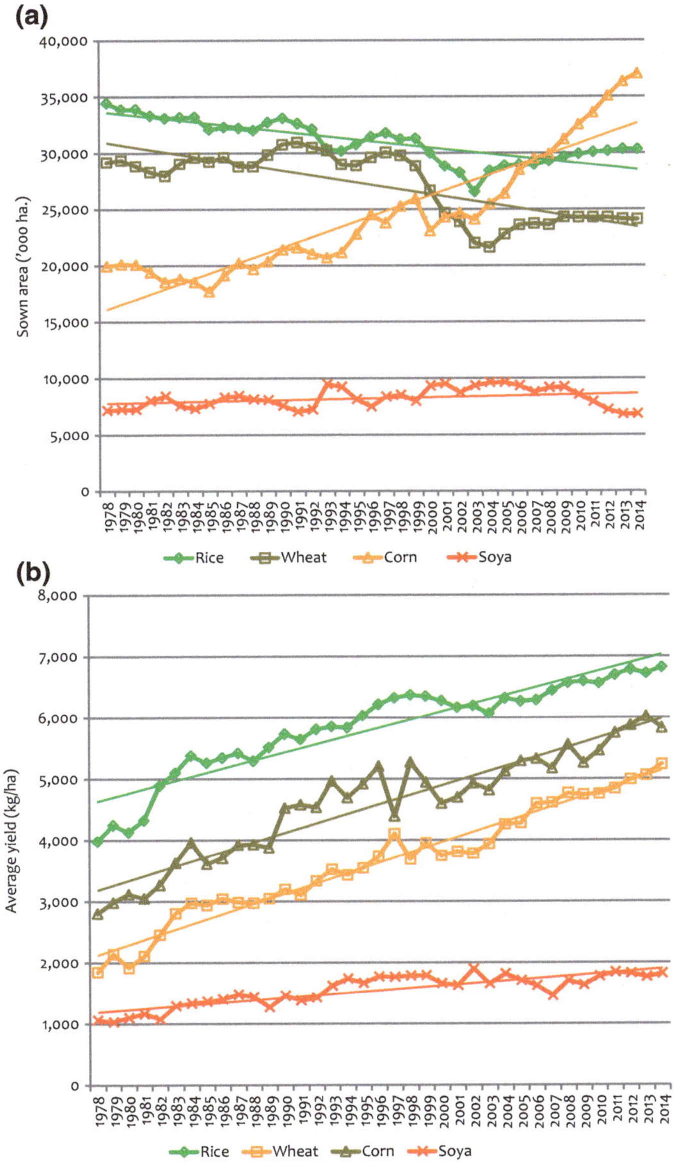

Fig. 12.3 (**a**) Changes in sown area under rice, wheat corn and soya (1978–2014). (**b**) Changes in average yield of rice, wheat, corn and soya (1978–2014). Sources: Sown area and total output estimates from China, National Bureau of Statistics, *Zhongguo tongji nianjian* (China Statistical Yearbook), 2016 and various previous issues. Yield estimates derived from total output and sown area data

1950s the framework by which it controlled the use of the agricultural surplus was the grain circulation—Central Purchase and Centre Supply (CPCS)—system whereby grain procured at a low price from farmers was made available even more cheaply to urban households. In effect, the government subsidised industrial workers and their families by squeezing farmers through manipulation of the "price scissors" (Ash, 2006; Knight, 1995; Sah & Stiglitz, 1987). Until the 1980s tight administrative controls through central planning mechanisms made it relatively easy to reallocate the agricultural surplus to the urban sector. However, as the economy was opened up to the market and price signals began to shape farmers' decision making, the government was forced to resort to compensatory measures in an attempt to prevent industrial costs from rising without threatening farm output growth. In short, it faced a major fiscal challenge of maintaining support for farmers without jeopardising subsidy protection for the urban sector (Du & Deng, 2017).

Already in 1985 the government had acknowledged the outmoded nature of the CPCS system and endorsed its replacement by market forces (Ash, 1993). But emerging problems in the farm sector forced a retreat, and at the beginning of the 1990s most grain and almost all cotton were still being sold through state commercial channels (Ash, 2001, p. 83). In 1993 a new initiative once more signalled the government's determination to sanction the use of markets as the main channel for transferring food from the rural to the urban sector. Yet again, however, such efforts were thwarted—in this case by soaring retail food price inflation—leading the government to re-impose control over grain farmers. But by the end of the 1990s the cumulative fiscal burden resulting from price support for farm producers had become unsustainable and was jeopardising fiscal balance. The government once more conceded that allowing a widening inter-sectoral price gap to facilitate a continued *de facto* rural–urban welfare transfer was unsustainable. Hence, in 1998, another reform initiative whereby farmgate procurement pricing responsibilities were relinquished to the Grain Bureau.

With the Grain Bureau in control, a steady decline in the real procurement price halted grain output growth. In 1998 total grain production was at a historic peak, but thereafter until 2003 China witnessed a decline in total and per capita output unprecedented since 1979 (see Fig. 12.2).

The government's response was to sanction wholesale liberalisation of the grain market and to abandon any suggestion of rural–urban transfers by introducing for the first time direct subsidies to grain farmers. From 2004 the focus of institutional changes in agriculture was to adjust protection prices for major crops in the main producing regions, while seeking to rebuild China's strategic grain reserve.

Before 1978 resources in both the rural and the urban sectors were tightly controlled by the central planned system. China's agricultural performance displays a strong correlation with major state economic plans. Farmers were prevented from leaving the agricultural sector under the dual constraints of central planning and the *hukou* (household registration) systems. As a result, there was a very clear demarcation between the agricultural and industrial sectors.

After 1978 the re-introduction of market forces blurred this boundary, facilitating inter-sectoral resource flows. The boom in non-state owned enterprises in eastern coastal provinces in the 1980s was a major source of labour demand, and encouraged the movement of labour out of farming into the industrial sector (including township and village enterprises). Until the mid-1990s, although jobs for university graduates continued to be allocated by the government, most of the labour needed by non-state-owned enterprises was provided by migrants from farming. As the agricultural and industrial sectors began to compete for labour, rural labour out-migration presented Chinese agriculture with a new challenge—one that impacted on the marginal product of farm labour. Between the early 1960s and the end of the 1970s, the urban share of total population remained quite constant at 17–18 per cent. But thereafter it steadily increased and in recent years has accelerated sharply, reaching more than 57 per cent in 2016. Such figures are striking, but the true effect of the labour outflow on farming was even more severe than they suggest. First, those who abandoned farming mainly comprised young and relatively better-educated labourers (Ji et al., 2016), resulting in a steady rise in the average age of Chinese farmers to around 60 years. Second, those working in privately owned enterprises in the countryside retained their *rural* household classification, despite being *de facto* industrial workers.

Despite this major loss of farm labour, grain output did not fall. On the contrary (Fig. 12.2), from the early 1980s to the present day the output of major grain crops has shown a strong trend increase. Given the decrease in labour input and with little change in the grain-sown area having taken place,[22] labour-saving technical change seems the most likely source of sustained output growth in post-1978 years. This is not to ignore the impact of institutional change. But it is to suggest that when viewed through the eyes of future analysts, the effect of such changes may seem to have been quite short-lived.

3.4 Concluding Remark

The reforms which were instituted at the end of 1978 constitute a watershed in China's agricultural development. Previously, central planning had made possible tight administrative control over all aspects of agricultural production, including the use of physical inputs. Restrictions on labour movements meant that farm labour supply was regulated by the rate of rural population growth. In effect, rural labour was trapped in an inefficient agricultural sector, which encouraged the adoption of highly labour-intensive production methods encapsulated in the Cultural Revolution slogan "In agriculture learn from Dazhai".

The major benefit of this system was that it enabled the state to control the surplus, but at the expense of gross inefficiency and low farm incomes. After 1978, as market forces and price signals began to make themselves felt, farmers' decisions were no longer led by planning imperatives, but were increasingly shaped by changing prices. Simultaneously, rapid urbanisation, accelerated industrial development and large-scale infrastructural construction encroached on an already limited arable land base, whilst also encouraging massive inter-regional labour flows.

Notes

1. An early twentieth-century Japanese source makes the point forcefully: "On the Manchus becoming the masters of China, they did not like to have their birthplace defiled by the subject nation, and forbade the Chinese to immigrate into it. This greatly retarded the economic progress

of the country [Manchuria]...[When Chinese migrants were subsequently allowed once more to settle in Manchuria] these immigrants carried with them the advanced knowledge of agriculture, and the intelligence and industry inborn in the great race" (Bank of Chosen, 1920, pp. 12–13). See also Naoto (1995).

2. Access to farmland outside China Proper was a major source of the increase in arable land. E.g. Kent Deng notes that "[t]he additional farmland supply in Manchuria and South Mongolia alone was equivalent to about one-sixth of China's total" and he adds that "China's farmland more than doubled in the first 100 years of the Qing rule" (Deng, 2015, p. 6).
3. Among those who have wrestled with these problems, often reaching different conclusions, are: Ho (1959: Chap. 6); Perkins (1969: esp. Appendix B, 217–240); and Kang Chao (1986: esp. Chap. 4).
4. Cf. Deng's (2003) estimate of 1.7 per cent p.a. population growth between 1734 and 1833 and the much lower 1.1 per cent growth rate (1943–1833) given by Ho (1959) and Perkins (1969). The difference reflects a wide disparity in the base year figures: Deng's population estimate for 1734 is 75.2 m; that of both Ho and Li, for 1741, is 143.4 m. Commenting on official Qing census data, Kent Deng argues that "the [Chinese] census-based series are fundamentally sound: institutionally, economically, sociologically and biologically (i.e., in terms of human reproductive parameters). The conclusion is that Chinese official census data are...more accurate and reliable than all the modern-day estimates or guesses" (Deng, 2004).
5. After 1850 political dislocation and the delegation of important fiscal and other responsibilities to provincial officials impacted on China's population registration system. Thus, "the century between 1851 and 1949...is practically a demographer's vacuum" characterised by the absence of any reliable provincial population estimates (Ho, 1959, pp. 97 and 246). The demographic impact of the Taiping Rebellion was catastrophic, according to some sources reducing the total population by one-sixth. Millions of lives were also lost as a result of natural disasters.
6. The gradual dissemination of paddy cultivation techniques had a huge pay-off, and laid the foundation for the eventual spread of wet rice culture throughout Southern China. Success in using wet-field rice farming techniques was critically dependent on access to water, especially between flowering and ripening of the rice-plant. No less important was the

introduction of new seed strains, the single most important of which was early ripening rice, whose shorter growing period made it possible to introduce a second (winter) crop, thereby extending double cropping over a much wider area and generating increased energy supplies (calories).

7. Compared with pre-industrial agricultural technologies available to European farmers, a major advantage of wet-field rice cultivation was its ability to maintain soil fertility at a high level, without the necessity of rotating crops. Its main challenge was, however, a high labour requirement.
8. Nor were they necessarily engaged full-time in farming: many pursued handicraft activities in the winter months when conditions made it impossible to work in the fields.
9. Although Shi is not explicit on this point, his estimates would appear to reflect the *arable* grain area and average yields per unit of *arable* land under grain.
10. Comparison of Shi's estimates of per capita output (1989, p. 66) with those of the post-1949 period is no less interesting, suggesting that the 1850 per capita level was not re-attained until into the 1980s in post-1949 China.
11. Cf. Perkins, who argued that domestic political upheavals acted as a safety valve that "helped delay a Malthusian day of reckoning for Chinese agriculture…Were it not for the Taiping Rebellion, rising population in the late nineteenth and early twentieth centuries might have outstripped the ability of Chinese agriculture to provide adequate food supplies" (1969, p. 29).
12. The focus of Myers' study was the two provinces of Hebei and Shandong.
13. Myers captures this well: "A study of Chinese agriculture on a global basis will always be complex and intractable. The huge size and diversity of China must make us cautious in theorizing about agriculture elsewhere in the country. In the famine-ridden northwest great masses of peasants were perpetually on the verge of starvation; the human spirit frequently broke under these conditions, and the family disintegrated. On the other hand, commerce was more developed and rural conditions were more prosperous and stable in the central provinces" (1970, pp. 294–295).
14. After an increase in the early Qing, the formal agricultural tax burden remained stable until towards the end of the Dynasty, when the Taiping

Rebellion led to a tax rise (Liu, 1912). Additional taxes were levied by local authorities to fund local expenditures.

15. An important distinction is that between "regular taxes" (*zheng shui*, 正税) and "supplementary taxes" (*fu shui*, 附税). The late 1920s and 1930s saw the introduction of an increasing number of new levies on farmers, the burden of which gradually outweighed that of "regular" taxes.
16. Hence the phenomenon of "permanent tenancy" (*yong dian*, 永典), reflecting the symbolic division of a piece of land between the "surface" and "bottom" rights to the land. Cf. the notion of emphyteusis in Roman Law.
17. Cf. J.L. Buck: "…it is the fashion in some places for the landlord to know as little as possible about his business, and any landlord who takes an interest in his holdings loses social status…In southern Kiangsu [Jiangsu], where there are many tenants of absentee landlords and of large resident landlords, the landlord looks upon his tenant as of the lowest order of humanity" (Buck, 1925, pp. 19 and 24).
18. One source suggests that in Jiangsu during the decade before the outbreak of war against Japan in 1937 rents rose substantially: "…in Baoshan [county] the bigger landlords have raised rents by nearly 50%… In Danyang and…villages near Shanghai they have doubled and even trebled them" (Zhang, 1957: Vol. 3, 256–257).
19. Elsewhere, Bianco is unequivocal in arguing that in the face of what he [Bianco] describes as "the most fundamental problem, the condition of the peasantry…the Kuomintang's failure was well-nigh total" (1971, p. 109).
20. There is of course a vast literature on the issues raised in this paragraph. Especially relevant are Walker (1968) and Ishikawa (1967).
21. Increasing affluence since the 1980s has allowed consumption to shift towards a more protein-rich diet, raising the "self sufficiency" benchmark to at least 400 kg.
22. The grain-sown area fell from 120.6 to a low of 99.4 m ha between 1978 and 2003. Although it subsequently recovered, in 2016 it was 113 m ha—still more than 6% below the 1978 level. Concealed in these aggregate figures were sown-area adjustments for individual grains, of which corn was the largest beneficiary, in response to burgeoning demand for animal feed (cf. Fig. 12.3a).

References

Ash, R. F. (1993). Agricultural Policy Under the Impact of Reform. In Y. Y. Kueh & R. F. Ash (Eds.), *Economic Trends in Chinese Agriculture: The Impact of Post-Mao Reforms* (pp. 11–45). Oxford: Clarendon Press.

Ash, R. F. (2001). China's Agricultural Reforms: A Twenty-Year Retrospective. In C. Chao & B. J. Dickson (Eds.), *Remaking the Chinese State: Strategies, Society, and Security* (pp. 76–100). London: Routledge.

Ash, R. F. (2006). Squeezing the Peasants: Grain Extraction, Food Consumption and Rural Living Standards in Mao's China. *The China Quarterly, 188*, 959–998.

Bank of Chosen. (1920). *Economic History of Manchuria. Chosen [Korea]*. Seoul: Bank of Chosen.

Bianco, L. (1971). *Origins of the Chinese Revolution*. Stanford, CA: Stanford University Press.

Bianco, L. (2001). *Peasants Without the Party: Grass-Roots Movements in Twentieth-Century China*. Armonk, NY: M.E. Sharpe.

Brandt, L. (1989). *Commercialisation and Agricultural Development: Central and Eastern China, 1870–1937*. Cambridge: Cambridge University Press.

Buck, J. L. (1925). *Farm Ownership and Tenancy in China*. Shanghai: Commercial Press.

Buck, J. L. (1964). *Land Utilisation in China: A Study of 16,786 Farms in 168 Localities, and 38,256 Farm Families in Twenty-Two Provinces in China, 1929–1933*. New York: Paragon Book Reprint Corp. First published in 1937.

Cao, S. (2009). *Zhongguo Renkou Shi [A History of the Chinese Population]*. Shanghai: Fudan University Press.

Chao, K. (1986). *Man and Land in Chinese History: An Economic Analysis*. Stanford, CA: Stanford University Press.

Cheung, S. (1969). *The Theory of Share Tenancy*. Chicago: University of Chicago Press.

China, National Bureau of Statistics (NBS). (2009). *Gaige Kaifang Sanshi Nian: Nongye Tongji Ziliao Huibian [Thirty Years of Reform and Opening: An Agricultural Statistical Compendium]*. Beijing: Zhongguo rongji chubanshe.

China, National Bureau of Statistics (NBS). (2017). Statistical communiqué of the People's Republic of China on the 2016 National Economic and Social Development. http://www.stats.gov.cn/english/PressRelease/201702/t20170228_1467503.html

China, National Bureau of Statistics (NBS). (annual publication). *Zhongguo Tongji Nianjian* (*China Statistical Yearbook*). Beijing: Zhongguo tongji chubanshe.

Dawson, O. (1970). *Communist China's Agriculture: Its Development and Future Potential*. New York: Praeger.

Deng, K. (2003). *Fact or Fiction? Re-examination of Chinese Premodern Population Statistics*. London: London School of Economics and Political Science, Economic History Working Paper Series, 76.

Deng, K. (2011). *China's Political Economy in Modern Times; Changes and Economic Consequences*. Abingdon: Routledge.

Deng, K. (2015). *China's Population Expansion and Its Causes During the Qing Period, 1644–1911*. London: London School of Economics and Political Science, Economic History Working Paper Series, 219.

Ding, C. (1985). *Guanyu Zhongguo jindai nongcun shangpin jingji fazhan de jige wenti* [Several Problems in Modern Chinese Rural Commercial Economic Development]. *Nankai Jingji Yanjiu [Nankai Economic Research], 3*, 42–47.

Du, J., & Deng, K. (2017). Getting Food Prices Right: The State Versus the Market in Reforming China, 1979–2006. *European Review of Economic History, 21*(3), 302–325.

Du, J., & King, C. (n.d.). *Unravelling China's food security puzzle*. National University of Singapore, East Asian Institute, East Asian Institute Working Papers, 167.

Elvin, M. (1973). *The Pattern of the Chinese Past*. Stanford, CA: Stanford University Press.

Fan, Q., & Nolan, P. (1994). *China's Economic Reforms: The Costs and Benefits of Incrementalism*. Basingstoke: Palgrave Macmillan.

Fan, S. (1991). Effects of Technological Change and Institutional Reform on Production Growth in Chinese Agriculture. *American Journal of Agricultural Economics, 73*, 337–369.

Ho, P. (1955). The introduction of American food plants into China. *American Anthropologist, 57*(2 Part 1), 191–201.

Ho, P. (1959). *Studies on the Population of China, 1368–1953*. Cambridge, MA: Harvard University Press.

Ho, S. P. S. (1975). *Economic Development of Taiwan, 1860–1970*. New Haven, CT: Yale University Press.

Huang, J., & Rozelle, S. (1996). Technological Change: Rediscovering the Engine of Productivity Growth in China's Rural Economy. *Journal of Development Economics, 49*(2), 337–369.

Huang, Z. (2009). *Minguo shiqi Gansu nongjia jingji yanjiu* [An Investigation of the Gansu Peasant Economy in the Republican Era], Part II. *Zhongguo Nongshi [Agricultural History of China], 28*(2), 47–55.

Ishikawa, S. (1967). Resource Flow Between Agriculture and Industry—The Chinese Experience. *The Developing Economies, 5*(1), 3–49.

Ji, X., Rozelle, S., Huang, J., Zhang, L., & Zhang, T. (2016). Are China's Farms Growing? *China and World Economy, 24*, 1.

Knight, J. (1995). Price Scissors and Inter-Sectoral Resource Transfers: Who Paid for Industrialization in China? *Oxford Economic Papers, 47*(1), 117–135.

Kuo, L. T. C. (1970). *The Technical Transformation of Agriculture in Communist China*. New York: Praeger.

Liang, F. (2008). *Zhongguo Lidai Hukou Tianfu Tiandi Tongji [The Statistics of Ancient Accounts, Land and Land Taxes of China]*. Beijing: Zhonghua Book Company.

Lin, J. (1989). An Economic Theory of Institutional Change: Induced and Imposed Change. *The Cato Journal, 9*, 1–33.

Liu, J. (1970). *China's Fertiliser Economy*. Chicago: Aldine Publishing Company.

Liu, Y. (2016). Tianfu, dizu yu Zhongguo chuantong shehui xiangcun jiegou bianqian: jiyu 20 shiji 20–30 niandai de fenxi [Land Tax, Land Rent and Rural Structural Change]. *Xueshu Yuekan [Academic Monthly], 48*(6), 52–67.

Myers, R. H. (1970). *The Chinese Peasant Economy: Agricultural Development in Hopei and Shantung, 1890–1949*. Cambridge, MA: Harvard University Press.

Na, Y. (n.d., mid-Qing). *Collections of Wenyi Lord Na Yancheng*, Vol. 77. (Reprint: *Xubian Siku Quanshu*, Vol. 497. Shanghai: Shanghai Classics Publishing House).

Naoto, K. (1995). 清代双城堡の屯墾について [A Study of Military Cultivation at Shuang Cheng Bao]. In H. Ishibashi (Ed.), *Problems of Qing China* (清代中国の諸問題) (pp. 141–158). Tokyo: Yamakawa Press.

Perkins, D. H. (1969). *Agricultural Development in China, 1368–1968*. Chicago: Aldine Publishing Co.

Perkins, D. H. (Ed.). (1975). *China's Modern Economy in Historical Perspective*. Stanford, CA: Stanford University Press.

Perkins, D. H. (1988). Reforming China's Economic System. *Journal of Economic Literature, XXVI*, 601–645.

Sah, R. K., & Stiglitz, J. E. (1987). Price Scissors and the Structure of the Economy. *Quarterly Journal of Economics, 102*(1), 109–134.

Sheng, B. (2002). *Ershi shiji 20–30 niandai Zhongguo nongcun jingji jiben tezheng tantao* [An Investigation of the Basic Characteristics of the Chinese Rural Economy, 1920s–1930s]. *Zhongguo Nongshi [Agricultural History of China], 21*(4), 59.

Shi, Z. (1989). Qingdai qianqi de gengdi mianji ji liangshi chanliang guji [An Estimation of the Cultivated Area and Grain Yields in the Early Qing Dynasty]. *Zhongguo Jingjishi Yanjiu [Chinese Economic History Research], 2*, 47–62.

Shi, Z. (2002). *Ershi shiji 30–40 niandai Huabei Pingyuan nongcun de tudi fenpei jiqi bianhua* [Changes in Land Distribution on the North China Plain, 1930s–1940s]. *Zhongguo Jingjishi Yanjiu [Chinese Economic History Research], 3*, 2–20.

Stavis, B. (1970). *The Politics of Agricultural Mechanisation in China*. Ithaca: Cornell University Press.

Vermeer, E. (1977). *Water Conservancy and Irrigation in China: Social, Economic and Agrotechnical Aspects*. Leiden: Leiden University Press.

Walker, K. R. (1968). Organisation for Agricultural Production. In A. Eckstein, W. Galenson, & T. C. Liu (Eds.), *Economic Trends in Communist China* (pp. 397–458). Chicago: Aldine Publishing Company.

Walker, K. R. (1984). *Food Grain Procurement and Consumption in China*. Cambridge: Cambridge University Press.

Wang, S. (1911). *Chronicles and Maps of Xinjiang*. Xinjiang: The Governor's Press.

Xu, D. (Ed.). (1983). *Zhongguo jindai nongye shengchan ji maoyi tongji ziliao* (*Statistical Materials on China's Agricultural and Trade in Recent Times*). Shanghai: Renmin chubanshe.

Zhang, Y. (1947). *Zhongguo jindai nongye shi ziliao [Source Materials on Modern Chinese Agricultural History]* (Vol. 3). Beijing: Sanlian chubanshe.

Zhang, Z. (2006). *1927–1937 Huabei tianfu zhengshou tizhi yu nongmin fudan* [1927–1937 North China's Agricultural Tax Collection System and the Burden on Peasants]. *Zhongguo Jingjishi Yanjiu [Research on Chinese Economic History], 3*, 142–148.

Zhu, K. (1972). *Zhongguo jin wuqian nianlai qihou bianqian de chubu yanjiu* [Preliminary research on climate change in China during the past 5,000 Years]. *Kaogu Xuebao [Acta Archaeologica Sinica], 1*, 15–38.

Robert Ash is a Professorial Fellow of the China Institute at the School of Oriental and African Studies (SOAS), University of London. From 1986 to 1995 he was Head of the Contemporary China Institute at SOAS; and from 1999 to 2013, Director of the SOAS Taiwan Studies Programme. During 1997–2001 he was Coordinator of the EU-China Academic Network. He has published widely on many aspects of China's economic development, and has held visiting research and teaching positions at universities in Australia, Hong Kong, France and Italy.

Jun Du is a Visiting Research Fellow in the East Asian Institute, National University of Singapore. Du has specialised in the political economy of Chinese agriculture, and sectoral relations between industry and agriculture and their evolution. The themes of her publications on Chinese agriculture have ranged from Mao's collectivisation to Deng's agricultural reforms, and the role of agriculture in China's return to the market. A current research focus is the historical development of China's agricultural economy and its relationship to modern industrialisation.

Cheng King is Associate Research Fellow at the Institute of Public Policy, South China University of Technology, and he is also a Visiting Fellow at the East Asian Institute, National University of Singapore. He received his PhD in Economics from SOAS, University of London. His major research foci include fiscal management in China between the seventeenth and nineteenth centuries, the agricultural history of ancient China, and the process of post-war economic catch-up in East and Southeast Asia.

Part IV

Latin America and the Settler Economies

13

The Goose That Laid the Golden Eggs? Agricultural Development in Latin America in the 20th Century

Miguel Martín-Retortillo, Vicente Pinilla, Jackeline Velazco, and Henry Willebald

This study has received financial support from Spain's Ministry of Science and Innovation, project ECO2015-65582-P and from the Government of Aragon, through the Research Group "Agri-food Economic History (nineteenth and twentieth Centuries)". The authors wish to thank Bernardo Mueller, Charles Mueller and participants at the Meeting "Agricultural development in the world periphery. A global economic history approach" (University of Zaragoza, April 2017) for their help and advice. The usual disclaimers apply.

M. Martín-Retortillo (✉)
Department of Economics, Universidad de Alcalá de Henares, Alcalá de Henares, Madrid, Spain

V. Pinilla
Department of Applied Economics and Economic History, Universidad de Zaragoza, Zaragoza, Spain

J. Velazco
Economics Deparment, Pontificia Universidad Católica del Perú, Lima, Peru

H. Willebald
Department of Economics, Universidad de la República, Montevideo, Uruguay

V. Pinilla, H. Willebald (eds.), *Agricultural Development in the World Periphery*, Palgrave Studies in Economic History, https://doi.org/10.1007/978-3-319-66020-2_13

1 Introduction

Given its productive and commercial capacity, agriculture in Latin America is called on to play a fundamental role in supplying food to the world, and in improving the situation of its farmers. The region needs responsive and efficient policies and programmes that will raise agricultural productivity in a sustainable and inclusive manner. To accomplish this objective, the Latin American countries have advanced not only in the formulation of sectoral policies, but also in the coordination of effort among the various organisations that make up the institutional architecture aimed at improving the sector's performance. (ECLAC-FAO-IICA, 2015). Supporting these expectations for the twenty-first century requires an adequate review and interpretation of the arguments, experiences, and learning derived from the agricultural history of the twentieth century.

Latin American agriculture is heterogeneous, reflecting the broad diversity of landscapes, climates, soils, and local conditions. However, some common characteristics offer a clear conceptual unity to the region (Solbrig, 2008). The first and most notable is the importance of agriculture in the economies of Latin America. Since colonial times, the region has depended on crops and livestock as major sources of production, employment, exports, and foreign currency. Second, the uneven distribution of land, the well-known latifundio–minifundio coupling, appears as a structural feature that has shaped the agricultural development of Latin America. Third, the persistence of a large sector of small farmers, poorly integrated into the economy and producing primarily food staples for local markets, is a characteristic that exerts its influence on the majority of countries of the region. Finally, in the agricultural export sector, only one (or, occasionally, a very few) products have prevailed in each country. This dependence on a small number of export products has exposed countries to the contingencies of the external markets, price fluctuations, and boom-and-bust cycles.

However, in spite of the importance of agriculture in most Latin American countries, the sector has not often been able to encourage the rest of the economy and create dynamic forward and backward linkages. From a world perspective, the twentieth century involved greater changes in the rural sector than at any other time in history (Federico, 2005). From very traditional and conservative modalities of production, agriculture has been transformed into a knowledge- and science-based enterprise. This process has augmented productivity and supported the expansion of production to keep up with an increased demand from a growing population. It has also altered the relation of people to the land because the industrialisation of farming has increased the linkages and dependence on manufacturing, made agriculture more vulnerable to foreign markets, and exacerbated the environmental consequences of farming (Solbrig, 2008). However, Latin America has been unable to benefit greatly from these changes in supply and demand, and institutional, and technological conditions. The reasons and consequences are discussed throughout this chapter, ordering our analysis and arguments according to the different development patterns that have dominated the Latin American economic evolution during the twentieth century.

2 Commodity Export-Led Growth

In the last third of the nineteenth century, Latin America seemed set for a period of relatively high economic growth rates, thanks to its capacity to integrate itself dynamically into the international economy. This process was the outcome of the confluence of two sets of external and internal factors (Bértola & Ocampo, 2012).

On the one hand, the impact on trade of the revolution in transport, led to significant reductions in maritime and overland shipping costs, narrowing the economic distance between Europe and the Americas (O'Rourke & Williamson, 2001). This effect was reinforced by the sustained expansion of the demand for raw materials and foodstuffs from the core of the world economy. On the other hand, factors derived from the political and institutional changes that had been taking place in most Latin American countries since their independence had significant influence in the so-called liberal economic reforms, whose introduction continued to run its course. Additionally, political power structures were consolidated, giving rise to greater institutional stability in several countries.

The combination of these factors encouraged a dynamic trajectory in Latin American exports and, although the export sector was not prominent, it induced backward linkages with the rest of the economy of varying power in different countries. Growth was also supported by considerable capital inflows and mass immigration from Europe and, to a lesser extent, Asia, although these flows were very unevenly distributed (Williamson, 2002).

In terms of economic policy, free trade, along with a certain degree of protection for domestic industry and foreign investment and immigration, was considered acceptable and generally encouraged. However, the implementation of a consistent set of economic policies was a recurring problem. Economic policy was concerned mainly with the needs of the export sector, and its influence on other activities of the economy remained uncertain. The (usually implicit) assumption was that export growth would enhance productivity growth and structural change throughout the economy.

This wave of economic growth was, to some degree, extensive, in as much as it translated into a marked expansion of the agricultural frontier and the settlement of new areas (Harley, 2007), especially in those parts of Latin America that were growing the fastest. Increased export activity in some regions led to a greater diversification of the production structure, which was manifested in the development of incipient manufacturing, communications, transport infrastructure, and financial services, together with rapid urbanisation.

2.1 Agricultural World Demand and Export-Led Growth

There is no question that the export sector set the pace and was the engine of growth for the entire economy during this time. It is also quite clear that this export pattern was based on agricultural and mining products, with manufactured goods and services playing a negligible role.

The period from the middle of the nineteenth century to WWI was characterised by the rise of new export products in response to the demands created by the Industrial Revolution. In major parts of Latin

America, new exports were of agricultural origin (Bulmer-Thomas, 2003): rubber, wool, henequen, cereals, meat, coffee, cocoa, bananas, quinine, quebracho extract, and Peruvian balsam, sugar, and tobacco.

As a result, and always considering a high degree of generalisation, on the eve of WWI the productive specialisation of Latin America as a whole was mostly dominated by tropical products (almost half of world exports), with temperate-climate products only being important in the Southern Cone (a quarter of total world exports, Bértola & Williamson, 2008).[1]

The introduction of new products did not necessarily lead to export diversification. On the contrary, the rise of new exports was often matched by the eclipse of traditional products, so export concentration remained extremely high. In 1870, the leading export commodity of each of the Latin American countries accounted, on average, for approximately 50 per cent of total exports. By 1913, this figure had dropped to 42 per cent, but it climbed back to 54 per cent by 1929 (Bértola & Ocampo, 2012). This clearly illustrates how important commodities were as an export base for the region, whose competitiveness was heavily dependent on access to a limited number of natural resources. The dependence on only a few export products made countries strongly contingent on the vagaries of external markets and vulnerable to price fluctuations and boom-and-bust cycles.

In terms of export markets, the statistics also indicate a high dependence on the four main industrialised countries (the USA, Great Britain, Germany, and France) with little evidence of intra-regional trade (Carreras-Marín, Badia-Miró, & Peres Cajías, 2013).

The worst situation was clearly one in which exports were concentrated in a single product and a single market and in which the productivity of the non-export sector was unaffected by the dynamism of the exports. It was highly probable that, under such circumstances, export-led growth failed. According to Bulmer-Thomas (2003), such cases were found all too often in Latin America, even during the so-called golden age of export-led growth.

The export-led model, therefore, needed to be extremely dynamic; new products and markets had to be found and introduced. Under these circumstances, it was possible to achieve a significant rise in living standards, provided that the dynamism of the export sector was also reflected in some increase in labour productivity in the non-export sector.

2.2 Export-Led Growth and the Supply Side

The competitiveness of exports was heavily dependent on access to a limited number of natural resources; a situation that the literature identifies with the concept of "commodity lottery" (Díaz-Alejandro, 1984). This concept must be viewed with caution, however, because it can give the impression that export capacity was a question of luck, whereas a broad range of economic and social factors did exist, offering logical cause-and-effect relationships to help understand historical patterns (Bértola & Ocampo, 2012).[2] The efficiency with which each factor functioned determines the results.

The increase in population experienced in the decades following independence deepened during this period. This was also a time in which migration was to play a prominent role. Latin America's population grew at an annual rate of 1.7 per cent in 1870–1929, which was above the world average; even so, of course, it was still a small continent in demographic terms (only 4.2 per cent of the world population). However, the annual increase in labour supply was never enough to satisfy the needs of the export sector for additional workers. The export sector therefore had to attract its labour supply either through internal or international migration (Bulmer-Thomas, 2003).

Internal mobility was historically restricted, and different modalities of coercion—a typical feature of the labour market in colonial times—were still found in different parts of Latin America on the eve of WWI. Many individuals shared the prevailing scorn for the lower classes found among the elite, and assumed that only international migration from Europe could solve the problem of labour shortages (in quantity and quality).

International migration was, in fact, of two kinds: selective and mass. Selective international migration did not mean a free market in labour; workers were imported for specific tasks. Mass immigration was only really important in Argentina, Cuba, Southern Brazil, and Uruguay.

Complaints of labour shortages persisted up to WWI (Bulmer-Thomas, 2003), and the inefficient way in which the labour market operated was certainly one explanation for the low rate of capital formation in certain countries.

The expansion of agricultural exports required access to new lands. No Latin American country suffered from a physical shortage of land, during this period, but access to land was another matter. Latin America suffered from two serious problems. First, inadequate modes of transport meant that large areas were practically inaccessible until the coming of the railways (Kuntz, 2015). Second, Latin America maintained a system of land tenure, inherited from the Iberian Peninsula, that left the ownership of land highly concentrated (Bértola & Ocampo, 2012; Frankema, 2009).

The incorporation of "new" lands over nearly a century was enormous and would have provided many opportunities to alter the concentration ratio if those lands in private ownership had been allocated more equally. The failure to do so responded not only to inherited colonial patterns, but also related to the balance of political power and to economic exigencies post-independence.

The exercise of political hegemony by the landowning class led to the manipulation of fiscal systems and factor markets, which marginalised much of the labour force in both economic and political terms.

Capital requirements were evident, although this input per unit of output was generally higher in mining than in agriculture. The growth of labour productivity in the export sector was made possible through the adoption of technical innovations that tended to be embodied in new capital equipment.

Commercial banking was an important contribution to mobilising resources, but it suffered from two main weaknesses. First, the volume of deposits attracted to commercial banks in most countries was modest. Second, commercial banking had a limited impact on resource allocation in general and on export diversification in particular. In fact, elites attempted to create distributional coalitions that would generate rents for bankers and a source of finance for states (Haber, 2012).

The institutional framework for investment in human capital was even more deficient in most countries (Engerman, Sokoloff, & Mariscal, 2012; Frankema, 2009). Some effort went into the creation of professional institutions for training labour in the new skills required. Schools for engineers were established, along with institutions specialising in plant breeding, agronomy, and livestock raising. At the university level, however, the situation was far from adequate, for neither the curricula nor the course structures had changed much since colonial times (Maloney & Valencia, 2014).

Given the difficulties encountered in mobilising domestic resources, it is not surprising that governments in every country turned to foreigners as a source of additional finance. Direct Foreign Investment (DFI) was attracted to those areas where technological barriers and access to capital restricted the entry of local firms. The bulk of the investment, therefore, flowed toward railways, public utilities, mining, banking, and shipping (Esteves, 2012; Stone, 1999), although the first two activities were by far the most important. However, above all in agricultural production for the home market, DFI played only a minor role in most countries.

2.3 Domestic-Use Agriculture

A successful export-led growth model implies a rapid rise in exports and in per-capita exports, coupled with increases in labour productivity in the export sector. Yet this is only the first, albeit very important, condition for a significant rise in real per-capita income. The second condition is the transfer of productivity gains in the export sector to the non-export economy.

Bértola and Ocampo (2012) propose exercises to examine the dynamics of exports and the domestic market in 1870–1929, and the differences between countries are very important. We consider the growth rates of real exports and domestic markets reported in this study and construct a ratio that represents the relative dynamics of both "sides" of the economy (Fig. 13.1). The ratio is calculated as follows: $[(x+1)/(g+1)]-1$. Where x is the real growth rate of exports and g is the real growth rate of GDP. When the export sector of the economy exhibited a more dynamic evolution than the domestic market, the indicator is positive, and the opposite happens when the ratio is negative. For the whole of Latin America, the external sector was clearly more dynamic than the domestic market. Brazil and Venezuela showed records around the regional average. The countries where the export sector showed a clearly dominant role were Peru, Cuba, and Colombia, and only the Southern Cone of South America—Uruguay, Argentina and, Chile—had truly dynamic domestic markets. In these cases, the domestic market growth was somewhat more stable than the export sector, and gave rise to important structural changes in terms of urbanisation, the development of public utilities, industrialisation, and the development of the state in various areas (Bértola & Ocampo, 2012).

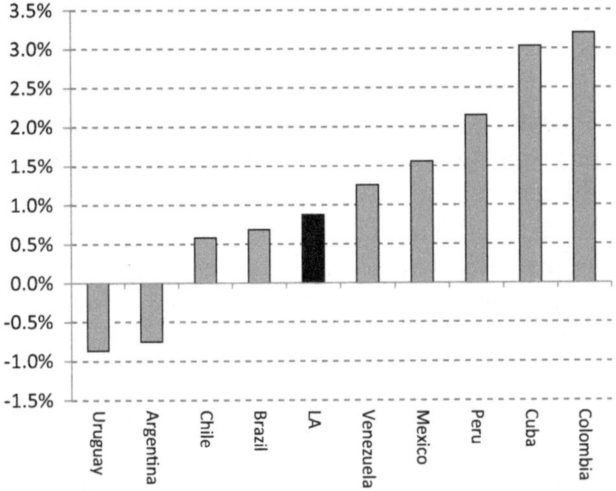

Fig. 13.1 Dynamics of exports and the domestic market, 1870–1929: exports/domestic market growth rates. Source: Bértola and Ocampo (2012, p. 100)

In terms of the labour force, the most important import-competing sector was domestic-use agriculture (DUA) (Bulmer-Thomas, 2003). This branch of agriculture employed everyone in the sector not producing exports, huge estates and tiny plots of land, owner-occupied farms and rented properties, and efficient and inefficient estates. In 1913, the labour force in DUA was the largest component of the economically active population (EAP) in practically all countries and produced an output, which, in principle, could be replaced by imports.

The transference of productivity gains from the export sector to DUA was often very difficult. According to Bulmer-Thomas (2003), first, in a few countries the export commodities were also the staples of the national diet; in these cases (e.g., wheat in Argentina and beef in Uruguay) it was almost inevitable that the technological changes that brought productivity gains to the export sectors would do the same for DUA. The Chilean case is more impressive. Despite the success of wheat exports, foreign-exchange earnings were derived mainly from minerals. Yet the productivity of Chilean farming could still benefit from mineral production because the concentration of workers around the nitrate mines in the deserts of northern Chile was a powerful stimulus to technological change and labour productivity in the fertile central valley. Second, labour productivity in DUA could expect to benefit from the lowering of transport costs, the growth of financial institutions linked to the export sector, and the rise of a more sophisticated division of labour, related to population growth and the expansion of the market. In general, DUA kept pace with the growth in demand but the majority of Latin American countries failed to transfer productivity gains. In a long tradition, Latin American structuralism identified this fact with the concept of "structural heterogeneity" (Pinto, 1965, 1970) and the conformation of dual economies.

The relationship between exports and real income per capita almost a century after independence is plotted in Fig. 13.2. Despite the fact that our data on exports includes all types of products, we assume that they represent a good proxy to agricultural exports. It is difficult to deny that export performance was an important determinant of the standard of living in Latin America before WWI (Bulmer-Thomas, 2003). Points above the line refer to countries—Argentina, Uruguay—whose real GDP per

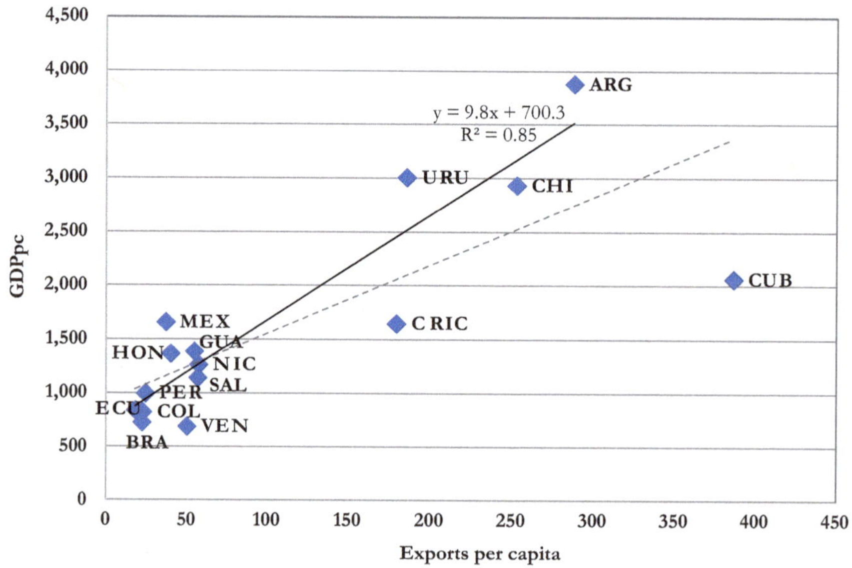

Fig. 13.2 Real GDP and exports per capita circa 1913. Source: Bértola and Ocampo (2012) and authors' own elaboration from Bulmer-Thomas (2003)

head is higher than predicted by export performance. Points below the line refer to countries—Costa Rica, Cuba—with income per head lower than predicted. Even when we exclude Cuba from the analysis, the best fit improves significantly showing the relevant "underperformance" of a country with noticeable characteristics of an enclave economy.[3]

3 The Inward-Looking Development Model: Agriculture Loses Its Leading Role, 1950–1973

The turbulence and problems for exporters of primary products in the years 1914–1945 had a severe impact on the strategies of economic growth followed during the second post-war period. The Great Depression, which began in 1929, was a great external shock for Latin America, the countries of the region having no capacity to control it. It seriously affected world trade, with falls in volume and prices. However, one of the principal sources of recovery in South America, following the worst years of the Depression, was the promotion of exports, which recovered from 1931 on. Many governments took active measures to try to ensure the survival of the export sector; these included devaluation, the creation of new financial institutions providing credit for exporting companies, moratoria on external debt, governmental purchase, and even the destruction of harvests to maintain prices, and the establishment of multiple exchange rates (Paiva Abreu, 2006, pp. 106–118).

World War II constituted a heavy blow for the Latin American agro-exporting economies. The war affected mostly those in which the foreign sectors had a greater weight, and whose exports were more oriented towards the European market. Paradoxically, peace did not improve the situation in the short term; in fact, it worsened it for some countries. The demand for strategic products declined, and so did the North American preference for Latin American goods, while the European countries did not substantially increase their imports in the short term. The difficulties of European countries, their shortage of hard currencies, and the non-convertibility of the pound sterling further complicated the situation.

The difficult situation of Europe during reconstruction, the maintenance of high levels of protectionism, and the generalised measures and support for agriculture in Europe, only increased the pessimism regarding the possibilities of the agro exporting model (Paiva Abreu, 2006, p. 121). The exclusion in 1947 of agricultural products from the GATT reinforced this pessimism, confirming the difficulties foreseen for the dismantling of the complex system of tariff and non-tariff protection, which the developed countries had progressively constructed since 1929 and developed further during the war and the early post-war years (Cárdenas, Ocampo, & Thorp, 2000, pp. 13–14).

These difficulties faced by Latin American export-led economies caused deep pessimism regarding the continuity of their model of growth. The United Nations Economic Commission for Latin America (ECLA), led by Raúl Prebisch, proposed, soon after its foundation in 1948, a new model of economic development for the region: the idea of import substitution industrialisation (ISI). In the original formulation of the ECLA to justify the ISI, the decline in the terms of trade for primary products, and the lack of markets with sufficient capacity to absorb them, played a crucial role in explaining the limits to growth imposed by the export-led development model.

Export-led agriculture was penalised by ISI policies, which were clearly biased against exports, giving place to support for industry while sidelining overseas trade in agricultural and food products (Krueger, Schiff, & Valdés, 1990). The resulting impact on agricultural prices was largely a sub-product of this development strategy, hurting the region's most competitive producers who received only meagre compensation in the form of official farm loans and fertiliser subsidies (Anderson & Valdés, 2008).

Policy now focused on measures to protect national output, including high tariff barriers, the imposition of occasional export taxes, indirect taxation of agriculture as a by-product of industrial protection, and overvaluation of the currency. These policies caused a major transfer of resources away from agriculture. The resulting net outflow between 1960 and 1984 has been estimated at 85 per cent of agricultural GDP in Argentina, 56 per cent in Chile and 42 per cent in Colombia (Krueger, Schiff, & Valdés, 1988). The goals, of course, were to hold down food prices, assure the domestic food supply in the cities, and foster the process of industrialisation.

These policies resulted in negative protection rates for agriculture, especially in the initial decades of the period considered. Reasonably reliable estimates exist of the impact of these polices on agriculture in a significant group of Latin American nations between 1965 and 2004. The figures are telling: the nominal rate of assistance (NRA), defined as "the percentage by which government policies have raised gross returns to producers above what they would be without government intervention (or lowered them, if the NRA is below zero)" was negative in weighted average terms in the Latin America nations examined (Argentina, Brazil, Chile, Colombia, the Dominican Republic, Ecuador, Mexico, and Nicaragua) between 1965 and 1989. Public policy depressed farm incomes by between 7 per cent and 21 per cent in this period. Support in the subsequent years was minimal, at no time exceeding 5 per cent of farm incomes. Even more striking was the substantial anti-trade bias. Breaking farm output down into import-competing and exportable products, we may observe that the former enjoyed significant, positive protection throughout practically the whole of the period (1965–2004), despite wide variations in actual levels of support, while the latter were unremittingly disadvantaged, despite a fall in the penalty from around 25 per cent in the 1980s to less than 5 per cent by the 1990s. Finally, the relative rate of assistance (RRA), constructed as the ratio between the NRAs for farm and non-farm products, reveals a strong anti-farm bias in the policies followed in Latin America until the 1980s (Anderson & Valdés, 2008, pp. 21–39).

In this context, significant output growth was achieved, driven by the expansion of domestic demand, the technological gains provided by the green revolution, and the protection afforded to products destined for consumption in the home market (Martín-Retortillo, Pinilla, Velazco, & Willebald, 2016). From a long-term standpoint, agricultural growth rates were above the world average and sometimes even higher in those countries where farmers enjoyed greater government support (Reca & Díaz-Bonilla, 1997). Output growth was exceptional in the case of products for which demand was rising in Latin America (oil seeds, vegetable oils, alcoholic beverages, meat, vegetables and fruit, and dairy products) but very slow for the main agro-export crops (caffeinated beverages and sugar). It would seem reasonable, then, to argue that ISI policies, resting on the competitiveness of Latin American agriculture and tariff barriers, caused a shift in farm output, subordinating the sector to the needs of the industrialisation process.

Consequently, Latin America lost significant weight among world exporters of agricultural products and food until the early 1990s (Serrano & Pinilla, 2014). This was due not only to policy changes and their bias against agrarian exports, but also to specialisation in products with limited demand and a low level of industrial transformation. Additional restrictions were caused by protectionist policies with respect to agricultural products from developed countries, especially from Europe, because trade was often carried out within zones of regional agreements (González, Pinilla, & Serrano, 2015; Serrano & Pinilla, 2016). However, support for agriculture was directed at the production of food or raw materials for the domestic market, particularly in the context of the demographic boom in Latin American countries.

Table 13.1 shows that the average annual growth of Latin American agriculture was moderately high (2.9 per cent) between 1950 and 1973. The countries that grew the most were Mexico, Venezuela and Brazil, with average rates of 5.2 per cent, 4.4 per cent, and 4.1 per cent, respectively. These countries have in common an integrationist approach to ISI, in which agriculture serves as a support for the industrialisation process and nourishes itself from it. Regarding the role of the State, it is actively involved in technological development (linked to the Green Revolution in some countries) and important institutional changes, such as those related to agrarian reform.

On the other hand, Argentina and Uruguay were the countries with the lowest growth rate for the entire period, below 1 per cent annually. In both countries, the 1950s and 1960s were dominated by a policy of industrial promotion, which involved the transfer of resources from the agricultural sector to the manufacturing sector (with profuse rent-seeking activities). Furthermore, a diversity of restrictions on imports of machinery and inputs that caused negative effects on the production of agricultural commodities was carried out.

Figure 13.3 plots the relationship between per-capita GDP and per-capita agricultural exports. For 1961 and 1973 the low level of adjustment, represented by the value of R^2, indicates that during this period, characterised by ISI and policies with anti-agrarian bias, agricultural exports would not have been one of the key factors explaining GDP growth. Moreover, the line of best fit seems to suggest a negative relationship between both variables.

4 The Foreign Debt Crisis and the Lost Decade, 1973–1992

Between 1973 and 1992, the time of economic crisis, the exhaustion of ISI and the foreign debt crisis created conditions for a change to a development model based on export growth (Bulmer-Thomas, 2003; Ffrench-Davis, Múñoz, & Palma, 1997).

The performance of Latin American agricultural production between 1973 and 1993 was the lowest of the second half of the twentieth century (Table 13.1). The generalised implementation of adjustment programmes adopted in the region had an impact upon agriculture. There was a fall in the funds allocated to rural development, the supply of subsidised inputs, state purchases with guaranteed prices, and technical assistance, as well as

Table 13.1 Agricultural gross production (annual growth rates, %)

	1950–1973	1973–1993	1993–2008	1950–2008
Argentina	0.7	1.6	3.0	1.6
Brazil	4.1	3.6	4.4	4.0
Chile	1.3	3.5	2.6	2.4
Colombia	2.5	2.9	2.2	2.6
Honduras	3.6	2.4	3.2	3.1
Mexico	5.2	2.6	2.6	3.6
Panama	3.3	2.3	3.4	3.0
Peru	2.1	1.3	5.6	2.7
Uruguay	0.4	1.3	2.7	1.3
Venezuela	4.4	2.9	2.7	3.4
Latin America	2.9	2.7	3.5	3.0

Source: Authors' elaboration, from FAOSTAT and FAO (1948–2004a). Triennial averages, except 1950

subsidised rural credit. Therefore, both private and public agricultural investment showed a declining trend. Although exchange rate policies tended to benefit agricultural and livestock product exporters, their impact was limited due to the constraints on access to foreign markets and the marked deterioration of international agricultural prices during this period (Serrano & Pinillla, 2011).

Despite the crisis that characterised this period and considering as a reference the year 1983, Fig. 13.3 shows that there is a positive relationship between GDP per capita and agricultural exports per capita. Although the adjustment level of R^2 is very low, suggesting that variations in agricultural exports per capita explain only 5 per cent of the variations in real GDP per capita, a change in the relationship is evident when compared with the previous years.

5 Structural Reforms and the Return to the International Markets of Agricultural Products, 1992–2015

The closing years of the twentieth century were characterised by an expansion of adjustment policies and structural reforms, applied in the late 1980s and early 1990s. As a consequence of the redefinition of the role of the state and the implementation of policies aimed at favouring the free market, the economy as a whole and agriculture in particular underwent changes in productive structure, competitiveness, productivity, and profitability. The new strategy consisted of mobilising resources in competitive export sectors, including agriculture. The outcome was an increase in agricultural exports and a change in their composition towards products with a greater degree of industrial transformation, or with more options for demand expansion. New products, such as fresh fruit and vegetables, vegetable oils, and fodder tended to compete with or replace traditional exports. Thus, the shift in development strategy that began in the 1980s was followed by significant changes in the composition of agricultural trade resulting from the move towards a strategy of reintegration in international markets.

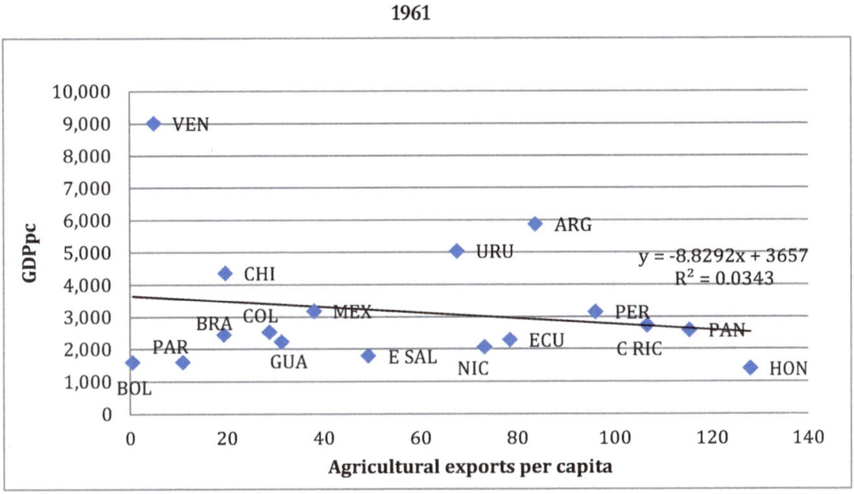

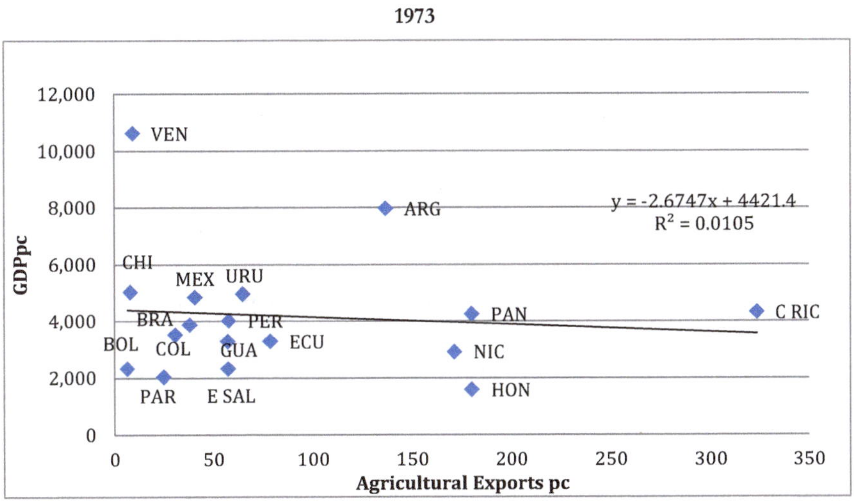

Fig. 13.3 Real agricultural GDP per capita and agricultural exports per capita, 1961–1983. Source: Authors' elaboration, from FAOSTAT database (2017), Maddison database (2010)

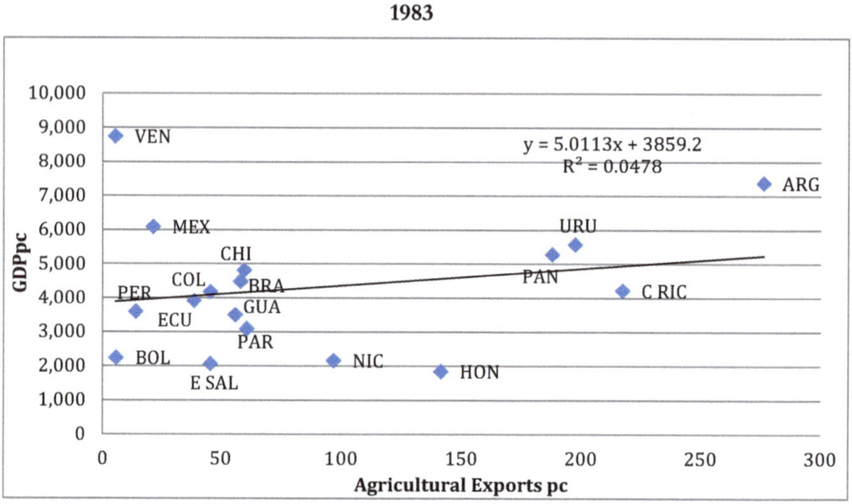

Fig. 13.3 (continued)

Therefore, from the 1990s onwards, Latin America tended to regain importance in international markets for agricultural products and food, as Table 13.2 shows. This was possible due to a change in the mix of exports, resulting in significant gains in the share of high-value products and a decline in the share of basic and, especially, plantation commodities. Moreover, regional integration initiatives began to fructify. Intra-regional trade in farm products grew rapidly at this time. The biggest success stories, however, were agreements like the Asia-Pacific Economic Cooperation (APEC) and Global System of Trade Preferences for developing countries (GSTP), between very different economic structures, which provided the opportunity to supply wider markets, driving technological progress and agro-industrial development.

In addition to this, the trade distortions implemented by the European Community (EC) were less severe than in the first period, with the result that agricultural exports from Latin American countries faced fewer protected markets and lower penalties in key destination markets. Meanwhile, the EU's relaxed agricultural protection resulted in a certain decline in agricultural output (Martín-Retortillo & Pinilla, 2015). The growing

Table 13.2 Latin America in the international trade of agricultural and food products (% of world trade in 1985 $US)

Agricultural exports	1961–63	1971–73	1981–83	1991–93	1998–2000
Latin America and Caribbean	16.52	15.07	14.66	11.20	13.32
Latin American participation by product group					
Basic products	9.61	8.09	7.86	7.14	10.67
Plantation products	44.26	41.53	40.90	23.70	24.75
High-value and processed foods	10.31	10.57	10.72	9.48	11.21
Other agricultural processed products	5.46	5.18	7.97	7.72	11.11

Source: Author's compilation from FAO (1948–2004b) and FAOSTAT

demand from Asia for agricultural or food raw materials also strengthened this impulse to the agro-exporting sector.

However, the prices of traditional agricultural exports from Latin America experienced an acute decline in real terms from 1976 onwards and thus their improvement in terms of volume was not reflected in a similar increase in their real value (Serrano & Pinilla, 2011).

The highest annual growth in Latin American agricultural production in the second half of twentieth century occurred between 1993 and 2008, at an average rate of 3.5 per cent, the leaders being Peru and Brazil (Table 13.1). In the former, the implementation of the stabilisation programme and state structural reforms modified the institutional framework and the conditions in which agricultural producers took part in market relations (Velazco & Pinilla, 2018). Meanwhile, Brazil consolidated an expansionary trajectory where, progressively, the extensive character that prevailed for decades gave rise to an increasing intensification in the use of productive factors and increased productivity (Mueller & Mueller, 2018).

On the other hand, the lowest increases were found in Colombia, Mexico, and Chile. Regarding Mexico, its agriculture as a whole did not expand sufficiently, with the exception of fruit and vegetable crops for export in the north of the country. This outcome can be largely attributed to the inability of a liberalising agricultural policy, highly inequitable in its support for farmers, to transform the agriculture of the country (Yúnez, 2010).

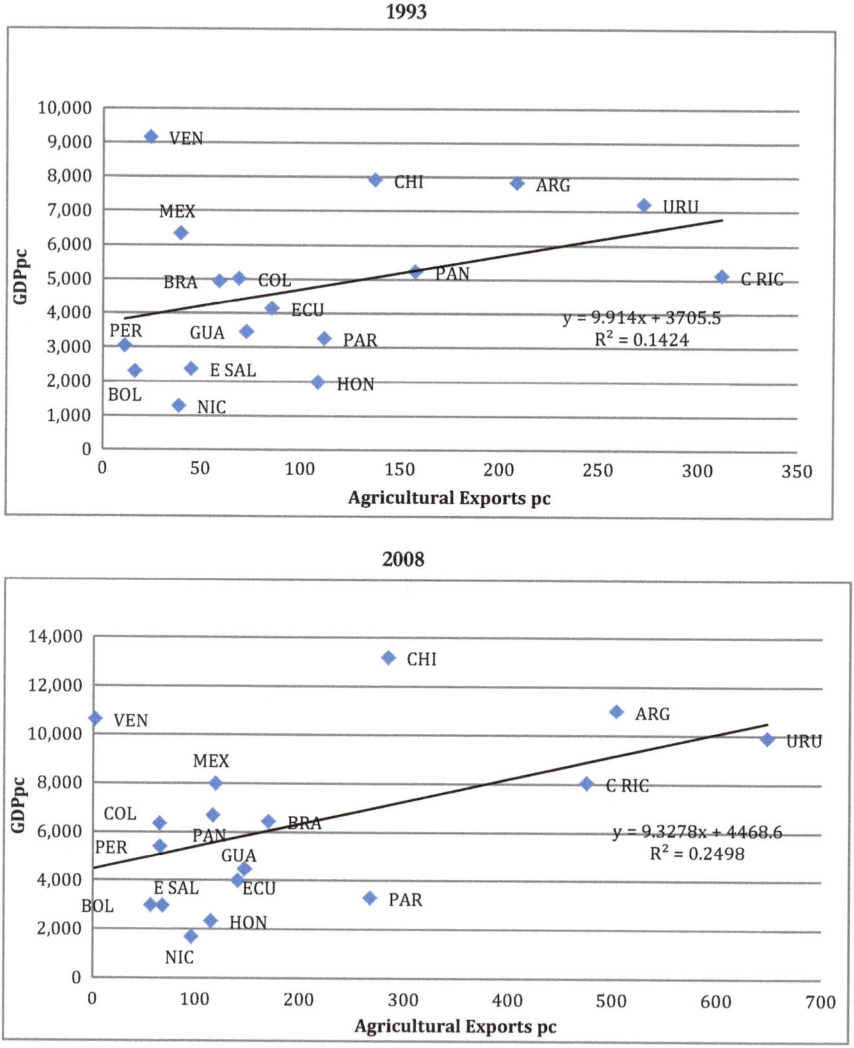

Fig. 13.4 Real agricultural GDP per capita and agricultural exports per capita, 1993 and 2008. Source: Authors' elaboration, from FAOSTAT database (2017) and Maddison database (2010)

In the Southern Cone, increasing international prices for cereals and soya encouraged a growth in the production of these crops. The adoption of transgenic seeds and other innovations such as direct sowing stimulated Argentinean production from the mid-1990s onwards, reaching its highest rates in the whole period (Barsky & Gelman, 2001). Therefore, foreign demand, as in the "belle époque", boosted this increase in production.

Finally, Fig. 13.4 compares, once more, the relationship between GDP per capita and agricultural exports per capita. The years of analysis are 1993 and 2008. It is observed that the relationship between both variables becomes stronger and positive. This result indicates that, in the context of the export-led model, the new dynamism of agricultural exports would become one of the driving forces behind the growth of Latin American economies.

6 Conclusions

Initially, we have described the commodity export-led growth model that extended from the last third of the nineteenth century to the 1920s, when a series of profound transformations in the world economy determined changes in the previous development trajectory. Although a large majority of the Latin American republics adopted these models of growth, their results were varied. Two extreme cases can be distinguished. On the one hand, the countries in which this strategy produced significant results in terms of economic development and per-capita income growth, mainly Argentina and Uruguay; and on the other hand, most of the countries in the region, especially those in the tropics, where the strategy was not successful, either because of too slow growth in exports or because linkages with the rest of the economy were very weak and there was no significant growth-spreading effect.

These changes led to the progressive creation of the so-called inward-looking development model, in which agriculture definitively lost its previous leading role. As a country develops, the economic importance of agriculture diminishes and its contribution to internal generation of value-added is reduced. This is because the income elasticity of demand for agricultural products is low; once people have satisfied their basic needs, their attention moves to the satisfaction of other wants. This type of argument supported the insistence of Latin American Structuralism of the 1940s–1950s, in the regional necessity of stimulating the industrialisation even—often times—at the expense of diminished agricultural growth. In this sense, the transference of resources from agriculture to manufacturing may have killed the goose that laid the golden egg. Usually, as an economy develops, the productivity of agriculture increases and the sector can be the driving force of the economy. A modern agriculture, in contrast with traditional farming, has many linkages with industry as a user of manufactured products (e.g., fertilisers, machinery), as a source of materials for industrial enterprises (e.g. fibres, raw food products) or as consumer of services (e.g., banking, transport, and research).

The inward-looking development model—ISI or state-led industrialisation—prevailed during the 1950s and 1960s in the majority of the Latin American countries, with the exception of the large economies—Argentina, Brazil, Mexico—that advanced through a second stage of the ISI in the 1970s. However, this last decade meant major changes in the world economy and we conceptualise another analytical period from 1973 to the beginning of the 1990s, characterised by the foreign debt crisis and the lost decade. Finally, the last period considered includes the structural reforms and the return to the international market of agricultural products, from the 1990s to 2015. The resulting new strategy involved mobilising resources in competitive export sectors, with increasing agricultural exports and a certain change in their composition towards products with a greater degree of industrial transformation, or with greater expectations from the point of view of demand. In this sense, we find a sort of long-run reversion of agricultural production in Latin America, with a renewed role for agriculture and the perception of many scholars and specialised technicians that we are witnessing a real resurrection of the goose that laid the golden egg.

Notes

1. For the composition of agricultural and food exports from South America in the first third of the twentieth century, see Pinilla and Aparicio (2015).
2. Willebald et al. (2015) discuss the endogeneity of natural resources.
3. When Cuba is included, the R^2 coefficient decreases to 0.61.

References

Anderson, K., & Valdés, A. (2008). *Distortions to Agricultural Incentives in Latin America*. Washington, DC: World Bank.

Barsky, O., & Gelman, J. (2001). *Historia del agro argentino. Desde la Conquista hasta fines del siglo XX*. Buenos Aires: Grijalbo.

Bértola, L., & Ocampo, J. A. (2012). *The Economic Development of Latin America Since Independence*. Oxford: Oxford University Press.

Bértola, L., & Williamson, J. (2008). Globalization in Latin America Before 1940. In V. Bulmer-Thomas, J. Coatsworth, & R. Cortes Conde (Eds.), *The Cambridge Economic History of Latin America. Volume 2. The Long Twentieth Century* (pp. 11–56). Cambridge and New York: Cambridge University Press.

Bulmer-Thomas, V. (2003). *The Economic History of Latin America Since Independence*. Oxford: Oxford University Press.

Cárdenas, E., Ocampo, J. A., & Thorp, R. (2000). Introduction. In E. Cárdenas, J. A. Ocampo, & R. Thorp (Eds.), *An Economic History of Twentieth-Century Latin America. Vol. 3: Industrialization and the State in Latin America. The Postwar Years* (pp. 1–35). New York: Palgrave.

Carreras-Marín, A., Badia-Miró, M., & Peres Cajías, J. (2013). Intraregional Trade in South America, 1912–1950: The Cases of Argentina, Bolivia, Brazil, Chile and Peru. *Economic History of Developing Regions, 28*(2), 1–26.

Díaz-Alejandro, C. (1984). Latin America in the 1930s. In R. Thorpe (Ed.), *Latin America in the 1930s. The Role of the Periphery in World Crisis* (pp. 17–49). London: Macmillan.

ECLAC-FAO-IICA. (2015). *The Outlook for Agriculture and Rural Development in the Americas: A Perspective on Latin America and the Caribbean: 2015–2016*. Santiago, Rome, and San Jose: Economic Commission for Latin America and the Caribbean (ECLAC), Food and Agriculture Organization of the United

Nations (FAO), and Inter-American Institute for Cooperation on Agriculture (IICA).

Engerman, S., Sokoloff, K., & Mariscal, E. (2012). The Evolution of Schooling: 1800–1925. In S. Engerman & K. Sokoloff (Eds.), *Economic Development in the Americas Since 1500. Endowments and Institutions* (pp. 121–167). New York: NBER/Cambridge University Press.

Esteves, R. (2012). *Between Imperialism and Capitalism: European Capital Exports Before 1914*. SSRN: https://doi.org/10.2139/ssrn.2024932 or https://ssrn.com/abstract=2024932

FAO. (1948–2004a). *Production Yearbook*. Rome: Food and Agriculture Organization of the United Nations Database.

FAO. (1948–2004b). *Trade Yearbook*. Rome: Food and Agriculture Organization of the United Nations Database.

FAOSTAT. (2017). *Food and Agricultural Organisation Database*. Retrieved November, 2016, from http://www.fao.org/faostat/en/#home

Federico, G. (2005). *Feeding the World: An Economic History of Agriculture, 1800–2000*. Princeton: Princeton University Press.

Ffrench-Davis, R., Múñoz, Ó., & Palma, J. G. (1997). Las economías latinoamericanas, 1950–1990. In L. Bethell (Ed.), *Historia de América Latina. Vol. 11, Economía y sociedad desde 1930* (pp. 83–161). Barcelona: Crítica.

Frankema, E. (2009). *Has Latin America Always Been Unequal? A Comparative Study of Asset and Income Inequality in the Long Twentieth Century*. Leiden & Boston: Brill.

González, A., Pinilla, V., & Serrano, R. (2015). International Agricultural Markets After the War, 1945–1960. In C. Martiin, J. Pan-Montojo, & P. Brassley (Eds.), *Agriculture in Capitalist Europe, 1945–1960. From Food Shortages to food Surpluses* (pp. 64–84). London: Routledge.

Haber, S. (2012). Politics and Banking Systems. In E. Stanley & K. Sokoloff (Eds.), *Economic Development in the Americas Since 1500. Endowments and Instittutions* (pp. 245–294). New York: NBER/Cambridge University Press.

Harley, K. (2007). Comments on Factor Prices and Income Distribution in Less Industrialized Economies, 1870–1939: Refocusing on the Frontier. *Australian Economic History Review, 47*(3), 238–248.

Krueger, A., Schiff, M., & Valdés, A. (1988). Agricultural Incentives in Developing Countries: Measuring the Effect of Sectoral and Economy wide Policy. *The World Bank Economic Review, 2*(3), 255–271.

Krueger, A., Schiff, M., & Valdés, A. (1990). *Economía política de las intervenciones agrícolas en América Latina*. San Francisco: Banco Mundial.

Kuntz, S. (2015). *Historia mínima de la expansión ferroviaria en América Latina*. México: El Colegio de México.

Maddison, A. (2010) *Historical Statistics of the World Economy: 1-2008 AD*. Retrieved February, 2013, from http://www.ggdc.net/maddison/Maddison.htm

Maloney, W., & Valencia, F. (2014). *Engineers, Innovative Capacity and Development in the Americas*. Policy Research Working Paper 6814, The World Bank, Development Research Group.

Martín-Retortillo, M., & Pinilla, V. (2015). Patterns and Causes of the Growth of European Agricultural Production, 1950–2005. *Agricultural History Review, 63*(1), 132–159.

Martín-Retortillo, M., Pinilla, V., Velazco, J., & Willebald, H. (2016). *The Dynamics of Latin American Agricultural Production Growth Since 1950*. Documentos de trabajo de la AEHE, 1610.

Mueller, C., & Mueller, B. (2018). From Backwardness to Global Agricultural Powerhouse: The Transition of Brazilian Agriculture. In V. Pinilla & H. Willebald (Eds.), *Agricultural Development in the World Periphery: A Global Economic History Approach*. New York: Palgrave Macmillan.

O'Rourke, K., & Williamson, J. (2001). *Globalization and History: The Evolution of a Nineteenth-Century Atlantic Economy*. Cambridge, MA: The MIT Press.

Paiva Abreu, M. (2006). The External Context. In V. Bulmer-Thomas, J. H. Coatsworth, & R. Cortés-Conde (Eds.), *The Cambridge Economic History of Latin America. Volume II. The Long Twentieth Century* (pp. 101–134). Cambridge: Cambridge University Press.

Pinilla, V., & Aparicio, G. (2015). Navigating in Troubled Waters: South American Exports of Food and Agricultural Products, 1900–1950. *Revista de Historia Económica—Journal of Iberian and Latin American Economic History, 33*(2), 223–255.

Pinto, A. (1965). Concentracion del progreso técnico y de sus frutos en el desarrollo de America Latina. *El Trimestre Económico, 32*(1), 125, 39–69.

Pinto, A. (1970). Naturaleza e implicaciones de la 'heterogeneidad estructural' de la America Latina. *El Trimestre Económico, 37*(1), 145, 83–100.

Reca, L., & Díaz-Bonilla E. (1997). *Changes in Latin American Agricultural Markets*. TMD Discussion Paper 24.

Serrano, R., & Pinilla, V. (2011). Terms of Trade for Agricultural and Food Products, 1951–2000. *Revista de Historia Económica—Journal of Iberian and Latin American Economic History, 29*(2), 213–243.

Serrano, R., & Pinilla, V. (2014). New Directions of Trade for the Agri-food Industry: A Disaggregated Approach for Different Income Countries, 1963–2000. *Latin American Economic Review, 23*(10), 1–22.
Serrano, R., & Pinilla, V. (2016). The Declining Role of Latin America in Global Agricultural Trade, 1963–2000. *Journal of Latin American Studies, 48*(1), 115–146.
Solbrig, O. (2008). Structure, Performance, and Policy in Agriculture. In V. Bulmer-Thomas, J. Coatsworth, & R. Cortes Conde (Eds.), *The Cambridge Economic History of Latin America. Volume 2. The Long Twentieth Century* (pp. 483–536). Cambridge and New York: Cambridge University Press.
Stone, I. (1999). *The Global Export of Capital from Great Britain, 1865–1914. A Statistical Survey*. London: Macmillan.
Velazco, J., & Pinilla, V. (2018). Development Models, Agricultural Policies and Agricultural Growth: Peru, 1950–2010. In V. Pinilla & H. Willebald (Eds.), *Agricultural Development in the World Periphery: A Global Economic History Approach*. New York: Palgrave Macmillan.
Willebald, H., Badía-Miró, M., & Pinilla, V. (2015). Introduction: Natural Resources and Economic Development. What Can We Learn from History? In M. Badía-Miró, V. Pinilla, & H. Willebald (Eds.), *Natural Resources and Economic Growth: Learning from History* (pp. 21–45). London & New York: Routledge.
Williamson, J. (2002). Land, Labor, and Globalization in the Third World, 1870–1940. *Journal of Economic History, 62*(1), 55–85.
Yúnez, A. (2010). Las transformaciones del campo y el papel de las políticas públicas: 1929–2008. In S. Kuntz (Ed.), *Historia económica general de México. De la colonia a nuestros días* (pp. 729–755). El Colegio de Mexico/Secretaría de Economía: México.

Miguel Martín-Retortillo is an Assistant Professor at Universidad de Alcalá (Spain). He has a PhD in Economics from the University of Zaragoza (2015). His research is focused on the agricultural production and productivity and economic development, especially in Europe and Latin America. He has written some articles and book chapters about these topics.

Vicente Pinilla is Professor of Economic History at the University of Zaragoza and a Fellow of the Instituto Agroalimentario de Aragón (IA2). His research interests lies in international trade in agricultural products, long-term agricultural changes, environmental history, and migration. He is the author of *Peaceful Surrender: The Depopulation of Rural Spain in the Twentieth Century*, and editor of the books *Agriculture and Economic Development in Europe since 1870*, *Markets and Agricultural Change in Europe from the Thirteenth to the Twentieth Century*, *Natural Resources and Economic Growth: Learning from History*, and *Wine Globalization: A New Comparative History*.

Jackeline Velazco is Associate Professor in Economics at Pontificia Universidad Católica del Perú, Peru. She pursued a Masters in Development Studies at the Institute of Social Studies (The Hague) and obtained a PhD in Economics from the University of Manchester (UK). Her research experience covers: (a) agricultural economics and rural development; (b) well-being and quality of life; and (c) household economics.

Henry Willebald is Professor of Economic History and Economic Development at the Universidad de la República, Uruguay. His research interests lie in natural resources, international trade, regional development and inequalities in the long run (nineteenth and twentieth centuries). He is an editor of the book *Natural Resources and Economic Growth: Learning from History*, has written chapters in books edited by international publishers and has published articles in the main economic history journals.

14

Agricultural Development in Australia: 1845–2015

Kym Anderson

Australia largest and longest improvement in its international terms of trade can be seen in Fig. 14.1. This improvement triggered the country's biggest mining investment boom ever, funded mostly by foreign capital. Mineral and energy exports, which accounted for 45 per cent of Australia's merchandise exports in 2000, rose to more than 70 per cent by 2011. The real exchange rate appreciated accordingly over the period, to a record height previously reached only briefly during 1973–1974. The rise in the nominal Australian dollar (AUD)–US dollar exchange rate was especially marked, with the AUD more than doubling from just under 50 US cents during 2001 to a peak of 108 US cents in February 2012.

A boom in one sector of the economy typically raises national income, but not everybody is certain to gain.[1] This is true regardless of whether the boom and currency strengthening is demand driven, by a terms of

Thanks are due to the editors and reviewers for critical comments. This chapter draws heavily on Anderson (2017).

K. Anderson (✉)
Department of Economics, University of Adelaide and Australian National University, Adelaide, SA, Australia

V. Pinilla, H. Willebald (eds.), *Agricultural Development in the World Periphery*, Palgrave Studies in Economic History, https://doi.org/10.1007/978-3-319-66020-2_14

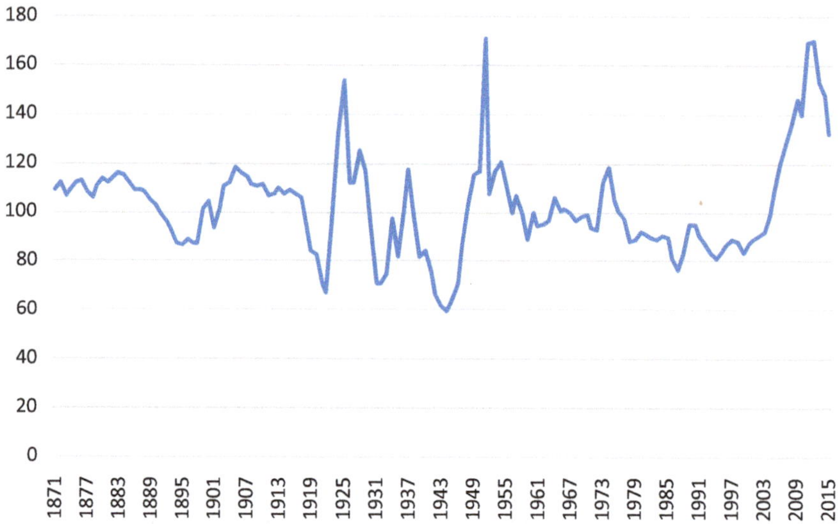

Fig. 14.1 International terms of trade, Australia, 1871 to 2015 (1967 = 100). Source: Gillitzer and Kearns (2005), updated for 2005–2015 from ABS Cat No 5206.0, Table 34

trade improvement, or supply driven by, for example, a new discovery of minerals. Either way, the real exchange rate appreciation resulting from a boom in one sector makes it more difficult for sectors producing other tradable goods and services to compete in domestic and foreign markets. In the absence of strong re-distributional policies, there are likely to be both gainers and losers when one sector of the economy booms. Conversely, a slump in international prices of a major export sector's outputs (or the exhaustion of natural resources) lowers national income but may cause a real exchange rate depreciation sufficient to benefit producers of other tradables.

The normal pattern of structural change in growing economies is for the primary sector's shares of GDP and employment to diminish as the industrial sector expands, and for manufacturing to subsequently diminish as service sectors increasingly dominate the economy (Kuznets, 1966; Syrquin, 1988; Syrquin & Chenery, 1989). In Australia's case, however, that normal pattern has been disrupted periodically by major fluctuations in the international terms of trade, and by spurts of discoveries of large reserves of minerals and energy raw materials (Blainey, 2003). Thus, its long-run sectoral trends have been shocked numerous times. The sectoral structure of the Australian economy also has been affected by a long-standing policy of protection from import competition, particularly for manufactures (Anderson & Garnaut, 1986; Lloyd, forthcoming; Lloyd & MacLaren, 2015). One result of high levels of protection has been to reduce the share of GDP traded internationally and the range of products traded, which has in turn contributed to fluctuations in the country's terms of trade.

This chapter—which benefits greatly from the pioneering research of Noel Butlin (1962, 1986)—seeks to shed light on the extent to which Australia's agricultural, mining and manufacturing sectors have altered their contributions to GDP, employment, and exports in the course of Australia's economic growth over the past two centuries, with a particular focus on periods of mining booms and slumps.[2] It begins by reviewing the branch of international trade theory that deals with sectoral comparative advantage changes in growing economies that are resource rich and subject to occasional mining booms. It then examines the extent to which data on Australia's sectoral trends and fluctuations are consistent with the theory of comparative advantage for countries with trade-restrictive policies. The data reveal a number of unusual patterns in the sectoral composition of Australia's economy. Understanding these patterns requires some Australian policy and institutional background, in addition to the variables suggested by standard trade theory such as trade costs, relative factor endowments, and international terms of trade.

1 Pertinent Theory

One of the best-known facts about growing economies is that their agricultural sector's shares of GDP and employment tend to fall over time. The reasons for those declines in a closed economy are well known: domestic prices and quantities of farm relative to non-farm products fall because of low and falling income elasticities of demand for food plus relatively rapid advances in farm production technologies. It is less obvious that the farm sector of a small *open* economy—especially one with an abundance of farmland relative to labour and capital—would have to face relative decline as its economy grows. The fact that it nonetheless almost always does is due to rising demand for non-tradable goods and especially services as incomes rise. Being non-tradable, more of those products can be produced only by drawing mobile resources from sectors producing tradables. Thus, agriculture's shares of national GDP and employment tend to fall with economic growth, even in open, land-abundant economies (Anderson, 1987a). Eventually even the absolute number of farm workers may shrink, but delays in labour out-migration from farming mean that agriculture's declining share of national employment typically exceeds the sector's declining share of GDP.

Agriculture's share of national *exports* depends on the country's comparative advantage, however, and so need not fall as the world economy expands. Indeed, the tradability of the sector's output is likely to increase as trade costs are lowered through investments in transport-related infrastructure. If a country's trade costs fall relative to the rest of the world, and if farm products gain more from the decline of trade costs than non-farm products, the country may strengthen its agricultural comparative advantage over time (Venables, 2004).

According to the workhorse theory of comparative advantage developed in the nineteenth and twentieth centuries, we should expect agricultural and mineral trade to occur between relatively lightly populated economies that are well-endowed with agricultural land and/or mineral resources and those that are densely populated with few natural resources per worker (Deardorff, 1984; Krueger, 1977). Leamer (1987) develops this model further and relates it to paths of economic development. If the stock of natural resources is unchanged, rapid growth of produced capital (physical plus human skills and technological knowledge) per unit of available labour tends to strengthen comparative advantage in non-primary products. By contrast, a discovery of minerals or energy raw materials would strengthen that country's comparative advantage in mining and weaken its comparative advantage in agricultural and other tradable products, *ceteris paribus*. It would also boost national income and hence the demand for non-tradables, which would cause mobile resources to move into the production of non-tradable goods and services, further reducing farm and industrial production (Corden, 1984). Conversely, a depletion or fall in the prices of minerals or energy would strengthen the comparative advantage of agricultural and other sectors producing tradables and weaken the demand for non-tradables.

At early stages of economic development, a country with high trade costs typically is agrarian, with most GDP and employment in the agricultural sector (when home-produced food is included in the GDP estimates). If such a country has a relatively small stock of agricultural land and other natural resources per worker, labour rewards will be low. It may be autarkic initially, but as its trade costs fall or governmental trade restrictions are removed, it will develop a comparative advantage in unskilled labour-intensive, standard-technology manufactures (as in Japan during the Meiji Restoration of 1868–1912). Then as the stock of industrial and human capital per worker grows, there will be a gradual move toward exporting manufactures that are relatively intensive in their use of physical capital, skills, and knowledge.

Natural resource-abundant economies, however, may attract migrants from more-densely populated countries who seek to become farmers or miners in frontier regions, thereby raising the settler economy's total if not per capita GDP. In such economies, the primary sector's share of GDP falls slower than in economies that are growing equally rapidly but are less abundant in natural resources. If resource-rich economies invest relatively more in capital (including new technologies) specific to primary production rather than manufacturing, they would not develop a comparative advantage in manufacturing or services until a later stage of development, at which time their exports from those sectors would be relatively capital intensive. This is all the more likely if new technologies developed for the primary sector become increasingly labour-saving as real wages rise—leading potentially to what are known as factor intensity reversals, whereby a primary industry in a high-wage country can retain competitiveness against a low-wage country by adopting capital-intensive new technologies. The primary sector's share of GDP would also decline slower if its productivity growth outpaced that of other sectors by more than the average global rate.

The above theory of sectoral changes and evolving comparative advantages (which has many similarities with the theory of trade, migration and a moving land frontier developed by Findlay, 1995, Chap. 5)[3] has been used successfully to explain the twentieth-century "flying geese" pattern of comparative advantage and then disadvantage in unskilled labour-intensive manufactures, as some rapidly growing economies expand their endowments of industrial capital per worker relative to the rest of the world—the classic example being clothing and textiles (Anderson, 1992; Ozawa, 2009). It has also been used to explain the evolving patterns and project future patterns of trade between Asia's resource-poor first- and second-generation industrialising economies and their resource-rich trading partners (Anderson & Smith, 1981; Anderson & Strutt, 2014).

A boom in one of the main tradable sectors has the effect of strengthening the real exchange rate. This, in turn, draws resources to that sector, and to the sectors producing non-tradables such as services, and thus away from other sectors producing tradables, *ceteris paribus*. It also raises national income and so boosts the domestic demand for both locally produced and imported products. Together those forces reduce the volume of exports from non-booming sectors and the domestic-currency price of those exports, and hence their aggregate value (Corden, 1984). Such a boom in a key export sector could be supply driven (e.g, the discovery of a mineral or energy raw material deposit), or demand driven (e.g., a rise in the international price of that sector's output). In the former case, it may attract immigrants and so expand the domestic economy, as with Australia's nineteenth-century gold rushes. In the latter case it will show up as an improvement in the country's international terms of trade and encourage new investment in the booming sector. The more capital funding for new investment comes in from abroad, the earlier and larger will be the initial appreciation in the real exchange rate. Later the exchange appreciation will reverse as the boom moves from its investment phase to its export phase and starts to return dividends and possibly capital to foreign investors (Freebairn, 2015).

The growth and commodity composition of a country's trade also depends on sectoral policies. In those industrialising economies whose growth has been accompanied by increases in protection from agricultural imports, demand for farm products from abroad is diminished, thereby reducing growth prospects for agricultural exporting countries (Anderson, 2009). In resource-rich economies that protect their manufacturers from import competition and ban some mineral exports—as Australia has done for much of its history—their primary product exports are dampened (Lerner, 1936).

2 Implications of the Theory for Australia

The above theory suggests Australia's very lightly populated antipodean continent would have had a strong comparative advantage in primary products from the outset, and have a high (low) share of GDP from, and employment in, primary (manufacturing) production relative to other high-income countries. Being relatively labour scarce and one of the world's highest wage countries (McLean, 2013), Australia also is likely to have been at the frontier of developing and adopting labour-saving technologies. That suggests the agricultural share of the workforce would not be as much above the agricultural share of GDP, relative to other high-income countries.

In the early decades of European settlement before mineral discoveries, Australia's international competitiveness was strongest in non-perishable agricultural products that were not labour intensive in their production (because real wages were high in this labour-scarce economy) and that had a high price per ton or per cubic metre (given the high cost of transport to the main markets in Europe) (Blainey, 1966). The discovery of mineral reserves and subsequent mining would have altered that picture for the nineteenth century only if mining outputs had high value-to-weight ratios, such as precious metals. A comparative advantage in bulky commodities such as coal, natural gas, and iron ore would not emerge until the 1970s when their historically low prices in international markets were to rise very substantially and new bulk shipping innovations lowered ocean transport costs.

These expectations from theory need to be amended, however, because of the extreme protectionist policies Australia adopted in the colonial period and increased during its first few decades as an independent Federation. (Lloyd, forthcoming; Lloyd & MacLaren, 2015). These tariffs were supplemented with binding import quotas between 1952 and early 1960, and were especially high for labour-intensive goods such as textiles, clothing, and footwear (Anderson & Garnaut, 1986). Australia also had a ban on iron ore exports from April 1938 until it was partially lifted in November 1960 and removed entirely in May 1966 (Lee, 2013). As well as these severe direct trade restrictions, myriad regulations affecting services sectors and labour markets discouraged services production and raised intermediate input costs for industries producing exportables.

As a consequence of these policy interventions, the decadal average of Australia's merchandise exports plus imports was barely 20 per cent of GDP from the 1930s to the 1970s. Policy reforms began to be implemented with an across-the-board 25 per cent cut to import tariffs in 1973 and then with far more comprehensive microeconomic reforms from 1984. The programme included not only a virtual phasing out of import tariffs and quotas and other direct industry-assistance measures but also a freeing up of markets for labour, capital, foreign currencies and various services, and the privatisation of major state-owned enterprises (Hatton & Withers, 2014; Productivity Commission, 2003). Goods exports plus imports as a share of GDP gradually rose from 21 per cent in the 1970s to 25 per cent in the 1980s, 28 per cent in the 1990s, and 32 per cent in the first sixteen years of the present century (or 41 per cent when services are included). Although other countries also experienced an increased trade propensity as globalisation has proceeded, the extent to which Australia experienced an increase in trade was much greater. Data from WTO (2015) reveal that during 2000–2014, international trade grew only marginally faster than world GDP, at 3.7 per cent per year compared with 3.2 per cent.

3 Empirical Evidence[4]

When Europeans settled in New South Wales in 1788, production of fresh food was the highest priority. For almost all of the next 60 years, agriculture accounted for more than 85 per cent of merchandise GDP (that is, ignoring services) at current prices. Up to 1830, whale and seal oil were the main exports, before the quality and quantity of wool was high enough to warrant exporting it to Britain (Shaw, 1990). With the discovery of gold in 1851, agriculture's share declined to just 26 per cent within a year. Mining's share peaked at 61 per cent in 1852 and stayed above 30 per cent until the mid-1860s. That first gold rush caused Australia's non-aboriginal population to rise by 140 per cent and real GDP to rise by 220 per cent in the 1850s. Mining's share of merchandise GDP averaged a more modest 15 per cent during 1870–1890, before returning to 25 per cent by the turn of the century because of a gold rush in Western Australia. But it had halved again by 1914, and from 1918 to 1971 it was never above 9 per cent and averaged just under 6 per cent.

It is not surprising that sectoral shares in Australia are different from those in other high-income countries. They are different in a number of ways that are consistent with the theory—and qualifications—made above. The features stressed here are:

- the manufacturing sector's share of the economy was as large as in other high-income countries until trade protectionism began to be cut in the 1970s;
- the service sector's share of GDP declined slightly over the 100 years following the first gold rush, contrary to the normal pattern in growing economies;
- the agricultural and mining sectors' shares of GDP and exports vacillated as the mining sector went through its occasional booms followed by much longer slumps;
- the agricultural sector's share of GDP remained relatively constant during 1860–1960 and even during the latest mining boom, whereas in most developed countries it has declined under similar circumstances; and
- the farm sector continued to enjoy a strong comparative advantage despite periodic spurts of growth in mining exports.

3.1 A Larger than Warranted Manufacturing Sector Up to the Early 1970s

Australian manufacturing's share of GDP and employment peaked by the early 1960s at rates little different from the average high-income country (both almost 30 per cent—see Anderson, 1987b, Fig. 7.1). Such a high share was possible despite Australia's strong comparative advantage in primary products only because the manufacturing sector was more highly protected than all other advanced economies except New Zealand (Anderson et al., 2009) and nearly as protected as Argentina (Norgés, 2011; Sturzenegger & Salazni, 2008). The extent of that support for manufacturing at the expense of primary products is shown in Fig. 14.2, which reveals the average nominal rates of assistance or NRA to those sectors (the percentage by which the average gross value of output has been raised by government policies such as protection from imports). The huge gap between those sectors' NRAs began

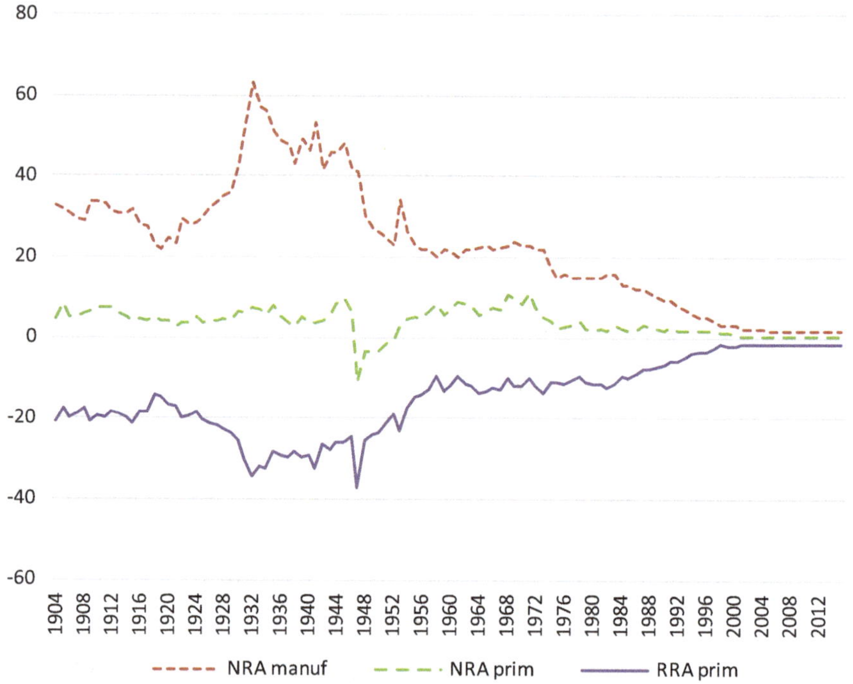

Fig. 14.2 Nominal rates of government assistance (NRA) to manufacturing and primary production and relative rate of assistance (RRA) to primary sectors, 1904 to 2015 (per cent). Source: Author's compilation based on data in Anderson, Lloyd, & MacLaren (2007) and Lloyd & MacLaren (2015) and assuming the NRA for mining was zero each year

to diminish only from the 1970s as policy reforms were gradually implemented. The impact of protection on incentives in the primary sectors is indicated by their relative rate of assistance (RRA), defined in percentage terms as:

$$\mathrm{RRA} = 100\left[\left(1 + \mathrm{NRAp}^{t}/100\right)/\left(1 + \mathrm{NRAm}^{t}/100\right) - 1\right]$$

where NRAp^{t} and NRAm^{t} are the weighted average percentage NRAs for the tradable parts of the primary and manufacturing sectors, respectively. The RRA suggests the policy regime reduced the gross rewards from primary production by approximately 20 to 30 per cent in the first half of the twentieth century relative to what would have been the case under free trade, and by about 10 per cent between the mid-1950s and mid-1980s before gradually being eliminated by the turn of the century.

The political economy forces that led to policies seeking to diversify and industrialise the economy, and to redistribute some of the gains from economic growth to wage-earners or encourage more immigration, were similar to those of other settler economies. In Australia the case was made more compelling by a report to the government that appeared to make an economic argument for such intervention (Brigden et al., 1929). Critics (e.g., Viner, 1929) argued it was not the first-best way to achieve those objectives, but supporters argued that first-best policies such as taxing land rents or incomes were not feasible administratively at that time. Anderson and Garnaut (1986, p. 31) point out that such a defence would have weakened over time, had it not been for the publication of the Stolper-Samuelson theorem which invited a conclusion favourable to protection (Samuelson, 1981 Stolper & Samuelson, 1941). It was not until the specific factors trade theory was popularised by Jones (1971, 1975) that a more appropriate model for the case of a resource-rich economy was available to argue against protection of manufacturing as a way to raise real wages.

Policy reforms in Australia had several impacts on tradable sectors. One was a faster shrinkage in Australia than in other high-income countries in the manufacturing sector's share of GDP. By 2000 that share had fallen to 13 per cent and by 2014 to just 7 per cent, compared with 18 and then 15 per cent for other high-income countries (Anderson, 2017, Fig. 4a). The share of the workforce employed in manufacturing had fallen commensurately, and was just 8 per cent in 2015. By contrast, the manufacturing employment share in other high-income countries has fallen by less than ten percentage points over the past 25 years. However, as noted below, the halving in Australia's manufacturing shares of GDP and employment after 2000 was in part due to the mining boom.

A related consequence of those policy reforms is that agriculture's share of GDP has remained well above that of most other high-income countries, and increasingly so in proportional terms since 1970—despite the recent mining boom (Anderson, 2017, Fig. 4b). The fluctuations in that GDP share are far larger for Australia than for other high-income countries, reflecting the greater abandonment of farm price stabilisation schemes in Australia than elsewhere since 1970 (Griffith & Watson, 2016).

Another consequence of the opening up of the economy was a non-trivial rise in the extent to which Australia's farm production was exported. During 1973–1979, the value of rural exports (which includes the post-farmgate costs of getting produce to the port and on ships) was 69 per cent of the gross value of farm production at current prices. This rose to 75 per cent in 1980–1999 and to 83 per cent in 2000–2015. In addition to an increase in the overall level of exports, there has been a much wider range of farm products exported, and, in some cases, products have switched from net import to net export status, despite the mining boom's recent impact on exchange rates (ABARES, 2015).

3.2 A Flat Trend in the Service Sector's Share of GDP for 100 Years

In contrast to the pattern that is usual in a growing economy, the share of services in Australian GDP declined slightly between 1860 and 1960. The sector's share rarely moved out of the 50–60 per cent range during those ten decades, before rising rapidly over the past half century to 80 per cent as in other high-income countries (Fig. 14.3). True, the initial share of around half of GDP was high by the standards of other high-income countries in the mid-nineteenth century, but not 100 years later

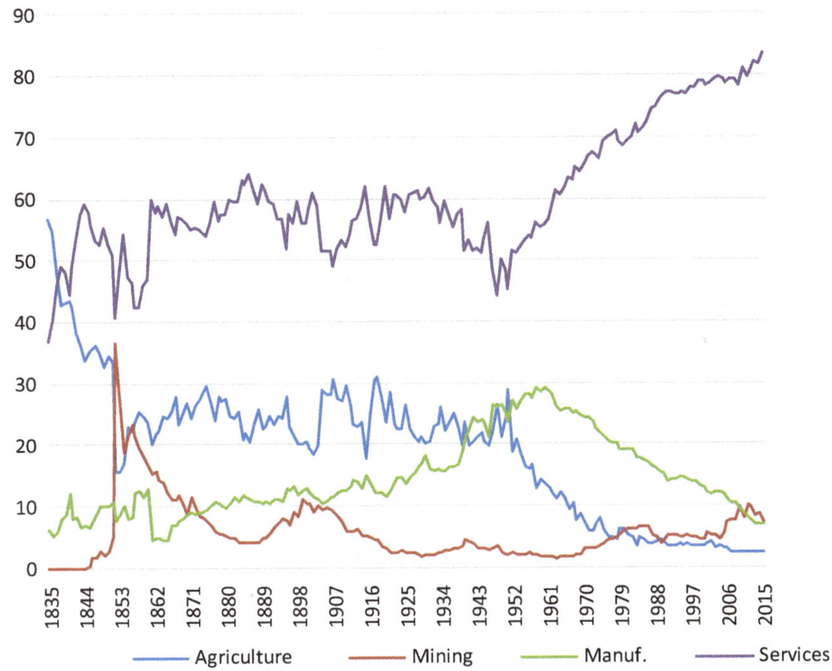

Fig. 14.3 Sectoral shares of total GDP at current prices, Australia, 1835 to 2015 (per cent). Source: Butlin, Dixon, & Lloyd (2014), updated for 2011–2015 from ABS Cat No 5204.0

(Kuznets, 1966, Table 3.1; Syrquin & Chenery, 1989). That slightly declining trend for services contrasts with the steep upward trend in the GDP share contributed by manufacturing, especially after 1910. The huge degree of government assistance to manufacturing leading up to and following Federation for decades, shown in Fig. 14.2, contributed to that large difference in the two sectors' growth rates.

3.3 The Fluctuating Importance of Agriculture and Mining

The most valuable mining output in the nineteenth century was gold, although there were numerous other ores mined as well (Blainey, 2003). The first gold rush was centred in Victoria from 1851, followed by one in

Western Australia in the 1890s. They show up very clearly as bulges in mining's share of GDP (Fig. 14.4). However, by the time of WWI, mining's importance had decreased, and its share of GDP remained relatively low for more than five decades. It began to grow again only after the ban on iron ore exports was gradually lifted during 1961–1966 and permits began to be issued by the Western Australian government to mine the ore and privately develop new rail and port facilities to allow exports. It grew even more after the OPEC cartel quadrupled the price of petroleum in 1973–1974 and then doubled it again in 1979–1980, as this made it economically feasible for thermal coal and subsequently natural gas to be exported from Australia to East Asia. Mining expanded even more from 2005 as Chinese demand for imports of coking coal and iron ore increased and ships capable of carrying loads of up to 250,000 tons of ore became available to transport these exports at relatively low cost. That latest expansion caused considerable de-industrialisation of the Australian economy, but relatively little de-agriculturalisation because farm product prices rose almost as much as mineral prices between 2005 and 2012.

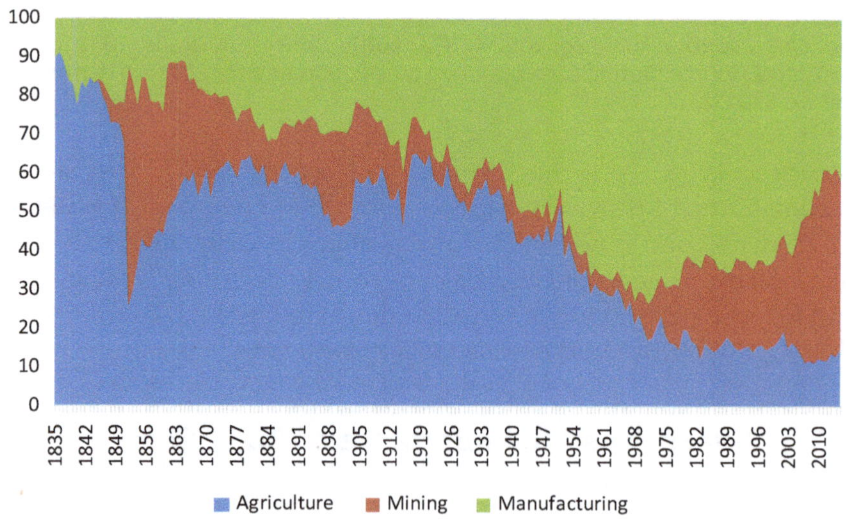

Fig. 14.4 Sectoral shares of merchandise-only GDP (i.e. excluding services) at current prices, Australia, 1835 to 2015 (per cent). Source: Butlin, Dixon, & Lloyd (2014), updated for 2011–2015 from ABS Cat No 5204.0

3.4 A Non-declining Trend in the Agricultural Sector's Share of GDP for 100 Years

Agriculture's share of GDP slumped sharply at the start of Victoria's gold rush in the early-1850s, as rural workers abandoned their farm activities and headed for the goldfields. But it soon recovered and remained within the 20–30 per cent range for the next 100 years (Fig. 14.4). It dipped only during Western Australia's 1890s gold rush and in WWI, and otherwise just fluctuated with the seasons and with international prices, for example declining during the severe economic depressions of the mid-1890s and early-1930s. That flat trend contrasts markedly with the downward trend in virtually all other high-income economies (Kuznets, 1966, Table 3.1). Even during the latest mining boom, agriculture's share of GDP was adversely affected far less than that of manufacturing, despite many farm regions being in a severe drought in the first decade of the century.

Nor did the mining booms of the nineteenth century depress the farm sector for long. That was because they were so large relative to total GDP at the time, and they stimulated major expansions of the economy. The 1850s, for example, saw the continent's non-aboriginal population nearly treble and real incomes per capita rise, so the domestic demand for farm products grew enormously, encouraging men to return from the gold fields to farming (Maddock & McLean, 1984) The high and rising level of real wages also encouraged the development and widespread adoption of labour-saving farm (and mining) technologies such that the shares of national employment in primary sectors kept in line with their GDP shares (Fig. 11.6), unlike in most other countries where slow labour adjustment has meant the employment share exceeds the GDP share (see, e.g., Axelsson & Palacio, 2018, Chap. 11 of this volume).

The relatively minor impact of the recent mining boom on farming was partly a result of international food prices rising at the same time as the price of mining products in those years. However, the price index of Australia's farm exports rose considerably less than the index for the country's mining exports (Anderson, 2017, Fig. 7), so that can not be the full explanation. An additional explanation is that a high level of public and private investments in rural research over many decades ensured very high productivity growth in farming, especially since the 1980s (Alston

& Pardey, 2016). Grafton, Mullen, & Williams (2015) report also that productivity growth since the turn of this century has been faster for agriculture than for both mining and manufacturing. Perhaps this, together with agricultural tertiary education colleges that began to be established as early as the 1880s (Shaw, 1990), was a more-important contributor in Australia than in the other settler economies analysed in this volume (see, e.g. Willebald & Juambeltz, 2018, Chap. 17 of this volume).

3.5 Retention of Agricultural Comparative Advantage

Australia's relatively rapid farm productivity growth also helped the rural sector maintain a high share of national exports. In the nineteenth century, agricultural exports were dominated by wool from the 1830s, which alone accounted for around half of all exports apart from during the two gold-mining booms (Fig. 14.5). Wool production was the farm enterprise that was perhaps least intensive in its use of scarce labour relative to

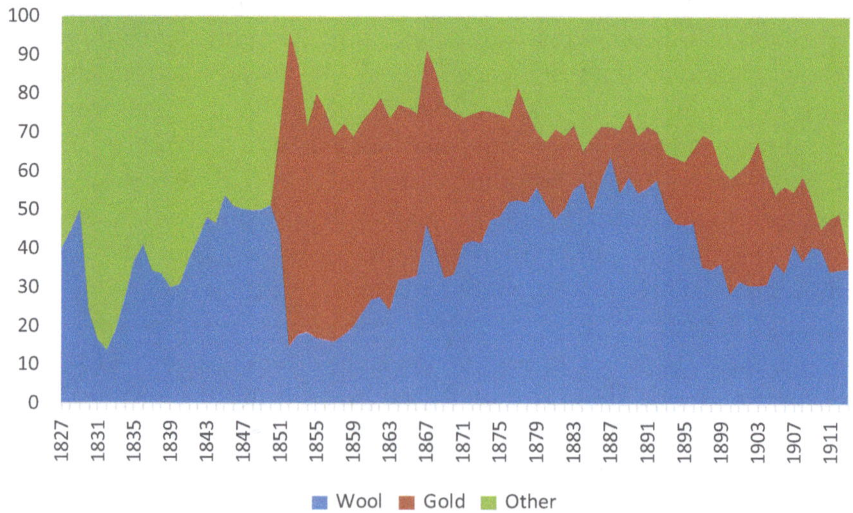

Fig. 14.5 Shares of wool and gold in Australia's merchandise exports, 1827 to 2013 (per cent). Source: Compiled by the author as reported in Anderson (2015, Sect. IV)

abundant grazing land (Davidson, 1981, Chap. 6). Together with gold it accounted for most of Australia's exports throughout the second half of the 1800s. Even though export concentration was not unusual among economies of the New World, it is clear from Fig. 14.6 that Australia had one of the highest concentrations.[5] During the five decades to 1960 Australia's exports became more diversified, but nonetheless around three-quarters of its value was contributed by the rural sector. Even in the

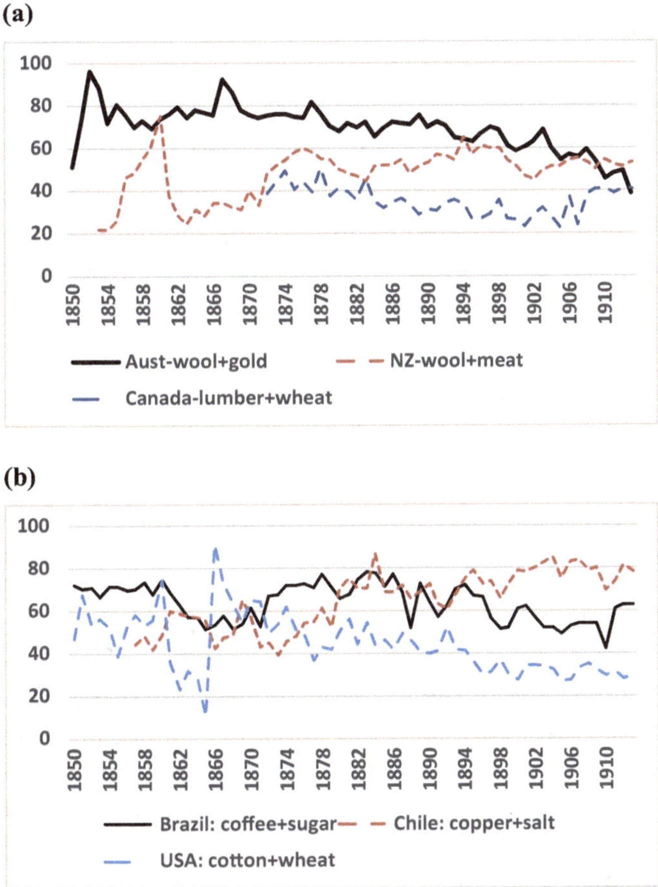

Fig. 14.6 Share of top two goods in settler economies' exports, 1850 to 1913 (per cent). **(a)** Australia, New Zealand and Canada. **(b)** Brazil, Chile and the USA. Source: Author's compilation based on data in Mitchell (2005)

following five decades the agricultural share of Australia's exports has been more than twice the global average, while the manufacturing share has always been well under half the global average.

4 Conclusion

This review of sectoral trends and shocks in the course of economic growth over the past two centuries reveals a number of unusual features of Australia's economy, yet they are fairly consistent with what trade theory would suggest once the country's policies and institutions are taken into account. The data underscore the resilience of Australian farmers in dealing with supply and demand shocks associated not only with their own product markets (due to variability of weather and farm product prices) but also with mining. Manufacturing has not fared as well over the past decade. Even with the recent ending of the country's latest mining investment boom and the associated depreciation of its real exchange rate, manufacturers will have to continue to contend with strong competition for labour and other mobile resources not only from the farm sector but also from those service sectors whose products are becoming increasingly tradable internationally. Future governments may still occasionally provide some direct assistance to struggling firms in marginal electorates, but much more efficient social safety nets—and, even better, trampolines (Trebilcock, 2014)—are now available to assist the losers from economic growth to adjust to future sectoral trends and shocks.

A key fact highlighted in this study—the persistence of agriculture in the overall economy for 100 years, and even during the latest mining boom—is due to several factors: a big land frontier that took more than a century for European settlers to exploit; declines in initially crippling domestic and ocean trade costs for farm products; innovations both by farmers and via a strong public agricultural R&D system; and reasonably sound macroeconomic policies that avoided the "resource curse" that afflicted so many other natural resource-rich economies. True, manufacturing protection policies reduced the prosperity of primary production, but for farmers and graziers that was at least somewhat offset by the ban on iron ore exports between the late 1930s and early 1960s and a boom in wool prices in the early 1950s.

Notes

1. National income is less likely to rise, the poorer the government's macroeconomic management and the more distorting are its sectoral and trade policies (Anderson, 1998). Adverse outcomes are so common among developing countries as to have given rise to the term "resource curse" (coined by Auty, 1993). Extensive reviews of that literature as it pertains to developing countries can be found in Smith (2015) and Venables (2016). See also Badía-Miró, Pinilla, & Willebald (2015).
2. It leaves aside the question of how these structural changes and shocks contributed to the growth and fluctuations in the country's *aggregate* output, employment, and income. The reasons for high per-capita income in Australia in the nineteenth century, and continued prosperity to date, is the subject of a study by McLean (2013).
3. See also Willebald & Juambeltz (2018), Chap. 17.
4. Historical macroeconomic and sectoral data on Australia's economy have been compiled by Vanplew (1987), and a subset of those data has been updated by Butlin, Dixon, & Lloyd (2014). Anderson (2015) has extended some of those series (and added the colonial/state data) by drawing on, among others, Butlin & Sinclair (1986), Sinclair (2009) and the *Statistical Registers* of each Colony.
5. Gold (not shown) contributed more than meat to New Zealand's exports prior to the 1880s. Argentina's exports also were highly concentrated on two products: wool and hides to the 1880s and wool and grain from then to WWI. Livestock products accounted for between 75 per cent and 90 per cent of Uruguay's exports right up to 1970.

References

Axelsson, T., & Palacio, A. (2018). Transforming Indonesia: Structural Change in a Regional Perspective 1968–2010. In V. Pinilla & H. Willebald (Eds.), *Agricultural Development in the World Periphery: A Global Economic History Approach*. London: Palgrave Macmillan.

ABARES. (2015). *Agricultural Commodities Statistics 2015*. Canberra: Australian Bureau of Agricultural and Resource Economics and Sciences.

Alston, J. M., & Pardey, P. G. (2016). Antipodean Agricultural and Resource Economics at 60: Agricultural Innovation. *Australian Journal of Agricultural and Resource Economics, 60*(4), 554–568.

Anderson, K. (1987a). On Why Agriculture Declines with Economic Growth. *Agricultural Economics, 1*(3), 195–207.

Anderson, K. (1987b). Tariffs and the Manufacturing Sector. In R. Maddock & I. McLean (Eds.), *The Australian Economy in the Long Run* (pp. 165–195). Cambridge: Cambridge University Press.

Anderson, K. (Ed.). (1992). *New Silk Roads: East Asia and World Textile Markets*. Cambridge: Cambridge University Press.

Anderson, K. (1998). Are Resource-Abundant Economies Disadvantaged? *Australian Journal of Agricultural and Resource Economics, 42*(1), 1–23.

Anderson, K. (Ed.). (2009). *Distortions to Agricultural Incentives: A Global Perspective, 1955–2005*. London and Washington, DC: Palgrave Macmillan and World Bank.

Anderson, K. (2017). Sectoral Trends and Shocks in Australia's Economic Growth. *Australian Economic History Review, 57*(1), 2–21.

Anderson, K. (with the assistance of N.R. Aryal) (2015). *Growth and Cycles in Australia's Wine Industry: A Statistical Compendium, 1843 to 2013*. Adelaide: University of Adelaide Press. Retrieved October 17, 2016, from URL and as Excel spreadsheets at www.adelaide.edu.au/databases

Anderson, K., & Garnaut, R. (1986). *Australian Protectionism: Extent, Causes and Effects*. Sydney: Allen & Unwin.

Anderson, K., Lloyd, P., & MacLaren, D. (2007). Distortions to Agricultural Incentives in Australia Since World War II. *Economic Record, 83*(263), 461–482.

Anderson, K., Lattimore, R., Lloyd, P., & MacLaren, D. (2009). Australia and New Zealand. In K. Anderson (Ed.), *Distortions to Agricultural Incentives: A Global Perspective, 1955–2005* (pp. 221–256). London and Washington, DC: Palgrave Macmillan and World Bank.

Anderson, K., & Smith, B. (1981). Changing economic relations between Asian ADCs and resource-exporting developed countries. In W. Hong & L. Krause (Eds.), *Trade and Growth in the Advanced Developing Countries* (pp. 293–338). Seoul: Korea Development Institute Press.

Anderson, K., & Strutt, A. (2014). Emerging Economies, Productivity Growth, and Trade with Resource-Rich Economies by 2030. *Australian Journal of Agricultural and Resource Economics, 58*(4), 590–606.

Auty, R. M. (1993). *Sustaining Development in Mineral Economies: The Resource Curse Thesis*. London: Routledge.

Badía-Miró, M., Pinilla, V., & Willebald, H. (Eds.). (2015). *Natural Resources and Economic Growth. Learning from History*. London and New York: Taylor and Francis Group.

Blainey, G. (1966). *The Tyranny of Distance: How Distance Shaped Australia's History*. Melbourne: Macmillan.
Blainey, G. (2003). *The Rush That Never Ended: A History of Australian Mining* (5th ed.). Melbourne: Melbourne University Press.
Brigden, J. R., Copeland, D. B., Dyason, E. C., Giblin, L. F., & Wickens, C. H. (1929). *The Australian Tariff: An Economic Enquiry*. Melbourne: Melbourne University Press.
Butlin, M., Dixon, R., & Lloyd, P. J. (2014). A statistical narrative: Australia, 1800–2010. In S. Ville & G. Withers (Eds.), *The Cambridge Economic History of Australia* (pp. 555–594). Cambridge: Cambridge University Press.
Butlin, N. G. (1962). *Australian Domestic Product, Investment and Foreign Borrowing 1861–1938/39*. Cambridge: Cambridge University Press.
Butlin, N. G. (1986). Contours of the Australian Economy 1788–1860. *Australian Economic History Review, 26*(2), 96–125.
Butlin, N. G., & Sinclair, W. A. (1986). Australian Gross Domestic Product 1788–1860: Sources and Methods. *Australian Economic History Review, 26*(2), 127–147.
Corden, W. M. (1984). Booming Sector and Dutch Disease Economics: Survey and Consolidation. *Oxford Economic Papers, 36*(3), 359–380.
Davidson, B. R. (1981). *European Farming in Australia: An Economic History of Australian Farming*. Amsterdam: Elsevier.
Deardorff, A. V. (1984). An Exposition and Exploration of Krueger's Trade Model. *Canadian Journal of Economics, 5*(4), 731–746.
Findlay, R. (1995). *Factor Proportions, Trade, and Growth*. Cambridge, MA: MIT Press.
Freebairn, J. (2015). Mining Booms and the Exchange Rate. *Australian Journal of Agricultural and Resource Economics, 59*(4), 533–548.
Gillitzer, C., & Kearns, J. (2005). *Long-Term Patterns in Australia's Terms of Trade. RDP2005-01*. Sydney: Reserve Bank of Australia.
Grafton, R. Q., Mullen, J., & Williams, J. (2015). *Australia's Agricultural Future: Returns, Resources and Risks*. Melbourne: Australian Council of Learned Academies.
Griffith, G., & Watson, A. S. (2016). Antipodean Agricultural and Resource Economics at 60: Agricultural Markets and Marketing Policies. *Australian Journal of Agricultural and Resource Economics, 60*(4), 594–609.
Hatton, T., & Withers, G. (2014). The labour market. In S. Ville & G. Withers (Eds.), *The Cambridge Economic History of Australia* (pp. 351–372). Cambridge: Cambridge University Press.

Jones, R. W. (1971). A Three-Factor Model in Theory, Trade, and History. Chap. 1, in J.N. Bhagwati, R. Jones, R. Mundell, & J. Vanek (Eds.), *Trade, Balance of Payments and Growth*. Amsterdam: North-Holland.

Jones, R. W. (1975). Income Distribution and Effective Protection in a Multicommodity Trade Model. *Journal of Economic Theory, 11*(1), 1–15.

Krueger, A. O. (1977). *Growth, Distortions and Patterns of Trade Among Many Countries*. Princeton, NJ: International Finance Section.

Kuznets, S. (1966). *Modern Economic Growth: Rate*. Structure and Spread, New Haven: Yale University Press.

Leamer, E. E. (1987). Paths of Development in the Three-Factor, n-Good General Equilibrium Model. *Journal of Political Economy, 95*(5), 961–999.

Lee, D. (2013). Reluctant Relaxation: The End of the Iron Ore Export Embargo and the Origins of Australia's Mining Boom, 1960–1966. *History Australia, 10*(3), 149–170.

Lerner, A. (1936). The symmetry between import and export taxes. *Economica, 3*(11), 306–313.

Lloyd, P.J. (forthcoming). The First Hundred Years of Tariffs in Australia: The Colonies. *Australian Economic History Review.*

Lloyd, P. J., & MacLaren, D. (2015). Relative Assistance to Australian Agriculture and Manufacturing Since Federation. *Australian Journal of Agricultural and Resource Economics, 59*(2), 159–170.

Maddock, R., & McLean, I. (1984). Supply-Side Shocks: The Case of Australian Gold. *Journal of Economic History, 44*(4), 1047–1067.

McLean, I. W. (2013). *Why Australia Prospered: The Shifting Sources of Economic Growth*. Princeton, NJ: Princeton University Press.

Mitchell, B. R. (2005). *International Historical Statistics*. Basingstoke: Palgrave Macmillan.

Norgés, J. (2011). *Agro e Industria: del centenario al bicentenario. [Agriculture and Industry: From the Centenary to the Bicentenary]*. Buenos Aires: Ciudad Argentina.

Ozawa, T. (2009). *The Rise of Asia: The 'Flying-Geese' Theory of Tandem Growth and Regional Agglomeration*. Cheltenham: Edward Elgar.

Productivity Commission. (2003). *From Industry Assistance to Productivity: 30 Years of 'The Commission*. Canberra: Productivity Commission.

Samuelson, P. A. (1981). Summing Up on the Australian Case for Protection. *Quarterly Journal of Economics, 96*(1), 147–160.

Shaw, A. (1990). Colonial Settlement 1788–1945. In D. B. Williams (Ed.), *Agriculture in the Australian Economy* (3rd ed., pp. 1–18). Sydney: University of Sydney Press.

Sinclair, W.A. (2009). *Annual Estimates of Gross Domestic Product: Australian Colonies/States 1861–1976/77*. Retrieved October 17, 2016, from URL http://arrow.monash.edu.au/hdl/1959.1/88855
Smith, B. (2015). The Resource Curse Exorcised: Evidence from a Panel of Countries. *Journal of Development Economics, 116*(1), 57–73.
Stolper, W., & Samuelson, P. A. (1941). Protection and Real Wages. *Review of Economic Studies, 9*(1), 58–73.
Syrquin, M. (1988). Patterns of Structural Change. In H. Chenery & T. N. Srinivasan (Eds.), *Handbook of Development Economics* (Vol. 1, pp. 203–273). Amsterdam: North-Holland.
Syrquin, M., & Chenery, H. (1989). Three Decades of Industrialization. *World Bank Economic Review, 3*(1), 145–181.
Trebilcock, M. J. (2014). *Dealing With Losers: The Political Economy of Policy Transitions*. London: Oxford University Press.
Vanplew, W. (1987). *Australians: Historical Statistics*. Sydney: Fairfax, Syme & Weldon.
Venables, A. J. (2004). Small, Remote and Poor. *World Trade Review, 3*(3), 453–457.
Venables, A. J. (2016). Using Natural Resources for Development: Why Has it Proven so Difficult? *Journal of Economic Perspectives, 30*(1), 161–184.
Viner, J. (1929). The Australian Tariff. *Economic Record, 5*(9), 306–315.
Willebald, H., & Juambeltz, J. (2018). Land Frontier Expansion in Settler Economies, 1830–1950: Was it a Ricardian Process? Chap. 17. In V. Pinilla & H. Willebald (Eds.), *Agricultural Development in the World Periphery: A Global Economic History Approach*. London: Palgrave Macmillan.
WTO. (2015). *International Trade Statistics 2015*. Geneva: World Trade Organization.

Kym Anderson is the George Gollin Professor of Economics at the University of Adelaide in Australia, where he has been affiliated since 1984. Previously he was a Research Fellow at the Australian National University (1977–1983), following graduate studies at the University of Chicago and Stanford University, and in 2012 he rejoined ANU part-time as a Professor of Economics in its Crawford School of Public Policy. He was on extended leave at the Economic Research division of the GATT (now WTO) Secretariat in Geneva during 1990–1992 and at the World Bank's Research Group in Washington DC as Lead Economist (Trade Policy) during 2004–2007. He is Chair of the Board of Trustees of the Washington DC-based International Food Policy Research Institute. He has published around 400 articles and 40 books.

15

From Backwardness to Global Agricultural Powerhouse: The Transition of Brazilian Agriculture

Charles C. Mueller and Bernardo Mueller

1 Introduction

In 2015 Brazilian GDP fell by 3.8 per cent and in 2016 a by further 3.6 per cent, making this one of the worst recessions in its history. The result was not worse because as other sectors stagnated, agriculture came to the rescue generating production, exports, jobs and foreign currency reserves. Today Brazil's agriculture is highly modernised and one of the most productive in the world for many commodities, making the country one of the major producers and exporters of a large list of agricultural and animal commodities. But this has not always been the case. Just a few decades back Brazilian agriculture was considerably more backward, unproductive and plagued by all manner of economic, technical and social problems. Since the mid-1970s, however, the sector has experienced a fourfold increase in production using basically the same amount of land and labour. How did this exceptional transition take place?

C.C. Mueller • B. Mueller (✉)
Department of Economics, University of Brasilia, Brasilia, DF, Brazil

V. Pinilla, H. Willebald (eds.), *Agricultural Development in the World Periphery*, Palgrave Studies in Economic History, https://doi.org/10.1007/978-3-319-66020-2_15

We answer this question in this chapter by analysing the economic history of Brazilian agriculture since the end of WWII. Until the early 1960s, frontier expansion had been the main determinant of agricultural growth, but starting in the early 1970s, modernisation accelerated substantially, and the expansion of the frontier assumed a subsidiary role. We consider the extent to which two often-cited theories of agricultural development explain the modernisation and transition of Brazilian agricultural. The first is the Hayami & Ruttan (1971) theory of induced innovation, in which technological change comes about as a natural response to resource endowments and the economic environment of the country. The second is the claim that the changes were fundamentally driven by enlightened technocrats who commanded the process of change.[1] We argue that the initial process of modernisation up to the 1990s can best be understood through the second of these approaches. Top-down technocratic policy imposed a series of reforms that sought to modernise the sector and remove the bottlenecks and inefficiencies that hindered agriculture and created obstacles with consequences for industry and the macroeconomy, which were the central objectives of the policymakers. We describe how these interventions succeeded in creating a productive agribusiness sector, for example by investing heavily in technology adapted to the realities of Brazilian agriculture. But at the same time the interventions also led to further distortions and inefficiencies in agriculture as it was used as an instrument for generating foreign exchange, controlling inflation and other subsidiary objectives. The final transformation into a major world agricultural producer only took place after the mid-1990s, once the country managed to control inflation and improve political institutions, which allowed a less interventionist policy, in which induced innovation could finally thrive.

2 Theories of Agricultural Development

Different theories have been proposed for understanding the transformation of agriculture in developing economies. We focus on two theories which have dominated the literature on Brazilian agriculture, but also address other approaches. The first assumes that, in the take-off stage, traditional agriculture fails to respond to the needs of development; the second considers that agriculture, even traditional, is essentially responsive, merely requiring the removal of obstacles and the provision of incentives to change. The first outlook usually prescribes deep restructuring—a broad agrarian reform—to achieve a satisfactory response; the other prescribes adequate market-oriented policies to trigger agricultural modernisation.

For the Brazilian structuralists, agricultural modernisation was precluded by the country's highly concentrated pattern of land ownership. This would explain the lack of motivation of large landowners, more interested in political power, and the paltry contribution of peasants—small farmers being too weak and oppressed to make a difference. Thus, the country's agriculture remained locked at the margin of modernisation. To eliminate this obstacle, a thorough land reform would be required. Their outlook had some similarities to that of Malthusian population theory. As shown by Boserup (1965), for Malthus agricultural expansion would inevitably fall behind that of population, generating scarcity and holding up development. In both cases, the removal of exogenous obstacles would require drastic measures—an agrarian reform for the structuralists, and drastic population control policies for the Malthusians.

Boserup's approach rejects such extreme outlooks; she contended that agriculture in developing countries was far from stagnant in the face of demand pressures. When demand is small and land abundant, its use tends to be extensive; however, as demand increases, intensification would emerge in various forms, helping to expand production.

Hayami & Ruttan (1971) presented a similar approach in Chap. 3 of their major opus, where they reviewed major models of agricultural development, each relevant to specific countries and situations: the *model of resource exploration*—pertinent to Brazil along the first economic surge; the *model of conservation*, the *model of localisation*, the *model of diffusion* and Theodore Schultz (1964)'s influential *model of modern inputs*.[2] In their book, Hayami & Ruttan proposed the *induced development model,* which uses aspects of these models but goes far beyond them. Their model is clearly in line with the second outlook mentioned above. They argue that in most countries that achieved agricultural advances, there was technical development, essentially induced by market forces. Reacting to deficiencies in the endowment of certain production factors, farmers, organised in rural pressure groups and operating in market economies, pressured for the development of means to overcome such deficiencies, leading to technological change.

3 Agricultural Expansion in the First Economic Boom and Beyond

From the end of WWII to the early 1970s, agricultural growth in Brazil went through a phase of horizontal expansion. As mentioned, the model relevant to this period was that of *resource exploration* (Hayami & Ruttan, 1971, Chap. 3). The growth of agricultural production resulted basically from the incorporation of areas in the agricultural frontier; outside limited islands of modernisation, agriculture remained essentially traditional, with low productivity. In the 1960s the agricultural frontier was still limited to the country's South and Southeast regions. There were huge areas in the centre and the North of Brazil (the Cerrado Savannas of central Brazil; the Amazon) lightly touched by agricultural ventures, but the availability of unused or underused potential land in the Southeast and South of Brazil had declined. To continue growing, agriculture depended on technological change.

Up to the early 1970s Brazil was basically an exporter of a few cursorily processed commodities. As shown by Miller Paiva, Rui, & de Freitas (1976, Table II.21), in 1970, 78.5 per cent of the value of agricultural exports originated from three products: coffee (59.7 per cent), cotton (10.7 per cent) and sugar (8.2 per cent). Until then, large portions the rural productive resources (especially land and labour) were devoted to the production of the main export crops, (coffee and cotton in the Southeast and South, and sugar in the Southeast and the Northeast), and to basic products, consumed domestically.

Brazil's economic history in the phase of horizontal expansion highlights, along with the coffee boom, the impact of the first economic import substitution industrialisation (ISI) surge. The modernisation of agriculture received very limited attention by the ISI strategy then implemented. Nevertheless, it succeeded in transferring income from agriculture to the urban–industrial sector, chiefly through the manipulation of relative prices against agriculture (Bacha, 1975; Oliveira, 1981). The foreign exchange—then primarily generated by agricultural exports—was maintained artificially overvalued, and the prices of agricultural products for the domestic market were compressed, in contrast to prices of industrial goods, which were subject to protectionist measures. But in the booming 1950s, the consistently overvalued foreign exchange did not hinder the income transfer; high international coffee prices compensated, to some extent, for the overvalued domestic currency. This commodity was responsible for an important portion of the country's export earnings, essential for input and equipment imports. Moreover, the performance of agriculture in meeting the demands of an expanding urban–industrial sector was satisfactory in that period. Production increased enough to assure that, by and large, the sectoral terms of trade would not negatively affect ISI, despite the rapid pace of import substitution and of the growth of urban demand for food; this was a by-product of the opening of the agricultural frontier (Mueller, 2011).

Agricultural modernisation policies were almost non-existent in the phase of horizontal expansion; an exception were initiatives to advance the production of coffee, cotton and sugar cane by the state government of São Paulo, the effects of which, although noteworthy, were limited mostly to that state (Pastore, Dias, Guilherme, & Castro, 1976). In fact, as documented by Nicholls (1970), the policy that favoured most agricultural expansion was road building; new and better roads widened the agricultural frontier, enabling production to grow with traditional methods. There were attempts at engendering technical change in other states, but with negligible results (Miller Paiva et al., 1976, Chap. 4).

The nature of the Brazilian agricultural expansion in the period emerges in the indicators calculated by Patrick (1975). Using shift-share analysis on the amount produced of Brazil's 23 major agricultural crops, he compared their 1947–1949 average physical production with that of 1967–1969. For Brazil as a whole, he estimated a 3.8 per cent annual rate of growth of production (4.3 per cent excluding coffee); he established that 91.9 per cent of that growth was due to the expansion of the area cultivated—the *area effect*—and only 20.2 per cent to the *yield effect*. In that period, agricultural expansion relied mainly on the expansion of the frontier; increases in yield had limited impact.

It is interesting to contrast Patrick's results for São Paulo, then the more advanced agricultural state, with those for the backward, drought-prone Northeast region. Of the 3.1 per cent 1947/1949–1967/1969 growth of São Paulo, 23.0 per cent was due to area expansion but 59.8 per cent to increases in yield; as for the Northeast, of the 3.8 per cent growth in production in the period, 123.6 per cent was due to the *area effect* and −16.4 per cent to the *yield effect*. In the period, São Paulo experienced the effects of its modernisation policies, while in the Northeast, area had to expand to overcome yield reductions.

Table 15.1 reveals the backward state of Brazilian agriculture in the phase of horizontal expansion. It shows the 1949–1951 and the 1969–1971 average yields of the country's main crops of the period. They are low both by international standards, and relative to the 2013–2015 yields. In most cases, they changed little over two decades. Crops such as potatoes, coffee and sugar cane may seem to contradict this, but the evolution of these crops was influenced by the mentioned technical changes in the State of São Paulo. The stagnant state of important crops such as rice, beans and maize reveals the poor technological progress of most of Brazilian agriculture along this period (soya bean cultivation was just beginning). This contrasts markedly with the 1970–2014 performance.

The livestock sector went through a similar state of affairs. Between 1950 and 1970, in the beef cattle industry the number of animals grew and the production of beef increased (see Table 15.2, below), but as shown by Mueller (1974, Chap. II), the beef cattle production was mostly extensive or ultra-extensive in the period. There were localised exceptions, but as a rule the main problems—which even in the early 1970s appeared intractable—were: inadequate sanitary control; animal diseases; low genetic quality of the heard; low calving indexes; large mortality of calves; low quality pastures; and poor management. Due to inadequate sanitary conditions, beef exports were minimal—in 1970, the value of beef cattle meat exports amounted to only 3 per cent of the total agricultural exports (Miller Paiva et al., 1976, Chap. 3.c). As we show in Table 15.2, however, changes afterwards were remarkable.

Table 15.1 Average yields of major crops, 1950, 1970 and 2014

Crop	I 1949–1951	II 1969–1971	III 2013–2015	% Δ I–II	% Δ II–III
Cotton (a)	–	2,028	3,752	–	85.0%
Rice	1,603	1,430	5,320	−10.8%	272.0%
Potatoes	4,814	7,260	28,336	50.8%	290.3%
Coffee	406	975	1,387	140.1%	42.3%
Beans	695	642	1,047	−7.6%	63.1%
Sugar-cane	38,921	45,926	73,387	18.0%	59.8%
Manioc	12,946	14,655	14,717	13.2%	0.4%
Corn	1,170	1,365	5,322	16.7%	289.9%
Soya beans (b)	1,483*	1,186	2,941	−20.0%	148.0%

Yields in kilograms/hectare. (a) 1949/1951 comparable data for cotton were not available; (b) data for soya beans available starting in 1952; *1952/1954 average

Source: IBGE, Estatísticas Históricas (1946–1971); IBGE, Sidra (2016)

Table 15.2 Brazil, livestock sector, 1961, 1970 and 2014

	1961	1970	2014
Cattle (million animals)	76.2	97.9	212.4
Animals slaughtered (million)	7.1	9.6	40.4
Production weight (million tonnes)	1.4	1.8	9.7
Carcass weight (kg/animal)	1,917	1,930	2,408
Chicken			
Animals slaughtered (million)	0.123	0.333	5690.7
Production weight (million tonnes)	0.123	0.366	12,519.5
Pig meat			
Animals slaughtered (million)	8.0	11.3	37.1
Production weight (million tonnes)	0.53	0.77	3.19
Carcass weight (kg/animal)	667	683	860
Fresh milk			
Dairy cattle (million)	7.4	9.5	23.0
Production (million tonnes)	5.2	7.3	35.1

Sources: fao.org/faostat, accessed 3/1/2017. IBGE (1990). IBGE sidra.org br. Accessed 5/1/17

During this period, the other livestock sectors—poultry, milk and pork—also exhibited very low technological performances. Suffice it to say that no exports of chicken and pig meat were recorded. Low productivity and sanitary problems strongly hindered external sales.

In sum, by the early 1970s Brazilian agriculture was still "traditional" almost everywhere. Production increased, due mostly to the incorporation of land and of traditional inputs. Because of the high priority given to ISI, there were negligible efforts to induce agricultural modernisation. As we show below, the situation changed remarkably afterwards.

4 Agricultural Expansion in the Phase of 'Conservative Modernisation'

From the 1970s onwards, there were noticeable increases and diversification in the production of the modern sector of agriculture. As can be seen in Fig. 15.1, the harvest of grains and oilseeds[3]—a proxy of Brazil's agricultural performance—experienced a strong growing trend.

Progress started modestly along the 1976/1977–1983/1984 harvests (production increased from 46.9 million to 52.4 million tonnes), and accelerated between 1983/1984–1999/2000 (production rose from 52.4 million to 83.0 million tonnes) and, quite remarkably between the turn of the century and the 2014/2015 harvests (from 83.0 million to 207.7 million tonnes).[4] In the 23 years between the 1976/1977 and the 1999/2000 harvests, production grew 77 per cent, from 46.9 million to 83.0 million tonnes; and it grew an outstanding 250.2 per cent in 13 years, between 1999/2000 and 2014/2015 harvests, reaching 207.7 million tonnes.

Figure 15.1 shows that growth in the 1976/1977–1999/2000 period took place with limited addition of cultivated area. The expansion of production occurred with very little addition of land under cultivation (from 37.3 million to 37.8 million ha). In the 1999/2000–2014/2015 period, the area cultivated increased 53.2 per cent. In the first period (1976–1999) production expanded mostly by means of a more intensive use of land in settled areas of the Southeast and South regions; in the 1999/2000–2014/2015 harvests, there was a significant incorporation of areas in the frontier—notably in the Cerrado savannahs of Central Brazil. The marked increase in output was due to gains in yield, made possible by technical change, both in the previously settled regions and in the Cerrado areas incorporated since the early 1970s (Rezende, 2003).

Table 15.1 shows the recent yields of major agricultural products; the contrast with those of the first phase is stark. Crops such as maize, then

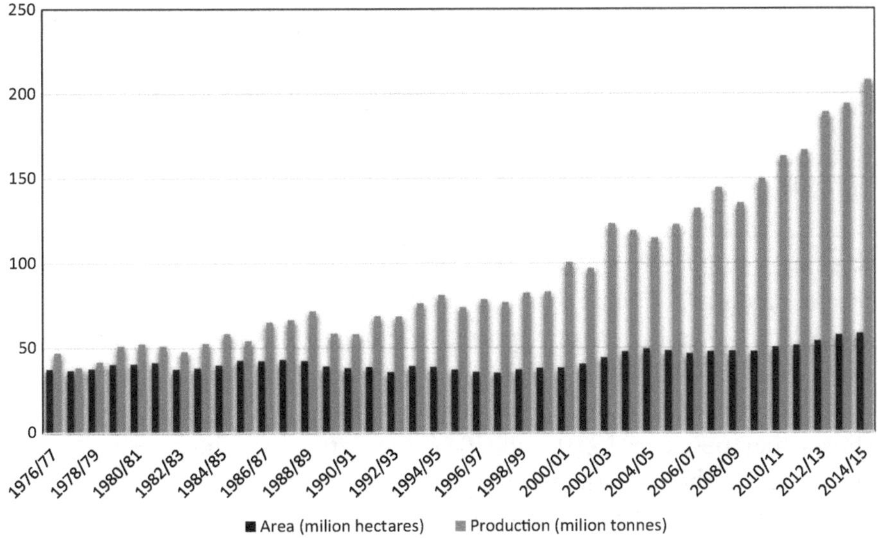

Fig. 15.1 Brazil, area cultivated and production of grains and oilseeds, 1976/1977–2014/2015. Source of the data: CONAB (2016)

grown mostly for internal use, became "internationalised" in the second phase; its yield increased from an average of 1365 kg/ha (kilograms per hectare) in 1969–1971 to an average of 5322 kg/ha in 2013/2015. The yield of sugar cane increased from an average of 45.9 tonnes/hectare in 1969/1971 to an average of 73.4 tonnes/ha in 2013/2015. The yield of soya beans showed an apparently modest rise, from an average of less than 1500 kg/ha in the first phase to an average of 2941 kg/ha in the 2013/2015 years. The cultivation of soya beans, which started relatively modernised in the South of Brazil, advanced rapidly—with increasing technology—in the Cerrado savannahs.

The advance of the crop sector was translated into a rapid increase and diversification of exports. Today Brazil is one of the main exporters of commodities such as soybeans (ranked 1st worldwide in 2013), sugar (ranked 1st), coffee (ranked 1st), and maize (ranked 3rd), as well as a major exporter of cotton, tobacco, and oranges juice, among other crops (faostat.fao.org, 2017).

There have also been outstanding changes in the beef, poultry, pork, eggs and milk sectors. The problems of the first phase were consistently tackled alongside the second phase, transforming the livestock sector into a leading world player. Table 15.2 presents features of this transformation. Starting with chicken meat, at the end of the 1st phase only 333,000 animals were slaughtered and 366,000 tonnes were produced. As mentioned, chicken meat exports were insignificant. By 2014 the changes in this segment were astounding. The number of animals slaughtered reached almost 5.7 billion, with a total weight of 12.6 million tonnes; in 2013 Brazil was the main exporter of chicken meat, with a total value exceeding US$ 7 billion.[5]

The beef cattle sector also experienced remarkable change. Table 15.2 shows that between 1970 and 2014 the cattle herd increased 117 per cent, the number of animals slaughtered 321 per cent and the total production weight 439 per cent—quite a substantial increment in productivity. In 2013 Brazil's total beef cattle exports ranked second (after India) totalling US$ 5.3 billion. As for pig meat, in the 1970–2014 period the number of animals increased 228 per cent, but the production weight rose 414 per cent, reflecting strong gains in productivity. In 1970 the idea of Brazilian pig meat exports would be considered absurd; but in 2013 the country was the fifth largest world exporter of the commodity.

As for milk, up to the mid-1980s, disruptions in production often turned Brazil into a net importer, but with technological improvements the situation changed. Table 15.2 shows a 142 per cent increase in the milk herd, and a sizable 381 per cent increment in production between 1970 and 2014. The sector also experienced marked qualitative improvements.

Across both periods the value of exports increased systematically, but there was a rise in the rate of increase in the second period. The volume of agricultural exports rose by 105 per cent from 1973 to 1999, but then it increased 483 per cent from 1999 to 2016.[6] The acceleration of agricultural exports is due both to the improvements in supply emphasised in this chapter and to the increased demand for agricultural and food products in the 2000s. It is beyond the scope of this paper to determine the relative importance of each of these factors regarding exports.

5 Foundations of Brazil's Recent Technological Advance

We focus now on two possible explanations of the modernisation which took place in Brazilian agriculture—a process that occurred with impressive results in a relatively short period. We examine first, whether these changes were brought about by market-forces-induced technological development, such as that of the Hayami & Ruttan (1971) theory. Incidentally, this theory was widely acknowledged in Brazil during the 1970s and 1980s.

According to Hayami & Ruttan, in most countries that achieved agricultural advances, technical development was brought about by market forces. Reacting to deficiencies in the endowment of certain production factors, farmers, organised in rural pressure groups and operating in free-market economies, pressured for the development of means to overcome such deficiencies, leading to technological change, and to increases in production and productivity.[7]

In corroboration of their theory, Hayami & Ruttan (1971, Part III) offer the cases of the USA and of Japan. For the USA, the main limitation was the scarcity of labour—strongly felt in in the nineteenth century. This was conducive to the development and diffusion of labour-saving mechanical technologies by agricultural R&D organisations. In Japan, the main deficiency was the scarcity of land. In the nineteenth century, development of effective land-saving chemicals and biological technical changes had already started. The events in both countries led to significant agricultural advances, not due to actions of enlightened planners, but brought about by pressure coming from farmers in the two countries—exerted through rural pressure organisations. These led to efforts in R&D fields that overcame the respective shortfalls in productive factors. In other words, change was induced by growing costs that the scarcity of the productive resources entailed. Market forces and farmer pressure brought about the development of mechanisation in the USA, and chemical and biological technologies in Japan. Thus, both countries avoided the problems of the shortfalls of productive factors, achieving noteworthy agricultural expansion.

We contend that the theory of induced development does not hold up in the case in Brazil. In the 1970s, when the technological development of agriculture started to accelerate, basically neither land nor labour were scarce. Of course, unused potential land in the old agricultural frontier was shrinking, but investments in transportation infrastructure could make additional potential land available in new frontier areas; and labour—at least unskilled—was far from scarce. Moreover, farmers' organisations that might effectively pressure for technological change were few. Such pressure certainly began taking place in the early twentieth century in the state of São Paulo, where the influence of coffee growers led to measures to overcome agronomic problems affecting them (Pastore et al., 1976). But there was no similar movement when the more recent effort for technical development began to unfold.

To a large extent, what took place starting in the late 1960s was the effect of actions and measures created by enlightened technocrats. The theory induced institutional innovation by Hayami and Ruttan (1971) had a great influence on agricultural economists and other agricultural experts. This view emphasized the importance and complexities of technical change in agriculture. In addition, several other changes were introduced in Brazil in the late 1960s and 1970s, as discussed below.

The import substitution strategy adopted after WWII, already mentioned above, was quite successful in promoting industrialisation and economic growth. Between 1947 and 1961 the Brazilian economy grew, in real terms, 128 per cent, and industry, 262 per cent (Baer, 2001, p. 63). The implementation of the strategy relied substantially on ad hoc measures; an instance was the above-mentioned transfers of income from agriculture in the first phase, achieved basically through artificially compressed agricultural prices and by the maintenance of an overvalued foreign exchange—to a large extent generated by agricultural exports.

Since growth involved the recourse to foreign capital (as loans and as direct investment), there were mounting balance-of-payment pressures (Baer, 2001, p. 69). Likewise, in this period the tax structure remained inadequate for the needs and subsidies of ISI, and there were growing fiscal deficits, financed by the creation of money, resulting in mounting inflation, which peaked in the early 1960s. Moreover, the Brazilian financial system was progressively out of tune with the needs of a modernised urban industrial sector; the country did not even have a Central Bank.[8]

In the early 1960s, however, the ISI strategy began losing its impetus. Due to a legacy of problems, growth decelerated, unemployment increased sharply, and balance-of-payment deficits got out of hand. And the economic problems intensified political conflicts, the main origin of which lay in two opposing views about the future of the Brazilian development: on one extreme was the left, demanding radical reforms; on the other, factions on the centre-right and right, rejected the radical stance, claiming that to recover growth the creation of institutions for the efficient functioning of a market economy was necessary.

Agricultural expansion offers an instance of the nature of this political confrontation. The left embraced the structuralist interpretation generated by agrarian and social studies (de Castro, 1979); it claimed that, by failing to grow adequately, agriculture was an obstacle to development; the root of the problem was Brazil's huge disparity of land distribution (which remains to the present). For the structuralists, the few owners of large farms—the "latifundistas"—were concerned with political power and land speculation and not with productivity and efficiency; as for the large number of landless peasants, they were regarded as too weak and oppressed to make a difference. The main structuralist policy prescription was that of agrarian reform, expropriating land from large landholdings, transferring it to small farmers and agricultural workers—groups regarded as more responsive to the requirements of development.[9] The opposite view, however, contended that what agriculture needed was institutional change, allowing it to grow with rising productivity. An agrarian reform would require excessive resources; besides, it would upset revered property rights.

In 1964 the confrontation between the extremes was resolved by a military coup crushing the radical reform attempts of the left and establishing the 1964–1984 authoritarian regime. And, as shown by Resende (1992), the main economic objectives of the new regime were: to induce economic growth, led by market forces; raise productive employment; contain inflation; lessen sectoral and regional imbalances; induce investments—public and private, domestic and foreign; revert the tendency of high balance-of-payment deficits; and curb the foreign debt. To control inflation the main instrument would be the reduction of fiscal deficits, through tax reform and cuts in public expenditures. And, in order to limit foreign sector distortions, a foreign exchange reform was prescribed (Corrêa do Lago, 1992).

The new regime claimed that it would maintain a free-market economy, but that, to create conditions for growth and modernisation, it would be necessary to impose economic reforms and significant central planning. Measures were deemed necessary for agricultural modernisation to take place; yet a radical agrarian reform was not considered necessary. This was, in a nutshell, the basis of the "conservative modernisation" strategy that was implemented.

The second half the 1960s saw the emergence of the *domain of technocracy*. Modernising reforms were imposed, establishing the environment for a rapid resumption of growth, under the heavy guidance of technocrats in all policy areas (Baer, 2001, Chap. 5; Resende, 1992). Technocrats substituted the political appointees of the past, establishing a strong tutelage over the "free-market" development process. After the imbalances of the past were addressed, the technocrats began implementing a vigorous import substitution strategy—at a quite higher level than that of the 1950s. It brought about a period of substantial growth and of structural transformation (de Castro, 1985). There was an important participation of the public sector in this, and of a burgeoning segment of public enterprises (Baer, 2001: Chap. 12).

It is important to consider that the nature of political institutions during this period facilitated the implementation of the agricultural policies we are describing. Many countries have had the intention of adopting similar policies to modernise agriculture but without achieving similar results. Brazil's authoritarian military regime that delegated policy implementation to technocratic bureaucracy provided the setting in which policymakers had both the intent and the power to implement the modernising reforms.

In the late 1970s and in the 1980s the strategy generated very high costs in terms of both an explosive foreign debt and of an accelerating inflation. The end of the military regime in 1984 and the return to democracy brought about the end of the *domain of technocracy,* but it left significant marks in the Brazilian economy.

We focus now on the nature and results of actions of the *domain of technocracy* to modernise agriculture. Promotion of industrialisation was the main goal of the military regime, but for this an adequate performance of agriculture, both for the adequate supply of products for growing urban–industrial markets, and for the provision of foreign exchange through exports, was deemed fundamental; the modernisation of agriculture was considered vital for this. We now turn to the actions undertaken.

6 The Construction of "Conservative Modernisation"

The central agents of agricultural modernisation were an active class of entrepreneurial farmers. If the typical agricultural producers of the 1970s and beyond had been the archetypal absentee landlords, the impacts of the modernisation measures undertaken would have been modest. However, in portions of the South and Southeast regions there already was a significant reserve of entrepreneurial farmers willing to innovate. These farmers, prompted by incentive policies, mobilized much land that was previously extensively used in the settled regions of the South and Southeast, as well as land in frontier areas that were made accessible by new transport infrastructure. These entrepreneurial farmers were fundamental for the modernised expansion of agriculture of the second phase.

The main foundations of the agricultural development strategy were:

- *Erection of an effective research system in tropical agriculture*. The first steps towards this were taken in the late 1960s, and efforts were intensified in the 1970s and afterwards. The construction of this system required the assembly of ample research facilities, the hiring and training of the personnel, and the institution of a scheme to coordinate, manage and make the system expand. For this, the federal government established a public entity, EMBRAPA (*Empresa Brasileira de Pesquisa Agropecuária*—The Brazilian Enterprise for Agricultural Research)

(Martha Jr, Contini, & Alves, 2012). In view of Brazil's geographical size and of the diversity of the country's habitats and social design, EMBRAPA was instituted as a decentralised research system, composed of units spread throughout the country, together with special thematic centres. Furthermore, the organisation enlisted the collaboration of other organisations involved in agricultural research (state research units, universities—in Brazil and abroad—and private organisations).

- As indicated above, results began to be felt already in the 1970s; initially new technologies emphasised improvements in production processes, but with time more complex developments took place, such as the creation of plant varieties adapted to the conditions of specific regions. Modernisation, which accelerated during the 1980s and beyond, owes a lot to this approach to technilogical change that significantly advanced the green revolution in Brazil.
- *Inducement policies*. From the start, inducements were deemed necessary for the adoption of modern agricultural technologies. The modernisation strategy made substantial financial resources increasingly available to agricultural producers willing to follow this path. The main policies to this effect were:

  – *The establishment of the National System of Rural Credit (NSRC)*. The NSRC began, in the late 1960s, to provide abundant financing, in very generous terms, to modernising farmers. Among other things it financed the purchase of modern inputs (equipment, fertilisers, pesticides and insecticides, selected seeds), much of which was initially imported, but gradually also provided domestically. The NSRC credit was highly subsided; its interest rates were maintained far lower than the growing rates of inflation, and the principal tended not to be corrected for inflation.
  Agricultural credit expanded noticeably in the 1970s, reaching US$ 16 billion in 1974 and staying above US$ 20 billion every year of the 1975–1982 period.[10] Until the mid-1980s, the ultimate source of the financial resources for the credit policy was the Treasury, and it made use of its access to the Central Bank to create money for this.

The credit bonanza was maintained up to the mid-1980s. Cutbacks in subsidised agricultural credit occurred thereafter, and provisions for the correction of amounts due for inflation became the norm. Brazil was then, frequently, at the brink of hyperinflation and international insolvency (Carneiro & Modiano, 1992; Modiano, 1992). Moreover, in 1986 the almost automatic link between the Treasury and the Central Bank was eliminated and the use of federal funds was limited.

– *Improvement and expansion of the minimum price policy*. In the 1970s an already existing minimum price apparatus was reformed and the role of the policy increased; however, until the mid-1980s credit policy was dominant in the modernisation strategy. Changes in this policy and the determination to continue extending financial incentives to agriculture led, increasingly, to the use of the minimum price policy (Goldin & Castro de Rezende, 1993; Rezende, 2003: Chap. 1). However, in the second half of the 1980s and the early 1990s, there were swelling problems in the administration of the policy. Sharply growing public expenditure with minimum prices and the substantial accumulation of inventories of products together with ensuing logistical problems, led to restrictions in the use of the policy.

In the late 1980s, minimum prices became an instrument of regional development (Rezende, 2003). Setting up nationally unified—and usually remunerative—minimum prices of crops such as soya beans and cotton, the expansion of agriculture in Brazil's large savannahs (the *Cerrado*) was stimulated. The *tropicalisation* of such crops, achieved by EMBRAPA, contributed to their successful cultivation in areas previously considered unsuitable (Cunha et al., 1994). An obstacle for expansion in that area was high transportation costs resulting from a deficient transportation infrastructure. To overcome this, official minimum prices offered the Cerrado producers nearly the same compensation as those of farmers located near markets; in most of the new Cerrado areas minimum prices substantially exceeded market prices after transportation costs were deducted, and producers there tended to sell their output to the minimum price organisation. Over the second half of the 1980s, considerable portions of the output of the Cerrado (mainly soya beans) became publicly owned and the government subsidised the growing costs of transportation and storage of products, which then were being disposed with substantial losses.[11]

- *Inducements for the expansion of a dynamic agribusiness sector.* The import substitution strategy encouraged the growth of a dynamic agribusiness sector, which became an important factor in agricultural growth and modernisation. An agribusiness comprises a set of economic activities operating in tandem with agricultural or livestock production. It involves enterprises and activities providing inputs and services to farms; the agricultural activity proper; and businesses purchasing, transporting, processing, transforming and selling the products generated by the agribusiness. In the mid-1970s, the more advanced agricultural areas of the state of São Paulo and of the south of Brazil already had incipient agribusiness complexes, linked to a few agricultural or livestock segments. From this period onwards, several new agribusiness complexes were formed and expanded, stirred by market conditions, by incentives provided by import substitution policies, and by the spread of modern technologies in increasingly diversified agricultural segments of wider geographical areas, reaching new agricultural and livestock fields. Many of the major agribusiness complexes have an important participation of foreign multinationals, and there have also emerged large Brazilian-led agribusinesses.

Finally, if in the 1970s, apart from a few commodities such as coffee, there were no Hayami & Ruttan-type farm organisations to pressure for the measures demanded by farmers as modernisation unfolded, this gradually changed (Mueller, 2009); but such organisations were not important for the conformation of the modernisation strategy.

7 The Consolidation *of Modernisation*

The picture we presented above describes a hectic agricultural policy setting, which was engendering turbulence for the agricultural sector in the 1980s and early 1990s. As shown by Dias & Moitinho Amaral (2000) and Rezende (2003), it was brought about chiefly by macroeconomic constraints and changing priorities. The efficacy of the credit policy for inducing output growth had weakened, the system became regarded as wasteful and distorting, and as an obstacle for the implementation of monetary policy (da Mata, 1982). The public sector became unable to continue funding an increasingly complex and diversified modern agriculture.[12] There was, therefore, a gradual but substantial change in direction of the agricultural strategy.

An important feature in the consolidation of modernisation was the liberalising trend of the 1990s (Mueller & Mueller, 2016). In the decade, Brazilian productive sectors—including its agriculture—were increasingly exposed to international competition. Tariffs were reduced, export prohibitions and import quotas ceased to be employed and the foreign trade bureaucracy was streamlined.

The main changes in agricultural financing were: as mentioned, the *direct* governmental funding of commercial agriculture was contained; official financing was channelled mostly to small farmers and to land-reform projects. For commercial agriculture, there emerged other sources of finance, mostly private. As for the minimum price policy, it ceased to transfer resources to producers, and the purchase of surpluses was limited. Modern, more agile instruments were created, avoiding the untenable practices of the past.

The policy changes of the 1990s evolved with ups and downs, bringing turmoil for the sector. Starting in 1994, for instance, a measure implemented by the administration of the Real Plan was an officially induced growing appreciation of the value of the Real (Baer, 2001: chap. 10). This adversely affected agricultural exports and stimulated imports, in a period of slack international commodity prices. But from 1999 onwards, agriculture received an important boost; the foreign exchange rate was allowed to float freely, producing a sharp depreciation of the Real. This, and favourable world commodity prices, contributed to the expansion and diversification of agricultural production and exports.

It is interesting that, instead of being contained by the "hands off" policy changes, modern agriculture—prompted by a favourable institutional setting—became increasingly driven by market conditions. Between 1991 and 1998, encompassing the period of foreign exchange appreciation, the annual rate of growth of real agricultural GDP averaged a modest 2.4 per cent, similar to the rate of growth of GDP for the economy (2.8 per cent annually). But from 1999 to 2004, the annual agricultural growth rate averaged an impressive 5.4 per cent; and growth was substantial in almost every year of the period (Mueller & Mueller, 2016). As seen above, agricultural expansion continued even in the more recent period of declining trends in international commodity prices. In effect, this period since 2000 can be thought of as a third period in Brazilian agricultural history, of more market-based growth and modernisation.[13]

Notes

1. Other theories are mentioned below but have not been very influential in the literature on Brazilian agriculture.
2. Hayami & Ruttan emphasised the contribution of this author to their model.
3. Data on grain and oilseed production from CONAB (2016). Crops included: canola, rye, barley, beans, sunflower seeds, mamona, corn (maize), soya beans, sorghum, wheat and triticale.
4. It should be noted that the expansion of the modern sector in the first five years of the millennium occurred in years of very favourable external markets; undoubtedly this favoured the adoption of technology. But this continued to take place when commodity prices dipped.
5. Data on 2013 livestock exports, from fao.org/faostat/en, 2017.
6. These numbers were calculated using agicultural export indices from Brandão (2001) and from CEPEA (*Centro de Estudos Avançados em Economia Aplicada*) http://www.cepea.esalq.usp.br/br/indicador/serie-indices-de-exportacao-do-agronegocio.aspx.

7. For a critique of the Hayami–Ruttan induced innovation theory see Olmstead and Rhodes (1993).
8. Central bank functions were carried out precariously by the federally owned Banco do Brasil; this was opportune for the creation of money to cover growing fiscal deficits.
9. At the time this outlook represented a significant portion of urban public opinion. The structuralist argument was destroyed by Antonio Barros de Castro (1979), once ideologically aligned with it. He identified inconsistencies of the structuralist approach, showing how it was contradicted by the observed performance of agriculture in the 1950s and early 1960s.
10. Values expressed in current US$ dollars (no correction for the US inflation). Series obtained by Goldin and Castro de Rezende (1993).
11. The dumping of part of the surpluses on markets was also used to help contain inflation.
12. This was magnified by changes introduced by the Constitution approved in 1988. It drastically reduced the capacity of the federal government to transfer resources to agriculture in the manner of the past.
13. For a detailed analysis of this period of Brazilian agriculture see Mueller & Mueller, 2016.

References

Bacha, E. L. (1975). O café na economia brasileira. In E. L. Bacha (Ed.), *Os mitos de uma década*. Rio de Janeiro: Paz e Terra.

Baer, W. (2001). *The Brazilian Economy: Growth and Development*. Westport, CT: Praeger Publishers.

Boserup, E. (1965). *The Conditions of Agricultural Growth: The Economics of Agrarian Change Under Population Pressure*. London: Allen and Unwin.

Brandão, Antonio Salazar P. (2001). Aumento de produtividade e exportação: uma análise exploratória. Cadernos de Ciência e Tecnologia (EMBRAPA), v. 18, n.3.

Carneiro, D., & Modiano, E. (1992). Ajuste externo e desequilíbrio interno e desequilíbrio interno: 1980–1984. In M. de Paiva Abreu (Ed.), *A ordem do progresso, cem anos de política econômica republicana: 1889–1989* (pp. 323–346). Rio de Janeiro: Campus.

de Castro, A. B. (1979). *Sete Ensaios Sobre a Economia Brasileira—Volume I*. Rio de Janeiro: Forense, sessão 2.
de Castro, A. B. (1985). Ajustamento x transformação—a economia brasileira de 1974 a 1984. In A. B. de Castro & F. E. Pires de Souza (Eds.), *A economia brasileira em marcha forçada* (pp. 13–82). São Paulo: Paz e Terra.
CONAB. (2016). *Produção e área de cerais—séries históricas*. Brasília: Ministério da Agricultura, Pecuária e Abastecimento.
Corrêa do Lago, L. A. (1992). A retomada do crescimento e as distorções do "milagre": 1967–1973. In M. de Paiva Abreu (Ed.), *A ordem do progresso, cem anos de política econômica republicana: 1889–1989* (pp. 233–294). Rio de Janeiro: Campus.
Cunha, A., Mueller, C., Alves, E., & da Silva, E. (1994). *Uma Avaliação da Sustentabilidade da Agricultura no Cerrado* (Vol. 1). Brasília: IPEA.
Dias, G. L. da S., & Moitinho Amaral, C. (2000). Mudanças estruturais na agricultura brasileira, 1980–98. In R. Baumann (Ed.), *Brasil: Uma Década em Transição*. Rio de Janeiro: CEPAL/CAMPUS.
Goldin, I., & Castro de Rezende, G. (1993). *A Agricultura Brasileira na Década de 1980: Crescimento numa Economia em Crise*. Brasília: IPEA.
IBGE. (1990). *Estatísticas Históricas do Brasil, 2ª. Edição revista e atualizada do vol. 3 de Séries Estatísticas Retrospectivas*. Rio de Janeiro: IBGE.
IBGE. (2016). www.sidra.ibge.gov.br. Retrieved December 27, 2016 in March 1, 2017.
faostat.fao.org. Retrived March 1, 2017.
Hayami, Y., & Ruttan, W. V. (1971). *Agricultural Development: An International Perspective*. Baltimore: Johns Hopkins University Press.
Martha, G., Jr., Contini, E., & Alves, E. (2012). Embrapa: Its Origins and Changes. In W. Baer (Ed.), *The Regional Impacts of National Policies—The Case of Brazil* (pp. 204–226). Massachusetts: Edward Elgar Publishing Inc..
da Mata, M. (1982). Credito rural: caracterização do sistema e estimativas dos subsídios implícitos. *Revista Brasileira de Economia, 36*(3), 215–245.
Modiano, E. (1992). A opera dos três cruzados: 1985–1989. In M. de Paiva Abreu (Ed.), *A ordem do progresso, cem anos de política econômica republicana: 1889–1989* (pp. 347–386). Rio de Janeiro: Campus.
Mueller, B., & Mueller, C. (2016). The Political Economy of the Brazilian Model of Agricultural Development: Institutions Versus Sectoral Policy. *The Quarterly Review of Economics and Finance, 62*, 12–20.
Mueller, C. C. (1974). *Factors Affecting the Productivity of Central Brazil's Beef Cattle Industry*. PhD thesis, Department of Economics, Vanderbilt University.

Mueller, C. C. (2009). Agricultural, Agrarian and Environmental Policy Formation Under Lula: The Role of Policy Networks. In J. Love & W. Baer (Eds.), *Brazil Under Lula—Economy, Politics and Society Under the Worker-President* (pp. 135–150). New York: Palgrave Macmillan.

Mueller, C. C. (2011). Inflation and Income Transfers During the Golden Phase of Import Substitution Industrialization of the 1950s: The Contribution of an Expanding Agricultural Frontier. In S. Ranincheski, C. Mueller, & C. Negri (Eds.), *The Brazilian Economy in Historical Perspective* (pp. 41–52). Brasília: Verbena Editora.

Nicholls, W. (1970). The Brazilian Agricultural Economy: Recent Performance and Policy. In R. Roett (Ed.), *Brazil in the Sixties* (pp. 147–184). Nashville (Tenn.): Vanderbilt University Press.

Oliveira, J. do C. (1981). *An Analysis of Transfers from Agricultural Sector and Brazilian Development, 1950–1974*. PhD thesis, University of Cambridge.

Olmstead, A. L., & Rhode, P. (1993). Induced Innovation in American Agriculture: A Reconsideration. *Journal of Political Economy, 101*(1), 100–118.

Paiva, M., Rui, S. S., & de Freitas, C. T. (1976). *Setor Agrícola do Brasil: comportamento Econômico, Problemas e Possibilidades*. Rio de Janeiro and São Paulo: Editora Forense-Universitária and Editora da Universidade de São Paulo.

Pastore, J., Dias, S., Guilherme, L., & Castro, M. C. (1976). Condicionantes da produtividade da pesquisa agrícola no Brasil. *Estudos Econômicos, 6*(3), 147–181.

Patrick, G. (1975). Fontes de crescimento na agricultura brasileira: o setor de culturas. In C. Contador (Ed.), *Tecnologia e Desenvolvimento Agrícola* (pp. 89–110). Rio de Janeiro: IPEA/INPES.

Resende, A. L. (1992). Estabilização e reforma: 1964–67. In M. de Paiva Abreu (Ed.), *A ordem do progresso, cem anos de política econômica republicana: 1889–1989* (pp. 213–231). Rio de Janeiro: Campus.

Rezende, G. de C. (2003). *Estado, Macroeconomia e Agricultura No Brasil*. Porto Alegre: Editora UFRGS/IPEA.

Schultz, T. W. (1964). *Transforming Traditional Agriculture*. New Haven: Yale University Press.

Charles C. Mueller has been Emeritus Professor of Economics at the University of Brasilia since 1974. He has a PhD in Economics from Vanderbilt University from 1974. He was president of the Brazilian Census Bureau IBGE from 1988 to 1989. His research is on agricultural economics and environmental economics.

Bernardo Mueller has been a professor of Economics at the University of Brasilia since 1995. He has a PhD in Economics from the University of Illinois at Champaign-Urbana (1994), and has been a visiting scholar at the University of Colorado (2005) and Indiana University (2016). His interests are new institutional economics, development and complexity theory. His latest book is *Brazil in Transition: Beliefs, Leadership and Institutional Change* (with Alston, Melo & Pereira), published by Princeton University Press.

16

Development Models, Agricultural Policies and Agricultural Growth: Peru, 1950–2010

Jackeline Velazco and Vicente Pinilla

1 Introduction

The economic importance of the agricultural sector in Peru has decreased noticeably in the last half-century. Changes in the distribution of gross domestic product (GDP) and employment by economic sectors, based on the national population censuses (1961, 1972, 1981, 1993 and 2007), show a downward trend in the weight of agricultural production and

This study has received financial support from Spain's Ministry of Science and Innovation, project ECO2015-65582 and from the Government of Aragon, through the Research Group 'Agri-food Economic History (nineteenth and twentieth Centuries)'. The authors wish to thank Montserrat López-Jérez and participants at the Meeting "Agricultural development in the world periphery. A global economic history approach" (University of Zaragoza, April 2017) for their help and advice. The usual disclaimers apply.

J. Velazco (✉)
Economics Department, Pontificia Universidad Católica del Perú, Lima, Peru

V. Pinilla
Department of Applied Economics and Economic History, Universidad de Zaragoza, Zaragoza, Spain

V. Pinilla, H. Willebald (eds.), *Agricultural Development in the World Periphery*, Palgrave Studies in Economic History, https://doi.org/10.1007/978-3-319-66020-2_16

employment. At present, the agricultural sector contributes 9 per cent to GDP and represents 24.7 per cent of the economically active population (EAP), according to the 2007 census, and 65.5 per cent of the EAP in rural areas (INEI, 2008). Peruvian agriculture shows low levels of labour productivity, partly explained by the fragmentation of land ownership, the lack of private and public assets available to farmers, rural poverty, and the limited development of agrarian markets (labour, credit, technical assistance, information, insurance, and so on). Agriculture is also the sector with the highest poverty levels, affecting 53.8 per cent of the total EAP occupied in agriculture in 2010, compared to only 16.4 per cent among the non-agricultural occupied EAP (Velazco & Velazco, 2012).

Furthermore, agriculture in Peru is heterogeneous, both in terms of its articulation with the markets and in its levels of profitability and sustainability. Thus, we see the coexistence of modern, highly technical agriculture alongside small family farms, oriented to both local and international markets. The linkage between small-scale agriculture and the export agro-industry occurs through markets, in that agricultural goods are the raw materials for agribusiness, the renting of land, and the labour market (Figueroa, 1996).

From a geographical perspective, we must take into account the characteristics that determine Peru's three natural regions: *costa* (coast), *sierra* (highlands), and *selva* (forest). The coast is the centre of the country's industrial, commercial, and agricultural activity. Lima, the political and economic capital, is on the coast and is home to about a third of the total population. The highlands consist of the Andes, high plateaus (*altiplanos*), and mountain valleys, covering 27 per cent of the country. The forest is the largest but least populated area of Peru. Tropical rainforest covers 60 per cent of the national territory. Small farms are found in all three regions, but are most common in the highlands.

Peru is an interesting case for studies of the effects of development strategies and agricultural policies, having experienced a major socio-economic transformation in the twentieth century, like many other developing countries. In 1940, when the first census of the century was conducted, the country's population was mainly rural (65 per cent) and resident in the highlands (63 per cent). By 2007, the date of the latest census (at the time of writing), most of the population (77 per cent) was living in the cities, and most settlements (55 per cent) of any size were on the coast (INEI, 2008). Over this period, the country experimented with a variety of economic policies.

In this context, this chapter has a two-fold aim: to identify the salient characteristics of the development models and policies affecting Peruvian agriculture since the mid-twentieth century, and to identify what effect they have had on agricultural production and productivity, and on the sources of growth of agricultural output, based on an estimation of total-factor productivity (TFP) for the 1950–2010 period. Evidently, it is not only economic development strategies that affect results in the agricultural sector; changes in the international economy also play an important role, although they are outside the scope of this work.

This chapter is organised into six sections. Section 2 explains the economic development models implemented, with a particular interest in the export-led growth model (focusing on the promotion of both traditional and non-traditional export products), and the import-substitution industrialisation model. Agrarian reform policy and its effects on agrarian structure are discussed in Sect. 3. Section 4 analyses changes in production and labour productivity in the agriculture sector, and the results of estimating TFP are presented in Sect. 5. We outline our conclusions in Sect. 6.

2 Economic Development Models in the Second Half of the Twentieth Century in Peru

Throughout its history, Peru, as a small open economy, has undergone cycles of crisis and recovery, usually linked to fluctuations in the international market. The Peruvian economy has always been an exporter of primary products and an importer of manufactured goods (Thorp & Bertram, 1978). Development strategy models have ranged from the diversification of primary exports (until the late 1950s) to import-substitution industrialisation (1960–1975) and the promotion of non-traditional exports; this pattern has held since the early 1990s and is current today.

Until the late 1950s, agriculture was a key sector of the Peruvian economy, and could be described as the sector leading growth (Escobal, 1993). Agriculture was an axis of accumulation for the economy in the context of the model of primary exports of agricultural products (cotton and sugar) and minerals.

The economic history of Peru is marked by recurring export booms. Products such as guano, rubber, sugar, cotton, silver, gold, and others, have succeeded each other in dominating the export structure since the nineteenth century, reflecting the role of many countries on the periphery of the first globalisation, as suppliers of agricultural products and raw materials for the industrialised countries of Europe.

The political independence of the Spanish colonial government in the nineteenth century did not lead to a bourgeois transformation of the colonial structure, and the *hacienda* and peasant communities continued to be the predominant forms of Peruvian agrarian structures.

Capitalist development of agriculture took place in the twentieth century, with foreign capital playing an important part in this new process. As a result, the coastal hacienda evolved into a modern enterprise, leading to the consolidation of the larger haciendas and their sugar and cotton plantations. These were typically characterised by production for export, a high level of capital investment, centralised administration, and the use of modern technology (Byerlee & Viswanathan, 2018, Chap. 4). The wage-labour system also became the norm in sugar-producing haciendas. Thus, agricultural development was driven by a growth model based on exports, in which the sugar sector was one of the leaders, its influence spreading over the northern highlands in areas such as Cajamarca, benefiting from its mainly peasant labour resources, and livestock farming.

This development model changed in the late 1950s, as in many other Latin American countries, with a turn toward models based on import-substitution industrialisation (ISI) (Bulmer-Thomas, 1994). The growth of agriculture then became dependent on the expansion of industry. It went from generating to demanding foreign currency, with food being imported to meet the growing domestic demand. The pace of growth of agricultural production for the internal market was not fast enough to meet the increased demand for food caused by population growth and rising incomes. This meant that Peru became a net importer of the food products that made up the urban diet. In 1960, the country imported 70 per cent of the wheat it consumed, 35 per cent of the food oil, and 22 per cent of the dairy products (Rojas, 1993).

During the 1960s, there were major economic, political, and social changes in Peru. In economics, there was an attempt to reduce the vulnerability of growth driven by exports, by promoting industrialisation.[1] Although the economy's dependence on metal exports as the main source of growth remained substantial (its weight in the export structure went from 48.4 per cent in 1970 to 40.2 per cent in 1989), there was a transformation in the export structure. Agricultural products were overtaken by fuels and by manufactured products, and minerals continued to be the main source of foreign revenue.

In the ISI implementation scenario, from 1960 to 1975, the macroeconomic policy to promote industrial growth created conditions that were hostile to agricultural development. Tax and price-control policies had a negative effect on the sector's profitability and growth. In this context of support for national industry, there were two main elements of agricultural policy during the military government of 1969–1979: implementing agrarian reform (promoting the creation of cooperatives) and guaranteeing the low cost of the food basket (Álvarez, 1983). According to Alberts (1983), agricultural policies were extremely biased in favour of urban consumers. Price-control policies and the overvalued exchange rate discriminated against agricultural exports and incentivised food imports.

The 1980s were marked by an agrarian counter-reform, reflected in the disappearance of associative forms of production and the expansion of smallholdings. This was accompanied by the emergence of politically motivated violence in rural areas, which later spread to coastal cities, a situation which was finally controlled in the early 1990s.

The macroeconomic scenario was characterised by the effects of the external debt crisis and the application of orthodox policies, driving a change to a market-based strategy centred on privatisation and private investment, trade liberalisation, and the rerouting of state investments into economic infrastructure to support private enterprise. The orthodox programme failed due to difficulties and inconsistencies in its application, and to external factors (deterioration in the terms of trade, external credit being cut off, and adverse weather conditions caused by El Niño)

(Wise & Pastor, 1992). Given this scenario, 1985 saw the rise to power of the American Popular Revolutionary Alliance (APRA), a political party that implemented a heterodox policy rooted in the Latin American structuralism tradition.

The APRA government diagnosed the agricultural problem as one of low profitability and implemented a set of measures to raise agricultural prices, lower costs, and increase productivity. Substantial injections of cash were used to subsidise loans and basic inputs, such as fertilisers and pesticides (Escobal, 1989). The results were positive until 1987, reflected in increased production. The main beneficiaries of this policy were the modern farms in the coastal and forest regions.

The populist policies of the ARPA government under García, from 1985 to 1990, increased aggregate demand and imports, leading to a fiscal deficit in 1988/1989 and a balance of payments crisis, which led in turn to hyperinflation and recession. In mid-1990s, Fujimori launched a stabilisation programme in order to control inflation, with basic elements including restricting monetary variables, price adjustments, and public tariffs. Other measures included the elimination of subsidies, increased tax pressure, lower public expenditure, and free-floating exchange and interest rates. These measures were complemented by a set of structural reforms intended to manage resources efficiently through deregulation and market liberalisation, along with the reduction of the business role of the government through privatisations and the closure of state companies (León, 1994).[2]

The sectoral measures affecting the performance of agriculture were the elimination of subsidies and price controls on agricultural products and inputs, and free trade with the external market. In the case of imports, these measures took the form of variable import tariffs that, to some extent, provided protection from the subsidies of the main exporter countries and the overvaluing of the local currency against the dollar.[3]

On the financial market side, the interest rate was liberalised, and credit for the sector was reduced drastically when the *Banco Agrario del Perú* (Agricultural Bank, BAP) was liquidated. Alongside this, the main institutional measures were the liberalisation of the land and water markets and the end of the State monopoly on the purchase of agricultural inputs and products.

The Banco Agrario began reducing the cultivated hectares from the 1988/1989 cropping season, when it helped finance 800,000 ha, and the previous one where its coverage reached 1,200,000 ha (Escobal, 1989). This situation was exacerbated by the disappearance of the *Banca de Fomento* (Development Bank) and increased interest rates. To identify the groups that were the most negatively affected by these measures, it is enough to remember that BAP funding tended to favour coastal products. For example, in the 1980–1988 period, funding for cotton was 22.6 per cent of the total, and for rice, 32.2 per cent of the allocated funds (Banco Agrario, annual reports).[4]

The 1990s were a period of far-reaching changes in the economic performance of agriculture (Escobal, 1999; Valcárcel, 2002; Von Hesse, 2000). The implementation of the stabilisation programme and the State's structural reforms changed the institutional environment and the conditions of participation in market relationships for farmers. A key point, in the context of those reforms, was the explicit policy of encouraging investment in the sector by declaring the development of agro-industry to be in the national interest. The role of the State changed with this new approach; its functions were redefined and its participation in promoting and guiding economic development was limited. The State assumed a regulatory and subsidiary role, and private enterprise became a fundamental driver of development (Eguren, 2003; Von Hesse, 2000).

However, the bias favouring the promotion of export agriculture meant that small-scale agriculture and the peasant economy were excluded from the development agenda, unless they were able, with non-governmental support, to successfully insert themselves into the export agriculture production chain (Eguren, 2003)

According to Kay (1994), from a Latin American perspective, the link between agriculture and the world market was strengthened after the 1980s, with the change from an import-substitution strategy to a more export-oriented approach. This trend was consolidated with the introduction of structural adjustment programmes, as the expansion of export agriculture was prioritised as an alternative solution to the permanent shortage of foreign currency. Thus, as part of the economic globalisation process, transnational agricultural corporations and local investors became the predominant players on the Latin American scene. With the use of new technology enabling improvements in storage, agro-industrial processing, preservation, transport, communications, and industrial organisation, these companies achieved advantages in the production of fruit, vegetables, and flowers. Peru was no exception to this process. The structural reforms of the 1990s, particularly the policies promoting the development of agro-industry, created favourable conditions for non-traditional export agriculture to expand and consolidate.[5]

Since 2000, there have been changes in agricultural activity in Peru, due to such factors as greater openness to trade with the international markets (at present Peru has free trade agreements with several countries); the growing international demand for healthy, high-quality food; the addition of new farmland; the increasing interest in bio-fuels; higher incomes for Peruvians (who now demand greater variety and higher quality in their food); the expansion of private investment in agriculture, and so on. These changes in agricultural activity have influenced the link between farmers and the agricultural product and factor markets.

The positive impact of measures favouring agro-industry can be seen in the levels of exports and employment in the productive regions.

Since the 1990s, there have been significant changes in the mix of crops at the national level, explained by internal factors (higher income of the population, changes in consumption patterns, new regulations favouring investment in agriculture, greater openness to trade) and by external factors (a growing world population with higher incomes, and an increasing consumer preference for healthy and organic food). Crops for the internal market represent 45 per cent of farmland, with an average annual growth rate of 3.7 per cent. The proportion of farmland devoted to traditional Andean crops for regional and local markets fell by 3.9 percentage points in the 1990–2009 period. Industrial crops represented 16.1 per cent of farmland and showed moderate growth in the 1990–2009 period.

Export-oriented crops represent the greatest dynamism in terms of farmland use. Coffee, cocoa, asparagus, mango, beans, plantain, grapes, artichoke, and paprika were the crops with the greatest expansion in farmland. The increase in farmland allocated to non-traditional crops for export is due to increased international demand; new laws favouring the sector such as the *Ley de Promoción del Sector Agrario* (Law of Promotion of the Agrarian Sector), which offer incentives for companies; optimal environmental conditions for cultivating these crops; the ability to supply goods while production is decreasing elsewhere in the world; the development of transport infrastructure that delivers products in better condition; and the implementation of Free Trade Agreements (FTAs) between Peru and the rest of the world, including FTAs with the USA, Thailand, Singapore, and China (PROINVERSIÓN, 2007). The output for export is not only provided by large companies—small, medium, and large farmers have all established individual arrangements for dealing with major corporations—and some companies are vertically integrated with their suppliers through contracts establishing their supervision of farming activities, financing, and conditions of sale (the quantity and quality of the product, prices, place of delivery, and penalties).

The expansion of agricultural frontiers based on irrigation in coastal areas creates the opportunity for greater growth of exportable production and employment, but this brings with it environmental problems and questions as to the sustainability of agricultural activity, as in the case of the exhaustion of groundwater in Ica, a situation which may threaten the availability of water for human consumption (RedGE, 2012).

Another problem to take into account, and which the 2008 financial crisis has made evident, is the heavy dependency of exports on the economic cycles of the importing countries. It is expected that the demand for fruit and vegetables among high-income segments of the population will not fall significantly when there are negative income shocks. Based on agricultural labour employment records and information on exports in 2009–2011, Gamero (2012) concludes that the loss of employment in Peru due to the impact of the 2008 economic crisis is elastic in relation to exports. In other words, registered agricultural jobs fell more than exports. However, during the recovery phase, 2010–2011, employment appears to be inelastic to rising exports. This situation shows that employment is the adjustment variable when there are changes in the international market, and reveals vulnerability and a lack of protection for wage labourers when adverse changes arise in external demand.

In the 1960s, more than half of the economically active population was engaged in agriculture, so access to land was an important factor in the performance of the Peruvian economy. Consequently, the following section will briefly discuss the main characteristics of the agrarian reform implemented in 1969, as well as its effects on the distribution of land and the agrarian structure.

3 1969 Agrarian Reform and Its Impact on Land Ownership

The military government of General Velasco (1969–1975) implemented an extensive programme of agrarian reform in 1969. The attempted reforms of earlier governments were limited in scope. An international context dominated by the Cold War and the Cuban revolution, and an internal front with a growing peasant movement in the 1950s and 1960s, put agrarian reform back on the government's agenda (de Janvry, 1994). The priority was the formation of agricultural cooperatives and associations: *Cooperativas Agrarias de Producción* (CAP), *Cooperativas Comunales, Sociedades Agrarias de Interés Social* (SAIS), and others (Bourque & Palmer, 1975). The main beneficiaries were wage labourers in the large estates that were in the process of being expropriated.[6] According to Alberts (Alberts, 1983; Figueroa, 1990), the bias can be explained by three factors. The first is political: by implementing this agrarian reform, the government expected to immediately dismantle the power of the Peruvian oligarchy, and the expropriation of these *haciendas*, and transferring them to the wage labourers who worked on them, was an effective way to do so. The second factor is connected to the motto "la tierra es para quien la trabaja"—"the land to the tiller"—reacting to the exploitative nature of the worker-owner relationship and making the point that exorbitant rents were being extracted from the peasants. The third and last factor relates to administrative convenience: it was easier to strip power from the large landowners by handing their land directly to the wage labourers, and reorganising the rural population's access to the land later.

From the economic point of view, the Agrarian Reform was considered a measure for developing the internal market and supporting the industrialisation process. Thus, it was assumed that eliminating the former oligarchy would allow the peasants to integrate more fully in the national economy, and the surpluses generated in the modern agricultural sector could be funnelled into industrial investment and expansion (Valderrama, 1976).

Peru's agrarian problem in the 1950s and 1960s was defined by highly concentrated land ownership. The agrarian reform implemented in 1969, characterised by changes in ownership structure, did not significantly alter the original agricultural structure. The haciendas were transformed into agricultural cooperatives and SAIS, with that becoming the dominant form of organisation in Peruvian agriculture until they were gradually dissolved in the 1980s. Only a small part of the expropriated land was directly allocated to private family farms (Kay, 2002). This is confirmed when we compare the agricultural censuses for 1961 and 1972. In 1961, small farms—under 5 ha—comprised 83.2 per cent of the total number of farms, corresponding to 5.7 per cent of the land. In 1972, farms under 5 ha comprised 78 per cent of agricultural units, but were only 6.6 per cent of the land. Mid-sized farms—20 to 100 ha—now had a larger share than before. This sector represented 2.9 per cent of agricultural farm units and owned 5.3 per cent of all farmland in 1961. After the agrarian reform, this group constituted 6.3 per cent of all farms and held 11.7 per cent of the land (INEI, 2009).

In the 1980s, the organisation and functions of the CAPs and SAIS collapsed, due to problems in their administration and their internal management, while their members were working less and production costs were rising, making the companies economically unviable.[7] The coastal CAPs, except for the sugar-producing cooperatives, decided to dissolve the companies and distribute the land among their members. In the highlands, most lands owned by SAIS associations were taken over by peasant communities (Burneo, 2011). As a result of this process, which was accelerated by land transfers through inheritance, farmland was fragmented and smallholdings became the most numerous group. Farmers were more interested in concentrating their efforts on their own land, and pressed for the recognition of their individual deeds of ownership (Binswanger-Mkhize, Bourguignon, & van den Brink, 2009).

Table 16.1, based on the farming censuses of 1961, 1972, 1994, and 2012, shows the distribution of farms by number and size (hectares). At the national level, in 1961, farms under 5 ha represented 83 per cent of all farms, but had access to only 5.7 per cent of farmland. The results of the

Table 16.1 Peru: number and size of farming units according to 1961, 1972, 1994 and 2012 farming surveys

	1961		1972		1994		2012	
	Number of farms (%)	Size (area) (%)	Number of farms (%)	Size (area) (%)	Number of farms (%)	Size (area) (%)	Number of farms (%)	Size (area) (%)
Under 1 Ha.	34.1	0.7	34.7	0.8	24.2	0.5	37.6	0.8
1–5 Ha.	49.1	5	43.2	5.8	46.1	5.3	41.7	5.1
5–20 Ha.	12.6	4.7	16.7	8.7	22.2	9.6	15.2	7.6
20–100 Ha.	2.9	5.3	4.3	9.3	6.3	11.7	4.5	9.5
100–500 Ha.	0.9	8.7	0.8	9.1	1.1	10.4	0.8	8.4
500–1000 Ha.	0.2	5.7	0.1	4.6	0.1	5	0.1	4.3
1000–2500 Ha.	0.1	8.9	0.1	7.4	0.1	8.4	0.1	7.3
Over 2500 Ha.	0.1	61	0.1	54.3	0.1	49.1	0.1	57
Total (%)	100	100	100	100	100	100	100	100
Total (absolute value)	851,957	18,604,500	1,390,877	23,545,147	1,745,773	35,381,808	2,213,506	38,742,465

Source: 1st, 2nd, 3rd and 4th National Farming Surveys, 1961, 1972, 1994 and 2012 (INEI)

2012 census confirm the predominance of very small farms, which nevertheless represent a tiny proportion of farmland. The first phase of the agrarian reform produced a small reduction in the concentration of land, with the Gini coefficient passing from 0.94 in 1961 to 0.88 in 1972. In 1994, the coefficient dropped to 0.5 because of the land fragmentation process taking place during the 1980s (Zegarra, 1999). Estimates seem to indicate a pattern of greater equality in land distribution (Velazco, 2001). From 1961 to 1994, we can also see declining numbers of large farms and the growth of mid-sized holdings (INEI, 2013). However, when comparing the results of the 2012 farm census, processes of fragmentation and concentration of land are identified. The first process leads to the predominance of small-scale units, while the second refers to the fact that land has been acquired by a few agents (either for productive or speculative purposes). A more dynamic land market has enhanced land transactions.

Since the 1990s, the central government, in coordination with certain sub-national governments, has promoted and financed irrigation projects on the *costa*. These new lands were auctioned off and transferred to economic groups specialising in export agriculture (Escobedo, 2015). The regional analysis of the land concentration based on the Gini coefficient for the 2012 census allows us to distinguish a more pronounced dynamic on the *costa* than in the *sierra* and *selva*. Therefore, the Gini is 0.75 for the *costa*, 0.68 for the *sierra*, and 0.53 for the *selva* (Bourliaud & Eresue, 2015). This process is associated with the expansion of large-scale agro-export farms in the *costa*.

Returning to the discussion of the agriculture output performance, the next two sections deal with the trend in agricultural production and the estimation of the TFP.

4 Trends in Agricultural Production and Productivity

When we analyse the growth in agricultural production (Table 16.2), we can see that the periods of greatest growth are at the beginning and end of the study period: 1950–1970 and 1991–2007. Fast growth coincides with the end of the export agriculture era around 1960 and the first

Table 16.2 Annual average growth rates of agricultural production by destination markets (at constant 1994 soles)

Periods	Agricultural GDP Total	Internal market	External market	% External market In Agricultural GDP
1950–1960	2.32	1.23	7.56	19.31
1961–1970	3.41	4.12	0.86	21.32
1971–1980	0.15	0.27	−0.34	17.61
1981–1990	1.76	1.94	1.38	14.92
1991–2000	5.46	5.62	4.96	13.23
2001–2007	3.62	3.49	4.78	14.12
Entire period 1950–2007	2.74	2.74	3.12	17.23

Source: Authors' calculations based on estimations by Tello (2009) of the destination markets of agricultural products. The external agricultural GDP was calculated based on the sum of the value of achiote, unprocessed cotton, cocoa, coffee, sugar cane, onion, asparagus, mandarin oranges, mango, dried lima bean, avocado, and grapes

decade of the ISI, and again when the model changed to greater liberalisation and opening up to outside trade in 1991, and the subsequent economic expansion. The most critical period coincides with the economic crisis of the 1970s and the "lost decade" of Latin America in the 1980s.

Figure 16.1 also clearly shows Peru's unfavourable economic situation in the intermediate period, when it was unable to recover the 1977 level of GDP per capita until 2005. The same graph highlights the fact that until the mid-1970s, agricultural production grew at the same rate as the population, slowing down from the mid-1970s to the mid-1990s, and then growing at a significantly higher rate after 1995. The intermediate stage is considered to be a period of crisis in Peruvian agriculture, defined in terms of the agricultural output growing more slowly than domestic demand (Escobal, 1993).

The breakdown of agricultural production by destination market, whether domestic or export, and the share of exports in total production also show which market has been the main driver of growth in agricultural GDP. The strong growth of the first two decades was based on the external market in the 1950s (when the export agriculture model was still current) and on the internal market in the 1960s, after the switch to ISI. This change in policy had a notable effect on agricultural exports, which

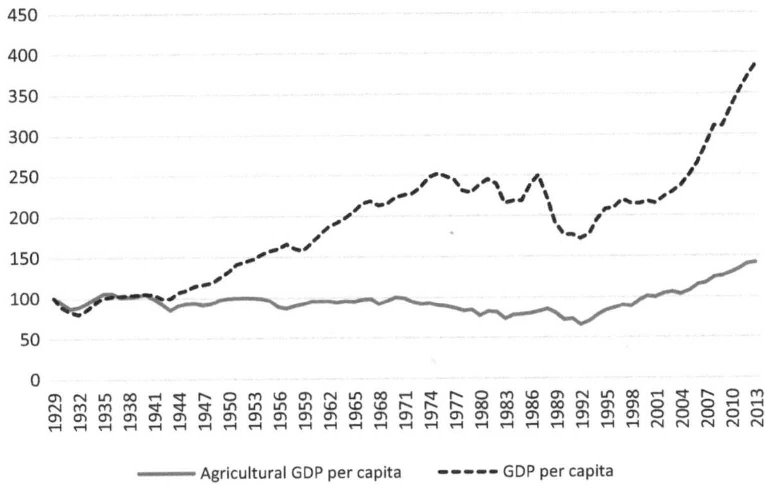

Fig. 16.1 Evolution of GDP per capita and agricultural GDP per capita, 1929–2011 (at constant 1994 Soles, index number 100 = 1929). Source: Authors' calculations based on statistics from the Central Reserve Bank of Peru, available at www.bcrp.gob.pe. GDP information is at constant 1994 Soles (national currency of Peru)

were much less dynamic from 1961 and 1991, due to the reduced profitability of the sector, lower levels of investment, and a decline in the terms of trade.[8] Also, ecological limits appear on the exploitation of raw materials such as sugar and cotton (Rojas, 1993).

The return to rapid growth of agricultural GDP from 1991 rested equally on the external and internal markets, although exports had a much lower weight in the total agricultural GDP than at the end of the export agriculture period.

Table 16.3 shows that labour productivity growth was very slow from the early 1960s to early 1990s. Productivity convergence with other economic activities was very modest. However, from the mid-1990s, growth was extremely rapid, with notable convergence.

This poor growth in productivity can also be explained by the meagre growth in agricultural production from the early 1970s to the early 1990s, while the sector's workforce continued to grow in absolute terms until the twenty-first century, when inter-sectoral labour mobility began to change, and the absolute collapse of the agricultural EAP became evident (Banco Mundial, 2010).

Table 16.3 Estimated labour productivity (at constant 1994 Soles) (index number 1961 = 100 and % of agricultural labour productivity over the economy as a whole)

	1961	1972	1981	1993	2007
Agriculture	100	136	124	128	218
Agriculture/total	23.8	21.4	19.4	29.8	37.4

Source: Authors' calculations based on statistics from the Central Reserve Bank of Peru and the National Population and Housing Census (INEI) of 1961, 1972, 1981, 1993, and 2007

In recent years, improvements in agricultural productivity, and in the economy in general, have had a significant effect on poverty levels. Estimates based on the National Household Survey (ENAHO) show that the national poverty rate was 54.3 per cent in 2002, and had fallen to 40.4 per cent by 2007. For the same years, the rural poverty rate was 77.1 per cent and 64 per cent respectively, and urban poverty declined from 42.1 per cent to 27.7 per cent.

Although poverty has decreased overall, the impact on urban areas, where 70 per cent of the country's population lives, has obviously been more favourable. The growth elasticity of poverty is higher in urban than rural areas, and higher in rural coastal areas than the rural highlands or forest (Escobal & Ponce, 2008). The decrease in rural poverty is highly concentrated in rural coastal areas. This trend is confirmed by the growth of annual household expenditure from 2004 to 2007: 6.4 per cent for the urban coast, 3.9 per cent for the rural coast, and 1.9 per cent for the rural highlands (Vakis, Herrera, & Escobal, 2008). The evidence suggests that not all households in rural areas have benefited from growth, and there are different patterns and dynamics of growth on the rural coast and in the rural highlands.

5 Trends in Total-Factor Productivity in Agriculture

This section presents the results of the estimation of TFP in Peruvian agriculture for the period 1950–2010. The aim of this approach is to identify the sources of growth of agricultural output, depending on the contribution of factors and changes in productivity.

TFP is defined as the ratio of total output (Y) to total input (X). Thus, TFP can be shown as:

$$\mathrm{TFP} = \mathrm{Y} / \mathrm{X} \tag{1}$$

Changes in TFP over time are estimated by comparing the change in output with the change in input. Equation (1) expressed in logarithms is:

$$\frac{d\ln(TFP)}{dt} = \frac{d\ln(Y)}{dt} - \frac{d\ln(X)}{dt} \tag{2}$$

Assuming a Cobb-Douglas production function with constant returns to scale, Eq. (2) becomes:

$$\ln\left(\frac{TFP_t}{TFP_{t-1}}\right) = \ln\left(\frac{Y_t}{Y_{t-1}}\right) - \sum_j S_j \ln\left(\frac{X_{j,t}}{X_{j,t-1}}\right) \tag{3}$$

where S_j is the cost structure of input *j*. The inputs considered are labour, land, machinery, stock of cattle, and fertiliser.[9] In order to assess the robustness of the estimates, two scenarios are taken into account. The first consists of assuming constant input shares for the whole period of analysis. The weights correspond to the case of Brazil reported by Avila and Evenson (1995). The weights are: 0.43 for labour; 0.22 for the land; 0.14 for the stock of cattle; 0.14 for machinery, and 0.07 for fertilisers. The alternative corresponds to variable input shares by decades. Input shares were calculated from the Brazilian Agricultural Censuses of 1970, 1985, 1996 and 2006 and reported by Fuglie (2012). Velazco (2001) estimated the shares of land, labour, machinery and fertiliser for the period 1970–1995, using a Cobb-Douglas function. The relative importance of those input shares is similar to the Brazilian weights, these being preferred for application to the Peruvian case.[10] Table 16.5 shows the factor shares used for the variable input share scenario.

There is a substantial empirical literature that estimates TFP using various approaches, such as the translog production function, stochastic frontier analysis, and data envelopment analysis (DEA), among others. In the context of international comparative analysis of changes in agricultural TFP, the case of Peru has been considered as part of a sample of countries for estimating this. The database used is from the FAO and the analysis period begins in 1960 (Avila, Romano, & Garagorry, 2010; Bravo-Ortega & Lederman, 2004; Coelli & Rao, 2005; Fuglie, 2012; Ludena, 2010; Nin-Pratt & Yu, 2009; Pfeiffer, 2003, among others).

Tables 16.4 and 16.5 show the sources of agricultural growth for the analysis periods. The contribution of the TFP index and the input index (land, livestock, labour, machinery, and fertiliser) is estimated. Outcomes with constant-input shares and variable-input shares provide similar trends, showing some discrepancy only in the 1976–1990 period. In general, results denote that the TFP shows poor performance during 1950–1959, with output being explained largely by input accumulation. The ISI period, 1960–1975, was characterised by a recovery in the TFP contribution to output growth, ranging from 18.18 per cent to 20.08 per cent. During the next sub-period, 1976–1990, the external debt crisis, the spread of political violence, and hyperinflation caused by the economic crisis undermined output growth. This was largely explained by

Table 16.4 Factor accumulation and productivity contributions to output growth, 1950–2010 (annual average growth rate in percent) (with constant input shares)

Periods	National context	Output growth (%)	Input growth (%)	TFP growth (%)	TPF relative to output
1950–1959	Export-oriented policies	1.67	3.03	−1.36	−81.44
1960–1975	ISI policies	2.64	2.16	0.48	18.18
1976–1990	Internal/debt crisis	1.17	0.90	0.27	23.08
1991–2001	Export-oriented policies Stabilisation programmes and structural reforms	5.10	2.01	3.09	60.59
2002–2010	Economic expansion	4.26	0.93	3.33	78.17
Total period 1950–2010		2.60	1.66	0.94	36.15

Source: Authors' calculations

Table 16.5 Factor accumulation and productivity contributions to output growth, 1950–2010 (annual average growth rate in percent) (with variable input shares)

Periods	National context	Output growth (%)	Input growth (%)	TFP growth (%)	TPF relative to output
1950–1959	Export-oriented policies	1.67	2.08	−0.41	−24.55
1960–1975	ISI policies	2.64	2.11	0.53	20.08
1976–1990	Internal/debt crisis	1.17	1.19	−0.02	−1.71
1991–2001	Export-oriented policies Stabilisation programme and structural reforms	5.10	3.29	1.81	35.49
2002–2010	Economic expansion	4.26	0.94	3.32	77.93
Total period 1950–2010		2.60	1.79	0.81	31.15

Source: Authors' calculations

input accumulation—77 per cent according to the constant-input share scenario and 100 per cent for the variable-input shares scenario. The following two sub-periods witnessed remarkable output growth. From the 1990s, productivity in Peruvian agriculture recovered significantly, growing at an annual average rate of 3.09 per cent and 3.33 per cent during the fourth and fifth sub-periods, respectively, for the constant-input share context, and 1.81 per cent and 3.32 per cent for the variable-input share scenario.

Regarding the input trends, the higher growth rates were associated with arable land and permanent crops (2.09 per cent for the entire period), fertiliser use (4.3 per cent), and use of agricultural tractors (2.97 per cent). On the other hand, the lowest rate of growth corresponds to the size of the economically active population in agriculture (1.01 per cent) and the number of livestock units (0.86 per cent).

The estimation of TFP suggests that significant changes have taken place in Peruvian agriculture in the last two decades. These were due to the increasing openness to international markets (Peru currently has free trade agreements with a range of countries), as well as other factors: the growing international demand for healthy, high-quality food; the incorporation of new land for farming; the growing interest in bio-fuels; the increased income of Peruvians who demand a more varied, higher-quality food supply; and the expansion of private investment in agriculture, among other factors (Velazco & Velazco, 2012).

Finally, from a Latin American perspective, the outstanding performance of the Peruvian case since the 1990s is not an isolated case. Further, as discussed in Martín-Retortillo et al. (2018) (Chap. 13), Peru follows the patterns identified in the whole region.

6 Conclusions

This chapter, based on gathering and analysing secondary sources, examines the consequences of diverse growth models and agrarian policies for Peruvian agricultural production and productivity from 1950 to 2010.

A long-term view, 1929–2011, of total GDP per capita and agricultural GDP per capita allows us to compare the growth dynamics of total and sectoral output in relation to the demand component of population growth. Taking into account Peru's history of growth over the long term, it becomes obvious that the current accelerated growth of GDP is, in fact, a return to the growth trends of past decades. A long period has been identified in which agricultural production was stagnant, lagging behind population growth. However, this trend changed in the early 1990s, and since then, agriculture has grown steadily.

Throughout its history, Peru, as a small open economy, has undergone cycles of crisis and recovery, usually linked to fluctuations in the international market. The Peruvian economy has always been an exporter of primary products and an importer of manufactured goods (Thorp & Bertram, 1978). Development strategy models have ranged from the diversification of primary exports, to import-substitution industrialisation, and the promotion of non-traditional exports, which is the current model. These strategies have determined the outcome for agriculture. The sector was an axis of accumulation for the economy in the context of the model of primary exports of agricultural products (cotton and sugar) and minerals. This situation changed radically in the late 1950s, when an ISI process was encouraged. This marked a turning point, when the growth of agriculture became dependent on the expansion of industry. The evidence discussed, particularly the growth in agricultural labour productivity and the performance of TFP, seems to suggest another change in the 1990s, in how agriculture related to and connected with other economic sectors. The structural reforms of the 1990s, particularly the policies promoting the development of agro-industry, created favourable conditions for non-traditional export agriculture to expand and consolidate. This growth was led by the coastal region, thanks to its climate, access to the best land, proximity to the markets, and infrastructure. And its expansion has revitalised the wage-labour market.

Notes

1. Concern over industrialisation is part of an old debate in the economic history of Peru. The subject arose in the political arena every time there was a crisis in the export sector. These periods can be identified in the 1880s, after the War of the Pacific; in the Great Depression; and in WWII.
2. For a detailed analysis of the stabilisation policy and macroeconomic performance of agriculture, see León (1994) and Dancourt and Mendoza (1994).
3. Dancourt and Mendoza (1994) discuss the implications and effectiveness of import tariffs on agricultural products.
4. Despite these trends, it should be borne in mind that the BAP's coverage did not reach all farms, and this was most noticeable in small-scale agriculture. Data from the National Survey of Rural Households (Encuesta Nacional de Hogares Rurales; Portocarrero, 1987) show that in 1984, only 7.6 per cent of farms had access to loans from the BAP. This information is crucial when considering the importance of alternative, informal sources of agricultural credit and the impact on interest rates.
5. This expansion of the agricultural export sector can be related to the trends identified in Latin America, as well as the ways capitalism can expand into agriculture, as described by de Janvry (1981), when considering commercial and contract farming as the predominant modes in the region. This subject has yet to be researched in the context of Peruvian agriculture. Some initial thoughts and hypotheses on this process can be found in Eguren (2003) and Valcárcel (2002).

6. The agrarian reform was executed mainly on the coast and in the highlands, the two regions with greater rural populations and greater areas of agricultural use. Between June 1969 and June 1979, 15,826 properties and more than 9 million ha were expropriated. Most of this area was transferred to 370,000 beneficiaries (Eguren, 2006).
7. Mejía (1982) provides some examples of the problems faced by these companies. A study carried out in 1977 by a High-Level Commission of the Ministry of Agriculture clearly revealed this fact. Of 1,388 existing companies at that time, 955 (68%) had no manager and 659 (47%) lacked accounting. At the same time, the problems of lack of human resources were classified as serious in 1,088 cases (78%); lack of training in 941 cases (68%); and lack of business organisation in 633 cases (48%).
8. Regarding the terms of term (ratio of export prices to import prices), a correlation coefficient between the terms of trade and an openness trade ratio (agricultural exports to agricultural GDP) for the period 1950–2010 is 0.61, suggesting a significant and positive relationship.
9. Further information about the sources of data for estimating TFP is found in Velazco & Pinilla (2017).
10. The Brazilian weights were preferred due to the fact that we used the same five inputs in our empirical analysis.

References

Alberts, T. (1983). *Agrarian Reform and Rural Poverty: A Case Study of Peru*. Boulder: Westview.

Alvarez, E. (1983). *Política Económica y Agricultura en el Perú, 1969–1979*. Lima: IEP.

Avila, A., & Evenson, R. (1995). Total Factor Productivity Growth in Brazilian Agriculture and the Role of Agricultural Research. In *Anais do XXXIII Congresso Brasileiro de Economia e Sociologia Rural* (Vol. 1, pp. 631–657). Curitiba, 31/07 a 03/09/95.

Avila, A., Romano, L., & Garagorry, F. (2010). Agricultural productivity in Latin American and the Caribbean and sources of growth. In E. Pingali & R. Evenson (Eds.), *Handbook of Agricultural Economics* (Vol. 4, pp. 3714–3768). North Holland: Elsevier.

Banco Mundial. (2010). *El Mercado Laboral Peruano Durante el Auge y Caída*. Washington, DC: Banco Mundial.

Binswanger-Mkhize, H., Bourguignon, C., & van den Brink, R. (2009). *Agricultural Land Redistribution: Toward Greater Consensus*. Washington, DC: World Bank.

Bourliaud, J., & Eresue, M. (2015). La (re)concentración de las tierras en la costa. *La Revista Agraria, 169*, 3–5.

Bourque, S., & Palmer, D. (1975). Transforming the Rural Sector: Government Policy and Peasant Response. In A. Lowental (Ed.), *The Peruvian Experiment* (pp. 179–219). Princeton: Princeton University Press.

Bravo-Ortega, C., & Lederman, D. (2004). Agricultural Productivity and Its Determinants: Revisiting International Experiences. *Estudios de Economía, 31*(2), 133–163.

Bulmer-Thomas, V. (1994). *La historia económica de América Latina desde la independencia*. México: Fondo de Cultura Económica.

Burneo, Z. (2011). *El Proceso de Concentración de la Tierra en el Perú*. Lima: CEPES.

Byerlee, D., & Viswanathan, P. K. (2018). Plantations and Economic Development in the Twentieth Century: End of an Era? In V. Pinilla & H. Willebald (Eds.), *Agricultural Development in the World Periphery: A Global Economic History Approach*. London: Palgrave Macmillan.

Coelli, T., & Rao, D. (2005). Total Factor Productivity Growth in Agriculture: A Malmquist Index Analysis of 93 Countries, 1980–2000. *Agricultural Economics, 32*(1s), 115–134.

Dancourt, O., & Mendoza, W. (1994). Agricultura y Política de Estabilización en el Perú. In O. Dancourt, E. Mayer, & C. Monge (Eds.). Perú and Lima: El problema agrario en debate. SEPIA V and SEPIA.

De Janvry, A. (1981). *The Agrarian Question and Reformism in Latín América*. Baltimore: The Johns Hopkins University Press.

De Janvry, A. (1994). Social and Economic Reforms: The Challenge of Equitable Growth in Latin American Agriculture. In E. Muchnik & A. Niño de Zepeda (Eds.), *Apertura Económica, Modernización y Sostenibilidad de la Agricultura* (pp. 79–98). Santiago de Chile: Asociación de Latinoamérica y del Caribe de Economistas Agrarios (ALACEA).

Eguren, F. (2003). Las Políticas Agrarias en la última década: Una Evaluación. Ponencia balance presentada al SEPIA X, Pucallpa (mimeo).

Eguren, F. (2006). Reforma agraria y desarrollo rural en el Perú. In F. Eguren (Ed.), *Reforma agraria y desarrollo rural en la región Andina* (pp. 11–32). Lima: CEPES.

Escobal, J. (1989). *Políticas de Precios y Subsidios Agrícolas: Impactos Macroeconómico y Sectorial.* Perú 1985–1989. Documento de Trabajo No.5, GRADE, Lima

Escobal, J. (1993). Relaciones de largo plazo entre el sector agrícola y en no agrícola: Un estudio de cointegración para la economía peruana. *Economía, XVI*(31), 71–89.

Escobal, J., & Ponce, C. (2008). *Dinámicas Provinciales de Pobreza en el Perú 1993–2005*. Working Papers 011. Santiago: Rimisp Latin American Center for Rural Development.

Escobedo, J. (2015). Concentración de tierras a la peruana. *La Revista Agraria, 169*, 6–9.

Figueroa, A. (1990). *Desarrollo agrícola en América latina: teoría y políticas.* Documentos de Trabajo/Working Papers 1990–88, Departamento de Economía—Pontificia Universidad Católica del Perú.

Figueroa, A. (1996). *Pequeña agricultura y agroindustria en el Perú*. Santiago de Chile: CEPAL.

Fuglie, K. (2012). Productivity Growth and Technology Capital in the Global Agricultural Economy. In K. Fuglie, S. Wang, & V. Ball (Eds.), *Productivity Growth in Agriculture: An International Perspective* (pp. 335–369). Oxfordshire: CAB International.

Gamero, J. (2012). *Derechos Laborales y Empleo en la Agroexportación*. Lima: RedGE and CEPES.

INEI. (2008). *Censos Nacionales 2007. XI de población y VI de vivienda. Primeros resultados*. INEI: Lima.

INEI. (2009). *Perú: Migraciones internas 1993–2007*. Lima: INEI.

INEI. (2013). *Resultados Definitivos. IV Censo Nacional Agropecuario 2012.* Lima: INEI.

Kay, C. (1994). *Rural Development and Agrarian Issues in Contemporary Latin America*. Working Paper No. 173, Institute of Social Studies. La Haya: ISS.

Kay, C. (2002). Agrarian Reform and the Neoliberal Counter-Reform in Latin America'. In J. Chase (Ed.), *The Spaces of Neoliberalism: Land, Place and Family in Latin America* (pp. 25–52). Bloomfield, CT: Kumarian Press.

Leon, J. (1994) Política de Estabilización y Crisis Agraria. In O. Dancourt, E. Mayer, & C. Monge (Eds.). *Perú: El problema agrario en debate. Sepia V.* Lima: Sepia.

Ludena, C. (2010). *Agricultural Productivity Growth, Efficiency Change and Technical Progress in Latin American and the Caribbean*. IDB Working Paper Series No.IDB-WP-186.

Martín-Retortillo, M., Pinilla, V., Velazco, J., & Willebald, H. (2018). The Goose That Laid the Golden Eggs? Agricultural Development in Latin America in the 20th Century. In V. Pinilla & H. Willebald (Eds.), *Agricultural Development in the World Periphery: A Global Economic History Approach*. London: Palgrave Macmillan.

Mejía, M. (1982). Perú 1969–1980. La penúltima reforma agraria latinoamericana. *Comercio Exterior, 32*(4), 441–446.

Nin-Pratt A., & Yu, B. (2009, August 16–22). *Getting Implicit Shadow Prices Right for the Estimation of the Malmquist Index: The Case of Agricultural Total Factor Productivity in Developing Countries*. Paper presented at the International Association of Agricultural Economists Conference, Beijing, China.

Pfeiffer, L. (2003). Agricultural Productivity Growth in the Andean Community. *American Journal of Agricultural Economics, 85*(5), 1335–1341.

Portocarrero, J. (Ed.). (1987). *Los hogares rurales en el Perú. Importancia y articulación con el desarrollo agrario. GAPA/PADI. Ministerio de Agricultura*. Lima: Fundación Friedrich Ebert.

PROINVERSIÓN. (2007). *Sembrando oportunidades*. Lima: PROINVERSION.

RedGe. (2012). *¿Más Exportaciones, Menos Agua? Exportación de Espárragos Amenaza el agua de Ica*. Alerta Urgente. No. 10, marzo, Lima.

Rojas, J. (1993). *El Perú hasta 1960. Políticas liberales en una economía abierta*. Documentos de Trabajo/Working Papers 1993-109, Departamento de Economía—Pontificia Universidad Católica del Perú.

Tello, M. (2009). *Impacto de los choques externos, ciclos económicos y arreglos preferenciales comerciales sobre la producción agropecuaria en el Perú, 1950–2007*. CISEPA, Pontificia Universidad Católica del Perú, Working Paper No. 277, Lima.

Thorp, R., & Bertram, G. (1978). *Peru 1890–1977: Growth and Policy in an Open Economy*. New York: Columbia University Press.

Vakis, R., Herrera, J., & Escobal, J. (2008). *Una mirada a la evolución reciente de la pobreza en el Perú: avances y desafíos*. Lima: Banco Mundial.

Valcárcel, M. (2002). *Agroexportación No Tradicional, sistema esparraguero, agricultura de Contrata y ONG*. Debate Agrario No. 34, CEPES, 29–44.

Valderrama, M. (1976). *7 años de reforma agraria peruana, 1969–1976*. Lima: Fondo Editorial PUCP.

Velazco, J. (2001). Agricultural production in Peru (1950–1995): Sources of growth. In L. Zepeda (Ed.), *Agricultural Investment and Productivity in Developing Countries. Economic and Social Development Paper No. 148*. Rome: FAO.

Velazco, J. & Pinilla, V. (2017). *Development Models, Agricultural Policies, and Agricultural Growth: Peru, 1950–2010*. SEHA Working Paper (forthcoming).

Velazco, J., & Velazco, J. (2012). Características del Empleo Agrícola en el Perú. In C. Garavito & I. Muñoz (Eds.), *Empleo y Protección Social en el Perú*. Lima: Fondo Editorial, Pontificia Universidad Católica del Perú.

Von Hesse, M. (2000). Aspectos Macroeconómicos. In M. Von Hesse, C. Trivelli, A. Diez, & L. Castillo (Eds.), *Desafíos del Desarrollo Rural en el Perú*. Consorcio de Investigación Económica y Social: Lima.

Wise, C., & Pastor, M. (1992). Peruvian Economic Policy in the 1980s: From Orthodoxy to Heterodoxy and Back. *Latin American Research Review., 27*, 83–117.

Zegarra, E. (1999). *El mercado de tierras rurales en el Perú. Vol. I Análisis institucional.* Santiago de Chile: CEPAL.

Jackeline Velazco is Associate Professor in Economics at Pontificia Universidad Católica del Perú, Peru. She pursued a Masters in Development Studies at the Institute of Social Studies (The Hague) and obtained a PhD in Economics from the University of Manchester (UK). Her research experience covers agricultural economics and rural development; well-being and quality of life; and household economics.

Vicente Pinilla is Professor of Economic History at the University of Zaragoza and Fellow at Instituto Agroalimentario de Aragón (IA2). His research interests lies in international trade in agricultural products, long-term agricultural changes, environmental history, and migration. He is the author of *Peaceful Surrender: The Depopulation of Rural Spain in the Twentieth Century*, and is an editor of the books *Agriculture and Economic Development in Europe since 1870*, *Markets and Agricultural Change in Europe from the Thirteenth to the Twentieth Century*, *Natural Resources and Economic Growth: Learning from History*, and *Wine Globalization: A New Comparative History*.

17

Land Frontier Expansion in Settler Economies, 1830–1950: Was It a Ricardian Process?

Henry Willebald and Javier Juambeltz

1 Introduction

The expansion of the Atlantic economy since the mid-nineteenth century until the First World War (WWI), the incorporation of new regions into the global economy and the formation of markets for goods and factors on a world scale are three of the main features of the

First versions were written as part of Willebald's PhD Thesis at Universidad Carlos III, Madrid, Spain. He thanks Instituto Laureano Figuerola for financial support. He is grateful for comments by his supervisor, L. Prados de la Escosura, and the members of the Thesis Committee: C. Lewis, B. Milanovic, P. Astorga, A. Herranz and I. Sanz-Villaroya. We thank the participants in the Workshop on "Comparative studies of the Southern Hemisphere in global economic history and development", RIDGE, Montevideo (Mar-2015)—especially L. Bértola, G. Austin, E. Frankema and O. Licandro—and the XVIIth World Economic History Congress, Kyoto (Jul-2015)—especially V. Pinilla and A. Booth—for their comments. We thank the collaboration of E. Riaño and V. Fernández in the initial data analysis with GIS software. We also thank the reviewers of our Chapter: V. Pinilla and A. Palacios. We are solely responsible for the remaining errors.

H. Willebald (✉)
Department of Economics, Universidad de la República, Montevideo, Uruguay

J. Juambeltz
Universidad del Trabajo del Uruguay (CETP-UTU), Montevideo, Uruguay

V. Pinilla, H. Willebald (eds.), *Agricultural Development in the World Periphery*, Palgrave Studies in Economic History, https://doi.org/10.1007/978-3-319-66020-2_17

First Globalisation. The new settlement economies followed parallel paths (Duncan & Fogarty, 1984) based on similar dynamic relations between waves of immigration, marginalisation of native people, European capital inflows, land abundance, free labour, socially useful political institutions and neo-European cultures (Lloyd & Metzer, 2013). These "temperate economies" include Argentina, Australia, Canada, Chile, New Zealand, South Africa, the USA and Uruguay (Lewis, 1983, p. 209), and Foreman-Peck (1995, p. 105) identifies this "club" with "the group of non-European countries which at the twentieth century can be classified as developed".

However, outcomes and evolutions varied within the "club" and these discrepancies have been explained by: the institutional matrix that produces a set of organisations, rights and privileges; the stability of the structure of exchange relationships in political and economic markets; and a state that provides the set of political rules and enforcement of rights. "In this characterization, the South American Southern Cone countries were the 'failure' in the settler club, with slower development paths and lower living standards" (Willebald, 2007, p. 295).

Settler economies benefited from the consequences of the Second Industrial Revolution (railways, refrigeration, decreasing transport costs) as their climate and fertile soils were especially suitable for producing wool, beef, mutton and cereals. Their natural endowments enabled them to take a fast track to expansion and, on the eve of the WWI, they reached levels of income per capita on a par with the richest economies. Their abundance of natural resources was understood as a "blessing" as these countries were able to participate in external trade with resources that were hitherto almost unexploited, and for which European demand was dynamic.

The domestic contribution to economic growth was the incorporation of "new" land into production, which had consequences for the structural change, income distribution and the intensity of the use of production factors. We focus on this process in order to understand one of the main explicative factors of the economic evolution of the settler economies (Argentina, Australia, Canada, Chile, New Zealand, South Africa and Uruguay) over a very long time that includes the mercantilist era of the 1830–1860s, the First Globalisation (1870–1910s) and the interwar and the post-WWII period (1920–1950s). For this, we use the notion of "land frontier expansion". This old idea has followed a path with many transformations along the twentieth century, from the original "frontier hypothesis" of Frederick Turner in 1893 and its application for diverse countries and historical contexts during the first half of the twentieth century, to renewed conceptual views of the last decades in terms of cultural encounters and the construction of collective imaginaries. In recent years, the interest in the frontier has reappeared following two paths. On the one hand, it complements the prolific line of research about the First Globalisation which authors such as Williamson, O'Rourke and Taylor have actively promoted. On the other hand, it reacts and challenges this vision with the introduction of new insights that place the land frontier expansion as a pivotal concept that makes it possible to connect technological progress and institutional configuration. This conceptual revival offers new arguments to explain the comparative economic performance of settler economies.

First, we present the concept of land frontier expansion and review the recent theoretical and empirical analysis in the literature (Sect. 2). We use an analytical model that considers the classical Ricardian approach in order to understand the land frontier expansion in terms of the extensive and intensive margins in agriculture (Sect. 3). After this, we discuss methods to measure the land frontier expansion considering the recent quantification efforts and present our strategy based on the use of Geographic Information Systems (GIS) (Sect. 4). After we explain the innovations introduced (different land aptitudes and distances to centres of gravity), we present our results (Sect. 5). On the one hand, our evidence supports the extensive margin in the land frontier expansion of Argentina, Uruguay and New Zealand, but rejects it for Canada, Australia and Chile where the geographical and historical conditions seem to determine a different pattern. The evidence for South Africa is not conclusive; it presents an intermediate situation. On the other hand, our evidence does not reject the intensive margin in the land frontier expansion for Argentina, Chile and Uruguay, but it does not support the hypothesis for Australasia and Canada. We conclude in Sect. 6.

Settler economies applied different modalities of land incorporation into the production and they faced different conditions than implied adopting extensive or intensive processes of expansion. Those settler economies that evolved intensively through the process of land frontier expansion applying labour as an intensification factor fell behind in the long-term performance and constituted the "impoverished cousins"[1] of the club: Argentina, Chile and Uruguay. Those countries where the land frontier expansion adopted a different pattern—probably based on capital intensification—consolidated as the rich-countries of the club: Australia, Canada and New Zealand. South Africa shared features of both groups.

2 Is the Land Frontier Expansion a Classical Concept that Came Back?

The most popular study about the importance of frontier expansion for economic development was written by Frederick Jackson Turner, who postulated what is known as the "Turner thesis". According to this, the frontier attracted a particular type of person, which was crucial in determining the development path of US society. The frontier promoted individualism, social mobility, economic equality and freedom, and it was decisive to the development of democratic institutions in a process of "perennial rebirth" (Turner, 1894).

Developed in the 1920s, this thesis came in for a wide range of remarkable empirical and theoretical criticisms, especially based on its overemphasis on a single determinant influence in the frontier environment (ignoring the class struggle, urbanisation, religion, gender, ethnic heterogeneity, slavery and the growth of international capitalism) (Furniss, 2006). However, and probably due to the connection with US nationalism, Turner's ideas remained influential in economic and socio-political thought for decades. It was not until the 1960s–1970s that academic interest in the frontier revived, and in the 1980s a new approach emerged to definitively challenge Turner's framework. The environment was seen not as a barrier to expansion but a factor that changed with human and cultural interaction, including conflicts and violence, and eventually resolved through domination and conquest.

These ideas have been applied in the rest of North America and in Australasia, South Africa, and Latin America (Hartz, 1964, Winks, 1971, 1981). According to Burt (1965), if Turner had looked north when he wrote, he might have discovered surprising evidence for his thesis in New France as "the westward movement was North American, not just American in the narrow sense of the word" (Mikesell, 1960, p. 68). Some authors take note of the interlocking nature of American and Canadian westward expansion while others play down the similarities (Sharp, 1955) and identify "several wests" in the overall expansion (Winks, 1971). The historiography has dealt with different topics and approaches and, in recent years, subjects related to the imaginary (Francis, 1992) and cultural issues have emerged (Higham & Thacker, 2006).

The frontier is one of the most pervasive images underlying the creation of a national identity in Australia. According to Davis (2006), the most influential interpretation of the Turner view was from Ward (1958) although previous contributions (Sharp, 1955) had employed similar concepts and reached pessimistic conclusions about the supposed imperial utopia. Subsequent studies followed one of two lines. On the one hand, there are considerations of several frontiers (Winks, 1971, 1981), in which New Zealand appears as a part of the process (Coleman, 1958) and they recognise a lasting impact on national identity in remote regions such as the Northern Territory (Loveday, 1991). On the other hand, the frontier is considered as a discursive trope that settler society produces to reinforce the formation of civil society and cultural hegemony.

Like North America, many parts of Latin America were conquered and settled by Europeans in a process that seems, at least on the surface, to be similar to what happened on the Anglo-American frontier. However, except for the case of Brazil and Argentina, Latin American academics have seldom seen the frontiers as important factors in institutional and identity formation (Weber & Rausch, 1994). Various authors in the early twentieth century argued that the shortage of "free land"—which caused the rigidity of social systems in Hispanic America (Belaúnde, 1923)—and the use of different institutions to deal with labour (missions, *encomiendas*) (Bolton, 1917) make it difficult to apply the thesis. It was not simply the physical environment that determined the impact of the frontiers on people, but the values that people brought to the physical environment. Hispanic colonisers wanted to incorporate those indigenous cultures into their own society, which is another reason why frontiers differed from those in North America (Zavala, 1965). This pattern changed in the nineteenth century when the countries achieved political independence and needed to define political boundaries with active settlement that legitimated the new states.

The most important of these movements was the wave of settlement which spread from the estuary of La Plata northward across Uruguay and westward across Argentina (Butland, 1966). This occupation of grazing lands, previously the habitat of hunting natives, by immigrants from Southern Europe, the construction of a railway network and the growth of the great cities (Buenos Aires, Rosario, Montevideo) are all in the Turner classical tradition. Other neglected lands range from the arid pampas of Atacama to the rain-drenched forest south of Chile's Bío-Bío river. In Atacama, the focus was a long-established form of mining, and in the forest there was a central European pattern of farming that occupied lands slowly won from the Araucanians. At the same time, profits to be made from sub-Antarctic pastoralism stimulated European penetration in the cold lands of Tierra del Fuego, and similarly, irrigation in agriculture brought about a more intensive settlement pattern from the Río Negro through the Andean regions of Mendoza and Tucumán.

In the recent literature about the expansion of the Atlantic economy during the nineteenth century and the first decades of the twentieth century, the Stolper-Samuelson theorem from the Heckscher-Ohlin trade theory is used to explain the performance of the New World. 1870–1913 was a real "golden age" for the settler economies. This expansion can be traced to the Industrial Revolution, a process that started in Britain in the eighteenth century and spread to other European countries, transmitting technological impulses from the core to peripheral regions. The studies by Lindert, O'Rourke, Taylor and Williamson on globalisation, growth and inequality have opened up a fruitful line of research and generated multiple debates.

The stimulus to development came from expanding markets in the world economy—expressed as rising prices—that led to an extension of the internal land occupation accompanied by considerable inflows of capital and labour. The expansion of the frontier has played a secondary role in the modern historical analysis of settler economies, in spite of the fact that the main "domestic contribution" to economic growth was precisely the incorporation of "new" land. Only recently academics have seriously returned to the notion of frontier expansion.

Land was not a fixed factor in these economies; at that time, large areas were incorporated into production and this enabled the settler economies to actively participate in international commodity markets (Arroyo Abad, 2013). The endogenous land frontier expansion constitutes a main factor in the explanation of settler development (Di Tella, 1982) and it could be taken as a pivotal concept in the analysis of changes in relative prices, inflows of labour and capital, structural change and movements in income distribution (Findlay & Lundahl, 2001). These analytical approaches can be considered complementary visions to the "mainstream" framework of the First Globalisation. However, there have been other approaches that are more critical.

As globalisation can be "defined as a shift from an economy where local supply and demand fluctuations dominated price fluctuations to one in which the economy became a price-taker to global forces" (Harley, 2007, pp. 240–241), nineteenth-century globalisation can be understood as a process in which peripheral economies were incorporated into the core of organised economic activity. In this approach, the consequences of the existence of a frontier depend on the nature of the political institutions which came into being in the early independence period (García-Jimeno & Robinson, 2011) and the way each economy incorporated the technological change that made it possible to increase production.

3 Conceptual Framework and Analytical Model

The role of land in economic theory has changed considerably over time. Originally, land used for agriculture was the main motivation for an economic treatment of national production. However, neoclassical economic theory gave less attention to land use, generally regarding it as a production factor of relatively little importance. Afterwards, specialised sub-fields within economics such as regional and urban economics met the demand for explicit spatial analysis including land use considerations. More recently, attention to environmental and resource problems has provided incentives for new perspectives in economic analysis. Within this long conceptual evolution, the idea of land frontier expansion is clearly represented in the Classical Economics because the dynamics of the expansion and the incorporation of new land into the production are the main concepts. The Ricardian Theory of Rent and the view of land presented by Johann von Thünen offer interesting insights.

In Ricardo's theory, there are two reasons for rent: unequal fertility and scarcity of land. Ricardo assumed a farm producing wheat by applying homogeneous labour to a fixed supply of land subject to diminishing returns. Land Represents an inexhaustible and non-reproducible factor, completely specialised in the production of one crop, and homogeneous except for differences in fertility and location (Blaug, 1997). These differences in fertility were the inspiration for his concept of the differential return because "land is not unlimited in quantity and uniform in quality, and because in the progress of population, land of an inferior quality, or less advantageously situated, is called into cultivation." (Ricardo, 1821 [2013], Chap. 2). If land was homogeneous in quality, the limitations of supply would create only scarcity of rents. The higher intensity in the production would exist even if all land were of equal fertility, as long as land was in scarce supply.

The rent is the difference between the yield of a plot and that of the marginal plot (which yields just enough to pay for the incurred costs). The differential arises when inferior grades of land are cultivated. Rent arises because good-quality land is scarce. If the demand for food and raw materials further increases—due to population growth or economic progress—farmers can adopt two possible courses of action. They can use less fertile land for cultivation or, alternatively, they can cultivate the most fertile plot more intensively by applying additional doses of labour and capital. In the first case, Ricardo identifies the rent on extensive margin and, in the second, he identifies the rent on intensive margin.

A different view was presented by von Thünen in 1826, who focused on distance as the central concept. He was interested in the pattern of agricultural production around a central town in an isolated state, in a homogeneous plain of equal fertility. He developed a system of concentric circles, in which perishable goods are produced closer to the city and durable goods are imported from a further distance. In this central town, the price of a product like grain is determined by the production and transportation costs from the most distant farms. Since grain must sell at the same price irrespective of its location of production, land rent is higher in the first concentric ring and decreases with distance (Blaug, 1997).

Therefore, when we analyse the land frontier expansion we should consider the triple impact of fertility, scarcity and location and how these factors influence the evolution of the incorporation of new land into the productive process.

We consider as the "best lands" those that combine conveniently fertility and location, which we call land of high quality (land No. 1 in Ricardian terminology) and set up the rest of the lands in terms of medium and low quality. We can represent the use of each one according to the following relationships:

$$\lambda_h = \frac{N_h}{\mathbb{N}_H} \quad (1)$$

$$\lambda_m = \frac{N_m}{\mathbb{N}_M} \quad (2)$$

$$\lambda_l = \frac{N_l}{\mathbb{N}_L} \quad (3)$$

Our indexes are calculated as the proportion of the land occupied (N_h, N_m, N_l) of each type of land on the total area (endowment) of each quality (N_H, N_M, N_L). Therefore,

$$N_h + N_m + N_l = N \quad \text{occupied area,} \quad (4)$$

$$\mathbb{N}_H + \mathbb{N}_M + \mathbb{N}_L = \mathbb{N} \quad \text{available area.} \quad (5)$$

We represent the shares of each type of land as,

$$w_i = \frac{\mathbb{N}_i}{\mathbb{N}} \tag{6}$$

where w_i is fixed and known.

Our indicator of land frontier expansion (λ) is the weighted sum of our land frontier expansion indexes,

$$w_H \lambda_h + w_M \lambda_m + w_L \lambda_l = \lambda \tag{7}$$

This indicator tends to unity when the occupation on the land closes the frontier.

On the one hand, whether land frontier expansion associated with the extensive margin followed the "Ricardian Model"—the best lands are cultivated first—our indicators would follow a pattern similar to that shown in Fig. 17.1. Each type of land is incorporated until it is available and, at this point, landowners put in production the following quality. On the left axis, we represent the evolution of the land frontier expansion indicators weighted by the corresponding land share. On the right axis, we represent the trajectory of the difference between high and medium + low quality components which we call "difference quality index" (Panel a).[2] However, this theoretical evolution does not result realistic. Usually, economies expand the frontier through different types of land simultaneously and we represent this fact in Panel (b).[3]

Therefore, a land frontier expansion according to the extensive margin shows an evolution where the high-quality land predominates and this means that the difference quality index is positive and follows an inverted-V curve. This indicator follows an increasing trend in the first stages of the land expansion and, when the high-quality land starts being scarce, the index shows a decreasing trend. This is our first working hypothesis.

On the other hand, considering the intensive margin—that concerned with cultivating the most fertile plot more intensively by applying additional

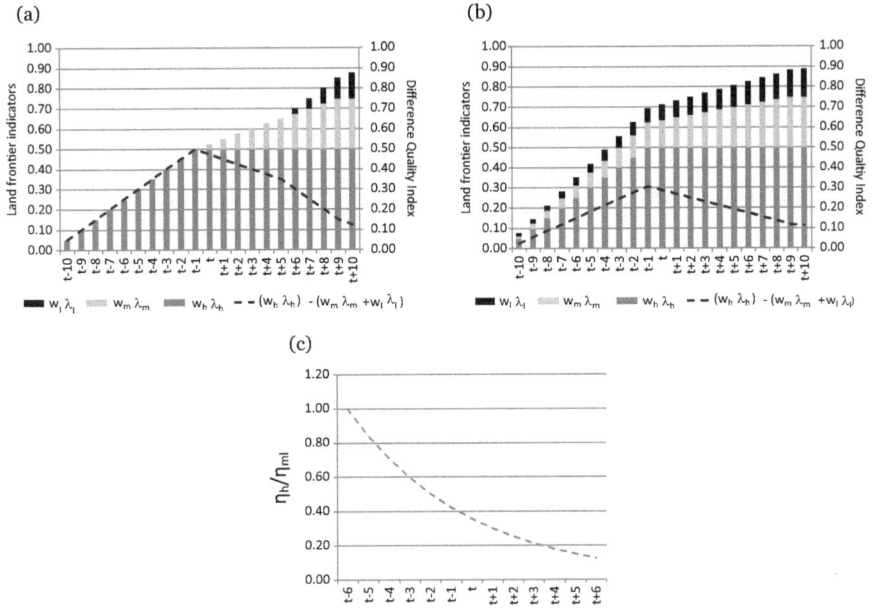

Fig. 17.1 Land frontier expansion and the Ricardian model. Panel (**a**): $w_H = 1/2$; $w_M = w_L = 1/4$; extensive margin. Panel (**b**): $w_H = 1/2$; $w_M = w_L = 1/4$; "realistic" extensive margin. Panel (**c**): $\eta_h = \eta_m$ in the initial moment; intensive margin

doses of production factors—we can assume as an indicator the relationship between the occupied lands and the population settled (as a proxy of labour) by type of land.

$$\eta_h = \frac{N_h}{L_h} \tag{8}$$

$$\eta_m = \frac{N_m}{L_m} \tag{9}$$

$$\eta_l = \frac{N_l}{L_l} \tag{10}$$

L_i represents the population settled by type of land ($i = h, m, l$) and η_i the land-labour ratios. When the intensive margin happens, the indicator

η_i decreases because the quantity of labour per unit of land increases. We expect more intensive labour doses in the best lands because they are capable of yielding relatively higher incomes than the worst lands (diminishing returns "appear later" in the best lands). If the intensive margin operated we could expect a decreasing relation between the ratio between high and the other land quality (medium+low). In analytical terms:

$$\frac{\partial \frac{\eta_h}{\eta_{ml}}}{\partial t} \leq 0 \tag{11}$$

In Fig. 17.1, Panel (c) we represent this argument, where the curve is convex and tends to zero in the long run. This is our second working hypothesis.[4]

4 Measuring Land Frontier Expansion

4.1 Antecedents

The literature about the frontier has been rather imprecise as to how the concept can be defined. In historical analysis, the conditions to define it are the presence of native communities not subject to state control, the absence of significant numbers of settlers and the inexistence of State institutions. However, there have been very few efforts to quantify the process.

On the one hand, in the Heckscher Ohlin Samuelson (H-O-S) framework approach, land frontier expansion is a concept introduced to consider changes in factor endowments, and the expansion itself is represented by the land/labour ratio (Williamson, 2002). In accordance with this framework, Arroyo Abad (2013) provides an analysis considering the institutional and political conditions that characterised the incorporation of new land and refers to the percentage of arable land transferred from public to private ownership. She, correctly, argues that *"land was not a fixed factor of production* [in Argentina, Mexico, Uruguay and Venezuela] *because large tracts of land were brought into production at various times"* (p. 44).

On the other hand, García-Jimeno & Robinson (2011) study the effects of the frontier on economic development but choose a different strategy. They estimate the proportion of land which was frontier (non-occupied territory) in each independent country in the Americas in 1850. They classify land with fewer than two people per square mile as frontier land. This threshold was employed by the US Census Bureau and was the criterion used by the US office that declared the country had a closed frontier in 1890.

In the neoclassical vision, the expansion of the frontier is important when it comes to conceptualising movements in factor endowments, but beyond this consideration it is only of secondary interest. García Jimeno & Robinson's approach focuses on the concept, and they propose a specific measurement using a new tool (GIS) to study land frontier from a historical perspective. Our approach is closer to this last idea.

4.2 Our Proposal

The starting point is to know how many inhabitants were settled in the territory. We assume that the presence of a relatively high level of population is the best proxy for land incorporated into economic activity.

We construct our indicators every 10 years during the period 1830–1950. Recent literature related to the negative effects of economic growth on the environment includes historical proxies to geographical location of people, consumption and production on a world scale. The "Netherlands Environmental Assessment Agency" has two programmes: "History Database of the Global Environment" and "Integrated Modelling of Global Environmental Change", and information about population is available on their website. GIS data refer to the population located in cells of 69.4 km^2 along the territory.

We can describe the movement of population into a territory, but it is important to consider how was the area effectively achievable by the new settlers. We do not take the total area of a country as a reference for the "maximum frontier" because this option is not consistent with the historical development. We can assume that colonisers settled in places suitable for human habitation. Geography, climate, lack of infrastructure and hostile indigenous populations limited access to many regions.

What exactly was the "wildness" that eighteenth- and nineteenth-century settlers had to face? Some concepts from environment and climate change literature can be useful to answer this question. Data representative of the world's "potential vegetation" are a proxy for the natural environment that people in settlement times had to confront. This concept refers to the vegetation that would most likely exist now in the absence of human activities (Ramankutty & Foley, 1999). We are interested in identifying land able to "support" settlers and potentially able to produce goods for international markets. A basic condition is to consider land that can be used to raise livestock, which in general coincides with the allocation of grassland. An alternative criterion would be to take arable land or land suitable for crops (typically wheat), but this would be an excessively rigorous criterion. Settler economies had extensive areas where it was (almost) impossible to cultivate the land but where cattle or sheep could be reared successfully.[5] We consider the distribution of biomes, which are defined by plant structures, leaf types, plant spacing and climate. The biome types that can be classed as grassland are shown in Table 17.1. Klein Goldewijk and Van Drecht (2006) construct a ranking including grassland and steppe, open shrubland, savannah, dense shrubland, tundra and several varieties of woodland.

Table 17.1 Biome types and the allocation of grassland

	Rank
Grassland/steppe	6
Open shrubland	5
Savannah	4
Dense shrubland	3
Tundra	2
Evergreen/deciduous mixed forest/woodland	1
Temperate broadleaved evergreen forest/woodland	1
Temperate deciduous forest/woodland	1
Temperate needle leaf evergreen forest/woodland	1
Tropical deciduous forest/woodland	1
Polar desert/rock/ice	0
Boreal deciduous forest/woodland	0
Boreal evergreen forest/woodland	0
Tropical deciduous forest/woodland	0
Hot desert	0

In Australia shrubland and savannah predominated and only a very small part was grassland/steppe. In New Zealand, grassland/steppe was the main biome (although with big differences between both islands). In South Africa, grassland, steppe and open shrubland dominate a big proportion of the landscape but the first colonisers settled in the dense shrubland. In Canada, there was grassland and open shrubland on the prairies but there were large swathes of tundra and boreal forest between this central region and the Atlantic and Pacific coasts. In the South American Southern Cone (SASC), grassland predominated in Argentina and Uruguay, and Chile presents a wide range of variation from hot desert in the north to polar desert in the south. We consider the "potential vegetation grassland" area of each country—rank 1 to 6—as that part of the territory suitable to graze livestock and, in consequence, it represents the concept N presented previously. This ranking enables us to distinguish three land types as having "high", "medium" or "low" aptitude for grassland: N_H:6,5; N_M:4,3; N_L:2,1, and we can construct the indicators presented in Eqs. (1), (2), and (3).

GIS data corresponding to biome types derive from Atlas of the Biosphere, a product of the Centre for Sustainability and the Global Environment (SAGE), part of the Nelson Institute for Environmental Studies at the University of Wisconsin, Madison.

In settler economies, the land quality not only depended on the agricultural aptitude but also on the distance from the production regions to the markets and, especially, to the ports because it meant the effective materialisation of the natural wealth. We estimate an indicator of "land quality" according to the agriculture aptitude "adjusted" by the distance to specific places that, given their economic, political or historical conditions, result in a sort of "centre of gravity".

Our geo-referenced database presents information in terms of grid cells, representing the distribution of population with a global 5 × 5 minute resolution; therefore, we have grid cells that have a surface area of 69.4 km^2. Theoretically, the cost of clearing land is an increasing function on the quantity of land incorporated into production (Findlay, 1995). We can apply this idea here and consider that each cell incorporated into production has a different area that depends on its distance from the centre of gravity. As a result, 69.4 km^2 would be an "average" of the closer cells (that have high values) and the distant cells (that have low values).

We multiply the area of each cell by the inverse of the minimum (air) distance to a centre of gravity and then we rescale the total surface of each type of land to maintain the true cell average (69.4 km^2).

Settler economies based their growth on external conditions so ports are natural candidates to be considered "centres of gravity". We assume that the producers decide to direct their products to the closest port in the region. In cases in which there is another type of "centre of gravity", we argue about the feasibility of our assumption (Table 17.2).

Table 17.2 Identification of Centres of gravity

Country	Criterion	Centres of gravity
Australia	We choose one port per state as reference	
		Sidney
		Melbourne
		Brisbane
		Adelaide
		Perth
		Darwin
		Hobart
Argentina	Land expansion developed along two axes: coastal and Pampas (pampeana) and the inland Andean (andino) regions	
		Buenos Aires
		Tucumán
Canada	The most important port in the east, and the demographic development of the middle areas of the country, close to the eastern border of the Canadian Prairies, and directly influenced by the railway expansion	
		Montreal
		Winnipeg
South Africa	The origin of the colonisation and specific demographic dynamics related to mineral discovers and exploitation in the inland territory	
		Cape Town
		Johannesburg
Chile	We choose one port per region (North, South and *Núcleo Central*)	
		Iquique
		Talcahuano
		Valparaiso
New Zealand	We choose one port per island	
		Auckland
		Bluff Harbour
Uruguay	We choose one port per region (South, North)	
		Montevideo
		Paysandú

5 Results

5.1 Land Frontier Expansion and the Extensive Margin

We present the evolution of the indicators λ_h, λ_m and λ_l (and λ as consequence). When an increasing trend is obtained, this means the incorporation of land in agrarian production with an economic orientation (and the consequent reduction of the frontier). Each type of land is presented considering the weight in the total expansion; i.e. $\lambda = w_H\lambda_h + w_M\lambda_m + w_L\lambda_l$ represents the weighted sum of different types of land and the corresponding weights w_i ($0 \leq w_h, w_m, w_l \leq 1$).

We find support for the Ricardian hypothesis (Fig. 17.2) in Argentina (Panel a), Uruguay (b) and New Zealand (c). The First Globalisation that characterised the period from the 1870s onwards encouraged the incorporation of "new" lands and, specially, those that presented better agrarian conditions and were relatively near to ports and large markets (centres of gravity).

These evolutions contrast with the other members of the club (Fig. 17.3). Australia (Panel a), Canada (b) and Chile (c) presented a significantly less intense process of land frontier expansion where the high land quality maintained a secondary role (our difference quality index presents negative values). However, the timing and the characteristics of the process differ. The expansion of the frontier in Australia occurred earlier (1830s–1860s) and before the clearest effects of the First Globalisation. Probably, this evolution was related with the mining expansion of those years (especially in the 1850s) and the "gold rush" era. In Chile, the frontier expansion was a moderate process and the clearest change corresponded to the period 1870–1880, which coincided with the incorporation of "new" territories (from Bolivia and Peru) and the expansion of the low-quality land (a region with arid climate and bad conditions for agriculture). Despite not presenting a Ricardian process, Canada showed a land frontier expansion that reacted to the stimulus of the First Globalisation. It started to "close" its frontier from 1870 onwards and this implied to advance through the three types of land to achieve the best lands and settling the "far west".

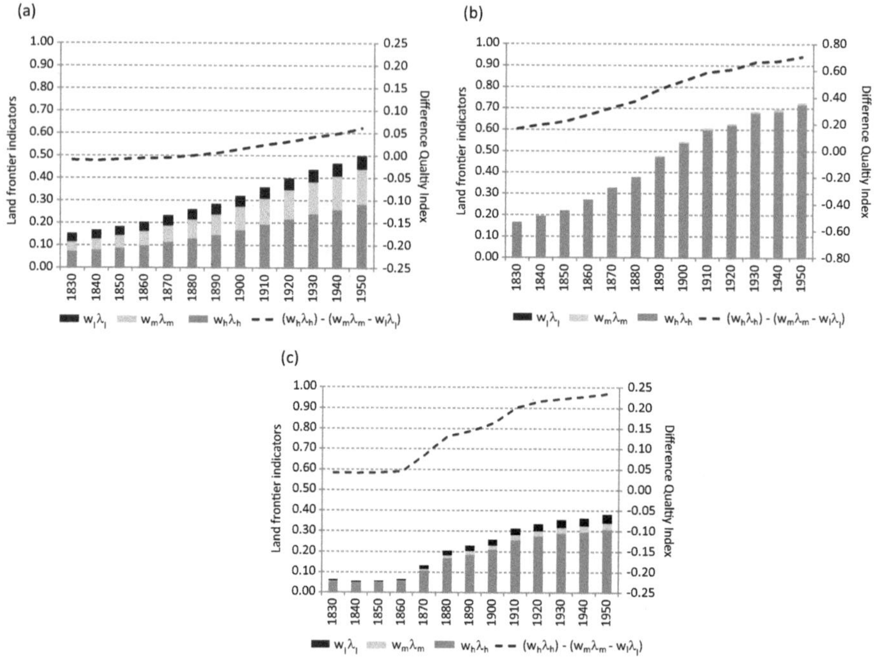

Fig. 17.2 Extensive margin not rejected. Panel **(a)** Argentina. Panel **(b)** Uruguay. Panel **(c)** New Zealand

Finally, South Africa (d) showed an intermediate evolution. Like the first group, it seemed to react to the effects of the First Globalisation and the low-quality land maintained a marginal role and, as in Canada, the expansion involved high- and medium-quality land with similar trajectories.

Several factors can explain the differences between both groups but it is evident that the evolution depends critically on the magnitude of the endowments. It is more likely to run out of a type of land when it is scarce in the economy. Table 17.3 presents the shares of each type of land ranked by "quality". The three economies with the lowest shares of high-quality land coincide with those that did not experience a Ricardian process—Canada, Chile and Australia—and, as before, South Africa presents an intermediate situation.

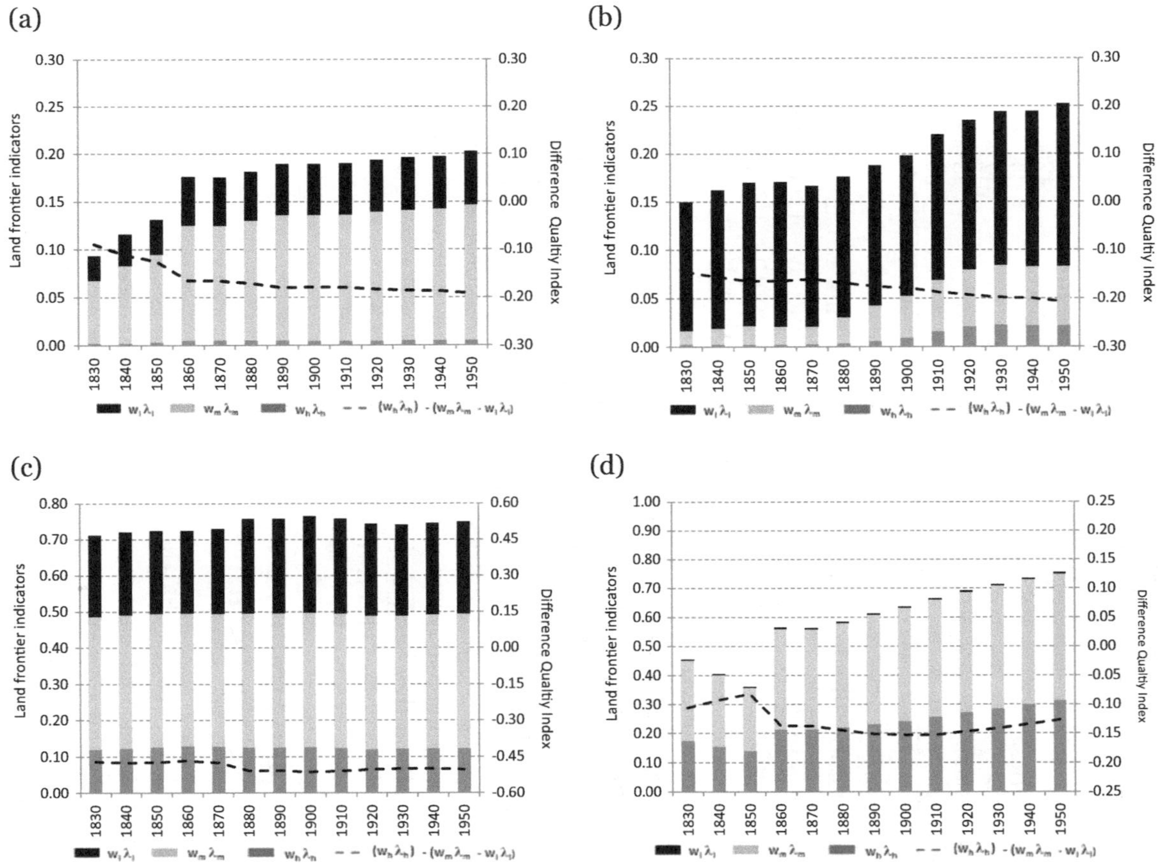

Fig. 17.3 Extensive margin rejected. Panel **(a)** Australia. Panel **(b)** Canada. Panel **(c)** Chile. Panel **(d)** South Africa

Table 17.3 Allocation of grassland

	According to quality		
	High	Medium	Low
Canada	6%	9%	86%
Chile	20%	38%	42%
Australia	23%	65%	12%
South Africa	53%	46%	1%
Argentina	61%	27%	12%
New Zealand	68%	9%	23%
Uruguay	99%	1%	0%

In addition, the location of the first settlements explains, at least partially, these differences. In Australia, the initial objective of the British colonisers was the creation of a penal colony and in South Africa the intention was the establishment of a secure place for the ships that traded with Asia. Production conditions were absolutely secondary in both cases. In Canada, the eastern coastal lands presented deficient conditions for grassland and the achievement of the best soils implied to face high costs in infrastructure and transport. The first European settlements in Chile were located in the best lands for grassland but the share of high-quality land ran out quickly.

Finally, another factor is the type of natural wealth that economies possess. These four countries relied on big endowments of mineral resources (gold, coal, diamonds, nitrates) whose discovery and exploitation significantly changed the political, social and demographic conditions of the colonies and early settler nations.

5.2 Land Frontier Expansion and the Intensive Margin

The relation between the land–labour ratios of high- and medium-low quality shows that agrarian producers would have applied increasing doses of labour more intensively in the first type of land in Argentina—from the 1870s onwards—(Panel a), Chile (b) and Uruguay (c). Therefore, our evidence does not reject the Ricardian hypothesis of intensive margin in these cases. The evolution in the other members of the "club" was different (Fig. 17.4). South Africa (c) and New Zealand (d)

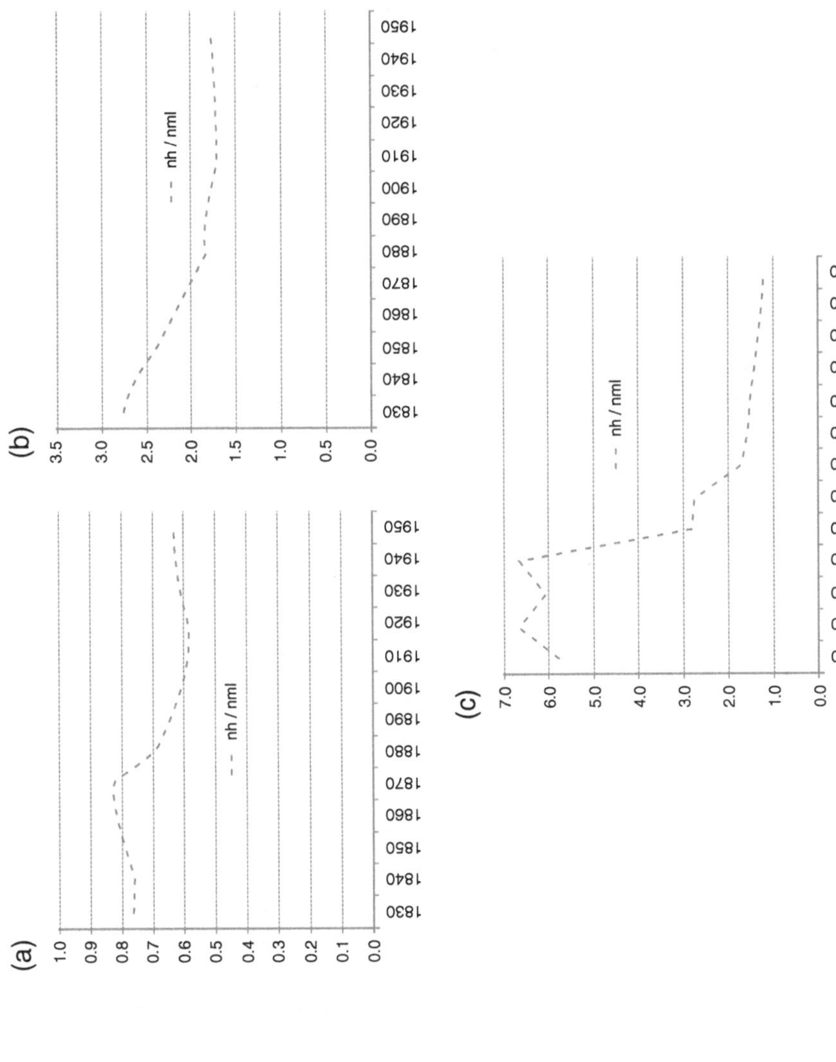

Fig. 17.4 Intensive margin not rejected. Panel **(a)** Argentina. Panel **(b)** Chile. Panel **(c)** Uruguay

present increasing trends in the indicators and Canada (b) and Australia (a) show curves with changeable slopes and rising paths during the First Globalisation (Fig. 17.5). Therefore, our evidence does not support the intensive margin for these countries. This result is particularly interesting considering the period from 1870 to the 1920s.

The SASC (Argentina, Chile and Uruguay) reacted to the First Globalisation by intensifying (relatively) production through higher doses of labour applied to the best lands. Australasia, Canada and South Africa did not do it. But this subject gives rise to the limitations of our exercise. We only consider the possibility of intensifying the use of land with the incorporation of more labour, but the landowners could have achieved a deeper intensification with higher doses of capital. In a previous paper (Willebald, 2015), we find evidence of increasing profits in agriculture in the last decades of the nineteenth century in Australia and Canada, and a similar evolution evidenced in New Zealand (see Alvarez, 2017). This process would have been a result of the increasing capitalisation of agrarian activity with the mechanisation of production, the construction of irrigation systems and the increasing use of fertilisers and special varieties of cereals. The option of the landowners could have been to intensify the use of production factors other than labour but our methodological approach is not capable of recognising this effect.

6 Conclusion

By the late nineteenth century settler economies were well integrated into the global economy and achieved levels of income per capita on a par with the richest economies. They benefited from the consequences of the Second Industrial Revolution as their natural endowments were especially suitable for the production of food and raw materials. The abundance of natural resources was understood as a "blessing" as these countries were able to participate in external trade with resources that were up till then almost unexploited and for which European demand was strong.

The domestic contribution to economic growth was the incorporation of "new" land, of variable quality, into production, and we use the notion of land frontier expansion to offer new arguments to explain the comparative

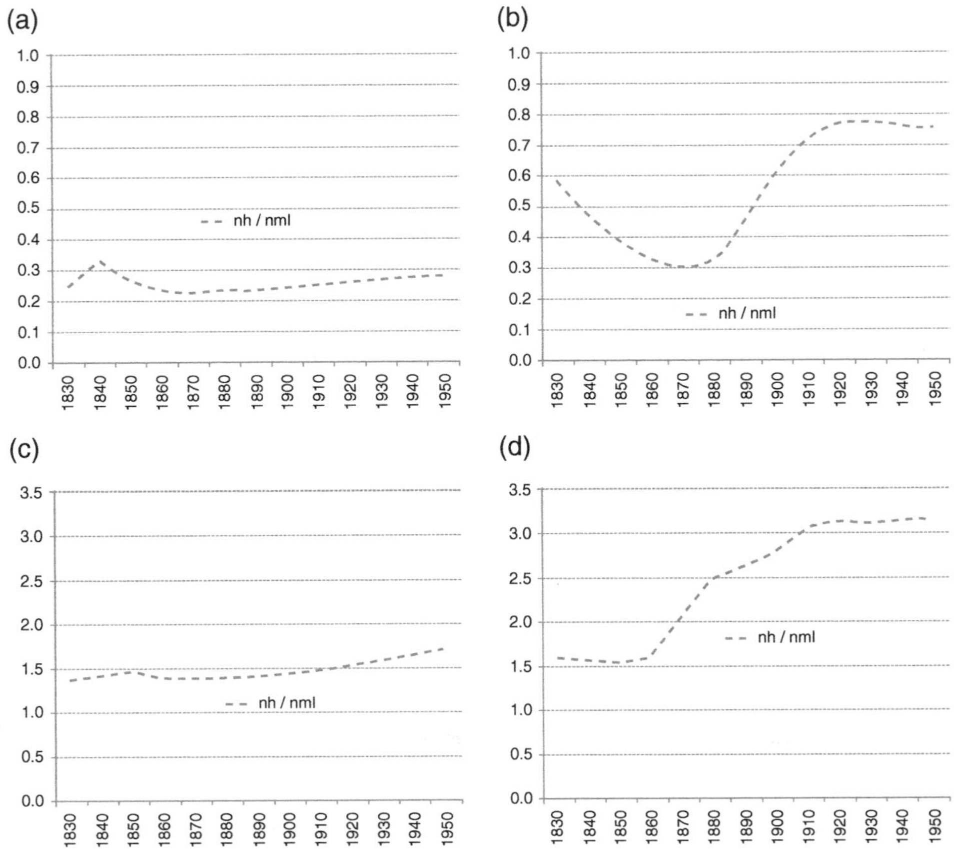

Fig. 17.5. Intensive margin rejected. Panel **(a)** Australia. Panel **(b)** Canada. Panel **(c)** South Africa. Panel **(d)** New Zealand

performance during the First Globalisation as a long-run process with roots in the previous period (1830–1870) and consequences in the following decades (until WWII).

We decided on proposing an analytical model that considers the classical Ricardian view in terms of the extensive and intensive margins. We used GIS tools to consider different land agrarian aptitudes and distances to centres of gravity to test our hypotheses. We understand "quality" as the combination of aptitude to grassland and (minimum) distance to ports and large markets.

On the one hand, our evidence supports the extensive margin in the land frontier expansion of Argentina, Uruguay and New Zealand but rejects it for Canada, Australia and Chile, where the geographical and historical conditions seem to determine a different pattern. The evidence for South Africa is not conclusive. The magnitude of the endowments, the location of initial settlements and the existence of mineral wealth are factors that transcend the Ricardian expectations and help to characterise more properly the process. On the other hand, our evidence does not support the intensive margin for Canada, Australia, New Zealand and South Africa but we do not reject this hypothesis for the SASC. The reaction to the effects of First Globalisation in these last economies meant the labour intensification in the use of the best lands while the other economies opted for alternatives (for instance, the use of higher doses of capital).

In brief, the land frontier expansion in Canada, Australia and South Africa does not fit with the model while Argentina and Uruguay presented a process close to the Ricardian expectation. New Zealand shows a land frontier expansion clearly Ricardian in terms of the extensive margin, but the intensification of the use of land included factors other than labour. In contrast, Chile did not expand the frontier in a Ricardian sense but increased the intensity of labour in the use of land as its River Plate neighbours made. Countries of the SASC falling behind the other members of the club (Willebald & Bértola, 2013) and, probably, this different type of intensification of land explain, at least partially, the differences. Those countries that faced the best conditions to expand the land frontier extensively or intensively via the labour factor performed worst in comparison with other members of the club. The intuition behind this result is that the best performance occurred when the land intensification happened with higher capital accumulation and technological change.

Notes

1. Here we paraphrase Alvarez et al. (2007).
2. We assume a country where a half of the land corresponds to high quality and the rest distributes equally between medium and low quality. We suppose a constant addition of land of 10 percentage points year by year.
3. We assume that the increases of high-, medium- and low-quality indicators are equivalent to 10, 5 and 2.5 percentage points to represent a higher dynamism corresponding to high-quality land.
4. We assume an initial moment where ηh and ηml coincide and where the first decreases 20 per cent each period and the second only 5 per cent.
5. A critique to our proposal is that it constitutes a static approach. The transformation of one type of land to another—typically from forest to grassland, steppe or savannah—is perfectly feasible and we do not capture this process. We will pay attention to this point in next steps of our research.

References

Álvarez, J., Bértola, L., & Porcile, G. (Comp.). (2007). *Primos Ricos y Empobrecidos. Crecimiento, distribución del ingreso e instituciones en Australia-Nueva Zelanda vs Argentina-Uruguay*. Montevideo: Ed. Fin de Siglo.

Arroyo Abad, L. (2013). Persistent Inequality? Trade, Factor Endowments, and Inequality in Republican Latin America. *The Journal of Economic History, 73*(1), 38–78.

Belaúnde V. (1923). The Frontier in Hispanic America. Rice Institute Pamphlets 10, October, 202–213. (Reprinted in D. Weber & J. Rausch, 1994). *Where Cultures Meet. Frontiers in Latin American History* (pp. 33–41). Wilmington, Delaware: Jaguar Books on Latin America, No 6.

Blaug, M. (1997). *Economic Theory in Retrospect*. Cambridge: Cambridge University Press.

Bolton, H. (1917). The Mission as a Frontier Institution in the Spanish-American Colonies. *The American Historical Review, 23*(1), 42–61.

Burt, A. L. (1965). If Turner Had Looked at Canada, Australia, and New Zealand When He Wrote About the West. In W. Wyman & C. Kroeber (Eds.), *The Frontier in Perspective* (pp. 59–79). Madison, WI: The University of Wisconsin Press.

Butland, G. J. (1966). Frontiers of Settlement in South America. *Revista Geográfica, 65*, 93–108.

Coleman, P. (1958). The New Zealand Frontier and the Turner Thesis. *Pacific Historical Review, 27*(3), 221–237.

Davis, R. (2006). Introduction: Transforming the Frontier in Contemporary Australia. In D. Bird Rose & R. Davis (Eds.), *Dislocating the Frontier. Essaying the Mystique of the Outback* (pp. 7–22). Canberra: The Australian National University Press.

Di Tella, G. (1982). The Economics of Frontier. In C. P. Kindleberger & G. Di Tella (Eds.), *Economics in the Long View, (1)*. London: Macmillan.

Duncan, T., & Fogarty, J. (1984). *Australia and Argentina. On Parallel Paths*. Melbourne: Melbourne University Press.

Findlay, R. (1995). *Factor Proportions, Trade, and Growth*. Cambridge: MIT Press.

Findlay, R., & Lundahl, M. (2001). Natural Resources and Economic Development: The 1870–1914 Experience. In R. Auty (Ed.), *Resource Abundance and Economic Development* (pp. 95–112). Oxford: Oxford University Press.

Foreman-Peck, J. (1995). *A History of the World Economy: International Economic Relations Since 1850*. London: Harvester Wheatsheaf.

Francis, D. (1992). *The Frontier and Images of the Canadian West in the Settlement Era*. Sophia University. Retrieved from http://repository.cc.sophia.ac.jp/dspace/bitstream/123456789/166/1/200000260873_000009000_19.pdf

Furniss, E. (2006). Imagining the Frontier: Comparative Perspectives from Canada and Australia. In D. Bird Rose & R. Davis (Eds.), *Dislocating the Frontier. Essaying the Mystique of the Outback* (pp. 7–22). Canberra: The Australian National University Press.

García-Jimeno, C., & Robinson, J. (2011). The Myth of the Frontier. In D. Costa & N. Lamoreaux (Eds.), *Understanding Long-Run Economic Growth: Geography, Institutions, and the Knowledge Economy* (pp. 49–88). Chicago: University of Chicago Press.

Harley, K. (2007). Comments on Factor Prices and Income Distribution in Less Industrialized Economies, 1870–1939: Refocusing on the Frontier. *Australian Economic History Review, 47*(3), 238–248.

Hartz, L. (1964). *The Foundations of New Societies. Studies in the History of the United States, Latin America, South Africa, Canada, and Australia*. New York: Hartcourt, Brace & World, Inc..

Higham, C., & Thacker, R. (Eds.). (2006). *One West, Two Myths II. Essays on Comparison*. Calgary, AB: University of Calgary Press.

Klein Goldewijk, K., & van Drecht, G. (2006, October). HYDE 3: Current and Historical Population and Land Cover. In A. F. Bouwman, T. Kram, &

K. Klein Goldewijk (Eds.), *Integrated Modelling of Global Environmental Change. An Overview of IMAGE 2.4* (pp. 93–111). Bilthoven: Netherlands Environmental Assessment Agency (MNP). MNP publication number 500110002/2006.

Lewis, A. (1983). *Crecimiento y fluctuaciones*. México: Fundación de Cultura Económica.

Lloyd, C., & Metzer, J. (2013). Settler Colonization and Societies in History: Patterns and Concepts. In C. Lloyd, J. Metzer, & R. Sutch (Eds.), *Settler Economies in World History* (pp. 1–34). Leiden: Brill Publishers.

Loveday, P. (1991). Political History of the North. In I. Moffatt & A. Webb (Eds.), *North Australian Research; Some Past Themes and New Directions* (pp. 146–172). Darwin: North Australia Research Unit.

Mikesell, W. (1960). Comparative Studies in Frontier History. *Annals of the Association of American Geographers, 50*, 62–74.

Nelson Institute for Environmental Studies. (n.d.). University of Wisconsin, Madison. Retrieved December 27, 2009, from http://www.sage.wisc.edu/atlas/

Netherlands Environmental Assessment Agency (MNP). (n.d.). Retrieved December 27, 2009, from http://www.pbl.nl/en/themasites/hyde/index.html

Ramankutty, N., & Foley, J. (1999). Estimating Historical Changes in Global Land Cover: Croplands from 1700 to 1992. *Global Biogeochemical Cycles, 12*(4), 997–1027.

Ricardo, D. (1821). *On the Principles of Political Economy and Taxation*. Library of Economics and Liberty. 2 October 2013. http://www.econlib.org/library/Ricardo/ricP1a.html

Sharp, P. (1955). Three Frontiers: Some Comparative Studies of Canadian, American, and Australian Settlement. *Pacific Historical Review*, 369–377.

Turner, F.J. (1894). *The Significance of the Frontier in American History*. Annual Report of the American Historical Association for 1893. Washington DC, 199–227. (Reprinted from *The Frontier in American History*, by F. J. Turner, 1920, New York: Henry Holt).

Ward, R. (1958). *The Australian Legend*. Melbourne: Oxford University Press.

Weber, D., & Rausch, J. (1994). *Where Cultures Meet. Frontiers in Latin American History*. Wilmington, Delaware: Jaguar Books on Latin America, No 6.

Willebald, H. (2007). Desigualdad y especialización en el crecimiento de las economías templadas de nuevo asentamiento, 1870–1940. *Revista de Historia Económica-Journal of Iberian and Latin American Economic History, 2*, 291–345.

Willebald, H. (2015). Distributive Patterns in Settler Economies: Agrarian Income Inequality During the First Globalization (1870–1913). *Historia Agraria. Revista de agricultura e historia rural, 66*, 75–104.

Willebald, H., & Bértola, L. (2013). Uneven Development Paths Among Settler Societies, 1870–2000. In C. Lloyd, J. Metzer, & R. Sutch (Eds.), *Settler Economies in World History* (pp. 105–140). Leiden: Brill Publishers.

Williamson, J. (2002). Land, Labour and Globalization in the Third World, 1870–1940. *Journal of Economic History, 62*(1), 55–85.

Winks, R. (1981). Australia, the Frontier, and the Tyranny of Distance. In G. Wolfskill & S. Palmer (Eds.), *Essays on Frontiers in World History* (pp. 121–146). College Station, TX: Texas A&M University Press.

Winks, R. (1971, Jan 21). *The Myth of the American Frontier. Its relevance to America, Canada and Australia*. Sir George Watson Lecture, University of Leicester.

Zavala, S. (1965). The Frontier of Hispanic America. In W. Wyman & C. Kroeber (Eds.), *The Frontier in Perspective* (pp. 35–58). Madison, WI: The University of Wisconsin Press.

Henry Willebald is Professor of Economic History and Economic Development at the Universidad de la República, Uruguay. His research interests lie in natural resources, international trade, regional development and inequalities in the long run (nineteenth and twentieth centuries). He is an editor of the book *Natural Resources and Economic Growth: Learning from History*, has written chapters in books edited by international publishers and has published articles in the main economic history journals.

Javier Juambeltz is a Technological Engineer (Electronics) from Consejo de Educación Técnico Profesional, Universidad del Trabajo del Uruguay (CETP-UTU). His main interest in economics and economic history fields are Python programming and geographic information systems application.

18

Technological Change and Productivity Growth in the Agrarian Systems of New Zealand and Uruguay (1870–2010)

Jorge Álvarez Scanniello

1 Introduction

In economic historiography the countries of the South American Southern Cone, especially Argentina and Uruguay, have been classed as new European settlement societies, as have two other countries in the southern hemisphere, Australia and New Zealand. The fact that these

This article summarizes some results of one chapter of my PhD dissertation in economic history. I would like to thank my tutor Luis Bértola for his guidance and ongoing support. I am also grateful for the valuable comments of the dissertation committee members: Geoff Bertram, Eduardo Miguez, Gabriel Oddone and Miguel Sierra. I would also like to thank the participants in the session "Agriculture and economic development in the periphery, 19th and 20th centuries", 17th World Economic History Congress, Kyoto, Japan, 3–7 August 2015, and the participants of the workshop "Agricultural development in the world periphery: a global economic history approach", Zaragoza, 29–30 March 2017, in which I presented a previous version of the text and received very useful comments and suggestions. I am grateful for the valuable comments of Vicente Pinilla, Miguel Martin-Retortillo and Henry Willebald that helped to improve the final version. Finally, I would like to thank the CSIC, University of the Republic, Uruguay and Stout Research Centre for New Zealand Studies, Victoria University of Wellington, New Zealand, for supporting my research activities.

J.Á. Scanniello (✉)
Social Sciences Faculty, University of the Republic, Montevideo, Uruguay

V. Pinilla, H. Willebald (eds.), *Agricultural Development in the World Periphery*, Palgrave Studies in Economic History, https://doi.org/10.1007/978-3-319-66020-2_18

four nations have so many characteristics in common yet have performed so differently in terms of economics in the long term makes them interesting cases for comparative analysis (Alvarez, Bértola, & Porcile, 2007; Denoon, 1983; Lloyd, Metzer, & Sutch, 2013; Nurske, 1961).

New Zealand and Uruguay may be viewed as suitable cases for comparison because they are similar in many ways, including size of population, size of markets, natural resource endowments, surface area devoted to agrarian production, patterns of production specialization, insertion into the world economy and the fact that both achieved a high level of income per capita at the start of the twentieth century. They are also very far from Europe, their main market for a long time. They have also exhibited long-term differences, which has aroused interest in both countries and has led to attempts to explain why they have diverged in various ways (Alvarez, 2014; Alvarez & Bértola, 2013; Alvarez, Bértola, & Porcile, 2007; Alvarez et al., 2011; Bertoni & Willebald, 2016; Kirby, 1975; Schlüter, 2014). The most obvious difference is in income per inhabitant. In 1870 Uruguay's gross domestic product (GDP) per capita stood at 72% of New Zealand's, but by the last quarter of the twentieth century and first decade of the twenty-first century it had fallen, on average, to only 48% (Fig. 18.1).

These two economies share the characteristic that their development was based on producing and exporting agrarian goods, especially leather, wool,

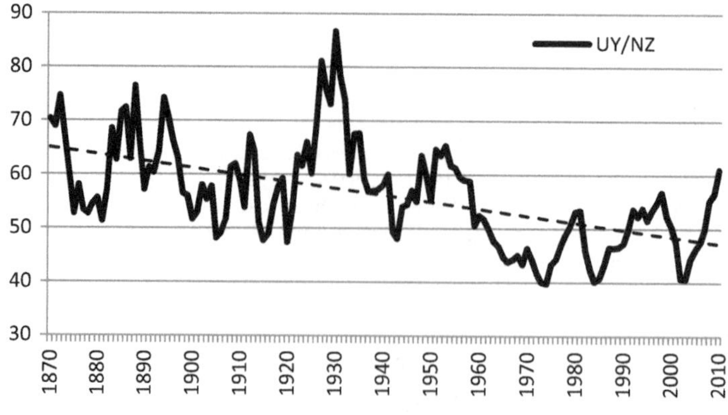

Fig. 18.1 Ratio of GDP per capita Uruguay/New Zealand (%), 1870–2010. Source: based on Maddison (2009), Maddison-Project (2013)

meat and dairy products, derived from livestock rearing. This pattern of production, specialization and trade was the result of a combination of opportunities that emerged during the first globalization of capitalism thanks to the transport revolution, refrigeration technology and the expansion of demand in Europe for temperate-climate products, as is explained in Aparicio et al. (2018) (Chap. 3 of this volume). These factors favoured the new European settlement economies of the periphery and contributed towards the moulding of a highly specialized production structure in New Zealand and Uruguay. Sutch (1969) calls this profile a monocultural economy, a system in which exports depend on a limited number of agrarian products. From 1870 to 1970 an average of more than 70% of New Zealand's exports and more than 80% of Uruguay's were derived from livestock rearing (Fig. 18.2).[1]

A logical outcome of this trade specialization pattern was that the two countries followed similar trends in respect of trade of terms (Alvarez, 2014, p. 63, Gráfico III.10). In spite of these shared trends, the growth of

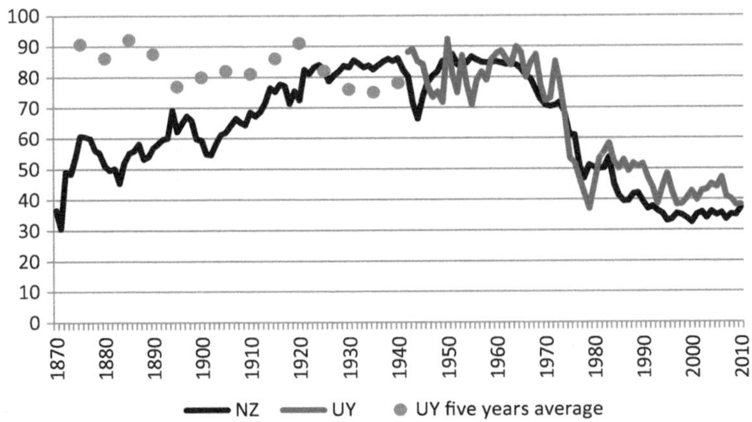

Fig. 18.2 Share of livestock products in total New Zealand and Uruguayan exports (%), 1870–2010. Source: based on: NZ, 1870–2006, Briggs (2003), 2007–2010, NZOYB (2012), http://www.stats.govt.nz/. UY: 1892–1941 five-year averages based on 1872–1890, Millot and Bertino (1996), Fig. IV.3, pp. 138; 1891–1941, Finch (2005), Fig. 4.4, p. 162; annual series based on 1942–1968, Instituto de Economía (1969), Fig. No. 39; 1969–1971, BCU (1973, p. 40, Fig. 15); 1972–1974 BCU (1975, p. 26, Fig. No. 11); 1975–1992, Central Bank of Uruguay, statistical bulletins for respective years series taken from FCS (2013); 1993–2010 Central Bank of Uruguay, series taken from INE (2013)

the two countries' export volumes began to diverge after 1930. Uruguay's exports stagnated, especially in the period 1930–1970, while New Zealand's continued a long-term growth trend, albeit at varying rates.[2]

Here we argue that these variations in export performance, which affected the two economies through different channels, reflect variations in the growth of physical productivity in livestock production (Fig. 18.3), especially in respect of the productivity of agrarian land (Fig. 18.4).

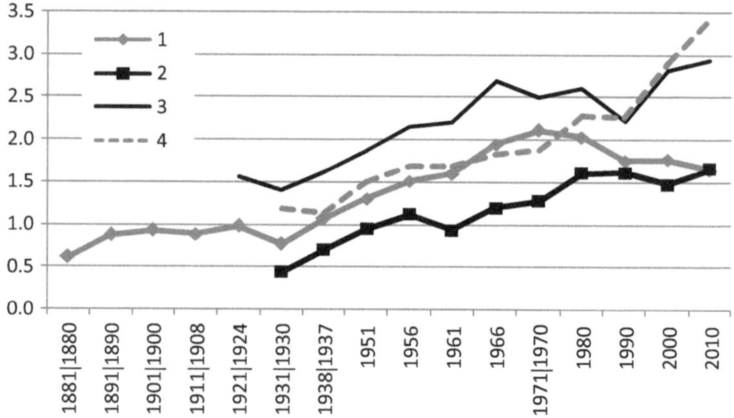

Fig. 18.3 Livestock production (ratio NZ/UY) meat equivalent per hectare, 1870–2010. Source: Alvarez (2014, pp. 149–159) (see Sources and methodological issues for details)

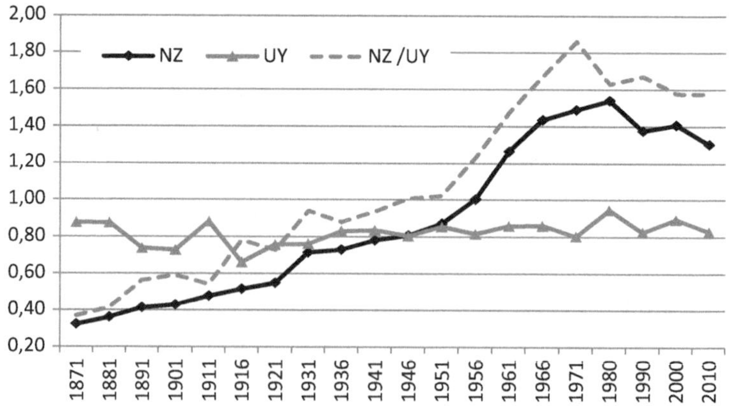

Fig. 18.4 Evolution of livestock units by hectare in New Zealand and Uruguay, 1870–2010. Source: Alvarez (2014, pp. 135–142) (see Sources and methodological issues for details)

A key factor in these variations was the different rates at which the two countries implemented technologies that improved the land. While in New Zealand the livestock system was based on transforming the soil and creating pasture land, in Uruguay livestock rearing was based on natural grassland, with only a low proportion of artificially produced or improved pasture land (Fig. 18.5).

There are two main questions that emerge from this evidence. Why did New Zealand develop technologies that improved the land and

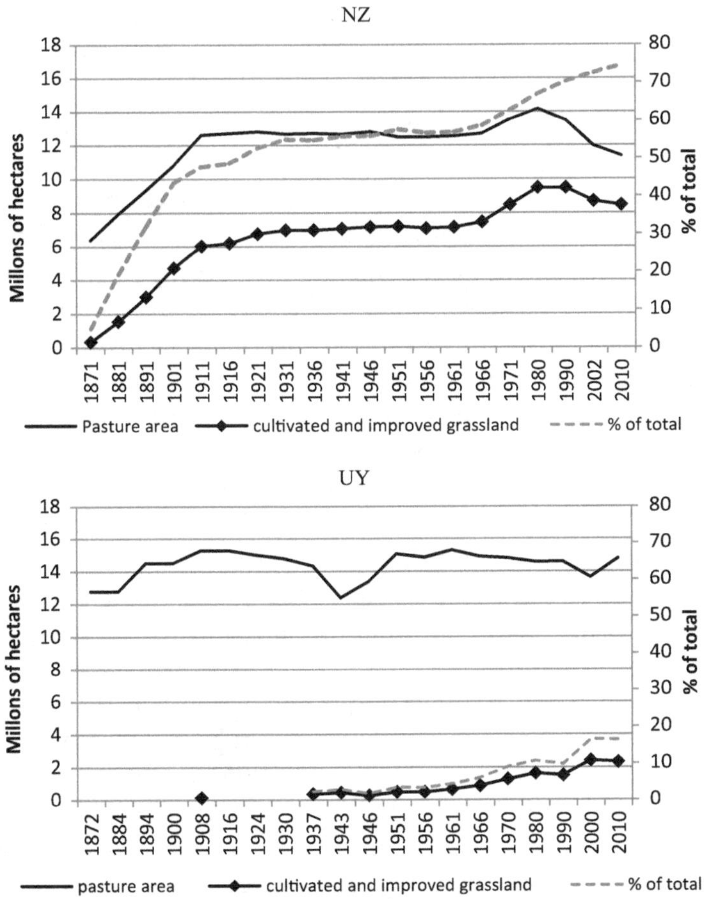

Fig. 18.5 Area of pasture land, artificial and improved grassland (million hectares) artificial and improved grassland as share of total area (%). Source: Alvarez (2014, p. 181, Fig. VI.1)

enabled it to maintain higher livestock productivity growth rates than Uruguay? Why did Uruguay not develop technologies to improve the land when the productive performance of its main export sectors for most of the twentieth century depended on it? These questions place technologies to improve the land at the centre of a comparative analysis of the livestock sector's development in these two countries.

To tackle these questions, our theoretical approach considers the main analytical contributions of evolutionist thought (Lundvall, 1992; Winter & Nelson, 1982) about the economic analysis of innovation and technological development (Schumpeter, 1934), especially the relation between technological change, the institutional context and economic performance (Perez, 2010).

It is well known that incorporating technology into agriculture requires a major adaptation effort. The adoption of technology is a complex process that involves considerable local research and learning on the part of rural producers because of the specific characteristics of animal and plant biological processes, the varying qualities and composition of soils and climate differences between regions and countries. This means that technology adoption processes depend on four main factors: first, the geographical conditions such as the quality of land for agricultural production; second, the role of public research and diffusion institutions in the framework of what we can call sector innovation systems; third, rural producers' capacity to interpret the new technology; and fourth, the economic efficiency of adopting the new technology. Diffusion processes tend to develop in an S-shaped logistical growth curve.

Our main hypothesis states that Uruguay had better natural conditions for livestock production, which became apparent in the nineteenth century, and therefore it had fewer incentives than New Zealand to develop technologies to improve the productivity of land that was devoted to livestock production. In other words, Uruguay suffered from some kind of "resource curse" (Sachs & Warner, 1995), or "*bendición diabólica*" (Barrán & Nahum, 1978),[3] that prevented it from developing soil amending technologies at the same rate as New Zealand. The divergence of the New Zealand and Uruguayan agrarian sectors in terms of production performance was the outcome of a long process of technological and institutional changes in specific geographical and historical contexts.

The main aim of this chapter is to identify and compare the long-term stages in the technological trajectories of the New Zealand and Uruguayan agrarian systems. For this reason, the focus is on the development of technological improvements to the land as a production resource. This approach involves considering the geographical peculiarities of the spaces in which each of these livestock production systems developed and the institutional contexts in which technologies to create and improve pasture emerged. We assume that the interaction among institutions (land market regulation), public policy (subsidy and credit schemes to stimulate the intensification of livestock production), agrarian innovation systems,[4] and the geographical context played a key role in the development of technology that improved the productivity of land devoted to livestock production in each country.

2 The Geographical Context of the Agrarian Systems in New Zealand and Uruguay

It is often pointed out that New Zealand and Uruguay are alike in many ways: they are both in the southern hemisphere, they have similar climate, similar average temperature (although there is more diversity in New Zealand), similar rainfall (but with marked differences in distribution, frequency and intensity) and a comparable surface area for production. However, they have geographical differences that have posed specific challenges and have conditioned the different evolutions of their agrarian systems.

The differences between the two countries in terms of natural land quality for livestock production are clearly explained in Willebald and Juambeltz (2018) (Chap. 17 of this volume). In addition, we may emphasize that New Zealand's surface area is 27 million hectares distributed between two main islands: North Island has 114,000 square kilometres and South Island has 151,000. The country's total productive area amounts to barely 50% of the land and is the result of a long process of modifying the native ecosystem. The main change is that the area of native forest has been reduced and the soil has been adapted for farming and livestock activities. This transformation began with the arrival of the first human settlers, who were of Polynesian origin, in about 1200 (McKinnon, Bradley, & Kirkpatrick, 1997), and it intensified when mass immigration from Europe started in the mid-nineteenth century.[5]

Uruguay has a surface area of 18.7 million hectares, of which an average of 16.5 million has been devoted to agrarian production. With nearly 90% of its land productive, Uruguay has one of the highest production to surface area ratios in the world (Berreta, 2003). While the landscape and original vegetation have undergone big changes since European colonization began, the transformation has not been as widespread or as profound as in New Zealand. The main changes to the grasslands were caused by continual livestock grazing, which has gone on since the beginning of the seventeenth century when Europeans introduced cattle and horses (Marchesi & Durán, 1969). The natural vegetation of more than 80% of the productive land is grasses, and there are relatively few trees (Berreta, 2003).

Besides their differences in the production area to surface area ratio and the original vegetation cover, the topography in which New Zealand and Uruguay developed their agrarian systems is very different. Uruguay is basically a gently undulating plain with little land rising above 200 metres; it forms a transitional area between the Argentine Pampas and the high lands in the south of Brazil. New Zealand, on the other hand, is predominantly mountainous, with 75% of its surface area over 200 metres and with mountain chains that rise as high as 3,700 metres (Charteris, Morris, & Matthew, 1999). These geographical differences influenced the two countries' respective technological and institutional dynamics, and gave their livestock systems specific characteristics that conditioned their long-term development.

3 Stages in the Development of the New Zealand and Uruguayan Agrarian Systems Associated with changes in the Land

Because of the geographical differences emphasized in the previous section, each country has had to face different challenges in developing a high productivity pastoral system.

Starting in the mid-nineteenth century, the geographical and historical conditions of agrarian expansion in New Zealand meant that the country had to overcome a series of challenges and restrictions that Uruguay did not have to face. Among the most serious of these were the low productivity of the natural grassland, mainly on the hills and mountains of South Island, and the need to radically change the landscape and native ecosystem of North Island, which was mainly covered in forest. These limitations gave an early impulse to efforts to find technologies to transform the soil, and these were developed and employed to improve the productivity of the land (Tennant, 1978).

Uruguay was quite different in that after the mid-nineteenth century the development of livestock rearing was based on the intensive use of the natural grassland. Until the WWI the country did not need to improve the soil in order to successfully maintain its position in the world agrarian products market. However, the early maturity of a technological trajectory, which was dynamic until the first decade of the twentieth century (Moraes, 2001), was followed by a long period of stagnation that continued until the 1980s. The country only began to emerge from this in the 1990s, and an intense process of improvement in agriculture only really got under way in the first decade of the twenty-first century.

The periodization that we propose considers both the main stages of the productive performance of the pastoral systems in New Zealand and Uruguay and the soil amending technologies that were applied in each country and stage to improve the productivity of land devoted to livestock.

3.1 New Zealand: The Transformation of the Natural Landscape and the Creation of an Agrarian System Based on the Production of Pasture

In New Zealand we can distinguish five broad stages in the agrarian sector's development from the mid-nineteenth century to the present day.

In the first (1840–1870), which was characterized by colonization and the occupation of land, livestock production was established on the natural grasslands of South Island. This was mainly the extensive rearing of sheep, and as this did not require large capital investment or the intensive use the labour, the ranchers quickly made big profits (Nightingale, 1992). By 1860 nearly all the available land on the plains of South Island was occupied by colonists, but these grasslands were under used because there was a high ratio of land to livestock (McAloon, 2009; Sinclair, 1988). In this stage the geographical conditions on North Island were unsuitable for livestock, because the land was largely covered in dense forest. In addition there was resistance from the Maori communities, who jealously defended their sovereignty and way of life (Belich, 1996; Boast, 2008).

The second stage (1870–1920) was of extensive growth, in which the occupation of the plains and grasslands of South Island was completed, the agrarian frontier expanded into the high lands and forests of North Island, and land improvements were developed that improved productivity on the grasslands . The increase in agrarian activity in this period was characterized by three main processes. First, there was a huge increase in livestock: the number of sheep doubled and the stock of cattle increased by a factor of 7.4 (Bloomfield, 1984). Second, the area of grazing land greatly expanded, with an increase from 6.4 to 12.5 million hectares. And third, there were land improvement efforts based on the introduction of foreign grasses (of British origin). The adoption of British pasture cultivation techniques was mainly driven by the revolutionary impact of the new technology of refrigeration (Belich, 2001; Sinclair, 1988; Tennant, 1978). The main results of these changes were that agrarian production diversified, with products of higher value such as meat and dairy produce (butter and cheese) being added; the area of cultivated pasture increased enormously from 1.4 to 5.7 million hectares between 1881 and 1911 (see Fig. 18.5), mainly in North Island; and trade links with Great Britain were reinforced. However, the British pasture production technique contributed to rapid exhaustion of the soil's natural fertility, a problem that was tackled with chemical and organic fertilizers such as guano, phosphates and bonemeal, which were commonly used at this time. However, fertilizers were costly and their effectiveness decreased over time; this stimulated research into the natural deficiencies of the soil and the development of domestic technologies for producing pasture.

The third stage (1920–1966) was of high growth. Production intensified because of the development of important technological innovations that greatly increased the productivity of agrarian land. Within this stage two sub-periods can be identified.

In the first (1920–1940), scientific knowledge of plants and soils advanced, and this made it possible to establish high-yield pasture on the country's plains and low lands. This development is associated with the scientific work of Alfred Cockayne and Bruce Levy, who were botanists from Canterbury University College and Victoria University College respectively (Nightingale, 1992). These innovations consisted of producing perennial strains of ryegrass with high nutritional value for animal feed, and combining cultivation with local varieties of clover, which increased the capacity to fix nitrogen in the soil and reduced the need for fertilizers. The combined impact of these two discoveries (the development of an autochthonous strain of ryegrass and combined cultivation with clover) was enormous. It showed that it was possible to develop permanent high-yield pasture in New Zealand and replace the traditional techniques such as extensive fodder crops and crop rotation on pasture, which were costly and gave decreasing returns. The next steps were to disseminate these innovations among producers and create a seed certification system that guaranteed high-quality pasture was sown.

In the second sub-period (1940–1966), especially after the WWII, there was greater productivity growth on livestock land. These results were the consequence of three processes. First, fertilization and sowing by aeroplanes (aerial topdressing) was used,[6] which meant the new techniques could be implemented in mountainous areas. Second, there was new investment in improving the soil in mountainous regions, especially by creating fields for the efficient use of improved pasture. Third, there were large investments in public works , such as roads, electrification, house-building and land distribution, all geared towards establishing livestock enterprises in regions of very low production.

In the fourth stage (1966–1980), the total area under pasture increased by 2.5 million hectares, as did the area of improved and artificial pasture. This new expansion was mainly in mountainous regions and was a response on the part of rural producers to the fall in wool prices on the world market. This process of expansion and intensification (MacLeod & Moller, 2006) made possible a marked increase in the stock of sheep and cattle for meat, and at the same time improved land productivity in terms of livestock units per hectare. It was also the result of incentive policies (financing and agro-subsidies) promoted by the government to stimulate domestic production and counteract very serious problems (Dalziel & Lattimore, 2004) caused by the fall in international prices for the country's exports and the impact of the oil crisis at the beginning of the 1970s. Expanding the area under pasture into mountainous regions called for considerable research into how pasture could be adapted to very sloping land. The result of these efforts was that the technology to produce and improve pasture was refined and, starting in the 1970s, a specific pasture management system for these regions was developed (Moot et al., 2009).

Since the 1980s New Zealand's agrarian system has moved into a new stage of intensification. The total area under pasture has been reduced by nearly 3 million hectares and the improved area by 1 million hectares (see Fig. 18.5). The sector most affected has been extensive ovine production, and there has been a considerable change in the composition of stock with an increase in meat and dairy livestock. There were two main reasons behind this reduction in pasture area. The first was that subsidies for the agrarian sector were discontinued (Nightingale, 1992) during reforms implemented by the Labour Party in the 1980s, in a move to liberalize and deregulate the economy (Wallace & Lattimore, 1987). The second was that the paradigm of New Zealand's agrarian system began to change, and the ecological sustainability of intensified production became a central aspect of agrarian development. This change of paradigm was consolidated in the 1990s when the focus shifted more towards the sustainability of the agrarian system based on a balance between intensification and biodiversity (MacLeod & Moller, 2006). There were some contradictions to this trend. On the one hand, an agrarian development model geared to biodiversity and environmental sustainability was gaining ground, and there was a shift towards agrarian diversification and changes were made in how the soil in high regions was used. But on the other hand, production in the most productive regions and those of easiest access was greatly intensified. This applied in particular to the dairy cattle sector, in which the use of nitrogenous and superphosphate fertilizers greatly increased, with negative impacts on the environment.

3.2 Uruguay: The Intensive Use of Natural Grassland and the Late Incorporation of Technologies to Improve the Land

Three broad stages of this sector's development in Uruguay can be identified, when considering the livestock sector's long-term production performance and the technological dynamics associated with improving the land.

Broadly speaking, we can identify a first stage that covered the last quarter of the nineteenth century and the first decade of the twentieth century. In this period, an increase in foreign demand led to rising production and productivity based on diversifying animal stocks and developing a collection of technological changes (enclosing land with wire fences, genetic improvements in livestock, British investment in infrastructure and transport). There were also institutional changes (legislation to consolidate ownership rights, strengthening of the State's political power and the creation of a factors market). One of the effects of these changes was that more efficient use could be made of the country's natural grasslands (Barrán & Nahum, 1977; Finch, 2005; Millot & Bertino, 1996; Moraes, 2001).

The second stage was from the second decade of the twentieth century to the 1980s. Natural grassland's maximum potential was reached around the time of the WWI, and from then until the 1980s the sector's performance was in a state of what has been defined as "dynamic stagnation"[7] (Barbato, 1981; Irigoyen, 1991; Moraes, 2001). The main cause of this was that although grassland had reached its maximum potential, technologies to improve the soil and overcome this restriction on growth were not developed or successfully adapted. In this long period of stagnation, three sub-periods can be identified that were associated with the development of different strategies oriented towards improving land productivity.

In the first sub-period (1914–1930) it became evident that the technological trajectory that made the sector very dynamic up to the WWI had matured. In this context, it was realized that the natural grasslands had reached their production limit, and this was one of the main restrictions on the expansion of livestock production. Various solutions to this problem were gestating (Finch, 1992), ranging from traditional agricultural fodder production to improving the natural grassland. The former line of research did not take account of the specificities of the climate or the soil's characteristics in Uruguay, neither of which were very favourable for the development of fodder agriculture. The latter research was into the country's soil and natural grassland, but this did not enjoy the public sector support it needed in order to be effectively developed.

From 1930 to 1950, improving natural grassland was explored as the most suitable solution in the Uruguayan environment, and an investment scheme to improve animal management was implemented (Astori, 1979; Campal, 1969; Reig & Vigorito, 1986). There were some studies in which sowing on cover to improve the quality of production on the grasslands was postulated, land plots were sub-divided, fields were made and sheep herding was rotated to take better advantage of natural pasture (Spangenberg, 1936). To do this, it was proposed that credits subsidized by the State should be made available to producers (Gallinal Heber, Bergalli, & Campal, 1938). The results of this initiative were limited in terms of raising land productivity, and the persistent stagnation of production led to this whole line of work being abandoned. Instead, there was a switch to exploring technological solutions imported from other livestock-rearing countries.

Starting in the 1950s there was an initiative to adopt the technological improvement and pasture cultivation package that had been successfully developed in New Zealand (Alvarez & Bortagaray, 2007; Astori, 1979; Campal, 1969; Moraes, 2001). The main measures taken included the introduction of a subsidies scheme for the use of fertilizers and a request to the World Bank and the United Nations Food and Agriculture Organization (FAO) for foreign technical assistance. This second initiative bore fruit in 1950, when a group of foreign specialists visited the country and jointly with local experts analysed the main problems in Uruguayan agriculture. In 1951 a team of experts was sent to Australia,

New Zealand and the United States to learn about those countries' agrarian technologies. The Uruguayan specialists reacted with varying degrees of intensity and enthusiasm. Their good impression of New Zealand's technological development of livestock production and especially of the technology to produce pasture and improve grassland, along with the influence of outstanding New Zealand specialists such as Dr McMeekan (Campal, 1969; Herrera, 2006), generated a favourable attitude toward adopting what later came to be called the "New Zealand technological package". The New Zealand experience was seen as offering a real solution and a possible technological horizon for Uruguayan agriculture.

This led to the implementation of some measures that were supported by foreign aid from the World Bank and the FAO as part of the Agriculture Plan. Despite the financial and technical aspects of the plan and a substantial expansion in the area of improved and implanted grassland, the adoption of this technology developed more slowly than expected, and the results were not what had been foreseen. In particular, there was not the expected impact in terms of helping to overcome the production stagnation in the sector. Diffusion of this technology stalled quite early, in the mid-1970s, and the process of adoption stopped at very low levels, affecting around 12% of the total pasture area. These results were certainly modest, and the impact of the changes implemented varied both from region to region and among the different livestock production segments (Paolino, Sosa, & Durán, 1987). Several different analyses found that this was because the high levels of investment involved meant a great risk for the producers, since the two countries' environments differed in respect of soil, climate and so on. There was also not enough accumulated knowledge about agronomy in Uruguay to be able to implement the new technology (Paolino, 1990; Reig & Vigorito, 1986), and the profitability of pasture production based on the New Zealand technological package was relatively low (Instituto de Economía, 1969; Pérez Arrarte, García, & Jarvis, 1982).

Although results were very poor in terms of the efficient application of the soil amending technology that was imported from New Zealand, this sub-period can be considered as a transition period to the next stage, because after a very intensive trial and error process, results crystallized in the later decades.

In the 1990s and the first decade of the twenty-first century there was a series of sweeping changes. These had a major impact on the sector's technological dynamics and the production performance of agriculture, and put an end to the long structural stagnation that had lasted most of the twentieth century (Buxedas, 2001; Mondelli & Picasso, 2001; Piñeiro & Moraes, 2008). Trends changed because of a number of factors, the most evident of which being higher levels of investment, a reduction in the area of natural grassland and an expansion in the area covered by improved pasture and fodder crops. The increase in investment was thanks to an increase in credit for the agrarian sector in an international context, which facilitated the flow of capital to the Uruguayan market and thus helped to create a favourable environment for producers, in which they were able to make efforts to improve productivity (Mondelli & Picasso, 2001). Indeed, a large part of this new investment went to raise land productivity : from 1990 to 2000 the area under fodder (improved fields, artificial grassland and fodder crops) jumped from 1.5 to 2.4 million hectares and at the same time the number of fields per establishment was increased. The combination of these two changes was that improvements in animal management could be introduced. In respect of technologies to produce pasture, the improvements were part of the same technological paradigm that had been tried in the 1960s (Paolino, 2001), and there were various regional and business sub-trajectories in the types and intensity of the innovations adopted (Mondelli & Picasso, 2001; Tommasino, 2010). In the first decade of the new century, farming production increased markedly not only in production volumes but also in the total area of land in use, and its share in exports overtook that of the traditional livestock sectors. Nevertheless, the intensification dynamics of livestock production gained strength (Errea et al., 2011). This expansion of farm agriculture meant a reduction in the area under pasture. This was mostly at the expense of natural grassland, although fodder production also decreased towards the end of the decade from its 2007 peak of 2.7 million hectares to 2.3 million hectares. Land productivity in terms of livestock units per hectare did not increase significantly, as there was a reduction in the ovine stock. The incorporation of other animal feed techniques based on the increasing use of concentrated fodder and feed lots made it possible to raise meat and milk production without a significant increase in the animal load per hectare.

3.3 An Overview of Trajectories and Technological Paradigms

In this analysis of the stages of development of livestock systems we can identify a sequence of three land improvement technological paradigms in New Zealand. The first was a cycle of formation, development and maturity (Pérez, 2009) that lasted from the 1880s to the 1920s, the second ran from the 1920s to the 1980s, and the third is still in its consolidation and expansion phase. In Uruguay, on the other hand, we find two broad technological paradigms. During the first, natural grassland was the main livestock production resource and technologies to improve the land were not introduced. This was the situation from 1860 until the WWI, and in practice it went on until the 1950s. The second phase came about when the second technological paradigm developed in New Zealand was imported and adapted in an attempt to narrow the technological gap between the two countries. Figure 18.6 is a schematic representation of the two countries' livestock production technological trajectories.

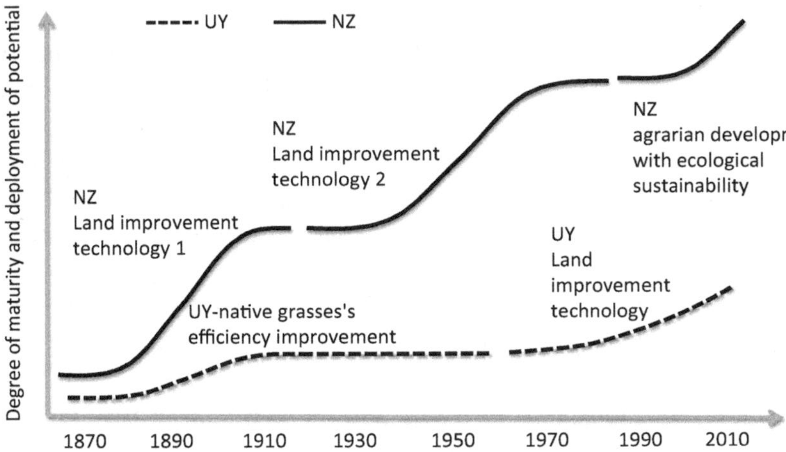

Fig. 18.6 Schematic model of the technological trajectories of the New Zealand and Uruguayan livestock systems, 1870–2010. Source: author's elaboration based on the technological trajectory model proposed by Pérez (2009)

4 Main Conclusions

Our aim in this chapter is to characterize the New Zealand and Uruguayan livestock systems with an analysis of their technological trajectories as they sought to raise land productivity. This was a key factor that determined the rate at which the two countries' livestock production grew in the long term and how their exports performed. Our main objective was to understand how their technological trajectories were initiated and developed in interaction with other important factors such as geographical environment, natural resource endowments and the institutional context in which technological innovations to raise land productivity were produced, disseminated and adapted.

In New Zealand, livestock, production changed relatively early from an extensive system to an intensive one. Besides developing and applying better technologies to improve the land on a large scale, this required raising the levels of capital investment and work to increase the sector's original production function. The growth in New Zealand's land productivity was based on three main pillars: first, the impact of refrigeration, which enabled the country to export new livestock products such as meat and milk; second, the production frontier in North Island expanded and forests were cleared to bring new land into livestock production, and the family farm system was consolidated; and third, scientific and technological knowledge was developed, making large-scale pasture production feasible and intensifying production. In all these stages, public policies played a key role in a variety of ways, including regulating the land market and introducing subsidy and credit schemes to stimulate the intensification of production.

In Uruguay, livestock production was based on the extensive use of natural grassland with low levels of capital investment and inputs, and while this system was very stable it suffered from inertia in the long run. Some technological solutions to improve the natural grassland were attempted, but they had little effect. In the mid-twentieth century it was decided to introduce pasture production technologies that had been developed in New Zealand. However, the results were disappointing and the new systems were not implemented consistently across the whole country. Then, in the 1990s, after a long period of trials and learning, the technological paradigm that had evolved in New Zealand in the 1920s crossed a dissemination threshold in Uruguay and the country was able to overcome, albeit to a modest degree, the stagnation of production in the sector.

This analysis of the two countries' long-term livestock system technological trajectories shows clearly that Uruguay lagged far behind New Zealand in the development of land improvement technologies.

5 Sources and Methodological Issues

5.1 Fig. 18.3

Meat equivalent per hectare = kg bovine meat/ha + kg ovine meat/ha + (kg wool/hax × transformation factor) + (litres of milk/hax × transformation factor).

Here four estimations based on different transformation coefficients are proposed:

1. Meat equivalent, classic coefficient (covers meat and wool)
2. Meat equivalent, specific coefficient (covers meat and wool)
3. Meat equivalent, classic coefficient (covers meat, wool and milk)
4. Meat equivalent, specific coefficient (covers meat, wool and milk)

Meat equivalent: is a homogenous indicator of the physical productivity of livestock that covers the production of the main livestock items: bovine meat, ovine meat, wool and milk. The indicator assumes a production cost of meat, wool and milk based on the fodder requirements of each animal species, so it is also a good indicator of land productivity.

Classic coefficient: the transformation coefficient most used in Uruguay considers that the production of one kilogram of wool demands 2.48 times more grassland than the production of one kilogram of meat (lamb or beef). The same coefficient is applied for New Zealand in this way:

Meat equivalent per hectare = kg bovine meat/ha + kg ovine meat/ha + (kg wool/hax × 2.48)

Specific coefficient: The classic coefficient has received strong criticism because it was estimated for calculating land productivity for tax collection purposes, based on the conditions of livestock production of 1970. If we used data from other years, the coefficient would change. Therefore, we estimate specific coefficients of transformation for each year considering the specific conditions of production of meat and wool in New Zealand and Uruguay.

We consider that the historical series that reflects the actual conditions of livestock production in the best way is the 4th series, which includes specific transformation coefficients, as well as milk production in addition to wool and meat. The different trends of the series after the 1990s that can be seen in Fig. 18.3 respond mainly to the kind of coefficients used and whether the indicator includes milk production. For a more detailed discussion see Alvarez (2014, pp. 149–159).

5.2 Fig. 18.4

The Livestock Unit indicator was constructed taking bovine livestock as a reference species. We applied dynamic bovine-ovine transformation coefficients considering the energy requirements of the two species in term of grass fodder and the specificities of each livestock system. In Uruguay, the coefficient is 1:5, which means that a Livestock Unit was habitually identified as 1 cow per 5 sheep. In both countries, different transformation coefficients have been used over time. Here we apply specific equivalence coefficients in each country and also in each period. The ranges of the transformation coefficients are from 1:5 to 1:6.67 for Uruguay and from 1:1.45 to 1:6.6 for New Zealand. For a more detailed discussion see Alvarez (2014, pp. 135–142).

Notes

1. After the 1970s the share of livestock production in total exports fell dramatically in both countries, because wool exports sank and because there was a substantial diversification of exports which increased the share of other agricultural products such as grains, horticulture, viticulture and forestry.
2. Between 1870 and 1930, the volume of exported goods of New Zealand and Uruguay grew in similar ways, on average 3.3 % annually for the

former and 3.4 % for the latter. But between 1930 and 1970 Uruguayan exports stagnated, showing a growth rate of −0.3 %, while New Zealand's exports grew at a rate of 2.5 %. Between 1970 and 2010 the performance of Uruguayan exports improved, but their growth rate remained lower than for New Zealand: 1.9 and 3.1 respectively, based on Alvarez (2014, p. 64, Graph III.11).

3. In English "diabolical blessing".
4. In an earlier paper we analysed the institutional framework of the agrarian innovation systems in New Zealand and Uruguay in the long run (Alvarez & Bortagaray, 2007). We show that agrarian innovation systems (interactions between agricultural research institutions, universities and the state) were denser in New Zealand than in Uruguay in term of functions and structure.
5. In the thirteenth century, New Zealand's native forests covered about 23 million hectares (approximately 85% of the surface area), but by the mid-nineteenth century this had been reduced to 15.4 million hectares (57% of the surface area). However, the greatest change has taken place in the last 150 years, when the area of forest has shrunk to 6.2 million hectares (23% of the surface area) and was largely replaced by grassland for livestock production (Taylor & Smith, 1997; Condliffe, 1959).
6. It is estimated that from 1950 and 1953 the area fertilized with this technique increased from 19,500 to 500,000 hectares, and by 1970 had reached 3.2 million hectares (Tennant, 1978, p. 192, Table 6.2).
7. Dynamic stagnation refers to the stagnation of agricultural production with important changes in the composition of livestock (sheep and cows), in the context of technological stagnation. These changes responded — among other factors—to the reaction of landowners to the evolution of the international prices of the main livestock products for export, such as beef and wool.

References

Alvarez, J. (2014). *Instituciones, cambio tecnológico y productividad en los sistemas agrarios de Nueva Zelanda y Uruguay. Patrones y trayectorias de largo plazo (1870–2010)*. PhD Thesis doctoral en Historia Económica, Universidad de la República, Montevideo.

Alvarez, J., & Bértola, L. (2013). So Similar, So Different: New Zealand and Uruguay in the World Economy. In C. Lloyd, J. Metzer, & R. Sutch (Eds.),

Settler Economies in World History (pp. 493–520). Leiden, The Netherlands: Brill.

Alvarez, J., Bértola, L., & Porcile, G. (2007). *Primos ricos y empobrecidos: crecimiento, distribución del ingreso e instituciones en Australia-Nueva Zelanda vs Argentina-Uruguay*. Montevideo: Editorial Fin de Siglo.

Alvarez, J., Bilancini, E., D'Alessandro, S., & Porcile, G. (2011). Agricultural Institutions, Industrialization and Growth: The Case of New Zealand and Uruguay in 1870–1940. *Explorations in Economic History, 48*(2), 151–168. https://doi.org/10.1016/j.eeh.2010.05.004.

Alvarez, J., & Bortagaray, I. (2007). El marco institucional de la innovación agropecuario en Nueva Zelanda y Uruguay en el largo plazo. In J. Álvarez, L. Bértola, & G. Porcile (Eds.), *Primos Ricos y Empobrecidos. Crecimiento, distribución del ingreso e instituciones en Australia-Nueva Zelanda vs Argentina-Uruguay* (pp. 233–272). Montevideo, Uruguay: Fin de Siglo.

Aparicio, G., González, Á., Pinilla, V., & Serrano, R. (2018). The World Periphery in Global Agricultural and Food Trade, 1900–2000. In V. Pinilla & H. Wilelbald (Eds.), *Agricultural Development in the World Periphery: A Global Economic History Approach*. London: Palgrave.

Astori, D. (1979). *La Evolución Tecnológica de la Ganadería Uruguaya 1930–1979*. Montevideo: EBO.

Banco de Datos – FCS. Retrieved June, 2013, from http://cienciassociales.edu.uy/bancosdedatos/

Barbato, C. (1981). *El proceso de generación, difusión y adopción de tecnología en la ganadería vacuna. Uruguay, 1950–1977*. Montevideo: CINVE.

Barrán, J. P., & Nahum, B. (1977). *Historia Rural del Uruguay Moderno. La civilización ganadera bajo Batlle (1905–1914)* (Vol. VI). Montevideo: EBO.

Barrán, J. P., & Nahum, B. (1978). *Historia rural del Uruguay Moderno. Agricultura, crédito y transporte bajo Batlle (1905–1914)* (Vol. Tomo VII). Montevideo: Ediciones de la Banda Oriental.

BCU. (1973). *Boletín Estadístico del Banco Central del Uruguay*, Montevideo: Uruguay.

BCU. (1975). *Boletín Estadístico del Banco Central del Uruguay*, Montevideo: Uruguay.

Belich, J. (1996). *Making Peoples: A History of the New Zealanders, from Polynesian Settlement to the End of the Nineteenth Century*. Auckland, New Zealand: Penguin Books.

Belich, J. (2001). *Paradise Reforged. A History of the New Zealanders from the 1880's to the Year 2000*. Auckland: Penguin Books.

Berreta, E. (2003). *Perfiles por País del Recurso Pastura/Forraje: Uruguay*. Rome: FAO.

Bertoni, R., & Willebald, H. (2016). Do Natural Energy Endowments Matter? New Zealand and Uruguay in a Comparative Perspective, 1870–1940. *Australian Economic History Review, 56*(1), 70–99. https://doi.org/10.1111/aehr.12092.

Bloomfield, G. T. (1984). *A Handbook of New Zealand Statistics* (Hall & Co ed.). Boston: Hall & Co.

Boast, R. (2008). *Buying the Land, Selling the Land: Governments and Maori Land in the North Island 1865–1921*. Wellington: Victoria University Press.

Briggs, P. (2003). *Looking at the Numbers: A View of New Zealand's Economic History*. Wellington: NZ Institute of Economic Research.

Buxedas, M. (2001). *El Uruguay ganadero: del auge a la aftosa* (Vol. Serie Seminario y Talleres). Montevideo: CIEDUR.

Campal, E. (1969). *La Pradera* (Vol. 28). Montevideo.

Charteris, P. L., Morris, S. T., & Matthew, P. N. P. (1999). *Pasture-Based Beef Production in New Zealand*. Palmerston North, New Zealand: WP Institute of Veterinary Animal and Biomedical Sciences Massey University.

Dalziel, P., & Lattimore, R. G. (2004). *The New Zealand Macroeconomy: Striving for Sustainable Growth with Equity*. Melbourne: Oxford University Press.

Denoon, D. (1983). *Settler Capitalism: The Dynamics of Dependent Development in the Southern Hemisphere*. Oxford: Clarendon Press.

Errea, E., Peyrou, J., Secco, J., & Souto, G. (2011). *Transformaciones en el agro uruguayo: nuevas instituciones y modelos de organización empresarial*. Montevideo: Universidad Católica del Uruguay.

Finch, H. (1992). *Economía y Sociedad en el Uruguay del siglo XX*. Montevideo: Departamento de Publicaciones de Facultad de Humanidades y Ciencias de la Educación, UdelaR.

Finch, H. (2005). *La economía política del Uruguay contemporáneo, 1870–2000*. Montevideo: Ediciones de la Banda Oriental.

Gallinal Heber, J. P., Bergalli, L. U., & Campal, E. (1938). *Estudios sobre praderas naturales del Uruguay* (Vol. Primera contribución). Montevideo: Germano Uruguaya

Herrera, M. (2006). The Development of Pastoral Farming in Uruguay 50 Years Following McMeekan; The Kiwi Trail. *Primary Industry Management, 9*(4), 33–36.

Instituto de Economía. (1969). *El proceso económico del Uruguay*. Montevideo: Departamento de publicaciones, Universidad de la República.

Instituto Nacional de Estadística – INE. Retrieved June, 2013, from http://www.ine.gub.uy/

Irigoyen, R. (1991). La racionalidad empresarial en la ganadería uruguaya. In D. Piñeiro (Ed.), *Nuevos y No Tanto. Los actores sociales para la modernización del agro uruguayo*. Montevideo: CIESU-EBO.

Kirby, J. (1975). On the Viability of Small Countries: Uruguay and New Zealand Compared. *Journal of Interamerican Studies and World Affairs, 17*(3), 259–280.

Lloyd, C., Metzer, J., & Sutch, R. (2013). *Settler Economies in World History*. Leiden, The Netherlands: Brill.

Lundvall, B.-A. (1992). *National Innovation System: Towards a Theory of Innovation and Interactive Learning*. London: Pinter.

MacLeod, C. J., & Moller, H. (2006). Intensification and Diversification of New Zealand Agriculture Since 1960: An Evaluation of Current Indicators of Land Use Change. *Agriculture, Ecosystems & Environment, 115*(1), 201–218.

Maddison, A. (2009). Historical Statistics of the World Economy: 1-2008 AD. Retrieved from www.ggdc.net/maddison/Historical_Statistics/horizontal-file_02-2010.xls

Maddison-Project. (2013). The Maddison Project Database. Retrieved from http://www.ggdc.net/maddison/maddison-project/home.htm

Marchesi, E., & Durán, A. (1969). *Suelos del Uruguay* (Vol. 18). Montevideo.

McAloon, J. (2009). The New Zealand Economy, 1792–1914. In G. Byrnes (Ed.), *The New Oxford History of New Zealand* (pp. 197–218). Melbourne, Australia: Oxford University Press.

McKinnon, M., Bradley, B., & Kirkpatrick, R. (1997). *New Zealand Historical Atlas: Visualising*. Auckland, New Zealand: Bateman.

Millot, J., & Bertino, M. (1996). *Historia Económica del Uruguay (1860–1910)*. Montevideo: Fundación de Cultura Universitaria.

Mondelli, M., & Picasso, V. (2001). *Trayectorias tecnológicas en la ganadería uruguaya: un enfoque evolucionista*. Montevideo: Universidad de la República.

Moot, D., Mills, A., Lucas, D., & Scott, W. (2009). *Country Pasture/Forage Resource Profiles*. Rome: FAO.

Moraes, I. (2001). *Las determinantes tecnológicas e institucionales del desempeño ganadero en el largo plazo, 1870–1970*. Tesis de maestría, Universidad de la República, Montevideo.

Nightingale, T. (1992). *White Collars and Gumboots: A History of the Ministry of Agriculture and Fisheries, 1892–1992*. Palmerston North: The Dunmore Press.

Nurske, R. (1961). *Equilibrium and Growth in the World Economy*. Cambridge, MA: Harvard University Press.

Paolino, C. (1990). *Estagnacao e dinamismo na agropecuaria uruguaia: uma abordagem heterodoxa.* Tesis de doctorado PhD, Universidade Estadual de Campinas, Sao Paulo. Retrieved from Biblioteca on-line Unicamp www.unicamp.br/bc/

Paolino, C. (2001). *Las tecnologías y la agroindustria en el Uruguay: ¿convergencia o divergencia?* Paper presented at the 1er Congreso Rioplatense de Economía Agrícola, Montevideo.

Paolino, C., Sosa, S., & Durán, H. (1987). El proceso tecnológico en la producción de leche. In C. Barbato & C. Paolino (Eds.), *Una década de cambio en la lechería uruguaya (1975–1985).* Montevideo: CINVE.

Pérez Arrarte, C., García, S., & Jarvis, J. (1982). *La ganadería de carne vacuna en el Uruguay.* Cali: Centro Internacional de Agricultura Tropical.

Perez, C. (2010). Technological Revolutions and Techno-Economic Paradigms. *Cambridge Journal of Economics, 34*(1), 185–202.

Pérez, C. (2009). *Technological Revolutions and Techno-Economic Paradigms.* Working Papers in Technology Governance and Economic Dynamics, 20.

Piñeiro, D., & Moraes, M. I. (2008). Los cambios en la sociedad rural durante el siglo XX. In EBO (Ed.), *El Uruguay del Siglo XX: La sociedad.* Montevideo: Benjamin Nahum.

Reig, N., & Vigorito, R. (1986). *Excedente ganadero y renta de la tierra. Uruguay 1930–1970.* Montevideo: EBO.

Sachs, J. D., & Warner, A. M. (1995). *Natural Resource Abundance and Economic Growth Working Paper* (Vol. 5398). Cambridge: National Bureau of Economic Research.

Schlüter, A. (2014). *Institutions and Small Settler Economies. A Comparative Study of New Zealand and Uruguay, 1870–2008.* New York: Palgrave Macmillan.

Schumpeter, J. A. (1934). *The Theory of Economic Development: An Inquiry into Profits, Capital, Credit, Interest, and the Business Cycle.* Cambridge: Harvard University Press.

Sinclair, K. (1988). *A History of New Zealand.* Auckland: Penguin.

Spangenberg, G. E. (1936). *El mejoramiento de las pasturas en la explotación extensiva del Uruguay* (Vol. 1). Montevideo

STATISTICS NEW ZEALAND. (2013). *New Zealand Official Yearbook, 2012.* (NZOYB 2012). Wellington: New Zealand.

Sutch, W. B. (1969). *Poverty and Progress in New Zealand: A Re-Assessment.* Wellington: Reed.

Tennant, D. B. (1978). *Soil-Amending Technology, Grassland Farming, and New Zealand Economic Development.* (PhD), Masseyt University, New Zealand.

Tommasino, H. (2010). 15 años de cambios en el agro uruguayo: impacto en la ganadería vacuna. *Anuario OPYPA*, 365–381.
Wallace, L. T., & Lattimore, R. (1987). *Rural New Zealand, what next?* Lincoln: Agribusiness & Economics Research Unit, Lincoln College.
Willebald, H., & Juambeltz, J. (2018). Land Frontier Expansion in Settler Economies (1830–1950): Was it a Ricardian Process? In V. Pinilla & H. Wilelbald (Eds.), *Agricultural Development in the World Periphery: A Global Economic History Approach*. London: Palgrave.
Winter, S. G., & Nelson, R. R. (1982). *An Evolutionary Theory of Economic Change*. Cambridge: The Belknap Press of Harvard University Press.

Jorge Álvarez Scanniello has an undergraduate degree in History and a PhD in Economic History. He is a Professor at the Economic and Social History Programme, Social Sciences Faculty, University of the Republic, Uruguay. His areas of research include the economic performance of the Uruguayan economy from a comparative perspective and the relation between institutions and development in settler economies. He has written two books and several articles and book chapters on the topic.

Index[1]

[1]Note: Page number followed by 'n' refer to notes.

V. Pinilla, H. Willebald (eds.), *Agricultural Development in the World Periphery*, Palgrave Studies in Economic History, https://doi.org/10.1007/978-3-319-66020-2

B

C

D

E

Kolibri 360 GmbH
Ferdinand-Jühlke-Straße 7
99095 Erfurt, Deutschland
produktsicherheit@kolibri360.de